Delphi for .NET
Developer's Guide

Xavier Pacheco

SAMS

800 East 96th Street, Indianapolis, Indiana 46240 USA

Delphi for .NET Developer's Guide

International Standard Book Number: 0-672-32443-1

Library of Congress Catalog Card Number: 2003116630

Printed in the United States of America

First Printing: May 2004

07   06   05   04   4   3   2   1

Trademarks

Warning and Disclaimer

Bulk Sales

Sams Publishing offers excellent discounts on this book when ordered in quantity for bulk purchases or special sales. For more information, please contact

U.S. Corporate and Government Sales
1-800-382-3419
corpsales@pearsontechgroup.com

For sales outside of the U.S., please contact

International Sales
1-317-428-3341
international@pearsontechgroup.com

Associate Publisher
Michael Stephens

Acquisitions Editor
Loretta Yates

Development Editor
Songlin Qiu

Managing Editor
Charlotte Clapp

Project Editor
George E. Nedeff

Copy Editor
Rhonda Tinch-Mize

Indexer
Erika Millen

Proofreader
Leslie Joseph

Technical Editor
Hallvard Vassbotn

Publishing Coordinator
Cindy Teeters

Multimedia Developer
Dan Sherf

Book Designer
Gary Adair

Page Layout
Bronkella Publishing

Contents at a Glance

Introduction 1

Part I   Introduction to the .NET Framework
1   Introduction to .NET 3
2   Overview of the .NET Framework 12

Part II   Delphi for .NET Programming Language
3   Introduction to Delphi for .NET and the New IDE 23
4   Programs, Units, and Namespaces 37
5   The Delphi Language 46

Part III The .NET Framework Class Library Development
6   Assemblies—Libraries and Packages 109
7   GDI+ Programming—Drawing in .NET 125
8   Mono—A Cross Platform .NET Project 166
9   Memory Management and Garbage Collection 187
10   Collections 197
11   Working with the String and StringBuilder Classes 221
12   File and Streaming Operations 239
13   Developing Custom WinForms Controls 261
14   Threading in Delphi for .NET 307
15   Reflection API 338
16   Interoperability—COM Interop and the Platform Invocation Service 356

Part IV   Database Development with ADO.NET
17   Overview of ADO.NET 401
18   Using the Connection Object 406
19   Using Command and DataReader Objects 412
20   DataAdapters and DataSets 429
21   Working with WinForms—DataViews and Data Binding ... 451
22   Saving Data to the Data Source 476
23   Working with Transactions and Strongly-Typed Datasets ... 504
24   The Borland Data Provider 523

Part V   Internet Development with ASP.NET
25   ASP.NET Fundamentals 534
26   Building ASP.NET Web Pages 551
27   Building Database Driven ASP.NET Applications 581
28   Building Web Services 620
29   .NET Remoting and Delphi 643

30   .NET Remoting in Action 669
31   Securing ASP.NET Applications 699
32   ASP.NET Deployment and Configuration 716
33   Caching and Managing State in ASP.NET Applications 738
34   Developing Custom ASP.NET Server Controls 763
      Index 791

Table of Contents

Introduction   1

1   **Introduction to .NET**   3

The .NET Initiative 4
    The .NET Vision 4
    The .NET Framework Components—the Common Language Runtime and Class
    Libraries 6
    Types of .NET Applications 7
    VCL for .NET Explained 8
Distributed Development through Web Services 8
    Web Services—Defined 8
    Web Service Clients 10
    Web Service Development Tools 11

2   **Overview of the .NET Framework**   12

From Development to Execution 12
The Common Language Runtime (CLR) 13
    Managed Modules 13
    Assemblies 14
    Managed and Unmanaged Code 14
    MSIL and JIT Compilation and Execution 14
The Common Type System (CTS) 17
    Value Types 17
    Reference Types 17
The Common Language Specification (CLS) 18
.NET Framework Class Library (FCL) 18
    Namespaces 18
    The System Namespace 18
    Primary Subsystem Namespaces 19

3   **Introduction to Delphi for .NET and the New IDE**   23

Delphi for .NET—a Bigger Picture 23
Introduction to the Integrated Development Environment (IDE) 24
    Welcome Page 24
    Designer 25
    Forms 27
    Tool Palette/Code Snippets 28
    Object Inspector 29
    Code Editor 29
    Project Manager 32
    Model View 33
    Data Explorer 33

Object Repository 34

Code Explorer 34

To-Do List 35

4   Programs, Units, and Namespaces   37

Managed Module Structures 37

The Program Structure 37

The Unit Structure 38

Uses Clause Syntax 40

Circular Unit References 41

Namespaces 42

Namespace Declaration 42

Using Namespaces 43

The Namespaces Clause 44

Resolving Generic Namespaces 44

Unit Aliases 45

5   The Delphi Language   46

It's All about .NET 46

Comments 47

Procedures and Functions 47

Parentheses in Calls 48

Overloading 48

Default Value Parameters 48

Variables 49

Constants 51

Operators 52

Assignment Operators 53

Comparison Operators 53

Logical Operators 53

Arithmetic Operators 54

Bitwise Operators 55

Increment and Decrement Procedures 55

Do-and-assign Operators 56

Delphi Language Types 56

Objects, Objects Everywhere! 56

A Comparison of Types 57

Characters 58

Variant Types 58

User-Defined Types 62

Arrays 62

Dynamic Arrays 63

Records 64

Sets 65

Unsafe Code 67
Pointers 68
Classes and Objects 71
Type Aliases 72
Typecasting and Type Conversion 72
String Resources 73
Testing Conditions 74
The if Statement 74
Using case Statements 75
Loops 75
The for Loop 76
The while Loop 76
repeat..until 77
The Break Statement 77
The Continue Statement 77
Procedures and Functions 78
Passing Parameters 79
Scope 81
Units and Namespaces 82
The uses Clause 83
Circular Unit References 84
Packages and Assemblies 84
Object-Oriented Programming 84
Using Delphi Objects 86
Declaration and Instantiation 86
Destruction 87
The Adam of Objects 87
Fields 87
Methods 88
Method Types 89
Class References 91
Properties 92
Events 92
Visibility Specifiers 95
"Friend" Classes 97
Class Helpers 97
Nested Types 98
Operator Overloading 98
Attributes 99
Interfaces 99

Structured Exception Handling 103
  Exception Classes 105
  Flow of Execution 106
  Reraising an Exception 108

6   Assemblies—Libraries and Packages   109
Core Assemblies 109
Viewing Assembly Contents and Dependencies 109
Ring the GAC 111
Building Assemblies 112
  Why Use Assemblies? 112
  Using Packages to Build Assemblies 113
  Using Libraries to Build Assemblies 117
Using Assemblies in Delphi 120
Using Delphi Assemblies in C# 121
Installing Packages into the Delphi IDE 122
Strong Naming Assemblies 122
Dynamically Loading Assemblies 123

7   GDI+ Programming—Drawing in .NET   125
Fundamental Concepts 125
  The GDI+ Namespaces 125
  The Graphics Class 126
  Windows Coordinate System 126
Drawing Lines 128
  The Pen and Brush Classes 128
  Drawing Lines 128
  Line Caps 130
  Joining Lines—The GraphicsPath Class 132
Drawing Curves 133
  The Cardinal Spline 134
  Bezier Spline 135
Drawing Shapes 138
  Drawing Rectangles 138
  Drawing Ellipses 139
  Drawing Polygons 139
  Drawing Pies 140
  More on the LinearGradientBrush 141
GraphicsPaths and Regions 142
  Drawing with the GraphicsPath Class 142
  Drawing with the Region Class 143
  Clipping Regions 144

Working with Images 147
    The Image Classes 148
    Loading and Creating Bitmaps 148
    Changing an Image's Resolution 149
    Drawing an Image 150
    Interpolation 151
    Drawing a Mirror Effect 151
    Using Transformation Methods 153
    Creating a Thumbnail 156
Revisiting Coordinate Systems 157
Animation Example 159

8   Mono—A Cross Platform .NET Project   **166**
Mono Features 166
History of Mono 167
Why Mono? 167
Mono's Roadmap 168
    Mono 1.0 Goals 168
    Mono 1.2 Goals 169
    Mono 1.4 Goals 169
Installation/Setup 170
    Mono Installation—Using Red Carpet 170
Creating Your First Mono Program 172
Running Delphi Generated Assemblies under Mono (on Linux) 173
Cross Platform ASP.NET 177
    ASP.NET Deployment to Mono 179
    XSP Configuration 179
    XSP Runtime Parameters 179
    Some Caveats and a Minor Extension of the Example 180
ADO.NET with Mono 181
Mono and Apache 184
Mono and System.Windows.Forms 186

9   Memory Management and Garbage Collection   **187**
How Garbage Collection Works 187
    Generational Garbage Collection 189
    Invoking the Garbage Collector 191
Constructors 192
Finalization 192
The Dispose Pattern—IDisposable 193
    IDisposable Example 193
    Automatically Implementing IDisposable 195
Performance Issues Regarding Finalization 196

10   Collections **197**

System.Collections Interfaces 197

IEnumerable Interface 198

ICollection Interface 199

IList Interface 199

IDictionary Interface 199

IEnumerator Interface 200

System.Collections Classes 200

The Stack Collection 200

The Queue Class 203

The ArrayList Class 206

The HashTable Class 209

Creating a Strongly-Typed Collection 212

Descending from CollectionBase 212

Using the Strongly-Typed Collection 216

Creating a Strongly-Typed Dictionary 216

Descending from DictionaryBase 216

Using the Strongly-Typed Dictionary 219

11   Working with the String and StringBuilder Classes **221**

The System.String Type 221

String Immutability in .NET 222

String Operations 224

Comparing Strings 224

The StringBuilder Class 228

StringBuilder Methods 228

StringBuilder Usage 229

String Formatting 230

Format Specifiers 231

Numeric Format Specifiers 231

Date and Time Format Specifiers 234

Enumeration Format Specifiers 237

12   File and Streaming Operations **239**

System.IO Namespace Classes 239

Working with the Directory System 240

Creating and Deleting Directories 241

Moving and Copying Directories 241

Examining Directory Information 243

Working with Files 244

Creating and Deleting Files 245

Moving and Copying Files 245

Examining File Information 245

Streams 246
    Working with Text File Streams 246
    Working with Binary File Streams 249
Asynchronous Stream Access 251
Monitoring Directory Activity 253
Serialization 255
    How Serialization Works 256
    Formatters 257
    A Serialization/Deserialization Example 257

13   Developing Custom WinForms Controls   261
Component Building Basics 262
    When to Write a Component 262
    Component Writing Steps 263
    Deciding on an Ancestor Class 263
    Creating a Component Unit 264
    Creating Properties 266
    Creating Events 277
    Creating Methods 282
    Constructors and Destructors 283
    Design-Time Behavior 284
    Testing the Component 285
    Providing a Component Icon 285
Sample Components 285
    ExplorerViewer: A UserControl Example 286
    SimpleStatusBars: Using Extender Providers 295
User Painting: The PlayingCard Control 299

14   Threading in Delphi for .NET   307
Processes 307
Threading 308
Threading .NET Style 309
AppDomain 310
The System.Threading Namespace 311
    The System.Threading.Thread Class 311
    System.Threading.ThreadPriority 316
    System.Threading.ThreadState 316
    System.Threading.ApartmentState Enumeration 317
    The System.Threading.ThreadPool Class 317
    The System.Threading.Timer Class 319
    Delegates 320

Writing Thread-safe Code .NET Style 322
    Locking Mechanisms 322
    Events 326
    Thread Local Storage 328
    Win32 Interprocess Communications 328
    Thread-safe .NET Framework Classes and Methods 328
User Interface Issues 329
    The System.Windows.Forms.Control.Invoke() Method 330
    The System.Windows.Forms.Control.InvokeRequired Property 330
    The System.Windows.Forms.Control.BeginInvoke() Method 331
    The System.Windows.Forms.Control.EndInvoke() Method 331
    The System.Windows.Forms.Control.CreateGraphics() Method 332
Threading Exceptions 334
    System.Threading.ThreadAbortException 334
    System.Threading.ThreadInterruptedException 337
    System.Threading.ThreadStateException 337
    System.Threading.SynchronizationLockException 337
Garbage Collection and Threading 337

15   Reflection API   338
Reflecting an Assembly 338
Reflecting a Module 341
Reflecting Types 342
Runtime Invocation of a Type's Members (Late Binding) 344
    Invoking the Member's Types for Efficiency 347
    Another Example of Member Invocation 348
Emitting MSIL Through Reflection 351
    Tools/Classes for Emitting MSIL 352
    The Emitting Process 352
    A System.Reflection.Emit Example 352

16   Interoperability—COM Interop and the Platform Invocation Service   356
Why Have Interoperability? 356
Common Interoperability Issues 357
Using COM Objects in .NET Code 358
    Late Bound Automation 358
    Value, Reference, and Optional Parameters 360
    Early Bound COM 362
    Interop Assemblies 364
    Creating an Interop Assembly 366
    What's in an Interop Assembly? 366
    Using COM Events 367
    COM Lifetime Control 369

Error Handling 369
Primary Interop Assemblies 369
Customizing Interop Assemblies and PIAs 371
Using .NET Objects in COM Code 372
Registering a .NET Assembly for Automation 373
Late Bound Automation 374
Interop Type Libraries 375
What's in an Interop Type Library? 375
Implementing Interfaces 376
Parameter Types and Marshaling 378
Error Handling 381
Using Win32 DLL Exports in .NET Code 381
Traditional Delphi Syntax 382
Custom Attribute Syntax 383
Parameter Types and Marshaling 384
Error Handling 387
Win32 Error Codes 388
HResult Error Codes 389
Performance Issues 391
Using .NET Routines in Win32 Code 395
Traditional Delphi Syntax 396
Parameter Types and Marshaling 397

17   Overview of ADO.NET   401
Design Principles 401
Disconnected Data Architecture 401
Integration with XML 402
Common Data Representation 402
Built on .NET Framework 402
Leverage Existing Technologies 402
ADO.NET Objects 402
Connected Classes 403
Disconnected Classes 404
.NET Data Providers 405

18   Using the Connection Object   406
Connection Functionality 406
Setting Up the ConnectionString Property 407
Specifying a SqlConnection.ConnectionString 407
Specifying an OleDbConnection.ConnectionString 408
Specifying an OdbcConnection.ConnectionString 408
Specifying an OracleConnection.ConnectionString 408

Opening and Closing Connections 408
Connection Events 409
Connection Pooling 411

19   Using Command and DataReader Objects   412
Executing Commands 412
    The IDbCommand Interface 412
Non-Query Commands 413
Retrieving Single Values 415
Executing Data Definition Language (DDL) Commands 416
Specifying Parameters Using IDbParameter 417
Executing Stored Procedures 419
Deriving Parameters 421
Querying for Resultsets Using DataReaders 422
    The IDataReader Interface 423
Querying a Resultset 423
Querying Multiple Resultsets Using DataReaders 424
Using DataReader to Retrieve BLOB Data 425
Using DataReader to Retrieve Schema Information 426

20   DataAdapters and DataSets   429
DataAdapters 429
    DataAdapter Composition 429
    Creating a DataAdapter 431
    Retrieving Query Results 432
    Mapping Query Results 434
Working with DataSets 436
    DataSet Composition 437
    DataSet Operations 438
Working with DataTables 440
    Defining Columns 440
    Defining Primary Keys 441
    Working with Constraints 442
    Working with DataRelations 445
    Manipulating Data—Working with DataRow 447
    Searching, Sorting, and Filtering Data 449

21   Working with WinForms—DataViews and Data Binding   451
Displaying Data Using DataView and DataViewManager 451
    The DataView Class 452
    The DataViewManager Class 453
    Example Projects Using DataView and DataViewManager 453
Data Binding 463
    The Data Binding Interfaces 463
    Simple Versus Complex Binding 464

WinForm Data Binding Classes 464
Building Data Bound Windows Forms 465

22   Saving Data to the Data Source   476
Updating the Data Source Using SQLCommandBuilder 476
Updating the Data Source Using Custom Updating Logic 479
Using a Command Class 479
Using the SqlDataAdapter Class 486
Updating Using a Stored Procedure 491
Handling Concurrency 497
Refreshing Data After It Is Updated 501

23   Working with Transactions and Strongly-Typed DataSets   504
Transaction Processing 504
A Simple Transaction Processing Example 505
Transactions When Using a DataAdapter 508
Isolation Levels 508
Savepoints 510
Nested Transactions 510
Strongly-Typed DataSets 511
Advantages/Disadvantages 511
Creating Strongly-Typed DataSets 512
Examining the Strongly-Typed DataSet .pas File 513
Using the Strongly-Typed DataSet 520

24   The Borland Data Provider   523
Architecture Overview 523
Borland Data Provider Classes 524
BdpConnection 525
BdpCommand 526
BdpDataReader 527
BdpDataAdapter 528
BdpParameter/BpdParameterCollection 529
BdpTransaction 530
Designers within the IDE 531
The Connections Editor 531
The Command Text Editor 531
Parameter Collection Editor 531
Data Adapter Configuration Dialog Box 532

25   ASP.NET Fundamentals   534
Web Technologies—How They Work 534
HTTP Protocol Overview 534
The HTTP Request Packet 535
The HTTP Response Packet 536

ASP.NET—How It Works 537
    A Simple Web Application 538
    ASP.NET Page Structure 538
    Event-Driven Communication 541
    VIEWSTATE and State Maintenance 542
    CodeBehind 542
ASP.NET Classes 544
    The HTTPResponse Class 544
    The HTTPRequest Class 547
    The HTTPCookie Class 548
    Handling Postback Events 549

26   Building ASP.NET Web Pages   551

Building Web Pages Using ASP.NET Controls 551
    Sample Download Request Form 552
    The Page Layout 553
    Creating a Form 553
    Processing the Load Event 554
    Saving Files from within an ASP.NET Application 555
    Event Processing Order for a Web Form 557
Pre-populating List Controls 557
Performing Web Form Validation 558
    Client Versus Server-side Validation 559
    BaseValidator Class 559
    RequiredFieldValidator 559
    CompareValidator 560
    RegularExpressionValidator 562
    RangeValidator 563
    CustomValidator 564
    ValidationSummary 565
Web Form Formatting 566
    WebControl Strongly-Typed Properties 566
    Cascading Style Sheets 567
    Using the Style Class 568
Navigating between Web Forms 568
    Passing Data via POST 569
    Using the Response.Redirect() Method and QueryString 569
    Using the Server.Transfer() Method 570
    Using Session Variables 571
Tips and Techniques 572
    Using the Panel Control for Multiform Simulation 572
    Uploading a File from the Client 574
    Sending an Email Response from a Form 575

Displaying Images 577
Dynamically Adding Controls—A Thumbnail Based Image Viewer 577

27   Building Database Driven ASP.NET Applications   581

Data Binding 581
   Simple Data Binding 581
   Complex Data Binding 586
Data Bound List Controls 586
   CheckBoxList Control 586
   DropDownList Control 588
   ListBox Control 590
   RadioButtonList Control 593
Data Bound Iterative Controls 595
   Repeater Control 595
   DataList Control 598
Working with the DataGrid 603
   Paging the DataGrid 604
   Editing the DataGrid 607
   Adding Items to the DataGrid 613
   Sorting the DataGrid 613
Database-Driven Download Request Form and Administrator 614

28   Building Web Services   620

Terms Related to Web Services 620
Web Service Construction 621
   The [WebService] Attribute 626
   Returning Data from a Web Service 627
   The [WebMethod] Attribute Explained 627
Consuming Web Services 630
   The Discovery Process 630
   Constructing a Proxy Class 630
   Using the Proxy Class 632
   Consuming a DataSet from a Web Service 635
   Invoking an Asynchronous Web Service Method 638
Securing Web Services 639

29   .NET Remoting and Delphi   643

Remoting Technologies Available Today 643
   Sockets 643
   RPC 644
   Java RMI 644
   CORBA 644

XML-RPC 645
DCOM 645
COM-Interop 645
SOAP 645
.NET Remoting 646
Distributed Architectures 646
Client/Server 647
Peer-to-peer 647
Multitier 648
Benefits of Multitier Application Development 649
Scalability and Fault Tolerance 649
Development and Deployment 650
Security 651
.NET Remoting Basics 651
Architectural Overview 651
Application Domains 651
The System.Runtime.Remoting Namespace 651
Remotable Objects 653
Object Activation 654
Leases and Sponsors 655
Proxies 656
Channels 656
Your First .NET Remoting Application 657
Setting Up the Project 657
Adding References 658
BankPackage.dll: Contract Between Clients and Servers 659
Implementing the Server 661
Implementing the Client 665

30   .NET Remoting in Action   669
Template Project 669
Tracing Messages 670
Analyzing the SOAP Packets 672
Client Activation 675
The Factory Pattern 675
The Example at Runtime 681
Problems of CAOs 682
Lifetime Management 683
Failing to Renew the Lease 686
Configuration Files 686
Server Configuration 688
Client Configuration 689

Switching from HTTP to TCP Communication 695
Switching from SOAP to Binary Remoting 695
Differences Between SOAP and Binary Encoding 697

31   Securing ASP.NET Applications   699
ASP.NET Security Methods 699
Authentication 700
     Configuring ASP.NET's Authentication Model 700
     Windows Authentication 700
     Forms-Based Authentication 702
     Passport Authentication 709
Authorization 710
     File Authorization 710
     URL Authorization—The <authorization> Section 711
     Role Based Authorization 712
     Impersonization 714
Signing Off 715

32   ASP.NET Deployment and Configuration   716
Deploying ASP.NET Applications 716
     Simple Deployment Considerations 716
     XCOPY Deployment 719
Configuration Settings 720
     The machine.config File 721
     The web.config File 721
Configuration Tips 727
     Handling Errors Redirection 727
     Worker Process Restarting 728
     Output Caching for Performance 730
     Monitoring the ASP.NET Process 731
     Tracing the Application 731
Adding/Retrieving Custom Configuration Settings 736
     Adding and Reading <appSettings> 736
     Adding and Reading Custom Configuration Sections 737

33   Caching and Managing State in ASP.NET Applications   738
Caching ASP.NET Applications 738
     Page Caching 738
     Page Fragment Caching 743
     Data Caching 743
     Cache File Dependencies 746
     Extending File Dependencies for Use in SQL Server 747
     Cache-Callback Methods 749

State Management in ASP.NET Applications 751
  Managing State with Cookies 751
  Working with ViewState 753
  Session State Management 756
  Storing Session Data in a Session State Server 757
  Storing Session Data in SQL Server 758
  Session Events 759
  Application State Management 760
  Using Cache Versus Application 762

34   Developing Custom ASP.NET Server Controls   763
User Controls 763
  A Very Simple User Control 764
  Examining the Simple Control 766
  A User Login User Control 769
Web Controls 771
  Building a Very Simple Web Control 771
  Persistent Values 773
  Adding Some Custom Rendering 775
  Determining the HTML Block Type 778
  Handling Post-back Data 778
  TPostBackInputWebControl 780
  Composite Controls 783
  Implementing a Composite Control—TNewUserInfoControl 784

Index   791

About the Author

Xavier Pacheco is the president of Xapware Technologies Inc., which he founded in January 1988. Xavier and the Xapware team help companies succeed at developing software through Xapware's product, Active! Focus, a team-based software development management suite. Xavier has over 16 years of professional experience in developing software solutions such as distributed systems, application architectures, and process and design methodologies. Xavier is an internationally recognized developer, author, consultant, and trainer. He has written several books on Delphi, frequently writes articles, and gives presentations at industry conferences. Xavier and his wife Anne live in Colorado Springs, Colorado, with their children Zachary and Jessica.

About the Contributing Authors

Steven Beebe is chief operating officer and senior consultant with Xapware Technologies Inc. provider of Active! Focus, a practical solution for managing a number of aspects of software projects. Steve has been developing software and managing the development of software for over 15 years. Steve's experience ranges from managing teams from 10 to 120 professionals, in both start-up and Fortune 20 companies. Steve and his wife Diane and daughters Hannah and Sarah live in Colorado Springs, Colorado.

Alessandro Federici is a highly recognized and respected member of the Delphi community. In 2002 he founded RemObjects Software Inc., which established itself as one of the key players in the Delphi remoting and data access arena. Alessandro has over 14 years of programming experience and currently specializes in the design and development of distributed systems and architectures. Of Italian origins (Milano), Alessandro now lives in Hoffman Estates, Illinois, with his wife and cats.

Nick Hodges is a Delphi consultant and trainer and the CTO of Lemanix Corporation. Nick is the author of numerous book chapters and magazine articles, as well as a frequent speaker at the Borland Conference. He is a member of Borland's TeamB and of the Borland Conference Advisory Board. Nick also has a MS in Information Technology Management from the Naval Postgraduate school. Nick and his family live in St. Paul, Minnesota.

Brian Long is a trainer and consultant for the Delphi, C++Builder, and NET communities and regularly speaks at international conferences. As well as authoring a Borland Pascal problem-solving book in 1994 and contributing to an early Delphi book, Brian has a Q&A column in the *Delphi Magazine* and contributes to other periodicals and `http://bdn.borland.com`. Brian was nominated for the Spirit of Delphi award in 2000 and was voted as Best Speaker at BorCon in May 2002.

Rick Ross is a Senior Consultant at PILLAR Technology Group, LLC, where he helps clients deliver solutions that best utlize technology. Over his 15 years of professional experience, Rick enjoys writing sophisticated applications such as distributed systems and multithreaded applications that address specific business challenges. Rick is the co-author of *Kylix 2 Development* and has written for *Delphi Informant*. He frequently gives presentations at conferences around the world. Rick and his family live in Brighton, Michigan.

Steve Teixeira is the CTO of Falafel Software, a software development consultancy. Previously, Steve held the positions of Director of Product Architecture at Zone Labs, a leading creator of Internet security solutions, and CTO for two other software consultancies. As an R&D software engineer at Borland, Steve was instrumental in the development of Delphi and C++Builder. Steve authored five award-winning books and numerous magazine articles on software development, and is a frequent speaker at industry events worldwide.

About the Technical Editor

Hallvard Vassbotn is a veteran Delphi programmer residing in Oslo, Norway. He works as a Senior Systems Developer at Infront AS, where he develops applications for realtime financial information over the Internet, see http://www.theonlinetrader.com/. Hallvard has written numerous articles for the *Delphi Magazine*. When not hacking around in Delphi or the FCL, he spends time with his three lovely girls; Nina, Ida, and Thea.

Dedication

This book is dedicated to my children, Amanda, Zachary, and Jessica. It is through them that I am reminded of the unfathomable love of my heavenly Father; that despite my inadequacies, He has entrusted these precious ones to my care.

Second, it is for the men and women who volunteer to serve in our armed forces, knowing that they might, one day, make the ultimate sacrifice so that we can enjoy our abundant freedoms. We don't deserve what you do for us.

Acknowledgments

This is my favorite part of writing a book because it is where I get to thank the people who REALLY made this book happen. Some of these people were directly involved with the work itself. Others were involved as supporters and cheerers. Both deserve more than mere mention. Both have my deepest gratitude and respect.

Invariably, because of my imperfect memory, I forget to mention by name many who contributed their share of hard work and support. Please forgive me for my oversight and accept my heartfelt thank you.

When I wrote my first book, *Delphi 1 Developer's Guide*, my wife Anne recalls going to bed and waking to the sound of typing. This time wasn't much different. Anne received little attention from me, but she paid utmost attention to me. I didn't talk much, but she did, to God, continually praying for me. She always cheered me on and encouraged me to write to the best of my ability. I can only hope that I live up to her example of Christ's love that she has shown me. This book exists because of her.

Thank you, Michael Stephens, for taking on this project and assigning to it a superb team to whom I am also grateful. These people are Loretta Yates, Songlin Qiu, George Nedeff, Rhonda Tinch-Mize, Dan Sherf, and the many people at Sams whom I've never met but whose excellent work I see in the final product.

I owe enormous gratitude to the contributing authors whose superior talents and expertise are reflected in the chapters they wrote. These are Steven Beebe, Alessandro Federici, Brian Long, Nick Hodges, Rick Ross, Steve Teixeira, and Hallvard Vassbotn. Hallvard deserves special mention. Hallvard was the technical reviewer for this book, but he did much more than that. Hallvard put many hours into making sure that this book was of the highest technical quality. You will find his words and code throughout each chapter—many of which I simply copied and pasted directly from his comments to me.

Writing this book is a demanding endeavor; there were those who supported my family and me during this time. First, I must thank my good friend and my brother Steven Beebe, his wife Diane, and their children Hannah and Sarah. Thank you for your help when Jessica was born; thank you for always being available, flexible, willing, and joyful when we needed you to lean on. I also want to thank my father-in-law Bob, who helped out with everything during Jessica's first days, giving me some time to work on this book. Thank you Rev. Joseph Wheat for your leadership, wisdom, and the Wednesday morning hikes. Many thanks to Bruce Beebe, Paul Adams, Rev. John Rantal, and Doug McIntire, my prayer warriors, sounding boards, and advisors. Thank you to the musicians, writers, and all involved in the Indelible Grace group (www.igracemusic.com) whose music was listened to while writing this book.

Most importantly, I cannot adequately thank the One to whom I owe my life, Jesus Christ—my Lord, my Savior and my God. You have given me all I have—my wife, children, work, skills, and my passion for programming and writing books such as this. You have blessed me with prosperity and trials, faithfully refining me and loving me. Thank You for Your gift of eternal life—my God; my King!

Soli Deo Gloria!

We Want to Hear from You!

As the reader of this book, *you* are our most important critic and commentator. We value your opinion and want to know what we're doing right, what we could do better, what areas you'd like to see us publish in, and any other words of wisdom you're willing to pass our way.

As an associate publisher for Sams Publishing, I welcome your comments. You can email or write me directly to let me know what you did or didn't like about this book—as well as what we can do to make our books better.

Please note that I cannot help you with technical problems related to the topic of this book. We do have a User Services group, however, where I will forward specific technical questions related to the book.

When you write, please be sure to include this book's title and author as well as your name, email address, and phone number. I will carefully review your comments and share them with the author and editors who worked on the book.

Email: feedback@samspublishing.com

Mail: Michael Stephens
Associate Publisher
Sams Publishing
800 East 96th Street
Indianapolis, IN 46240 USA

For more information about this book or another Sams Publishing title, visit our Web site at www.samspublishing.com. Type the ISBN (excluding hyphens) or the title of a book in the Search field to find the page you're looking for.

Introduction

*D*elphi for *.NET Developer's Guide* is a book about developing to .NET and specifically doing so using Delphi. This book doesn't rehash content covered in previous Delphi Developer's Guide books. With the exception of Chapter 5, "The Delphi Language," the material is all new. I've also taken a slightly different approach with this book than that of my previous works. Here, you will find more examples that illustrate a few or single concepts rather than larger listings that combine concepts. It will be easier for you to examine the technique without having to sift through unrelated code.

Additionally, I have intentionally avoided as much as possible using IDE's facilities. For instance, in the chapters on ADO.NET, you will see that I set properties programmatically. I did this so that you can see which properties are used and to avoid having to write out instructions on IDE usability that end up cluttering the text of the actual technique. However, because using the IDE is important to development productivity, Chapter 3 "Introduction to Delphi for .NET and the New IDE," highlights several of the IDE capabilities that help you to be productive when developing. Essentially, my goal was to write a book specifically about .NET that is technique oriented, using Delphi rather than a book about Delphi for .NET.

Who Should Read This Book

As the title of this book says, this book is for developers and, specifically, .NET developers using Delphi. In particular, this book is aimed at three groups of people:

- Professional Delphi developers who are looking to take their craft to the next level and start targeting .NET.

- .NET developers using another language who want to learn about how Delphi does .NET.

- Beginning programmers who want to learn .NET and want to do so using a powerful, intuitive language.

How This Book Is Organized

Delphi for .NET Developer's Guide is divided into five parts:

- Part I, "Introduction to the .NET Framework," provides some overview chapters about .NET in general and on Framework specifics.

- Part II, "Delphi for .NET Programming Language," covers specifics about Delphi for .NET, the IDE, and quite a bit about the Delphi language.

- Part III, "The .NET Framework Class Library Development," discusses core concepts when developing to the .NET Framework. For instance, in this section you will find chapters on threading, reflection, streaming, memory management, and so on.

- Part IV, "Database Development with ADO.NET," goes into the details of using Delphi along with ADO.NET to create database applications.

- Part V, "Internet Development with ASP.NET," delves into the various techniques for creating Web applications using ASP.NET.

What's on the Companion CD-ROM

You will find all the source code and project files on the CD-ROM accompanying this book, as well as source samples that we could not fit in the book itself. The source directory is divided up by chapter and further by example such as

```
\Code\Chapter 01\Ex01
\Code\Chapter 01\Ex02
\Code\Chapter 02\Ex01
. . .
```

Within the chapters and following each listing, you will find a reference showing where to locate the source for the listing on the CD.

On the CD, you will also find the entire *Delphi 6 Developer's Guide* book with individual .pdf files for each chapter. You'll find this under the folder \D6DG. The code for *Delphi 6 Developers Guide* is also included. In essence, you have two books in one. The code is located in the folder \D6DG\Code.

Finally, you will find numerous demos of third-party tools/components that you can use in developing Delphi for .NET applications.

Conventions Used in This Book

The following typographic conventions are used in this book:

- Code lines, commands, statements, variables, program output, and any text you see on the screen appears in a computer typeface with numbered lines for easy reference.

- Anything that you type appears in a bold computer typeface.

- Placeholders in syntax descriptions appear in an italic computer typeface. Replace the placeholder with the actual filename, parameter, or whatever element it represents.

- Boldface highlights technical terms when they first appear in the text, and italics is sometimes used to emphasize important points.

- Procedures and functions are indicated by open and close parentheses after the procedure or function name. Although this is not standard Pascal syntax, it helps to differentiate them from properties, variables, and types.

Within each chapter, you will encounter several Notes, Tips, and Cautions that help to highlight the important points and aid you in steering clear of the pitfalls.

Delphi for .NET Developer's Guide Web Site

The Web site for this book is located at www.DelphiGuru.com, where you will find updates, extras, and errata information for this book. You will also find a topical index to the book's various listings and code examples.

Introduction to .NET

PART I:
INTRODUCTION TO
THE .NET FRAMEWORK

CHAPTER 1   Introduction
to .NET

CHAPTER 2   Overview of the
NET Framework

IN THIS CHAPTER

- The .NET Initiative
- Distributed Development
through Web Services

The Internet is increasingly becoming a fundamental part of every aspect of our lives. Businesses rely on it. Education grows from it, and our personal lives are simplified by it. Modern Web sites are not only informational, but highly interactive.

For the individual, one can easily plan a trip, purchase an airline ticket, rent a hotel, and get information on events and spots to visit within minutes. One can even get reviews on various businesses, services, and locations.

Businesses can now reach and sell to broad, worldwide markets. The Internet is probably the most substantial source for up-to-date, real-time information critical to business decision makers.

With all this capability, it might seem peevish to infer that things could be better. The fact is that the Internet is still a hodgepodge of uncooperating technologies. How much better it would be if the services obtained through the Internet could work together overall improving the end-user experience and productivity.

Perhaps, for instance, your travel plans can include recommendations on restaurants based on your own personal tastes. From this, you might immediately reserve your table. Suppose that you are on a waiting list for a better flight. You might be alerted through your mobile device or PDA so that you can quickly make any adjustments to your schedule—real time. As a business user, you might not only want to know who has the lowest prices for a particular item, but also when a vendor offers an item at a lower cost without having to perform the manual research.

The truth is that, technically, this capability exists today. It is really a matter having such services developed and consumed so that they can become useable to the general community.

The .NET Initiative

According to Microsoft,

> ".NET is the Microsoft solution for Web Services, the next generation of software that connects our world of information, devices, and people in a unified, personalized way."

When Microsoft started talking about .NET (and even after its release), there was great confusion over exactly what it was. People weren't sure whether .NET was a new framework, operating system, or programming language. In reality, .NET is really a brand for Microsoft's vision for distributed development based on Microsoft's new technology. We call this technology the .NET Framework and it is through the .NET Framework that we develop Web Services.

Although it seems that building distributed systems on Web Services is the main objective of .NET, there is so much more to the .NET initiative. In the following sections, I attempt to shed some light and give a high-level overview of .NET and what it means to us developers, as well as to the end users of the systems we develop.

The .NET Vision

Certainly, there are many objectives to the .NET initiative. The following objectives appear to be more prominent in the Microsoft and other distributions, and they are covered in detail next:

- Faster, Easier Development
- Seamless Deployment of Applications
- Anytime, Anywhere Access to Services and Data
- Collaborating Apps

Faster, Easier Development

For developers, .NET is an exciting new development platform that overcomes many limitations of existing platforms. Overall, this new platform increases development productivity by helping developers become more efficient. In other words, development has been made easier, enabling developers to develop faster. This new platform is called the .NET Framework.

The .NET Framework encompasses a rich and extensible set of classes that give developers a wealth of powerful development tools. These classes make available everything from low-level system functions to elegant user-interface controls.

The .NET Framework goes much beyond just class libraries, however. Its core components allow developers to code for any device using any language that conforms to .NET specification. It frees the developer from having to worry about underlying tasks such as memory management and, with some .NET languages, type safety. It allows him to focus on the development solution. No other platform makes it as easy to share code between languages. Developers will no longer have to manually translate header files to use types from another language, for instance.

Microsoft .NET is also supported by more than 20 languages, including of course, the Delphi Language, also known as Object Pascal, which this book covers.

Seamless Deployment of Applications

Anyone who has done any reading on .NET has seen or heard the phrase "DLL Hell." Anyone who develops software for Windows knows exactly what these people are talking about. For some, like myself, hell is a trip to the shopping mall; for others, nothing can invoke terror like finding that important applications, or Windows itself, fail to run after having installed a new application on your system.

Windows, as well as the applications that run on it, uses and distributes Dynamic Link Libraries (DLLs). Other applications often use functions that reside in these DLLs. Problems occur when a user installs or updates an application that overwrites a DLL used by these other applications. When the new DLL's functionality is different from the original, other applications can misbehave.

Another feature of hell is writing and maintaining installation programs for Windows. I know this firsthand, having written installation programs and having to deal with the maze of Windows interdependencies. Registering server DLLs and dealing with the registry and user security on both personal computers and computers within a network domain are only a few of the battles you must deal with. Then, when your installation is finally working on a clean Windows installation running under a virtual machine (which mirrors nobody's system), you have to write an uninstall program to try to undo the mess you have created. Installation programs claim to solve this problem; however, they do not provide the means to perform low-level routines that you end up having to code for anyway.

With applications spewing pieces of themselves throughout your system, it's no wonder that Windows and Windows applications become unstable over time and have a reputation for being...buggy.

Microsoft .NET aims to solve this problem in how it deals with the deployment of .NET applications. This is another feature of the .NET Framework that I will discuss in Part III.

Anytime, Anywhere Access to Services and Data

Web Services are the component to .NET that Microsoft and others claim will revolutionize how developers build solutions and how users acquire and use these solutions. With the reality of powerful personal computers and other devices and the outlook of ubiquitous Internet access, such claims are not far-fetched. Three elements factor into this "anytime, anywhere" idea. First, the Internet is always accessible. Second, Web Services provide functionality via the Internet. Last, Web Services can target any device be it a personal computer, handheld organizer, mobile phone, or any other device designed to work with Web Services.

In general, developers can build solutions by incorporating existing functionality made available through Web Services. Therefore, instead of having to write or buy an accounting calculations package, developers can use one that exists from the Internet. By not having to program these and other functions in an online payroll package, for instance, developers can focus on the business solution and not so much on the internals of implementing it. Chapter 28, "Web Services," discusses building Web Services using Delphi for .NET.

Collaborating Apps

Web Services enables organizations to continue to use their existing automated services that currently cannot communicate with each other. Since Web Services are based on the XML technology, they can be used in integrating these proprietary systems. In many systems, the typical approach to integration involves exporting data to a file readable by customized code used to import into another system. By providing a collaborative layer through Web Services/XML, the proprietary nature of systems can be contained while exposing their functionality. Other systems can harness this functionality, enabling organizations to build complete enterprisewide business solutions.

The .NET Framework Components—the Common Language Runtime and Class Libraries

The .NET Framework is the core technology for building and running applications. It consists primarily of two components: the Common Language Runtime and Class Libraries.

NOTE

It would be impossible to cover the entire .NET Framework in this book. However, you will see key elements of the Framework discussed in this book's various chapters. Microsoft has complete documentation of the .NET Framework online at

`http://msdn.microsoft.com/library/`

- Common Language Runtime (CLR)—The CLR is a runtime environment that provides the services needed by all .NET applications. Some of these services include compilation, memory management, and garbage collection. The CLR also enforces a common type system. By having this within the CLR, the CLR can work with applications written in any .NET language. In fact, by the time the CLR deals with the code, it has already been compiled to a common, generic Intermediate Language (IL). Any CLR-compliant compiler can generate IL code. I will cover this process in more detail in Chapter 2, "Overview of the .NET Framework."

- Class Libraries—The .NET Framework includes a rich set of class library assemblies. These assemblies contain numerous types whose functionality is available to developers and with which they can develop any of the applications listed in the following section. Some of these technologies that you have probably heard of are ASP.NET and ADO.NET. Borland, with Delphi for .NET, has now introduced VCL for .NET, which extends the user interface component of the .NET Framework and makes the migration of existing Delphi applications faster and easier.

NOTE

The VCL for .NET is a port of Delphi's original Visual Component Library (VCL) to the .NET platform. Borland did this port to make developing .NET applications easier for existing Delphi developers since they will be able to get up and running with .NET using all the classes with which they are already familiar.

Types of .NET Applications

You can create several types of applications with the .NET Framework. These are Web Forms, Windows Forms, Web Services, and console applications. The following sections will discuss each of these.

Web Forms (ASP.NET)

Web Form Applications are applications whose GUI is based on dynamically generated HTML. Typically, the HTML display would have been generated through complex queries against database servers or from some other source. ASP.NET is the Microsoft server-based technology that enables you to develop dynamic and interactive Web pages. Part V of this book illustrates how to take advantage of ASP.NET using Delphi for .NET.

Windows Forms

When highly functional user interfaces are needed, .NET provides the powerful capabilities of the Windows desktop environment. Developers can separate the data and business from the presentation layer. Many of the examples used in the various chapters in this book demonstrate the general usage of Windows Forms. Chapter 13, "Windows Forms and VCL for .NET," discusses Windows forms specifically and also covers Borland's VCL for .NET components for creating Windows Forms applications.

Web Service Applications

Simply put, Web Services are remote procedure calls made over the Internet using XML as the communication message format and HTTP/HTTPS as the communication means. A Web Service can encompass specific functionality to be used in creating an application, or it can encompass an entire application. Either way, Web Services are considered applications in and of themselves. I will discuss Web Services a bit more in this chapter and throughout this book.

Console Applications

Occasionally, developers have the need to write simple applications/utilities that require no graphical/interactive user interface. In this case, you can develop console applications under .NET, or using Delphi for .NET, you can still resort to the Win32 compiler that will generate native executables not reliant on the .NET Framework or CLR.

Windows Service Applications

Windows Service Applications are applications that are required to run for a long period of time. They also run when nobody is logged on to the computer and are started when the computer boots up. It is possible to create such applications under .NET.

.NET Components

The .NET Framework contains components that you can use in building any of the aforementioned application types. Additionally, you, as a developer, can extend the .NET Framework by writing your own reusable components, allowing you to standardize functionality throughout your organization. Additionally, you can sell you components to the .NET community as many vendors are currently doing. Although components aren't specifically considered applications, they are a final product that is created by .NET Developers much like applications.

> **NOTE**
>
> Many third-party components extend the existing components already available in the .NET Framework. You can perform a google.com search on ".NET Components" or browse the CD accompanying this book, which contains many of these vendors' products.

VCL for .NET Explained

When Borland jumped onto the .NET bandwagon, one of the decisions the company made was to support its existing Delphi user base in migrating to .NET. It came up with a .NET implementation of the Visual Component Library. The VCL for .NET can be used advantageously in at least three areas. First, it can serve as a means to help existing Delphi developers learn about .NET. Second, it can be used to help you port existing VCL-based applications to the .NET Framework. Finally, it might be possible to write a single-source application that targets Win32, .NET, and possibly Linux (using Kylix and CLX). Chapter 13 discusses VCL for .NET in more detail.

Distributed Development through Web Services

The idea behind Web Services is not new. Ever since we have been dealing with distributed computing, it has been beneficial to break up the functional components of systems. This allows for better distribution of work loads, scalability, security, and so on.

Many models of distributed development are still based on tightly coupled and closed functional systems. Integration of systems is still dreadfully painful, yet the need is significant. An example would be integrating large-scale accounting systems with a process manufacturing system.

Through Web Services, functional components (which I will call Services from here on), are exposed to various consumers. A consumer, for instance, might be a Web site through which an individual can plan an entire vacation. This Web site would consume Services provided by other service providers. For instance, it might make use of Microsoft's MapPoint Web Service for obtaining maps and directions, somebody else's restaurant reservation service, and yet other services for flights, cabs, and so on.

Consumers do not have to be Web sites. A company's systemwide computing capability can be integrated through Services. Sales forces might have access to a CRM system in a Web interface. This same CRM system might integrate with Accounting's finance system, which users work with in a Web Forms application. This finance system might work with a separate inventory control system behind-the-scenes through more Web Services, and so forth.

The basic elements of Web Services are the services themselves, clients, developer tools, and servers.

Web Services—Defined

Web Services are discrete, decoupled, and reusable applications that expose their functionality through a Web interface. By Web interface, I don't mean a Web page. Instead, it communicates with the outside world through Remote Procedure Calls (RPC) over a protocol such as HTTP. The form of communication is the Extensible Markup Language (XML), and more specifically, the Simple Object Access Protocol (SOAP).

This idea of RPC over the Internet is nothing new. But what makes Web Services innovational is the idea that any client and any server can make use of such services regardless of their implementation language and device on which they reside. A Web Service can be developed in Delphi for .NET and can make available functionality residing in a Server for clients written in C#, Perl, or mobile WAP devices. Web Services are truly decoupled and disparate systems unlike other distributed technologies.

Web Services enable applications to share data and functionality in a revolutionary way in that it does not matter how these discrete applications were implemented, nor on which platform O/S or device they reside.

Web Service Universality

By using industry standard protocols, Web Services are universal when exposed through the Internet. These include XML, SOAP, and Universal Description, Discovery, and Integration (UDDI). Such standards are those defined by the World Wide Web Consortium (W3C).

> **NOTE**
>
> The World Wide Consortium (W3C) is a nonprofit membership-based authority for defining and developing technologies (specifications, guidelines, software, and tools) relevant to the use of the World Wide Web. Information on W3C can be obtained through its Web site at www.w3c.org.

You should be familiar with the following Web Services terms that are used throughout the book:

- XML—Extensible Markup Language. XML is a flexible text-based format originally derived from SGML for the purpose of electronic publishing. XML's richness and self-defining format make it ideal for use in passing messages between Web Service consumers.

- SOAP—Simple Object Access Protocol. SOAP is the protocol for Web Services based on the XML standard for invoking remote procedure calls over the Internet/intranet. SOAP specifies the format of the request and the format of parameters passed in the request. SOAP is only specific to the message and imposes no requirements on the implementation of the Web Service or of its consumer.

- WSDL—Web Service Description Language. WSDL is an XML based language that is used to describe the facilities of a Web Service. This includes all the various methods and their parameters as well as the location of the Web Service. Web Service consumers can understand WSDL and can determine the functionality provided by the Web Service.

- UDDI—Universal Description, Discovery, and Integration. UDDI is a public registry for storing information about and for publishing Web Services. You can visit UDDI at www.uddi.org.

Web Service Communication Benefits

Web Services offer a bridging component to disconnected applications enabling better integration of these discrete systems.

This integration enables organizations to integrate their internal systems much more seamlessly. By utilizing the .NET benefits such as language and platform independence, businesses can focus less on implementation and integration complexities and more on what information and functionality makes sense to integrate. Anybody who has ever participated in integrating systems understands the pains of dealing with different data formatting between systems. By shielding the implementation and definition details of these systems with a common communication medium, these issues can become transparent.

Organizations can also benefit by integrating with external resources. Consider a software company that develops and sells its own products. Instead of having to acquire or build an issue management system that integrates with its CRM package, the company might find a resource that provides the integration through Web Services.

Web Services also integrate with customers. Customers become Web Service consumers, for instance, when they start using Internet services that use Web Services. The previously mentioned example of the travel planning site is one example of what this might look like.

Web Service Clients

To get a feel of how applications communicate via Web Services, consider Figure 1.1.

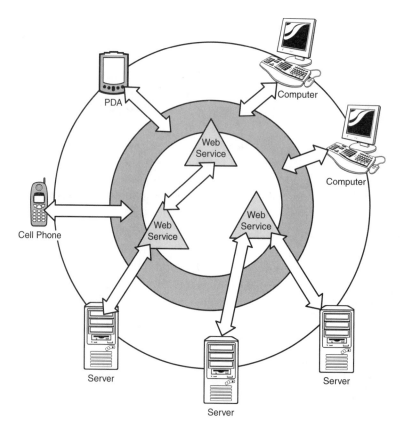

FIGURE 1.1   Web Service topology.

In Figure 1.1, you see clients connecting to Web Services that are connecting to servers. In the case of a client connecting to a Web Service to get data from a server, the client is a consumer of the Web Service. Also note that a server can make use of a Web Service for accessing data from another server. This also makes the invoking server a consumer. Finally, Web Services can make use of other Web Services. Although this illustrates a likely layout of a system, it does not illustrate how some of these Web Services can be internal whereas others are external. Eventually, the availability of Web Services will enable you to create highly complex business systems.

> **NOTE**
>
> Microsoft has introduced the notion of Smart Clients. Smart Clients are software products that make heavy use of Web Service technologies from both a standpoint of functionality and deployment. For instance, a Smart Client product might invoke calendaring/scheduling, contact management, and email management from three different Web Services. It might also perform self updates from a centralized server and still have the capability to work offline. All of this is foreseen to be device independent so that it would function on a PDA and with a desktop computer.

Web Service Development Tools

Delphi for .NET is one of the tools that developers can use to develop Web Services. Chapter 28 discusses how to use Delphi for .NET to develop both Web Services and the applications that consume them.

Reusability

By developing systems as disparate Web Services, development teams can take greater advantage of code reusability. This topic was a hot item when object-oriented programming became the hype. The idea was that a developer could develop a component that other developers could use by linking it into their source code. Web Services takes this concept to another level. Now, developers simply use the functionality provided by the Web Service through a common interface. By reusing internal and external Services, overall development productivity is increased.

Language Neutrality

Another benefit to Web Services (and .NET development in general) is their language neutrality. Developers need not concern themselves with how or in what language Web Services are developed. This is a benefit to large companies with multiple development teams that might use different development languages and databases. Through Web Services, communication/integration can occur across the enterprise without regard for these distinct systems.

Servers

To effectively provide a Web Service solution, you must understand how to deploy them and on what types of servers they must be deployed. If such servers are to meet the demands placed on them through Web Services, they must work intimately with the language of Web Services (XML) and be capable of being developed against with Web Service development tools such as Delphi for .NET.

IN THIS CHAPTER

- From Development to Execution
- The Common Language Runtime (CLR)
- The Common Type System (CTS)
- The Common Language Specification (CLS)
- .NET Framework and Base Class Library (FCL)

CHAPTER **2**

Overview of the .NET Framework

This chapter provides an overview of the core component of the .NET—the .NET Framework. The .NET Framework is the technical entity that enables developers to deliver on the business solutions discussed in Chapter 1, "Introduction to .NET."

From Development to Execution

In a simplified illustration, the steps to develop and execute a .NET application are

1. Write a program in your .NET language flavor of choice.

2. Compile your code to the Intermediate Language (IL) residing in a managed module.

3. Combine your managed modules to form an assembly.

4. Distribute/deploy your assembly to the target platform.

5. Invoke the CLR that loads, compiles, executes, and manages your code.

To make all this work, it takes several components of the .NET Framework. Figure 2.1 shows the Framework's components. These components are the .NET programming languages that appear in the top row of Figure 2.1. The Common Language Specification (CLS) are rules for .NET language developers such as Borland, the Framework Class Library (FCL), the Common Language Runtime (CLR), and development environments such as Delphi for .NET and Visual Studio .NET. This chapter discusses each component in greater detail.

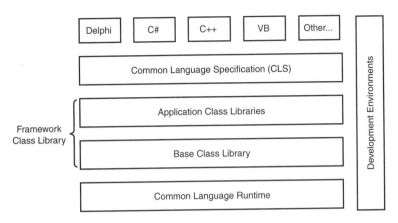

FIGURE 2.1   The .NET Framework.

The Common Language Runtime (CLR)

The Common Language Runtime (CLR) is a key component to the .NET Framework. The CLR handles the execution of .NET applications and provides necessary runtime services for these applications. The CLR, when invoked, performs the required operations to compile, allocate memory for, and manage the code of the invoking application. Although similar, in part, to the way that interpreted languages work, the CLR is anything but an interpreted system.

The CLR operates on an intermediate representation of the original code written in some .NET compliant languages such as Delphi or C#. This code, called the Microsoft Intermediate Language (MSIL) or simply Intermediate Language (IL), is contained in a file called a managed module. Managed modules contain other information required by the CLR, and are covered in the following subsections.

Managed Modules

Managed modules are generated by the .NET language compilers. A managed module is a Windows Portable Executable (PE) and consists for four pieces.

- PE Header—A standard Windows PE Header.

- CLR Header—Header information specific to the CLR and for use by the CLR.

- Metadata—Metadata consists of tables describing the types, members, and references to other modules.

- Managed Code—Managed code is in a common language that .NET compilers generate from .NET-compliant languages. This language is called the Microsoft Intermediate Language (MSIL).

Even though managed modules are Portable Executables, they require the CLR to execute and even so, they cannot be executed independently, but first must be incorporated into an assembly.

Assemblies

Assemblies are essentially a packaging and deployment unit for .NET applications. They can contain complete .NET applications or sharable functionality for other .NET applications. A .NET application is, in fact, an assembly.

Assemblies can contain one or more managed modules. Assemblies can also contain resource files such as images, html, and so on. Assemblies contain your .NET applications and enable better security around code access, type definition, scope, deployment, and versioning. Assemblies are similar to the classical Win32 executable (*.exe), dynamic link library (*.dll), and Delphi package (*.bpl) files. They are different in that they overcome many of the problems associated with Win32 specific files.

First, assemblies are versioned, and different versions can reside on the same system. Therefore, two applications might be using two different versions of an assembly—no more DLL hell.

Second, assemblies can run side-by-side, which is not easily possible when using DLLs.

Finally, installing assemblies is a matter of copying the file to the directory in which you want it to reside.

Chapter 6, "Assemblies," discusses the creation of assemblies and how to deploy them in detail.

Managed and Unmanaged Code

Code that is managed by the CLR is called managed code. Managed code relies on the CLR's runtime services such as type verification, memory management, and garbage collection. An advantage to managed code is that it enables the CLR to take care of many house-keeping tasks that the programmer would otherwise have to handle.

It is still possible, however, to write unmanaged code in a .NET application. By doing so, the responsibility to allocate and free memory falls on the programmer. Additionally, unmanaged code does not benefit from the runtime services offered to manage code. Nevertheless, sometimes it is necessary to write unmanaged code to handle low-level tasks or to use functionality only available outside of the CLR's services.

> **NOTE**
>
> The Delphi for .NET compiler (DCCIL) does not support unmanaged code. In fact, currently only Microsoft's C++.NET supports mixing managed and unmanaged code in the same module. You can, however, use Delphi 7 for Win32 to write unmanaged code in a separate DLL (exposing COM objects or plain routines). The routines in this DLL can be invoked from managed DCCIL code by using P/Invoke or COM Interop. Additionally, using unmanaged code essentially makes your code platform specific. COM Interop is covered in Chapter 16, "COM and COM+ Interoperability."

MSIL and JIT Compilation and Execution

The MSIL, sometimes called the Common Intermediate Language (CIL), is a format akin to assembly code but independent of any target platform/CPU. Languages such as Delphi and

C# are precompiled to MSIL. Because the MSIL gets distributed, developers can write .NET applications in a multitude of languages. In fact, the IL code, along with the metadata describing it, enables these languages to interact directly with any other .NET-compliant language. In other words, I can write a class in Visual Basic .NET that can be used directly by my Delphi for .NET or C# code. I will get into some specific examples of this later on.

Where the .NET/MSIL paradigm differs from interpreted technologies has to do with just-in-time (JIT) compilation. Consider Figure 2.2, which illustrates the load, compile, execute sequence of the CLR.

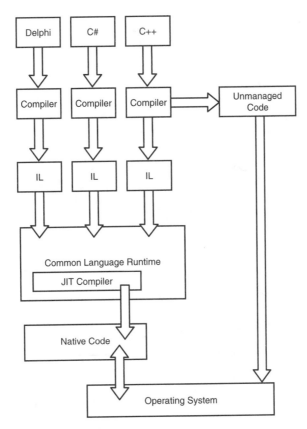

FIGURE 2.2 The CLR load, compile, execute sequence.

First, a programmer uses a .NET language compiler such as Delphi for .NET or C# to generate an assembly (IL code with metadata). When the code is executed, or more accurately stated, when the CLR executes the code, it handles some important tasks. The CLR loads the code (classes and their members), allocates and arranges memory, and performs type verification. Basically, the class loader prepares the code for compilation. The class loader does this using an on-demand mechanism. Therefore, classes are not loaded unless they are referenced. When this code is prepared, the JIT compiler is ready to compile the IL code into the native machine code. The JIT compiler also uses an on-demand mechanism in that it compiles methods only if they are referenced and if they have not already been compiled. Therefore, once a method is compiled to native CPU code, it does not have to be compiled again. Once compiled, the CLR's execution engine runs the compiled code. Also note that the loading of code and JIT compilation is initiated from the Execution Engine. The CLR might be sophisticated enough to inline the machine code generated directly at the point of invocation. This might result in smaller and/or faster code.

.NET EVERYWHERE?

Microsoft is currently providing CLR implementations for mobile units such as Pocket PC targeting a number of different CPU architectures such as ARM, MIPS, and SH3. Additionally, efforts are under way to port the .NET Framework to other platforms such as Linux, FreeBSD, and Unix. If these efforts succeed, it is likely that we will see the CLR running our same code on multiple machines, just as Java does today, but with much more efficiency.

Other subcomponents of the CLR are shown in Figure 2.3.

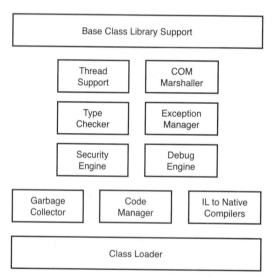

FIGURE 2.3   The CLR subcomponents.

These subcomponents work together to form the runtime services needed for .NET applications.

For instance, the Execution Engine is the component that handles the actual execution of managed code. It manages getting code compiled so that it can be executed. The execution engine of the CLR works in conjunction with the other CLR components such as the Garbage Collector (GC). The code manager allocates space on the managed heap for managed objects. When these objects are no longer referenced, the GC takes care of disposing of them and removing them from the heap. The GC changes what we are used to in dealing with memory management in Win32 Delphi development. Chapter 9, "Memory Management and Garbage Collection," discusses the GC in more detail.

The Common Type System (CTS)

The CTS is a rich standard set of types and operations within the CLR. According to Microsoft, the CTS supports complete implementation of most programming languages. Many languages will use some sort of naming alias to refer to a specific type within the CTS. For instance, the type System.Int32 in the CTS is an integer in Delphi, and an int in C#. Although named differently at the language level, they both map to the same underlying type. This aspect of the CTS contributes to language interoperability.

The benefits of having the CTS are at least three-fold. It provides a level of language interoperability. Second, because all types are derived from one base class, all types have a common interface. Finally, the CTS guarantees type safety with any code that you develop.

The CTS is built in to the CLR and defines, verifies, and manages the runtime use of these types. All types derive from a base class, System.Object. From this, types will fall in one of two categories: Value Types and Reference Types. Figure 2.4 depicts a chart showing the hierarchical relationship between these types.

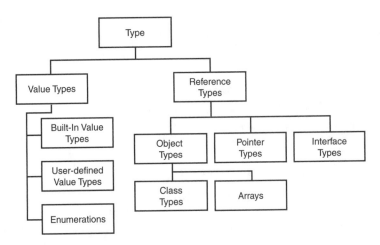

FIGURE 2.4   Types in the CTS.

Value Types

Value Types are simple data types that can be maintained on the stack and directly contain their data. Figure 2.4 shows that there are three derivations of the Value Type: Built-in, User-defined, and Enumerations.

Built-in Value Types are primitive data types such as integer, double, and bool. User-defined types are basically records. Because they are maintained on the stack, it makes sense to keep these small. An Enumeration is a set of named integer constants in which each constant represents a specified value within the set.

Reference Types

Reference Types are allocated on the heap. A Reference Type's variable stores the address to the actual type's heap instance. If you have developed with Delphi before, you will be very familiar with heap based types because they are practically synonymous with the Delphi TObject type. The three base Reference Types are Object Types, Pointer Types, and Interface Types. As shown in Figure 2.4, Class and Array Types are basically derivatives of the Object Type. You will occasionally hear Object Types referred to as self-describing.

The Common Language Specification (CLS)

The CLS defines a subset of the CTS rules around types, naming conventions, and other language implementation attributes that enable cross language integration. These rules are outlined in Partition I of the Common Language Infrastructure standardization proposal of the European Computer Manufactures Association (ECMA). These are the rules that language designers must adhere to if they want their languages to target the CLR and inter-act with other languages. This does not mean that languages or your applications that use such languages must adhere to CLS-only constraints. In fact, many language features, although valid in the CTS, are not valid in the CLS. If you desire to guarantee cross languages compatibility, you must code according to the CLS only the code that you intend to expose to other languages.

> **TIP**
>
> It is possible to check your code for CLS compliancy by using tools such as FxCop. FxCop is downloadable from
>
> `http://www.gotdotnet.com/team/fxcop/.`
>
> Additionally, information about the CLS can be obtained from
>
> `http://msdn.microsoft.com/net/ecma/.`

.NET Framework Class Library (FCL)

The .NET Framework Class Library (FCL) is a rich object-oriented library composed of classes, interfaces, types, and other elements for programming .NET applications. The FCL provides developers with preexisting code and functionality to perform common program-ming tasks. The FCL is similar in nature to the VCL in Delphi, the MFC in Visual C++, and other such libraries. One major difference is that the FCL is available to all .NET languages. Consider the benefit of a unified class library. Prior to .NET, Delphi developers could only use Visual C++ functionality if it was exposed through a DLL or COM. Now, if you learn the FCL, you will be able to directly use the classes provided by the FCL from any language. The following subsections discuss some of the main features of the FCL.

Namespaces

Namespaces in .NET are logical and organizational units of types. Namespaces enable the containment of types and functionality and are hierarchically grouped into levels of logical specificity.

The System Namespace

The System namespace contains base classes used by other classes in the framework. It also defines the value and reference data types, events, event handlers, interfaces, attributes, and exception processing. The System namespace declares the base of all classes, the `Object` class. All types in .NET ultimately derive from the Object class.

Primary Subsystem Namespaces

Table 2.1 shows the primary subsystem namespaces in the FCL. As you develop for .NET, you will become more familiar with the types within these names. Many of these types will be used in the examples throughout this book.

TABLE 2.1   FCL Namespaces

Name	Functional Containment
System.CodeDOM	Classes and interfaces representing the elements and structure of a source code document.
System.Collections	Classes and interfaces that define collection based objects (lists, queues, bit arrays, hash tables, and dictionaries).
System.ComponentModel	Classes and interfaces for supporting the design-time/runtime component implementation.
System.Configuration	Classes and interfaces for programmatically accessing .NET Framework and application configuration settings.
System.Data	Classes and interfaces that make up the ADO.NET framework for managing data from multiple data sources.
System.DirectoryServices	Classes for accessing the Active Directory through managed code.
System.Drawing	Access to GDI+ drawing functionality.
System.EnterpriseServices	COM+ accessibility.
System.Globalization	Classes for defining culture-related settings.
System.IO	Types for reading/writing files, streams, and file/directory manipulation.
System.Management	Accessibility to the Windows Management Instrumentation (WMI).
System.Messaging	Classes for accessing, monitoring, and administrating network message queues.
System.Net	Programming interface for network protocols.
System.Reflection	Classes and interfaces that provide runtime view and invocation of types, methods, and fields.
System.Resources	Classes and interfaces for managing culture-specific resources.
System.Runtime.CompilerServices	Access to runtime behavior of the CLR used by compiler writers.
System.Runtime.InteropServices	Access to COM objects.
System.Runtime.Remoting	Access to object and methods running in another AppDomain or machine.
System.Runtime.Serialization	Used for serializing objects to and from streams.
System.Security	Access to the underlying CLR security system.
System.ServiceProcess	Classes to support the creation and management of Windows services.
System.Text	Classes supporting text formatting capabilities.
System.Threading	Classes that enable multithreaded programming.
System.Timers	Timer functionality.
System.Web	Classes for browser/server communication. This is otherwise known as ASP.NET.
System.Windows.Forms	Classes to support Windows desktop applications.
System.XML	Support for XML programming.

Literally hundreds of types are defined within the namespaces described in Table 2.1. Depending on the type of development you are doing, you will likely use some more frequently than others. For instance, if you are developing GUI applications, you will use many of the types defined in the System.Windows.Forms namespace. If you are writing database applications, you will use the types contained in the System.Data namespace. Admittedly, this is only a high-level view of the FCL namespaces. As you become more familiar with the FCL, you will find that you will be able to navigate through the various namespace hierarchies to find the specific type you need for just about any programming task.

A simple example provided in Listing 2.1 illustrates using two namespaces from Table 2.1. These are the System.Windows.Forms and System.Drawing namespaces.

LISTING 2.1   First Delphi for .NET Example

```
1:    program d4dgCh2Ex1;
2:
3:    {%DelphiDotNetAssemblyCompiler '$(SystemRoot)\microsoft.net\framework\
      ➥v1.1.4322\System.Drawing.dll'}
4:    {%DelphiDotNetAssemblyCompiler '$(SystemRoot)\microsoft.net\framework\
      ➥v1.1.4322\System.Windows.Forms.dll'}
5:
6:    uses
7:      System.Windows.Forms,
8:      System.Drawing;
9:
10:   type
11:     TFirstForm = class(Form)
12:     private
13:       btnDrawRect: Button;
14:     public
15:       constructor Create;
16:       procedure btnDrawRectClick(Sender: TObject; E: EventArgs);
17:     end;
18:
19:   constructor TFirstForm.Create;
20:   begin
21:     inherited Create;
22:     Text := 'D4DN First example';
23:     Size := System.Drawing.Size.Create(400, 300);
24:
25:     btnDrawRect := Button.Create;
26:     btnDrawRect.Text      := 'Draw Rect';
27:     btnDrawRect.Parent    := self;
28:     btnDrawRect.Location := Point.Create(10, 10);
29:     btnDrawRect.Size      := System.Drawing.Size.Create(70, 25);
30:     btnDrawRect.add_Click(btnDrawRectClick);
31:   end;
32:
33:   procedure TFirstForm.btnDrawRectClick(Sender: TObject; E: EventArgs);
34:   var
35:     grGraphics: Graphics;
36:     rct: Rectangle;
37:     pn: Pen;
38:   begin
```

LISTING 2.1   Continued

```
39:    grGraphics := Graphics.FromHwnd(Handle);
40:    rct := Rectangle.Create(40, 40, 200, 200);
41:    pn := Pen.Create(Color.Red);
42:    grGraphics.DrawRectangle(pn, rct);
43: end;
44:
45: begin
46:   Application.Run(TFirstForm.Create);
47: end.
48:
49:
```

▶ Find the code on the CD: \Code\Chapter2\Ex01.

This simple example creates a Windows form with a button which, when pressed, draws a rectangle on the form's surface (see Figure 2.5).

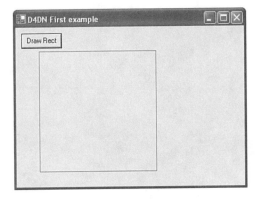

FIGURE 2.5   First Example Form—Drawing a rectangle.

If you have programmed in Delphi before, you should be familiar with this code, although there are a few subtle differences. If you have not dabbled in Delphi yet, hang in there until Part II, which covers the Delphi for .NET Programming Language. For now, I only want to point out how namespace classes are accessed in a Delphi for .NET program.

First, notice the code block,

```
uses
  System.Windows.Forms,
  System.Drawing;
```

This code tells the compiler, "Give me access to the classes contained in the System. Windows.Forms and System.Drawing namespaces." By doing this, I can use the classes, Application, Form, and Button, which are contained in the System.Windows.Forms namespace and the Graphics, Rectangle, Size, and Pen objects contained in the System.Drawing name-space. The click event for the Button object dynamically creates the objects I need and then uses them to draw a rectangle to the form's surface.

The Delphi for .NET compiler implicitly uses the .NET System namespace, which gives you access to the EventArgs class. Likewise, it always implicitly uses the Borland.Delphi.System unit, which gives you access to the TObject class. TObject is simply an alias for the System.Object class. You don't have to understand these details at this point. Much of this will be covered in Chapter 5, "The Delphi Language."

Much of .NET operates along these lines. That is, you get access to classes in namespaces and use them to perform the functionality you require—be it database access using components in System.Data or server-side Web page generation by using components in System.Web. Additionally, you can extend the framework by creating your own classes and placing them into their own namespaces. Later, in Chapter 6, you will learn how to deploy your own classes as assemblies, enabling you to extend the original framework with you own set of classes.

Introduction to Delphi for .NET and the New IDE

PART II:
DELPHI FOR .NET PROGRAMMING LANGUAGE

CHAPTER 3   Introduction to Delphi for .NET and the New IDE

CHAPTER 4   Programs, Units, and Namespaces

CHAPTER 5   The Delphi Language

IN THIS CHAPTER

- Delphi for .NET—a Bigger Picture
- Introduction to the Integrated Development Environment (IDE)

Borland's Delphi for .NET has been a long time coming—at least in the hearts and minds of the many loyal Delphi developers in the world. Borland has answered the call to create an integrated development environment for building .NET application in Delphi, and it has answered it well. This chapter introduces you to the Delphi for .NET product and how the new IDE enhances productivity.

Delphi for .NET—a Bigger Picture

So what exactly is Delphi for .NET? Delphi for .NET is one component of Borland's broad vision for how developers create business solutions. This vision has to do with providing the full Application Lifecycle Development (ALM) process onto the desks of development teams, giving them the full scope of tools needed to develop applications. These tools form a suite of products around this ALM concept, giving them what they need to define, design, develop, test, deploy, and manage software projects.

This book is focused on the "develop" stage of ALM, and Delphi for .NET is just one of the tools that Borland provides to serve that purpose. Nevertheless, because it is a good idea to know how Delphi for .NET fits into the grand scheme, it is recommended that you read the various whitepapers and articles on both the Borland's main site and community site.

> **TIP**
>
> Borland's Web site is `http://www.borland.com`. The community site is `http://bdn.borland.com/`. My site that will be dedicated to Delphi development and particularly .NET development in Delphi is `http://www.delphiguru.com`. This site will also be the location from which you can obtain code updates and errata sheets on this book.

Introduction to the Integrated Development Environment (IDE)

Much like previous versions of Delphi, its IDE is a powerful environment through which you design and develop applications. It includes the various tools needed to enable you to do this; plus it is extensible, enabling third-party vendors to enhance the IDE capabilities. This chapter goes over the key components of the IDE.

> **NOTE**
>
> This will be the only chapter in which I discuss how to use the IDE. In fact, in much of the code in this book, I make property assignments programmatically rather than setting them within the IDE. I do this so that it is clear what assignments have been made to the various properties. Normally, you would make such assignments using the IDE's Object Inspector. For further tips on IDE usability, you can visit http://www.delphiguru.com, where I will periodically post tutorials on using Delphi for .NET.

The main components to the Delphi IDE are

- Welcome Page
- Main Form
- Designer Surface
- Forms
- Tool Palette/Code Snippets
- Object Inspector
- Code Editor
- Project Manager
- Data Explorer
- Code Explorer
- To-Do List
- Object Repository

This chapter discusses each of these components and then gets you started with your first, simple Delphi for .NET application.

Welcome Page

The Welcome page is the first thing you see when the Delphi IDE is started (see Figure 3.1). This page serves as more of a quick launch center from which you can create new projects, open recent projects, and access various resources on Delphi for .NET.

> **TIP**
>
> If for some reason you lose the Welcome page, you can redisplay it by clicking View, Welcome Page.

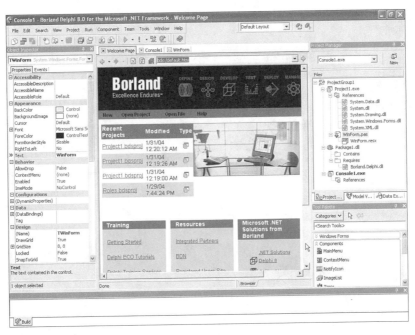

FIGURE 3.1   Welcome page.

Note that the Welcome page has an embedded Web browser. Therefore, you can type a valid URL into the URL combo to launch the Web site that you entered.

> **TIP**
>
> You can modify the `default.htm` file in the Welcome Page directory to customize your Welcome page—including your own links—change the shown picture, and so on.

Designer

The Designer is the area of the IDE that you see when you create either a new Windows Form, Web Form, or VCL Form application shown in the center pane and you have clicked the Design tab at the bottom of that pane (see Figure 3.2). The designer is the area where you perform your visual design within the IDE. You can drag and drop components from the Tool Palette onto your forms to visually design your applications. When working with VCL Forms, the designer looks and behaves differently. For instance, you'll notice that the right-click menu is different.

Some components are visual, whereas others are not. When you place visual components on a form, such as a TextBox, it is placed exactly where you positioned it on the form (Figure 3.2). Nonvisual components, such as the SqlDataAdapter and SqlConnection, are positioned on the Component Tray, which is the bottom portion of the Designer (see Figure 3.2). Such components are only visible at design time so that you can select them to modify their properties. Within the Designer's status bar, you'll see information about the status of the file on which you are working such as whether it has been modified. You'll also see your cursor position and whether the editor is in insert or overwrite mode. You'll also see the Macro recording buttons on the status bar, which is discussed momentarily.

Object Inspector   Main Form/Main Menu   Project Manager

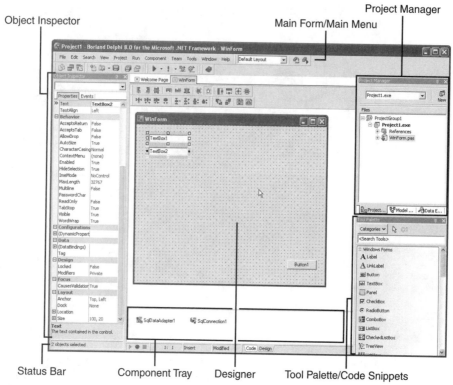

FIGURE 3.2   Designer.

Status Bar   Component Tray   Designer   Tool Palette/Code Snippets

When working within the design, you will want to make sure to take advantage of some of the features the IDE contains to enhance your productivity. Here are just a few:

- Locking Control—When you have positioned controls on the form the way you want them, it's often a good idea to lock them in place so that you don't accidentally move them as you select them with the mouse. To do this, simply right-click to invoke the local menu and select the Lock Controls option. This locking is per form. Also, the VCL designer only has a global Edit, Lock Controls for all forms.

- Tab Order—Something often forgotten is to set the tab order of controls. You can examine the tab order of controls on your form by right-clicking to invoke the local menu and selecting Tab Order. You can adjust the tab order of each control by clicking with your mouse anywhere on the control containing the tab order number.

- Be sure to take advantage of the Align, Position and Spacing toolbars to arrange controls on your form. These toolbars become enabled when you have multi-selected controls on the form.

- Docking—The IDE allows you to reposition/doc the various windows almost wherever you want. This great feature enables you to adjust your work space as you like.

- Layouts—There are three predefined desktop layouts: Default, Classic (for those of you who prefer the classic Delphi undocked layout), and Debug. The Default layout is shown in Figure 3.2. Figure 3.3 depicts the Debug layout, which shows various debugging windows (Call Stack, Watch List, and Local Variables). The IDE switches to the Debug layout whenever you start debugging an application. You can change and save your own custom layouts as well.

- Customizing the File Menu—You can now customize the File, New menu to add items that you frequently need to create. For instance, if you frequently need to create Web Forms, you can add a WebForm to the File, New menu directly so that you don't have to launch the Object Repository from which you would normally select this form.

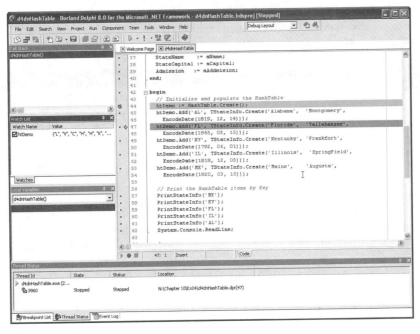

FIGURE 3.3   IDE Debug layout.

Forms

Forms are the main GUI entities that you create. They can be a window or dialog with which the user interacts or a Web page. In Delphi for .NET, you can work with three types of forms: Windows Forms, Web Forms, and VCL Forms.

Windows Forms enable you to use the classes within the .NET Framework to create functionally rich, Managed GUI applications. You create a Windows Forms application by selecting File, New, Windows Forms Application from the main menu. The IDE will then present you with a Windows Form surface on which you place the various user-interface controls from the tool palette to design the main form of the application. Typically, your applications will consist of numerous Windows Forms. This book uses many examples built upon Windows Forms.

Web Forms are the building blocks of ASP.NET Web applications. To create Web Forms, select File, New, ASP.NET Web Application from the main menu. The IDE will then present you with the Web Form designer, which is your workspace for your Web site pages. Part V, "Internet Development with ASP.NET," covers developing ASP.NET applications in detail.

VCL Forms are similar to Windows Forms in that they give you the tools and classes required to build managed GUI applications. However, VCL Forms make use of Borland's own set of native .NET classes. VCL Forms, being built on Borland's VCL framework, also enable you to easily port existing Win32 applications to managed .NET applications. Through VCL.NET, you will be able to create applications that target both the managed .NET runtime and native Win32. To create a VCL Forms application, select File, New, VCL Forms Application from the main menu. The IDE will present you with a form design surface onto which you can place components from the Tool Palette to build functionally interactive applications.

> **NOTE**
>
> The Mono project is an effort well under way to create an open source .NET runtime for the Linux Operating System. The goal of Mono is to be capable of running any managed assembly, and this includes Delphi assemblies. Theoretically, because of the Wine project used to emulate Win32 on Linux, there is hope to run VCL for .NET apps as is on Linux/Mono/Wine. As of now, this is not realized. You can find out about the Mono project at http://www.go-mono.com/.

Tool Palette/Code Snippets

By default, the Tool Palette is located at the lower-right pane (refer to Figure 3.2). Its contents depend on which view you happen to be working in. If you are working with the Designer display, the Tool Palette contains the various components that you can add to your form either by dragging and dropping them onto the form or by double-clicking them. The list of available components depends on what kind of file you are editing (Win Form, Web Form, VCL Form, or HTML file, for instance). If you are working in the Code Editor, the Tool Palette contains a list of code snippets.

Code snippets are small blocks of reusable code. You can add your own code snippets to the Tool Palette. Additionally, you can categorize the arrangement of your code snippets. To add a category, simply right-click within the Tool Palette and select Add New Category. Enter a category name and click OK. To add code from the code editor to your list of code snippets, highlight your code, press the Alt key, and drag onto the Tool Palette. To add code snippets to a new category, you must first add them to the default Code Snippets category. Once added there, they can be dragged to a custom category. The order is

1. Drag the code to the default Code Snippets category.

2. Right-click to Add New Category.

3. Alt+Drag the new snippet from Code Snippets to your new category.

Also, an empty category will be removed when the Tool Palette loses focus.

Object Inspector

Through the Object Inspector (refer to Figure 3.2), you modify the properties of components and attach event handlers to these components. This allows you to specify at design-time various attributes that affect the visual appearance and behavior of components. For example, after placing a Label component on a Windows Form, you can change its Text property to something more specific and its font color to red. This is done in the Properties Page of the Object Inspector. The Events page is where you attach code to various events of each component. For example, a Button component has a Click event that fires when the user clicks the button. By double-clicking in the edit portion of the Object Inspector for that event, the IDE automatically creates the event handler for you and places your cursor in that event handler within the Code Editor.

Various attributes of the Object Inspector, such as color and look and feel, are configurable. Simply right-click over the Object Inspector to invoke the local menu and select the Properties menu. This will launch the Object Inspector Properties dialog box shown in Figure 3.4.

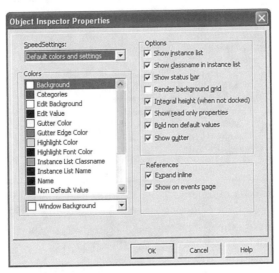

FIGURE 3.4 Object Inspector Properties dialog box.

Code Editor

If you have the opportunity to ever attend a Borland demonstration of one of its products, you'll always hear the claim about being able do great things with the products "without writing a single line of code." Well, the truth is, you really can't do anything useful without writing many lines of code. Fortunately, Borland delivers world class Code Editors with its development tools. The Delphi for .NET Code Editor does not fall short of this trend. Here are some handy features of the Code Editor:

- Code Folding—Hands down, this is one of the coolest features of the IDE. Within the Code Editor, you'll notice minus (·) and plus (+) signs to the right of code blocks. By clicking a minus sign, you'll collapse the block of code. By clicking a plus sign, you'll expand the block of code. Figure 3.5 shows both a collapsed and expanded block of code. Code folding is enabled automatically for functions, nested functions, structured types, and unit blocks.

TIP

The IDE provides some keyboard shortcuts for people tired of using the mouse (using the default keyboard mapping). These are

- Ctrl+Shift+K+U—Expands nearest block.
- Ctrl+Shift+K+E—Collapses nearest block.
- Ctrl+Shift+K+A—Expands all blocks in this file.
- Ctrl+Shift K+T—Toggles nearest block.
- Ctrl+Shift+K+O—Turns off/on code folding. (After turning it on, you must change to another file and back to see it.)

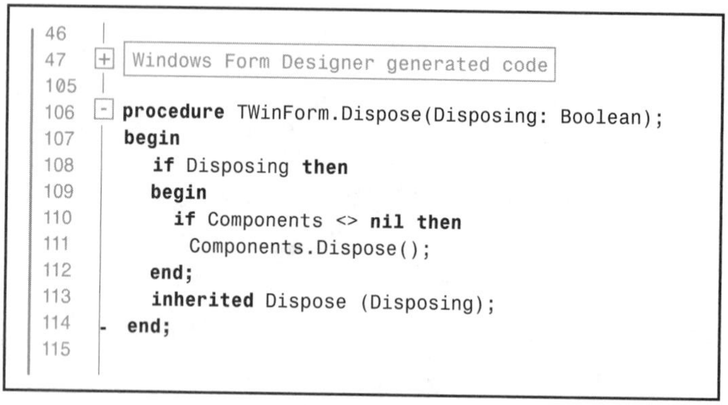

```
 46   |
 47   [+] | Windows Form Designer generated code
105   |
106   [-] procedure TWinForm.Dispose(Disposing: Boolean);
107       begin
108         if Disposing then
109         begin
110           if Components <> nil then
111             Components.Dispose();
112         end;
113         inherited Dispose (Disposing);
114   -   end;
115
```

FIGURE 3.5   Code folding.

- Regions—You can use the $REGION/$ENDREGION directives to specify your own code folding blocks. The syntax for using these directives is

```
{$REGION 'Region Title'}
code
{$ENDREGION}
```

Figure 3.6 shows how this looks in the IDE.

- Class Completion—This is a great productivity tool that allows you to define a class, and then through a shortcut key, the Code Editor will automatically create implementation methods for you. For instance, suppose that you define the class shown here:

```
TMyClass = class (System.Object)
private
  procedure Foo;
public
  property MyInt: Integer;
  property MyString: String;
end;
```

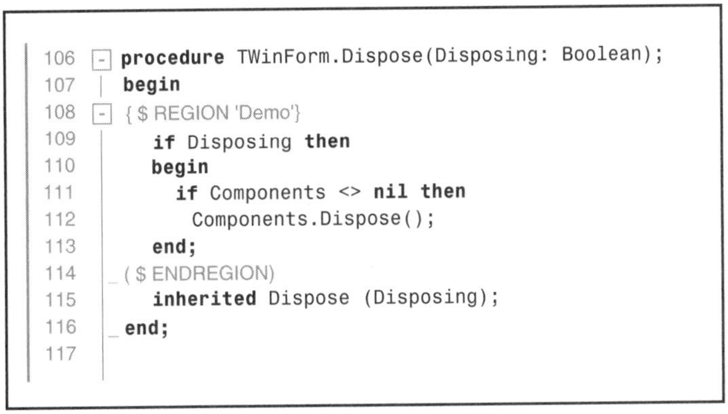

```
106 ⊟  procedure TWinForm.Dispose(Disposing: Boolean);
107 |   begin
108 ⊟    {$ REGION 'Demo'}
109         if Disposing then
110         begin
111           if Components <> nil then
112             Components.Dispose();
113         end;
114     ($ ENDREGION)
115         inherited Dispose (Disposing);
116     end;
117 |
```

FIGURE 3.6   Regions.

After pressing the Shift+Ctrl+C key combination, the Code Editor creates the following class declaration:

```
TMyClass = class (System.Object)
private
  procedure Foo;
public
  FMyString: &String;
  FMyInt: Integer;
  procedure set_MyInt(const Value: Integer);
  procedure set_MyString(const Value: &String);
public
  property MyInt: Integer read FMyInt write set_MyInt;
  property MyString: String read FMyString write set_MyString;
end;
```

You'll notice that the property accessor methods have been defined. The implementation of these methods is also created in the implementation section of the unit as shown here:

```
{TMyClass}
procedure TMyClass.Foo;
begin
end;

procedure TMyClass.set_MyInt(const Value: Integer);
begin
  FMyInt := Value;
end;

procedure TMyClass.set_MyString(const Value: &String);
begin
  FMyString := Value;
end;
```

- Code Block Indentation—Another IDE favorite is code block indent/un-indent. Simply highlight a block of code and use the Ctrl+K+I key combination to indent the selected block of code. Use Ctrl+K+U to un-indent a block of code. Alternatively, you can use Ctrl+Shift+I and Ctrl+Shift+U.

- Code Browsing—If you want to find the declaration of a particular function in code, simply hold down the Ctrl key while left-clicking with the mouse over the function call. Alternatively, you can use the Alt+Up Arrow key combination to accomplish the same. To quickly navigate from the definition of a function to its implementation, use the Shift+Ctrl+Up Arrow/Shift+Ctrl+Down Arrow combination. Also, the IDE maintains a history of browsed code links. Using Alt+Left and Alt+Right, you can move back and forth in the browsing history.

Project Manager

From the Project Manager, you manage the various files that are contained within your Project Groups. It contains three tabs—Project Manager, Model View, and Data Explorer. Figure 3.7 shows the Project Manager undocked.

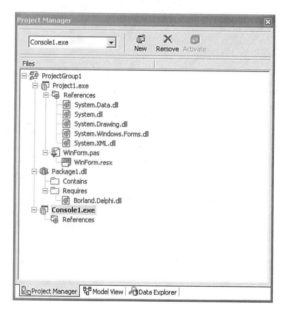

FIGURE 3.7   Project Manager (undocked).

A Project Group is a group of related projects. For instance, you have a project group composed of a project with multiple separate assembly projects. Figure 3.7 shows a Project Group, ProjectGroup1. It contains the projects Project1.exe, Package1.dll, and Console1.exe. The Project Manager tab allows you to manage projects groups by providing menu options to add/remove projects and to compile/build projects contained in the group.

The Project Manager tab also allows you to manage projects by providing menus to add/remove files as well as compilation options.

Model View

The Model View gives you a nested view of the projects units, classes, and other members contained within your projects. Figure 3.8 shows the Model View. Note that the Model Views is accessed within the Project Manager window by selecting its tab on the lower portion of the Project Manager Window.

FIGURE 3.8   Model View window.

Data Explorer

The Data Explorer (see Figure 3.9) is also accessible from within the Project Manager window.

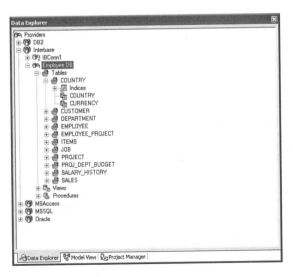

FIGURE 3.9   The Data Explorer displays connections.

From the Data Explorer, you can manage various connections to data sources through Database Providers. You can perform various functions such as creating new connections, creating projects from connections, browsing databases, and more. The online Delphi for .NET help provides examples of performing such functions. Developing database applications is covered in greater detail in Part IV, "Database Development with ADO.NET."

Object Repository

The Object Repository is the location from which you can use reusable items within your applications. From the Object Repository, you can select a type of application or elements that you will use within your application, such as Windows Forms, ASP.NET Forms, classes, and so on. To open the Object Repository, simply select File, New, Other, which launches the form shown in Figure 3.10.

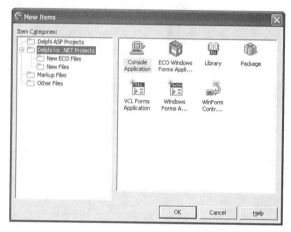

FIGURE 3.10   Object Repository is used to select reusable items.

This list on the left represents the various categories of items that you can select from. The view on the right displays the items for a selected category. For instance, by selecting the category Delphi for .NET Projects, you will see a list of the various projects you can create in Delphi for .NET, such as Window Forms Application, VCL Forms Application, Package, Library, and so on. When you select an item that creates a new application, the IDE will create the application and application files for you. If you select an element such as a form, the IDE will create that item for you and will add it to your existing application on which you are currently working.

Code Explorer

The Code Explorer can be useful for navigating through large units of source code. The Code Explorer displays the structural layout of a unit including classes, methods, components, and so on. To navigate to a particular item, simply double-click it, and it will position the cursor on the code in which the item appears. The Code Explorer is shown in Figure 3.11.

FIGURE 3.11   Use the Code Explorer to navigate through a unit.

To-Do List

The To-Do list is a convenient way to keep track of to-dos. They are listed in a dockable window and are maintained in your source files.

To use To-Dos, simply right-click anywhere in the Code Editor and select Add To-Do Item from the local menu. Doing so will invoke the Add To-Do Item dialog box.

When you press OK after adding the To-Do, the To-Do will be added to the To-Do list that appears at the bottom of the IDE (see Figure 3.12). If the To-Do list is not displayed, select View, To Do List from the main menu.

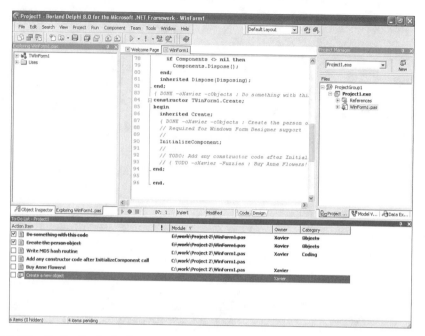

FIGURE 3.12   To-Do list is displayed at the bottom of the IDE.

CHAPTER 4

Programs, Units, and Namespaces

IN THIS CHAPTER

- Managed Module Structures
- Namespaces

All Delphi for .NET applications are structured around the classic Delphi, Program-unit construct. Some of the "Delphi" terms are matched with .NET terms. For example, a Delphi unit defines a .NET namespace, and a Delphi program is a .NET managed module. Although the matches "loosely" exist structurally, the Delphi programming language has been greatly extended to conform to the .NET paradigm. In this chapter, I will discuss how to construct the various programs using Delphi for .NET. I will use the .NET terminology to explain the various pieces.

Managed Module Structures

Delphi applications compile to managed modules. The following sections discuss the structure of a Delphi program.

The Program Structure

A program is the base unit that forms an application; we call this the main module. Typically, a program can consist of many units and can also use code from libraries and/or packages. To use .NET terminology, a Delphi program can directly link code from any number of units and import code from one or more assemblies.

> **NOTE**
>
> A feature of Delphi for .NET, which does not exist in other .NET languages, is the capability to link code from a Delphi assembly directly into your managed module. This capability simplifies deployment even more because you would only have to deploy a single executable. This is particularly useful with regard to third-party components written in Delphi. I will talk more on this in the chapter covering assemblies.

Listing 4.1 shows an example of a skeleton program file.

LISTING 4.1   Skeleton Program File (Main Module)

```
1:   program MyProgram;
2:   {$APPTYPE CONSOLE}
3:   uses
4:      SysUtils;
5:   var
6:      s: String;
7:   begin
8:      s := 'lower case string';
9:      Console.Writeline(UpperCase(s));
10:     Console.Readline;
11:  end.
```

▶ Find the code on the CD: \Code\Chapter4\Ex01\.

The program file consists of a heading, a uses clause, and the declaration/execution block. The program heading simply states the name of the program (also called the project default namespace, but more on this later). In this example, the name of this program is MyProgram. The uses clause specifies the units whose code will be linked into MyProgram. In this example, I am linking code that is contained in the SysUtils unit, which gives me access to the UpperCase() function used in the execution block.

> **NOTE**
>
> The Borland.Delphi.System unit (or namespace) is automatically linked into your source files. Adding it explicitly is prohibited by the DCCIL compiler.

The program declaration/execution block begins with the keyword var and ends with the end keyword. The code that gets executed appears between the begin..end statements. In this example, the code is very simple.

The Unit Structure

Delphi units are organizational containers for classes, types, routines, variables, constants, and other language constructs. When a program, or another unit, adds a unit name to its uses clause, it is telling the compiler to make the constructs contained within the used unit available locally. Listing 4.2 shows a unit containing a string writer class.

LISTING 4.2   An Example Unit—MyUnit.pas

```
1:   unit MyUnit;
2:   interface
3:
4:   type
5:     TMyStringWriter = class(TObject)
6:       procedure WriteMyString(aMyString: String);
7:     end;
8:   var
9:     msw: TMyStringWriter;
10:
11:  implementation
12:
13:  procedure TMyStringWriter.WriteMyString(aMyString: String);
```

LISTING 4.2   Continued

```
14:  begin
15:    Console.Writeline(aMyString);
16:  end;
17:
18:  initialization
19:    msw := TMyStringWriter.Create;
20:
21:  finalization
22:    msw.Free;
23:  end.
```

▶ Find the code on the CD: \Code\Chapter4\Ex02\.

NOTE

In a pure .NET context, the msw.Free statement on line 22 is unnecessary. For cross-platform code (to Win32) or if the TMyStringWriter class had implemented the IDisposable interface (by having an explicit destructor), the Free call would make sense. It is used here for illustrating the finalization section only.

The Unit Header

Like the program file, the unit consists of various sections. The unit header names the unit with the identifier following the unit keyword (line 1, Listing 4.2).

The Interface Section

The interface exists between the interface and implementation keywords (lines 2–11 in Listing 4.2). It is within this section that you define elements that you want to expose to users of your unit. Listing 4.3 shows this concept.

LISTING 4.3   Example Program Using MyUnit.pas

```
1:   program MyProgram;
2:   {$APPTYPE CONSOLE}
3:
4:   uses
5:     MyUnit;
6:   var
7:     s: String;
8:   begin
9:     s := 'Hello .NET!';
10:    msw.WriteMyString(s);
11:  end.
```

▶ Find the code on the CD: \Code\Chapter4\Ex02\.

This code is similar to that in Listing 4.1. Listing 4.3 contains MyUnit in the uses clause. This tells the compiler to make available types contained in MyUnit's interface section to MyProgram. You can see in the code block that I actually use the variable msv, which is declared in MyUnit's interface section. The interface section is where you declare types and classes. Their implementation is done in the appropriately named implementation section.

The Implementation Section

The implementation section appears between the `implementation` and `initialization` keywords. The implementation section contains the code for any routines, classes, and so on that are declared in the interface section. The implementation section can also declare types, routines, and so on, which are not declared in the interface section, thus making those unexposed to external units but accessible to the declaring unit.

The interface section's uses clause lists those units whose declarations are available to both the interface and implementation sections. Note that this does not expose any used units to the external module. Therefore, even though `MyOtherUnit` is included in `MyUnit`, the types contained in `MyOtherUnit` are not exposed to `MyProgram`. `MyProgram` would have to include `MyOtherUnit` in its own uses clause for access to its types.

The implementation section can contain its own uses clause. If so, it would appear as

```
implementation
uses
  UnitA, UnitB, UnitC;
```

The implementation section's uses clause lists those units whose declarations are only available to the implementation section.

The Initialization and Finalization Sections

The initialization section is an optional section where you can provide code that is executed when the program is launched. Likewise, the finalization section (also optional) is executed when the program shuts down.

> **CAUTION**
>
> When writing initialization and finalization blocks, it is best not to place dependencies on other units' initialization and finalization. This is particularly true of finalization. The Delphi compiler/linker and the RTL determine the order of execution for the different units' initialization and finalization blocks. The order is ultimately determined by the program's uses clause order and the units' own uses clause orders. So although the order is deterministic, it is not easy or obvious how to control the execution order. The timing of the finalization execution is tied to the `System.AppDomain.CurrentDomain.ProcessExit` event. This event fires when the default application domain's parent process exits.

Uses Clause Syntax

The uses clause can occur in program files, library files, and units. In a unit, it might appear in both the interface and implementation sections. A uses clause can contain as many unit references as required. Each entry is separated by a comma with the last being terminated with a semicolon:

```
Uses UnitA, UnitB, UnitC, UnitD;
```

Disambiguating Types

Suppose that you had the following uses clause in a program:

```
Uses UnitA, UnitB;
```

Also suppose that both units declared two different types that were named TMyType. Finally, suppose that you need to reference the TMyType declared in UnitA in a variable declaration:

```
Var
  Mt: TMyType;
```

The problem here is that the TMyType being used is the one contained in UnitB because it is the last in the list of used units. This ambiguity can be solved by prepending the unit name followed by a period (.) to the type identifier anywhere it is referenced. Therefore, your variable declaration would be written as

```
Var
  Mt: UnitB.TMyType;
```

Circular Unit References

Occasionally, you will run into a situation in which UnitA uses UnitB which uses UnitC which uses UnitA—all from within the interface section. This is called a circular unit reference, and the Delphi compiler complains at this. Typically, it means that you have modularized your code incorrectly.

In a simpler example, we could say that UnitA uses a type in UnitB (TypeZ). UnitB, needs to use a type in UnitA (TypeY). This circular unit reference is depicted in Figure 4.1.

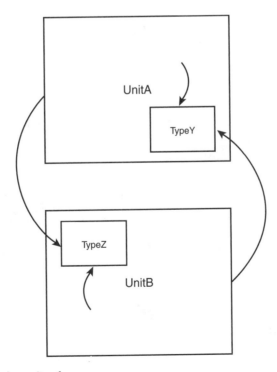

FIGURE 4.1   A circular unit reference.

To solve this, you would move TypeY from UnitA to a new unit, UnitC, see Figure 4.2. Now, both UnitA and UnitB can use UnitC without the circular reference because UnitC uses neither UnitA nor UnitB.

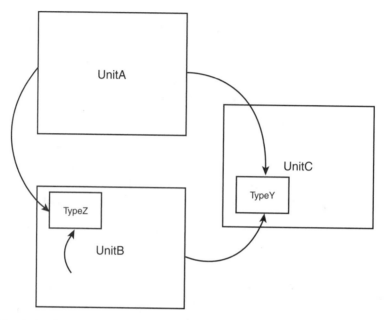

FIGURE 4.2   A circular unit reference corrected.

Namespaces

Delphi units provide the capability to physically group logical types into separate files. Namespaces take this grouping further by proving a way to hierarchically contain Delphi units. This fits well within the .NET way of doing this because native NET types are already grouped in this manner. The benefits to this are

- Namespaces can be nested to form a logical hierarchy of types.
- Namespaces can be used to disambiguate types with the same name.
- Namespaces can be used to disambiguate units with the same name that reside in different packages.

Namespace Declaration

A project file declares its own default namespace, which we call the project default name-space. Therefore, a project declared as

```
program MyProject.MyIdeas;
```

creates the namespace MyProject, whereas the statement

```
program MyProject.MyIdeas.FirstIdea
```

declares the namespace `MyProject.MyIdeas`. Notice that the dot (.) is used to create a hierarchy within namespaces. In the preceding statement, `FirstIdea` is a member of `MyIdeas`, which is a member of `MyProject`.

Units declare their namespace in the unit header statement. For example,

```
unit MyProject.MyIdeas.MyUnitA
```

declares a unit that is a member of the `MyProject.MyIdeas` namespace.

Consider the following program and unit file headings:

```
program MyProject.MyIdeas;
unit MyProject.MyIdeas.FirstIdea;
unit MyProject.MyIdeas.SecondIdea;
unit MyProject.MyIdeas.ThirdIdea;
unit MyProject.MyTasks.Task1;
unit MyProject.MyTasks.Task1.SubTask1;
unit MyProject.MyTasks.Task2;
```

These units would form a namespace hierarchy, as shown in Figure 4.3.

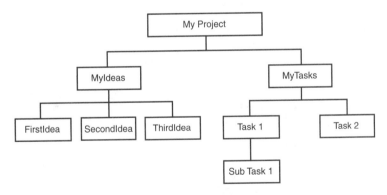

FIGURE 4.3   A namespace hierarchy.

A generic unit is a unit that does not explicitly declare its own namespace.

Using Namespaces

Namespacesare brought into the context of a unit through the unit's uses clause. Therefore, to use the types in `MyProject.MyIdeas.FirstIdea`, a unit's uses clause should contain

```
uses
  MyProject.MyIdeas.FirstIdea;
```

Types that are declared in `MyProject.MyIdeas` are not available; this would require an explicit inclusion of that namespace in the unit's uses clause:

```
uses
  MyProject.MyIdeas;
  MyProject.MyIdeas.FirstIdea;
```

Likewise, having `MyProject.MyIdeas` in a uses clause does not bring its member namespaces (`FirstIdea`, `SecondIdea`, ...) into the context of the using unit.

Once a namespace is used within a unit, you can access type identifiers in the usual way. However, given a type of the same name within two different namespaces to which you have access, you must prepend the fully qualified namespace name to the ambiguous identifier:

```
writeln(MyProject.MyIdeas.Identifier1);
```

The Namespaces Clause

A project can declare a list of namespaces separated by commas and terminated with a semicolon for the compiler to search when resolving identifier names from generic units. This declaration appears in the project file following the program (or package) declaration:

```
program MyProject.MyIdeas;
namespaces MyProject.HerIdeas, MyProject.HisIdeas;
```

This clause must precede any other clause within the project file.

Resolving Generic Namespaces

The Delphi compiler must resolve identifiers used from other units to their containing unit. It does this by iterating through the units listed in the uses clauses. For units that have fully qualified namespaces, finding the unit is simple because the unit's scope is known. For generic units, the compiler resolves identifier names by going through the following search order:

1. Current unit namespace (if exists)

2. Project default namespace (if exists)

3. The project's namespaces clause (in reverse order as they appear in the clause)

4. Namespaces in the compiler options

Given a unit with a uses clause of

```
unit MyProject.MyIdeas.FirstIdea;
uses MyProject.MyIdeas.SecondIdea, BadIdeas, GoodIdeas;
```

The search order for `BadIdeas` would be

1. BadIdeas

2. MyProject.MyIdeas

3. MyProject (starting point for a generic unit)

4. MyProject.HisIdeas

5. MyProject.HerIdeas

6. Compiler Options

Unit Aliases

It is possible that your hierarchies will become quite deep. In this case, you can declare unit aliases to provide a shorter name that can be used when qualifying identifiers within your source code. The following line of code illustrates this:

```
uses MyProgram.MyFramework.MyClasses.FileClasses as aFC;
```

The statement as aFC creates a shorter name that can be used in your source code:

```
MyFile := aFC.File.Create;
```

This statement is equivalent to the following statement:

```
MyFile := MyProgram.MyFramework.MyClasses.FileClasses.File.Create;
```

Keep in mind that unit aliases must not conflict with another identifier.

IN THIS CHAPTER

- It's All about .NET
- Comments
- Procedures and Functions
- Variables
- Constants
- Operators
- Delphi Language Types
- User-Defined Types
- Typecasting and Type Conversion
- String Resources
- Testing Conditions
- Loops
- Procedures and Functions
- Scope
- Units and Namespaces
- Packages and Assemblies
- Object-Oriented Programming
- Using Delphi Objects
- Structured Exception Handling

CHAPTER **5**

The Delphi Language

by Steve Teixeira

This chapter covers Delphi's underlying language, Object Pascal. First, you'll receive an introduction to the basics of the Delphi language, such as language rules and constructs. Then, you'll learn about some of the more advanced aspects of the Delphi language, such as classes and exception handling. This chapter assumes that you have some experience with other high-level computer languages. Therefore, it does not teach the concepts associated with programming languages, but rather on how to express those concepts in Delphi. By the time you're finished with this chapter, you'll understand how programming concepts such as variables, types, operators, loops, cases, exceptions, and objects work in Delphi and how many of these elements relate to the underlying .NET Framework. To provide additional practical grounding, we will draw comparisons where appropriate with Delphi's more widely used .NET cousins, C# and Visual Basic .NET.

It's All about .NET

Delphi 8 produces applications that run completely within the context of the Microsoft .NET Framework. Therefore, the capabilities and features of Delphi 8's compiler must be subject to the capabilities and features of the underlying .NET Framework. This notion might be vaguely disconcerting for those coming into the .NET from the native code world. A native code compiler can essentially do anything it wants—its capabilities limited only by the desires of the compiler vendor. In .NET development, literally everything one might do—even something as trivial as adding two integers together—boils down to the compiler generating code that manipulates features and types of the .NET Framework.

Rather than producing native code, a .NET compiler such as Delphi 8 produces code in a format called Microsoft Intermediate Language, or MSIL, which is the lowest-level representation of application instructions.

Chapter 2 discusses the just-in-time (JIT) compilation nature of the .NET Framework. Now might be a good time to review that information.

Comments

The Delphi language supports three types of comments: curly brace comments, parenthesis/asterisk comments, and double backslash comments. Examples of each type of comment follow:

```
{ Comment using curly braces }
(* Comment using paren and asterisk *)
// double backslash comment
```

The first two types of comments are virtually identical in behavior. The compiler considers the comment to be everything between the open-comment and close-comment delimiters. For double backslash comments, everything following the double backslash until the end of the line is considered a comment.

You cannot nest comments of the same type. Although it is legal syntax to nest comments of different types inside one another, we don't recommend the practice. Here are some examples:

```
{ (* This is legal *) }
(* { This is legal } *)
(* (* This is illegal *) *)
{ { This is illegal } }
```

Another handy technique for disabling a body of code, particularly when different kinds of comments are used in the code, is to use the $IFDEF compiler directive. For example, the following code uses $IFDEF to comment out a block of code:

```
{$IFDEF DONTCOMPILEME}
// imagine a bunch of code here
{$ENDIF}
```

Because the DONTCOMPILEME identifier is not defined, the code inside the $IFDEF is effectively commented out.

Procedures and Functions

Because procedures and functions are fairly universal topics as far as programming languages are concerned, we won't go into a great deal of detail here. We just want to fill you in on a few unique or little-known features in this area.

Functions with no return value (a void return in C# parlance) are called procedures, while functions returning some value are referred to as functions. Often, the term routine will be used to describe both procedures and functions, and the term method describes a routine within a class.

Parentheses in Calls

One of the lesser-known features of the Delphi language is that parentheses are optional when calling a procedure or function that takes no parameters. Therefore, the following syntax examples are both valid:

```
Form1.Show;
Form1.Show();
```

Granted, this feature isn't one of those things that sends chills up and down your spine, but it's particularly nice for those who split their time between Delphi and a language like C#, where parentheses are required. If you're not able to spend 100% of your time in Delphi, this feature means that you don't have to remember to use different function-calling syntax for different languages.

Overloading

The Delphi language supports the concept of function overloading, that is, the ability to have multiple procedures or functions of the same name with different parameter lists. All overloaded methods are required to be declared with the overload directive, as shown here:

```
procedure Hello(I: Integer); overload;
procedure Hello(S: string); overload;
procedure Hello(D: Double); overload;
```

Note that the rules for overloading methods of a class are slightly different and are explained in the section "Method Overloading."

Default Value Parameters

Also supported in the Delphi language are default value parameters—that is, the ability to provide a default value for a function or procedure parameter and not have to pass that parameter when calling the routine. In order to declare a procedure or function that contains default value parameters, follow the parameter type with an equal sign and the default value, as shown in the following example:

```
procedure HasDefVal(S: string; I: Integer = 0);
```

The HasDefVal() procedure can be called in one of two ways. First, you can specify both parameters:

```
HasDefVal('hello', 26);
```

Second, you can specify only parameter s and use the default value for i:

```
HasDefVal('hello');  // default value used for I
```

You must follow several rules when using default value parameters:

- Parameters having default values must appear at the end of the parameter list. Parameters without default values cannot follow parameters with default values in a procedure or function's parameter list.

- Default value parameters can be of an ordinal, string, floating point, pointer, or set type. Class, interface, dynamic array, procedural, and class references are also supported, but only when the default value is made equal to `nil`.

- Default value parameters must be passed by value or as `const`. They cannot be reference (`var`, `out`) or untyped parameters.

One of the biggest benefits of default value parameters is in adding functionality to existing functions and procedures without sacrificing backward compatibility. For example, suppose that you publish a unit containing a revolutionary function called `AddInts()` that adds two numbers:

```
function AddInts(I1, I2: Integer): Integer;
begin
  Result := I1 + I2;
end;
```

In order to keep up with the competition, you feel you must update this function so that it has the capability for adding three numbers. However, you're loathe to do so because adding a parameter will cause existing code that calls this function to not compile. Thanks to default parameters, you can enhance the functionality of `AddInts()` without compromising compatibility. Here's an example:

```
function AddInts(I1, I2: Integer; I3: Integer = 0);
begin
  Result := I1 + I2 + I3;
end;
```

> **TIP**
>
> Generally, you should look to overloaded routines when choosing between the addition of default values or overloaded routines as a means to add new features without breaking backward compatibility. Overloads are executed a bit more efficiently and are more compatible with other .NET languages because default value parameters are not supported in C# or managed C++.

Variables

You might be used to declaring variables off the cuff: "I need another integer, so I'll just declare one right here in the middle of this block of code." This is a perfectly reasonable notion if you're coming from another language such as C# or Visual Basic .NET. If that has been your practice, you're going to have to retrain yourself a little in order to use variables in the Delphi language. Delphi requires you to declare all variables up front in their own section before you begin a procedure, function, or program. Perhaps you used to write freewheeling code like this:

```
public void foo()
{
  int x = 1;
  x++;
  int y = 2;
  float f;
```

```
//... etc ...
}
```

In Delphi, any such code must be tidied up and structured a bit more to look like this:

```
procedure Foo;
var
  x, y: Integer;
  f: Double;
begin
  x := 1;
  inc(x);
  y := 2;
  //... etc ...
end;
```

CASE SENSITIVITY AND CAPITALIZATION

The Delphi language—like Visual Basic .NET, but unlike C#—is not a case sensitive language. Upper- and lowercase is used for clarity's sake, so use your best judgment, as the style used in this book indicates. If the identifier name is several words mashed together, remember to camel-cap for clarity by capitalizing the first letter of each word in the identifier. For example, the following name is unclear and difficult to read:

```
procedure thisprocedurenamemakesnosense;
```

This code is quite readable, however:

```
procedure ThisProcedureNameIsMoreClear;
```

You might be wondering what all this structure business is and why it's beneficial. You'll find, however, that the Delphi language's structured style of variable declaration lends itself to code that's more readable, maintainable, and less buggy than other languages that rely on convention rather than rule to enforce sanity.

Notice how Delphi enables you to group more than one variable (or formal parameter, for that matter) of the same type together on the same line with the following syntax:

```
VarName1, VarName2: SomeType;
```

Using this feature tends to make code much more compact and readable compared to a language such as C#, where every variable or parameter must have the type spelled out.

Remember that when you're declaring a variable in Delphi, the variable name precedes the type, and there's a colon between the variables and types. For local variables, the variable initialization is always separate from the variable declaration.

Delphi permits initialization of global variables inside a var block. Here are some examples demonstrating the syntax for doing so:

```
var
  i: Integer = 10;
  S: string  = 'Hello world';
  D: Double  = 3.141579;
```

5

NOTE

Preinitialization of variables is only allowed for global variables, not variables that are local to a procedure or function.

ZERO INITIALIZATION

The CLR sees to it that all variables are automatically zero-initialized. When your application starts or a function is entered, all integer types will hold 0, floating-point types will hold 0.0, objects will be nil, strings will be empty, and so forth. Therefore, it isn't necessary to zero-initialize variables in your source code.

Unlike Win32 versions of Delphi, this is true for variables local to functions as well as global variables.

Constants

Constants in Delphi are defined in a const clause, which behaves similarly to the C#'s const keyword. Here's an example of three constant declarations in C#:

```
public const float ADecimalNumber = 3.14;

public const int i = 10;

public const String ErrorString = "Danger, Danger, Danger!";
```

The major difference between C# constants and Delphi language constants is that Delphi, like Visual Basic .NET, doesn't require you to declare the constant's type along with the value in the declaration. The Delphi compiler automatically allocates the appropriate type for the constant based on its value, or, in the case of scalar constants such as Integer, the compiler keeps track of the values as it works, and space never is allocated. Here's an example:

```
const
  ADecimalNumber = 3.14;
  i = 10;
  ErrorString = 'Danger, Danger, Danger!';
```

Optionally, you can also specify a constant's type in the declaration. This provides you with full control over how the compiler treats your constants:

```
const
  ADecimalNumber: Double = 3.14;
  I: Integer = 10;
  ErrorString: string = 'Danger, Danger, Danger!';
```

THE TYPE SAFETY OF TYPED CONSTANT

Typed constants have one distinct advantage over the untyped variety: Untyped constants' lack of strict compile-time typing prevents them from supporting object method calls. For example, the following code is legal:

```
const
  I: Integer = 19710704;
  S: string;
```

```
begin
  S := I.ToString;
```

Whereas the following code will not compile:

```
const
  I = 19710704;
  S: string;
begin
  S := I.ToString;
```

The Delphi language permits the usage of compile-time functions in `const` and `var` declarations. These routines include `Ord()`, `Chr()`, `Trunc()`, `Round()`, `High()`, `Low()`, `Abs()`, `Pred()`, `Succ()`, `Length()`, `Odd()`, `Round()`, `Trunc()`, and `SizeOf()`. For example, all of the following code is valid:

```
type
  A = array[1..2] of Integer;

const
  w: Word = SizeOf(Byte);

var
  i: Integer = 8;
  j: SmallInt = Ord('a');
  L: Longint = Trunc(3.14159);
  x: ShortInt = Round(2.71828);
  B1: Byte = High(A);
  B2: Byte = Low(A);
  C: Char = Chr(46);
```

CAUTION

For backward compatibility, the compiler provides a switch that enables typed constants to be assignable, just like variables. This switch is accessible via the Compiler page of the Project, Options dialog box, or using the $WRITEABLECONST (or $J) compiler directive. However, this behavior should be officially deemed icky, and it should be avoided by leaving this functionality at its default disabled state.

NOTE

Like C# and Visual Basic .NET, the Delphi language doesn't have a preprocessor as does the C language. There's no concept of a macro in Delphi and, therefore, no Delphi equivalent for C's #define for constant declaration. Although you can use Delphi's $define compiler directive for conditional compiles similar to C's #define, you cannot use it to define constants. Use `const` in Delphi where you would use #define to declare a constant in C.

Operators

Operators are the symbols in your code that enable you to manipulate all types of data. For example, there are operators for adding, subtracting, multiplying, and dividing numeric data. There are also operators for addressing a particular element of an array. This section explains some of the Delphi operators and their correlation with C# and CLR counterparts.

Assignment Operators

Unless you have some experience with Pascal, Delphi's assignment operator might be one of the toughest things to get used to. To assign a value to a variable, use the := operator as you would use the = operator in C# or Visual Basic .NET. Delphi programmers often call this the gets or assignment operator, and the expression

```
Number1 := 5;
```

is read either "Number1 *gets* the value 5," or "Number1 *is assigned* the value 5."

Comparison Operators

If you've already programmed in Visual Basic .NET, you should be very comfortable with Delphi's comparison operators because they're virtually identical. These operators are fairly standard throughout programming languages, so they're covered only briefly in this section.

The Delphi language uses the = operator to perform logical comparisons between two expressions or values. Delphi's = operator is analogous to the C# == operator, so a C# expression written as

```
if (x == y)
```

is written like this in Delphi:

```
if x = y
```

> **NOTE**
>
> Remember that in the Delphi language, the := operator is used to assign a value to a variable, and the = operator compares the values of two operands.

Delphi's "not equal to" operator is <>, and its purpose is identical to C#'s != operator. To determine whether two expressions are not equal, use this code:

```
if x <> y then DoSomething
```

Logical Operators

Delphi uses the words and and or as logical "and" and "or" operators, whereas C# uses the && and ¦¦ symbols, respectively, for these operators. The most common use of the and and or operators is as part of an if statement or loop, as demonstrated in the following two examples:

```
if (Condition 1) and (Condition 2) then
  DoSomething;

while (Condition 1) or (Condition 2) do
  DoSomething;
```

Delphi's logical "not" operator is `not`, which is used to invert a Boolean expression. It's analogous to the C#'s `!` operator. It's also often used as a part of `if` statements, as shown here:

```
if not (condition) then (do something);   // if condition is false then...
```

Table 5.1 provides an easy reference of how Delphi operators map to corresponding C# and Visual Basic .NET operators.

TABLE 5.1   Assignment, Comparison, and Logical Operators

Operator	Delphi	C#	Visual Basic .NET
Assignment	:=	=	=
Comparison	=	==	= or Is*
Not equal to	<>	!=	<>
Less than	<	<	<
Greater than	>	>	>
Less than or equal to	<=	<=	<=
Greater than or equal to	>=	>=	>=
Logical and	and	&&	And
Logical or	or	||	Or
Logical not	not	!	Not
Logical xor	xor	^	Xor

Arithmetic Operators

You should already be familiar with most Delphi language arithmetic operators because they're generally similar to those used in most common languages. Table 5.2 illustrates all the Delphi arithmetic operators and their C# and Visual Basic .NET counterparts.

TABLE 5.2   Arithmetic Operators

Operator	Delphi	C#	Visual Basic .NET
Addition	+	+	+
Subtraction	-	-	-
Multiplication	*	*	*
Floating-point division	/	/	/
Integer division	div	/	\
Modulus	mod	%	Mod
Exponent power	None	None	^

You might notice that Delphi and Visual Basic .NET provide different division operators for floating-point and integer math, although this isn't the case for C#. The `div` operator automatically truncates any remainder when you're dividing two integer expressions.

In Visual Basic .NET, the `Is` comparison operator is used for objects, whereas the `=` comparison operator is used for other types.

> **NOTE**
>
> Remember to use the correct division operator for the types of expressions with which you're working. The Delphi compiler gives you an error if you try to divide two floating-point numbers with the integer `div` operator or assign to an integer the result of two integers divided with the floating-point / operator, as the following code illustrates:
>
> ```
> var
>   i: Integer;
>   d: Double;
> begin
>   i := 4 / 3;        // This line will cause a compiler error
>   d := 3.4 div 2.3;  // This line also will cause an error
> end;
> ```
>
> If you must divide two integers using the / operator, you can assign the result to an integer if you convert the expression to an integer using the `Trunc()` or `Round()` functions.

Bitwise Operators

Bitwise operators enable you to modify individual bits of a given integral variable. Common bitwise operators enable you to shift the bits to the left or right or to perform bitwise "and," "not," "or," and "exclusive or" (xor) operations with two numbers. The Shift-left and Shift-right operators are `shl` and `shr`, respectively, and they're much like the C# << and >> operators. The remainder of Delphi's bitwise operators is easy enough to remember: and, not, or, and xor. Table 5.3 lists the bitwise operators.

TABLE 5.3   Bitwise Operators

Operator	Delphi	C#	Visual Basic .NET
And	and	&	And
Not	not	~	Not
Or	or	¦	Or
Xor	xor	^	Xor
Shift-left	shl	<<	None
Shift-right	shr	>>	None

Increment and Decrement Procedures

Increment and decrement operators provide a convenient means to add to or subtract from a given integral variable. Delphi doesn't really provide honest-to-gosh increment and decrement operators similar to the C# ++ and -- operators, but Delphi does provide procedures called `Inc()` and `Dec()` intended for this very purpose.

You can call Inc() or Dec() with one or two parameters. For example, the following two lines of code increment and decrement `variable`, respectively, by 1:

```
Inc(variable);
```

```
Dec(variable);
```

The following two lines increment or decrement `variable` by 3:

```
Inc(variable, 3);
```

```
Dec(variable, 3);
```

Table 5.4 compares the increment and decrement operators of different languages.

TABLE 5.4   Increment and Decrement Operators

Operator	Delphi	C#	Visual Basic .NET
Increment	`Inc()`	`++`	*None*
Decrement	`Dec()`	`--`	*None*

Note that the C# `++` and `--` operators return a value, whereas `Inc()` and `Dec()` do not. Delphi's `Succ()` and `Pred()` functions do return a value; however, these do not modify the parameter.

Do-and-assign Operators

Not present in the Delphi language are handy do-and-assign operators like those found in C#. These operators, such as `+=` and `*=`, perform an arithmetic operation (in this case, an add and a multiply) before making the assignment. In Delphi, this type of operation must be performed using two separate operators. Therefore, this code in C#:

```
x += 5;
```

becomes this in Delphi:present in the Delphi language are handy do-and-assign

```
x := x + 5;
```

Delphi Language Types

One of the Delphi language's greatest features is that it's strongly typed, making it an excellent fit for the .NET platform. This means that actual variables passed to procedures and functions must be of the same type as the formal parameters identified in the procedure or function definition—very little is done for you in terms of implicit type conversion. Delphi's strongly-typed nature enables it to perform a sanity check of your code—to ensure that you aren't trying to put a square peg in a round hole. After all, the easiest bug fixes are the ones the compiler tells you to perform!

Objects, Objects Everywhere!

One of the most important notions regarding fundamental types in the .NET version of the Delphi compiler is that they are all value types capable of implicit conversion to classes. This conversation between value and object and back again is known as boxing and unboxing in .NET parlance. Integers, strings, floating points, and all of the rest are not implemented as primitive concepts in the compiler, as in Win32, but instead map to value types provided either by the .NET Framework or by Borland's RTL or VCL. Unlike Win32 Delphi, these value types can have their own procedures and functions in addition to those available in corresponding classes created by the implicit boxing and unboxing of these types. This allows for a kind of syntax that might be foreign for those coming from native compilers (although perhaps familiar for those experienced with languages such as Java or SmallTalk):

```
var
  S: string;
  I: Integer;
begin
  I := 42;
  S := I.ToString;   // can call a method on an Integer!
end;
```

> **NOTE**
>
> The string type is used heavily in development. This is not to say that other types are not, but there are some special considerations when using strings. Chapter 11 addresses strings specifically; therefore, you will not see detailed coverage of them here.

A Comparison of Types

Delphi surfaces most of the primitive types available in the CLR. Table 5.5 compares and contrasts the base types of the Delphi language with those of C# and the CLR. This table also indicates whether each type is compliant with the CLS.

TABLE 5.5   A Delphi-to-C#-to-CLR Type Comparison

Variable range	Delphi	C#	CLR	CLS Compliant?
8-bit signed integer	ShortInt	sbyte	System.SByte	No
8-bit unsigned integer	Byte	byte	System.Byte	Yes
16-bit signed integer	SmallInt	short	System.Int16	Yes
16-bit unsigned integer	Word	ushort	System.UInt16	No
32-bit signed integer	Integer	int	System.Int32	Yes
32-bit unsigned integer	Cardinal	uint	System.UInt32	No
64-bit signed integer	Int64	long	System.Int64	Yes
64-bit unsigned integer	UInt64	ulong	System.UInt64	No
single precision float	Single	float	System.Single	Yes
double precision float	Double	double	System.Double	Yes
fixed-point decimal	None	decimal	System.Decimal	Yes
Delphi fixed-point decimal	Currency	None	None	No
date/time	TDateTime*	None	System.DateTime	Yes
variant	Variant, OleVariant	None	None	No
1-byte character	AnsiChar	None	None	No
2-byte character	Char, WideChar	char	System.Char	Yes
Fixed-length byte string	ShortString	None	None	No
Dynamic 1-byte string	AnsiString	None	None	No
Dynamic 2-byte string	string, WideString	string	System.String	Yes
Boolean	Boolean	bool	System.Boolean	None

*TDateTime is a record that wraps a System.DateTime with methods and operator overloads that makes it behave very much like System.DateTime, but with additional behavior to be compatible with Win32 Delphi's TDateTime type.

Characters

Delphi provides three character types:

- WideChar—This CLS-compatible character is two bytes in size and represents a Unicode character.

- Char—This is an alias for WideChar. In Win32 versions of Delphi, Char was an AnsiChar.

- AnsiChar—An old school one-byte ANSI character.

Never assume the size of a Char (or any other type, for that matter), in your code. Instead, you should use the SizeOf() function where appropriate.

> **NOTE**
>
> The SizeOf() standard procedure returns the size, in bytes, of a type or variable.

Variant Types

The Variant class provides an implementation of a type capable of serving as a kind of container for many other types. This means that a variant can change the kind of data to which it refers at runtime. For example, the following code will compile and run properly:

```
var
  V: Variant;
  I: IInterface;
begin
  V := 'Delphi is Great!';  // Variant holds a string
  V := 1;                    // Variant now holds an Integer
  V := 123.34;               // Variant now holds a floating point
  V := True;                 // Variant now holds a boolean
  V := I;                    // Variant now holds an interface
end;
```

Variants support a wide variety of types, including complex types such as arrays and interfaces. The following code from the Borland.Vcl.Variants unit shows the various supported types, which are identified by values known as TVarTypes:

```
type
  TVarType = Integer;
```

```
const                     // Decimal ¦ Other names for this type
  varEmpty    = $0000; // = 0    ¦ Unassigned, Nil
  varNull     = $0001; // = 1    ¦ Null, System.DBNull
  varSmallInt = $0002; // = 2    ¦ I2, System.Int16
  varInteger  = $0003; // = 3    ¦ I4, System.Int32
  varSingle   = $0004; // = 4    ¦ R4, System.Single
  varDouble   = $0005; // = 5    ¦ R8, System.Double
  varCurrency = $0006; // = 6    ¦ Borland.Delphi.System.Currency
  varDate     = $0007; // = 7    ¦ Borland.Delphi.System.TDateTime
  varString   = $0008; // = 8    ¦ WideString, System.String
  varError    = $000A; // = 10   ¦ Exception, System.Exception
  varBoolean  = $000B; // = 11   ¦ Bool, System.Boolean
  varObject   = $000C; // = 12   ¦ TObject, System.Object
```

```
varDecimal   = $000E; // = 14   ¦ System.Decimal
varShortInt  = $0010; // = 16   ¦ I1, System.SByte
varByte      = $0011; // = 17   ¦ U1, System.Byte
varWord      = $0012; // = 18   ¦ U2, System.UInt16
varLongWord  = $0013; // = 19   ¦ U4, System.UInt32
varInt64     = $0014; // = 20   ¦ I8, System.Int64
varUInt64    = $0015; // = 21   ¦ U8, System.UInt64
varChar      = $0016; // = 22   ¦ WideChar, System.Char
varDateTime  = $0017; // = 23   ¦ System.DateTime;

varFirst     = varEmpty;
varLast      = varDateTime;

varArray     = $2000; // = 8192 ¦ System.Array, Dynamic Arrays
varTypeMask  = $0FFF; // = 4095
varUndefined = -1;
```

As a function of value assignment, variants are capable of coercing themselves into other types, as needed. For example:

```
var
  V: Variant;
  I: Integer;
begin
  V := '1';  // V hold string '1'
  I := V;    // Implicitly converts to Integer, I is now 1
end;
```

Typecasting Variants

You can explicitly typecast expressions to type `Variant`. For example, the expression

```
Variant(X);
```

results in a `Variant` type whose type code corresponds to the result of the expression x, which must be an integer, floating point, currency, string, character, date/time, class, or Boolean type.

You can also typecast a variant to that of a simple data type. For example, given the assignment

```
V := 1.6;
```

where v is a variable of type `Variant`, the following expressions will have the following results shown:

```
S := string(V);   // S will contain the string '1.6';
// I is rounded to the nearest Integer value, in this case: 2.
I := Integer(V);
B := Boolean(V);  // B contains True, since V is not equal to 0
D := Double(V);   // D contains the value 1.6
```

These results are dictated by certain type-conversion rules applicable to `Variant` types. These rules are defined in detail in the Delphi Language Guide.

By the way, in the preceding example, it isn't necessary to typecast the variant to another data type to make the assignment. The following code would work just as well:

```
V := 1.6;
S := V;
I := V;
B := V;
D := V;
```

When multiple variants are used in an expression, there can be much more behind-the-scenes code logic attached to these implicit type coercions. In such cases, if you're sure of the type a variant contains, you're better off explicitly typecasting it to that type in order to speed up the operation.

Variants in Expressions

You can use variants in expressions with the following operators: +, =, *, /, div, mod, shl, shr, and, or, xor, not, :=, <>, <, >, <=, and >=. The standard `Inc()`, `Dec()`, `Trunc()`, and `Round()` functions are also valid with variant expressions.

When using variants in expressions, Delphi knows how to perform the operations based on the types contained within a variant. For example, if two variants, V1 and V2, contain integers, the expression V1 + V2 results in the addition of the two integers. However, if V1 and V2 contain strings, the result is a concatenation of the two strings. What happens if V1 and V2 contain two different data types? Delphi uses certain promotion rules in order to perform the operation. For example, if V1 contains the string '4.5' and V2 contains a floating-point number, V1 will be converted to a floating point and then added to V2. The following code illustrates this:

```
var
  V1, V2, V3: Variant;
begin
  V1 := '100';  // A string type
  V2 := '50';   // A string type
  V3 := 200;    // An Integer type
  V1 := V1 + V2 + V3;
end;
```

Based on what we just mentioned about promotion rules, it would seem at first glance that the preceding code would result in the value 350 as an integer. However, if you take a closer look, you'll see that this is not the case. Because the order of precedence is from left to right, the first equation executed is V1 + V2. Because these two variants refer to strings, a string concatenation is performed, resulting in the string '10050'. That result is then added to the integer value held by the variant V3. Because V3 is an integer, the result '10050' is converted to an integer and added to V3, thus providing an end result of 10250.

Delphi promotes the variants to the numerically largest type in the equation in order to successfully carry out the calculation. However, when an operation is attempted on two variants of which Delphi cannot make any sense, an EVariantTypeCast exception is raised. The following code illustrates this:

```
var
  V1, V2: Variant;
```

```
begin
  V1 := 77;
  V2 := 'hello';
  V1 := V1 / V2;  // Raises an exception.
end;
```

As stated earlier, it's sometimes a good idea to explicitly typecast a variant to a specific data type if you know what that type is and if it's used in an expression. Consider the following line of code:

```
V4 := V1 * V2 / V3;
```

Before a result can be generated for this equation, each operation is handled by a runtime function that goes through several gyrations to determine the compatibility of the types the variants represent. Then the conversions are made to the appropriate data types. This results in a large amount of overhead and code size. A better solution is obviously not to use variants. However, when necessary, you can also explicitly typecast the variants so the operations are resolved at compile time:

```
V4 := Integer(V1) * Double(V2) / Integer(V3);
```

Keep in mind that this assumes you know the data types to which the variants can be successfully converted.

Empty and Null

Two special values for variants merit a brief discussion. The first is Unassigned, which means that the variant has not yet been assigned a value. This is the initial value of the variant as it comes into scope. The other is Null, which is different from Unassigned in that it actually represents the value Null as opposed to a lack of value. This distinction between no value and a Null value is especially important when applied to the field values of a database table. You will learn about database programming in Part IV, "Database Development with ADO.NET."

Another difference is that attempting to perform operations with a variant containing an Unassigned value will result in the value being converted to 0 for numeric operations or an empty string for string operations. The same isn't true of variants containing a Null value, however. When a variant involved in an equation contains a Null value, operating on the variant with that value might result in an EVariantTypeCast exception being raised.

If you want to assign or compare a variant to one of these two special values, the System.Vcl.Variants unit defines two variants, appropriated called Unassigned and Null, which can be used for assignment and comparison.

CONTROLLING VARIANT BEHAVIOR

You can control whether an exception is raised when performing an arithmetic operation with a Null variant by setting the Variant.NullStrictOperations property to True. The other Variant flags controlling Null behavior and string and Boolean conversions include

```
NullEqualityRule: TNullCompareRule;
NullMagnitudeRule: TNullCompareRule;
NullAsStringValue: string;
```

```
NullStrictConvert: Boolean;
BooleanToStringRule: TBooleanToStringRule;
BooleanTrueAsOrdinalValue: Integer;
```

User-Defined Types

Integers, strings, and floating-point numbers often are not enough to adequately represent variables in the real-world problems that programmers must try to solve. In cases like these, you must create your own types to better represent variables in the current problem. In Delphi, these user-defined types usually come in the form of records or classes; you declare these types using the Type keyword.

Arrays

The Delphi language enables you to create arrays of any type of variable. For example, a variable declared as an array of eight integers reads like this:

```
var
  A: Array[0..7] of Integer;
```

This statement is equivalent to the following C# declaration:

```
int A[8];
```

It's also equivalent to this Visual Basic .NET statement:

```
Dim A(8) as Integer
```

Delphi arrays have a special property that differentiates them from other languages: They don't have to be based at a certain number. You can therefore declare a three-element array that starts at 28, as in the following example:

```
var
  A: Array[28..30] of Integer;
```

Because Delphi arrays aren't guaranteed to begin at 0 or 1, you must use some care when iterating over array elements in a for loop. The compiler provides built-in functions called High() and Low(), which return the lower and upper bounds of an array variable or type, respectively. Your code will be less error prone and easier to maintain if you use these functions to control your for loop, as shown here:

```
var
  A: array[28..30] of Integer;
  i: Integer;
begin
  for i := Low(A) to High(A) do  // don't hard-code for loop!
    A[i] := i;
end;
```

To specify multiple dimensions, use a comma-delimited list of bounds:

```
var
  // Two-dimensional array of Integer:
  A: array[1..2, 1..2] of Integer;
```

To access a multidimensional array, use commas to separate each dimension within one set of brackets:

```
I := A[1, 2];
```

Dynamic Arrays

Dynamic arrays are dynamically allocated arrays in which the dimensions aren't known at compile time. To declare a dynamic array, just declare an array without including the dimensions, like this:

```
var
  // dynamic array of string:
  SA: array of string;
```

Before you can use a dynamic array, you must use the SetLength() procedure to allocate memory for the array:

```
begin
  // allocate room for 33 elements:
  SetLength(SA, 33);
```

Once memory has been allocated, you can access the elements of the dynamic array just like a normal array:

```
  SA[0] := 'Pooh likes hunny';
  OtherString := SA[0];
```

> **NOTE**
>
> Dynamic arrays are always zero-based.

Dynamic arrays are lifetime managed by the .NET runtime, so there's no need (and, in fact, no way) to free them when you're through using them because they will be garbage collected at some point after leaving scope. However, there might come a time when you want to request that the .NET runtime remove the dynamic array from memory before it leaves scope (if it uses a lot of memory, for example). To do this, you need only assign the dynamic array to nil:

```
SA := nil;  // requests release of SA
```

Note that assigning to nil does not release SA; it only releases a reference to it, as there could be more than one variable referencing the array indicated by SA. When the last reference to SA is released, the .NET garbage collector will release the memory occupied by the array during the next garbage collection.

Dynamic arrays are manipulated using reference semantics rather than value semantics like a normal array. Here's a quick test: What is the value of A1[0] at the end of the following code fragment?

```
var
  A1, A2: array of Integer;
begin
```

```
   SetLength(A1, 4);
   A2 := A1;
   A1[0] := 1;
   A2[0] := 26;
```

The correct answer is 26 because the assignment A2 := A1 doesn't create a new array but instead provides A2 with a reference to the same array as A1. Therefore, any modifications to A2 will also affect A1. If you want instead to make a complete copy of A1 in A2, use the Copy() standard procedure:

```
A2 := Copy(A1);
```

After this line of code is executed, A2 and A1 will be two separate arrays initially containing the same data. Changes to one will not affect the other. You can optionally specify the starting element and number of elements to be copied as parameters to Copy(), as shown here:

```
// copy 2 elements, starting at element one:
A2 := Copy(A1, 1, 2);
```

Dynamic arrays can also be multidimensional. To specify multiple dimensions, add an additional array of to the declaration for each dimension:

```
var
   // two-dimensional dynamic array of Integer:
   IA: array of array of Integer;
```

To allocate memory for a multidimensional dynamic array, pass the sizes of the other dimensions as additional parameters to SetLength():

```
begin
   // IA will be a 5 x 5 array of Integer
   SetLength(IA, 5, 5);
```

You access multidimensional dynamic arrays the same way you do normal multidimensional arrays; each element is separated by a comma with a single set of brackets:

```
IA[0,3] := 28;
```

C-style sytanx for multidimensional array access is also supported:

```
IA[0][3] := 28;
```

Records

A user-defined structure is referred to as a record in the Delphi language, and it's the equivalent of C#'s struct or Visual Basic .NET's Type. As an example, here's a record definition in Delphi as well as equivalent definitions in C# and Visual Basic .NET:

```
{ Delphi }
Type
   MyRec = record
      i: Integer;
      d: Double;
   end;
```

```
/* C# */
public struct MyRec
{
  int i;
  double d;
}
```

```
'Visual Basic
Type MyRec
  i As Integer
  d As Double
End Type
```

When working with a record, you use the dot symbol to access its fields. Here's an example:

```
var
  N: MyRec;
begin
  N.i := 23;
  N.d := 3.4;
end;
```

Methods, operator overloads, and interfaced implementations are also supported for records. This capability was not supported on previous versions of the Delphi compiler. These topics are covered in more detail, along with class types, later in this chapter. However, the following code example shows the syntax for using these elements with records:

```
IBlah = interface
  procedure bar;
end;

Foo = record(IBlah)  // record implements IBlah interface
  AField: Integer;
  procedure bar;
  class operator Add(a, b: Foo): Foo;  // overload + operator
end;
```

Sets

Sets are a uniquely Delphi type that have no equivalent in C# or Visual Basic .NET. Sets provide an efficient and convenient means of representing a collection of ordinal, AnsiChar, or enumerated values. You can declare a new set type using the keywords set of followed by an ordinal type or subrange of possible set values. Here's an example:

```
type
  TCharSet = set of AnsiChar;        // possible members: #0 - #255

  TEnum = (Monday, Tuesday, Wednesday, Thursday, Friday);
  TEnumSet = set of TEnum;  // can contain any combination of TEnum members

  TSubrangeSet = set of 1..10; // possible members: 1 - 10
```

Note that a set can only contain up to 256 elements. Additionally, only ordinal types can follow the set of keywords. Therefore, the following declarations are illegal:

```
type
  TIntSet = set of Integer;  // Invalid: too many elements
  TStrSet = set of string;   // Invalid: not an ordinal type
```

Sets store their elements internally as individual bits, which makes them very efficient in terms of speed and memory usage.

NOTE

If you are porting Win32 code to .NET, bear in mind that chars are 2-bytes in the .NET world and 1-byte in Win32. This means that a set of Char declaration in .NET is demoted by the compiler to a set of AnsiChar, which can potentially change the meaning of code. The compiler will issue a warning to this effect, recommending that you explicitly use set of AnsiChar.

Using Sets

Use square brackets when constructing a literal set value from one or more elements. The following code demonstrates how to declare set type variables and assign them values:

```
type
  TCharSet = set of AnsiChar;      // possible members: #0 - #255

  TEnum = (Monday, Tuesday, Wednesday, Thursday, Friday, Saturday, Sunday);
  TEnumSet = set of TEnum;  // can contain any combination of TEnum members

var
  CharSet: TCharSet;
  EnumSet: TEnumSet;
  SubrangeSet: set of 1..10; // possible members: 1 - 10
  AlphaSet: set of 'A'..'z'; // possible members: 'A' - 'z'

begin
  CharSet := ['A'..'J', 'a', 'm'];
  EnumSet := [Saturday, Sunday];
  SubrangeSet := [1, 2, 4..6];
  AlphaSet := [];  // Empty; no elements
end;
```

Set Operators

The Delphi language provides several operators for use in manipulating sets. You can use these operators to determine set membership, union, difference, and intersection.

Membership   Use the in operator to determine whether a given element is contained in a particular set. For example, the following code would be used to determine whether the CharSet set mentioned earlier contains the letter 'S':

```
if 'S' in CharSet then
  // do something;
```

The following code determines whether `EnumSet` lacks the member `Monday`:

```
if not (Monday in EnumSet) then
  // do something;
```

Union and Difference   Use the + and - operators or the `Include()` and `Exclude()` procedures to add and remove elements to and from a set variable:

```
Include(CharSet, 'a');        // add 'a' to set
CharSet := CharSet + ['b'];   // add 'b' to set
Exclude(CharSet, 'x');        // remove 'z' from set
CharSet := CharSet - ['y', 'z']; // remove 'y' and 'z' from set
```

> **TIP**
>
> When possible, use `Include()` and `Exclude()` to add and remove a single element to and from a set rather than the + and – operators, as the former is more efficient.

Intersection   Use the * operator to calculate the intersection of two sets. The result of the expression `Set1 * Set2` is a set containing all the members that `Set1` and `Set2` have in common. For example, the following code could be used as an efficient means for determining whether a given set contains multiple elements:

```
if ['a', 'b', 'c'] * CharSet = ['a', 'b', 'c'] then
  // do something
```

Unsafe Code

Right about now, those with previous experience in Delphi for Win32 might be thinking, "this all sounds fine so far, but what happened to the pointers?" Although pointers are in the language, they are considered unsafe from a .NET standpoint because they allow for direct access to memory. Therefore, in order to employ pointers in your applications, you will need to let the compiler know that it should permit unsafe code. In order to write unsafe code, you must

1. Include the `{$UNSAFECODE ON}` directive in the unit containing the unsafe code.

2. Mark functions containing unsafe code with the `unsafe` keyword.

The following unsafe code will successfully compile in Delphi:

```
{$UNSAFECODE ON}

procedure RunningWithScissors; unsafe;
var
  A: array[0..31] of Char;
  P: PChar;   // PChar is an unsafe type
begin
  A := 'safety first';   // fill character array
  P := @A[0];            // point to first element
  P[0] := 'S';           // change first element
  MessageBox.Show(A);    // show changed array
end;
```

Note the use of Delphi's @, or address of operator, to obtain the address of a bit of data.

You can assume that the code in this portion of the chapter must be compiled using the $UNSAFECODE and unsafe directives.

Pointers

A pointer is a variable that contains a memory location. You already saw an example of a pointer in the PChar type earlier in this chapter. Delphi's generic pointer type is called, aptly, Pointer. A Pointer is sometimes called an untyped pointer because it contains only a memory address, and the compiler doesn't maintain any information on the data to which it points. That notion, however, goes against the grain of Delphi's type-safe nature, so pointers in your code will usually be typed pointers.

> **NOTE**
>
> In .NET, the System.IntPtr type is used to represent an opaque, untyped pointer.

Typed pointers are declared by using the ^ (or pointer) operator in the Type section of your program. Typed pointers help the compiler keep track of exactly what kind of type a particular pointer points to, thus enabling the compiler to keep track of what you're doing (and can do) with a pointer variable. Here are some typical declarations for pointers:

```
Type
  PInt = ^Integer;        // PInt is now a pointer to an Integer
  Foo = record            // A record type
    GobbledyGook: string;
    Snarf: Double;
  end;
  PFoo = ^Foo;            // PFoo is a pointer to a foo type
var
  P: Pointer;             // Untyped pointer
  P2: PFoo;               // Instance of PFoo
```

> **NOTE**
>
> C/C++ programmers will notice the similarity between Delphi's ^ operator and C's * operator. Delphi's Pointer type corresponds to the C/C++ void * type.

Remember that a pointer variable only stores a memory address. Allocating space for whatever the pointer points to is your job as a programmer. Previous versions of Delphi had many functions that enabled a developer to allocate and deallocate memory; however, because direct memory allocation is so rare in .NET, it is typically accomplished only via the `System.Runtime.InteropServices.Marshal` class. The following code demonstrates how to use this class to create and free a block of memory, as a well as copy some array data in and out of the block.

```
{$UNSAFECODE ON}

type
  TArray = array[0..31] of Char;

procedure ArrayCopy; unsafe;
var
  A1: TArray;
  A2: array of char;
  P: IntPtr;
begin
  A1 := 'safety first';  // fill character array
  SetLength(A2, High(TArray) + 1);
  P := Marshal.AllocHGlobal(High(TArray) + 1);
  try
    Marshal.Copy(A1, 0, P, High(TArray) + 1);  // copy A1 to temp
    Marshal.Copy(P, A2, 0, High(TArray) + 1);   // copy temp to A2
    MessageBox.Show(A2);   // show changed array
  finally
    Marshal.FreeHGlobal(P);
  end;
end;
```

If you want to access the data that a particular pointer points to, follow the pointer variable name with the ^ operator. This method is known as dereferencing the pointer. The following code illustrates working with pointers:

```
procedure PointerFun; unsafe;
var
  I: Integer;
  PI: ^Integer;
begin
  I := 42;
  PI := @I;                   // points to I
  PI^ := 24;                  // changes I
  MessageBox.Show(I.ToString);
end;
```

The Delphi compiler employs strict type checking on pointer types. For example, the variables a and b in the following example aren't type compatible:

```
var
  a: ^Integer;
  b: ^Integer;
```

By contrast, the variables a and b in the equivalent declaration in C are type compatible:

```
int *a;
int *b
```

The Delphi language creates a unique type for each pointer-to-type declaration, so you must create a named type if you want to assign values from `a` to `b`, as shown here:

```
type
  PtrInteger = ^Integer;  // create named type

var
  a: PtrInteger;
  b: PtrInteger;    // now a and b are compatible
```

> **NOTE**
>
> When a pointer doesn't point to anything (its value is zero), its value is said to be `nil`, and it is often called a nil or null pointer.

Null-Terminated Strings

Earlier, this chapter mentions that Delphi has three different null-terminated string types: `PChar`, `PAnsiChar`, and `PWideChar`. As their names imply, each of these represents a null-terminated string of each of Delphi's three character types. In .NET, `PChar` is an alias for `PWideChar`, whereas `PChar` is an alias for `PAnsiChar` in Win32. In this chapter, we refer to each of these string types generically as `PChar`. The `PChar` type in Delphi exists mainly for backward compatibility with previous versions. A `PChar` is defined as a pointer to a string followed by a null (zero) value. Because it is a raw, unmanaged, unsafe pointer, memory for `PChar` types isn't automatically allocated and managed by .NET.

In the Win32 flavor of Delphi, `PChar`s are assignment compatible with `string`s. However, in .NET, these types are no longer compatible, which makes their use far less common in the .NET world.

Variant Records

The Delphi language also supports variant records, which enable different pieces of data to overlay the same portion of memory in the record. Not to be confused with the `Variant` data type, variant records enable each overlapping data field to be accessed independently. If your background is C, you'll recognize variant records as being the same concept as a `union` within a C `struct`. The following code shows a variant record in which a `Double`, `Integer`, and `Char` all occupy the same memory space:

```
type
  TVariantRecord = record
    NullStrField: PChar;
    IntField: Integer;
    case Integer of
      0: (D: Double);
      1: (I: Integer);
      2: (C: Char);
  end;
```

> **NOTE**
>
> The rules of the Delphi language state that the variant portion of a record cannot be of any life-time-managed type. This includes classes, interfaces, variants, dynamic arrays, and strings.

Here's the C equivalent of the preceding type declaration:

```c
struct TUnionStruct
{
  char * StrField;
  int IntField;
  union u
  {
    double D;
    int i;
    char c;
  };
};
```

Because variant records deal with explicit memory layout, they also are considered unsafe types.

> **NOTE**
>
> Record memory layout can be controlled by the developer in .NET using the `StructLayout` and `FieldOffset` attributes.

Classes and Objects

A class is a value type that can contain data, properties, methods, and operators. Delphi's object model is discussed in much greater detail later in the "Using Delphi Objects" section of this chapter, so this section covers just the basic syntax of Delphi classes. A class is defined as follows:

```delphi
Type
  TChildObject = class(TParentObject)
  public
    SomeVar: Integer;
    procedure SomeProc;
  end;
```

This declaration is equivalent to the following C# declaration:

```csharp
public class TChildObject: TParentObject
{
  public int SomeVar;
  public void SomeProc() {};
}
```

Methods are defined in the same way as normal procedures and functions (which are discussed in the section "Procedures and Functions"), with the addition of the classname and the dot symbol:

```delphi
procedure TChildObject.SomeProc;
begin
  { procedure code goes here }
end;
```

Delphi's . symbol is similar in functionality to C# and Visual Basic .NET's . operator when referencing members.

Type Aliases

The Delphi language has the capability to create new names, or aliases, for types that are already defined. For example, if you want to create a new name for an `Integer` called `MyReallyNiftyInteger`, you could do so using the following code:

```
type
  MyReallyNiftyInteger = Integer;
```

The newly defined type alias is compatible in all ways with the type for which it's an alias, meaning, in this case, that you could use `MyReallyNiftyInteger` anywhere in which you could use `Integer`.

It's possible, however, to define strongly-typed aliases that are considered new, unique types by the compiler. To do this, use the `type` reserved word in the following manner:

```
type
  MyOtherNeatInteger = type Integer;
```

Using this syntax, the `MyOtherNeatInteger` type will be converted to an `Integer` when necessary for purposes of assignment, but `MyOtherNeatInteger` will not be compatible with `Integer` when used in `var` and `out` parameters. Therefore, the following code is syntactically correct:

```
var
  MONI: MyOtherNeatInteger;
  I: Integer;
begin
  I := 1;
  MONI := I;
```

On the other hand, the following code will not compile:

```
procedure Goon(var Value: Integer);
begin
  // some code
end;

var
  M: MyOtherNeatInteger;
begin
  M := 29;
  Goon(M);  // Error: M is not var compatible with Integer
```

In addition to these compiler-enforced type compatibility issues, the compiler also generates runtime type information for strongly-typed aliases. This enables you to create unique property editors for simple types, as you'll learn in Chapter 8, "Mono—A Cross Platform .NET Project."

Typecasting and Type Conversion

Typecasting is a technique by which you can force the compiler to view a variable of one type as another type. Because of Delphi's strongly-typed nature, you'll find that the compiler is very picky about types matching up in the formal and actual parameters of a function call. Hence, you occasionally will be required to cast a variable of one type to a variable of another type to make the compiler happy. Suppose, for example, that you need to assign the value of a character to a Word variable:

```
var
  c: char;
  w: Word;
begin
  c := 's';
  w := c;   // compiler complains on this line
end.
```

In the following syntax, a typecast is required to convert c into a Word. In effect, a typecast tells the compiler that you really know what you're doing and want to convert one type to another:

```
var
  c: Char;
  w: Word;
begin
  c := 's';
  w := Word(c);   // compiler happy as a clam on this line
end.
```

> **NOTE**
>
> You can typecast a variable of one type to another type only if the data size of the two variables is the same. For example, you cannot typecast a Double as an Integer. To convert a floating-point type to an integer, use the Trunc() or Round() functions. To convert an integer into a floating-point value, use the assignment operator: FloatVar := IntVar. You can also convert between types when implicit or explicit conversion operators are defined for a class (more on operator overloading later).

The Delphi language also supports a special variety of typecasting between objects using the as operator. The as operator functions identical to a standard typecast, except that it yields null rather than raising an exception on failure.

String Resources

Delphi provides the capability to place string resources directly into Delphi source code using the resourcestring clause. String resources are literal strings (usually those displayed to the user) that are physically located in a resource attached to the application or library rather than embedded in the source code. Your source code references the string resources in place of string literals. By separating strings from source code, your application can be translated more easily by added string resources in a different language. String resources are declared in the form of *identifier = string literal* in the resourcestring clause, as shown here:

```
resourcestring
  ResString1 = 'Resource string 1';
  ResString2 = 'Resource string 2';
  ResString3 = 'Resource string 3';
```

Syntactically, resource strings can be used in your source code in a manner similar to a function returning a string:

```
resourcestring
  ResString1 = 'hello';
  ResString2 = 'world';

var
  String1: string;

begin
  String1 := ResString1 + ' ' + ResString2;
  .
  .
  .
end;
```

Testing Conditions

This section compares `if` and `case` constructs in Delphi to similar constructs in C# and Visual Basic .NET. We assume that you've used these types of programmatic constructs before, so we don't spend much time explaining them to you.

The if Statement

An `if` statement enables you to determine whether certain conditions are met before executing a particular block of code. As an example, here's an `if` statement in Delphi, followed by equivalent definitions in C# and Visual Basic .NET:

```
{ Delphi }
if x = 4 then y := x;

/* C# */
if (x == 4) y = x;

'Visual Basic
If x = 4 Then y = x
```

> **NOTE**
>
> If you have an `if` statement that makes multiple comparisons, make sure that you enclose each set of comparisons in parentheses for code clarity. Do this:
>
> `if (x = 7) and (y = 8) then`
>
> However, don't do this (it causes the compiler displeasure):
>
> `if x = 7 and y = 8 then`

Use the `begin` and `end` keywords in Delphi almost as you would use { and } in C#. For example, use the following construct if you want to execute multiple lines of text when a given condition is true:

```
if x = 6 then begin
  DoSomething;
  DoSomethingElse;
```

```
  DoAnotherThing;
end;
```

You can combine multiple conditions using the `if..else` construct:

```
if x =100 then
  SomeFunction
else if x = 200 then
  SomeOtherFunction
else begin
  SomethingElse;
  Entirely;
end;
```

Using case Statements

The `case` statement in Delphi works in much the same way as a `switch` statement in C#. A `case` statement provides a means for choosing one condition among many possibilities without a huge `if..else if..else if` construct. Here's an example of Delphi's `case` statement:

```
case SomeIntegerVariable of
  101 : DoSomething;
  202 : begin
      DoSomething;
      DoSomethingElse;
    end;
  303 : DoAnotherThing;
  else DoTheDefault;
end;
```

> **NOTE**
>
> The selector type of a case statement must be an ordinal type. It's illegal to use nonordinal types, such as strings, as case selectors. Other .NET languages, such as C#, do permit strings to be used as selectors.

Here's the C# `switch` statement equivalent to the preceding example:

```
switch (SomeIntegerVariable)
{
  case 101: DoSomeThing(); break;
  case 202: DoSomething();
            DoSomethingElse(); break
  case 303: DoAnotherThing(); break;
  default: DoTheDefault();
}
```

Loops

A loop is a construct that enables you to repeatedly perform some type of action. Delphi's loop constructs are very similar to what you should be familiar with from your experience with other languages, so we don't spend any time teaching you about loops. This section describes the various loop constructs you can use in Delphi.

The for Loop

A for loop is ideal when you need to repeat an action a predetermined number of times. Here's an example, albeit not a very useful one, of a for loop that adds the loop index to a variable 10 times:

```
var
  I, X: Integer;
begin
  X := 0;
  for I := 1 to 10 do
    inc(X, I);
end.
```

The C# equivalent of the preceding example is as follows:

```
void main()
{
  int x = 0;
  for(int i=1; i<=10; i++)
    x += i;
}
```

Here's the Visual Basic .NET equivalent of the same concept:

```
Dim X As Integer
For I = 1 To 10
  X = X + I
Next I
```

The while Loop

Use a while loop construct when you want some part of your code to repeat itself while some condition is true. A while loop's conditions are tested before the loop is executed, and a classic example for the use of a while loop is to repeatedly perform some action on a file as long as the end of the file isn't encountered. Here's an example demonstrating a loop that reads one line at a time from a file and writes it to the screen:

```
program FileIt;

{$APPTYPE CONSOLE}

var
  f: TextFile;  // a text file
  s: string;
begin
  AssignFile(f, 'foo.txt');
  Reset(f);
  try
    while not EOF(f) do
    begin
      readln(f, S);
      writeln(S);
    end;
  finally
```

```
      CloseFile(f);
  end;
end.
```

Delphi's while loop works basically the same as C#'s while loop or Visual Basic .NET's Do While loop.

repeat..until

The repeat..until loop addresses the same type of problem as a while loop but from a different angle. It repeats a given block of code until a certain condition becomes True. Unlike a while loop, the loop code is always executed at least once because the condition is tested at the end of the loop. Delphi's repeat..until is roughly equivalent to C#'s do..while loop, except that the break condition is reversed.

For example, the following code snippet repeats a statement that increments a counter until the value of the counter becomes greater than 100:

```
var
  x: Integer;
begin
  X := 1;
  repeat
    inc(x);
  until x > 100;
end.
```

The Break Statement

Calling Break from inside a while, for, or repeat loop causes the flow of your program to skip immediately to the end of the currently executing loop. This method is useful when you need to leave the loop immediately because of some circumstance that might arise within the loop. Delphi's Break statement is analogous to C#'s break and Visual Basic .NET's Exit statement. The following loop uses Break to terminate the loop after five iterations:

```
var
  i: Integer;
begin
  for i := 1 to 1000000 do
  begin
    MessageBeep(0);          // make the computer beep
    if i = 5 then Break;
  end;
end;
```

The Continue Statement

Call Continue inside a loop when you want to skip over a portion of code and the flow of control to continue with the next iteration of the loop. Note in the following example that the code after Continue isn't executed in the first iteration of the loop:

```
var
  i: Integer;
```

```
begin
  for i := 1 to 3 do
  begin
    writeln(i, '. Before continue');
    if i = 1 then Continue;
    writeln(i, '. After continue');
  end;
end;
```

Procedures and Functions

As a programmer, you should already be familiar with the basics of procedures and functions. A procedure is a discrete program part that performs some particular task when it's called and then returns to the calling part of your code. A function works the same except that a function returns a value after its exit to the calling part of the program.

Listing 5.1 demonstrates a short Delphi program with a procedure and a function.

LISTING 5.1   An Example of a Function and a Procedure

```
1:  program FuncProc;
2:
3:  {$APPTYPE CONSOLE}
4:
5:  procedure BiggerThanTen(I: Integer);
6:  { writes something to the screen if I is greater than 10 }
7:  begin
8:    if I > 10 then
9:      writeln('Funky.');
10: end;
11:
12: function IsPositive(I: Integer): Boolean;
13: { Returns True if I is 0 or positive, False if I is negative }
14: begin
15:   Result := I >= 0;
16: end;
17:
18: var
19:   Num: Integer;
20: begin
21:   Num := 23;
22:   BiggerThanTen(Num);
23:   if IsPositive(Num) then
24:     writeln(Num, ' Is positive.')
25:   else
26:     writeln(Num, ' Is negative.');
27: end.
```

RESULT

The local variable Result in the IsPositive() function deserves special attention. Every Delphi function has an implicit local variable called Result that contains the return value of the function. Note that unlike C#'s return statement, the function doesn't terminate as soon as a value is assigned to Result.

If you want to duplicate the behavior of C#'s return statement, you can call `Exit` immediately after assigning to `Result`. The `Exit` statement immediately exits the current routine.

You also can return a value from a function by assigning the name of a function to a value inside the function's code. This is standard Delphi syntax and a holdover from previous versions of Borland Pascal. If you choose to use the function name within the body, be careful to note that there is a huge difference between using the function name on the left side of an assignment operator and using it somewhere else in your code. If on the left, you are assigning the function return value. If somewhere else in your code, you are calling the function recursively!

Note that the implicit `Result` variable isn't allowed when the compiler's Extended Syntax option is disabled in the Project, Options, Compiler dialog box or when you're using the `{$EXTENDEDSYNTAX OFF}` (or `{$X-}`) directive.

Passing Parameters

Delphi enables you to pass parameters by value or by reference to functions and procedures. The parameters you pass can be of any basic or user-defined type or an open array. (Open arrays are discussed later in this chapter.) Parameters also can be constant if their values will not change in the procedure or function.

Value Parameters

Value parameters are the default mode of parameter passing. When a parameter is passed by value, it means that a local copy of that variable is created, and the function or procedure operates on the copy. Consider the following example:

```
procedure Foo(I: Integer);
```

When you call a procedure in this way, a copy of `Integer` `I` will be made, and `Foo()` will operate on the local copy of `I`. This means that you can change the value of `I` without having any effect on the variable passed into `Foo()`.

Reference Parameters

Delphi enables you to pass variables to functions and procedures by reference; parameters passed by reference are also called variable parameters. Passing by reference means that the function or procedure receiving the variable can modify the value of that variable. To pass a variable by reference, use the keyword `var` in the procedure's or function's parameter list:

```
procedure ChangeMe(var x: longint);
begin
  x := 2;  { x is now changed in the calling procedure }
end;
```

Instead of making a copy of `x`, the `var` keyword causes the address of the parameter to be copied so that its value can be directly modified.

Using `var` parameters is equivalent to passing variables by reference in C# using the `ref` keyword or in Visual Basic .NET using the `ByRef` directive.

Out Parameters

Like `var` parameters, `out` parameters provide a means for a routine to return a value to the caller in the form of a parameter. However, although `var` parameters must be initialized to a valid value prior to calling the routine, out parameters make no assumption about the validity of the incoming parameter. For reference types, this means that the reference will be completely discarded on entering the routine.

```
procedure ReturnMe(out O: TObject);
begin
  O := SomeObject.Create;
end;
```

Here's a rule of thumb: Use var for in/out parameters and out for out only parameters.

Constant Parameters

If you don't want the value of a parameter passed into a function to change, you can declare it with the const keyword. Here's an example of a procedure declaration that receives a constant string parameter:

```
procedure Goon(const s: string);
```

Open Array Parameters

Open array parameters provide you with the capability for passing a variable number of arguments to functions and procedures. You can either declare open arrays of some homogenous type or const arrays of differing types. The following code declares a function that accepts an open array of integers:

```
function AddEmUp(A: array of Integer): Integer;
```

You can pass to open array routines variables, constants, or expressions of any array type (dynamic, static, or incoming open). The following code demonstrates this by calling AddEmUp() and passing a variety of different elements:

```
var
  I, Rez: Integer;
const
  J = 23;
begin
  I := 8;
  Rez := AddEmUp([I, I + 50, J, 89]);
```

You can also directly pass an array to an open array routine as shown here:

```
var
  A: array of integer;
begin
  SetLength(A, 10);
  for i := Low(A) to High(A) do
    A[i] := i;
  Rez := AddEmUpConst(A);
```

In order to work with an open array inside the function or procedure, you can use the High(), Low(), and Length() functions to obtain information about the array. To illustrate this, the following code shows an implementation of the AddEmUp() function that returns the sum of all the numbers passed in A:

```
function AddEmUp(A: array of Integer): Integer;
var
  i: Integer;
begin
  Result := 0;
  for i := Low(A) to High(A) do
    inc(Result, A[i]);
end;
```

The Delphi language also supports an `array of const`, which allows you to pass heterogeneous data types in an array to a routine. The syntax for defining a routine that accepts an `array of const` is as follows:

```
procedure WhatHaveIGot(A: array of const);
```

You could call the preceding procedure with the following syntax:

```
WhatHaveIGot(['Tabasco', 90, 5.6, 3.14159, True, 's']);
```

The compiler passes each element of the array as a `System.Object`, so it can easily be handled as such in the receiving function. As an example of how to work with `array of const`, the following implementation for `WhatHaveIGot()` iterates through the array and shows a message to the user indicating what type of data was passed in which index:

```
procedure WhatHaveIGot(A: array of const);
var
  i: Integer;
begin
  for i := Low(A) to High(A) do
    WriteLn('Index ', I, ': ', A[i].GetType.FullName);
  ReadLn;
end;
```

Scope

Scope refers to some part of your program in which a given function or variable is visible to the compiler. A global constant is in scope at all points in your program, for example, whereas a variable local to some procedure only has scope within that procedure. Consider Listing 5.2.

LISTING 5.2   An Illustration of Scope

```
1:   program Foo;
2:
3:   {$APPTYPE CONSOLE}
4:
5:   const
6:     SomeConstant = 100;
7:
8:   var
9:     SomeGlobal: Integer;
10:    D: Double;
11:
```

LISTING 5.2   Continued

```
12: procedure SomeProc;
13: var
14:    D, LocalD: Double;
15: begin
16:    LocalD := 10.0;
17:    D := D - LocalD;
18: end;
19:
20: begin
21:    SomeGlobal := SomeConstant;
22:    D := 4.593;
23:    SomeProc;
24: end.
```

SomeConstant, SomeGlobal, and D have global scope—their values are known to the compiler at all points within the program. Procedure SomeProc() has two variables in which the scope is local to that procedure: D and LocalD. If you try to access LocalD outside of SomeProc(), the compiler displays an unknown identifier error. If you access D within SomeProc(), you'll be referring to the local version; but if you access D outside that procedure, you'll be referring to the global version.

Units and Namespaces

Units are the individual source code modules that make up a Delphi program. A unit is a place for you to group functions and procedures that can be called from your main program. To be a unit, a source module must consist of at least three parts:

- A unit statement—Every unit must have as its first noncomment, nonwhitespace line a statement saying that it's a unit and identifying the unit name. The name of the unit must always match the filename, excluding the file extension. For example, if you have a file named FooBar.pas, the statement would be

  unit FooBar;

- The interface part—After the unit statement, a unit's next functional line of code should be the interface statement. Everything following this statement, up to the implementation statement, are the types, constants, variables, procedures, and functions that you want to make available to your main program and to other units. Only declarations—never routine bodies—can appear in the interface. The interface statement should be one word on one line:

  interface

- The implementation part—This follows the interface part of the unit. Although the implementation part of the unit contains primarily procedures and functions, it's also where you declare any types, constants, and variables that you don't want to make available outside of this unit. The implementation part is where you must define any functions or procedures that you declared in the interface part. The implementation statement should be one word on one line:

  implementation

Optionally, a unit can also include two other parts:

- An `initialization` part—This portion of the unit, which is located near the end of the file, contains any initialization code for the unit. This code will be executed before the main program begins execution, and it executes only once.

- A `finalization` part—This portion of the unit, which is located in between the `initialization` and `end.` of the unit, contains any cleanup code that executes when the program terminates. The `finalization` section was introduced to the language in Delphi 2.0. In Delphi 1.0, unit finalization was accomplished by adding a new exit procedure using the `AddExitProc()` function. If you're porting an application from Delphi 1.0, you should move your exit procedures into the finalization part of your units.

A unit also implies a namespace. A namespace provides a logical, hierarchical means to organize an application or library. Dot notation can be used to create nested namespaces to prevent name collisions. It's common practice to nest namespaces three levels: `company.product.area`; for example, `Borland.Delphi.System` or `Borland.Vcl.Controls`.

> **NOTE**
>
> When several units have `initialization`/`finalization` code, execution of each section proceeds in the order in which the units are encountered by the compiler (the first unit in the program's uses clause, then the first unit in that unit's uses clause, and so on). Also, it's a bad idea to write initialization and finalization code that relies on such ordering because one small change to the uses clause can cause some difficult-to-find bugs!

The uses Clause

The `uses` clause is where you list the namespaces that you want to include in a particular program or unit. For example, if you have a program called `FooProg` that uses functions and types in two namespaces, `UnitA` and `UnitB`, the proper `uses` declaration is as follows:

```
program FooProg;

uses UnitA, UnitB;
```

Units can have two `uses` clauses: one in the `interface` section and one in the `implementation` section.

Here's code for a sample unit:

```
unit FooBar;

interface

uses BarFoo;

  { public declarations here }

implementation

uses BarFly;
```

```
  { private declarations here }
  {definition of routines declared in interface section}

initialization
  { unit initialization here }
finalization
  { unit clean-up here }
end.
```

> **NOTE**
>
> The uses clause might have the fully qualified namespaces, or Delphi permits using just the inner-most namespace name in the uses clause for backward compatibility (for example, Controls) using the namespace prefixes control of the Tools, Options, Delphi Options, Library dialog.

Circular Unit References

Occasionally, you'll have a situation in which UnitA uses UnitB and UnitB uses UnitA. This is called a circular unit reference. The occurrence of a circular unit reference is often an indication of a design flaw in your application; you should avoid structuring your program with a circular reference. The optimal solution is often to move a piece of data that both UnitA and UnitB need to use out to a third unit. However, as with most things, sometimes you just can't avoid the circular unit reference. Note that circular references in both the interface or implementation section are illegal. Therefore, in such a case, move one of the uses clauses to the implementation part of your unit and leave the other one in the interface part. This usually solves the problem.

Packages and Assemblies

Delphi packages enable you to place portions of your application into separate modules, which can be shared across multiple applications as .NET assemblies.

Packages and Assemblies are described in detail in Chapter 6, "Assemblies: Libraries and Packages."

Object-Oriented Programming

Volumes have been written on the subject of object-oriented programming (OOP). Often, OOP seems more like a religion than a programming methodology, spawning arguments about its merits (or lack thereof) that are passionate and spirited enough to make the Crusades look like a slight disagreement. We're not orthodox OOPists, and we're not going to get involved in the relative merits of OOP; we just want to give you the lowdown on a fundamental principle on which Delphi's language is based.

OOP is a programming paradigm that uses discrete objects—containing both data and code—as application building blocks. Although the OOP paradigm doesn't necessarily lend itself to easier-to-write code, the result of using OOP traditionally has been easy-to-maintain code. Having objects' data and code together simplifies the process of hunting down bugs, fixing them with minimal effect on other objects, and improving your program one part at a time. Traditionally, an OOP language contains implementations of at least three OOP concepts:

- Encapsulation—Deals with combining related data fields and hiding the implementation details. The advantages of encapsulation include modularity and isolation of code from other code.

- Inheritance—The capability to create new objects that maintain the properties and behavior of ancestor objects. This concept enables you to create object hierarchies such as VCL—first creating generic objects and then creating more specific descendants of those objects that have more narrow functionality.

  The advantage of inheritance is the sharing of common code. Figure 5.1 presents an example of inheritance—how one root object, fruit, is the ancestor object of all fruits, including the melon. The melon is ancestor of all melons, including the watermelon. You get the picture.

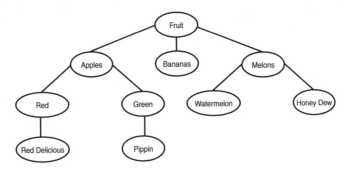

FIGURE 5.1   An illustration of inheritance.

- Polymorphism—Literally, polymorphism means "many shapes." Calls to virtual methods of an object variable will call code appropriate to whatever instance is actually in the variable at runtime.

Note that the .NET CLR does not support the concept of C++-style multiple inheritance, and neither does the Delphi language.

You should understand the following three terms before you continue to explore the concept of objects:

- Field—Also called field definitions or instance variables, fields are data variables contained within objects. A field in an object is just like a field in a Delphi record. In C#, fields sometimes are referred to as data members.

- Method—The name for procedures and functions belonging to an object. Methods are called member functions in C#.

- Property—An entity that acts as an accessor to the data and code contained within an object. Properties work similar to fields with attached logic to insulate the end user from the implementation details of an object.

Using Delphi Objects

As mentioned earlier, classes are entities that can contain both data and code. Objects are created instances of those classes. Delphi classes provide you with all the power of object-oriented programming in offering full support of inheritance, encapsulation, and polymorphism.

Declaration and Instantiation

Of course, before using an object, you must have defined it using the `class` keyword. As described earlier in this chapter, classes are declared in the `type` section of a unit or program:

```
type
  TFooObject = class;
```

In addition to a class declaration, you usually also will have a variable of that class type, or instance, declared in the `var` section:

```
var
  FooObject: TFooObject;
```

You create an instance of an object in Delphi by calling one of its constructors. A constructor is responsible for creating an instance of your object and allocating any memory or initializing any fields necessary so that the object is in a usable state upon exiting the constructor. Delphi objects always have at least one constructor called `Create()`—although it's possible for an object to have more than one constructor. Depending on the type of object, `Create()` can take different numbers of parameters. This chapter focuses on the simple case in which `Create()` takes no parameters.

Object constructors in the Delphi language aren't called automatically, and it's incumbent on the programmer to call the object constructor. The syntax for calling a constructor is as follows:

```
FooObject := TFooObject.Create;
```

Notice that the syntax for a constructor call is a bit unique. You're referencing the `Create()` constructor of the class by the type rather than the instance, as you would with other methods. This might seem odd at first, but it does make sense. `FooObject`, a variable, is undefined at the time of the call, but the code for `TFooObject`, a type, is static in memory. A static call to its `Create()` constructor is therefore totally valid.

The act of calling a constructor to create an instance of an object is often called instantiation.

> **NOTE**
>
> When an object instance is created using the constructor, the CLR will ensure that every field in your object is zero-initialized. You can safely assume that all numbers will be initialized to 0, all objects to `nil`, all Boolean values to `False`, and all strings will be empty.

Destruction

All .NET classes inherit a method called `Finalize()`, which can be overridden to perform any necessary class cleanup. `Finalize()` is called automatically for each instance by the .NET garbage collector. Note however, that there is no guarantee as to when `Finalize()` will actually be called or even that it will execute in its entirety in certain circumstances. For these reasons, it is not recommended that critical or limited resources—such as large memory buffers, database connections, or operating system handles—be released in the `Finalize()` method. Instead, Delphi developers should use the Disposable Pattern by overriding the `destructor Destroy()` of an object to free valuable resources. How to do this is discussed in Chapter 9, "Memory Management and Garbage Collection."

The Adam of Objects

You might be asking yourself how all these methods got into your little object. You certainly didn't declare them yourself, right? Right. The methods just discussed actually come from .NET's base `System.Object` class. Delphi's `TObject` class is an alias for `System.Object`. In .NET, all objects are always descendants of `TObject` regardless of whether they're declared as such. Therefore, the declaration

```
type
  TFoo = class
  end;
```

is equivalent to the declaration

```
type
  TFoo = class(TObject)
  end;
```

Fields

Adding fields to a class is accomplished with syntax very similar to declaring variables in a `var` block. For example, the following code adds an `Integer`, `string`, and `Double` to class `TFoo`:

```
type
  TFoo = class(TObject)
    I: Integer;
    S: string;
    D: Double;
  end;
```

The Delphi language also supports static fields—that is, fields whose data is shared among all instances of a given class. This is accomplished by adding one or more `class var` blocks to a class declaration. To illustrate, the following code adds three static fields to the TFoo class:

```
type
  TFoo = class(TObject)
    I: Integer;
    S: string;
    D: Double;
    class var
      I_Static: Integer;
      S_Static: string;
      D_Static: Double;
  end;
```

Note that it is also legal (although syntactically unnecessary) to have a var block in a class definition that defines normal fields.

The class var block is identical in function to the static keyword in C#. Note that a class var or var block is terminated by any of the following elements:

- Another class var or var block

- A property declaration

- Any method declaration

- A visibility specifier

Methods

Methods are procedures and functions belonging to a given object: They give an object behavior rather than just data. Two important methods of the objects you create are the constructor and the destructor methods, which we just covered. You can also create custom methods in your objects to perform a variety of tasks.

Creating a method is a two-step process. You first must declare the method in the object type declaration, and then you must define the method in the code. The following code demonstrates the process of declaring and defining a method:

```
type
  TBoogieNights = class
    Dance: Boolean;
    procedure DoTheHustle;
  end;

procedure TBoogieNights.DoTheHustle;
begin
  Dance := True;
end;
```

Note that when defining the method body, the fully qualified name—consisting of the class and method names—must be used. It's important also to note that the object's Dance field can be accessed directly from within the method.

Method Types

A class type's methods can be declared as normal, `static`, `virtual`, `class static`, `class virtual`, `dynamic`, or `message`. Consider the following example object:

```
TFoo = class
  procedure IAmNormal;
  class procedure IAmAClassMethod;
  class procedure IAmAStatic; static;
  procedure IAmAVirtual; virtual;
  class procedure IAmAVirtualClassMethod; virtual;
  procedure IAmADynamic; dynamic;
  procedure IAmAMessage(var M: TMessage); message WM_SOMEMESSAGE;
end;
```

Regular Methods

`IAmNormal()` is a regular method. This is the default method type, and it works similarly to a regular procedure or function call. The compiler knows the address of these methods, so when you call a static method, it's capable of statically linking that information into the executable. Static methods execute the fastest; however, they don't have the capability to be overridden to provide polymorphism.

Class Methods

`IAmAClassMethod()` is a special, Delphi-specific type of static method. Class methods may be called without an instance, and the implementation of class methods are shared among all instances of the given class. However, class methods have a special implicit and hidden `Self` parameter that is passed by the compiler that allows for the calling of polymorphic (virtual) class methods. Class methods can be plain or virtual. Nonclass or nonstatic elements may not be accessed from within a class method.

Static Methods

`IAMStatic()` is a true, .NET-compatible static method. Like static fields, the implementation of static methods are shared among all instances of the given class. As such, nonstatic elements may not be accessed from within a static method. No `Self` parameter is passed for static methods, meaning that nonstatic methods may not be called from static methods.

Virtual Methods

`IAmAVirtual()` is a virtual method. Virtual methods are called in the same way as static methods, but because virtual methods can be overridden, the compiler doesn't know the address of a particular virtual function when you call it in your code. The .NET JIT compiler, therefore, builds a Virtual Method Table (VMT) that provides a means to look up function addresses at runtime. All virtual method calls are dispatched at runtime through the VMT. An object's VMT contains all its ancestor's virtual methods as well as the ones it declares.

Dynamic Methods

`IAmADynamic()` is a dynamic method. The .NET compiler maps dynamic methods to virtual methods, unlike the Win32 compiler, which provides for a separate dynamic method dispatching mechanism.

Message Methods

`IAmAMessage()` is a message-handling method. The message directive creates a method that can respond to dynamically dispatched messages. The value after the `message` keyword dictates what message the method will respond to. In VCL, message methods are used to create an automatic response to Windows messages, and you generally don't call them directly.

Overriding Methods

Overriding a method is the Delphi language's implementation of the OOP concept of polymorphism. It enables you to change the behavior of a method from descendant to descendant. Delphi methods can be overridden only if they're first declared as `virtual`, `dynamic`, or `message`. To override a `virtual` or `dynamic` method, just use the `override` directive instead of `virtual` or `dynamic` in your descendant object type. To override a message method, the message directive must be repeated and the same message ID used in the ancestor class. For example, you could override the `IAmAVirtual()`, `IAmADynamic()`, and `IAmAMessage()` methods as shown here:

```
TFooChild = class(TFoo)
  procedure IAmAVirtual; override;
  procedure IAmADynamic; override;
  procedure IAmAMessage(var M: TMessage); message WM_SOMEMESSAGE;
end;
```

The `override` directive replaces the original method's entry in the VMT with the new method. If you had redeclared `IAmAVirtual` and `IAmADynamic` with the `virtual` or `dynamic` keyword instead of `override`, you would have created new methods rather than overriding the ancestor methods. This will normally result in a compiler warning unless you suppress the warning by adding the `reintroduce` directive (described shortly) to the method declaration. Also, if you attempt to override a normal method in a descendant type, the static method in the new class hides the method from users of the descendent class.

Method Overloading

Like regular procedures and functions, methods can be overloaded so that a class can contain multiple methods of the same name with differing parameter lists. Overloaded methods must be marked with the `overload` directive, although the use of the directive on the first instance of a method name in a class hierarchy is optional. The following code example shows a class containing three overloaded methods:

```
type
  TSomeClass = class
    procedure AMethod(I: Integer); overload;
    procedure AMethod(S: string); overload;
    procedure AMethod(D: Double); overload;
  end;
```

Reintroducing Method Names

Occasionally, you might want to add a method to one of your classes to replace a virtual method of the same name in an ancestor of your class. In this case, you don't want to override the ancestor method but instead obscure and completely supplant the base class method. If you simply add the method and compile, you'll see that the compiler will produce a warning explaining that the new method hides a method of the same name in a base class. To suppress this error, use the reintroduce directive on the method declaration in the descendant class. The following code example demonstrates proper use of the reintroduce directive:

```
type
  TSomeBase = class
    procedure Cooper; virtual;
  end;

  TSomeClass = class
    procedure Cooper; reintroduce;
  end;
```

Self

An implicit variable called Self is available within all object methods. Self is a reference to the class instance that was used to call the method. Self is passed by the compiler as a hidden parameter to all methods. Self is analogous to this in C# and Me in Visual Basic .NET.

Class References

Although normal class variables hold a reference to an object, class references provide a means to hold a reference to a class type. Using a class reference, you call class or static methods of a class or create instances of the class. The following code illustrates the syntax for declaring a new class called SomeClass and a class reference type for SomeClass:

```
type
  SomeClass = class
    constructor Create; virtual;
    class procedure Foo;
  end;

  SomeClassRef = class of SomeClass;
```

Using these types, you could call the SomeClass.Foo() class method through the SomeClassRef class reference type like this:

```
var
  SCRef: SomeClassRef;
begin
  SCRef := SomeClass;
  SCRef.Foo;
```

Similarly, an instance of SomeClass can be created from the class reference:

```
var
  SCRef: SomeClassRef;
  SC: SomeClass;
begin
  SCRef := SomeClass;
  SC := SCRef.Create;
```

5

Note that creating a class via a class reference requires that the class have at least one virtual constructor. Virtual constructors are a feature somewhat unique to the Delphi language, allowing classes to be created by class references, where the specific type of class is not known at compile time.

Properties

It might help to think of properties as special accessor fields that enable you to modify data and execute code contained within your class. For components, properties are those things that show up in the Object Inspector window when published. The following example illustrates a simplified Object with a property:

```
TMyObject = class
private
  SomeValue: Integer;
  procedure SetSomeValue(AValue: Integer);
public
  property Value: Integer read SomeValue write SetSomeValue;
end;

procedure TMyObject.SetSomeValue(AValue: Integer);
begin
  if SomeValue <> AValue then
    SomeValue := AValue;
end;
```

TMyObject is an object that contains the following: one field (an integer called SomeValue), one method (a procedure called SetSomeValue), and one property called Value. The sole purpose of the SetSomeValue procedure is to set the value of the SomeValue field. The Value property doesn't actually contain any data. Value is an accessor for the SomeValue field; when you ask Value what number it contains, it reads the value from SomeValue. When you attempt to set the value of the Value property, Value calls SetSomeValue to modify the value of SomeValue. This is useful for a few reasons: First, it allows the developer to create natural side effects of getting or setting a property (such as recalculating an equation or repainting a control). Second, it allows you to present the users of the class with a simple variable without burdening them with the class's implementation details. Finally, you can allow the users to override accessor methods in descendant classes for polymorphic behavior.

Like static fields and methods, the Delphi language also supports static properties using the class keyword. The following code shows a class with a static property that accesses a static field:

```
TMyClass = class(TObject)
  class var FValue: Integer;
  class procedure SetValue(Value: Integer); static;
  class property Value: Integer read FValue write SetValue;
end;
```

Note that static properties can employ only static fields and methods as getter and setters.

Events

The Delphi language supports two different kinds of events: singleton and multicast.

Singleton events have been in the Delphi language since the beginning. They are declared as a property whose type is a procedure type with read and write accessors. Singleton events may have zero or one event listeners. The assignment operator is used to hook a listener to the event, and nil is assigned to remove the listener from the event. Listing 5.3 provides a demonstration of the declaration and use of a singleton event.

LISTING 5.3   Singleton Event Demonstration

```
1:    program singleevent;
2:
3:    {$APPTYPE CONSOLE}
4:
5:    type
6:      TMyEvent = procedure (Sender: TObject; Msg: string) of object;
7:
8:      TClassWithEvent = class
9:      private
10:       FAnEvent: TMyEvent;
11:     public
12:       procedure FireEvent;
13:       property AnEvent: TMyEvent read FAnEvent write FAnEvent;
14:     end;
15:
16:     TListener = class
17:       procedure EventHandler(Sender: TObject; Msg: string);
18:     end;
19:
20:   { TClassWithEvent }
21:
22:   procedure TClassWithEvent.FireEvent;
23:   begin
24:     if Assigned(FAnEvent) then
25:       FAnEvent(Self, '*singleton event*');
26:   end;
27:
28:   { TListener }
29:
30:   procedure TListener.EventHandler(Sender: TObject; Msg: string);
31:   begin
32:     WriteLn('Event was fired. Message is: ', Msg);
33:   end;
34:
35:   var
36:     L: TListener;
37:     CWE: TClassWithEvent;
38:   begin
39:     L := TListener.Create;          // create objects
40:     CWE := TClassWithEvent.Create;
41:     CWE.AnEvent := L.EventHandler;  // assign event handler
42:     CWE.FireEvent;                  // cause event to fire
43:     CWE.AnEvent := nil;             // disconnect event handler
44:     ReadLn;n
45:   end.
```

The output of the program shown in Listing 5.3 is

```
Event was fired. Message is: *singleton event*
```

Multicast events have been added to the language to support .NET's capability of having multiple listeners for a given event. A multicast event is a property whose type is a procedure type and requires both add and remove accessors. Multicast events can have any number of listeners. The Include() and Exclude() procedures are used to add and remove listeners from a multicast event.

Listing 5.4 provides an example of declaring and using a multicast event.

LISTING 5.4   Multicast Event Demonstrationn

```
1:   program multievent;
2:
3:   {$APPTYPE CONSOLE}
4:
5:   uses
6:     SysUtils;
7:
8:   type
9:     TMyEvent = procedure (Sender: TObject; Msg: string) of object;
10:
11:    TClassWithEvent = class
12:    private
13:      FAnEvent: TMyEvent;
14:    public
15:      procedure FireEvent;
16:      property AnEvent: TMyEvent add FAnEvent remove FAnEvent;
17:    end;
18:
19:    TListener = class
20:      procedure EventHandler(Sender: TObject; Msg: string);
21:    end;
22:
23:  { TClassWithEvent }
24:
25:  procedure TClassWithEvent.FireEvent;
26:  begin
27:    if Assigned(FAnEvent) then
28:      FAnEvent(Self, '*multicast event*');
29:  end;
30:
31:  { TListener }
32:
33:  procedure TListener.EventHandler(Sender: TObject; Msg: string);
34:  begin
35:    WriteLn('Event was fired. Message is: ', Msg);
36:  end;
37:
38:  var
39:    L1, L2: TListener;
40:    CWE: TClassWithEvent;
41:  begin
```

LISTING 5.4 Continued

```
42:    L1 := TListener.Create;                  // create objects
43:    L2 := TListener.Create;
44:    CWE := TClassWithEvent.Create;
45:    Include(CWE.AnEvent, L1.EventHandler);   // assign event handler
46:    Include(CWE.AnEvent, L2.EventHandler);   // assign event handler
47:    CWE.FireEvent;                           // cause event to fire
48:    Exclude(CWE.AnEvent, L1.EventHandler);   // disconnect event handler
49:    Exclude(CWE.AnEvent, L2.EventHandler);   // disconnect event handler
50:    ReadLn;
51: end
```

The output of the program shown in Listing 5.4 is

```
Event was fired. Message is: *multicast event*
Event was fired. Message is: *multicast event*
```

Note that attempts to use Include() to add the same method more than once to the listener list will result in the method being called multiple times.

In order to maintain compatibility with other .NET CLR languages, the Delphi compiler will implement multicast semantics even for singleton events, creating add and remove accessors for the singleton event. In this implementation, the add() method will result in an overwrite of the existing value.

Visibility Specifiers

The Delphi language offers you further control over the behavior of your objects by enabling you to declare fields and methods with directives such as private, strict private, protected, strict protected, public, and published. The syntax for using these directives is as follows:

```
TSomeObject = class
private
  APrivateVariable: Integer;
  AnotherPrivateVariable: Boolean;
strict private
  procedure AStrictPrivateMethod;
protected
  procedure AProtectedProcedure;
  function ProtectMe: Byte;
strict protected
  procedure AStrictProtectedMethod;
public
  constructor APublicContructor;
  destructor Destroy; override;  // a public destructor
published
  property AProperty: Integer
 read APrivateVariable write APrivateVariable;
end;
```

You can place as many fields or methods as you want under each directive. Style dictates that you should indent the specifier the same as you indent the classname. The meanings of these directives follow:

- `private`—These parts of your object are accessible only to code in the same unit as your object's implementation. Use this directive to hide implementation details of your objects from users and to prevent users from directly modifying sensitive members of your object.

- `strict private`—Members are accessible within the declaring class and not within the same unit. Used for more strict data encapsulation than `private`.

- `protected`—Your object's `protected` members can be accessed by descendants of your object. This capability enables you to hide the implementation details of your object from users while still providing maximum flexibility to descendants of your object.

- `strict protected`—Members are accessible only within the declaring class and ancestors and not within declaring units. Used for more strict data encapsulation than `protected`.

- `public`—These fields and methods are accessible anywhere in your program. Object constructors and destructors always should be `public`.

- `published`—Identical to `public` from a visibility standpoint. Published has the additional benefit of adding the `[Browsable(true)]` attribute to properties contained within, which causes them to be displayed in the Object Inspector when used in the form designer. Attributes are discussed later in this chapter.

> **NOTE**
>
> The meaning of `published` represents a fairly substantial departure from the Win32 implementation of the Delphi language. In Win32, Runtime Type Information (RTTI) was generated for published properties. The .NET equivalent of RTTI is Reflection; however, Reflection is possible on all class elements, regardless of visibility specifier.

Here, then, is code for the `TMyObject` class that was introduced earlier, with directives added to improve the integrity of the object:

```
TMyObject = class
private
  SomeValue: Integer;
  procedure SetSomeValue(AValue: Integer);
published
  property Value: Integer read SomeValue write SetSomeValue;
end;

procedure TMyObject.SetSomeValue(AValue: Integer);
begin
  if SomeValue <> AValue then
    SomeValue := AValue;
end;
```

Now, users of your object will not be able to modify the value of `SomeValue` directly, and they will have to go through the interface provided by the property `Value` to modify the object's data.

"Friend" Classes

The C++ language has a concept of friend classes (that is, classes that are allowed access to the private data and functions in other classes). This is accomplished in C++ using the friend keyword. .NET languages, such as Delphi and C#, have a similar concept, although the implementation is different. Non-strict, private, and protected members of a class are visible and accessible to other classes and code declared within the same unit namespace.

Class Helpers

Class helpers provide a means to extend a class without modifying the actual class. Instead, a new class, the helper, is created and its methods effectively bolted on to the original class. This enables users of the original class to call methods of the helper class as if they were methods of the original class.

The following code example creates a simple class and class helper and demonstrates calling a method on the helper class:

```
program Helpers;

{$APPTYPE CONSOLE}

type
  TFoo = class
    procedure AProc;
  end;

  TFooHelper = class helper for TFoo
    procedure AHelperProc;
  end;

{ TFoo }

procedure TFoo.AProc;
begin
  WriteLn('TFoo.AProc');
end;

{ TFooHelper }

procedure TFooHelper.AHelperProc;
begin
  WriteLn('TFooHelper.AHelperProc');
  AProc;
end;

var
  Foo: TFoo;
begin
  Foo := TFoo.Create;
  Foo.AHelperProc;
end.
```

5

> **CAUTION**
>
> Class helpers are an interesting feature, but not a feature that generally lends itself to good soft-
> ware design. This feature is in the language mostly because Borland needed it to hide the differ-
> ences between standard .NET classes and similar classes in Win32 Delphi. The occasion should be
> rare when a good design involves the use of class helpers.

Nested Types

The Delphi language allows for a `type` clause to appear with a class declaration, effectively
nesting types within a class. Such nested types are referenced using a `NestedType.OuterType`
syntax, as shown in the following code example:

```
type
  OutClass = class
    procedure SomeProc;

    type
      InClass = class
        procedure SomeOtherProc;
      end;

  end;


var
  IC: OutClass.InClass;
```

Operator Overloading

The Delphi language supports the overloading of select operators for classes and records.
The syntax for overloading an operator is as straightforward as declaring a class method
with a specific name and signature. A complete list of overloadable operators can be found
in the Delphi online help under the Operator Overloads topic; however, the following
code example demonstrates how you might overload the + and - operators of a class:

```
OverloadsOps = class
private
  FField: Integer;
public
  class operator Add(a, b: OverloadsOps): OverloadsOps;
  class operator Subtract(a, b: OverloadsOps): OverloadsOps;
end;

class operator OverloadsOps.Add(a, b: OverloadsOps): OverloadsOps;
begin
  Result := OverloadsOps.Create;
  Result.FField := a.FField + b.FField;
end;

class operator OverloadsOps.Subtract(a, b: OverloadsOps): OverloadsOps;
begin
  Result := OverloadsOps.Create;
  Result.FField := a.FField - b.FField;
end;
```

Note that the overloaded operators are declared as `class operator` and take the declaring class as parameters. Because the + and - operators are binary, they also return the declaring class.

Once declared, the operators can be used in a manner similar to that shown here:

```
var
  O1, O2, O3: OverloadsOps;
begin
  O1 := OverloadsOps.Create;
  O2 := OverloadsOps.Create;
  O3 := O1 + O2;
end;
```

Attributes

One of the more exciting features of .NET platform is the realization of attribute-based development, which had been on the drawing board of a few different programming languages for the past several years. Attributes provide a means to tie metadata to language elements such as classes, properties, methods, variables, and so on that provide extended information about those elements to their consumers.

Attributes are declared using square bracket notation before the element to be augmented. For example, the following code demonstrates the use of the `DllImport` attribute, which signals to .NET that the method should be imported from the specified DLL:

```
[DllImport('user32.dll')]
function MessageBeep(uType : LongWord) : Boolean; external;
```

Attributes are used liberally in .NET. For example, the `Browsable` attribute on a property determines whether it should be displayed in the Object Inspector:

```
[Browsable(True)]
property Foo: string read FFoo write FFoo;
```

.NET's attribute system is quite extensible because attributes are implemented as classes. This allows you to extend the attribute system without limit because you can create your own attributes either from scratch or by inheriting from existing attribute classes and use these new attributes in other classes.

Interfaces

The Delphi language contains native support for interfaces, which, simply put, define a set of functions and procedures that can be used to interact with an object. The definition of a given interface is known to both the implementer and the client of the interface—acting as a contract of sorts for how an interface will be defined and used. A class can implement multiple interfaces, providing multiple known "faces" by which a client can control an object.

As its name implies, an interface defines only, well, an interface by which object and clients communicate. It's the job of a class that supports an interface to implement each of the interface's functions and procedures.

> **NOTE**
>
> Unlike Win32 Delphi, .NET interfaces to not implicitly descend from `IInterface` or `IUnknown`. As such, they no longer implement `QueryInterface()`, `_AddRef`, or `_Release()`. Typecasting is now used for type identity, and reference counting is built in to the .NET platform.

Defining Interfaces

The syntax for defining an interface is very similar to that of a class. The primary difference is that an interface can optionally be associated with a globally unique identifier (GUID), which is unique to the interface. The following code defines a new interface called `IFoo`, which implements one method called `F1()`:

```
type
  IFoo = interface
    function F1: Integer;
  end;
```

Note that GUIDs are not required for .NET interface definitions, but they are required for Win32. Therefore, the use of GUID is only recommended when you need to maintain a multiplatform code base or want to engage in .NET COM Interop to interoperate between .NET and COM.

> **TIP**
>
> The Delphi IDE will manufacture new GUIDs for your interfaces when you use the Ctrl+Shift+G key combination.

The following code defines a new interface, `IBar`, which descends from `IFoo`:

```
type
  IBar = interface(IFoo)
    function F2: Integer;
  end;
```

Implementing Interfaces

The following bit of code demonstrates how to implement `IFoo` and `IBar` in a class called `TFooBar`:

```
type
  TFooBar = class(TObject, IFoo, IBar)
    function F1: Integer;
    function F2: Integer;
  end;

function TFooBar.F1: Integer;
begin
  Result := 0;
end;

function TFooBar.F2: Integer;
begin
  Result := 0;
end;
```

Note that multiple interfaces can be listed after the ancestor class in the first line of the class declaration to implement multiple interfaces. The binding of an interface function to a particular function in the class happens when the compiler matches a method signature in the interface with a matching signature in the class. A compiler error will occur if a class declares that it implements an interface but the class fails to implement one or more of the interface's methods.

INTERFACE METHODS MADE EASY

Let's face it, interfaces are great, but all of that typing to implement interface methods in a class can be a bummer! Here's an IDE trick to implement all the interface methods in just a few keystrokes and mouse clicks:

1. Add the interfaces you want to implement to the class declaration.

2. Place the cursor somewhere in the class and press the Ctrl+Spacebar keystroke combination to invoke code completion. The yet unimplemented methods show in red in the code completion window.

3. Select all the red-colored methods in the list by holding down the Shift key and using the keyboard arrow keys or mouse.

4. Press the Enter key, and the interface methods will be added automatically to the class definition.

5. Press the Ctrl+Shift+C keystroke combination to complete the implementation portion of the new methods.

6. Now all that is left to do is fill in the implementation portion of each method!

If a class implements multiple interfaces that have methods of the same signature, you must alias the same-named methods as shown in the following short example:

```
type
  IFoo = interface
    function F1: Integer;
  end;

  IBar = interface
    function F1: Integer;
  end;

  TFooBar = class(TObject, IFoo, IBar)
    // aliased methods
    function IFoo.F1 = FooF1;
    function IBar.F1 = BarF1;
    // interface methods
    function FooF1: Integer;
    function BarF1: Integer;
  end;

function TFooBar.FooF1: Integer;
begin
  Result := 0;
end;
```

```
function TFooBar.BarF1: Integer;
begin
  Result := 0;
end;
```

> **NOTE**
>
> The `implements` directive from Win32 Delphi is not available in the current version of the .NET Delphi compiler.

Using Interfaces

A few important language rules apply when you're using variables of interface types in your applications. Like other .NET types, interfaces are lifetime managed. The garbage collector will release an object when all reference to the object and its implemented interfaces have been released or go out of scope. Before use, an interface type is always initialized to `nil`. Manually setting an interface to `nil` releases the reference to its implementation object.

Another unique rule of interface variables is that an interface is assignment compatible with objects that implement the interface. However, this compatibility is only one way: You can assign an object reference to an interface reference, but not the other way around. For example, the following code is legal using the `TFooBar` class defined earlier:

```
procedure Test(FB: TFooBar)
var

  F: IFoo;
begin

  F := FB;  // supported because FB supports IFoo
  .
  .
  .
```

If `FB` did not support `IFoo`, the code would still compile, but the interface reference would be assigned `nil`. Any subsequent attempt to use that reference would result in `NullReferencedException` being raised at runtime.

Finally, the `as` typecast operator can be used to query a given interface variable for another interface on the same object. This is illustrated here:

```
var
  FB: TFooBar;
  F: IFoo;
  B: IBar;
begin
  FB := TFooBar.Create;
  F := FB;  // supported because FB supports IFoo
  B := F as IBar;  // cast for IBar
  .
  .
  .
```

If the requested interface isn't supported, the expression returns nil.

Structured Exception Handling

Structured exception handling (SEH) is a method centralizing and normalizing error handling, providing both non-invasive error handling within source code as well as the capability to gracefully handle nearly any kind of error condition. The Delphi language's SEH is mapped to that provided in the CLR by .NET.

Exceptions are, at the most basic level, merely classes that happen to contain information about the location and nature of a particular error. This makes exceptions as easy to implement and use in your applications as any other class.

.NET provides predefined exceptions for many dozens of program-error conditions, such as out of memory, divide by zero, numerical overflow and underflow, and file I/O errors. Borland provides even more exception classes within Delphi's RTL and VCL. And of course, there is nothing to prevent you from defining your own exception classes as you see fit in your applications.

Listing 5.5 demonstrates how to use exception handling during file I/O.

LISTING 5.5   File I/O Using Exception Handling

```
1:   program FileIO;
2:
3:   {$APPTYPE CONSOLE}
4:
5:   uses System.IO;
6:
7:   var
8:     F: TextFile;
9:     S: string;
10:  begin
11:    AssignFile(F, 'FOO.TXT');
12:    try
13:      Reset(F);
14:      try
15:        ReadLn(F, S);
16:        WriteLn(S);
17:      finally
18:        CloseFile(F);
19:      end;
20:    except
21:      on System.IO.IOException do
22:        WriteLn('Error Accessing File!');
23:    end;
24:    ReadLn;
25:  end
```

In Listing 5.5, the inner try..finally block is used to ensure that the file is closed regardless of whether any exceptions come down the pike. What this block means in English is "Hey, program, try to execute the statements between the try and the finally. Whether you finish them or run into an exception, execute the statements between the `finally` and the `end` in any case. If an exception does occur, move on to the next exception-handling block." This means that the file will be closed and the error can be properly handled no matter what error occurs.

The outer `try..except` block is used to handle the exceptions as they occur in the program. After the file is closed in the `finally` block, the `except` block prints a message to the console informing the user that an I/O error occurred.

One of the key advantages that exception handling provides over more old school methods of check-the-function-return-value-error-handling is the capability of distinctly separating the error-detection code from the error-correction code. This is a good thing primarily because it makes your code easier to read and maintain by enabling you to concentrate on one distinct aspect of the code at a time.

The fact that you cannot trap any specific exception by using the `try..finally` block is significant. When you use a `try..finally` block in your code, it means that you don't care what exceptions might occur. You just want to perform some tasks when they do occur to gracefully get out of a tight spot. The `finally` block is an ideal place to free any resources you've allocated (such as files or Windows resources) because it will always execute in the case of an error. In many cases, however, you need some type of error handling that's capable of responding differently depending on the type of error that occurs. You can trap specific exceptions by using a `try..except` block, which is again illustrated in Listing 5.6.

LISTING 5.6   A try..except Exception-Handling Block

```
1:   program HandleIt;
2:
3:   {$APPTYPE CONSOLE}
4:
5:   var
6:     D1, D2, D3: Double;
7:   begin
8:     try
9:       Write('Enter a decimal number: ');
10:      ReadLn(D1);
11:      Write('Enter another decimal number: ');
12:      ReadLn(D2);
13:      Writeln('I will now divide the first number by the second...');
14:      D3 := D1 / D2;
15:      Writeln('The answer is: ', D3:5:2);
16:    except
17:      on System.OverflowException do
18:        Writeln('Overflow in performing division!');
19:      on System.DivideByZeroException do
```

LISTING 5.6   Continued

```
20:        Writeln('You cannot divide by zero!');
21:      on Borland.Delphi.System.EInvalidInput do
22:        Writeln('That is not a valid number!');
23:    end;
24: end
```

Although you can trap specific exceptions with the `try..except` block, you also can catch other exceptions by adding the catchall `else` clause to this construct. The syntax of the `try..except..else` construct follows:

```
try
  Statements
except
  On ESomeException do Something;
else
  { do some default exception handling }
end;
```

> **CAUTION**
>
> When using the `try..except..else` construct, you should be aware that the `else` part will catch *all* exceptions—even exceptions you might not expect, such as out-of-memory or other runtime-library exceptions. Be careful when using the `else` clause, and use it sparingly. You should always reraise the exception when you trap with unqualified exception handlers. This is explained in the section "Reraising an Exception."

You can achieve the same effect as a `try..except..else` construct by not specifying the exception class in a `try..except` block, as shown in this example:

```
try
  Statements
except
  HandleException  // almost the same as else statement
end;
```

Exception Classes

Exceptions are merely special instances of objects. These objects are instantiated when an exception occurs and are destroyed when an exception is handled. The base exception object is .NET's `System.Exception` class.

One of the more important elements of the `Exception` object is the `Message` property, which is a string that provides more information or explanation on the exception. The information provided by `Message` depends on the type of exception that's raised.

> **CAUTION**
>
> If you define your own exception object, make sure that you derive it from a known exception object such as `Exception` or one of its descendants. This is so that generic exception handlers will be able to trap your exception.

When you handle a specific type of exception in an except block, that handler also will catch any exceptions that are descendants of the specified exception. For example, System.ArithmeticException is the ancestor object for a variety of math-related exceptions, such as DivideByZeroException, NotFiniteNumberException, and OverflowException. You can catch any of these exceptions by setting up a handler for the base ArithmeticException class, as shown here:

```
try
  Statements
except
  on EMathError do  // will catch EMathError or any descendant
    HandleException
end;
```

Any exceptions that you don't explicitly handle in your program eventually will continue to unwind the stack until handled. In a .NET Winform or Webform application, a default exception handler performs some work to display the error to the user. In VCL applications, the default handler will put up a message dialog box informing the user that an exception occurred.

When handling an exception, you sometimes need to access the instance of the exception object in order to retrieve more information on the exception, such as that provided by its Message property. There are two ways to do this: The preferable method is to use an optional identifier with the on SomeException construct. You can also use the ExceptObject() function, but this technique is not recommended and has been deprecated.

You can insert an optional identifier in the on ESomeException portion of an except block and have the identifier map to an instance of the currently raised exception. The syntax for this is to preface the exception type with an identifier and a colon, as follows:

```
try
  Something
except
  on E:ESomeException do
    ShowMessage(E.Message);
end;
```

The identifier (E in this case) receives a reference to the currently raised exception. This identifier is always of the same type as the exception it prefaces.

The syntax for raising an exception is similar to the syntax for creating an object instance. To raise a user-defined exception called EBadStuff, for example, you would use this syntax:

```
raise EBadStuff.Create('Some bad stuff happened.');
```

Flow of Execution

After an exception is raised, the flow of execution of your program propagates up to the next exception handler until the exception instance is finally handled and destroyed. This process is determined by the call stack and therefore works program-wide (not just within one procedure or unit). Listing 5.7 is a VCL unit that illustrates the flow of execution of a program when an exception is raised. This listing is the main unit of a Delphi application that consists of one form with one button. When the button is clicked, the `Button1Click()` method calls `Proc1()`, which calls `Proc2()`, which in turn calls `Proc3()`. An exception is raised in `Proc3()`, and you can witness the flow of execution propagating through each `try..finally` block until the exception is finally handled inside `Button1Click()`.

> **TIP**
>
> When you run this program from the Delphi IDE, you'll be able to see the flow of execution better if you disable the integrated debugger's handling of exceptions by unchecking Tools, Options, Debugger Options, Borland .NET Debugger, Language Exceptions, Stop on Language Exceptions.

LISTING 5.7   Main Unit for the Exception Propagation Project

```
 1:  unit Main;
 2:
 3:  interface
 4:
 5:  uses
 6:    Windows, Messages, SysUtils, Variants, Classes, Graphics, Controls, Forms,
 7:    Dialogs;
 8:
 9:  type
10:    TForm1 = class(TForm)
11:      Button1: TButton;
12:      procedure Button1Click(Sender: TObject);
13:    end;
14:
15:  var
16:    Form1: TForm1;
17:
18:  implementation
19:
20:  {$R *.nfm}
21:
22:  type
23:    EBadStuff = class(Exception);
24:
25:  procedure Proc3;
26:  begin
27:    try
28:      raise EBadStuff.Create('Up the stack we go!');
29:    finally
30:      ShowMessage('Exception raised. Proc3 sees the exception');
31:    end;
32:  end;
33:
34:  procedure Proc2;
35:  begin
36:    try
37:      Proc3;
38:    finally
39:      ShowMessage('Proc2 sees the exception');
40:    end;
```

LISTING 5.7   Continued

```
41:  end;
42:
43:  procedure Proc1;
44:  begin
45:    try
46:      Proc2;
47:    finally
48:      ShowMessage('Proc1 sees the exception');
49:    end;
50:  end;
51:
52:  procedure TForm1.Button1Click(Sender: TObject);
53:  const
54:    ExceptMsg = 'Exception handled in calling procedure. The message is "%s"';
55:  begin
56:    ShowMessage('This method calls Proc1 which calls Proc2 which calls Proc3');
57:    try
58:      Proc1;
59:    except
60:      on E:EBadStuff do
61:        ShowMessage(Format(ExceptMsg, [E.Message]));
62:    end;
63:  end;
64:
65:  end
```

Reraising an Exception

When you need to perform special exception handling for a statement inside an existing try..except block and still need to allow the exception to flow to the block's outer default handler, you can use a technique called reraising the exception. Listing 5.8 demonstrates an example of reraising an exception.

LISTING 5.8   Reraising an Exception

```
1:   try              // this is outer block
2:     { statements }
3:     { statements }
4:     ( statements )
5:     try            // this is the special inner block
6:       { some statement that may require special handling }
7:     except
8:       on ESomeException do
9:       begin
10:        { special handling for the inner block statement }
11:        raise;     // reraise the exception to the outer block
12:      end;
13:    end;
14:  except
15:    // outer block will always perform default handling
16:    on ESomeException do Something;
17:  end;
```

CHAPTER 6

Assemblies—Libraries and Packages

by Steve Teixeira

Assemblies were introduced in Chapter 2, "Overview of the .NET Framework," as discrete deployment modules for .NET applications and libraries. Physically, assemblies are PE-format files containing .NET IL code intended for execution. Logically, assemblies form boundaries for scope, type, version, and security in the .NET Framework.

Assemblies can be executable modules (.exe files) or shared libraries (.dll files). Any program, library, or package you create with Delphi is an assembly.

Core Assemblies

The best place to begin a discussion on assemblies is probably with those that provide the basic services to your applications. All .NET applications use the mscorlib.dll assembly. Among other things, this assembly houses all the basic .NET types, as well as the base Exception class, key attributes, and a few other important items.

Borland's core assembly is Borland.Delphi.dll, which houses the Borland.Delphi.System unit namespace. Most of Delphi's core types, described in the previous chapter, are implemented in this assembly.

Viewing Assembly Contents and Dependencies

The .NET SDK, which is freely available from Microsoft, contains a tool called ILDASM (Intermediate Language Disassembler) that allows you to peer inside an assembly to view its contents and dependencies. An assembly can be opened within ILDASM by passing its name on the command

PART III: THE .NET FRAMEWORK CLASS LIBRARY DEVELOPMENT

CHAPTER 6 Assemblies: Libraries and Packages

CHAPTER 7 GDI+ Programming: Drawing in .NET

CHAPTER 8 Mono - A Cross Platform .NET Project

CHAPTER 9 Memory Management and Garbage Collection

IN THIS CHAPTER

- Core Assemblies
- Viewing Assembly Contents and Dependencies
- Ring the GAC
- Building Assemblies
- Using Assemblies in Delphi
- Using Delphi Assemblies in C#
- Installing Packages into the Delphi IDE
- Strong Naming Assemblies
- Dynamically Loading Assemblies

line when launching ILDASM or by selecting File, Open from the main menu. Figure 6.1 shows the main window of ILDASM viewing a very simple Windows Forms application.

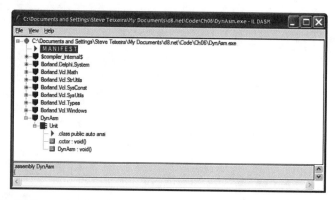

FIGURE 6.1   Inspecting a simple WinForm application with ILDASM.

As shown in Figure 6.1, every assembly contains a manifest, which is a collection of metadata that details dependencies on other assemblies as well as various attributes of the assembly and module. Double-clicking on the manifest item in the ILDASM tree view creates a new window that provides a view of the manifest contents. This window is shown in Figure 6.2.

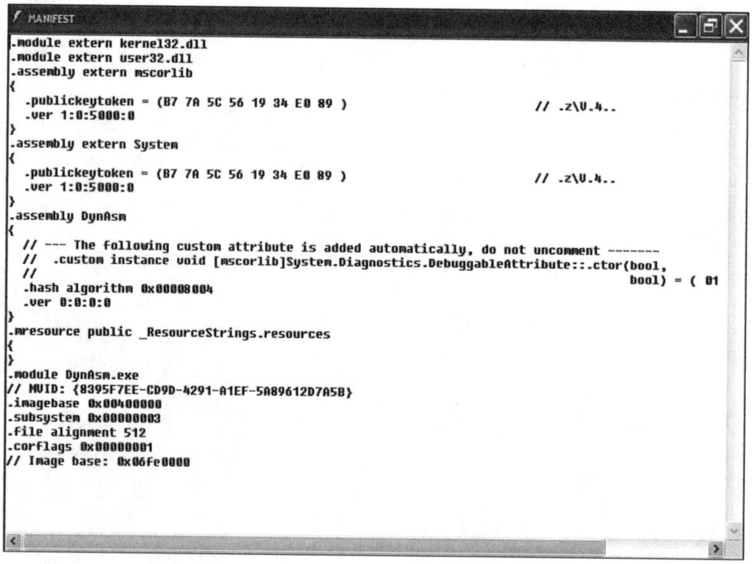

FIGURE 6.2   Viewing the contents of an assembly manifest.

As shown in Figure 6.2, the simple WinForm application contains dependencies on the mscorlib, System, System.Windows.Forms, and System.Drawing assemblies. The version and publickeytoken entries found for each of these assemblies is the secret sauce that enables the end of "DLL Hell" in the .NET world; assemblies bind to their dependencies not just by filename, as in the Win32 world, but by version number and cryptographic key. This is discussed in greater detail as a part of strong naming later in this chapter.

> **NOTE**
>
> Applications built with Delphi will always require one or more Microsoft and Borland assemblies. These dependent assemblies must be deployed to any other machines on which you intend to use your assembly. The Microsoft assemblies must be deployed as a part of the .NET Framework redistributable package (see http://www.microsoft.com/net), whereas the Borland assemblies can be deployed more granularly. See the deploy.txt file in your Delphi directory or on your product CD for details on deploying Borland packages.

Ring the GAC

When one assembly is dependent upon another, the CLR manages the loading of the dependent assemblies into the application domain. The CLR expects to find the assembly either listed in a sort of registry for assemblies called the Global Assembly Cache (GAC for short) or using Win32 rules for locating a library on disk (looking in current, windows, and windows system directories, as well as on the path). When deploying an application requiring custom assemblies, therefore, you can either place the assembly in one of these locations or drop them into any old directory and register them in the GAC. GAC registration is the preferred method of deployment when the assemblies are required by multiple disparate applications.

The GAC can be manipulated via the .NET Framework Configuration tool. You can invoke this tool by bring up the Windows Control Panel, launching the Administrative Tools applet, and then invoking the Microsoft .NET Framework Configuration tool. This application is shown in Figure 6.3.

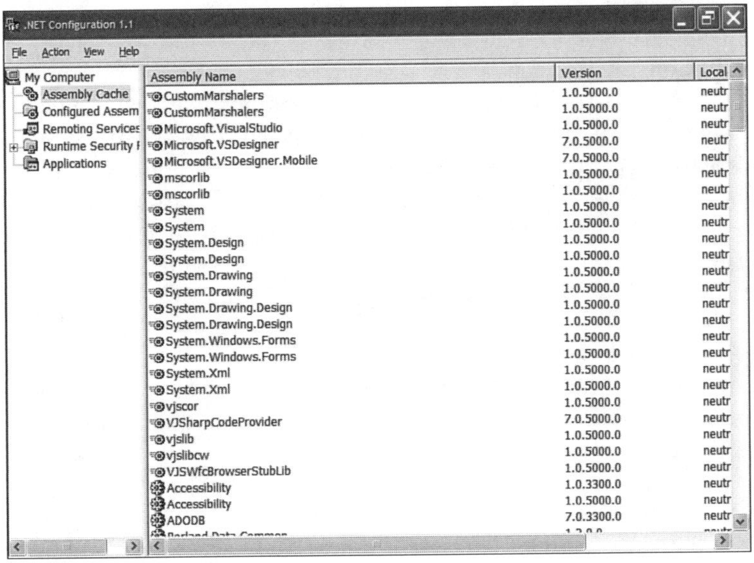

FIGURE 6.3   Managing the Global Assembly Cache (GAC).

Real-world applications would most likely leverage an installer utility's capability to simultaneously install an assembly and place it in the GAC rather than requiring the GAC to be directly edited.

Building Assemblies

The remainder of this chapter focuses on building and using .dll assemblies. In Object Pascal, .NET library assemblies can be developed using either the package or the library keywords.

The reason Delphi maintains two methods of assembly creation has more to do with legacy than practicality. Win32 versions of Delphi used library to create Win32 Dynamic Link Libraries and package to create Borland Packages, DLL-like modules usable only in Delphi and C++Builder. In .NET, these things both boil down to assemblies—with only slight syntactical differences separating the two.

> **NOTE**
>
> The package syntax is preferred for creating and maintaining assemblies because package semantics most closely match those of .NET assemblies. The library syntax is primarily a vehicle for backward compatibility.

Why Use Assemblies?

There are several reasons why you might want to use assemblies, including

- Smaller distribution
- Application partitioning
- Component containment

Smaller Distribution

It's a rather common situation to have multiple applications that share some types or other libraries in common. In such cases, it can be efficient to place this shared code in assemblies to be used by the various applications. For example, consider that many programs are available over the Internet as full-blown applications, downloadable demos, or updates to existing applications. Consider the benefit of giving users the option of downloading smaller versions of the application when pieces of the application might already exist on their systems, such as when they have a prior installation.

Application Partitioning

By partitioning your applications using assemblies, you not only divide modules physically based on logical organization, but you also allow your users to obtain updates to only those parts of the application that they need.

Component Containment

Probably one of the most common reasons for using assemblies is the distribution of third-party components. If you are a component vendor, you must know how to create assemblies because certain design-time elements—such as component and property editors, wizards, and experts—are all provided by assemblies.

Using Packages to Build Assemblies

If you know how to create Object Pascal units and compile an application, you already know all you need to know to create assemblies using packages. Using the IDE Wizard to create a new package and adding a new unit to that package generates a file similar to the one shown in Listing 6.1. This file is viewable by right-clicking the package node in the Project Manager and selecting View Source from the local menu.

LISTING 6.1   A Sample Package File

```
1:   package Package2;
2:
3:
4:   {$ALIGN 0}
5:   {$ASSERTIONS ON}
6:   {$BOOLEVAL OFF}
7:   {$DEBUGINFO ON}
8:   {$EXTENDEDSYNTAX ON}
9:   {$IMPORTEDDATA ON}
10:  {$IOCHECKS ON}
11:  {$LOCALSYMBOLS ON}
12:  {$LONGSTRINGS ON}
13:  {$OPENSTRINGS ON}
14:  {$OPTIMIZATION ON}
15:  {$OVERFLOWCHECKS OFF}
16:  {$RANGECHECKS OFF}
17:  {$REFERENCEINFO ON}
18:  {$SAFEDIVIDE OFF}
19:  {$STACKFRAMES OFF}
20:  {$TYPEDADDRESS OFF}
21:  {$VARSTRINGCHECKS ON}
22:  {$WRITEABLECONST OFF}
23:  {$MINENUMSIZE 1}
24:  {$IMAGEBASE $400000}
25:  {$IMPLICITBUILD OFF}
26:
27:  requires
28:    borland.delphi;
29:
30:  [assembly: AssemblyDescription('')]
31:  [assembly: AssemblyConfiguration('')]
32:  [assembly: AssemblyCompany('')]
33:  [assembly: AssemblyProduct('')]
34:  [assembly: AssemblyCopyright('')]
35:  [assembly: AssemblyTrademark('')]
36:  [assembly: AssemblyCulture('')]
37:
38:
39:  // The Delphi compiler controls the AssemblyTitleAttribute via the
40:  // ExeDescription. You can set this in the IDE via the Project Options.
41:  // Manually setting the AssemblyTitle attribute below will override the
```

LISTING 6.1   Continued

```
42:  // IDE setting.
43:  // [assembly: AssemblyTitle('')]
44:
45:
46:  //
47:  // Version information for an assembly consists of the following four
➥values:
48:  //
49:  //      Major Version
50:  //      Minor Version
51:  //      Build Number
52:  //      Revision
53:  //
54:  // You can specify all the values or you can default the Revision and Build
55:  // Numbers by using the '*' as shown below:
56:
57:  [assembly: AssemblyVersion('1.0.*')]
58:
59:  //
60:  // In order to sign your assembly you must specify a key to use. Refer to
61:  // the Microsoft .NET Framework documentation for more information on
62:  // assembly signing.
63:  //
64:  // Use the attributes below to control which key is used for signing.
65:  //
66:  // Notes:
67:  //   (*) If no key is specified, the assembly is not signed.
68:  //   (*) KeyName refers to a key that has been installed in the Crypto
69:  //       Service Provider (CSP) on your machine. KeyFile refers to a file
70:  //       which contains a key.
71:  //   (*) If the KeyFile and the KeyName values are both specified, the
72:  //       following processing occurs:
73:  //       (1) If the KeyName can be found in the CSP, that key is used.
74:  //       (2) If the KeyName does not exist and the KeyFile does exist, the
75:  //           key in the KeyFile is installed into the CSP and used.
76:  //   (*) In order to create a KeyFile, you can use the sn.exe (Strong Name)
77:  //       utility. When specifying the KeyFile, the location of the KeyFile
78:  //       should be relative to the project output directory. For example,
79:  //       if your KeyFile is located in the project directory, you would
80:  //       specify the AssemblyKeyFile attribute as
81:  //       [assembly: AssemblyKeyFile('mykey.snk')], provided your output
82:  //       directory is the project directory (the default).
83:  //   (*) Delay Signing is an advanced option - see the Microsoft .NET
84:  //       Framework documentation for more information on this.
85:  //
86:  [assembly: AssemblyDelaySign(false)]
87:  [assembly: AssemblyKeyFile('')]
88:  [assembly: AssemblyKeyName('')]
89:  end.
```

▶ Find the code on the CD: \Code\Chapter 06.

Examining this file from the top down, we can break it down as follows:

- The `package` directive dictates that this module is a package assembly project (line 1).

- The `requires` clause lists which assemblies are required by this package (lines 27–28).

- The `contains` clause lists the units that will be compiled into this assembly (not shown in this listing).

- Several `assembly` attributes allow the user to enter various bits of information about this assembly that will ultimately be placed in the manifest (lines 30–36).

- The `AssemblyTitle` and `AssemblyVersion` assembly attributes (line 43 and line 57, respectively) enable the user to control this assembly's title and version number.

- Finally, there are a few more `assembly` attributes that provide control over how the assembly is signed for strong naming. More on this is discussed shortly (lines 86–88).

> **NOTE**
>
> Irrespective of what assemblies are contained in the package's `requires` clause, all packages implicitly require the `mscorlib.dll` assembly.

Table 6.1 lists and describes the types of package-specific files based on their file extensions.

TABLE 6.1 Package Files

File Extension	File Type	Description
`.dpk`	Package source file	This file is created when you invoke the Package Editor. You can think of this as you might think of the `.dpr` file for a Delphi project.
`.pas`	Unit source file	A package consists of one or more Object Pascal units containing the shared code.
`.bdsproj`	Project settings file	File used by the IDE to store project settings.
`.cfg`	Project configuration file	Configuration file generated for use by command line compiler.
`.dcpil`	IL compiled package symbol file	This is the IL compiled version of the package that contains the symbol information for the package and its units.
`.dcuil`	Compiled unit	An IL compiled version of a unit contained in a package. One `.dcuil` file will be created for each unit contained in the package.
`.dll`	Assembly	This is the final assembly file that contains code usable by any .NET programming language.

Listings 6.2 and 6.3 show the `.dpk` and `.pas` files that make up a package assembly. This package will be used by other applications shortly.

LISTING 6.2 D8DG.TestPkg: A Test Package Project

```
1:    package D8DG.TestPkg;
2:
```

LISTING 6.2   Continued

```
3:
4:    {$ALIGN 0}
5:    {$ASSERTIONS ON}
6:    {$BOOLEVAL OFF}
7:    {$DEBUGINFO ON}
8:    {$EXTENDEDSYNTAX ON}
9:    {$IMPORTEDDATA ON}
10:   {$IOCHECKS ON}
11:   {$LOCALSYMBOLS ON}
12:   {$LONGSTRINGS ON}
13:   {$OPENSTRINGS ON}
14:   {$OPTIMIZATION ON}
15:   {$OVERFLOWCHECKS OFF}
16:   {$RANGECHECKS OFF}
17:   {$REFERENCEINFO ON}
18:   {$SAFEDIVIDE OFF}
19:   {$STACKFRAMES OFF}
20:   {$TYPEDADDRESS OFF}
21:   {$VARSTRINGCHECKS ON}
22:   {$WRITEABLECONST OFF}
23:   {$MINENUMSIZE 1}
24:   {$IMAGEBASE $400000}
25:   {$IMPLICITBUILD OFF}
26:
27:   requires
28:     Borland.Delphi;
29:
30:   contains
31:     D8DG.PkgUnit in 'D8DG.PkgUnit.pas';
32:
33:   [assembly: AssemblyDescription('')]
34:   [assembly: AssemblyConfiguration('')]
35:   [assembly: AssemblyCompany('')]
36:   [assembly: AssemblyProduct('')]
37:   [assembly: AssemblyCopyright('')]
38:   [assembly: AssemblyTrademark('')]
39:   [assembly: AssemblyCulture('')]
40:
41:   [assembly: AssemblyVersion('1.0.*')]
42:
43:   [assembly: AssemblyDelaySign(false)]
44:   [assembly: AssemblyKeyFile('')]
45:   [assembly: AssemblyKeyName('')]
46:   end
```

▶ Find the code on the CD: \Code\Chapter 06.

LISTING 6.3   D8DG.PkgUnit: A Unit Within the Package

```
1:    unit D8DG.PkgUnit;
2:
3:    interface
4:
```

LISTING 6.3   Continued

```
5:   type
6:     TBlandClass = class
7:     private
8:       FTheString: string;
9:     public
10:      function TheMethod: Integer;
11:      property TheString: string read FTheString write FTheString;
12:    end;
13:
14:  procedure IAmProcedural;
15:
16:  implementation
17:
18:  procedure IAmProcedural;
19:  begin
20:    // do nothing
21:  end;
22:
23:  { TBlandClass }
24:
25:  function TBlandClass.TheMethod: Integer;
26:  begin
27:    Result := 3;
28:  end;
29:
30:  end.
```

▶ Find the code on the CD: \Code\Chapter 06.

Note that the unit contains both a class (line 6) and a standalone procedure (line 14) that is not a member of a class.

> **TIP**
>
> Namespaces are created simply by using dot notation on a unit name.

Using Libraries to Build Assemblies

The process of building assemblies as libraries is very similar to doing so using packages. The differences are small; as a starting point, the new library wizard is used instead of the new package wizard, and the syntax is slightly different. Listings 6.4 and 6.5 show a library file very similar to the package already created.

LISTING 6.4   D8DG.TestLib.dpr: A Test Library Project

```
1:   library D8DG.TestLib;
2:
3:   {%DelphiDotNetAssemblyCompiler 'c:\program files\common files\
   ➥borland shared\bds\shared assemblies\2.0\Borland.Vcl.dll'}
4:
5:   uses
6:     System.Reflection,
```

LISTING 6.4   Continued

```
 7:     D8DG.LibU in 'D8DG.LibU.pas';
 8:
 9:     [assembly: AssemblyTitle('')]
10:     [assembly: AssemblyDescription('')]
11:     [assembly: AssemblyConfiguration('')]
12:     [assembly: AssemblyCompany('')]
13:     [assembly: AssemblyProduct('')]
14:     [assembly: AssemblyCopyright('')]
15:     [assembly: AssemblyTrademark('')]
16:     [assembly: AssemblyCulture('')]
17:
18:     //
19:     // Version information for an assembly consists of the following
20:     // four values:
21:     //
22:     //      Major Version
23:     //      Minor Version
24:     //      Build Number
25:     //      Revision
26:     //
27:     // You can specify all the values or you can default the Revision and
28:     // Build Numbers by using the '*' as shown below:
29:
30:     [assembly: AssemblyVersion('1.0.*')]
31:
32:     //
33:     // In order to sign your assembly you must specify a key to use.
34:     // Refer to the Microsoft .NET Framework documentation for more
35:     // information on assembly signing.
36:     //
37:     // Use the attributes below to control which key is used for signing.
38:     //
39:     // Notes:
40:     //    (*) If no key is specified, the assembly is not signed.
41:     //    (*) KeyName refers to a key that has been installed in the
42:     //        Crypto Service Provider (CSP) on your machine. KeyFile
43:     //        refers to a file which contains a key.
44:     //    (*) If the KeyFile and the KeyName values are both specified,
45:     //        the following processing occurs:
46:     //        (1) If the KeyName can be found in the CSP, that key is
47:     //            used.
48:     //        (2) If the KeyName does not exist and the KeyFile does
49:     //            exist, the key in the KeyFile is installed into the CSP
50:     //            and used.
51:     //    (*) In order to create a KeyFile, you can use the sn.exe (Strong
52:     //        Name) utility. When specifying the KeyFile, the location of
53:     //        the KeyFile should be relative to the project output
54:     //        directory. For example, if your KeyFile is located in the
55:     //        project directory, you would specify the AssemblyKeyFile
56:     //        attribute as [assembly: AssemblyKeyFile('mykey.snk')],
57:     //        provided your output directory is the project directory
58:     //        (the default).
59:     //    (*) Delay Signing is an advanced option - see the Microsoft .NET
```

LISTING 6.4   Continued

```
60:  //        Framework documentation for more information on this.
61:  //
62:  [assembly: AssemblyDelaySign(false)]
63:  [assembly: AssemblyKeyFile('')]
64:  [assembly: AssemblyKeyName('')]
65:
66:  type
67:    TLibClass = class
68:      procedure AProc;
69:    end;
70:
71:  procedure LibProc;
72:  begin
73:    // nothing
74:  end;
75:
76:  function LibFunc: Integer;
77:  begin
78:    Result := 3;
79:  end;
80:
81:  { TSomeClass }
82:
83:  procedure TLibClass.AProc;
84:  begin
85:    // Nothing
86:  end;
87:
88:  begin
89:  end
```

▶ Find the code on the CD: \Code\Chapter 06.

LISTING 6.5.   D8DG.LibU.pas: A Test Unit for the Library

```
1:   unit D8DG.LibU;
2:
3:   interface
4:
5:   type
6:     TSomeClass = class
7:       procedure AProc;
8:     end;
9:
10:  procedure foobar;
11:  procedure barfoo;
12:  procedure BlahBlah;
13:
14:  implementation
15:
16:  { TSomeClass }
17:
18:  procedure TSomeClass.AProc;
```

LISTING 6.5 Continued

```
19:  begin
20:    // Nothing
21:  end;
22:
23:  procedure BlahBlah;
24:  begin
25:    // Nothing
26:  end;
27:
28:  procedure foobar;
29:  begin
30:    // nothing
31:  end;
32:
33:  procedure barfoo;
34:  begin
35:    // nothing
36:  end;
37:
38:  end.
```

▶ Find the code on the CD: \Code\Chapter 06.

Like the package assembly, this library assembly contains both object-oriented and procedural code. The key points of difference between library and package assemblies include

- Library project files use the %DelphiDotNetAssemblyCompiler directive (as shown on line 3 of Listing 6.4) to enable the IDE and compiler to keep track of what assemblies are required by this assembly, whereas package files use the requires clause.

- A library can contain code in the .dpr file, including code in the begin..end section that will run when the library is first loaded. This is shown in Listing 6.4 from line 66 on.

- A library can export flat routines to Win32 applications—this is a powerful way of leveraging the .NET Framework in existing Win32 applications.

- A library is smart-linked by the Delphi compiler. This means that the code for any class not directly or indirectly used will not be linked into compiled binary. In a package assembly, all code in the contained units will be linked into the package.

> **NOTE**
>
> The exports directive in a library is used by the .NET compiler to export routines to native Win32 applications. Libraries exporting such routines must have unsafe code enabled using the {$UNSAFECODE ON} directive. All symbols in the library file or in unit interface sections are automatically exported in the assembly for use by .NET applications.

Using Assemblies in Delphi

Using assemblies similar to the ones just shown is a straightforward process. The first step is to add a reference to the assembly in the project by selecting Project, New Reference from the main menu or right-clicking in the Project Manager and selecting Add Reference. After the reference is added, the appropriate namespaces can be added to the uses clause. Listing 6.6 shows a sample project unit that uses both the package and library assemblies created previously. Code from these assemblies is referenced on lines 13 and 14 of the listing.

LISTING 6.6   Using Assemblies in Delphi

```
1:    program TestApp;
2:
3:    {$APPTYPE CONSOLE}
4:
5:    {%DelphiDotNetAssemblyCompiler 'D8DG.TestPkg.dll'}
6:    {%DelphiDotNetAssemblyCompiler 'D8DG.TestLib.dll'}
7:
8:    uses
9:      D8DG.PkgUnit,
10:     D8DG.LibU;
11:
12:   begin
13:     D8DG.LibU.Unit.BlahBlah;
14:     D8DG.PkgUnit.TBlandClass.Create;
15:   end.
```

▶ Find the code on the CD: \Code\Chapter 06.

Using Delphi Assemblies in C#

The process for using Delphi-written assemblies from any other .NET language is remarkably similar to using them from Delphi; just add the references to the project and access the namespaces directly. Listing 6.7 illustrates how our assembly examples could be called from C#.

LISTING 6.7   Using a Delphi Assembly from C#c

```
1:    using System;
2:
3:    namespace DelAsmUser
4:    {
5:        /// <summary>
6:        /// Summary description for Class.
7:        /// </summary>
8:        class Class
9:        {
10:           /// <summary>
11:           /// The main entry point for the application.
12:           /// </summary>
13:           [STAThread]
14:           static void Main(string[] args)
15:           {
16:               new D8DG.LibU.TSomeClass();
17:               D8DG.PkgUnit.Unit.IAmProcedural();
```

LISTING 6.7   Continued

```
18:          }
19:       }
20:    }
```

Listing 6.7 can be compiled using the Microsoft C# compiler with the following command line:

```
csc DelAsmUser.cs /r:D8DG.TestLib.dll;D8DG.TestPkg.dll
```

> **NOTE**
>
> Note that procedural (for example, nonobject) elements can be accessed as static class methods of a compiler-manufactured class called Unit.

Installing Packages into the Delphi IDE

If you have a VCL component that you want to install into the Delphi IDE, it is a matter of selecting Component, Install VCL Component. This will allow you to add the component unit to a new or existing package assembly and install that assembly into the IDE, thereby making it available on the component palette.

Strong Naming Assemblies

Strong naming an assembly is a process whereby public key encryption is added to the assembly. A strong name doesn't actually make any assurances about the trustworthiness of the assembly, but it is instead a vehicle to help to verify name uniqueness, prevent name spoofing, and provide callers with some identity when a reference is resolved.

> **NOTE**
>
> Any assembly you ship to the public should be strong named.

The process of strong naming involves generating a key pair and then using that key pair in the assembly attributes.

To create a key pair, use the sn.exe utility from the Microsoft .NET SDK with the -k switch:

```
sn -k newkeypair.snk
```

Then pass this filename to the AssemblyKeyFile attribute in the package file:

```
[assembly: AssemblyKeyFile('newkeypair.snk')]
```

Once strong named, you will see the public key in the assembly manifest as shown in Figure 6.4.

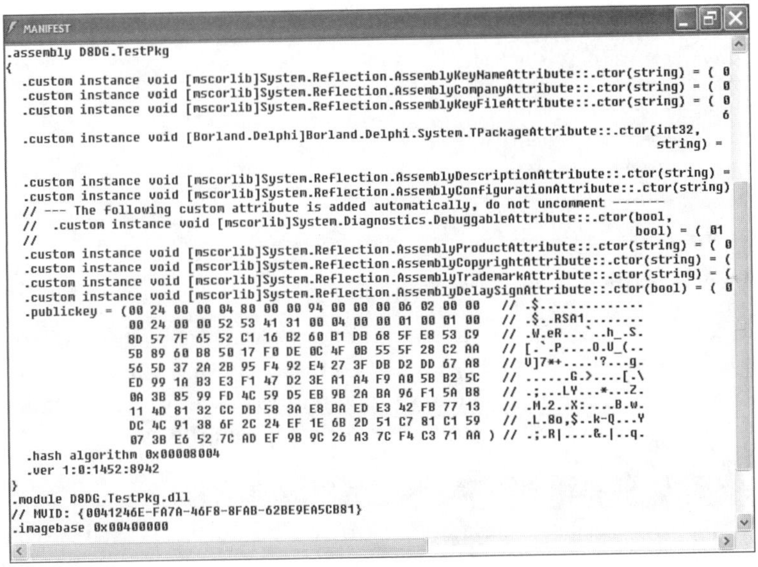

FIGURE 6.4   Viewing the public key in the assembly manifest.

Dynamically Loading Assemblies

One of the more powerful features of assemblies is that they can be loaded not just statically as a reference from another assembly but also dynamically at runtime. This is accomplished by using .NET reflection to load the file from disk, find and create objects, and invoke methods. Listing 6.8 shows how this is done.

LISTING 6.8   Dynamically Loading a Package

```
1:  program DynAsm;
2:
3:  {$APPTYPE CONSOLE}
4:
5:  {%DelphiDotNetAssemblyCompiler '$(SystemRoot)\microsoft.net\framework\
 ➥v1.1.4322\System.dll'}
6:
7:  uses
8:    System.Reflection;
9:
10: var
11:   a: Assembly;
12:   typ: System.Type;
13:   meth: MethodInfo;
14:   o: System.Object;
15: begin
16:   // load the assembly based on the file name
17:   a := Assembly.LoadFrom('D8DG.TestPkg.dll');
18:   // use reflection to obtain an object type from the assembly
19:   typ := a.GetType('D8DG.PkgUnit.TBlandClass');
20:   // get the method off of the object
```

LISTING 6.8   Continued

```
21:     meth := typ.GetMethod('TheMethod');
22:     // create an instance of the object
23:     o := Activator.CreateInstance(typ);
24:     // invoke the method on the object
25:     WriteLn(meth.Invoke(o, nil));
26:     ReadLn;
27:   end.
```

▶ Find the code on the CD: `\Code\Chapter 06`.

As Listing 6.8 shows, it's quite straightforward not only to dynamically load an assembly, as shown on line 17, but also to pull types and methods out of the assembly, as demonstrated on lines 19 and 21. Lines 23 and 25 show that it isn't much more work to create instances and invoke methods on these things reflected from the assembly.

CAUTION

Dynamically loaded packages and reflection are very powerful features, but you should be judicious in employing them. Because most of the work is done at runtime using strings, the compiler doesn't have the opportunity to find bugs for you prior to running. Because of this, your code is much more likely to exhibit errors or raise exceptions at runtime.

To avoid these problems and still benefit from dynamically loading assemblies, use interfaces or abstract base classes defined in a common assembly used by both the application and the dynamically loaded assembly. This way, you make your code type safe while improving the performance considerably compared to reflection and Invoke calls.

CHAPTER 7

GDI+ Programming— Drawing in .NET

IN THIS CHAPTER

- Fundamental Concepts
- Drawing Lines
- Drawing Curves
- Drawing Shapes
- GraphicsPaths and Regions
- Working with Images
- Revisiting Coordinate Systems
- Animation Example

Graphics programming is a lot of fun. Admittedly, it was difficult to stay serious while writing this chapter. There is quite a bit to the GDI+ library, and this chapter presents some of these capabilities. You will see how to work with drawing lines and shapes. This chapter illustrates the use of the Brush and Pen classes. You will see how to create special effects such as gradient coloring and line caps. Drawing curves and working with GraphicsPaths, Regions, and transformations are covered. You'll see how to manipulate images, and finally, the chapter wraps up with an animation demo.

Fundamental Concepts

Before delving into the examples, let's go over a few fundamental concepts about GDI+ programming.

The GDI+ Namespaces

The GDI+ related classes are defined in the following namespaces:

- System.Drawing—Provides basic graphics classes such as Bitmap, Font, Brushes, Graphics, Icon, Image, Pen, Region, etc.

- System.Drawing.Drawing2D—Provides advanced two-dimensional and vector graphics classes such as the LinearGradientBrush and the Matrix classes.

- System.Drawing.Imaging—Provides advanced imaging functionality classes.

- System.Drawing.Printing—Provides classes dealing with printing.

- System.Drawing.Text—Contains classes with typography support.

This chapter only covers classes contained in the first two namespaces listed. It does not cover classes contained in the latter two namespaces listed.

The Graphics Class

The Graphics class will be used heavily throughout this chapter and throughout your development in GDI+. This class encapsulates the drawing surface and contains all the supporting methods to perform various rendering operations.

Windows Coordinate System

The Windows coordinate system is simple. The surface is basically a grid composed of pixels. The origin of this grid is the upper-left pixel. Therefore, its coordinate using the x, y axis would be [x=0, y=0]. Figure 7.1 illustrates this concept in an 8x8 grid. It is composed of a line that extends from coordinate [0, 0] to coordinate [7, 7].

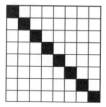

FIGURE 7.1   Line extending from [0, 0] to [7, 7].

This explanation is one way to think about *a* coordinate system. GDI+ actually relies on three different coordinate systems. These are the world, page, and device coordinate systems. When you draw to the screen, you typically specify an x, y coordinate for points on your drawing surface. These points are represented in world coordinates. This is basically an abstract drawing space. These coordinates must then be translated into page coordinates. Page coordinates usually represent some drawing surface such as a form. Finally, the page coordinates must get translated to device coordinates that represent the actual device on which rendering occurs (monitor, printer, and so on). Later in this chapter, I'll present an example that illustrates this concept.

A simple illustration will clarify this. Imagine that you have a sheet of graph paper lying on your desk. Establishing the fact that the box in the upper left position [0, 0] makes this graph paper much like the device when referring to device coordinates. Position [x=0, y=0] on your 1024x768 monitor is also in the upper left side of your monitor. The x coordinate increases and you move right along the paper as does the y coordinate when you move down. Now, suppose the you were to take a stencil, the same size as your paper, but with a smaller cutout somewhere in the middle. Figure 7.2 illustrates this—the grey area is covered by the stencil. The white area is the exposed area.

The exposed (white) area on the paper represents the page in the page coordinate system. This would be equivalent to any drawing surface on your screen, such as a form's client area. When we draw to the client area of a form, we usually refer to its upper corner as [0, 0]. Now, these are actually in world coordinates, but for now consider that they are page coordinates for this illustration. It is clear by looking at Figure 7.2 that position [0, 0] in page coordinates is not position [0, 0] in device coordinates. In fact, it's probably some other value as shown in Figure 7.2. The only time at which page coordinates match the device coordinates is when the upper left corner of the page is exactly over the upper left corner of the device. The translation between page to device coordinates is something that is handled between GDI+ and the device driver. You will not have to deal with this.

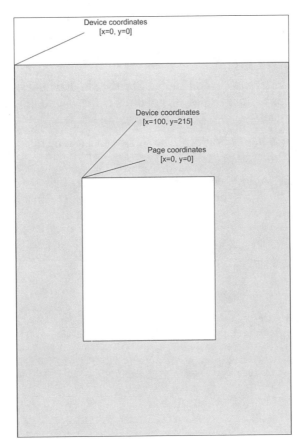

FIGURE 7.2   Device and page coordinates.

On the other hand, you might need to deal with the translation between world and page coordinates. It is mere convenience that the origin of world and page coordinates is in the same spot and uses the same unit of measure, the pixel. When you issue a command such as

```
MyGraphics.DrawLine(10, 10, 10, 100);
```

You are saying to the computer, "Computer, draw me a line in world coordinates from the pixel point 10, 10, to the pixel point 10, 100." The computer will determine the page coordinate for the first point, which just happens to be 10, 10 in page coordinates, and will draw a line to the second point after converting all points along the line to page coordinates. But what if world and page coordinates were not exactly matched? Well, that's a topic for later in this chapter when I deal with transformations. You will see how we can shift world coordinates along the page plane and how we can use different units of measurement when telling GDI+ what to draw. So, without further ado, grab your paintbrush; let's do some painting.

Drawing Lines

Having the ability to draw lines is fundamental to graphics development. GDI+ provides two key classes for line rendering. These are the Pen and Brush classes.

The Pen and Brush Classes

You use Pens to draw lines, shapes, and curves. The Pen can draw lines of different widths. You can also apply caps to lines (styles of endpoints to lines), and lines can be joined to form more complex shapes.

Brushes are used to fill a drawing surface. The surface area can be filled with a color, pattern, image, and texture.

This section covers various line techniques. In the example, there is a helper function that I'll point out before I illustrate the various drawing samples. The first is a helper routine used to clear my drawing surface. This is shown in Listing 7.1.

LISTING 7.1   ClearCanvas() Helper Routine

```
1:    procedure TWinForm.ClearCanvas;
2:    var
3:      MyGraphics: Graphics;
4:    begin
5:      MyGraphics := Graphics.FromHwnd(Panel1.Handle);
6:      MyGraphics.FillRectangle(Brushes.White, Panel1.ClientRectangle);
7:      MyPen.DashStyle := DashStyle.Solid;
8:      MyPen.Color := Color.Black;
9:      MyPen.StartCap := LineCap.Flat;
10:     MyPen.EndCap   := LineCap.Flat;
11:     MyPen.Width := 10;
12:   end;
```

▶ Find the code on the CD: \Code\Chapter 07\Ex01.

This routine simply initializes a Graphics class (line 5) for a Panel control. This Panel will serve as the drawing surface for the form. Additionally, it uses a standard Brush to fill the Panel's surface with a white background. This has the effect of erasing the surface. It does this by invoking the MyGraphics.FillRectangle() method (line 6), which takes a Brush and Rectangle parameter. Controls have a ClientRectangle property that refers to their client area. Finally, the routine sets various properties of a Pen object, MyPen, which I'll use throughout the example application.

Drawing Lines

When drawing lines, you can give them varying attributes such as color, line width, and so on. Additionally, using different brushes, you can vary the line's texture and color. Listing 7.2 illustrates some of these techniques.

LISTING 7.2   Line Drawing Techniques

```
1:    procedure TWinForm.PaintLines;
2:    var
3:      wdth: Integer;
4:      yPos: integer;
5:      lgBrush: LinearGradientBrush;
6:      txBrush: TextureBrush;
7:      img: Image;
8:    begin
9:      MyPen.Color := Color.Red;
10:     yPos := 10;
11:
12:     // draw different sized of lines.
13:     for wdth := 1 to 5 do
14:     begin
15:       MyPen.Width := wdth;
16:       MyGraphics.DrawLine(MyPen, 10, yPos, Panel1.Width-10, yPos);
17:       inc(yPos, 20);
18:     end;
19:
20:     // draw a line using a different brush
21:     MyPen.Width := 20;
22:     lgBrush := LinearGradientBrush.Create(Point.Create(0, yPos),
23:       Point.Create(Panel1.Width-10, 10), Color.Black, Color.Yellow);
24:     MyPen.Brush := lgBrush;
25:     MyGraphics.DrawLine(MyPen, 10, yPos, Panel1.Width-10, yPos);
26:
27:
28:     // draw a line using a pattern
29:     yPos := yPos + 40;
30:     img := Image.FromFile('Stucco.bmp');
31:     txBrush := TextureBrush.Create(img);
32:     MyPen.Brush := txBrush;
33:     MyGraphics.DrawLine(MyPen, 10, yPos, Panel1.Width-10, yPos);
34:   end;
```

▶ Find the code on the CD: \Code\Chapter 07\Ex01.

Lines 13–18 illustrate how to draw lines of differing widths. This is done by simply changing the width of the Pen used to draw the line. The Graphics.DrawLine() method is used to actually render the line to the drawing surface. The method shown here is one of the four overloaded versions of DrawLine(). In this example, DrawLine() takes the Pen and the x,y coordinate pairs representing the beginning and ending points for the line. The top five lines (which are in the color red when you run the program) in Figure 7.3 show the output of this loop.

Lines 21–25 illustrate how to draw lines using a different brush. In this case, I am using a LinearGradientBrush. This brush is capable of rendering a range of colors across the drawing surface. There are more complex ways to use this type of brush. Later, I'll demonstrate some. Other brushes that you can use are shown in Table 7.1.

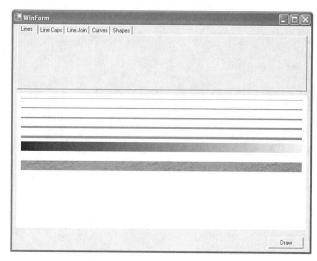

FIGURE 7.3   Output of the PaintLines() method.

TABLE 7.1   Brush Types

Brush Type	Description
HatchBrush	Draws using a hatch style, foreground color, and background color.
LinearGradientBrush	Draws using two color gradients or custom multicolor gradients.
PathGradientBrush	Draws a GraphicsPath using gradient colors.
SolidBrush	Draws using a single color.
TextureBrush	Draws using an image as the texture of the Brush.

Lines 29–33 illustrate using the TextureBrush class to draw a line. Here, a bitmap is used to specify the texture of the Brush. The output of this method is shown in Figure 7.3.

Line Caps

You can also apply start and end caps to lines to embellish them or to give joined lines a smoother appearance at their connection points. To achieve this, you assign one of the LineCap enumerations to the Pens's StartCap and EndCap properties. The possibilities are Flat, Square, SqaureAnchor, Round, RoundAnchor, AnchorMask, ArrorAnchor, Custom, DiamondAnchor, NoAnchor, and Triangle. Listing 7.3 shows the method that demonstrates LineCaps.

LISTING 7.3   Applying LineCap

```
1:    procedure TWinForm.PaintLineCaps;
2:    var
3:      endPoint: Point;
4:    begin
5:      MyPen.Color := Color.Black;
6:      MyPen.Width := 15;
7:
8:      if rbtnFlat.Checked then MyPen.EndCap := LineCap.Flat
9:      else if rbtnSq.Checked then MyPen.EndCap := LineCap.Square
```

LISTING 7.3   Continued

```
10:    else if rbtnSqAnc.Checked then MyPen.EndCap := LineCap.SquareAnchor
11:    else if rbtnRound.Checked then MyPen.EndCap := LineCap.Round
12:    else if rbtnRoundAnc.Checked then MyPen.EndCap := LineCap.RoundAnchor;
13:
14:    endPoint := DrawAngle(MyGraphics, MyPen, Point.Create(10,
15:      Panel1.Height-10),  200, 45.0);
16:    endPoint := DrawAngle(MyGraphics, MyPen, endPoint, 200, 315.0);
17:    endPoint := DrawAngle(MyGraphics, MyPen, endPoint, 200, 45.0);
18:    endPoint := DrawAngle(MyGraphics, MyPen, endPoint, 200, 315.0);
19:  end;
```

▶ Find the code on the CD: \Code\Chapter 07\Ex01.

Lines 8–12 determine which LineCap to apply based on the user's selection from the dialog box. Then, four lines are drawn at alternating angles to demonstrate how the end caps impact connected lines.

Consider Figure 7.4, which shows lines connecting using a Pen with Flat LineCaps.

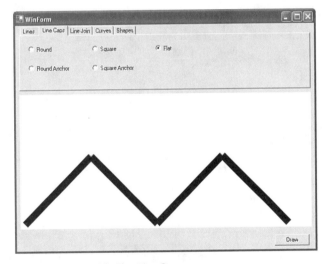

FIGURE 7.4   Connecting Lines with Flat LineCaps.

Now look at Figure 7.5. In this example, the LineCap.Round property has been assigned to the MyPen.EndCap property, and you can see how the connections have been brought together to give them a smoother appearance.

In Listing 7.3, I use a DrawAngle() method. This is a helper method that I use to draw an angle given a starting point, a line length, and the desired degree. This method is shown in Listing 7.4.

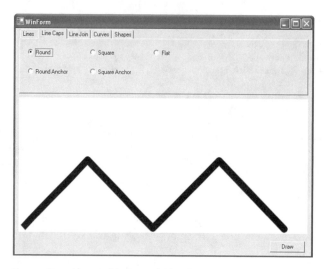

FIGURE 7.5   Connecting Lines with Round LineCaps.

LISTING 7.4   Applying LineCaps

```
1:    function TWinForm.DrawAngle(aGraphics: Graphics; aPen: Pen;
2:      aFromPt: Point; aLength: Integer; aTheta: Double): Point;
3:    var
4:      ToX, ToY: Integer;
5:    begin
6:      // convert degrees to radians
7:      aTheta := -aTheta*Math.PI/180;
8:
9:      // calculate points along a circle at radius R
10:     ToX := aFromPt.X + Convert.ToInt32(aLength * Math.Cos(aTheta));
11:     ToY := aFromPt.Y + Convert.ToInt32(aLength * Math.Sin(aTheta));
12:
13:     Result := Point.Create(ToX, ToY);
14:     aGraphics.DrawLine(aPen, aFromPt, Result);
15:   end;
```

▶ Find the code on the CD: \Code\Chapter 07\Ex01.

Joining Lines—The GraphicsPath Class

The GraphicsPath class is used to combine graphical shapes including lines. I'll get more into the GraphicsPath later. For now, just assume that the lines built in the following example are part of a combined collection. Listing 7.5 shows this.

LISTING 7.5   Joining Lines with GraphicsPath

```
1:    procedure TWinForm.PaintLineJoins;
2:    var
3:      MyPath: GraphicsPath;
4:    begin
5:      MyPath := GraphicsPath.Create;
```

LISTING 7.5   Continued

```
6:      MyPen.Color := Color.Black;
7:      MyPen.Width := 10;
8:
9:      MyPath.AddLine(10, 10, 300, 10);
10:     MyPath.AddLine(300, 10, 10, 200);
11:     MyPath.AddLine(10, 200, 300, 200);
12:
13:     if rbBevel.Checked then MyPen.LineJoin := LineJoin.Bevel
14:     else if rbMiter.Checked then MyPen.LineJoin := LineJoin.Miter
15:     else if rbRound.Checked then MyPen.LineJoin := LineJoin.Round
16:     else if rbMiterClipped.Checked then MyPen.LineJoin :=
17:       LineJoin.MiterClipped;
18:
19:     MyGraphics.DrawPath(MyPen, MyPath);
20: end;
```

▶ Find the code on the CD: \Code\Chapter 07\Ex01.

In this example, we use the `GraphicsPath` class to define three lines (lines 9–11). These lines, by virtue of belonging to the `GraphicsPath`, are part of a single unit. However, much like the previous `LineCaps` demo, they are drawn with the `LineCap.Flat` as the default. You can specify to use a `LineJoin` attribute for the `Pen`. This attribute can be `Bevel`, `Miter`, and `Round`. Figure 7.6 illustrates the affect of using `LineJoin.Miter`.

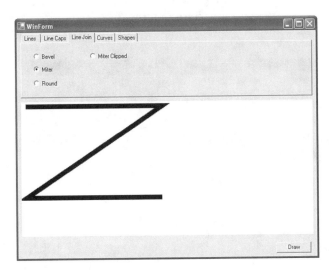

FIGURE 7.6   Using LineJoin.Miter when joining lines.

Drawing Curves

.NET supports two forms of curves. These are the cardinal spline and the Bezier spline. In general, curves are represented by a line passing through points on the drawing surface in a particular direction. Curve tension is based on the pull from points outside of the curve's line.

The Cardinal Spline

The cardinal spline is defined by a line that passes directly through the array of points. A tension value determines the bend of the line. When the tension is lower, the curve's bend will be flatter. Listing 7.6 shows the code for drawing a cardinal spline.

LISTING 7.6   Drawing the Cardinal Spline

```
1:    procedure TWinForm.paintCardinal;
2:    var
3:      MyPointsAry: array[0..2] of Point;
4:    begin
5:      MyPen.Color := Color.Blue;
6:      MyPen.Width := 8;
7:
8:      MyPointsAry[0] := Point.Create(10, 200);
9:      MyPointsAry[1] := Point.Create(150, 75);
10:     MyPointsAry[2] := Point.Create(500, 200);
11:     MyGraphics.DrawCurve(MyPen, MyPointsAry, TrackBar1.Value / 10)
12:    end;
```

▶ Find the code on the CD: \Code\Chapter 07\Ex01.

This example is fairly straightforward. The method declares an array of three points (line 3), populates it with points (lines 8–10), and calls the Graphics.DrawCurve() method (line 11). The final parameter of the method shown here takes the tension value. This value is determined by the value in a TrackBar control on the form. Figure 7.7 shows the impact of increasing the tension value.

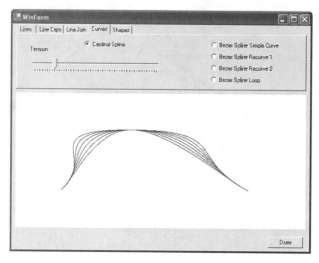

FIGURE 7.7   Increasing tension on a cardinal spline.

Bezier Spline

The Bezier spline is particularly interesting and has many uses, including CAD/CAM, animation, and postscript printing, just to name a few. I will demonstrate a simple curve, two recurves, and a loop using the Bezier.

Listing 7.7 shows the code for the various forms of the Bezier curve.

LISTING 7.7 Bezier Curve Example

```
 1: procedure TWinForm.paintBezier;
 2: var
 3:   MyPointsAry: array[0..4] of Point;
 4: begin
 5:   if rbtnBSC.Checked then // Simple curve
 6:   begin
 7:     MyPointsAry[0] := Point.Create(10, 200);
 8:     MyPointsAry[1] := Point.Create(100,100);
 9:     MyPointsAry[2] := Point.Create(250, 100);
10:     MyPointsAry[3] := Point.Create(500, 200);
11:   end
12:   else if rbtnBSR1.Checked then // Recurve 1
13:   begin
14:     MyPointsAry[0] := Point.Create(10, 200);
15:     MyPointsAry[1] := Point.Create(500, 10);
16:     MyPointsAry[2] := Point.Create(10, 180);
17:     MyPointsAry[3] := Point.Create(500, 200);
18:   end
19:   else if rbtnBSR2.Checked then // Recurve 2
20:   begin
21:     MyPointsAry[0] := Point.Create(10, 150);
22:     MyPointsAry[1] := Point.Create(250, 10);
23:     MyPointsAry[2] := Point.Create(200, 265);
24:     MyPointsAry[3] := Point.Create(450, 100);
25:   end
26:   else if rbtnBSL.Checked then // Loop
27:   begin
28:     MyPointsAry[0] := Point.Create(10, 10);
29:     MyPointsAry[1] := Point.Create(500, 265);
30:     MyPointsAry[2] := Point.Create(10, 200);
31:     MyPointsAry[3] := Point.Create(80, 15);
32:   end;
33:
34:   MyPen.Color := Color.Blue;
35:   MyPen.Width := 8;
36:
37:   // Draw the curve
38:   MyGraphics.DrawBezier(MyPen, MyPointsAry[0], MyPointsAry[1],
39:     MyPointsAry[2], MyPointsAry[3]);
40:
41:   // draw a lines to show the begin..end and control points.
42:   MyPen.Width := 4;
43:   MyPen.Color := Color.Red;
44:   MyPen.DashStyle := DashStyle.DashDotDot;
45:   MyPen.StartCap := LineCap.RoundAnchor;
```

LISTING 7.7   Continued

```
46:   MyPen.EndCap := LineCap.ArrowAnchor;
47:   MyGraphics.DrawLine(MyPen, MyPointsAry[0], MyPointsAry[1]);
48:
49:   MyPen.Color := Color.Green;
50:   MyPen.StartCap := LineCap.RoundAnchor;
51:   MyPen.EndCap := LineCap.ArrowAnchor;
52:   MyGraphics.DrawLine(MyPen, MyPointsAry[3], MyPointsAry[2]);
53: end;
```

▶ Find the code on the CD: \Code\Chapter 07\Ex01.

Lines 5–32 set up the various array points for the curve. The first element is the origin point of the curve. The last element is the destination point for the curve. The second and third points are control points that are control points for the origin and destination points, respectively. In line 38, the Graphics object renders the curve by calling the DrawBezier() method. As the curve moves along the line, it is pulled by the control points, which influence its shape. Figure 7.8 illustrates the simple Bezier curve.

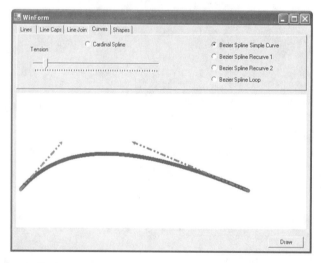

FIGURE 7.8   A simple Bezier curve.

I've drawn two additional lines to illustrate the relationship of the control points to the origin/destination points. When a Bezier curve has a change in direction as a result of at least one of the points, it is known as a recurve and thus why recurve bow is called such. Figures 7.9 and 7.10 illustrate two types of a recurve Bezier. Figure 7.11 illustrates how you can form a loop with this curve.

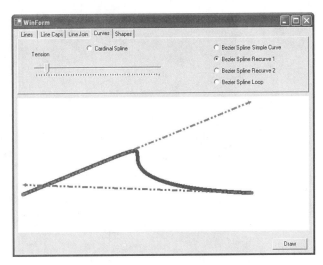

FIGURE 7.9   Recurve Bezier 1.

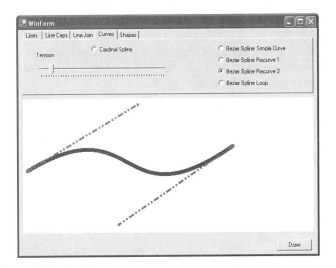

FIGURE 7.10   Recurve Bezier 2.

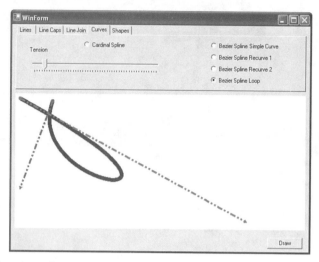

FIGURE 7.11　Forming a loop.

Drawing Shapes

Graphics drawing wouldn't be graphics drawing if you couldn't draw shapes. GDI+ supports the Rectangle, Ellipse, Polygon, and Pie shapes and also gives you the ability to draw other shapes that don't fit these common ones.

Drawing Rectangles

Drawing rectangles is simple. You use the Rectangle class to define the rectangle boundaries, and then you draw it using whatever Pen and Brush you choose. Listing 7.8 shows the code for drawing a rectangle.

LISTING 7.8　Drawing a Rectangle

```
1:    procedure DrawRectangle(aBrush: Brush);
2:    var
3:      MyRect: Rectangle;
4:    begin
5:      MyPen.Width := 5;
6:      MyRect := Rectangle.Create(10, 10, 500, 250);
7:      MyGraphics.DrawRectangle(MyPen, MyRect);
8:      if Assigned(aBrush) then
9:        MyGraphics.FillRectangle(aBrush, MyRect);
10:   end;
```

▶ Find the code on the CD: \Code\Chapter 07\Ex01.

You'll notice that line 9 optionally fills the rectangle with a specified brush. If you were to pass a SolidBrush or one of the other Brush variations, your rectangle would be filled with the brush you defined as illustrated in Figure 7.12, which shows a hatch-filled rectangle.

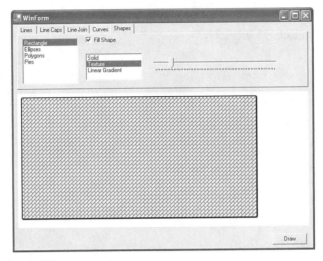

FIGURE 7.12   A hatch-filled rectangle.

Drawing Ellipses

Drawing ellipses is almost identical to drawing a rectangle. In fact, you use the `Rectangle` class to define the boundaries of the ellipsis. Listing 7.9 illustrates this.

LISTING 7.9   Drawing Ellipses

```
1:   procedure DrawEllipse(aBrush: Brush);
2:   var
3:     MyRect: Rectangle;
4:   begin
5:     MyPen.Width := 5;
6:     MyRect := Rectangle.Create(10, 10, 500, 250);
7:     MyGraphics.DrawEllipse(MyPen, MyRect);
8:     if CheckBox1.Checked then
9:        MyGraphics.FillEllipse(aBrush, MyRect);
10:  end;
```

▶ Find the code on the CD: `\Code\Chapter 07\Ex01`.

You'll notice that the only difference between drawing an ellipsis and drawing a rectangle is the call to `DrawEllipse()`/`FillEllipse`.

Drawing Polygons

A polygon is a closed plane that is bounded by at least three sides. To draw a polygon, you supply an array of points to the `DrawPolygon()`/`FillPolygon()` methods of the `Graphics` class. Listing 7.10 shows this technique.

LISTING 7.10   Drawing a Polygon

```
1:   procedure DrawPolygon(aBrush: Brush);
2:   var
```

LISTING 7.10   Continued

```
3:     MyPointAry: array[0..6] of Point;
4:   begin
5:     MyPen.Width := 5;
6:     MyPointAry[0] := Point.Create(200, 50);
7:     MyPointAry[1] := Point.Create(250, 100);
8:     MyPointAry[2] := Point.Create(250, 150);
9:     MyPointAry[3] := Point.Create(200, 200);
10:    MyPointAry[4] := Point.Create(150, 150);
11:    MyPointAry[5] := Point.Create(150, 100);
12:    MyPointAry[6] := Point.Create(200, 50);
13:    MyGraphics.DrawPolygon(MyPen, MyPointAry);
14:    if CheckBox1.Checked then
15:      MyGraphics.FillPolygon(aBrush, MyPointAry);
16:  end;
```

▶ Find the code on the CD: \Code\Chapter 07\Ex01.

Drawing Pies

With GDI+, you can draw your pie and eat it too. Given that an ellipse is bound by a rectangle and that a pie is simply a wedge from an ellipse (most often a circle), it would seem that we should be able to get our slice of pie from the same rectangle.

It's true; you can. Listing 7.11 shows this.

LISTING 7.11   Drawing a Pie

```
1:   procedure DrawPie(aBrush: Brush);
2:   var
3:     MyRect: Rectangle;
4:   begin
5:     MyPen.Width := 5;
6:     MyRect := Rectangle.Create(10, 10, 250, 250);
7:     // top right
8:     MyGraphics.DrawPie(MyPen, MyRect, 0, -90);
9:     // bottom right
10:    MyGraphics.DrawPie(MyPen, MyRect, -270, -90);
11:    // bottom left
12:    MyGraphics.DrawPie(MyPen, MyRect, -180, -90);
13:    // top left
14:    MyGraphics.DrawPie(MyPen, MyRect, -90, -90);
15:
16:    if CheckBox1.Checked then
17:      MyGraphics.FillPie(aBrush, MyRect, 0, -90);
18:  end;
```

▶ Find the code on the CD: \Code\Chapter 07\Ex01.

This example draws a pie with four segments. Line 17 shows how, by using a brush, you can fill your pie with a filling of choice. Figure 7.13 shows one segment of the pie filled.

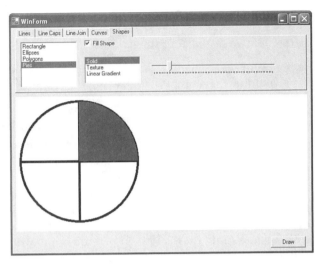

FIGURE 7.13   Drawing a pie.

More on the LinearGradientBrush

The line of code that creates the `LinearGradientBrush` is

```
B := LinearGradientBrush.Create(Panel1.ClientRectangle,
  Color.Blue, Color.Crimson, TrackBar2.Value);
```

You'll notice that the last parameter is obtained from the value of a `TrackBar` control. This parameter is an orientation angle, represented in degrees, clockwise from the x-axis. Figure 7.14 shows this effect, although statically. You'll have to run the application to get the full effect.

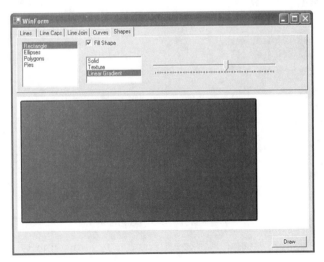

FIGURE 7.14   Drawing with a LinearGradientBrush.

GraphicsPaths and Regions

GraphicsPaths and Regions are two distinct but similar classes.

GraphicsPaths represent a list of independent figures. A GraphicsPath can, for example, contain different shapes and line drawings. When drawing the GraphicsPath, all figures are drawn at once.

A Region is an enclosed area representing a shape in which you can perform various drawing operations. Regions can, like the GraphicsPath, have disconnected elements.

Drawing with the GraphicsPath Class

Earlier, it was said that the GraphicsPath class is used to combine graphical shapes including lines. The following example illustrates how a GraphicsPath can be composed of lines and shapes that might not even be connected. What's convenient about the graphics path is that you can define what you want to draw and then perform the drawing of it in one swoop. Listing 7.12 shows this code.

LISTING 7.12   Drawing a Graphics Path

```
1:   procedure TWinForm.btnCreatePath_Click(sender: System.Object;
2:     e: System.EventArgs);
3:   var
4:     gp: GraphicsPath;
5:     MyPen: Pen;
6:   begin
7:     ClearCanvas;
8:     MyPen := Pen.Create(Color.Black, 2);
9:     gp := GraphicsPath.Create;
10:    gp.AddLine(10, 200, 50, 300);
11:    gp.AddLine(50, 300, 500, 250);
12:    gp.AddLine(500, 250, 260, 80);
13:
14:    gp.StartFigure;
15:    gp.AddLine(400, 10, 400, 60);
16:    gp.AddLine(400, 60, 450, 60);
17:    gp.AddLine(450, 60, 450, 10);
18:
19:    gp.StartFigure;
20:    gp.AddBezier(10, 50, 10, 55, 300, 70, 300, 250);
21:    if cbPathClosed.Checked then
22:      gp.CloseAllFigures;
23:    if cbPathFilled.Checked then
24:      MyGraphics.FillPath(Brushes.Bisque, gp);
25:    MyGraphics.DrawPath(MyPen, gp);
26:  end;
```

▶ Find the code on the CD: \Code\Chapter 07\Ex02.

You have already seen how to add lines to a GraphicsPath. Notice line 14. By using the StartFigure() method of the GraphicsPath class, you can create subpaths that are disconnected from one another but are still contained by the GraphicsPath. In this example, we create two figures composed of lines and a Bezier curve. When DrawPath() is called on line 25, all the figures are drawn. Figure 7.15 shows this output while filling the areas.

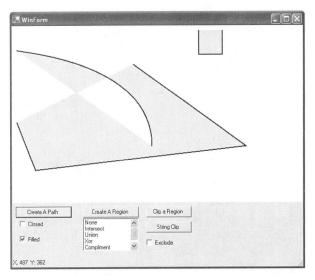

FIGURE 7.15 Drawing the elements of a graphics path.

You might have noticed that the FillPath() method worked even through the figures within the GraphicsPath were not closed. FillPath() knows how to determine the path to close each figure and assumes that when filling.

Drawing with the Region Class

When creating Regions, you are defining an area in which you will perform drawing operations. Listing 7.13 shows the code that illustrates how to use the Region class.

LISTING 7.13 Using the Region Class

```
1:   procedure TWinForm.btnCreateRegion_Click(sender: System.Object;
2:     e: System.EventArgs);
3:   var
4:     r: Rectangle;
5:     r2: Rectangle;
6:     MyPen: Pen;
7:     rg: System.Drawing.Region;
8:   begin
9:     ClearCanvas;
10:    MyPen := Pen.Create(Color.Black, 2);
11:    r := Rectangle.Create(20, 40, 400, 50);
12:    r2 := Rectangle.Create(100, 10, 50, 200);
13:    rg := System.Drawing.Region.Create(r);
14:
15:    case ListBox1.SelectedIndex of
16:      1: rg.Intersect(r2);
17:      2: rg.Union(r2);
```

LISTING 7.13   Continued

```
18:      3: rg.&Xor(r2);
19:      4: rg.Complement(r2);
20:      5: rg.Exclude(r2);
21:    end; // case
22:
23:    MyGraphics.FillRegion(Brushes.Indigo, rg);
24:    MyGraphics.DrawRectangle(Pens.Black, r);
25:    MyGraphics.DrawRectangle(Pens.Black, r2);
26: end;
```

▶ Find the code on the CD: \Code\Chapter 07\Ex02.

In this example, two Rectangles are created that will cross over each other. The first is used in creating the region (line 13). The second is combined with the Region by calling one of the operations that perform combinations of a Region with another artifact such as a Rectangle, another Region, or a GraphicsPath. The operations perform the functions as their names imply. Figure 7.16 is an example of a Region that has been Xored with another Rectangle.

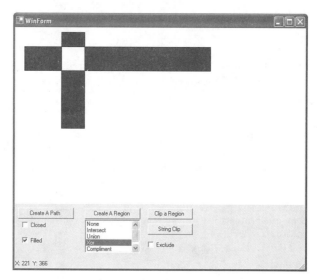

FIGURE 7.16   Region Xored with a Rectangle.

Figure 7.17 shows the same Region and Rectangle combined but intersected. This is the inverse of the Xor operation.

Clipping Regions

You've seen how Regions can be used to define an area in which drawing will be performed. You have also seen how certain operations on a region look when a Region is drawn with another, overlaying shape. Regions can also be used to prohibit drawing outside of, or within, itself. Listing 7.14 illustrates this.

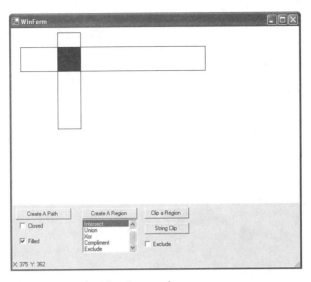

FIGURE 7.17   Region intersected with a Rectangle.

LISTING 7.14   Clipping a Region

```
 1:  procedure TWinForm.btnClipRegion_Click(sender: System.Object;
 2:    e: System.EventArgs);
 3:  var
 4:    gp: GraphicsPath;
 5:    r: Rectangle;
 6:  begin
 7:    ClearCanvas;
 8:    gp := GraphicsPath.Create;
 9:    r := Rectangle.Create(20, 40, 400, 200);
10:    gp.AddEllipse(r);
11:    MyGraphics.DrawPath(Pens.Black, gp);
12:    MyGraphics.SetClip(gp, CombineMode.Replace);
13:    MyGraphics.DrawString('Delphi 8',
14:      System.Drawing.Font.Create('Comic Sans MS',124),
15:      Brushes.Red, Point.Create(20, 20), StringFormat.GenericTypographic);
16:  end;
```

▶ Find the code on the CD: \Code\Chapter 07\Ex02.

This example draws an ellipse to the surface using a GraphicsPath. It then calls the Graphics.SetClip() method (line 12) to establish a clipping region. The second parameter, which is a CombineMode enumeration, determines the type of clipping to take effect. The CombineMode enumeration has the same impact on the region as do the combination operations when intersecting Regions. Figure 7.18 shows the output of this function. You'll see that the drawing of the string was prevented from going beyond the boundaries defined by the clipping region.

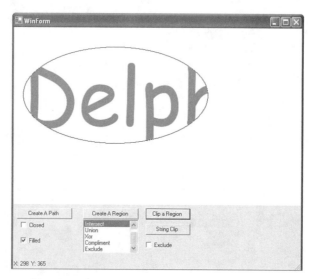

FIGURE 7.18   Displaying a clipping Region.

To illustrate some of the power of clipping regions, look at Listing 7.15.

LISTING 7.15   Clipping a String

```
1:    procedure TWinForm.btnClipString_Click(sender: System.Object;
2:      e: System.EventArgs);
3:    var
4:      gp: GraphicsPath;
5:    begin
6:      ClearCanvas;
7:      gp := GraphicsPath.Create;
8:      gp.AddString('Delphi 8', FontFamily.Create('Comic Sans MS'),
9:        Integer(FontStyle.Bold or FontStyle.Italic), 144,
10:       Point.Create(10, 20), StringFormat.GenericTypographic);
11:
12:     MyGraphics.DrawPath(Pens.Black, gp);
13:     if cbxExclude.Checked then
14:       MyGraphics.SetClip(gp, CombineMode.Exclude)
15:     else
16:       MyGraphics.SetClip(gp);
17:     MyGraphics.DrawImage(Bitmap.Create('USFlag.gif'),
18:       Panel1.ClientRectangle);
19:   end;
```

▶ Find the code on the CD: \Code\Chapter 07\Ex02.

This example adds a string to the GraphicsPath (lines 8–10). After drawing the GraphicsPath, the example sets a clipping region on the contents of the GraphicsPath using the CombineMode determined by the selection of a CheckBox control. When the CheckBox control is unchecked, the output is as shown in Figure 7.19. Otherwise, the clipping region is inversed and the output appears as shown in Figure 7.20.

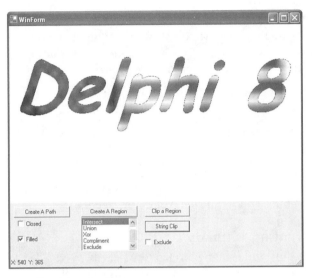

FIGURE 7.19   Output of a string Region.

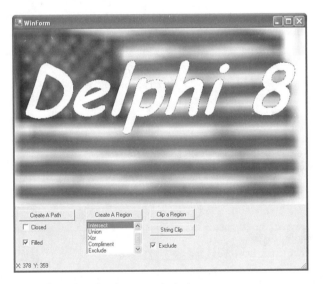

FIGURE 7.20   Output of a string Region—excluded.

Working with Images

No graphics library would be complete without the tools to work on images. GDI+ provides an abundance of capabilities for image manipulation. The following section illustrates some of these.

The Image Classes

There are two classes that you will work with when manipulating images. These are the Bitmap and the MetaFile classes. Both of these classes descend from Image, which is the abstract class providing functionality common to both.

The Bitmap class is used for manipulating raster-based images, which are images consisting of pixel data.

The Metafile class holds a recording of graphic rendering operations that get played back when it is drawn.

The following examples illustrate some of the Bitmap manipulations that you can do with GDI+. Of course, I can only touch the surface of GDI+'s capabilities within the space given. Hopefully, this will entice you to further explore this technology.

Loading and Creating Bitmaps

The methods for loading and creating bitmaps are heavily overloaded, so I won't attempt to write about all the various ways to create them. Instead, I discuss the methods I use in the remaining examples in this chapter.

I created a single application that demonstrates some of the image manipulation capabilities. This app contains a single method to load images from a file. This is shown in Listing 7.16.

LISTING 7.16   Loading Images for the Sample App

```
1:   procedure TWinForm1.LoadBitmap(aBm: String);
2:   begin
3:     MyBitmap:= Bitmap.Create(aBm);
4:     MyBitmap.SetResolution(120, 120);
5:     MyGraphics := Graphics.FromImage(MyBitmap);
6:     MyGraphics.DrawImage(MyBitmap, Rectangle.Create(0, 0, MyBitmap.Width,
7:       MyBitmap.Height));
8:     WriteStats;
9:     Invalidate;
10:  end;
```

▶ Find the code on the CD: \Code\Chapter 07\Ex03.

This procedure receives a parameter containing the path to the image it is to load. The image is loaded using the Bitmap.Create() constructor, which accepts a filename as a parameter.

MyBitmap and MyGraphics are private Bitmap and Graphics fields that are used in the various routines in this sample app.

Finally, MyGraphics draws the image to the screen as seen in Figure 7.21. The WriteStats() method is simply a method that writes out information about the image, as shown in the ListBox in Figure 7.21.

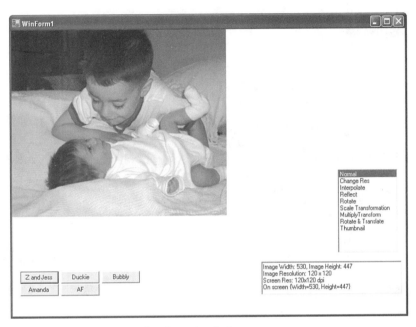

FIGURE 7.21   Image seen after it has been loaded.

Changing an Image's Resolution

You can change the resolution of an image by calling the SetResolution() method. Listing 7.17 illustrates using this method.

LISTING 7.17   Using the SetResolution() Method

```
1:   procedure TWinForm1.ChangeResolution(g: Graphics);
2:   var
3:    tmpBm1: Bitmap;
4:    tmpBm2: Bitmap;
5:   begin
6:    tmpBm1 := Bitmap.Create(MyBitmap);
7:    tmpBm2 := Bitmap.Create(MyBitmap);
8:
9:    tmpBm1.SetResolution(600, 600);
10:   tmpBm2.SetResolution(120, 120);
11:
12:   g.DrawImage(tmpBm1, 0, 0);
13:   g.DrawImage(tmpBm2, 100, 0);
14:   WriteStats;
15:  end;
```

▶ Find the code on the CD: \Code\Chapter 07\Ex03.

The output from the code used in Listing 7.17 is shown in Figure 7.22.

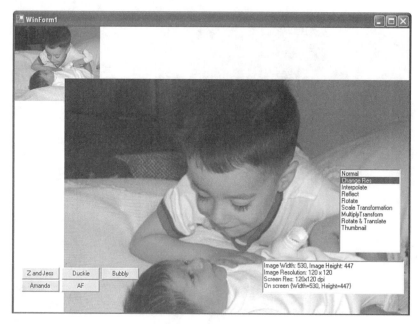

FIGURE 7.22   Output of calling the SetResolution() method.

When changing the resolution, you'll notice that the image is scaled to a different size when it is drawn. Figure 7.22 depicts this. When the resolution is increased, the image is drawn smaller on the screen. When the resolution in decreased, the image is drawn larger. This is because GDI+ uses the resolution of the image to factor how it will be scaled when drawn. So, for instance, an image that is 600 pixels wide with a resolution of 120 dpi will be drawn so that it is approximately 5 inches wide. That is,

5 in = 600/120

The same is true for the image's height. If you want an image to be rendered to a specific height/width regardless of its resolution, you must call the appropriate DrawImage() method that takes the boundaries you desire.

Drawing an Image

You've already seen how to render an image to a surface. Just to reiterate, you use the DrawImage() method of the Graphics class as shown here:

```
g.DrawImage(MyBitmap, 0, 0);
```

This method renders an image at coordinates [0,0] on the drawing surface. The image is drawn in using its default resolution. Again, GDI+ will determine how the image scales. DrawImage() is heavily overloaded. One of several versions of DrawImage(), which allows you to specify the physical size that it gets drawn, takes both the image and a Rectangle class representing the boundaries in which the image is drawn. This version can be called as

```
g.DrawImage(MyBitmap, Rectangle.Create(0, 0, 100, 100));
```

The DrawImage() method is documented well in the online help shipping with Delphi and at www.msdn.microsoft.com.

Interpolation

Interpolation is the process by which GDI+ determines fill pixel colors to use when an image is enlarged. Consider that an image is a two-dimensional representation of pixels. Each pixel holds a specific color. When an image is drawn on the same device, but larger, it will require more pixels. How GDI+ determines the fill color that the pixels use varies in complexity—the output of which affects image quality. A complex algorithm will interpolate the pixels more precisely, resulting in a higher quality image. A less complex algorithm will result in a lower quality image. Why not just use the best algorithm? The more complex algorithms take longer to process. If you're creating images on-the-fly for display on a Web site, you might not want to consume all the processor time creating high quality images. The property of the Graphics class that determines which algorithm is used is InterpolationMode. The values that can be used from highest quality to lowest are HighQualityBicubic, Bicubic, HighQualityBilinear, Bilinear, and NearestNeighbor. Listing 7.18 demonstrates using the lowest and highest. Figure 7.23 shows its output.

LISTING 7.18   Setting the Interpolation Mode

```
1:   procedure TWinForm1.Interpolate(g: Graphics);
2:   var
3:     tmpBm: Bitmap;
4:   begin
5:     tmpBm := Bitmap.Create(MyBitmap);
6:     tmpBm.SetResolution(45, 45);
7:     g.InterpolationMode := InterpolationMode.NearestNeighbor;
8:     g.DrawImage(tmpBM, 0, 0);
9:     g.InterpolationMode := InterpolationMode.HighQualityBicubic;
10:    g.DrawImage(tmpBm, 200, 0);
11:  end;
```

▶ Find the code on the CD: \Code\Chapter 07\Ex03.

Line 6 decreases the resolution resulting in the image being drawn so that it is larger. Lines 7 and 9 set different InterpolationMode values. In Figure 7.23, the differing quality of the two images can easily be made out.

Drawing a Mirror Effect

Ever had your photos developed and found that they were in the wrong direction, rotated that is? Fortunately, with digital images, you can rotate them yourself by using the Bitmap.RotateFlip() method as shown here:

```
tmpbm.RotateFlip(RotateFlipType.RotateNoneFlipX);
g.DrawImage(tmpBm, 290, 0);
```

▶ Find the code on the CD: \Code\Chapter 07\Ex03.

The RotateFlip() method performs various rotation/flipping operations on images based on one of the RotateFlipType enumeration values given it. The possible values are as shown in Table 7.2.

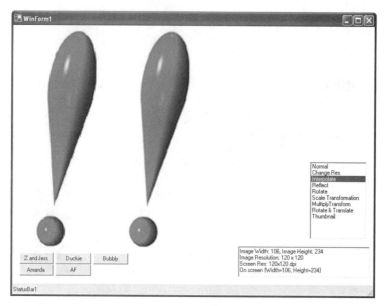

FIGURE 7.23   Images drawn using two different interpolation modes.

TABLE 7.2   RotateFlipType Enumeration Values

Value	Description
Rotate180FlipNone	Rotate 180 degrees, no flipping.
Rotate180FlipX	Rotate 180 degrees, flip horizontally.
Rotate180FlipXY	Rotate 180 degrees, flip horizontally and vertically.
Rotate180FlipY	Rotate 180 degrees, flip vertically.
Rotate270FlipNone	Rotate 270 degrees, no flipping.
Rotate270FlipX	Rotate 270 degrees, flip horizontally.
Rotate270FlipXY	Rotate 270 degrees, flip horizontally and vertically.
Rotate270FlipY	Rotate 270 degrees, flip vertically.
Rotate90FlipNone	Rotate 90 degrees, no flipping.
Rotate90FlipX	Rotate 90 degrees, flip horizontally.
Rotate90FlipXY	Rotate 90 degrees, flip horizontally and vertically.
Rotate90FlipY	Rotate 90 degrees, flip vertically.
RotateNoneFlipNone	Do not rotate, do not flip.
RotateNoneFlipX	Do not rotate, flip horizontally.
RotateNoneFlipXY	Do not rotate, flip horizontally and vertically.
RotateNoneFlipY	Do not rotate, flip vertically.

Figure 7.24 shows the resulting output of this operation, which you can see accomplishes a mirror-like effect when flipping.

You can also rotate a bitmap using the RotateTransform() method, which takes the degrees of the desired rotation as a parameter. Code to perform this operation is shown here:

```
g.RotateTransform(20);
g.DrawImage(MyBitmap, 250, -50);
```

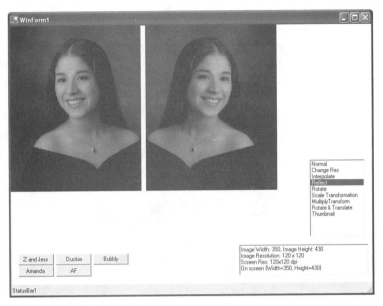

FIGURE 7.24   Flipping a bitmap.

The output of this code is shown in Figure 7.25.

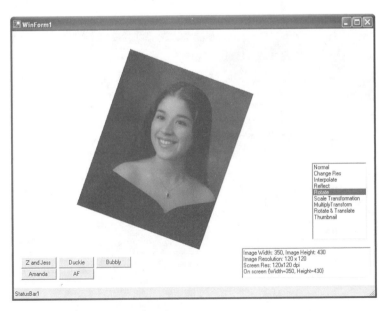

FIGURE 7.25   Rotating a bitmap by 20 degrees.

Using Transformation Methods

In GDI+, several methods exist that you can use to apply transformations to images. The transformations that you can use fall into the classifications of rotation, scaling, shearing, and translation. Rotation transformations involve rotating the images about a certain point. To accomplish rotation transformations, use the `Graphics.RotateTransform()` method. Scaling transformations involve resizing the image and require using the `Graphics.ScaleTransform()` method. Translation transformations involve shifting the image to another point. Use the `Graphics.TranslateTransform()` method to accomplish translation transformation.

The aforementioned methods are provided by GDI+ to make the more common transformation methods easily accessible. Transformation algorithms involve the use of matrix multiplication to achieve the results desired. You can still do this using the `MultiplyTransform()` method that makes shearing transformations possible. This method receives a `Matrix` class, which encapsulates the 3x3 matrix on which the necessary mathematics is applied to achieve the transformation. I won't present a lesson on matrix multiplication here, but I will demonstrate the use of `MultiplyTransform()` to skew an image, giving it a motion-like affect.

Let's look at a scale transformation first. This one is simple. The following code illustrates this:

```
g.ScaleTransform(1.5, 0.3);
g.DrawImage(MyBitmap, 0, 1000);
```

Here, we're setting a scale factor of 1.5 times the images width and 0.3 times the images height. The resulting output is shown in Figure 7.26.

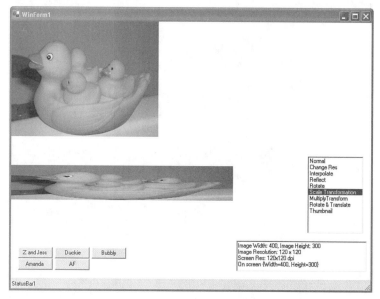

FIGURE 7.26   Result of ScaleTransformation().

I'll demonstrate the use of the `TranslateTransform()` and `RotateTransform()` methods simultaneously. Listing 7.19 contains code that makes use of both these methods.

LISTING 7.19   Translate and Rotate Transformation Demo

```
1:  procedure TWinForm1.RotateTransform(g: Graphics);
2:  var
3:    angle: Double;
4:  begin
5:    angle := 0.0;
6:    while angle < 360.0 do
7:    begin
8:      g.ResetTransform;
9:      g.TranslateTransform(275, 250);
10:     g.RotateTransform(angle);
11:     g.DrawString('Right round baby right round',
12:       System.Drawing.Font.Create('Times New Roman', 14),
13:       Brushes.Black, 25, 0);
14:     angle := angle + 45.0;
15:   end;
16: end;
```

▶ Find the code on the CD: \Code\Chapter 07\Ex03.

This example, although it doesn't work specifically with an image, demonstrates the use of the methods. It draws the same string to the form at an angle, which is incremented by 45% for each drawing. The TranslateTransform() method is used to position the subsequent graphics calls at the x, y coordinate specified (line 9). Then, the RotateTransform() method is called to set the rotation angle (line 10). Finally, the string is drawn. The output of this example is shown in Figure 7.27.

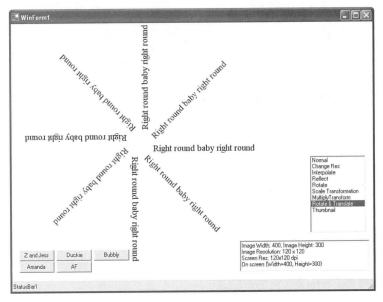

FIGURE 7.27   Translate and rotate transformation output.

The MultiplyTransform() method can be used to skew an image. The values placed in the Matrix object, which gets passed to the MultiplyTranform() method, will determine the resulting shape. Listing 7.20 shows how to use this method.

LISTING 7.20   Using the MultiplyTransform() Method

```
1:   procedure TWinForm1.MultiplyTransform(g: Graphics);
2:   var
3:     mx: Matrix;
4:   begin
5:     DrawNormal(g);
6:     mx := Matrix.Create(1, 0, 0, 1, 0, 0);
7:     mx.Shear(-0.65, 0);
8:     g.MultiplyTransform(mx);
9:     g.DrawImage(MyBitmap, 200, 200);
10:    mx := Matrix.Create(1, 0, 1.5, 1, 0, 1);
11:    g.MultiplyTransform(mx);
12:    g.DrawImage(MyBitmap, 250, 50);
13:  end;
```

▶ Find the code on the CD: \Code\Chapter 07\Ex03.

This example draws the image normally and then creates two versions of the skewed image. The Matrix values used in line 6 result in the image appearing as through it is moving forward. The values entered in line 10 present a breaking appearance. Figure 7.28 shows this.

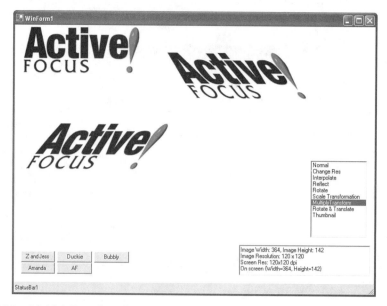

FIGURE 7.28   MultiplyTransform() output.

Creating a Thumbnail

Occasionally, you'll want to generate a thumbnail for an image. Some images have the capability of including their thumbnails. The Bitmap.GetThumbnailImage() method returns the thumbnail contained in an image. If a thumbnail does not exist, it is created and returned. This code is invoked as shown here:

```
procedure TWinForm1.Thumb(g: Graphics);
var
  tn: Image;
  tmpBm: Bitmap;
begin
  tn := MyBitmap.GetThumbnailImage(75, 75, nil, nil);
  tmpBm := Bitmap.Create(tn);
  g.DrawImage(tmpBm, 10, 10);
end;
```

Revisiting Coordinate Systems

Listing 7.19 gives a brief example of dealing with the Graphics.TranslateTransform() method. Internally, the TranslateTransform() method uses a Matrix class to represent the world transformation matrix used in calculating position, angle, and so on of where drawing occurs. A simple example of shifting where point [0, 0] on world coordinates appears on page coordinates is shown in Listing 7.21.

LISTING 7.21   Shifting World Origin Using TranslateTransform()

```
 1:   procedure TWinForm.DrawBasicTransform(g: Graphics);
 2:   var
 3:     MyPen: Pen;
 4:   begin
 5:     MyPen := Pen.Create(Color.Black, 3);
 6:     g.DrawLine(MyPen, 50, 50, 300, 50);
 7:     g.DrawLine(MyPen, 50, 50, 50, 300);
 8:
 9:     g.TranslateTransform(100, 100);
10:     g.DrawLine(MyPen, 50, 50, 300, 50);
11:     g.DrawLine(MyPen, 50, 50, 50, 300);
12:   end;
```

▶ Find the code on the CD: \Code\Chapter 07\Ex04.

Lines 6–7 draw a horizontal and a vertical line. Line 9 uses the TranslateTransform() method to effectively shift where GDI+ sees the world's origin. When the DrawLine() method is called again, with the same parameter values, you'll see in Figure 7.29 that they are drawn at a different location in page coordinates.

You can also change the unit of measure used in world coordinates. For example, let's say that you want to tell GDI+, "Draw me a line starting at one inch from the top of the page and one inch from the left of the page. Oh, and make it two inches long."

Well, you can do that. Consider the code

```
var
  MyPen: Pen;
begin
  MyPen := Pen.Create(Color.Black, (1/g.DpiX)*3);
  g.PageUnit := GraphicsUnit.Inch;
  g.DrawLine(myPen, 1, 1, 1, 3);
end;
```

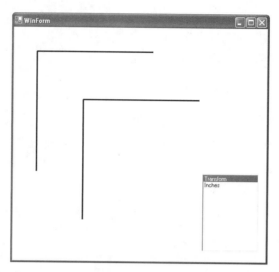

FIGURE 7.29   Result of shifting origin using TranslateTransform().

The Graphics.PageUnit property holds a GraphicsUnit enumeration value. This value determines how the page coordinates are interpreted by GDI+. Therefore, with GraphicsUnit.Inch, point [x=1, y=2] is interpreted as one inch from the left and two inches from the top of the page's origin. With GraphicsUnit.Pixel, the same values are interpreted as 1 pixel from the left and 2 pixels from the top. Both, of course, would result in two completely different results. In fact, you won't likely see the 2 pixel long line drawn with the Pixel option. Figure 7.30 shows the output from the preceding code. It should be a line about one inch from the left and top of the page, extending downward for about two inches.

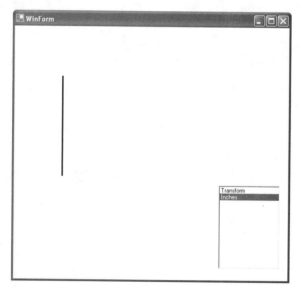

FIGURE 7.30   Using PageUnit to change the unit of measure to inches.

Animation Example

The animation demo for this section is one in which a background, a clear night's sky, is invaded by a flying saucer that bounces about, probably looking for someone to abduct. The program is actually quite simple—in fact, much simpler than the Win32 version, which involved using a series of BitBlt() and masking operations to achieve transparency.

> **NOTE**
>
> The Win32 Version of the application is still around and compiled under VCL.NET. You'll find it under the CD directory:
>
> \Code\Chapter 07\AnimateVCL

First, let's look at the class that contains the sprite, the flying saucer. This is shown in Listing 7.22.

LISTING 7.22   Declaration of the Sprite

```
1:   type
2:
3:      TSpriteDirection  = (sdLeft, sdRight, sdUp, sdDown);
4:      TSpriteDirections = set of TSpriteDirection;
5:
6:      TSprite = class
7:      private
8:      public
9:        Width: integer;
10:       Height: integer;
11:       Left: integer;
12:       Top: integer;
13:       Saucer: Bitmap;
14:       Direction: TSpriteDirections;
15:      public
16:        constructor Create;
17:      end;
18:   ...
19:
20:   constructor TSprite.Create;
21:   begin
22:     inherited;
23:     Saucer  := Bitmap.Create('saucer2.bmp');
24:     Saucer.SetResolution(72, 72);
25:     Left := 0;
26:     Top := 0;
27:
28:     Height := Saucer.Height;
29:     Width  := Saucer.Width;
30:     Direction := [sdRight, sdDown];
31:   end;
```

▶ Find the code on the CD: \Code\Chapter 07\Ex05.

I only included the code relevant to this discussion in this listing and will do the same in the remaining listings. The TSprite class encapsulates the properties that I need for the saucer. Specifically, I need its position, size, and also the direction of movement. The direction is maintained by a set of TSpriteDirection enumerations. The sprite is simply a bitmap that is stored on disk. It is loaded, and I've set a resolution of 72, which I do on all bitmaps in this demo for consistency (line 24). The sprite's direction is then initialized in line 30. The main form of this application will maintain an instance of this sprite. Listing 7.23 shows the main form's declaration.

LISTING 7.23   Main Form Declaration

```
1:   TWinForm = class(System.Windows.Forms.Form)
2:   strict private
3:     procedure Timer1_Tick(sender: System.Object; e: System.EventArgs);
4:     procedure Step1_Click1(sender: System.Object; e: System.EventArgs);
5:     procedure Step2_Click(sender: System.Object; e: System.EventArgs);
6:     procedure ClearSky_Click(sender: System.Object; e: System.EventArgs);
7:     procedure Animate_Click(sender: System.Object; e: System.EventArgs);
8:   strict protected
9:     procedure MoveSaucer;
10:    procedure ClearSky;
11:    procedure Step1_Erase(aDemo: Boolean);
12:    procedure Step2_DrawSaucerTrans(aDemo: Boolean);
13:    procedure Step3_DrawSaucerPos(aDemo: Boolean);
14:  private
15:    // Drawing is done to FSkyImage
16:    FSkyImage: Bitmap;
17:    // FClearSkyImage retains the clean sky
18:    FClearSkyImage: Bitmap;
19:    // FSkyGraphic is refers to FSkyImages
20:    FSkyGraphic: Graphics;
21:    // CanvasGraphic refers to the form
22:    CanvasGraphic: Graphics;
23:
24:    FSaucer: TSprite;
25:    FAnimate: Boolean;
26:    FStep: Integer;
27:  public
28:    constructor Create;
29:  end;
```

▶ Find the code on the CD: \Code\Chapter 07\Ex05.

Lines 3–7 are event handlers for the various buttons on the form. Lines 9–13 are the various procedures that are called by the Timer1_Tick() event handler to perform the animation. FSkyImage is a Bitmap on which all drawing will be performed. This Bitmap is drawn to in memory, which allows us to manipulate the Bitmap without causing refreshing of the display. This in-memory Bitmap manipulation is what allows us to perform these drawing operations efficiently. Drawing directly to the form would result in slower movement and flicker. FClearSkyImage is a clean copy of the sky bitmap. It is used to erase the dirty sky, FSkyImage. FSkyGraphics is the Graphics object that will be used to perform the drawing operations upon FSkyImage. CanvasGraphics is the Graphics object referring to the form. FSaucer is an instance of the TSprite class containing the saucer bitmap. FAnimate is used to determine whether to perform the animation, and FStep holds the number of pixels to move the saucer per movement operation. Listing 7.24 shows the implementation of the main form.

LISTING 7.24   Animation Demo Implementation

```
1:  implementation
2:
3:  procedure TWinForm.Step1_Click1(sender: System.Object;
4:    e: System.EventArgs);
5:  begin
6:    Step1_Erase(True);
7:  end;
8:
9:  procedure TWinForm.Step2_Click(sender: System.Object;
10:   e: System.EventArgs);
11: begin
12:   MoveSaucer;
13:   Step2_DrawSaucerTrans(True);
14: end;
15:
16: procedure TWinForm.ClearSky_Click(sender: System.Object;
17:   e: System.EventArgs);
18: begin
19:   ClearSky;
20: end;
21:
22: procedure TWinForm.Animate_Click(sender: System.Object;
23:   e: System.EventArgs);
24: begin
25:   FAnimate := not FAnimate;
26:   if FAnimate then
27:     Button4.Text := 'Stop'
28:   else
29:     Button4.Text := 'Animate';
30: end;
31:
32: procedure TWinForm.Timer1_Tick(sender: System.Object;
33:   e: System.EventArgs);
34: begin
35:   if FAnimate then
36:   begin
37:     Step1_Erase(false);
38:     MoveSaucer;
39:     Step2_DrawSaucerTrans(false);
40:     Step3_DrawSaucerPos(false);
41:   end;
42: end;
43:
44: constructor TWinForm.Create;
45: begin
46:   inherited Create;
47:   InitializeComponent;
48:
```

LISTING 7.24   Continued

```
49:     FAnimate := False;
50:
51:     FSkyImage := Bitmap.Create('sky2.bmp');
52:     FSkyImage.SetResolution(72, 72);
53:     FSkyGraphic := Graphics.FromImage(FSkyImage);
54:
55:     FStep := 2;
56:     FClearSkyImage := FSkyImage.Clone(Rectangle.Create(0, 0,
57:       FSkyImage.Width,  FSkyImage.Height), PixelFormat.Format32bppArgb);
58:     FClearSkyImage.SetResolution(72, 72);
59:
60:     FSaucer := TSprite.Create;
61:     CanvasGraphic := Graphics.FromHwnd(Handle);
62:   end;
63:
64:   procedure TWinForm.MoveSaucer;
65:   begin
66:     // Save the old values
67:     if (sdLeft in FSaucer.Direction) then
68:       if FSaucer.Left > 0 then
69:         FSaucer.Left := FSaucer.Left - FStep
70:       else
71:         FSaucer.Direction := FSaucer.Direction - [sdLeft] + [sdRight];
72:
73:     if (sdDown in FSaucer.Direction) then
74:       if FSaucer.Top+FSaucer.Height < FSkyImage.Height then
75:         FSaucer.Top := FSaucer.Top + FStep
76:       else
77:         FSaucer.Direction := FSaucer.Direction - [sdDown] + [sdUp];
78:
79:     if (sdUp in FSaucer.Direction) then
80:       if FSaucer.Top > 0 then
81:         FSaucer.Top := FSaucer.Top - FStep
82:       else
83:         FSaucer.Direction := FSaucer.Direction - [sdUp] + [sdDown];
84:
85:     if (sdRight in FSaucer.Direction) then
86:       if FSaucer.Left+FSaucer.Width < FSkyImage.Width then
87:         FSaucer.Left := FSaucer.Left + FStep
88:       else
89:         FSaucer.Direction := FSaucer.Direction - [sdRight] + [sdLeft];
90:   end;
91:
92:   procedure TWinForm.ClearSky;
93:   begin
94:     FSkyGraphic.DrawImage(FClearSkyImage, 0, 0);
95:     CanvasGraphic.DrawImageUnScaled(FSkyImage, 0, 0);
96:   end;
97:
98:   procedure TWinForm.Step1_Erase(aDemo: Boolean);
99:   begin
100:    // Copy portion of the stored sky to the in-mem image
101:    FSkyGraphic.DrawImage(FClearSkyImage,
```

LISTING 7.24 Continued

```
102:      Rectangle.Create(FSaucer.Left-2, FSaucer.Top-2, FSaucer.Width+2,
103:      FSaucer.Height+2), FSaucer.Left-2, FSaucer.Top-2, FSaucer.Width+2,
104:      FSaucer.Height+2, GraphicsUnit.Pixel);
105:
106:    if aDemo then
107:        CanvasGraphic.DrawImageUnscaled(FSkyImage, 0, 0);
108:  end;
109:
110:  procedure TWinForm.Step2_DrawSaucerTrans(aDemo: Boolean);
111:  var
112:    imAttr: ImageAttributes;
113:  begin
114:    ImAttr := ImageAttributes.Create;
115:    ImAttr.SetColorKey(Color.Black, Color.Black, ColorAdjustType.Default);
116:    FSkyGraphic.DrawImage(FSaucer.Saucer, Rectangle.Create(FSaucer.Left,
117:      FSaucer.Top, FSaucer.Width, FSaucer.Height), 0, 0,
118:      FSaucer.Width, FSaucer.Height, GraphicsUnit.Pixel, imAttr);
119:    if aDemo then
120:        CanvasGraphic.DrawImageUnScaled(FSkyImage, 0, 0);
121:  end;
122:
123:  procedure TWinForm.Step3_DrawSaucerPos(aDemo: Boolean);
124:  begin
125:      CanvasGraphic.DrawImageUnscaled(FSkyImage, 0, 0);
126:  end;
127:
128:  end.
```

▶ Find the code on the CD: \Code\Chapter 07\Ex05.

The Step1_Click() and Step2_Click() methods (lines 3–14) are used to step through procedure calls that the Timer1_Timer() event handler does. The Boolean variable that is passed to the procedures Step1_Erase() and Step1_DrawSaucerTrans() methods tell the methods to draw the result of the operation to the form after doing this. This allows me to illustrate the operation step-by-step. When actually animating, drawing to the screen is not done for the reason about performance and flicker mentioned previously. The event handler for the animate button Animate_Click() (lines 22–30) enables the timer to do its thing and invoke the various procedures that perform the animation.

Let's assume that the starting point for the animation is as shown in Figure 7.31.

The first action that occurs while animating is Step1_Erase(). This method (lines 98–108) copies a rectangle from the clean image that occupies the same space as the saucer and copies it over the dirty image (FSkyImage). This accomplishes erasing the saucer from the image. Figure 7.32 shows the results of this step.

Next, Timer1_Timer() calls MoveSaucer(). This method evaluates the saucer's direction and position relative to the drawing surface. It then determines whether the saucer needs to change direction. It is written so that the saucer bounces off the sky boundaries.

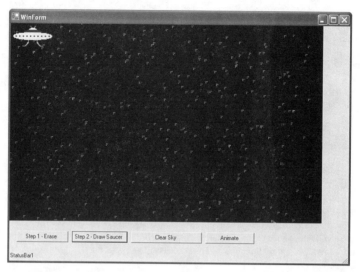

FIGURE 7.31   Starting point for the animation.

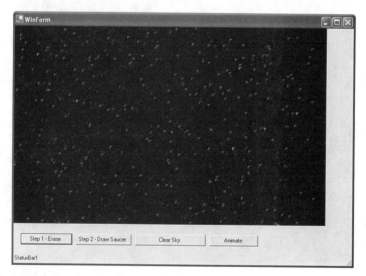

FIGURE 7.32   Saucer has been erased.

Step2_DrawSaucerTrans() calls the Graphics.DrawImage() method, but this time passes an ImageAttribute object as the last parameter to DrawImage(). With this class, defined in the System.Drawing.Imaging namespace, you can specify complex operations on how images are rendered such as color adjustments, grayscaling, gamma adjustments, and so on. In this example, its SetColorKey method is called, which sets the transparency color range. The color surrounding the flying saucer in the actual bitmap is black. Therefore, setting this as the color key range accomplishes making anything that is black transparent. The saucer with these attributes is then drawn to the now clean sky. Because the MoveSaucer() method had been called, the saucer is relocated.

By just pressing the Draw Saucer button, both the MoveSaucer() and DrawSaucerTrans() methods are called. In other words, the erasing operation is skipped. Figure 7.33 shows what this would look like. Although not the desired results, it does depict the saucer's movement.

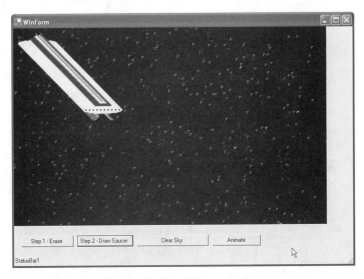

FIGURE 7.33   Saucer moving when not erased.

Finally, Step3_DrawSaucerPos() is called which draws the background bitmap, FSkyImage, to the forms surface overwriting the original. For each saucer movement, one write is written to the form's surface.

For the purposes of illustration, this example uses a poor man's animation approach by using a timer. Realistically, you'd use a threading model of sorts.

IN THIS CHAPTER

- Mono Features
- History of Mono
- Why Mono?
- Mono's Roadmap
- Installation/Setup
- Creating Your First Mono Program
- Running Delphi Generated Assemblies under Mono (on Linux)
- Cross Platform ASP.NET
- ADO.NET with Mono
- Mono and Apache
- Mono and System.Windows.Forms
- Get Involved with Mono

CHAPTER **8**

Mono—A Cross Platform .NET Project

by Steven Beebe

Mono is an open source implementation of the .NET Framework. The Mono Project provides a mechanism to realize the high productivity of .NET development in a multiplatform environment. With goals similar to Java, Mono ups the ante in the "write once, run anywhere" game. This chapter introduces you to Mono and its features, history, and goals. It shows you how to get Mono set up so that you can test it. This chapter also illustrates how you can use Delphi for .NET to target multiplatforms over Mono. Finally, you'll see how to learn more about and get involved with Mono.

Mono Features

The Mono implementation includes

- A Common Language Infrastructure (CLI) runtime that provides JIT compilation, class loading, and garbage collection

- A class library that works with any language that targets the CLR

- A compiler for the C# language

- An implementation of the .NET class libraries

- An implementation of the .NET Remoting infrastructure

- A Visual Basic .NET compiler

- A JScript compiler

- Linux/Unix specific features: GNOME specific class libraries, Mono.Posix, GTK#

THE MONO PROJECT'S OBJECTIVE

The Mono Project FAQ states the project objective as

The Mono Project is an open development initiative sponsored by Ximian that is working to develop an open source Unix version of the Microsoft .NET development platform. Its objective is to enable Unix developers to build and deploy cross-platform .NET applications. The project will implement various technologies developed by Microsoft that have now been submitted to the ECMA for standardization.

This quote is found at the following URL:

(www.go-mono.com/faq.html#basics)

History of Mono

The Mono Project was initiated by Miguel de Icaza, founder of the open source GNOME Project in 2001. Miguel was employed by Ximian Incorporated, producer of a business-oriented GNOME desktop (Ximian Desktop) and publishers of Evolution, a popular open source email client/PIM. Miguel was arguably the first in the open source community to recognize the potential of the .NET platform to drive development productivity. The GNOME Project had a long history of commitment to language independence. Miguel's initial attraction to .NET was to the elegance of the .NET technical solution for language independence; something the GNOME Project had been focused on from the very early days. After further investigation, he became convinced of the powerful productivity of the platform. In February 2002, Miguel explained his thinking in a popular newsgroup posting entitled "The Long Reply":

> The .NET Framework is really about productivity: Even if Microsoft pushes these technologies for creating Web Services, the major benefit of these is increased programmer productivity.
>
> Excerpt from Miguel de Icaza: "Mono and Gnome. The Long Reply."

NOTE

The preceding posting can be located by performing a Google search on "Miquel de Icaza" + "The Long Reply."

Miguel, and others, saw the .NET Framework as a more productive development solution than the current architecture in GNOME. Mono was the way to bring these benefits to the open source community. As the project has grown, the goals have expanded to recognize the potential for cross platform development and deployment.

Why Mono?

As a Windows developer, why should you be interested in Mono? Primarily because of the flexibility that Mono provides. Whether you are providing solutions for a single company or developing solutions to be used by a number of companies, Mono provides additional options for deploying solutions. Mono runs on a variety of hardware and operating system platforms. Mono platforms include Windows, Linux, Solaris, FreeBSD, HP-UX, and Mac OS X.

Mono separates the development platform decision from the production platform decision. The development platform can be selected and optimized for development productivity. The deployment platform can be selected to optimize operational cost, stability, and security. The optimal answers will vary by organization and perhaps by project. Mono provides additional flexibility that will give better answers to a broader set of organizations than .NET on Windows on its own.

Mono also provides additional database connectivity, expanding on the options provided by ADO.NET. Mono provides cross platform libraries for data access, targeting

- Postgress
- MySQL
- IBM DB2
- Sybase
- Oracle
- Microsoft SQL Server
- Firebird
- OLE DB
- ODBC
- GNOME's GDA

The correct way to view Mono is not as a replacement for .NET, but an extension of .NET that provides additional deployment flexibility. As a provider of internal solutions, you can separate the development platform decision from the operating platform decision. As a provider of solutions to the marketplace, Mono allows you to target an expanded customer base by allowing your solutions to run on a variety of platforms.

Mono's Roadmap

At the time of this writing, Mono's publicized roadmap covers releases through 2005. Generally, Mono releases are planned to track evolving functionality in .NET. Mono release packages will include a stable build that has features suitable for production and an unstable build, including a snapshot of features still under development.

While these plans are forward looking and subject to revision as progress is made, Mono offers real capabilities today (several months before the planned delivery of Mono 1.0). The Mono C# compiler is very complete and is currently used to build Mono. The Mono ASP.Net implementation is already functional enough to run the IBuySpy .NET demo without modification.

Mono 1.0 Goals

Mono 1.0 will deliver broad components of functionality from the .NET Framwork 1.1 API and provide a separate package to provide .NET 1.0 API compatibility. Mono 1.0 will not deliver a complete .NET 1.1 API implementation, but will implement enough of the framework to be able to deploy applications on top of Mono.

The 1.0 release of Mono is targeted for the second quarter of 2004, and at the time of this writing is planned to include

- C# compiler

- Virtual machine, with JIT and pre-compiler

- IL assembler, disassembler

- Core libraries: `mscorlib`, `System`, `System.XML`

- `System.Data` and Mono database providers

- `System.Web`: Web applications platform and Apache integration module

- `System.Web.Services`: client and server support

- `System.Drawing`

- `System.DirectoryServices`

- JIT support: x86 and PPC architectures (interpreter available for other architectures)

- Java integration through IKVM, a JVM that runs on top of Mono (`www.ikvm.net`)

- Embedding interface for the runtime

See `www.go-mono.com/mono-1.0.html` for a listing of assemblies, languages, and virtual machines that will be delivered with Mono 1.0.

Mono 1.2 Goals

The 1.2 release of Mono is planned to add features and improvements from the Whidbey release of the .NET Framework by Microsoft. Mono 1.2 is expected to include

- Core API for .NET Framework 1.2.

- ASP.NET 2.0 improvements.

- Remoting improvements from Whidbey.

- XML improvements from Whidbey.

- Compiler support for Visual Basic .NET and JScript.

- System.Windows.Forms with the .NET 1.0 API. Unstable will include the 1.1 and 1.2 APIs.

Mono 1.2 is planned for the end of 2004.

Mono 1.4 Goals

In 2005, the Mono team is planning the 1.4 release—with the focus of moving features from unstable to stable and continuing to track with the development of the .NET 1.2 API.

Installation/Setup

For our purposes, we will only be installing the Mono runtime environment. If you have an interest in understanding Mono in more depth, I encourage you to install the source and build Mono with its own C# compiler, mcs.

The Mono runtime environment is most quickly set up on Linux through an RPM distribution. Packages for various versions of Red Hat, Fedora, Mandrake, and SuSe are available through Novell/Ximian's Red Carpet installation utility. There is also a Windows installer if you'd like to try out Mono on Microsoft Windows. If you want to run Mono with Apache, install Apache before proceeding with the Mono installation. The Apache configuration will be covered later in this chapter. Mono supports Apache 1.3 and Apache 2.0.

The Mono installation process is described next, utilizing Red Carpet.

Mono Installation—Using Red Carpet

Ximian offers both a paid and free version of the Red Carpet service. The paid service offers higher bandwidth connections; however, for installing and maintaining a mono installation, the free service is adequate. Installing Red Carpet is done through the www.ximian.com Web site.

1. Navigate to http://www.ximian.com/products/redcarpet/download.html.

2. Select your distribution.

3. Download the packages shown in Table 8.1 to a suitable location, such as ~/downloads.

TABLE 8.1   Red Carpet Packages

Package	Description
rcd-{version}.{arch}.rpm	the Red Carpet daemon
red-carpet-{version}.{arch}.rpm	the Red Carpet gui (not available for all distributions)
rug-{version}.{arch}.rpm	the Red Carpet command line update program

4. Open a terminal window and navigate to ~/downloads (or the directory you selected for the Red Carpet rpms).

5. su to the root user, providing the root password when prompted.

6. Issue the following command at the command prompt:

   ```
   $ rpm -Uvh red-carpet-{version}.{arch}.rpm rcd-{version}.{arch}.rpm rug-
   {version}.{arch}.rpm
   ```

7. Start the Red Carpet daemon.

   ```
   $ rcd
   ```

8. Test the installation by pinging the Red Carpet daemon with the following command:

   ```
   $ rug ping
   ```

You should see output similar to the following:

```
Daemon identified itself as:
   Red Carpet Daemon 2.0.1
   Copyright (C) 2000-2003 Ximian Inc.
```

9. Launch the Red Carpet GUI. For a Red Hat 9.0 distribution, the rpm installation will generate a menu entry for Red Carpet in System Tools, Red Carpet of the main menu. You will be prompted for the root password.

If you do not find a menu entry, enter the following at the command prompt (as root):

```
$ red-carpet&
```

If your distribution did not come with a Red Carpet GUI (shown in Figure 8.1), the following steps can be completed using rug from the command line. The following provides a list of commands that can be used to complete the remaining steps:

```
$ rug —help
```

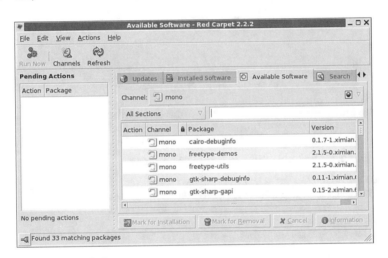

FIGURE 8.1 Red Carpet GUI.

10. Select the Channels icon from the toolbar.

11. Select the Mono Channel.

12. Select the Available Software tab.

13. Select the packages shown in Table 8.2.

TABLE 8.2 Mono Packages

Package	Description
mono	The Mono CIL runtime.
mono-wine	Patched version of Wine that supports System.Windows.Forms.
monodoc	Documentation browser for Mono.

TABLE 8.2   Continued

Package	Description
xsp	Small Web server for hosting the System.Web classes.
*-debuginfo	debug information for each of the aforementioned packages in this table.
mod-mono	Apache module that interfaces with Mono for running ASP.NET pages. This package is required if you intend to use Mono with Apache.

As you select packages, you will see them added to the Pending Actions panel.

14. Select Run Now from the toolbar. A dependency resolution dialog box will be briefly displayed.

15. The results of dependency resolution will be displayed for your review. When satisfied, select Continue.

16. The Processing Transaction dialog box will be displayed as packages are downloaded, verified, and installed. The dialog box will display Transaction Finished when processing is complete. Exit Red Carpet at this time.

17. Verify the installation of mono at the command prompt:

```
$ mono -V
```

You should see output similar to

```
Mono JIT compiler version 0.29, (C) 2002, 2003 Ximian, Inc.
```

18. Verify the Mono C# compiler using the following at the command prompt:

```
$ mcs —about
```

This should generate an output that looks similar to

```
The Mono C# compiler is (C) 2001, 2002, 2003 Ximian, Inc.
The compiler source code is released under the terms of the GNU GPL
For more information on Mono, visit the project Web site
    http://www.go-mono.com
The compiler was written by Miguel de Icaza, Ravi Pratap and Martin Baulig
```

Creating Your First Mono Program

This section shows you how to create a short program in C# that will do a more complete test of the mono environment. Open an editor on the Linux machine: For this example, we will use gedit; however, any editor will do. (If you prefer, type command_line_applications, run vi, or emacs at the command prompt). Enter the following code:

```
using System;
class Hello
{
  public static void Main(String[] args) {
    Console.WriteLine("Mono is working...");
    for (int i = 0; i < args.Length; i++)
      Console.WriteLine("{0}. Hello {1}!", i, args[i]);
```

```
    }
}
```

▶ Find the Code on the CD: \Code\Chapter 08\Ex01.

Save the file as `hello.cs`, and open a terminal window. Navigate to the location of `hello.cs` and execute

```
$ mcs hello.cs
```

If all is well, you will see Compilation Succeeded echoed to the terminal. If you have errors, make changes as necessary based on the compiler messages in the terminal window. A successful compile will generate a .NET assembly that can be run by the .NET runtime environment. Mono uses the same `.exe` extension convention as used on the Windows platform, although file extensions do not carry the same significance in Linux as they do in Windows. To verify that the assembly has been produced, do a directory list (`ls` command) and locate `hello.exe` in the listing. Next, we will run the assembly in the Mono runtime environment. At the command prompt, execute

```
$ mono hello.exe {name1} {name2}
```

Substitute the names of two of your favorite people for *{name1}* and *{name2}*. The output should look similar to the following:

```
Mono is working...
0. Hello Hannah!
1. Hello Sarah!
```

> **NOTE**
>
> You can remove the `.exe` extension from `hello.exe` and still run mono hello *{name1}* *{name2}*. Linux does not use the file extension to determine the file type. The `.exe` extension is used for portability in this case.

Congratulations! You have just written and run a C# program on Linux. For a simple demonstration of the potential of .NET and Mono together, copy `hello.exe` to a Windows machine with the .NET runtime environment installed. Execute `hello.exe` at the Windows command prompt. The results should match the following (with the possible exception of the names):

```
C:\>hello diane hannah sarah
Mono is working...
0. Hello diane!
1. Hello hannah!
2. Hello sarah!
C:\>
```

Running Delphi Generated Assemblies under Mono (on Linux)

Now we will get back to Delphi for .NET. Start a new console application by selecting File, New, Other, Console Application in the Delphi for .NET Projects folder. You will be presented with a blank project.

You will notice that Delphi includes the following uses clause by default:

```
Uses
  Sysutils;
```

Although this is desirable for a Win32 application, this will cause runtime errors on Mono. Many of Borland's VCL classes contain references to Win32 specific classes and native imports and therefore cannot be run on Mono. Remove the reference to SysUtils and avoid the urge to add other VCL units to the example.

The console application consists of the following: text based menu, request for user input, validation of user input, and processing of user input. The core part of the application is shown in Listing 8.1.

LISTING 8.1   MonoMenu .NET Console Application

```
1:    program MonoMenu;
2:
3:    {$APPTYPE CONSOLE}
4:
5:    uses
6:      MonoFuncs in 'MonoFuncs.pas';
7:
8:    var
9:      MainMenu: String;
10:     UserResponse: Integer;
11:     PossibleResponses: array of Char;
12:
13:
14:   begin
15:
16:     // the core of the app
17:     MainMenu :=
18:       'Welcome to Cross Platform Development - Are you:'+#10#13+#10#13+
19:       '1. Curious as to how this is going to work?'+#10#13+
20:       '2. A skeptic?'+#10#13+
21:       '3. Thinking this rocks?'+#10#13+#10#13+
22:       'Enter a number (1-3):';
23:
24:     // identify valid responses
25:     SetLength(PossibleResponses, 3);
26:     PossibleResponses[0] := '1';
27:     PossibleResponses[1] := '2';
28:     PossibleResponses[2] := '3';
29:
30:     // ask for a respone, ensuring we get an answer we want
31:     repeat
32:       UserResponse := GetInput(MainMenu, PossibleResponses);
33:     until UserResponse >= 0;
34:
35:     // acknowledge the answer with some encouragement
36:     Case UserResponse+1 of
37:       1:  WriteLn('Just watch, you will be impressed');
38:       2:  WriteLn('So am I.  But this is cool.');
```

LISTING 8.1 Continued

```
39:    3:  WriteLn('It does.');
40:    end; // case
41: end.
```

▶ Find the code on the CD: \Code\Chapter 08\Ex02.

Lines 17–22 define the string representing the main menu of the application. In lines 25–28, an array is created and loaded with valid responses. In line 32, GetInput is called to handle the processing of user input that is independent of the current specific example. To ensure that a valid response is obtained, GetInput is wrapped in a repeat-until loop.

The GetInput method will be created in a separate unit. Add a new unit to the project and create the GetInput shown in Listing 8.2.

LISTING 8.2 MonoFuncs Unit

```
1:  unit MonoFuncs;
2:
3:  interface
4:
5:  function GetInput(aConsoleMessage: String;
6:    aPossibleResponses: Array of Char):Integer;
7:
8:  implementation
9:
10: function GetInput(aConsoleMessage: String;
11:    aPossibleResponses: Array of Char):Integer;
12: var
13:   Response: String;
14:   i: Integer;
15: begin
16:   // establish a default result
17:   Result := -1;
18:
19:   // request user input
20:   WriteLn('');
21:   WriteLn(aConsoleMessage);
22:   Write('  > ');
23:
24:   // read input
25:   ReadLn(Response);
26:
27:   // determine if input is in expected result set
28:   for i := 0 to High(aPossibleResponses) do
29:     if Response = aPossibleResponses[i] then
30:       Result := i;
31: end;
32:
33: end.
```

▶ Find the code on the CD: \Code\Chapter 08\Ex02.

Using two parameters, GetInput displays a message, reads user input, and returns an integer. In line 17, a default result of -1 is assigned. Lines 20–22 display the contents of the aConsoleMessage parameter. Next, the response is read (line 25) and then evaluated against the values in the aPossibleResponses array parameter. If the response is found in aPossibleResponses, a return Result is assigned (line 30).

Compile the project to produce the MonoMenu.exe file. Open a Windows console session and execute the application. You should see output like that shown in Figure 8.2.

FIGURE 8.2   MonoMenu in action.

Copy the MonoMenu.exe file to the Linux computer running Mono.

> **NOTE**
>
> If you are going to do any serious work between a Windows computer and Linux computer, you will need to have Samba installed to support file sharing. I highly recommend either Webmin or SWAT as GUI configuration tools to simplify setting up Samba. Detailed Samba configuration is beyond the scope of this book. See www.samba.org for complete details on Samba installation and configuration.

Execute the file on Linux with the following command:

```
$ mono MonoMenu.exe
```

If all has gone well, your results should look identical to Figure 8.3—with the exception of the command prompt and possibly your response.

This example illustrates the Mono JIT compiler working with the .NET intermediate language code produced by Delphi for .NET. In other words, you have just run Delphi code on Linux.

Forgetting to remove or avoid VCL classes will result in compiler errors when running on Mono. You will see output similar to the following:

```
[steve@schroeder cs]$ mono MonoMenu.exe

(MonoMenu.exe:311): WARNING **: Failed to load function GetVersionEx
➥from kenel32.dll
(MonoMenu.exe:311): WARNING **: Failed to load function GetVersionEx
```

```
➥from kenel32.dll
Unhandled Exception: System.TypeInitializationException: An exception was
➥throw by the type initializer for MonoMenu.Unit  — ->
➥System.TypeInitializationExcepton: An exception was thrown by
➥the type initializer for Borland.Vcl.SysUtils.Unt  — ->
➥System.MissingMethodException: A missing method exception has occurred.

in <0x00042> (wrapper managed-to-native) Borland.Vcl.Windows.Unit:GetVersionEx Borland.Vcl.Win-
dows._OSVERSIONINFO&)
in <0x0006c> Borland.Vcl.SysUtils.Unit:InitPlatformId ()
in <0x00053> Borland.Vcl.SysUtils.Unit:Borland.Vcl.SysUtils ()
in <0x006b8> Borland.Vcl.SysUtils.Unit:.cctor ()
—· End of inner exception stack trace —·
in (unmanaged) /usr/lib/libmono.so.0(mono_raise_exception+0x20) [0x400acef7]
in (unmanaged) /usr/lib/libmono.so.0(mono_runtime_class_init+0x2c3) [0x400a9860
in (unmanaged) /usr/lib/libmono.so.0 [0x400afde8]
in <0x0001d> System.Runtime.CompilerServices.RuntimeHelpers:
➥RunClassConstructor(System.RuntimeTypeHandle)
in <0x00026> MonoMenu.Unit:.cctor ()
—· End of inner exception stack trace —·
```

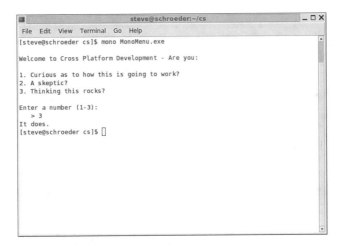

FIGURE 8.3   MonoMenu running on Linux.

Cross Platform ASP.NET

The example application for ASP.NET will be a simple one page application using code-behind and responding to simple user interaction. The application will ask the user to enter a name and select a date. Upon clicking the button on the form, the user's entries will be presented back.

Run Delphi and create a new ASP.NET (File, New, ASP.NET Web Application). The example application is called MonoASP.

> **TIP**
>
> I will be running this example on IIS on Windows; however, either IIS or Cassini will be sufficient to verify the functioning of the example application before deploying to Mono.

Select an appropriate directory for the application. Change the page layout property of the Document to `FlowLayout`. This is done through selecting Document in the object inspector and modifying the `PageLayout` property. `FlowLayout` will allow the browser to determine relative positioning on the page. An alternative approach is used in the Chapter 26 example to maintaining proper relative control positioning across HTML rendering engines. The initial Web form is saved as `MainGreeting.aspx`.

From the Web Controls category of the Tool Palette, place a `Label` and a `TextBox` on the first line. Using `FlowLayout`, you structure a page in much the same way as you would in using a word processor. For example, new page lines are inserted using the Enter or Return key. Insert a new line in `MainGreeting` by selecting the end of the first line (immediately behind the `TextBox`) and press Enter. For the next three lines, place a `Label`, `Calendar`, `Button`, and `Label`. Modify the control properties to resemble the Web form as shown in Figure 8.4.

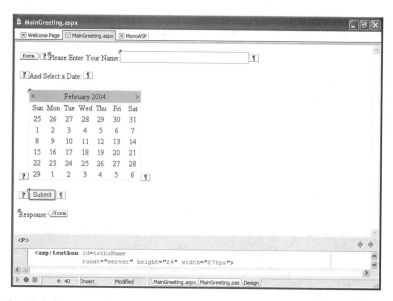

FIGURE 8.4   MainGreeting.aspx form layout.

Add a `Click` event handler for the `Button` and enter the following code:

```
procedure TWebForm1.Button1_Click(sender: System.Object;
  e: System.EventArgs);
begin
  lblResponse.Text := lblResponse.Text + ' Hello, '+txtbxName.Text+'!'+
    ' You have selected ' + Calendar1.SelectedDate.ToString'.';
end;
```

▶ Find the code on the CD: \Code\Chapter 08\Ex03.

Compile and run the application on Windows, correcting any compile errors. Enter a name, select a date, and click Submit. The page should reload with a response reflecting your selections.

Now we will run the application on Mono.

ASP.NET Deployment to Mono

Mono ASP.NET includes both Web Forms and Web services. Mono offers two options for Web servers:

- XSP—A lightweight Web server, primarily intended for testing, written in C#

- Apache—A production grade Web server

XSP is similar to Cassini in that it provides hosting for the System.Web namespace, but does not provide a feature set sufficient for serving a production Web site.

XSP Configuration

Using XSP will keep installation and configuration issues to a minimum. XSP is run by the following command:

```
$ mono {path to xsp}/xsp.exe
```

XSP Runtime Parameters

You should be familiar with certain runtime parameters that you might need to configure. They are discussed in the following sections.

Web Root

The Web root for XSP will be the directory from which xsp is run. To specify a Web root, add the --root {path} parameter when executing XSP. In the following example, the xsp.exe file is located in the /usr/bin directory, and the Web root is in /usr/share/doc/xsp/test/mono:

```
$ mono /usr/bin/xsp.exe --root /usr/share/doc/xsp/test/mono
```

The default installation by Red Carpet will place xsp.exe in both /usr/bin and /usr/share/doc/xsp/test. Sample applications are included in the test directory.

Application Root

XSP handles both a virtual and physical application root. By default, the virtual '/' directory is mapped to the physical directory from which xsp was run. XSP will expect .aspx files to be in the current directory and the .dll files to be the bin subdirectory. To specify a different application root, use the --applications parameter when running xsp as shown in the following command:

```
$ mono /usr/bin/xsp.exe —applications {virtual path}:{physical path}
```

Specifying multiple application root directories is accomplished by passing a semicolon delimited list of virtual/physical path pairs as the --applications parameter. To simplify transferring files to and from Windows and Linux, create a directory in your home directory on Linux, such as `monoapps`. `monoapps` will be exposed to Windows through a standard Samba `homes` share, allowing files to be copied using Windows file explorer. The following example will run `xsp` with two application root directories: the `xsp` installation directory and the `monoapps` subdirectory of my `home` directory:

```
$ mono /usr/bin/xsp.exe —application /:/usr/share/doc/xsp/test;/
➥monoapps:/home/steve/monoapps
```

Port and Address

XSP will listen on port 8080 by default.

XSP will listen on address 0.0.0.0 by default. If the XSP deployment test machine is exposed to the Internet, you will want to change the defaults for port and IP address.

The root and application directories specified will need to have `+rx` permissions for the user running XSP.

Create an appropriate directory for the `MonoASP` file on the machine running mono with a `bin` subdirectory. (I am using `monoapps` and `monoapps/bin`.) Copy the `MainGreeting.aspx` and `MonoApp.dll` created by Delphi for .NET to the machine running mono. In a console window, run XSP, including `monoapps` as an application root. You should see output similar to the following:

```
Listening on port: 8080
Listening on address: 0.0.0.0
Root directory: /usr/share/doc/xsp/test
Hit Return to stop the server.
```

Launch a browser on the Linux machine and type in **localhost:8080/MainGreeting.aspx** in the location bar. You should be presented with a page that looks remarkably similar to what you saw on Windows. Type in a name, select a date, and verify that the code-behind functions properly. Launch a browser on the Windows computer and enter **http://{ip address}:8080/MainGreeting.aspx** in the location bar. The page should appear exactly the same as when run from within Delphi.

Some Caveats and a Minor Extension of the Example

At this point, our example works on both Windows and Linux. An alternative approach would have been to use a `TDateTime` variable and the `DateToStr` function to process the calendar selection. By modifying the `Button_Click` event handler to resemble the following:

```
procedure TWebForm1.Button1_Click(sender: System.Object;
  e: System.EventArgs);
var
  lDate: TDateTime;
begin
  lDate := Calendar1.SelectedDate;
  lblResponse.Text := lblResponse.Text + '  Hello, '+
    txtbxName.Text+'!'+'  You have selected ' + DateToStr(lDate)+'.';
end;
```

You will need to add SysUtils to the uses clause.

When running the application in Windows, you should receive the same results as when using `Calendar1.SelectedDate.ToString`. However, when running under Mono, this code will generate a runtime error. A stack trace will be displayed in the browser, showing a `System.TypeInitializationException` attempting to initialize `Borland.Vcl.SysUtils.Unit`.

The point being made here is that the best path to portability is to target the CLR, using classes within the .NET namespaces, and to avoid including Borland runtime library assemblies.

ADO.NET with Mono

Our next example application demonstrates a Web application accessing information in a database, combining the capabilities of ASP.NET, ADO.NET, and Mono. The example consists of a Login Web form to establish database access and an Employees Web form to display the information from the database. The example requires access to MS SQL Server and the Northwind database.

> **NOTE**
>
> In the example, the user is asked for SQL server login information. This is purely for illustrative purposes. In a production application, you should establish application specific login information that can be validated. Once a user's access is validated, the ASP.NET application can access SQL Server through an Application Role. The Application Role is configured to provide the permissions necessary and also limited to the permissions required for the application.

Create a new ASP.NET application in Delphi. I named the application `MonoADO`. Using `FlowLayout`, place Web controls on the login form as shown in Figure 8.5.

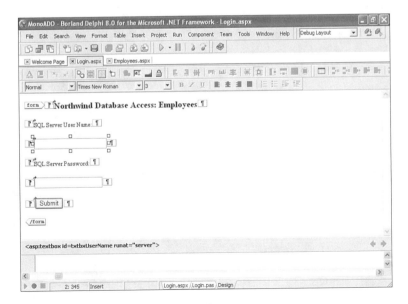

FIGURE 8.5   Northwind database access form layout.

Add a constant declaration and `btnSubmit_Click()` event handler as shown here:

```
const
  c_UrlStr = 'Employees.aspx?UserName={0}&Password={1}';
...
procedure TWebForm1.btnSubmit_Click(sender: System.Object;
  e: System.EventArgs);
begin
  if IsPostBack then
  Response.Redirect(System.String.Format(c_UrlStr, [txtbxUserName.Text,
    txtbxPassword.Text]));
end;
```

▶ Find the code on the CD: `\Code\Chapter 08\Ex04`.

This will call the second page in our application, passing the `UserName` and `Password` provided in the URL. Save the form as **Login.aspx**.

Add a new ASP.NET page to the project. This form will display employee information from the Northwind database. Place a `Label`, `Repeater`, and a `Label` each on a separate line. The top label will serve as a header, and the bottom label will display the time of the report. The `Repeater` will display employee data and is configured similarly to example 10 in Chapter 27. (Find the code on the CD: `\Code\Chapter 27\Ex10`). For this example, the `Title` and `HireDate` columns have been added.

The `Page_Load()` method creates the components needed to establish database connectivity and establishes the binding for the Repeater component. The code appears in Listing 8.3.

LISTING 8.3   Page_Load() Event Handler for Database Example

```
 1:    procedure TWebForm1.Page_Load(sender: System.Object; e: System.EventArgs);
 2:    const
 3:      c_sel  = 'select * from employees';
 4:      c_cnstr = 'server=192.168.0.102;database=Northwind;'+
 5:        'Trusted_Connection=No;User ID={0};Pwd={1}';
 6:    var
 7:      sqlcn: SqlConnection;
 8:      sqlDA: SqlDataAdapter;
 9:      ds: DataSet;
10:      dt: DataTable;
11:      lDateTime: TDateTime;
12:      lConnectionStr: String;
13:    begin
14:      // establish the connection string from page request
15:      lConnectionStr :=   System.String.Format(c_cnstr,
16:        [Request.QueryString['UserName'],
17:        Request.QueryString['Password']]);
18:
19:      sqlcn := SqlConnection.Create(lConnectionStr);
20:      sqlDA := SqlDataAdapter.Create(c_sel, sqlcn);
21:      ds := DataSet.Create;
22:      sqlDA.Fill(ds, 'employees');
23:      try
24:        dt := ds.Tables['employees'];
```

LISTING 8.3   Continued

```
25:      Repeater1.DataSource := dt.DefaultView;
26:      DataBind;
27:      lDateTime := System.DateTime.Now;
28:      lblProducedOn.Text := lblProducedOn.Text+' '+lDateTime.ToString;
29:   finally
30:      sqlcn.Close;
31:  end;
32: end
```

▶ Find the Code on the CD: \Code\Chapter 08\Ex04.

Note the c_cnstr connection string constant (line 4). This example specifies an IP address and includes the SQL Server login information in the connection string, as the application will be run from a different machine from the database. The UserName and Password components of the connection string will be built from information passed to the Employees.aspx page in the URL (line 15); again, this is not to be done in a production environment.

Compile and run the application, providing a valid SQL Server username and password. After submitting, you should see the screen shown in Figure 8.6.

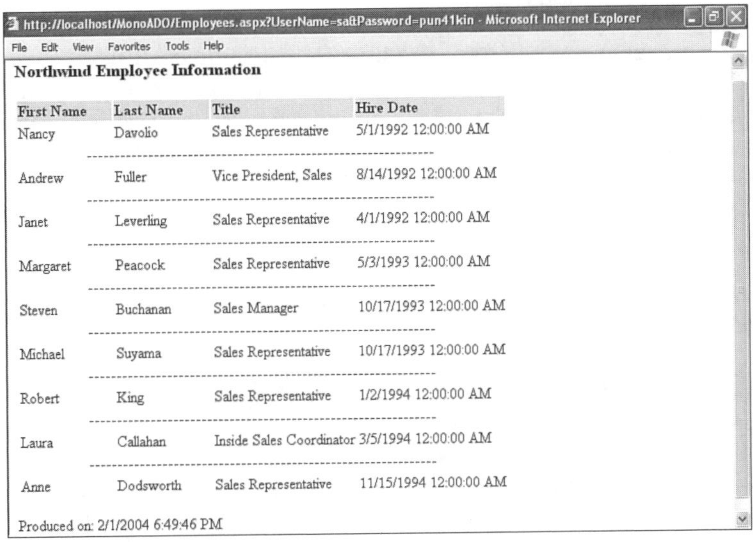

FIGURE 8.6   Results of a successful login.

To run MonoADO under Mono, identify or create an appropriate application root directory. I will be reusing monoapps from the ASP.NET example. Copy the Login.aspx and Employees.aspx files to the XSP application root directory on Linux. Copy MonoADO.dll to the bin directory. Then launch a browser pointed at localhost:8080/Login.aspx. Alternatively, point the browser on your Windows computer at XSP. The view of Microsoft SQL Server data on a Linux browser is shown in Figure 8.7.

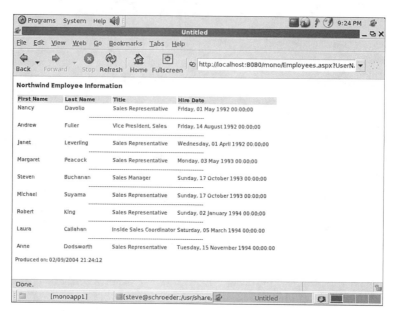

FIGURE 8.7   Northwind Employees table on Linux.

This is truly phenomenal. Although the example we have implemented is somewhat trivial, I challenge you to pick any other toolset and construct a Web application on Windows that can be directly deployed to a Linux Web server and retrieve data from MS SQL Server—and do it in less than 30 minutes.

Mono and Apache

Although XSP is more than adequate for development and testing purposes, it is not intended for production deployment. Mono makes the Apache (www.apache.org) HTTP Server accessible to .NET developers.

WEB SERVER SURVEY

In Netcraft's February 2004 Web Server Survey, of the over 47 million Web servers captured in the survey, 67.21% were running Apache. Development began on the core of what was to become the Apache Web server at the National Center for Supercomputing Applications (NCSA), University of Illinois, Urbana-Champaign, in the early '90s. When the key developer left NCSA, a small group of Webmasters who had patched and extended NCSA's work banded together to form the original Apache core team. From 1995–1996, Apache experienced meteoric growth and, since May 1996, has dominated all other Web servers in Netcraft's survey.

Apache provides a number of benefits: robustness, security, price/performance scalability, and platform flexibility being some of the key ones. This world class deployment platform is now available to Delphi developers creating ASP.NET applications.

Mono provides the mod_mono module and mod-mono-server for use with Apache, hosting both the Mono and ASP.NET runtimes, allowing Apache to serve ASP.NET pages and support code-behind. mod_mono supports both Apache 1.3 and Apache 2.0. Apache binaries are included with all major Linux distributions. Alternatively, the source can be easily down-loaded (you can locate a download mirror from `www.apache.org`) and built.

Apache needs to be configured to use `mod_mono`. Start with adding the following lines to `httpd.conf` (usually found in `/etc/httpd/conf/`):

```
AddType application/x-asp-net .aspx .ashx .asmx .ascx .asax .config
LoadModule mono_module modules/mod_mono.so
MonoUnixSocket /tmp/mod_mono_server
```

The `AddType` directive identifies file extensions to a specified content type—in this case, `x-asp-net`. The `LoadModule` directive causes Apache to load `mod_mono` at startup. Adjust the path in this entry to reflect the path to `mod_mono` of your installation. If unsure, execute locate `mod_mono.so` at a command prompt.

You might also want to change Apache to listen on the same port as XSP 8080 by adding `Listen 8080` in `httpd.conf`. To test Apache and `mod_mono` with the Mono examples, add

```
Alias /mono "/usr/share/doc/xsp/test"
```

to `httpd.conf`. This will redirect any requests to *{your test machine ip}*/mono to the directory containing Mono examples. Again, adjust the path to `xsp/test` if needed for your distribution.

To test the server configuration, begin by running `mod-mono-server.exe`. (Red Carpet will place this in `/usr/bin`, as well as `/usr/share/doc/xsp/test`.)

```
cd /usr/share/doc/xsp/test
mono /usr/bin/mod-mono-server.exe –root . –applications /mono:.
```

These commands will run the server with the `web` root in `/usr/share/doc/test/xsp` and direct requests to `/mono` to the same directory. The parameters for `mod-mono-server` are the same as for XSP. Running `mod-mono-server.exe` will create the Unix socket file `/tmp/mod_mono_server`. Both Apache and `mod-mono-server` must have write permissions to this file. There are two ways to accomplish this:

- For testing purposes, this can be done by running `mod-mono-server` and issuing `chmod 666 /tmp/mod_mono_server` at the command prompt before running or restarting Apache.

- In a production setting, it will be preferable to run both

    ```
    mod-mono-server and apache under the same user.
    ```

For the purposes of this test, `chmod` the permissions on `/tmp/mod_mono_server`. Start or restart Apache with a command such as

```
/usr/sbin/apachectl –k (re)start
```

or

```
/etc/init.d/httpd (re)start
```

Watch for error messages; if all is well, launch a browser and point it to `http://127.0.0.1:8080/mono/index.aspx`. Omit the `:8080` if you did not include `Listen 8080` in `httpd.conf`. You should see the initial page of the Mono examples. For more information on `mod_mono` and Apache, see `www.go-mono/asp-net.html`.

You can now test the examples from this chapter by copying the `.aspx` files to `/usr/share/doc/xsp/test` and the `.dll` files to `/usr/share/doc/xsp/test/bin`.

Mono and System.Windows.Forms

Mono is also implementing the `System.Windows.Forms` (SWF) component of .NET, although development in this area is proceeding significantly slower than other parts of the framework. This is in part because of technical issues with the implementation of SWF. However, real promise and therefore the focus for cross platform development lie with ASP.NET and ADO.NET. Browser-based applications provide a natural platform independence on the client side, avoiding a number of complex technical issues of a native GUI application. Nonetheless, work is continuing on SWF for Mono.

At the time of this writing, Mono's implementation of `System.Windows.Forms` is undergoing structural changes (mono-0.30) and is not functional. `System.Windows.Forms` is currently taking two tracks:

1. SWF implementation on top of Wine, an open source implementation of the Windows API for X

2. SWF implementation using GTK#, which provides C# bindings for GTK+

Fundamentally, I don't see this as a strong path for Windows developers looking to develop for multiple platforms. But the excellent work that has been on Mono warrants keeping an eye on this part of the project

---

GET INVOLVED WITH MONO

The open source community is built on the precept that a small contribution from each member yields ever increasing returns—the snowball effect, if you will. The best way to get involved generally involves a progression. Start by using Mono. Ask questions through online forums and mailing lists. Learn about the capabilities and how to deploy them. Report bugs and needed features. Begin to provide answers to others just getting started.

If you never progress beyond the point of contributing back what you have learned, the community will continue to thrive. However, let me warn you. Although it is tremendously exciting to experience the power of new development technologies such as .NET, it is somewhat intoxicating to contribute to its development. When you find that bug, fix it. Or when you find that badly needed feature, contribute it.

Whether you choose to get involved or not, know that the Mono project provides a powerful framework for leveraging your Delphi for .NET development skills into a multiplatform world.

LEARN MORE ABOUT MONO

The majority of resources for learning about Mono can be found through the `www.got-mono.com` Web site. For tracking development progress and assistance with deployment issues, Mono maintains a number of mailing lists. They all offer the option to receive a daily summary, minimizing nuisance traffic.

CHAPTER 9

Memory Management and Garbage Collection

IN THIS CHAPTER

- How Garbage Collection Works
- Constructors
- Finalization
- The Dispose Pattern— IDisposable
- Performance Issues Regarding Finalization

One of the primary causes of buggy programs is the improper management of memory by developers. Possibly the most common errors are that of not freeing up memory no longer needed or referring to memory that has already been released. The .NET Framework provides the Garbage Collector (GC), which is responsible for the management of memory—thus freeing the developer of this task. This chapter discusses some of the mechanics of how the GC works and then covers some practical usage of memory management in your code. For Delphi developers in particular, the GC imposes some different ways of thinking for resource management and cleanup.

How Garbage Collection Works

Two types of resources must be managed with which you should be familiar. These are managed resources and unmanaged resources. Managed resources are those about which the CLR knows how to manage because they are defined within the type specifications of the CLR. Unmanaged resources are those that the CLR will not know how to manage. Examples of such resources are those that require a Handle, such as a file or Windows resource (bitmap, icon, mutex, and so on).

The GC follows a simple mechanism for freeing heap memory of objects that are no longer being used within the application. Consider Figure 9.1.

This figure represents the heap containing some objects allocated from an application. When the GC kicks in, it refers to some internal tables created by the JIT compiler that store references to objects called roots. You can think of roots as storage locations such as global and static objects, objects on the thread stack, objects referred to by the FReachable queue, objects referred to by CPU registers, and so on. In other words, roots are objects that are still referred to by the application in which the GC cannot release. The GC then builds its own structure, matching roots to the objects in the heap. When finished, the unreachable memory on the heap is released and the reachable objects are compacted on the heap, as shown in Figure 9.2. The GC must also adjust the root references because the objects to which they refer have been relocated.

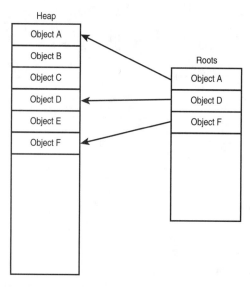

FIGURE 9.1   Objects in the heap.

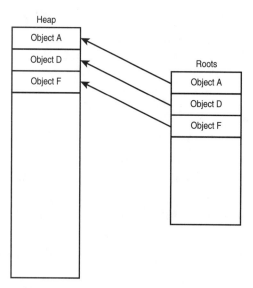

FIGURE 9.2   Compacted heap.

This is a simplified explanation of how the GC works. There is obviously much more to this; much of which is beyond what can be covered here. For instance, nested references must also be treated as live references—that is, objects that are referred to by other objects. This is not depicted in Figures 9.1 or 9.2, but you can imagine that when a relationship such as Object D references Object F, Object F must be treated as live by the GC in the same way as Object D is treated in the collection/compacting process.

One aspect of how the GC manages memory is that it relies on a generational algorithm.

Generational Garbage Collection

If the GC were to use the simplified description just presented, its performance would be unacceptable given the number of objects and memory shifting that would go on in a single pass-through. For this reason, the GC is based on a generational paradigm that improves performance since the GC, the majority of the time, will only be performing its magic on a small portion of the heap during a given run.

In the generational scheme, the heap is arranged as shown in Figure 9.3.

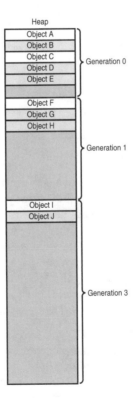

FIGURE 9.3   Generational heap.

Figure 9.3 roughly represents how the heap is. This representation is not exact, but it serves this illustrative purpose.

For instance, suppose that in our application we have a number of objects that we just created. They might appear as shown in Figure 9.4.

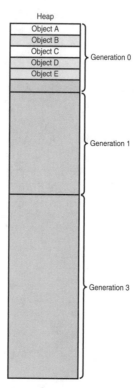

FIGURE 9.4   Generational heap—prior to collection.

These objects would be the first generation of objects in the heap. They are generation 0 because they have never survived a GC cycle. In Figure 9.4, the shaded objects are those that are no longer being referred to by the application. In other words, they are no longer used. Each generation has a maximum threshold with generation 0 having the smallest and generation 2 having the largest. When this threshold is exceeded, the GC kicks in. The GC will find unreferenced objects and free up the heap space they occupy. Now the GC compacts the heap so that it appears as in Figure 9.5. Figure 9.5 also shows some additional objects that have been allocated since the initial GC pass. The objects that survived the GC cycle are now considered generation 1 objects. The newly allocated objects are generation 0.

Once again, when generation 0 is full, the GC will kick in and perform its cleanup of generation 0, making objects that survive the pass generation 1 objects. This process continues until a point at which the maximum threshold of generation 1 has been exceeded and cannot hold any more objects. The GC must now perform the same type of steps against the objects in generation 1, finding those no longer being used and freeing up the memory. Those that survive this pass become generation 2 objects.

You should be able to see that the majority of the time, the GC will only work on generation 0. By ignoring objects in generation 1 and 2, the GC's performance is increased. Although it is not necessary for you to understand how the Garbage Collector works to develop .NET applications, it is helpful because there are implications in how you write your code that will be addressed momentarily.

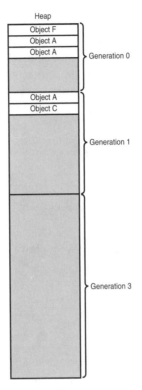

FIGURE 9.5   Generational heap after first GC pass.

Invoking the Garbage Collector

It is not likely that you will ever need to programmatically invoke the GC. The System.GC class defines various methods that you can use to start or determine information about the GC.

The two methods you can call to force collection by the GC are as follows:

```
Collect(Generation: integer);
Collect();
```

The former takes the generation you wish to collect as an integer parameter. This forces an inclusive collection, so by passing 2, generations 0–2 will be collected. The latter method performs a collection on generations 0–System.GC.MaxGeneration. System.GC.MaxGeneration holds the total number of generations supported by the GC. Currently, it returns the value 2. It is possible that GC might support more generations at some point.

There are a few additional informational methods from System.GC:

GetGeneration() takes a System.Object parameter and returns the generation of the object.

GetTotalMemory() returns the number of bytes thought to be allocated.

Constructors

One simple rule about constructors in Delphi for .NET is different from Delphi Win32. You cannot access class members from inherited classes prior to calling the inherited constructor. This will result in a compile-time error. You can access members of the class itself. So, for the given classes, the comments annotate the valid and invalid statements within the constructor.

```
TMyBase = class(TObject)
  FBaseField: integer;
end;

TMyObject = class(TMyBase)
  FMyObjectField: integer;
  constructor Create;
end;
```

The implementation of the preceding constructor above would be

```
constructor TMyObject.Create;
begin
  FBaseField := 3; // error
  FMyObjectField := 3; // valid
  inherited;
  FBaseField := 3; // valid
  FMyObjectField := 3; // valid
end;
```

Finalization

The freeing up of resources used by objects in the .NET world is different from what Delphi developers are used to. We already know that the GC will free managed resources from the heap when they are not used. It is still necessary to free unmanaged resources such as a file handle explicitly because the GC will not know how to do this.

In the past, freeing resources using Delphi relied on the destructor, which was called whenever the Free() method was invoked on the object. The destructor looked something like this:

```
destructor TMyObject.Destroy;
begin
  FreeResource;
  inherited;
end;
```

You still have the constructor in Delphi for .NET, but it does something different now. Before getting into how this is different, let's look at the .NET way of releasing unmanaged resources.

An object that contains unmanaged resources should override a Finalize() method, which every .NET object contains. In this method is the location where you would release any unmanaged resources. For instance, a critical section is an unmanaged resource. The following is the declaration of a class that will wrap this unmanaged resource:

```
TCriticalSection = class(TObject)
private
  FSection: TRTLCriticalSection;
strict protected
  procedure Finalize; override;
public
  constructor Create;end;
```

This is obviously an incomplete wrapper for a critical section intended to simply illustrate how the finalizer would be implemented. The implementation of the `Finalize()` method is shown here:

```
procedure TCriticalSection.Finalize;
begin
  DeleteCriticalSection(FSection);
  inherited;
end;
```

It assumes that `FSection` was initialized elsewhere, such as in the `constructor`. How is this different from the destructor pattern that all Delphi developers are used to? The `Finalize()` method is invoked by the GC; it is not directly accessed when an object is no longer being referenced. So, when an instance of the `TCriticalSection` object is no longer referenced, the GC will invoke the `Finalize()` method in the process of releasing the object from the heap. This is the way to ensure that your unmanaged resources will be properly cleaned up. Although this is convenient, you must consider whether the unmanaged resource is one that can hang around until the GC kicks in. For instance, you might be holding onto a file handle, unnecessarily preventing access to this file. This is where the dispose pattern comes in.

> **NOTE**
>
> Most application level code should never have to wrap raw, unmanaged resources and thus should never need to override `Finalize()`. Only existing FCL classes and low-level third-party component and class code would typically have to do this. The most used unmanaged resources have already been wrapped by the FCL classes (`FileStream`, `Control`, `Monitor`, and so on).

The Dispose Pattern—IDisposable

The dispose pattern gives developers an explicit mechanism to release unmanaged resources immediately rather than relying on a GC cycle. This is accomplished by implementing the `IDisposable` interface.

IDisposable Example

Consider the `TCriticalSection` class from the previous section. The following is its reworked definition that implements `IDisposable`:

```
TCriticalSection = class(TObject, IDisposable)
private
  FSection: TRTLCriticalSection;
  FCSValid: Boolean;
strict protected
```

```
      procedure Finalize; override;
  public
    constructor Create;
    procedure Dispose;
  end;
```

You should notice that the object now implements the IDisposable interface and its Dispose() procedure. Also, an FCSValid Boolean field will be initialized to False and set to True when the critical section is allocated. Additionally, the Finalize() procedure is kept. An explanation as to why Finalize() is kept will follow. The implementation of Dispose() is shown here:

```
procedure TCriticalSection.Dispose;
begin
  if FCSValid then
  begin
    DeleteCriticalSection(FSection);
    GC.SuppressFinalize(Self);
    FCSValid := False;
  end;
end;
```

The Dispose() method releases the unmanaged resource and then calls the Garbage Collector's SuppressFinalize() method. SuppressFinalize() prevents the GC from calling the Finalize() method on the specified object. Finally, FCSValid is set to False. The re-coded Finalize() method is shown here:

```
procedure TCriticalSection.Finalize;
begin
  if FCSValid then
    DeleteCriticalSection(FSection);
  inherited;
end;
```

Both the Finalize() and Dispose() methods evaluate the value of the FCSValid field to determine if there is a valid reference to the unmanaged resource; if so, it calls the method to release that resource.

The question might arise as to why we need the Finalize() method when we have just provided a Dispose() method that accomplishes the same. The reason is that the Finalize() method is guaranteed to be called by the GC. The Dispose() method is not. The Dispose() method is not guaranteed to be called. It is only called if the Free() method of the object itself is called using the standard Delphi method of resource protection as shown here:

```
cs := TCriticalSection.Create;
try
  // use cs
finally
  cs.Free;
end;
```

In other words, it is possible that a developer will forget to call the destructor of your object, which is likely unless she knows that she is supposed to. Given this scenario,

`Dispose()` would not be called, and the object would still be tagged for finalization by the GC because `GC.SuppressFinalize()` would not have been called. Also, `FCSValid` would still be true unless the handle was never allocated. GC will call the `Finalize()` method, and the critical section will be properly released, ultimately. So, you can see that having both the `Dispose()` and `Finalize()` methods is the safest approach. If `Dispose()` is explicitly invoked, the resource is released immediately and the GC will not have to deal with the finalization of this object, which, by the way, is a performance benefit for the GC. If `Dispose()` is not called, at least the resource will be released, eventually.

Automatically Implementing IDisposable

Now that you have seen the long way of implementing `IDisposable`, this section shows how to do this using the destructor construct, which is familiar to Delphi developers and the method recommended by Borland.

By writing a destructor that follows the specific format of

```
destructor Destroy; override;
```

the Delphi for .NET Compiler will automatically implement the `IDisposable` interface for your class. Let's take a look at the final version of the `TCriticalSection` class declaration:

```
TCriticalSection = class(TObject)
private
  FSection: TRTLCriticalSection;
  FCSValid: Boolean;
strict protected
  procedure Finalize; override;
public
  constructor Create;
  destructor Destroy; override;
end;
```

It should not surprise you that the implementation looks exactly like the `Dispose()` method with the exception of an additional `inherited` statement:

```
destructor TCriticalSection.Destroy;
begin
  if FCSValid then
  begin
    DeleteCriticalSection(FSection);
    GC.SuppressFinalize(Self);
    FCSValid := False;
  end;
  inherited;
end;
```

If it's practically the same, why all the fuss about using a destructor construct versus explicitly implementing `IDisposable`? For one thing, it gives existing Delphi developers the "warm fuzzies" that accompany familiarity. More importantly, it enables developers to write objects that target both the .NET and Win32 platforms without having to differentiate between those that are garbage collected and those that are not.

Here are a few rules that you should know when using this destructor/dispose pattern:

- The destructor name must be Destroy.

- The destructor must be overridden by using the override directive.

- The destructor must be paremeterless.

- You cannot have both the IDisposable interface and the Destroy() destructor implemented by your object.

The point to remember about the Destroy() destructor pattern is that like Dispose(), Destroy() is not called automatically and must be invoked by calling the object's Free() method. If an object encapsulates one or more inner objects that implement IDispose or have destructors, the outer object should also do so, forwarding Dispose calls from the class's users. This is why a WinForm project always includes the Dispose method, for instance.

Performance Issues Regarding Finalization

The GC, although it makes life easier for programmers, requires that programmers follow certain guidelines with regard to finalizers.

When an object has a finalizer, it is kept in a global list called the finalization list. The GC uses the list to determine which objects need to have their Finalize() method called during garbage collection. During an initial run of the GC on generation 0, the GC will enumerate through the finalization list to determine if any unreferenced objects can be released. If so, a reference to them is placed into the Freachable Queue and the reference in the Finalization List is removed. The Freachable Queue (pronounced "F-reachable" and meaning finalize-reachable) is a separate list of references to objects needing their Finalize() method invoked. The act of adding a reference to an object in this Freachable Queue deems the object reachable and thus, uncollectible. There is now a root to the object. This is a temporary state for objects in the Freachable Queue. The GC, after going through a GC cycle, will launch a special high priority thread that is responsible for enumerating through the Freachable Queue, removing the object references and invoking their Finalize() method. Once that is done, the object is now truly unreachable and can be collected upon the next GC run. All this work should show you that objects with finalizers can be expensive. They consume memory and require two collection cycles to release their memory.

Developers should implement finalizers judiciously in small classes that wrap unmanaged resources only. Note that if these classes maintain references to other classes, the contained classes will not be GCed because they are still referenced from the live roots in the Freachable Queue. Therefore, it is best to try to use existing FCL classes instead of wrapping unmanaged resources in your own classes when possible.

Also, code in the Finalize() method cannot call other objects because it is running in a very restricted thread. No memory allocations or typecasts that would box objects are valid. Within the Finalize() method, you can refer to objects that are members of itself; it cannot be guaranteed that these objects have not already had their own Finalize() method called, and thus they could be in an invalid state.

CHAPTER 10

Collections

IN THIS CHAPTER

- System.Collections Interfaces
- System.Collections Classes
- Creating a Strongly-Typed Collection
- Creating a Strongly-Typed Dictionary

At some point, all programmers will have to work with lists. The types of lists can vary in many ways. For instance, they might vary in how they are constructed. They might vary in what they contain. Some lists contain heterogeneous data, whereas others are limited to a specific type. Lists might vary in how you extract data from them as well as the method by which we iterate through them. If you are a Delphi user, you are probably familiar with the TList, TStrings, TStringList, and TCollection classes. You still have access to these classes; however, in .NET you also have the System.Collections namespace, which provides its own interfaces and types. This chapter delves into the topic of collections and enumerators to illustrate the .NET way of working with lists using Delphi for .NET.

The System.Collections namespace contains interfaces that define and classes that provide functionality around collections of objects. These classes are lists, queues, stacks, arrays, hash-tables, and dictionaries.

System.Collections Interfaces

Figure 10.1 depicts the hierarchy of interfaces defined within the System.Collections namespace.

Table 10.1 gives a brief description of each of these interfaces.

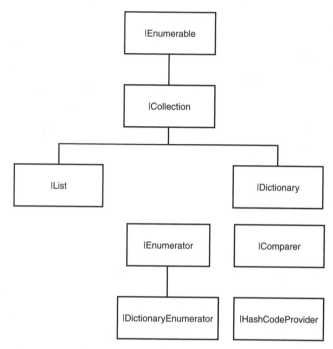

FIGURE 10.1   Interfaces in System.Collections.

TABLE 10.1   System.Collections Interfaces

Interface	Description
IEnumerable	Exposes an enumerator interface whose implementor iterates uni-directionally over a collection.
ICollection	Defines size and synchronization methods for collections. Inherits the IEnumerable methods.
IList	Defines a collection whose items are accessible via an index.
IDictionary	Defines a key-value pair collection.
IEnumerator	Defines method for uni-directional iteration over a collection.
IDictionaryEnumerator	Defines enumeration over a Dictionary.
IComparer	Defines a method for comparing two objects.
IHashCodeProvider	Defines the method for returning the hash code for a specified object.

Each of these interfaces defines its own set of methods that are implemented by the collection classes. Tables 10.2–10.6 describe methods for the primary interfaces listed in Table 10.1.

IEnumerable Interface

Table 10.2 describes the method in the IEnumerable interface.

TABLE 10.2   IEnumerable Method

Method	Description
GetEnumerator()	Returns an IEnumerator instance used to iterate over a Collection.

ICollection Interface

Table 10.3 describes the properties and methods in the ICollection interface.

TABLE 10.3   ICollection Properties and Methods

Property/Method	Description
Count	Returns the number of elements contained in the Collection.
IsSynchronized	Returns true if the Collection is thread-safe; otherwise returns false.
SyncRoot	Returns an object that can provide thread-safe access to the Collection.
CopyTo()	Copies the objects contained in the Collection to the specified Array starting at a specified index.

IList Interface

Table 10.4 describes the properties and methods in the IList interface.

TABLE 10.4   IList Properties and Methods

Property/Method	Description
IsFixedSize	Indicates if the IList has a fixed size.
IsReadOnly	Indicates if the IList grants read-only access to its elements.
Item	Returns the IList element by the specified index.
Add()	Adds the specified item to the IList.
Clear()	Empties the IList.
Contains()	Indicates whether the IList contains the specified value.
IndexOf()	Returns the index of the specified item.
Insert()	Inserts an item into the IList at a specified position.
Remove()	Removes the first occurrence of a specified item.
RemoveAt()	Removes the item at the specified index.

IDictionary Interface

Table 10.5 describes the properties and methods in the IDictionary interface.

TABLE 10.5   IDictionary Properties and Methods

Property/Method	Description
IsFixedSize	Determines if IDictionary is of a fixed size.
IsReadOnly	Determines if IDictionary elements are read-only.
Item	Gets/sets element with a specified Key.
Keys	Returns an ICollection of the IDictionary Keys.
Values	Returns an ICollection of the IDictionary Values.
Add()	Adds a specified element with the specified Key.
Clear()	Empties the IDictionary.
Contains()	Determines if IDictionary contains the element with the specified Key.
Remove()	Removes the element with the specified Key.

10

IEnumerator Interface

Table 10.6 describes the properties and methods in the `IEnumerator` interface.

TABLE 10.6   IEnumerator Properties and Methods

Property/Method	Description
Current	Returns the current element in the Collection tied to the `IEnumerator` instance.
MoveNext()	Advances the position of the current element in the Collection to which the `IEnumerator` refers.
Reset()	Repositions the `IEnumerator` to its initial position (just before the first element in the Collection).

The classes within the `System.Collections` namespace implement these interfaces. These are not the only classes that implement these interfaces. For instance, the `IList` interface is implemented by numerous UI and database classes. It is beneficial to examine how these classes implement these interfaces—then you will also know how to use all other classes that implement them. This chapter discusses the classes that exist within the `System.Collections` namespace.

System.Collections Classes

The `System.Collections` namespace includes several prebuilt classes that you can use to manage lists of various sorts. The following sections cover them.

The Stack Collection

The `Stack` collection stores objects according to a first-in-last-out (FILO) basis. To add objects, one pushes them onto the `Stack`. To remove them, one pops them from the `Stack`.

The Stack implements the `ICollection`, `IEnumerable`, and `ICloneable` interfaces.

> **NOTE**
>
> The `ICloneable` interface is not a member of the `System.Collections` namespace. It is a member of the System namespaces, and it defines the `Clone()` method which is used to create a new, identical object.

Stack Properties and Methods

The methods that you will primarily be using with the `Stack` are `Push()`, `Pop()`, and `Peek()`. Table 10.7 lists the methods for the `Stack` collection not already listed in previous tables for the interfaces that `Stack` implements.

TABLE 10.7   Stack Collection Method

Method	Description
Peek()	Returns the topmost element of the Stack without removing it from the `Stack`.
Pop()	Returns and removes the topmost element from the `Stack`.
Push()	Adds an element to the `Stack`. This element becomes the topmost element.
Syncronized()	Returns a thread safe wrapper for the `Stack`.
ToArray()	Copies the elements in the Stack to a new `ArrayList` class.

Stack Constructor

To create a `Stack` instance, you would use one of its three constructors as shown in the following examples.

> To create an empty `Stack` with a default initial capacity of 10, use the following construction:
>
> ```
> MyStack := Stack.Create();
> ```
>
> To create an empty Stack with a specified capacity, pass the desired capacity to the `Stack`'s constructor as a parameter:
>
> ```
> MyStack := Stack.Create(20);
> ```
>
> To create a `Stack` that contains elements from another `Collection` whose capacity is that of the collection or the default initial capacity (whichever is greater) use the following construction:
>
> ```
> MyStack := Stack.Create(AnotherCollection);
> ```
>
> where `AnotherCollection` is an object that implements the `ICollection` interface.

Stack Usage

Listing 10.1 illustrates using the `Stack` class. It also illustrates how to use an instance of an `IEnumerator` to iterate through the `Stack` so that one can print the `Stack`'s contents.

LISTING 10.1   Stack Example

```
1:   program d4dnStack;
2:   {$APPTYPE CONSOLE}
3:
4:   uses
5:     System.Collections;
6:
7:   procedure ShowCollection(Collection: IEnumerable);
8:   var
9:     enumMyStack: IEnumerator;
10:  begin
11:    enumMyStack := Collection.GetEnumerator;
12:    System.Console.WriteLine;
13:    while enumMyStack.MoveNext do
14:      System.Console.Write(enumMyStack.Current.ToString+'    ');
15:    System.Console.WriteLine;
16:  end;
17:
18:  var
19:    MyStack: Stack;
20:    i: integer;
21:  begin
22:    // Initialize and populate the Stack
23:    MyStack := Stack.Create;
24:    for i := 1 to 5 do
25:      MyStack.Push('Item '+i.ToString);
26:    ShowCollection(MyStack);
27:
28:    // Pop the topmost item
```

LISTING 10.1   Continued

```
29:     System.Console.Write('Pop:   '+MyStack.Pop.ToString);
30:     ShowCollection(MyStack);
31:
32:     // Peek at the topmost item
33:     System.Console.Write('Peek: '+MyStack.Peek.ToString);
34:     ShowCollection(MyStack);
35:
36:     // Pop the two topmost items
37:     System.Console.WriteLine('Pop:   '+MyStack.Pop.ToString);
38:     System.Console.Write('Pop:   '+MyStack.Pop.ToString);
39:     ShowCollection(MyStack);
40:
41:     // Push another item
42:     System.Console.Write('Push: Item 6');
43:     MyStack.Push('Item 6');
44:     ShowCollection(MyStack);
45:
46:     // Clear the stack
47:     MyStack.Clear;
48:     System.Console.WriteLine('Stack cleared');
49:
50:     // Push another item
51:     System.Console.Write('Push: Item 7');
52:     MyStack.Push('Item 7');
53:     ShowCollection(MyStack);
54:
55:     System.Console.Readline;
56: end.
```

▶ Find the code on the CD: \Code\Chapter 10\Ex01\.

The code in Listing 10.1 is a simple console application that initializes a stack, populates it, and performs some basic Stack operations on it. The output of this program is written to the screen as shown in Figure 10.2.

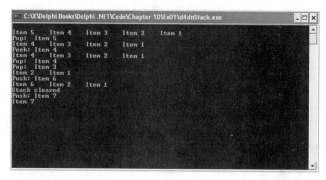

FIGURE 10.2   Stack output.

Lines 25–45 initialize and populate the Stack with five items. The procedure ShowCollection() (lines 7–16) is used to print out the Stack's contents and is invoked after each Stack operation.

`ShowCollection()` uses an instance of the `IEnumerator` interface to iterate through the `Stack`'s contents. Note how the `IEnumerator` is retrieved through the `GetEnumerator` method of the `IEnumerable` parameter in line 11. Using the `IEnumerator` instance, one is able to iterate through each item in the `Stack` by calling the `IEnumerator.MoveNext()` method. As the name implies, the `Current()` method returns the current item in the collection. Notice that `ShowCollection()` takes an `IEnumerable` interface as a parameter. `IEnumerable` is the interface that defines the `GetEnumerator()` function. By using this interface, the `ShowCollection()` method can be reused with any class that implements `IEnumerable`, such as the `Queue`, which you will see next.

The code in the main program block contains basic Stack operations that illustrate its usage. Examine each operation along with the screen output.

The Queue Class

The `Queue` collection stores objects according to a FIFO basis. To add objects, one performs an `Enqueue()` operation. To remove them, one performs a `Dequeue()` operation.

Similar to the `Stack` class, the `Queue` class implements the `ICollection`, `IEnumerable`, and `ICloneable` interfaces.

Queue Properties and Methods

The methods that you will primarily be using with the `Queue` are `Enqueue ()`, `Dequeue ()`, and `Peek()`. Table 10.8 lists the methods for the `Queue` collection.

TABLE 10.8   Queue Collection Methods

Method	Description
Enqueue()	Adds an element to the Queue. When added, this is the last element to be removed from the Queue unless others are added behind it.
Dequeue()	Removes and returns the first element at the beginning of the Queue.
Peek()	Returns the element at the beginning of the Queue. This operation does not remove the element from the Queue.
Syncronize()	Returns a thread-safe wrapper for the Queue.
ToArray()	Copies the elements in the Queue to a new ArrayList class.
TrimToSize()	Sets the Queue's capacity to the number of elements it contains.

Queue Constructor

When initializing a `Queue`, you have the option of specifying the `Queue`'s initial capacity and growth factor. The initial capacity is simply the starting size for the queue. The growth factor is the amount that the initial capacity is multiplied by when expansion is needed in the `Queue`. Therefore, a `Queue` with an initial capacity of 10 and a growth factor of 2 will double in size when needed.

To create a `Queue` instance, you would use one of its four constructors as shown in the following examples.

> To create an empty `Queue` with a default initial capacity of 32 and a default growth factor of 2, use the following construction:
>
> ```
> MyQueue := Queue.Create();
> ```

10

To create an empty `Queue` with a specified capacity and the default growth factor of 2, pass the initial capacity to the Queue's constructor as a parameter:

```
MyQueue := Queue.Create(20);
```

To create an empty `Queue` with a specified capacity and the specified growth factor, pass both the initial capacity and growth factor to the Queue's constructor as parameters:

```
MyQueue := Queue.Create(20, 3);
```

To create a `Queue` that contains elements from another `Collection` whose capacity is that of the collection or the default initial capacity (whichever is greater) and the default growth factor, use the following construction:

```
MyQueue := Queue.Create(AnotherCollection);
```

where `AnotherCollection` is an object that implements the `ICollection` interface.

Queue Usage

Listing 10.2 illustrates using the `Queue` object. Similar to the `Stack`, the `Queue` also uses an `IEnumerator` to iterate through its elements.

LISTING 10.2   Queue Example

```
1:    program d4dnQueue;
2:    {$APPTYPE CONSOLE}
3:
4:    {%DelphiDotNetAssemblyCompiler '$(SystemRoot)\microsoft.net\framework\
➥v1.1.4322\system.drawing.dll'}
5:
6:    uses
7:      System.Collections;
8:
9:    procedure ShowCollection(Collection: IEnumerable);
10:   var
11:     enumMyStack: IEnumerator;
12:   begin
13:     enumMyStack := Collection.GetEnumerator;
14:     System.Console.WriteLine;
15:     while enumMyStack.MoveNext do
16:       System.Console.Write(enumMyStack.Current.ToString+'     ');
17:     System.Console.WriteLine;
18:   end;
19:
20:   var
21:     MyQueue: Queue;
22:     i: integer;
23:   begin
24:     // Initialize and Enqueueulate the Queue
25:     MyQueue := Queue.Create();
26:     for i := 1 to 5 do
27:       MyQueue.Enqueue('Item '+i.ToString());
28:     ShowCollection(MyQueue);
29:
```

LISTING 10.2 Continued

```
30:     System.Console.Write('Dequeue:   '+MyQueue.Dequeue.ToString);
31:     ShowCollection(MyQueue);
32:
33:     System.Console.Write('Peek: '+MyQueue.Peek.ToString);
34:     ShowCollection(MyQueue);
35:
36:     System.Console.WriteLine('Dequeue:   '+MyQueue.Dequeue.ToString);
37:     System.Console.Write('Dequeue:   '+MyQueue.Dequeue.ToString);
38:     ShowCollection(MyQueue);
39:
40:     System.Console.Write('Enqueue: Item 6');
41:     MyQueue.Enqueue('Item 6');
42:     ShowCollection(MyQueue);
43:
44:     MyQueue.Clear();
45:     System.Console.WriteLine('Queue cleared');
46:
47:     System.Console.Write('Enqueue: Item 7');
48:     MyQueue.Enqueue('Item 7');
49:     ShowCollection(MyQueue);
50:     System.Console.ReadLine;
51:
52:  end.
```

▶ Find the code on the CD: \Code\Chapter 10\Ex02\.

The code in Listing 10.2 is similar to that of Listing 10.1 for the Stack. These two objects are quite similar in usage. Where they differ is in the order items are removed from the collection. The output of this program is written to the screen as shown in Figure 10.3.

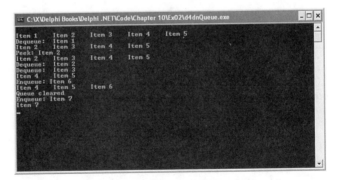

FIGURE 10.3 Queue output.

In the listing, lines 25–27 initialize the Queue with data. The rest of the main block then performs some Dequeue() and Enqueue() operations against it. Notice the difference in how the data is removed from the Queue during the Dequeue() operation. Unlike the Stack, the item removed is always the item at the beginning of the collection (the foremost item added); whereas in the Stack, it is always the last item added.

The ArrayList Class

ArrayList is probably the most versatile class in the System.Collections namespace. The Stack and Queue classes allow you to modify the objects they contain, not the actual reference, but the fields and properties of the objects. ArrayList allows you to actually overwrite existing elements with new references. This is a minor, but important distinction. It also has support for other useful operations that enable sorting, reverse ordering, range operations, element locating, and binary searching.

The ArrayList implements the IList, ICollection, IEnumerable, and ICloneable interfaces.

ArrayList Constructor

To create an ArrayList instance, you would use one of its three constructors as shown in the following examples.

> To create an empty ArrayList with a default initial capacity of 16, use the following construction:
>
> MyArrayList := ArrayList.Create();

> When the ArrayList needs to be expanded, its capacity will be double of the initialized capacity.

> To create an empty ArrayList with a specified capacity, pass the desired capacity to the ArrayList's constructor as a parameter:
>
> MyArrayList := ArrayList.Create(20);

> To create an ArrayList that contains elements from another Collection whose capacity is that of the collection or the default initial capacity (whichever is greater), use the following construction:
>
> MyArrayList := ArrayList.Create(AnotherCollection);

where AnotherCollection is an object that implements the ICollection interface.

ArrayList Properties and Methods

Table 10.9 lists the properties and methods for the ArrayList collection that are not listed in its interfaces.

TABLE 10.9   ArrayList Collection Properties and Methods

Property/Method	Description
Capacity	Number of items the ArrayList can contain before growing.
Adapter()	Creates an ArrayList adaptor, or wrapper, for an IList.
AddRange()	Adds elements from an ICollection to the end of an ArrayList.
BinarySearch()	Performs a binary search on a sorted ArrayList for a specified element.
FixedSize()	Returns a list wrapper with a fixed size. Elements of this list can be modified, but not added or removed.
GetEnumerator()	Returns an IEnumerator instance used to iterate over the ArrayList.
GetRange()	Returns a range (subset of the ArrayList), which itself is an ArrayList.
InsertRange()	Inserts elements from an ICollection at the specified index.
LastIndexOf()	Returns the last occurrence of an element within an ArrayList or a portion of the ArrayList.
ReadOnly()	Returns a list wrapper that is read-only.

TABLE 10.9   Continued

Property/Method	Description
RemoveRange()	Removes the specified subset of elements from the ArrayList.
Repeat()	Returns a copy of the ArrayList. This is not a shallow copy. Therefore, the elements are copies of the original elements. See Clone().
Reverse()	Reverses the order of all or a range of the items in the ArrayList.
SetRange()	Copies an ICollection over a specified range in the ArrayList.
Sort()	Sorts the ArrayList.
Syncronized()	Returns a thread-safe wrapper for the ArrayList.
ToArray()	Copies elements in the ArrayList to another ArrayList.
TrimToSize()	Sets the Capacity of the ArrayList equal to the Count (items actually contained in the ArrayList).

ArrayList Usage

Listing 10.3 illustrates using the ArrayList object. This example illustrates populating, enumerating, sorting, and working with ranges in an ArrayList.

LISTING 10.3   ArrayList Example

```
1:    program d4dnArrayList;
2:    {$APPTYPE CONSOLE}
3:
4:    uses
5:      System.Collections;
6:
7:    var
8:      ClassicCars: ArrayList;
9:      SubList: ArrayList;
10:     SubList2: ArrayList;
11:
12:   procedure ShowArrayListItems(aName: String; aArrayList: ArrayList);
13:   var
14:     i: integer;
15:   begin
16:     System.Console.WriteLine;
17:     System.Console.Write(aName+': ');
18:     for i := 0 to aArrayList.Count - 1 do
19:       System.Console.Write(' {0}', [aArrayList[i].ToString]);
20:     System.Console.WriteLine;
21:   end;
22:
23:   begin
24:     // Initialize and populate the arraylist
25:     ClassicCars := ArrayList.Create;
26:     ClassicCars.Add('Camaro');
27:     ClassicCars.Add('Mustang');
28:     ClassicCars.Add('Chevelle');
29:     ClassicCars.Add('Nova');
30:     ClassicCars.Add('Corvette');
31:     ClassicCars.Add('Thunderbird');
32:     ClassicCars.Add('Firebird');
```

10

LISTING 10.3   Continued

```
33:      ClassicCars.Add('Satellite');
34:
35:      ShowArrayListItems('ClassicCars', ClassicCars);
36:
37:      // sort the arraylist
38:      ClassicCars.Sort;
39:      ShowArrayListItems('ClassicCars', ClassicCars);
40:
41:      // reverse the ArrayList
42:      ClassicCars.Reverse;
43:      ShowArrayListItems('ClassicCars', ClassicCars);
44:
45:      // retrieve a range of items, but leave them in the original ArrayList
46:      SubList := ClassicCars.GetRange(2,3);
47:      ShowArrayListItems('SubList', SubList);
48:      ShowArrayListItems('ClassicCars', ClassicCars);
49:
50:      // create a new arraylist and add it to ClassicCars
51:      SubList2 := ArrayList.Create(3);
52:      SubList2.Add('GTO');
53:      SubList2.Add('Malibu');
54:      SubList2.Add('El-Camino');
55:      ClassicCars.AddRange(SubList2);
56:      ShowArrayListItems('ClassicCars', ClassicCars);
57:
58:      // re-sort the arraylist
59:      ClassicCars.Sort;
60:      ShowArrayListItems('ClassicCars', ClassicCars);
61:
62:      // Output the count and capacity
63:      System.Console.WriteLine('ClassicCars count: {0}',
64:        [ClassicCars.Count.ToString]);
65:      System.Console.WriteLine('ClassicCars capacity: {0}',
66:        [ClassicCars.Capacity.ToString]);
67:
68:      // Trim to size
69:      ClassicCars.TrimToSize;
70:      // Output the count and capacity
71:      System.Console.WriteLine('After trimmed—-');
72:      System.Console.WriteLine('ClassicCars count: {0}',
73:        [ClassicCars.Count.ToString]);
74:      System.Console.WriteLine('ClassicCars capacity: {0}',
75:        ClassicCars.Capacity.ToString);
76:      System.Console.ReadLine;
77:
78:  end.
```

▶ Find the code on the CD: \Code\Chapter 10\Ex03\.

In the listing, lines 8–10 declare three ArrayList objects—alClassicCars (cars that I'd like to own) and two additional arrays to demonstrate the use of range operations. ShowArrayListItems() is the procedure that prints the output to the console. Figure 10.4 shows the output of this program.

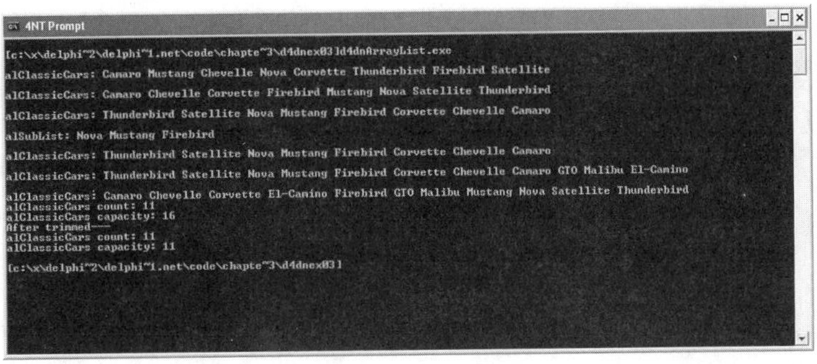

FIGURE 10.4   ArrayList output.

Lines 25–33 create and populate alClassicCars. Lines 42–43 demonstrate sorting and reversing the order of the ArrayList, which you can see in the console output. In line 46, the program retrieves a subset of the ArrayList into alSubList. alSubList will contain three items from alClassicCars beginning at index two. Because this is a zero-based array, this subset will begin at the third item in the list.

Lines 51–55 create another ArrayList, alSubList2, and populate it with three items not contained in alClassicCars. These items are added to the main list, alClassicCars, using the AddRange() method. In lines 63 and 66, alClassicCars' Count and Capacity are written. These properties display the number of items the collection contains and the space allocated, respectively. Line 69 invokes the TrimToSize() method to set the Capacity to that of Count.

The HashTable Class

The HashTable class is one you would use when you want to retrieve stored items by a key value. The HashTable internally converts the key to a hash code, which is a unique numeric index that the HashTable ultimately uses to retrieve the requested element. Elements are stored in buckets. A bucket is subgrouping of items stored within the collection. Items whose keys generate the same hash code are stored in the same bucket. The HashTable thus uses the hash code to identify the bucket, which it then searches for the requested item. Ideally, there would only be one item in each bucket, thus making the HashTable very efficient in searching with a search time of O(1).

The HashTable implements the IDictionary, ICollection, IEnumerable, and ISerializable and ICloneable interfaces. Instead of being defined in the System.Collections namespace, the ISerializable interface is defined in the System.Runtime.Serialization namespace. ISerializable defines the interface for serializing and deserializing classes.

HashTable Constructor

The HashTable can be constructed in one of several ways. The alternative constructors allow you to either specify or use the default capacity, load factor, hash code provider, and comparer. Additionally, you can specify another IDictionary instance from which to copy elements and serialization/streaming objects for streaming customization. The specific parameters are

capacity as Integer—Determines the number or buckets to be allocated based on the load factor.

loadFactor as Single—Specifies the maximum ratio of elements to buckets. The default is 1.0.

10

`hcp as IHashCodeProvider`—Generates hash codes for keys.

`comparer as IComparer`—Compares and determines whether two keys are equal.

`d as IDictionary`—Elements from the `IDictionary` parameter are copied to the `HashTable`.

`info as SerializationInfo`—Object that contains information needed to serialize the `HashTable`.

`context as StreamingContext`—Describes the source and destination of the serialized stream for the `HashTable`.

HashTable Properties and Methods

Table 10.10 lists the properties and methods for the `HashTable` collection that are not listed in its interfaces.

TABLE 10.10   HashTable Collection Properties and Methods

Property/Method	Description
ContainsKey()	Determines whether the HashTable contains the specified key.
ContainsValue()	Determines whether the HashTable contains the specified value.
GetObjectData()	Returns the data required to serialize the HashTable by having implemented ISerializable.
Syncronized()	Returns a thread-safe wrapper for the HashTable.
OnDeserialization()	Raises a deserialization event when deserialization is complete. Implements the ISerializable interface.

HashTable Usage

Listing 10.4 illustrates using the `HashTable` object. Whereas the previous examples stored strings, this example illustrates how to populate a `HashTable` with a custom class containing information on U.S. states.

LISTING 10.4   HashTable Example

```
1:   program d4dnHashTable;
2:   {$APPTYPE CONSOLE}
3:
4:   uses
5:     System.Collections,
6:     Borland.Vcl.SysUtils;
7:
8:   type
9:
10:    // Define a class to store in the HashTable
11:    TStateInfo = class
12:      StateName: String;
13:      StateCapital: String;
14:      Admission: TDateTime;
15:      constructor Create(aName, aCapital: String; aAddmision: TDateTime);
16:    end;
17:
18:  var
19:    htDemo: HashTable;
```

LISTING 10.4   Continued

```
20:
21:   procedure PrintStateInfo(aKey: String);
22:   var
23:     si: TStateInfo;
24:   begin
25:     // First retrieve the TStateInfo item from the HashTable
26:     si := htDemo[aKey] as TStateInfo;
27:     // Print out its contents
28:     Console.WriteLine(Format('State: %s, Capital: %s, Admission: %s',
29:       [si.StateName, si.StateCapital, DateTostr(si.Admission)]));
30:   end;
31:
32:   { TStateInfo }
33:   constructor TStateInfo.Create(aName, aCapital: String;
34:     aAddmision: TDateTime);
35:   begin
36:     inherited Create;
37:     StateName    := aName;
38:     StateCapital := aCapital;
39:     Admission    := aAddmision;
40:   end;
41:
42:   begin
43:     // Initialize and populate the HashTable
44:     htDemo := HashTable.Create();
45:     htDemo.Add('AL', TStateInfo.Create('Alabama',  'Montgomery',
46:       EncodeDate(1819, 12, 14)));
47:     htDemo.Add('FL', TStateInfo.Create('Florida',  'Tallahassee',
48:       EncodeDate(1845, 03, 15)));
49:     htDemo.Add('KY', TStateInfo.Create('Kentucky', 'Frankfort',
50:       EncodeDate(1792, 06, 01)));
51:     htDemo.Add('IL', TStateInfo.Create('Illinois',  'SpringField',
52:       EncodeDate(1818, 12, 03)));
53:     htDemo.Add('ME', TStateInfo.Create('Maine',     'Augusta',
54:       EncodeDate(1820, 03, 15)));
55:
56:     // Print the HashTable items by Key
57:     PrintStateInfo('ME');
58:     PrintStateInfo('KY');
59:     PrintStateInfo('FL');
60:     PrintStateInfo('IL');
61:     PrintStateInfo('AL');
62:     System.Console.ReadLine;
63:
64:   end.
```

▶ Find the code on the CD: \Code\Chapter 10\Ex04\.

Listing 10.4 illustrates how to store an object (TStateInfo) and how to retrieve that object using a sting key. Lines 11–16 contain the definition of the TStateInfo class, which defines basic information fields for U.S. states. Lines 44–54 initialize and populate the HashTable with data. The procedure, PrintStateInfo(), accepts a string as a parameter, and uses the parameter as a key to extract a TStateInfo instance from the HashTable. Upon getting the TStateInfo instance, PrintStateInfo() writes that state's data to the screen as shown in Figure 10.5.

FIGURE 10.5   HashTable output.

Creating a Strongly-Typed Collection

The collections you have been looking at in this chapter are generic in that they can store heterogeneous instances of any object type or boxed value type. Most likely, you might need to create a collection that stores data of only one type. This is called a strongly typed collection.

Descending from CollectionBase

The System.Collections namespace contains an abstract class, CollectionBase, from which your custom collection might descend in order to create strongly-typed collections. Internally, the CollectionBase uses an ArrayList instance to store elements. Access to the ArrayList is through an IList interface provided by the List property. CollectionBase also defines the methods that need to be overridden and enforce the type you want to store. Listing 10.5 shows a strongly-typed collection that stores the state information from the previous example.

LISTING 10.5   Strongly-Typed Collection

```
1:    unit d4dnDevGuide.StateCollection;
2:    interface
3:    uses
4:      System.Collections;
5:
6:    type
7:
8:      // Define a class to store in the Collection
9:      TStateInfo = class
10:       StateName: String;
11:       StateCapital: String;
12:       Admission: DateTime;
13:       constructor Create(aName, aCapital: String; aAddmision: DateTime);
```

LISTING 10.5   Continued

```
14:    end;
15:
16:    // Define the strongly-typed collection
17:    TStateInfoCollection = class(CollectionBase)
18:    private
19:      function GetStateInfo(Index: Integer): TStateInfo;
20:      procedure SetStateInfo(Index: Integer; const Value: TStateInfo);
21:      procedure VerifyType(Value: TObject);
22:    strict protected
23:      // Type checking events
24:      procedure OnInsert(index: integer; value: TObject); override;
25:      procedure OnSet(index: integer; oldValue: TObject;
26:        newValue: TObject); override;
27:      procedure OnValidate(value: TObject); override;
28:    public
29:      constructor Create;
30:      function Add(value: TStateInfo): Integer;
31:      function IndexOf(value: TStateInfo): Integer;
32:      procedure Insert(index: integer; value: TStateInfo);
33:      procedure Remove(value: TStateInfo);
34:      function Contains(value: TStateInfo): Boolean;
35:      procedure PrintItems;
36:      property StateInfo[Index: Longint]: TStateInfo read GetStateInfo
37:        write SetStateInfo;
38:    end;
39:
40:  implementation
41:
42:  { TStateInfo }
43:  constructor TStateInfo.Create(AName, ACapital: String;
44:    AAddmision: DateTime);
45:  begin
46:    inherited Create();
47:    StateName    := AName;
48:    StateCapital := ACapital;
49:    Admission    := AAddmision;
50:  end;
51:
52:  { TStateInfoCollection }
53:
54:  constructor TStateInfoCollection.Create;
55:  begin
56:    inherited Create;
57:  end;
58:
59:  function TStateInfoCollection.GetStateInfo(Index: Integer): TStateInfo;
60:  begin
61:    Result := List[Index] as TStateInfo;
62:  end;
63:
64:  procedure TStateInfoCollection.SetStateInfo(Index: Integer;
65:    const Value: TStateInfo);
66:  begin
```

LISTING 10.5   Continued

```
67:    List[Index] := Value;
68:  end;
69:
70:  procedure TStateInfoCollection.OnInsert(Index: integer; Value: TObject);
71:  begin
72:    VerifyType(Value);
73:  end;
74:
75:  procedure TStateInfoCollection.OnSet(Index: integer; OldValue:
76:    TObject; NewValue: TObject);
77:  begin
78:    VerifyType(NewValue);
79:  end;
80:
81:  procedure TStateInfoCollection.OnValidate(Value: TObject);
82:  begin
83:    VerifyType(Value);
84:  end;
85:
86:  function TStateInfoCollection.Add(Value: TStateInfo): Integer;
87:  begin
88:    Result := List.Add(Value);
89:  end;
90:
91:  function TStateInfoCollection.IndexOf(Value: TStateInfo): Integer;
92:  begin
93:    Result := List.IndexOf(Value);
94:  end;
95:
96:  procedure TStateInfoCollection.Insert(Index: integer; Value: TStateInfo);
97:  begin
98:    List.Insert(Index, Value);
99:  end;
100:
101: procedure TStateInfoCollection.Remove(Value: TStateInfo);
102: begin
103:   List.Remove(Value);
104: end;
105:
106: function TStateInfoCollection.Contains(Value: TStateInfo): Boolean;
107: begin
108:   result := List.Contains(Value);
109: end;
110:
111: procedure TStateInfoCollection.PrintItems;
112: const
113:   fmt = 'State: {0}, Capital: {1}, Admission: {2}';
114: var
115:   i: Integer;
116:   si: TStateInfo;
117: begin
118:   for i := 0 to Count -1 do
119:   begin
```

LISTING 10.5   Continued

```
120:      si := TStateInfo(List[i]);
121:      System.Console.WriteLine(System.String.Format(fmt, [si.StateName,
122:        si.StateCapital, si.Admission.ToShortDateString()]));
123:    end;
124: end;
125:
126: procedure TStateInfoCollection.VerifyType(Value: TObject);
127: begin
128:    if not (Value is TStateInfo) then
129:      raise ArgumentException.Create('Invalid Type');
130: end;
131:
132: end.
```

▶ Find the code on the CD: \Code\Chapter 10\Ex05\.

This is a unit that will be used in a project to be discussed momentarily. This unit defines two types: the TStateInfo class (lines 9–14) and the TStateInfoCollection class (lines 19–40). As the names imply, TStateInfoCollection is the strongly-typed collection that will store TStateInfo instances.

The steps required to implement this collection are

1. Create an indexed property to retrieve items in the Collection.

2. Override type-checking events OnInsert, OnSet, and OnValidate and add code to raise an exception given an invalid type (a type that is not a TStateInfo class).

3. Implement methods for working with the collection, using the same standard names as IList and ArrayList do.

The StateInfo property (lines 36–37) is the indexed property for TStateInfoCollection. Its getter and setter methods, GetStateInfo() and SetStateInfo(), both utilize the internal list to retrieve and store elements.

As you examine the code, notice that TStateInfoCollection basically exposes methods that internally perform the equivalent functions against the internal IList instance. For example, the TStateInfoCollection.Contains() method simply invokes the same method on List:

```
108:    result := List.Contains(value);
```

Most other methods do a similar function.

Notice that the three type-checking events determine whether the item being manipulated is of the type TStateInfo by passing it to the VerifyType() procedure. When a different type is used, these events raise an appropriate exception.

Finally, the PrintItems() function (lines 111–124) simply loops through the collection and writes its output to the console.

Using the Strongly-Typed Collection

Listing 10.6 illustrates a Delphi application that uses this collection. Note that it is no different than using any of the other collections discussed in this chapter.

LISTING 10.6　Delphi for .NET Program Using `TStateInfoCollection`

```
 1:  program d4dnStateCollDemo;
 2:  {$APPTYPE CONSOLE}
 3:
 4:  uses
 5:    d4dnDevGuide.StateCollection;
 6:
 7:  var
 8:    sicDemo: TStateInfoCollection;
 9:
10:  begin
11:    sicDemo := TStateInfoCollection.Create();
12:    sicDemo.Add(TStateInfo.Create('Alabama',  'Montgomery',
13:      DateTime.Create(1819, 12, 14)));
14:    sicDemo.Add(TStateInfo.Create('Florida',  'Tallahassee',
15:      DateTime.Create(1845, 03, 15)));
16:    sicDemo.PrintItems();
17:    System.Console.ReadLine;
18:  end.
```

▶ Find the code on the CD: \Code\Chapter 10\Ex05\.

Creating a Strongly-Typed Dictionary

As with the Collection, it is likely that you might need a strongly-typed `Dictionary`. In the `HashTable` example presented in this chapter, the data stored could have been any type descending from `System.Object`. The following section illustrates how to create a `Dictionary` that enforces the `TStateInfo` type.

Descending from DictionaryBase

The `System.Collections` namespace defines the `DictionaryBase` class. From this class, you should derive your strongly-typed dictionary classes. Listing 10.7 shows such a class.

LISTING 10.7　Strongly-Typed Dictionary

```
 1:  unit d4dnDevGuide.StateDictionary;
 2:  interface
 3:
 4:  uses
 5:    System.Collections;
 6:
 7:  type
 8:
 9:    // Define a class to store in the dictionary
10:    TStateInfo = class
11:      StateName: String;
12:      StateCapital: String;
```

LISTING 10.7   Continued

```
13:      Admission: DateTime;
14:      constructor Create(AName, ACapital: String; AAddmision: DateTime);
15:    end;
16:
17:    // Define the strongly-typed dictionary
18:    TStateInfoDictionary = class(DictionaryBase)
19:    private
20:      function GetStateInfo(key: String): TStateInfo;
21:      procedure SetStateInfo(key: String; const Value: TStateInfo);
22:      function GetKeys: ICollection;
23:      function GetValues: ICollection;
24:      procedure VerifyType(Value: TObject);
25:    strict protected
26:      // Type checking events
27:      procedure OnInsert(key: TObject; value: TObject); override;
28:      procedure OnSet(Key: TObject; OldValue: TObject;
29:        NewValue: TObject); override;
30:      procedure OnValidate(key: TObject; value: TObject); override;
31:    public
32:      constructor Create;
33:      procedure Add(key: String; value: TStateInfo);
34:      procedure Remove(key: String);
35:      function Contains(key: String): Boolean;
36:
37:      procedure PrintItems;
38:
39:      property StateInfo[key: String]: TStateInfo read GetStateInfo
40:        write SetStateInfo;
41:      property Keys: ICollection read GetKeys;
42:      property Values: ICollection read GetValues;
43:    end;
44:
45:  implementation
46:
47:  { TStateInfo }
48:  constructor TStateInfo.Create(AName, ACapital: String;
49:    AAddmision: DateTime);
50:  begin
51:    inherited Create();
52:    StateName    := AName;
53:    StateCapital := ACapital;
54:    Admission    := AAddmision;
55:  end;
56:
57:  { TStateInfoDictionary }
58:
59:  constructor TStateInfoDictionary.Create;
60:  begin
61:    inherited Create;
62:  end;
63:
64:  procedure TStateInfoDictionary.OnInsert(key: TObject; value: TObject);
65:  begin
```

LISTING 10.7   Continued

```
66:    VerifyType(Value);
67: end;
68:
69: procedure TStateInfoDictionary.OnSet(Key: TObject; OldValue:
70:    TObject; NewValue: TObject);
71: begin
72:    VerifyType(NewValue);
73: end;
74:
75: procedure TStateInfoDictionary.OnValidate(key: TObject; Value: TObject);
76: begin
77:    VerifyType(Value);
78: end;
79:
80: procedure TStateInfoDictionary.Add(key: String; value: TStateInfo);
81: begin
82:    Dictionary.Add(key, value);
83: end;
84:
85: procedure TStateInfoDictionary.Remove(key: String);
86: begin
87:    Dictionary.Remove(key);
88: end;
89:
90: function TStateInfoDictionary.Contains(key: String): Boolean;
91: begin
92:    result := Dictionary.Contains(key);
93: end;
94:
95: procedure TStateInfoDictionary.PrintItems;
96: const
97:    fmt = 'State: {0}, Capital: {1}, Admission: {2}';
98: var
99:    si: TStateInfo;
100:   enum: IDictionaryEnumerator;
101: begin
102:   enum := GetEnumerator;
103:   while enum.MoveNext() do
104:   begin
105:     si := TStateInfo(enum.Value);
106:     writeln(System.String.Format(fmt, [si.StateName, si.StateCapital,
107:       si.Admission.ToShortDateString()]));
108:   end;
109: end;
110:
111: function TStateInfoDictionary.GetStateInfo(key: String): TStateInfo;
112: begin
113:   Result := Dictionary[key] as TStateInfo;
114: end;
115:
116: procedure TStateInfoDictionary.SetStateInfo(key: String;
117:   const Value: TStateInfo);
118: begin
```

LISTING 10.7   Continued

```
119:   Dictionary[key] := Value;
120: end;
121:
122: function TStateInfoDictionary.GetKeys: ICollection;
123: begin
124:   Result := Dictionary.Keys;
125: end;
126:
127: function TStateInfoDictionary.GetValues: ICollection;
128: begin
129:   Result := Dictionary.Values;
130: end;
131:
132: procedure TStateInfoDictionary.VerifyType(Value: TObject);
133: begin
134:   if not (Value is TStateInfo) then
135:     raise ArgumentException.Create('Invalid Type');
136: end;
137:
138: end.
```

▶ Find the code on the CD: \Code\Chapter 10\Ex06\.

You will notice that the code contained here is very similar to that in Listing 10.5. Therefore, I will not go over this again except to say that this implementation internally uses a Dictionary rather than a List as with the strongly-typed collection. Do note that the same validation events and additional methods are implemented here and differ slightly in their parameters because it is working with a Dictionary.

Using the Strongly-Typed Dictionary

Listing 10.8 shows a Delphi program that uses the strongly-typed Dictionary defined previously.

LISTING 10.8   Delphi for .NET Program Using TStateInfoDictionary

```
1:   program d4dnStateDicDemo;
2:   {$APPTYPE CONSOLE}
3:
4:   uses
5:     d4dnDevGuide.StateDictionary in 'd4dnDevGuide.StateDictionary.pas';
6:
7:   var
8:     sicDemo: TStateInfoDictionary;
9:
10: begin
11:   sicDemo := TStateInfoDictionary.Create();
12:   sicDemo.Add('AL', TStateInfo.Create('Alabama',  'Montgomery',
13:     DateTime.Create(1819, 12, 14)));
14:   sicDemo.Add('FL', TStateInfo.Create('Florida',  'Tallahassee',
15:     DateTime.Create(1845, 03, 15)));
16:   sicDemo.PrintItems();
```

LISTING 10.8   Continued

```
17      Console.ReadLine();
18:  end.
```

▶ Find the code on the CD: \Code\Chapter 10\Ex06\.

Again, this code is practically identical to that for using the TStateCollection class and therefore will not be elaborated on.

> **NOTE**
>
> It is not necessary to derive from CollectionBase or DictionaryBase to create derivatives that are strongly typed. You could create your own objects that implement the ICollection, IEnumerable, IList, and IDictionary interfaces. However, these two classes already do this and, therefore, save you the effort.

CHAPTER 11

Working with the String and StringBuilder Classes

IN THIS CHAPTER

- The System.String Type
- The StringBuilder Class
- String Formatting
- Format Specifiers

Chapter 5, "The Delphi Language," deals with the Delphi language from a viewpoint of .NET data types. Strings, although they are a type, have some special characteristics such as formatting, immutability, operating with them, and more. When developing .NET applications, Strings are probably of one type on which you will rely most. These unique String characteristics are discussed in the sections contained in this chapter. This chapter discusses the System.String and the System.Text.StringBuilder classes. This chapter also covers the formatting of text.

The System.String Type

Suffice it to say that the System.String type is likely the most widely used data type. In the Delphi language, the String type maps directly to the WideString. A WideString is a Unicode string meaning that each character is two bytes in width. In fact, the WideString data type is an *alias* for the System.String type in .NET. This mapping of the String/WideString Delphi type to a .NET System.String data type is an implementation detail. The Delphi String type at the language level does not behave identically to System.String. The behavior (or implementation) is the same only if you cast a Delphi String to a System.String. One of these differences is that Delphi strings are initially empty (' ') with a zero length. System.Strings initially reference nil.

CAUTION

When casting a Delphi String to a System.String, you must be careful to handle the case in which the System.String will be nil (when the Delphi String is empty).

For the purpose of discussion, this chapter, when referring to `strings`, is talking about the `System.String` data type.

The CLR defines a `System.String` as being zero indexed. However, the following reveals that the Delphi is doing some voodoo to make the `System.String` behave like a Delphi `String`:

```
var
  ds: String;
  ss: System.String;
begin
  ds := 'ABC';
  ss := 'ABS';
  Console.WriteLine(ds[1]);
  Console.WriteLine(ss[1]);
end;
```

Both `WriteLine()` statements output the character `"A"`. You would have expected the second `WriteLine()` to write `"A"` instead. This is not a defect, but rather by design—probably to maintain backward compatibility with Delphi strings. You can still zero index a `System.String` by using the default indexer

```
Console.WriteLine(SS.Chars[1]);
```

which outputs `"B"` as expected.

String Immutability in .NET

What exactly is meant by strings being immutable? It means that once you instantiate a `String` type, you cannot change its value. This is not saying that the following code will fail:

```
procedure TWinForm.Button1_Click(sender: System.Object; e: System.EventArgs);
var
  s: System.String;
begin
  s := 'Classic Cars';
  s := s.ToUpper;
  s := s.ToLower;
end;
```

It is saying that the preceding code requires two string instances (or memory allocations) even though they both are being referred to by the same variable. Consider the IL code generated for the preceding string assignments:

```
.maxstack 1
.locals (String V_0)
L_0000: ldstr "Classic Cars"
L_0005: stloc.0
L_0006: ldloc.0
L_0007: call String.ToUpper
L_000c: stloc.0
L_000d: ldloc.0
L_000e: call String.ToLower
```

```
L_0013: stloc.0
L_0014: ret
```

Look particularly at the two calls to `String.ToUpper` and `String.ToLower`. The implementation of these two functions ultimately will allocate memory for the strings on which they will operate. This operation is one that actually performs a string allocation. This is equivalent to invoking the `newobj` IL instruction, which creates a type instance. The point being made is that you cannot assign or change the value of a string. The code might appear as though a string variable has been modified. In reality, a second string is being allocated. When s is assigned the result from `ToUpper`, it refers to a new `String` instance in memory. The original, referring to `"Classic Cars"`, is now available for the garbage collector to reclaim.

Operations such as the following show that performing various operations do not change the original string:

```
s := 'Xavier Pacheco';
Console.WriteLine(s.ToUpper);
Console.WriteLine(s);
```

The output would be

```
XAVIER PACHECO
Xavier Pacheco
```

Consider the following statement:

```
s := 'Chmh';
s := s.Insert(4, 'ro').Replace('h', 'a').ToUpper;
```

Figure 11.1 illustrates what's actually in memory.

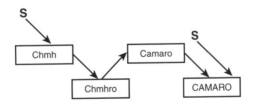

FIGURE 11.1   Memory allocation with String operations.

First, memory is allocated for the string `'Chmh'`. Next, the `Insert()` method causes another memory allocation for the string `'Chmhro'`. The `Replace()` method causes yet another memory allocation to hold the string `'Camaro'`. Finally, one last memory allocation is made to hold the string `'CAMARO'` and the variable s is set to reference that final string. Four memory allocations were made in this operation.

Despite all the memory allocations, the CLR handles `String` management quite efficiently. For the most part, you shouldn't have to worry about the allocations as the garbage collector will take care of them. However, if you are doing a lot of string manipulation—perhaps in a loop where the results would be many allocations—you'll want to use the

StringBuilder class, which is discussed momentarily. To illustrate the efficiency of the CLR, consider the following code:

```
var
  s1, s2: String;
begin
  s1 := 'delphi';
  s2 := 'delphi';
  Console.WriteLine(System.Object.ReferenceEquals(s1, s2));
  Console.ReadLine;
end.
```

The System.ReferenceEquals() function returns True if two variables refer to the same object instance. True is returned because of the way the CLR handles literal strings. This technique is called string interning.

Another benefit of string immutability is that strings are thread safe. Because strings cannot be modified, there are no thread-synchronization issues to deal with.

Now that you understand the nature of .NET Strings, it's time to examine the various string operations.

String Operations

There are numerous operations that you can perform on the String class through its many methods. This section covers some of these operations.

> **NOTE**
>
> The Delphi Runtime Library contains its own string manipulation routines. You might look under the Delphi online help for information on such methods.

Comparing Strings

The easy way to compare strings is to simply use the equality operator as shown here:

```
if s1 = s2 then
  Console.WriteLine('Strings are equal');
```

Alternatively, you can use the String.Compare() method:

```
if (System.String.Compare(s1, s2) = 0) then
  Console.WriteLine('Strings are equal');
```

The return value of the Compare() method, if less than zero, indicates that s1 is less than s2. A value of zero indicates equality. Finally, a value of greater than zero indicates that s1 is greater than s2.

The String.CompareOrdinal() function compares two strings according to the numeric value of each character within the string. This is different from the String.Compare() method, which is based on a language or alphabetic comparison.

> **NOTE**
>
> The language level compare operator (=) calls @WStrCmp in the Borland.Delphi.System unit. This function performs a character-by-character compare in a custom loop. The closest matching .NET string function is System.String.CompareOrdinal(). Your best chance at writing portable code would be to stick with the .NET version.

Consider the following case:

```
s1 := 'delphi';
s2 := 'Delphi';
r1 := System.String.CompareOrdinal(s1, s2);
Console.WriteLine(r1);

r2 := System.String.Compare(s1, s2, False);
Console.WriteLine(r2);
```

The output that you would see here is

```
32
-1
```

The first value indicates that s1 is greater than s2. The second value indicates that s1 is less than s2.

Another interesting case involves string comparisons using different cultures. Consider

```
s1 := 'delphi';
s2 := 'DELPHI';
r1 := System.String.Compare(s1, s2, True, CultureInfo.Create('en-US'));
Console.WriteLine(r1);
r2 := System.String.Compare(s1, s2, True, CultureInfo.Create('tr-TR'));
Console.WriteLine(r2);
```

In this example, the Boolean parameter tells the function to ignore the case of the strings. However, look at the output:

```
0
1
```

In this example, when using the US culture, the strings are the same. However, when using the Turkish culture, they are not. The reason has to do with the letters *I* and *i*. In the English language, without case sensitivity, they are the same. In the Turkish language, they are different as indicated by the comparison. Without getting into the differences in cultures, it is important to understand that when dealing with strings, such idiosyncrasies exist.

Several overloaded versions of the Compare() and CompareOrdingal() methods allow you to specify case honoring, use of culture information, substring comparisons, and so on. You might research these overloaded options under the Microsoft documentation for the String class.

GLOBALIZATION/LOCALIZATION

When designing an application for the worldwide community, it is important to take into account the different way that various languages handle the formatting and presentation of certain elements. Examples of this are character classifications, date and time formatting, numeric, currency and measurement conventions, sorting criteria, and so on. The process of making your application function in many cultures/locales is called globalization. The process of adapting a globalized application to a specific culture/locale is called localization. In the .NET Framework, the System.Globalization namespace contains the classes that handle culture related information. One of these classes is the CultureInfo class, which you see passed to many text formatting routines. It would be a good idea to peruse the many articles on the msdn.microsoft.com Web site about globalization.

String Modification Routines

The String.Concat() method is anther heavily overloaded method. The following code demonstrates the version of the Concat() method that concatenates the string representations of varying objects when an array of object is passed as a parameter.

```
var
  s: System.String;
  i: Integer;
  d: double;
  ObjAry: Array[0..2] of System.Object;
begin
  s := 'X';
  i := 55;
  d := 23.23;

  ObjAry[0] := s;
  ObjAry[1] := System.Object(i);
  ObjAry[2] := System.Object(d);
  Console.WriteLine(System.String.Concat(ObjAry));
end.
```

The output shown here would be "X5523.23" unless you're in Norway; in which case, it reads "X5523,23".

This example shows how to concatenate two strings together:

```
s1 := '1967 ';
s2 := 'Camaro';
Console.WriteLine(System.String.Concat(s1, s2));
```

You might look at the other variations of the Contact() function. Of course, the simplest way to concatenate strings is to use the plus (+) operator. An alternate form of the preceding example would be

```
s1 := '1967 ';
s2 := 'Camaro';
Console.WriteLine(s1 + s2);
```

You've already seen the `String.Insert()` function in use. Basically, you provide a starting position and a String to insert as shown here. Keep in mind that Strings are zero based when using `System.String` functions that take an index parameter.

```
s1 := '1967 Camaro';
s2 := S1.Insert(5, 'Z28 ');
```

This code produces the string, `"1967 Z28 Camaro"`.

You can also use the `String.Remove()` function to remove a specified number of characters from a specified location within a string:

```
s1 := '1967 Z28 Camaro';
s2 := S1.Remove(5, 4);
```

This code produces the string, `"1967 Camaro"`.

The `String.Replace()` method replaces a specified string with another string. For instance, the following code

```
s1 := '1967 Z28 Camaro';
s2 := S1.Replace('Z28', 'SS');
```

produces the string, `"1967 SS Camaro"`.

The `String.Split()` function is handy to use when you need to separate two strings by a delimiter. For instance, when given the name/value pair, it is usually represented as `"Name=Value"`. The following code illustrates how you might use this function:

```
var
  nv: System.String;
  sAry: array of System.String;
begin
  nv := 'Name=Xavier Pacheco';
  sAry := nv.Split(['=']);
end;
```

The `String.Split()` function separates the strings and returns them into a string array.

You can convert a string to all uppercase characters using the `String.ToUpper()` function and, conversely, change all characters to lowercase using the `String.ToLower()` function.

Other String Operations

To determine the length of a `String`, use the `String.Length` property.

To copy a string, simply assign one string to another,

```
s2 := s1;
```

or use the `String.Copy()` function:

```
s2 := System.String.Copy(s1);
```

Note that there is a slight difference between these two operations. Executing the following line after performing the operations reveals the difference:

```
Console.WriteLine(System.Object.ReferenceEquals(s1, s2));
```

Essentially, when using the assignment operator (:=), you are making a reference assignment. That is, both variables s1 and s2 will reference the same memory space holding the string. The `String.Copy()` function creates an additional allocation for the string and copies the contents from the first allocation to the second allocation.

There are three functions for trimming a string—`String.Trim()`, `String.TrimStart()`, and `String.TrimEnd()`. The `Trim()` function removes all occurrences of a set of characters from the beginning and end of a `String`. `TrimStart()` and `TrimEnd()` do the same but only from the beginning and end, respectively. The following code

```
s := '%^ This string has extraneous characters. *)(';
s := s.Trim(['%', '(', ')', ' ', '*', '^']);
```

removes the characters specified in the character array from the initial `String`.

The `String.PadLeft()` and `String.PadRight()` functions left and right align a specified character to a string for a specified length. So, for instance, the code

```
s := 'The String';
Console.WriteLine(s.PadLeft(20, '.'));
```

shows ".........The String".

The StringBuilder Class

Whereas the `String` class represents an immutable string, the `StringBuilder` class represents a mutable string. It is recommended that you use the `StingBuilder` class when you need to manipulate a string often. The `StringBuilder` class is defined in the `System.Text` namespace.

Constructing a `StringBuilder` is done by using one of its many overloaded constructors. The constructors' parameters allow you to specify values for the following four properties:

- `Capacity`—The `Capacity` property specifies the initial size of the character array member contained by the `StringBuilder` class. The default value is `16`. The `StringBuilder` doubles the size of the character array when the existing size is smaller than needed by an operation such as appending. Because such operations impose a performance hit, it is recommended to allocate the size needed if known during the construction of the `StringBuilder`.

- `Length`—Refers to the length of the string in this instance.

- `MaxCapacity`—The `MaxCapacity` property specifies the maximum number of characters that can be contained by the current instance of the `StringBuilder` class. By default, this value is `Int32.MaxValue`. The `StringBuilder.MaxCapacity` property cannot be changed once the `StringBuilder` is created.

- `Chars`—The `Chars` property is the indexer property for the internal character array being maintained by the `StringBuilder`. `Chars` uses zero-based indexing.

StringBuilder Methods

The `StringBuilder` class offers the methods shown in Table 11.1.

TABLE 11.1 StringBuilder Methods

Method	Description
Append()	A heavily overloaded method that appends the string representation of the specified object to the string maintained by the StringBuilder.
AppendFormat()	Similar to the Append() functionality, but uses the provided format specifiers and culture information.
EnsureCapacity()	Guarantees that the character array is at least of the specified capacity.
Equals()	Compares two StringBuilder classes (or objects) that have the same MaxCapacity, Capacity, Length, and character array contents.
Insert()	Inserts the String representation of a specified Object into the position specified.
Remove()	Removes a specified range of characters.
Replace()	Replaces occurrences of a specified character or string with another specified String.
ToString()	Converts the mutable StringBuilder to an immutable String.

StringBuilder Usage

The following code is just a simple example of how to use the StringBuilder class. The various operations change the internal string maintained by the StringBuilder. The final statement converts the contents of the StringBuilder to an immutable String class instance.

```
var
  sb: StringBuilder;
  s: System.String;
begin
  sb := StringBuilder.Create('Xavier');
  sb.AppendFormat('LastName: {0}', 'Pacheco');
  Console.WriteLine(sb);
  sb.Replace('rL', 'r L');
  Console.WriteLine(sb);
  sb.Insert(0, 'FirstName: ');
  Console.WriteLine(sb);
  s := sb.ToString;
  Console.WriteLine(s);

  Console.ReadLine;

end.
```

STRINGBUILDER ON STEROIDS

It might appear that the StringBuilder class is limited in its functionality by looking at the list of methods it supports. It is unknown why Microsoft didn't go to town on making the StringBuilder as functionally complete as possible. Fortunately, Hallvard Vassbotn certainly went to town and built his own StringBuilder. Hallvard's version shows that it is possible to extend the StringBuilder class in Delphi (despite it being sealed) with a goal of making this useful class available for Win32. Hallvard's StringBuilder on steroids was initially written about in *The Delphi Magazine*. The source for this charm can be found on the accompanying CD's directory for this chapter entitled: \HallvardGoesToTown.

String Formatting

The `String` class has a static `Format()` function that you use to format strings similar to the `Format()` function in the Delphi RTL. The type of formatting it uses is called composite formatting. The commonly used version of the overloaded `string.Format()` function takes a format string and values that it applies to the format string. The format string consists of fixed text and indexed placeholders.

The simplest form of `string.Format()` is declared as

```
Format(format: System.String; arg0: System.Object);
```

which would be used as

```
S :=  System.String.Format('You are {0} years old', System.Object(age));
```

with `age` being an integer variable. The following code illustrates the more common use, which takes an array of arguments to fill the placeholders in the format string:

```
const
  fStr = 'Name: {0}, age: {1}, Shoe size: {2}';
...
begin
  age := 23;
  S :=  System.String.Format(fStr, ['Xavier Pacheco', 38, 8.5]);
```

The preceding code produces the string `"Name: Xavier Pacheco, age: 38, Shoe size: 8.5"`.

Let's examine the use of the format string in a bit more detail.

The indexed placeholders each correspond to one of the values in the value array. The format item placeholders take the following syntax:

```
{index[,alignment][:formatString]}
```

The placeholder must begin and end with opening and closing curly braces ({}), respectively. To display curly braces in the string, they must be doubled: {{ and }}.

The index component identifies the corresponding parameter in the parameter list. For example, had the format string shown in the preceding code snippet been written as

```
fStr = 'Name: {2}, age: {0}, Shoe size: {1}';
```

The resulting string when used in the `String.Format()` function would have been `"Name: 8.5, age: Xavier Pacheco, Shoesize: 38"`. You can even specify the same parameter more than once in the format string such as

```
fStr = 'Name: {2}, age: {2}, Shoe size: {2}';
```

The alignment component is an integer value that specifies the field width and either right or left alignment based on its signed value. A positive value indicates right alignment, whereas a negative value indicates left alignment. Consider the following code:

```
Console.WriteLine(System.String.Format('{0,15} \ {1,15}',
  ['Blue', 'Crayon']));
```

```
Console.WriteLine(System.String.Format('{0,15} \ {1,15}',
   ['Yellow', 'Chalk']));
```

This produces the output of

```
        Blue \        Crayon
      Yellow \         Chalk
```

Notice how the strings are right aligned. If the values were negative, the output would be

```
Blue          \ Crayon
Yellow        \ Chalk
```

If the length of the string value exceeds the alignment value, the alignment value is ignored.

The optional formatstring can be a standard or custom format specifier.

Format Specifiers

Format specifiers are strings that specify how to apply formatting to a base type. They are typically used with formatting functions such as String.Format() or the ToString() method. Format specifiers can be used alone or with a format provider, which is discussed later. The .NET Framework provides a set of standard format specifiers for numeric, date, time, and enumeration types. When the standard format specifiers do not meet the need, you can apply custom format specifiers to the formatting functions.

Numeric Format Specifiers

Standard numeric format specifiers are used to format numeric types to string in predefined patterns. The format specifier takes the following form:

Ann

Where A is an alphabetic format specifier and nn is an option precision specifier represented as an integer. The precision specifier, when supplied, might range from 0–99 and typically specifies the number of significant digits to the right of the decimal.

Table 11.2 shows the various numeric format specifiers that can be used with formatting functions. Details about these format specifiers can be found in the Microsoft online documentation.

TABLE 11.2 Numeric Format Specifiers

Format Specifier	Name
C or c	Currency
D or d	Decimal
E or e	Scientific (exponential)
F or f	Fixed-point
G or g	General
N or n	Number
P or p	Percent
R or r	Round-trip
X or x	Hexadecimal

Listing 11.1 illustrates the usage of numeric specifiers.

LISTING 11.1   Use of Numeric Format Specifiers

```
1:    program NumFmtSpec;
2:
3:    {$APPTYPE CONSOLE}
4:
5:    var
6:      MyCurrency: Currency;
7:      MyDecimal: System.Int32;
8:      MyDouble:   System.Double;
9:      MyPercent:   System.Double;
10:
11:   begin
12:     MyCurrency := 23.12;
13:     MyDecimal   := 8654;
14:     MyDouble    := 87;
15:     MyPercent   := 0.25;
16:
17:     Console.Writeline('Currency: {0:C2}', MyCurrency);
18:     Console.Writeline('Decimal: {0:D4}',      System.Object(MyDecimal));
19:     Console.Writeline('Scientific: {0:E10}', System.Object(MyDouble));
20:     Console.Writeline('Fixed-point: {0:F3}', System.Object(MyDouble));
21:     Console.Writeline('General: {0:G3}', System.Object(MyDouble));
22:     Console.Writeline('Number: {0:N3}',   System.Object(MyDouble));
23:     Console.Writeline('Percent: {0:P0}', System.Object(MyPercent));
24:     Console.Writeline('Round-trip: {0:R}', System.Object(MyDouble));
25:     Console.Writeline('Hexadecimal: {0:X}', System.Object(MyDecimal));
26:
27:     Console.ReadLine;
28:   end.
```

▶ **Find the code on the CD:** \Code\Chapter 11\Ex01.

Lines 12–15 initialize the variables used in the program. Lines 17–25 display these variables with different formatting. The output of this program is

```
Currency: $23.12
Decimal: 8654
Scientific: 8.7000000000E+001
Fixed-point: 87.000
General: 87
Number: 87.000
Percent: 25 %
Round-trip: 87
Hexadecimal: 21CE
```

When the standard formatting specifiers do not meet the need for numeric formatting, you can use the custom formatting strings. Table 11.3 shows the list of custom numeric format specifiers.

TABLE 11.3   Custom Numeric Format Specifiers

Custom Format Specifier	Name
0	Zero placeholder.
#	Digit placeholder.
.	Decimal point.
,	Thousand separator and number scaling.
%	Percent placeholder.
E0, E+0, E-0, e0, e+0, e-0	Scientific notation.
'AAA', "AAA"	Literal string.
;	Section separator.
Other characters	All other characters are used literally.

Listing 11.2 shows how some of these custom format specifiers can be used. For detailed information on these format strings, you can refer to the Microsoft online help.

LISTING 11.2   Example of Custom Numeric Format Specifiers

```
1:    program CustNumFmtSpec;
2:
3:    {$APPTYPE CONSOLE}
4:
5:    var
6:      MyDecimal: System.Int32;
7:      MyDouble:  System.Double;
8:      MyPercent:  System.Double;
9:
10:   begin
11:     MyDouble  := 123456.78;
12:     MyDecimal := 12;
13:     MyPercent := 0.25;
14:
15:     Console.Writeline('Format {{A:#####}}: {0:#####}',
16:       System.Object(MyDouble));
17:     Console.Writeline('Format {{A:00000}}: {0:00000}',
18:       System.Object(MyDouble));
19:     Console.Writeline('Format {{A:###-##-####}}: {0:###-##-####}',
20:       System.Object(MyDouble));
21:     Console.Writeline('Scientific: {0:E10}', System.Object(MyDouble));
22:     Console.Writeline('Fixed-point: {0:F3}', System.Object(MyDouble));
23:     Console.Writeline('General: {0:G3}', System.Object(MyDouble));
24:     Console.Writeline('Number: {0:N3}',  System.Object(MyDouble));
25:     Console.Writeline('Percent: {0:P0}', System.Object(MyPercent));
26:     Console.Writeline('Round-trip: {0:R}', System.Object(MyDouble));
27:     Console.Writeline('Hexadecimal: {0:X}', System.Object(MyDecimal));
28:     Console.ReadLine;
29:   end.
```

▶ Find the code on the CD: \Code\Chapter 11\Ex02.

Lines 6–8 initialize the variables used by the program. Lines 15–28 use these values in demonstrating different ways of formatting their display.

Date and Time Format Specifiers

Standard date and time format specifiers are used to format date and time types to string in predefined patterns. The format specifier is a single character.

Table 11.4 shows the various date/time format specifiers that can be used with formatting functions. Details about these format specifiers can be found in the Microsoft online documentation.

TABLE 11.4   Date/Time Format Specifiers

Format Specifier	Name	Description
d	Short date pattern	Displays pattern according to `DateTimeFormatInfo.ShortDatePattern`.
D	Long date pattern	Displays pattern according to `DateTimeFormatInfo.LongDatePattern`.
t	Short time pattern	Displays pattern according to `DateTimeFormatInfo.ShortTimePattern`.
T	Long time pattern	Displays pattern according to `DateTimeFormatInfo.LongTimePattern`.
f	Full date/time pattern (short time)	Displays a combination of long date and short time patterns.
F	Full date/time pattern (long time)	Displays pattern according to `DateTimeFormatInfo.FullDateTimePattern`.
g	General date/time pattern (short time)	Displays a combination of short date and short time patterns.
G	General date/time pattern (long time)	Displays a combination of short date and long time patterns.
M or m	Month day pattern	Displays pattern according to `DateTimeFormatInfo.MonthDayPattern`.
R or r	RFC1123 pattern	Displays pattern according to `DateTimeFormatInfo.RFC1123Pattern`.
s	Sortable date/time pattern (ISO 8601)	Displays pattern according to `DateTimeFormatInfo.SortableDateTimePattern`.
u	Universal sortable date/time pattern	Displays pattern according to `DateTimeFormatInfo.UniversalSortableDateTimePattern`.
U	Universal sortable date/time pattern	Displays pattern according to `DateTimeFormatInfo.FullDateTimePattern`.
Y or y	Year month pattern	Displays pattern according to `DateTimeFormatInfo.YearMonthPattern`.

The code in Listing 11.3 shows some examples of using the date/time format specifiers.

LISTING 11.3   Use of Date/Time Format Specifiers

```
1:   var
2:     MyDateTime:  System.DateTime;
3:     ci: CultureInfo;
4:     ccName: String;
5:
6:   begin
7:     MyDateTime := System.DateTime.Now;
8:     ccName := CultureInfo.CurrentCulture.Name;
9:     ci := CultureInfo.Create('cs-CZ');
10:
11:    Console.WriteLine('d (cs-CZ): '+MyDateTime.ToString('d', ci));
12:    Console.WriteLine(System.String.Format('d ({0}): {1}', [ccName,
13:      MyDateTime.ToString('d')]));
```

LISTING 11.3   Continued

```
14:   Console.WriteLine(System.String.Format('D ({0}): {1}', [ccName,
15:     MyDateTime.ToString('D')]));
16:   Console.WriteLine(System.String.Format('t ({0}): {1}', [ccName,
17:     MyDateTime.ToString('t')]));
18:   Console.WriteLine('t (cs-CZ): '+MyDateTime.ToString('t', ci));
19:   Console.WriteLine(System.String.Format('T ({0}): {1}', [ccName,
20:     MyDateTime.ToString('T')]));
21:   Console.WriteLine('T (cs-CZ): '+MyDateTime.ToString('T'), ci);
22:   Console.WriteLine(System.String.Format('f ({0}): {1}', [ccName,
23:     MyDateTime.ToString('f')]));
24:   Console.WriteLine('f (cs-CZ): '+MyDateTime.ToString('f', ci));
25:   Console.WriteLine(System.String.Format('g ({0}): {1}', [ccName,
26:     MyDateTime.ToString('g')]));
27:   Console.WriteLine(System.String.Format('G ({0}): {1}', [ccName,
28:     MyDateTime.ToString('G')]));
29:   Console.WriteLine(System.String.Format('m ({0}): {1}', [ccName,
30:     MyDateTime.ToString('m')]));
31:   Console.WriteLine(System.String.Format('r ({0}): {1}', [ccName,
32:     MyDateTime.ToString('r')]));
33:   Console.WriteLine(System.String.Format('s ({0}): {1}', [ccName,
34:     MyDateTime.ToString('s')]));
35:   Console.WriteLine(System.String.Format('u ({0}): {1}', [ccName,
36:     MyDateTime.ToString('u')]));
37:   Console.WriteLine(System.String.Format('U ({0}): {1}', [ccName,
38:     MyDateTime.ToString('U')]));
39:   Console.WriteLine('U (cs-CZ): '+MyDateTime.ToString('U', ci));
40:   Console.WriteLine(System.String.Format('y ({0}): {1}', [ccName,
41:     MyDateTime.ToString('y')]));
42:   Console.ReadLine;
43: end.
```

▶ Find the code on the CD: \Code\Chapter 11\Ex03.

The output produced by this application is shown here:

```
d (cs-CZ): 4.1.2004
d (en-US): 1/4/2004
D (en-US): Sunday, January 04, 2004
t (en-US): 10:13 PM
t (cs-CZ): 22:13
T (en-US): 10:13:29 PM
T (cs-CZ): 10:13:29 PM
f (en-US): Sunday, January 04, 2004 10:13 PM
f (cs-CZ): 4. ledna 2004 22:13
g (en-US): 1/4/2004 10:13 PM
G (en-US): 1/4/2004 10:13:29 PM
m (en-US): January 04
r (en-US): Sun, 04 Jan 2004 22:13:29 GMT
s (en-US): 2004-01-04T22:13:29
u (en-US): 2004-01-04 22:13:29Z
U (en-US): Monday, January 05, 2004 5:13:29 AM
U (cs-CZ): 5. ledna 2004 5:13:29
y (en-US): January, 2004
```

> **NOTE**
>
> The output displayed here will vary depending on the current locale.

In this example, I display the date according to the locale in which the program is executed. Line 8 retrieves the name of the current culture. To make it more interesting, I used the CultureInfo for the Czech Republic so that you can see how using different cultures might and most likely will result in different formatting. This was done wherever you see cs-cz as the name of the culture in the displayed output, such as in lines 11 and 21.

Sometimes the standard date/time formatting specifiers do not suit the need—at which point, you can use custom date/time format specifiers. Table 11.5 shows the various custom date/time format specifiers.

TABLE 11.5   Custom Date/Time Format Specifiers

Format Specifier	Description
d	Current day of the month displayed without leading zeros (1–31).
dd	Current day of the month displayed with leading zeros (01–31).
ddd	Abbreviated day of the month.
dddd	Full name of the day of the month.
f-fffff	Fractions of seconds displayed with the number of digits indicated by the number of f specifiers.
g, gg, ggg, ...	Displays the era (AD).
h	Displays the hour (1–12) for both a.m. and p.m. without leading zeros.
hh	Displays the hour (01–12) for both a.m. and p.m. with leading zeros for single digit hours.
H	Displays the hour in the 24-hour clock format (0–23) without leading zeros.
HH	Displays the hour in the 24-hour clock format (00–23) with leading zeros for single digit hours.
m	Displays the minute in the range 0–59 without leading zeros.
mm	Displays the minute in the range 00–59 with leading zeros for single digit minutes.
M	Displays the month (1–12) without leading zeros.
MM	Displays the month (01–12) with leading zeros for single digit months.
MMM	Displays the abbreviated month name.
MMMM	Displays the full month name.
s	Displays the seconds in the range 0–59 without leading zeros.
ss	Displays the seconds in the range 00–59 with leading zeros for single digit seconds.
t	Displays the first character of the a.m., p.m. designation.
tt	Displays both characters of the a.m., p.m. designation.
y	Displays the year as a maximum two-digit number. If a single digit, it is displayed as a single digit.
yy	Displays the year as a maximum two-digit number. If a single digit, it has a leading zero (03).
yyyy	Displays the full year including the century.
z	Displays the time zone offset in whole hours only without leading zeros if a single digit.
zz	Displays the time zone offset in whole hours only with leading zeros if a single digit.

TABLE 11.5   Continued

Format Specifier	Description
zzz	Displays the time zone offset in hours and minutes.
:	Time separator.
/	Date separator.

The following code illustrates using custom date/time specifiers:

```
var
  MyDateTime:    System.DateTime;
begin
  MyDateTime := System.DateTime.Now;
  Console.WriteLine('ddd: '+MyDateTime.ToString('ddd'));
  Console.WriteLine('yyyy: '+MyDateTime.ToString('yyyy'));
  Console.WriteLine('zz: '+MyDateTime.ToString('zz'));
  Console.WriteLine('ggg: '+MyDateTime.ToString('ggg'));
  Console.ReadLine;
end.
```

▶ Find the code on the CD: \Code\Chapter 11\Ex04.

This code will produce the following output, which might vary depending on the current locale:

```
ddd: Sun
yyyy: 2004
zz: -07
ggg: A.D.
```

Enumeration Format Specifiers

When dealing with Enum types, there are four format specifiers that you can use, as shown in Table 11.6.

TABLE 11.6   Enum Format Specifiers

Format String	Description
G or g	Displays the enumeration as a string value. If not possible, displays the integer value. If the Flags attribute is set, the enumeration values are concatenated.
F or f	Displays the enumeration as a string value. If not possible, displays the integer value. Displays a summation of the values if possible with string values being concatenated and separated by a comma.
D or d	Displays the enumeration as an Integer value.
X or x	Displays the enumeration as a hexadecimal value.

Given an enumeration defined as

```
type
  [Flags]
  TMyColor = (Red=0, Green=1, Blue=2, Black=4, White=8, Orange=16);
```

The following code illustrates the use of each of the enumeration format specifiers:

```
MyColor := TMyColor.Green or  TMyColor.Black;
Console.WriteLine(Enum(MyColor).ToString('G'));
Console.WriteLine(Enum(MyColor).ToString('F'));
Console.WriteLine(Enum(MyColor).ToString('D'));
Console.WriteLine(Enum(MyColor).ToString('X'));
```

▶ **Find the code on the CD:** \Code\Chapter 11\Ex05.

This code would produce the following output:

```
Green, Black
Green, Black
5
05
```

> **NOTE**
>
> In the preceding example, you would expect to be able to declare the TMyColor enumeration as
> TMyColor = (Red, Green, Blue, Black, White, Orange);
>
> However, doing so reveals a bug in the compiler. Basically, the compiler ignores the [Flags]
> attribute and assigns sequential numeric values to the enums (0, 1, 2, 3, 4, 5). The compiler
> should use bit-flag values (0, 1, 2, 4, 8, 16). By hard-coding the bit-flag values for each enum
> value as illustrated previously, we can work around this problem and get the expected results.

CHAPTER 12

File and Streaming Operations

IN THIS CHAPTER

- System.IO Namespace Classes
- Working with the Directory System
- Working with Files
- Streams
- Asynchronous Stream Access
- Monitoring Directory Activity
- Serialization

Invariably, at some point all developers have to work with the file system. The System.IO namespace provides the various classes for reading and writing files. It also provides the streaming classes and classes for working with the Windows directory system. This chapter covers the classes defined in the System.IO namespace that deal with working with files and streams.

System.IO Namespace Classes

Several classes in the System.IO namespace provide the ability to perform both asynchronous and synchronous IO. The directory and file-related classes deal with the directories and files as they exist on disk. Streams deal with reading and writing data to other mediums (including files). For instance, a stream can be a file, memory, or a network share. Table 12.1 lists the various classes for dealing with directories and files.

TABLE 12.1 Directory and File Classes from System.IO

Class	Purpose
Directory	Provides static methods for performing directory operations such as copying, moving, renaming, creating, and deleting. Methods in the Directory class perform a security check. Therefore, if you intend to perform more than one operation, use the DirectoryInfo class instead.
DirectoryInfo	Provides instance methods for performing directory operations such as copying, moving, renaming, creating, and deleting. These methods do not perform a security check. Therefore, this is the optimal class to use if you are performing numerous operations.

TABLE 12.1   Continued

Class	Purpose
File	Provides static methods for file operations such as copying, moving, deleting, opening, and closing. These methods perform a security check; therefore, if you intend to perform numerous operations, use the `FileInfo` class.
FileInfo	Provides instance methods for file operations such as copying, moving, deleting, opening, and closing. These methods do not perform a security check; therefore, this is the optimal class to use if you are performing numerous operations.
FileSystemInfo	Base class for the `DirectoryInfo` and `FileInfo` classes.
Path	Enables for cross-platform processing of directory strings.

Table 12.2 lists the various classes in `System.IO` that deal with streaming operations.

TABLE 12.2   Stream Classes in System.IO

Class	Purpose
BufferedStream	Adds buffering to other streams to improve reading and writing performance of the stream. A `BufferedStream` caches data via memory to reduce operating system calls.
MemoryStream	Provides a store for streaming data to memory.
NetworkStream	Provides the ability to stream over a network connection. The `NetworkStream` is actually contained in the `System.Net.Sockets` namespace.
FileStream	Provides the ability to read/write data from/to files randomly through a `Seek()` method. `FileStream` can be used both asynchronously and synchronously.
BinaryReader	Provides the ability to read primitive data from a stream.
BinaryWriter	Provides the ability to write primitive data to a stream.
StringReader	Reads characters from strings.
StringWriter	Writes characters to strings.
StreamReader	Provides the ability to read characters from a stream using a specific encoding for the byte/character conversion.
StreamWriter	Provides the ability to write characters to a stream using encoding for the character/byte conversion.
TextReader	Base class for the `StringReader` and `StreamReader` classes.
TextWriter	Base class for the `StringWriter` and `StreamWriter` classes.
Stream	`Stream` is the abstract base class for all other `Stream` classes. This is the type to use as a parameter when you want to accept a `Stream` object.

The following sections illustrate the use of some of the classes listed in Tables 12.1 and 12.2.

Working with the Directory System

To work with directories, you use the `Directory` or `DirectoryInfo` classes. The `Directory` class provides static methods and is convenient in that you do not have to create an instance of the class to use it. However, each call invokes a security check; therefore, it might be inefficient. In this case, you would use the `DirectoryInfo` class. These classes provide the methods to manipulate (create, delete, move, copy) directories and to enumerate through the directory hierarchies.

Creating and Deleting Directories

The following code shows how to create a directory using the `DirectoryInfo` class:

```
dirInfo := DirectoryInfo.Create('c:\ddgtemp');
if not dirInfo.Exists then
  dirInfo.&Create;
```

First, an instance of `DirectoryInfo` is created and assigned to the variable `dirInfo`. By passing a valid path to the `Create()` constructor, you are associating that directory with the `DirectoryInfo` object; however, you are not creating the directory. To actually create the directory, you must call the `Create()` method. Also, note the usage of the `DirectoryInfo.Exists()` method, which checks for the existence of the directory with which it is associated.

> **NOTE**
>
> When the Delphi compiler sees names of methods and types such as Create(), type, begin, and so on, it assumes that these refer to the Delphi language constructs and not .NET constructs. You can turn off this behavior by prefixing an ampersand character (&) in front of the name.

Alternatively, you can use the `CreateDirectory()` method of the `Directory` class as shown here:

```
if not Directory.Exists('c:\ddgtemp') then
  dirInfo := Directory.CreateDirectory('c:\ddgtemp')
else
  dirInfo := DirectoryInfo.Create('c:\ddgtemp');
```

You'll also notice that the `Directory.Exists()` method takes the path parameter. Because `Directory` is providing static methods, you must pass information as parameters to those methods.

To delete a directory, you can call the `Directory.Delete()` method, which takes the directory path and a `Boolean` value indicating whether to delete subdirectories. If the recursive delete parameter is `false`, an exception is raised if subdirectories or files exist within the directory you are attempting to delete. The following code shows what this call would look like:

```
Directory.Delete('c:\ddgtemp', True); // remove subdirectories and files
```

Alternatively, you can call the `Delete()` method of the `DirectoryInfo` class, which only requires the recursive indicator:

```
dirInfo.Delete(True);
```

▶ Find the code on the CD: \Code\Chapter 12\Ex01\.

Moving and Copying Directories

Occasionally, you'll need to copy and/or move directories. The `Directory` and `DirectoryInfo` classes contain methods to move but not copy directories. This section illustrates how to use the built-in `Move()` method, as well as a technique for copying directories.

Moving a directory is a simple one-line statement:

```
Directory.Move('c:\source', 'c:\target');
```

The Move() method takes two parameters—a source and a target directory. Copying a directory takes a bit more work. Without having a built-in method for this, you must roll your own procedure. Listing 12.1 illustrates one way you can accomplish this.

LISTING 12.1   A CopyDirectory() Procedure

```
1:   procedure CopyDirectory(SourceDir, TargetDir: String);
2:   var
3:     FilesToCopy: array of String;
4:     i: integer;
5:     fa: FileAttributes;
6:     srcFile: String;
7:     tgtFile: String;
8:   begin
9:     if (SourceDir = '') or (TargetDir = '') then
10:      Exit;
11:
12:     // fix up directory separator char
13:     if SourceDir[SourceDir.Length-1] <> Path.DirectorySeparatorChar then
14:       SourceDir := SourceDir + Path.DirectorySeparatorChar;
15:
16:     if TargetDir[TargetDir.Length-1] <> Path.DirectorySeparatorChar then
17:       TargetDir := TargetDir + Path.DirectorySeparatorChar;
18:
19:   { Alternatively, you can use
20:
21:     SourceDir := SysUtils.IncludeTrailingPathDelimiter(SourceDir);
22:     TargetDir := SysUtils.IncludeTrailingPathDelimiter(TargetDir);
23:   }
24:     if Directory.Exists(SourceDir) and not
25:       SameFileName(SourceDir, TargetDir) then
26:     begin
27:       FilesToCopy := Directory.GetFileSystemEntries(SourceDir);
28:       for i := Low(FilesToCopy) to High(FilesToCopy) do
29:       begin
30:         srcFile := FilesToCopy[i];
31:
32:         fa := System.IO.File.GetAttributes(srcFile);
33:         if (fa and FileAttributes.Directory) = FileAttributes.Directory then
34:         begin
35:           tgtFile := TargetDir+Path.GetFileName(srcFile);
36:           if not Directory.Exists(tgtFile) then
37:             Directory.CreateDirectory(tgtFile);
38:           // Since it's a directory, recurse it.
39:           CopyDirectory(srcFile, tgtFile);
40:         end else // otherwise, copy the file.
41:           System.IO.File.Copy(srcFile, tgtFile, True)
42:       end;
43:     end;
44:   end;
```

▶ Find the code on the CD: \Code\Chapter 12\Ex01\.

The idea behind this code is to iterate through the source directory and subdirectories and to create the matching directory and subdirectories at the target location. The goal is also to copy nondirectory files in the process. This recursive function accomplishes this. It also illustrates some additional methods from System.IO classes.

The function first ensures that both the source and target directory paths end with the directory separator char. This occurs in lines 13–17 by appending the character returned from Path.DirectorySeparatorChar property. Using this property ensures that you will retrieve the platform specific character, which happens to be a slash (\) in Windows.

> **TIP**
>
> Note that you can also use the IncludeTrailingPathDelimiter() function from the SysUtils unit as well.

The remainder of the function iterates through all the files in the source directory, having retrieved a list of these files through the Directory.GetFileSystemEntries() method (line 27). This method returns the list of all filenames, including directories within a specified directory. As the code iterates through the array, it checks each file to determine if it is a directory by examining its FileAttribute (line 32–33). A FileAttribute is an enumeration that can be a combination of one or more of the values listed in Table 12.3.

TABLE 12.3   FileAttributes Enumeration Values

Value	Description
Archived	File's archived status for backup or removal.
Compressed	File is compressed.
Device	Unused/Reserved
Directory	File is a directory.
Encrypted	Determines that the file is encrypted (if referring to a file) or that newly created files in this directory will be encrypted (if referring to a directory).
Hidden	File is hidden. It will not be included in a normal directory listing.
Normal	File is normal; no other attributes may be set.
NotContentIndexed	File may not be indexed by the context indexing service of the operating system.
Offline	File is offline, and data is not immediately available.
ReadOnly	File is read-only.
ReparsePoint	File contains a reparse point, a user-defined block of data associated with another file or directory.
SparseFile	File is a sparse file containing mostly zeros.
System	File is an operating system file, or it is used by the operating system exclusively.
Temporary	File is a temporary file.

If the file is a directory, the directory is created in the target location, and the source directory is recursively walked. This process continues until the file is not a directory—in which case, it is copied to the target location using the File.Copy() method.

Examining Directory Information

The DirectoryInfo class inherits from FileSystemInfo various properties that contain information about the directory. These properties are listed in Table 12.4.

TABLE 12.4   FileSystemInfo Properties

Property	Description
Attributes	Refers to the FileAttribute enumeration (See Table 12.1).
CreationTime	Time the file was created.
CreationTimeUtc	Time the file was created in Coordinated Universal Time (UTC).
Extension	File extension.
Exists	Specifies whether the file exists.
FullName	Full pathname of the file or directory.
LastAccessTime	Last time that the file or directory was accessed.
LastAccessTimeUtc	Last time that the file or directory was accessed in UTC time.
LastWriteTime	Last time the file or directory was written to.
LastWriteTimeUtc	Last time the file or directory was written to in UTC time.
Name	Returns the name of the file if a file. Returns the last name in a directory hierarchy (if it exists and is a directory).

Listing 12.2 presents an example procedure that shows some of this information in a ListBox.

LISTING 12.2   Examining Directory Information

```
 1:    procedure TWinForm.btnGetDirInfo_Click(sender: System.Object;
 2:      e: System.EventArgs);
 3:    begin
 4:      ListBox1.Items.Add(dirInfo.FullName);
 5:      ListBox1.Items.Add(dirInfo.Name);
 6:      ListBox1.Items.Add(System.String.Format('Creation time: {0}',
 7:        [dirInfo.CreationTime.ToString]));
 8:      ListBox1.Items.Add(System.String.Format('Last Accessed: {0}',
 9:        [dirInfo.LastAccessTime.ToString]));
10:      ListBox1.Items.Add(System.String.Format('Last Written to: {0}',
11:        [dirInfo.LastWriteTime.ToString]));
12:      ListBox1.Items.Add('Attributes: ');
13:      ListBox1.Items.Add('  '+Enum(dirInfo.Attributes).ToString);
14:    end;
```

▶ Find the code on the CD: \Code\Chapter 12\Ex02\.

There's not much to explain here other than to point out the requirement to typecast the dirInfo.Attributes property so that its ToString() method can be invoked (line 13).

Working with Files

Like the Directory and DirectoryInfo classes, File and FileInfo classes exist in the System.IO namespace that provide the functionality for manipulating files. Because the directory and file classes descend from the same base class, they contain some of the same properties, and using them is almost identical.

Creating and Deleting Files

There are more than a few ways to create a file. One is to use the `File.CreateText()` method to create a text file. This method returns a `StreamWriter` that allows you to write to the file. This technique is illustrated here:

```
var
  sw: StreamWriter;
begin
  if not System.IO.File.Exists('c:\deleteme.txt') then
  begin
    sw := System.IO.File.CreateText('c:\deleteme.txt');
    try
      sw.Write('hello world');
    finally
      sw.Close;
    end;
  end;
end;
```

The `StreamWriter` class is a descendant of the `TextWriter` class and is used to write a series of characters to a stream. I talk more about streams later in this chapter. For now, just consider that this code created the file specified and wrote to it a stream of characters.

To delete a file, simply use the `File.Delete()` method:

```
if System.IO.File.Exists('c:\deleteme.txt') then
  System.IO.File.Delete('c:\deleteme.txt');
```

▶ Find the code on the CD: \Code\Chapter 12\Ex03\.

Moving and Copying Files

To move a file to a different location, use the `File.Move()` method:

```
if System.IO.File.Exists('c:\deleteme.txt') then
  System.IO.File.Move('c:\deleteme.txt', 'c:\deleteme2.txt');
```

This method takes two parameters—a source file and a target file. To copy a file is just as simple.

```
if System.IO.File.Exists('c:\deleteme.txt') then
  System.IO.File.Copy('c:\deleteme.txt', 'c:\copy_deleteme.txt');
```

Examining File Information

Examining a file's information is identical to examining directory information. Listing 12.3 illustrates this.

LISTING 12.3   Examining File Information

```
1:   if OpenFileDialog1.ShowDialog = System.Windows.Forms.DialogResult.Ok then
2:   begin
3:     fi := FileInfo.Create(OpenFileDialog1.FileName);
4:     TextBox1.Clear;
```

LISTING 12.3   Continued

```
5:     TextBox1.AppendText(OpenFileDialog1.FileName);
6:     TextBox1.AppendText(crlf+'Created: '+fi.CreationTime.ToString);
7:     TextBox1.AppendText(crlf+'Last Accessed: '+fi.LastAccessTime.ToString);
8:     TextBox1.AppendText(crlf+'Last Written: '+fi.LastWriteTime.ToString);
9:     TextBox1.AppendText(crlf+'Length: '+fi.Length.ToString);
10:    TextBox1.AppendText(crlf+'Extension: '+fi.Extension);
11:    TextBox1.AppendText(crlf+'Attributes: '+Enum(fi.Attributes).ToString);
12:  end;
```

▶ Find the code on the CD: \Code\Chapter 12\Ex03\.

Line 3 retrieves the `FileInfo` class instance for the filename passed to the `FileInfo` constructor. The remaining code (lines 5–11) adds the various property values to a `TextBox`. To manipulate a file's contents, you use the stream objects from `System.IO`, which the next section discusses.

Streams

When using streams, it is best to think of the different types of streams in an abstract sense. They are all a stream or a block of data that you can write to or read from. The medium that holds this data differentiates the different stream classes. Therefore, a `FileStream` hosts a block of data in a file; a `MemoryStream` hosts a block of data in memory. The methods by which you read from and write to a stream are the same. The following examples will use a `FileStream`; however, using a `MemoryStream` or `NetworkStream` will be, for the most part, identical.

Whereas the streaming classes encapsulate the block of data, one requires readers and writers to read from a stream and to write to a stream, respectively. For a text-based stream, these are the `StreamReader` and `StreamWriter` classes. For binary data, these are the `BinaryReader` and `BinaryWriter` classes. Their usage will be illustrated in the following sections.

Working with Text File Streams

Writing to a text stream, a `FileStream` specifically, requires a `FileStream` object and a `StreamWriter` object. Listing 12.4 illustrates this technique.

LISTING 12.4   Creating and Writing Text to a `FileStream`

```
1:   var
2:     MyFileStream: FileStream;
3:     MyStreamWriter: StreamWriter;
4:   begin
5:     // Create and write the file
6:     MyFileStream := FileStream.Create('c:\ddgdemo.txt',
7:       FileMode.OpenOrCreate, FileAccess.Write);
8:     try
9:       MyStreamWriter := StreamWriter.Create(MyFilestream);
10:      try
11:        MyStreamWriter.BaseStream.Seek(0, SeekOrigin.End);
```

LISTING 12.4   Continued

```
12:        MyStreamWriter.WriteLine('Hello Delphi for .NET');
13:        MyStreamWriter.WriteLine('Delphi for .NET Developer's Guide');
14:     finally
15:        MyStreamWriter.Close;
16:     end;
17:     finally
18:        MyFileStream.Close;
19:     end;
20:  end.
```

► Find the code on the CD: \Code\Chapter 12\Ex04\.

Lines 6–7 illustrate the use of the FileStream.Create() constructor. This constructor is overloaded, and the version used here takes a path, as well as FileMode and FileAccess parameters.

> **NOTE**
>
> Listing 12.4 shows how to append to a file by the FileMode.OpenOrCreate flag. This is for illustration only. The easiest way to append to a file is to use the FileMode.Append attribute instead of FileMode.OpenOrCreate.

FileMode instructs the operating system how the file should be opened. Table 12.5 lists the various FileMode values.

TABLE 12.5   FileMode Values

Value	Description
Append	Opens or creates a file and seeks to the end of the file. Attempts to read result in an exception. Must be used in conjunction with FileAccess.Write. Requires FileIOPermissionAccess.Append.
Create	Creates a new file, overwriting an existing file. Requires FileIOPermissionAccess.Write and FileIOPermissionAccess.Append.
CreateNew	Creates a new file. If the file already exists, raises an exception. This requires FileIOPermissionAccess.Write.
Open	Opens an existing file. FileMode.Access must enable the opening of this file. Raises an exception if file does not exist. Requires FileIOPermissionAccess indicated by the FileMode parameter.
OpenOrCreate	Opens the file if it exists. Creates a new file if it does not exist. Requires FileIOPermissionAccess indicated by the FileMode parameter.
Truncate	Opens an existing file and sets its size to zero. Truncate requires FileIOPermissionAccess.Write.

> **NOTE**
>
> The FileIOPermissionAccess enumeration is not part of the System.IO namespace but rather part of the System.Security.Permissions. This namespace defines classes that have to do with controlling access to system operations and resources. Such permissions are defined using the Code Access Security (CAS) system. Administrators can grant permissions to code and users using the .NET Configuration Tool. For more information on CAS, visit www.msdn.Microsoft.com and search on "Code Access Security."

12

The other parameter passed to the `FileStream.Create()` constructor was `FileAccess`, which determines the type of access allowed. Table 12.6 lists the various values that may be passed.

TABLE 12.6   FileAccess Values

Value	Description
Read	Data can be read from the file.
ReadWrite	File can be read from and written to.
Write	File can be written to.

The file stream can then be passed to the `StreamWriter`'s constructor to retrieve the `StreamWriter` instance for the specified `Stream`. At this point, the `StreamWriter` can be used to write data to the stream.

When dealing with streams, there is the concept of a current position from which data is read, or to which data is written, within the data block of the stream. This could either be at the beginning of the stream, the end of the stream, or somewhere in-between. This is represented by the `SeekOrigin` enumeration. You can set the current position of a stream by using its `Seek()` method, which takes an offset and a `SeekOrigin` value. The `SeekOrigin` values are listed in Table 12.7.

TABLE 12.7   SeekOrigin Values

Value	Description
Begin	Represents the beginning of the stream.
Current	Represents the current position of the stream.
End	Represents the end of the stream.

The `offset` parameter is a position relative to `SeekOrigin`. Therefore, as shown in line 11 of Listing 12.4, the `SeekOrigin` passed is `End` with an offset of zero (`0`). This sets the current position of the stream to exactly the end. Therefore, any data written to the stream will effectively be appended to it (see previous note on using `Filemode.Append()`. In fact, running this demo twice illustrates this. Writing to the stream requires using the `StreamWriter.Write()` or `StreamWriter.WriteLine()` methods.

Writing to a `FileStream` does not actually write the data to the underlying file until either the `StreamWriter.Close()` or `StreamWriter.Flush()` method is called. `Close()` writes the data to the underlying stream and closes, thus preventing any further write operations. `Flush()` simply writes the data to the underlying stream.

Reading from a stream, specifically a `FileStream`, is similar to writing. Listing 12.5 illustrates this.

LISTING 12.5   Creating and Reading Text from a FileStream

```
1:    var
2:      MyFileStream: FileStream;
3:      MyStreamReader: StreamReader;
4:    begin
```

LISTING 12.5   Continued

```
5:    //  Create and read from the file
6:    MyFileStream := FileStream.Create('c:\demo.txt', FileMode.OpenOrCreate,
7:      FileAccess.Read);
8:    try
9:      MyStreamReader := StreamReader.Create(MyFilestream);
10:     try
11:       MyStreamReader.BaseStream.Seek(0, SeekOrigin.Begin);
12:       while MyStreamReader.Peek <> -1 do
13:         Console.WriteLine(MyStreamReader.ReadLine);
14:     finally
15:       MyStreamReader.Close;
16:     end;
17:   finally
18:     MyFileStream.Close;
19:   end;
20: end.
```

▶ Find the code on the CD: \Code\Chapter 12\Ex04\.

In this example, note that we are using a `StreamReader` instead of a `StreamWriter`. Also, line 11 uses a `SeekOrigin` of `Begin`, which makes sense because the intent is to read from the stream. However, it isn't needed because the file position is already at the beginning of the file having just opened it. It is shown for illustrative purposes. The `StreamReader` has a few methods worthy of mention here, not necessarily shown in the example code. `Peek()` looks at the next character in the stream, but does not advance the stream position. When `Peek()` returns a value of `-1`, the end of the stream has been reached. `Read()` reads the next character (or an array of characters using the overloaded version of `Read()`) and advances the stream's position. `ReadLine()` reads and returns a `String` containing an entire line within a `TextStream`. The position is also advanced to the position following the line. `ReadToEnd()` reads from the current position to the end of the stream. `ReadBlock()` allows you to specify a number of characters in a stream to read.

With this understanding of `FileStream`, you should be able to manipulate text streams of any sort. The next section illustrates working with binary streams.

Working with Binary File Streams

To work with binary streams, you use different reader and writer classes. These are the `BinaryWriter` and `BinaryReader` classes. This writer/reader pair functions similarly to their text counterparts. However, they contain various methods for writing/reading primitive types. Listing 12.6 illustrates writing binary data to a `FileStream`. .

LISTING 12.6   Writing Binary Data to a FileStream

```
1:   const
2:     cAry: array[1..8] of char = ('o', 'h', ' ', 'y', 'e', 'a', 'h', '!');
3:   var
4:     MyFileStream: FileStream;
5:     MyBinWriter: BinaryWriter;
6:   begin
7:
```

LISTING 12.6   Continued

```
 8:    MyFileStream := FileStream.Create('ddgdemo.dat', FileMode.OpenOrCreate,
 9:      FileAccess.ReadWrite);
10:    try
11:      MyBinWriter := BinaryWriter.Create(MyFileStream);
12:      try
13:        MyBinWriter.Write(True);
14:        MyBinWriter.Write('Unten Gleeben Globbin Globin');
15:        MyBinWriter.Write(23);
16:        MyBinWriter.Write(23.23);
17:        MyBinWriter.Write(cAry);
18:      finally
19:        MyBinWriter.Close;
20:      end;
21:    finally
22:      MyFileStream.Close;
23:    end;
24:  end;
```

▶ Find the code on the CD: \Code\Chapter 12\Ex05\.

You will notice here that the main difference between StreamWriter and BinaryWriter is the use of the heavily overloaded Write() method (lines 13–17). Different versions of the Write() method write different primitive types. In the example, you see Boolean, String, Integer, Double, and an array of char being written to the file.

To read from a stream containing binary data, you must read using the corresponding ReadXXXX() methods. This is demonstrated in Listing 12.7.

LISTING 12.7   Reading Binary Data from a FileStream

```
 1:  var
 2:    MyFileStream: FileStream;
 3:    MyBinReader: BinaryReader;
 4:    MyCharAry: array of Char;
 5:    i: integer;
 6:  begin
 7:    MyFileStream := FileStream.Create('demo.dat', FileMode.Open,
 8:      FileAccess.Read);
 9:    try
10:      MyBinReader := BinaryReader.Create(MyFileStream);
11:      try
12:        Console.WriteLine('Boolean: {0}', [MyBinReader.ReadBoolean]);
13:        Console.WriteLine('String: {0}', [MyBinReader.ReadString]);
14:        Console.WriteLine('Integer: {0}', [MyBinReader.ReadByte]);
15:        Console.WriteLine('Double: {0}', [MyBinReader.ReadDouble]);
16:        MyCharAry := MyBinReader.ReadChars(8);
17:        for i := Low(MyCharAry) to High(MyCharAry) do
18:          Console.Write(MyCharAry[i]);
19:      finally
20:        MyBinReader.Close;
21:      end;
22:    finally
```

LISTING 12.7   Continued

```
23:      MyFileStream.Close;
24:    end;
25:  end;
```

▶ Find the code on the CD: \Code\Chapter 12\Ex05\.

You'll note that several different ReadXXXX() methods exist for reading data from the stream (lines 12–16). The ReadChars() method is interesting in that it allows you to read a specific number of chars from the stream.

Asynchronous Stream Access

In some applications, it is useful to enable the user to continue working with the application while some processing is happening in the background. Chapter 14, "Threading in Delphi for .NET," covers Threads in detail and how parallel processing is accomplished. Based on the treading model, streams provide the ability to allow asynchronous access to the underlying stream. Listing 12.8 illustrates this technique for reading a FileStream asynchronously.

LISTING 12.8   Asynchronous File Access

```
1:   unit WinForm;
2:
3:   interface
4:
5:   uses
6:     System.Drawing, System.Collections, System.ComponentModel,
7:     System.Windows.Forms, System.Data, System.IO, System.Threading;
8:
9:   type
10:
11:     TWinForm = class(System.Windows.Forms.Form)
12:     strict private
13:       procedure Button1_Click(sender: System.Object; e: System.EventArgs);
14:     private
15:       { Private Declarations }
16:       procedure MyCallback(result: IAsyncResult);
17:     end;
18:
19:     TByteArray = array of Byte;
20:
21:     TFileState = class(System.Object)
22:     public
23:       FFilePath: String;
24:       FByteArray: TByteArray;
25:       FFStream: FileStream;
26:     public
27:       constructor Create(aFilePath: String; aByteArraySize: Integer;
28:         aFileStream: FileStream);
29:       property FilePath: String read FFilePath;
30:       property FStream: FileStream read FFStream;
31:       property ByteArray: TByteArray read FByteArray;
```

LISTING 12.8   Continued

```
32:    end;
33:
34:  implementation
35:
36:  procedure TWinForm.Button1_Click(sender: System.Object;
37:    e: System.EventArgs);
38:  var
39:    MyFileStream: FileStream;
40:    MyFileState: TFileState;
41:    MyFileInfo: FileInfo;
42:  begin
43:    MyFileStream := FileStream.Create('c:\ddgdemo.txt', FileMode.Open,
44:      FileAccess.Read, FileShare.Read, 1, True);
45:    try
46:      MyFileInfo := FileInfo.Create('c:\ddgdemo.txt');
47:      MyFileState := TFileState.Create('c:\ddgdemo.txt', MyFileInfo.Length,
48:        MyFileStream);
49:      MyFileStream.BeginRead(MyFileState.ByteArray, 0, MyFileInfo.Length,
50:        MyCallBack, MyFileState);
51:    finally
52:      MyFileStream.Close;
53:    end;
54:  end;
55:
56:  procedure TWinForm.MyCallback(result: IAsyncResult);
57:  var
58:    MyState: TFileState;
59:    i: integer;
60:  begin
61:    MyState := result.AsyncState as TFileState;
62:    for i := 1 to 10 do
63:    begin
64:      ListBox1.Items.Add(System.String.Format('In callback for File {0}',
65:        [MyState.FilePath]));
66:      Thread.Sleep(1500);
67:    end;
68:    MyState.FStream.Close;
69:  end;
70:
71:  { TFileState }
72:
73:  constructor TFileState.Create(aFilePath: String; aByteArraySize: Integer;
74:    aFileStream: FileStream);
75:  begin
76:    inherited Create;
77:    FFilePath := aFilePath;
78:    SetLength(FByteArray, aByteArraySize);
79:    FFStream := aFileStream;
80:  end;
81:
82:  end.
```

▶ Find the code on the CD: \Code\Chapter 12\Ex06\.

Listing 12.8 is a partial listing of the example on the CD. The `Stream` classes such as `FileStream` have two methods for asynchronous reading and writing of a file—`BeginRead()` (line 49) and `BeginWrite()`. Listing 12.8 demonstrates the use of the `BeginRead()` method. `BeginWrite()` functions similarly but performs write operations. `BeginRead()` takes the parameters listed in Table 12.8.

> **CAUTION**
>
> Before you can run this program, you must create the file `c:\ddgdemo.txt` or modify the code to work with an existing text file.

TABLE 12.8   BeginRead() Parameters

Parameter	Description
Buffer	The buffer to read data into
Offset	A byte offset in the buffer, which is the starting point to which data will be written
Count	Maximum bytes to read
Callback	A callback function that will be invoked when the read operation is complete
State	An object that is used to distinguish read requests

The basic operation is one in which you invoke `BeginRead()` on a stream. You specify the parameters listed in Table 12.8, optionally passing a callback function that will get called when the operation is complete. As the operation is happening, in the background, the user can continue performing other functions within the application. In this example the parameter passed as the `CallBack` is the `MyCallback` method of the main form. To show that this is in fact an asynchronous operation, this method writes to a `ListBox` on the form and then sleeps for about a second and a half. During this time, the user is still able to type into the `TextBox` on the form.

The `TFileState` class is used to contain the file information including the buffer parameter of the `BeginRead()` function.

Monitoring Directory Activity

`FileSystemWatcher` is a useful class for monitoring events that occur on a file or within a directory. This class invokes certain events whenever the directory or file is created, modified, renamed, or deleted. You provide the event handlers that occur when one of these events is raised. Listing 12.9 is a simple application that demonstrates capturing these events and outputting the type of change to the user.

LISTING 12.9   FileSystemWatcher Example

```
1:   unit WinForm1;
2:
3:   interface
4:
5:   uses
6:     System.Drawing, System.Collections, System.ComponentModel,
7:     System.Windows.Forms, System.Data, System.IO;
8:
```

LISTING 12.9   Continued

```
 9:   type
10:     TWinForm1 = class(System.Windows.Forms.Form)
11:     private
12:       { Private Declarations }
13:       procedure OnChanged(source: System.Object; e: FileSystemEventArgs);
14:       procedure OnRenamed(source: System.Object; e: RenamedEventArgs);
15:     public
16:       fsw: FileSystemWatcher;
17:       constructor Create;
18:     end;
19:
20:   implementation
21:
22:   constructor TWinForm1.Create;
23:   begin
24:     inherited Create;
25:     InitializeComponent;
26:     fsw := FileSystemWatcher.Create('c:\work\');
27:     fsw.NotifyFilter := NotifyFilters.Attributes or
28:       NotifyFilters.CreationTime or NotifyFilters.DirectoryName or
29:       NotifyFilters.FileName or NotifyFilters.LastAccess or
30:       NotifyFilters.LastWrite or NotifyFilters.Size;
31:     fsw.Filter := '*.*';
32:     Include(fsw.Changed, OnChanged);
33:     Include(fsw.Created, OnChanged); // Use the OnChanged event handler
34:     Include(fsw.Deleted, OnChanged); // Use the OnChanged event handler
35:     Include(fsw.Renamed, OnRenamed);
36:     fsw.EnableRaisingEvents := True;
37:   end;
38:
39:   const
40:     crlf = #13#10;
41:
42:   procedure TWinForm1.OnChanged(source: TObject; e: FileSystemEventArgs);
43:   begin
44:     TextBox1.Text := TextBox1.Text +
45:       System.String.Format('Change Type: {0}, File: {1}'+crlf,
46:       [e.ChangeType, e.FullPath]);
47:   end;
48:
49:   procedure TWinForm1.OnRenamed(source: TObject; e: RenamedEventArgs);
50:   begin
51:     TextBox1.Text := TextBox1.Text +
52:       System.String.Format('Change Type: {0}, Renamed From: {1} To: {2}'
53:         +crlf, [e.ChangeType, e.OldFullPath, e.FullPath]);
54:   end;
55:
56:   end.
```

▶ Find the code on the CD: \Code\Chapter 12\Ex07\.

> **CAUTION**
>
> Before you can run the program from Listing 12.9, you must create a directory, `c:\work`, or modify the code to work in an existing directory.

Listing 12.9 is partial code to the example on the CD. The `FileSystemWatcher` constructor takes a directory path to monitor. An overloaded version of this constructor allows you to optionally specify certain file types to monitor. The `NofityFilter` property contains the `NofityFilters` enumerations, which specify the types of changes to monitor. These can be bitwise or'ed together (lines 27–30). Table 12.9 lists the `NotifyFilters` values.

TABLE 12.9   NotifyFilters Values

Value	Description
Attributes	Changes to the file or folder attributes.
CreationTime	Changes to the time the file or folder is created.
DirectoryName	Changes to the directory name.
FileName	Changes to a filename.
LastAccess	Changes to the date the file or folder was last accessed/opened.
LastWrite	Changes to the date the file or folder was written to.
Security	Changes to the file or folders security settings.
Size	Changes to the size of the file or folder.

The `FileSystemWatcher.Filter` property lets you specify file types based on their extension or name (line 31). Finally, you assign the events that you want to monitor. Because the `FileSystemWatcher`'s `Changed`, `Created`, and `Deleted` events are of the same type, this example reuses the `OnChanged` event handler for all three (lines 32–34). The `FileSystemWatcher` events are listed in Table 12.10.

TABLE 12.10   FileSystemWatcher Events

Event	Description
Changed	Fires when a file or directory has been changed in the monitored directory.
Created	Fires when a file or directory has been created in the monitored directory.
Deleted	Fires when a file or directory has been deleted in the monitored directory.
Renamed	Fires when a file or directory has been renamed in the monitored directory.

The `Changed`, `Created`, and `Deleted` events pass a `FileSystemEventArgs` parameter from which you can determine information about the change such as the filename and change type. The `Renamed` event passes a `RenamedEventArgs` parameter, which differs from the `FileSystemEventArgs` type. `RenamedEventArgs` contains additional data about the old filename, such as `OldFullPath` and `OldName`. When you run the application, you will see how changes within the directory are monitored.

Serialization

Up to this point, this chapter has covered how to work with files and streams. There is obviously great utility in being able to write data to various media such as disk and memory. There is greater utility in being able to write your .NET types, including their state to the same media. This is possible by using `serialization`. Serialization is a process that converts classes to a stream of bytes that can be persisted or transferred to another process and even another computer. `Deserialization` is the reverse process of reading the stream of bytes from a file or from a remote computer and reconstructing the class it contains, including its state.

Consider the possibilities. You can create your own custom class, create an instance, and save that instance, class definition, and data to a file. Later, you can load that class and reconstruct it to the exact state it was before you saved it. You can also send your class across the wire to another computer sitting in another country, where it is reconstructed and used. In fact, this second example is a simple description of how ASP.NET remoting works. Remoting will be covered in Chapters 29, ".NET Remoting and Delphi," and 30, ".NET Remoting in Action," of this book.

How Serialization Works

A class can be serializable by one of two ways. It can be declared with the `[Serializable]` attribute, or it can implement the `ISerializable` interface. This chapter discusses the former and easier method of applying the `[Serializable]` attribute. You can visit `http://www. DelphiGuru.com` for an example of `ISerializable` implementation in Delphi for .NET.

Consider the following class:

```
[Serializable]
TClassicCar = class(System.Object)
public
  CarName: String;
  Manufacturer: String;
  YearIntroduced: DateTime;
end;
```

In this example, the class `TClassicCar` contains three fields—two of which are `String`, and one of which is a `DateTime`. When serializing a class, the CLR not only knows how to handle the base class, `TClassicCar`, but it also knows how to serialize classes with which it is related. If you serialize a object, its members, provided they are also serializable, will also be serialized. It is possible to prevent a member from being serialized by applying the `[NonSerialized]` attribute as shown here:

```
[Serializable]
TClassicCar = class(System.Object)
public
  CarName: String;
  [NonSerialized]
  Manufacturer: String;
  YearIntroduced: DateTime;
end;
```

In the preceding case, the field, `CarName`, will not be persisted with the class.

Internally, when a class is serialized, the CLR builds an object graph. An object graph is a way that the CLR can store objects with their associative objects. Each object is assigned an identifier. When the object is serialized, objects to which it refers are associated with the main object by their identifier. During the reconstruction phase, when an object is deserialized, it can reference an object that has not yet been deserialized, yet it retains an identifier to the referenced object. Once the CLR encounters the matching object during deserialization, it can fix up the references by matching identifiers. This enables the serialization process to persist objects to the stream in any order rather than having to persist objects inline with one another.

Formatters

Once you have declared a class to be serializable, you have to decide upon a format to use when persisting the object. The .NET framework includes two formats—binary and SOAP. It is possible to create your own custom format as well. To save classes in binary format, you must use the `BinaryFormatter`, which is contained in the `System.Runtime.Serialization.Formatters.Binary` namespace. To use the SOAP format, you must use the `SoapFormatter`, which is contained in the `System.Runtime.Serialization.Formatters.Soap` namespace.

> **NOTE**
>
> The `BinaryFormatter` exists in the `mscorlib.dll` assembly. You only have to add its namespace to your uses clause to use it. The `SoapFormatter` exists in the `System.Runtime.Serialization.Formatters.Soap.dll` assembly. You must add this reference through the Add Reference dialog box in addition to adding the namespace to the uses clause before being able to use the `SoapFormatter` class.

The formatter converts objects to the format they will be serialized as. The formatter also rebuilds the objects from the underlying format. It is even possible (but fairly involved) to create a custom formatter of your own.

A Serialization/Deserialization Example

Listing 12.10 shows partial code for an example on the CD that illustrates the serialization and deserialization process.

LISTING 12.10   Serialization/Deserialization Example

```
1:   program Serialize;
2:
3:   {$APPTYPE CONSOLE}
4:
5:   {%DelphiDotNetAssemblyCompiler '$(SystemRoot)\microsoft.net\framework\
➡v1.1.4322\System.Runtime.Serialization.Formatters.Soap.dll'}
6:
7:   uses
8:     SysUtils,
9:     System.IO,
10:    System.Runtime.Serialization.Formatters.Soap,
11:    System.Runtime.Serialization.Formatters.Binary;
12:
13:  type
14:
```

LISTING 12.10   Continued

```
15:    [Serializable]
16:    TClassicCar = class(System.Object)
17:    public
18:      FCarName: String;
19:      [NonSerialized]
20:      FManufacturer: String;
21:      FYearIntroduced: DateTime;
22:    public
23:      constructor Create(aCar, aMan: String; aYearIntro: DateTime); override;
24:      property YearIntroduced: DateTime read FYearIntroduced;
25:      property CarName: String read FCarName;
26:      property Manufacturer: String read FManufacturer;
27:    end;
28:
29:    TClassicCarArray = array[1..2] of TClassicCar;
30:
31:  { TClassicCar }
32:
33:  constructor TClassicCar.Create(aCar, aMan: String; aYearIntro: DateTime);
34:  begin
35:    inherited Create;
36:    FCarName := aCar;
37:    FManufacturer := aMan;
38:    FYearIntroduced := aYearIntro;
39:  end;
40:
41:  const
42:    carOutput = 'Model: {0}, Mfg: {1}, Year: {2}';
43:  var
44:    MyFileStream: FileStream;
45:    MySoFormatter: SoapFormatter;
46:    MyClassicCar: TClassicCar;
47:    MyClassicCarArray: TClassicCarArray;
48:    i: integer;
49:  begin
50:    // Add one classic car
51:    MyClassicCar := TClassicCar.Create('Camaro', 'Chevrolet',
52:      EncodeDate(1967, 1, 1));
53:    MyClassicCarArray[1] := MyClassicCar;
54:
55:    // Add another classic car
56:    MyClassicCar := TClassicCar.Create('Mustang', 'Ford',
57:      EncodeDate(1964, 1, 1));
58:    MyClassicCarArray[2] := MyClassicCar;
59:
60:    MyFileStream := FileStream.Create('c:\car.xml', FileMode.Create);
61:    try
62:      MySoFormatter := SoapFormatter.Create;
63:      MySoFormatter.Serialize(MyFileStream, MyClassicCarArray);
64:    finally
65:      MyFileStream.Close;
66:    end;
67:
```

LISTING 12.10   Continued

```
68:    // Read back the serialized object
69:    MyFileStream := System.IO.File.OpenRead('c:\car.xml');
70:    try
71:      MySoFormatter := SoapFormatter.Create;
72:      MyClassicCarArray :=
73:        TClassicCarArray(MySoFormatter.Deserialize(MyFileStream));
74:      for i := Low(MyClassicCarArray) to High(MyClassicCarArray) do
75:        Console.WriteLine(System.String.Format(carOutput,
76:          [MyClassicCarArray[i].CarName, MyClassicCarArray[i].Manufacturer,
77:            MyClassicCarArray[i].YearIntroduced]));
78:    finally
79:      MyFileStream.Close;
80:    end;
81:
82:    Console.ReadLine;
83: end.
```

▶ Find the code on the CD: \Code\Chapter 12\Ex08\.

Lines 16–27 define the TClassicCar class, which is declared as a serializable class by its [Serializable] attribute on line 15. This class contains three members that will also be serialized along with their containing class.

Line 29 declares a two-dimensional array of TClassicCar. This listing will serialize the array, which in turn will serialize any TClassicCar instances that it contains.

Lines 50–58 perform the setup of the TClassicCar instances and assign them to the array.

Lines 60–66 illustrate how the array is serialized. In line 63, we call the Serialize method of the SoapFormatter instance, passing it the output FileStream and the array to serialize. Again, this converts the array and its related objects to the serialized format—in this case, SOAP. Had we used the BinaryFormatter class, the format would be a binary format. Figure 12.1 shows the contents of the car.xml file as it loaded in Internet Explorer.

The second part of this program, lines 69–80, illustrates the process of deserializing the array from the file. The SoapFormatter.Deserialize() method accepts a file stream as a parameter. It returns an Object type and therefore must be typecast to the appropriate class type expected. In this case, it is expecting an array of TClassicCar. Lines 96–99 simply write the contents of the array to the Console.

CAUTION

On line 73, the hard-cast to TClassicCarArray is needed because the Delphi compiler does not allow an as-cast to a static array type. The hard-cast is implemented as an isinst IL instruction. This means that if the serialized object is not an array of TClassicCar, no exception will be raised, but nil will be returned. Any de-referencing of the MyClassicCarArray variable will result in a NullReferenceException being raised. In this specific example, we know what the file contains; but in the general case, one should check whether MyClassicCarArray is assigned.

12

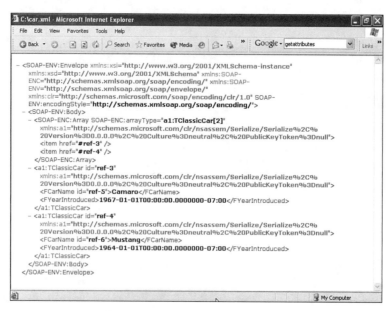

FIGURE 12.1   Car.xml—a serialized object.

Serialization is a simple yet very powerful mechanism for not only saving, but transferring objects and their state to other processes.

CHAPTER **13**

Developing Custom WinForms Controls

By Steve Teixeira

IN THIS CHAPTER

- Component Building Basics
- Sample Components
- User Painting: The PlayingCard Control

Delphi's VCL pioneered the combination of RAD with native component building. The ability to create and consume components within the context of a common object-oriented component framework and RAD IDE set Delphi apart from other tools in terms of productivity. The designers of the .NET Framework clearly understood this, and in the end they created a highly productive platform in which components and applications can leverage a common framework in the context of a RAD environment. The ability in Delphi 8 to write custom .NET components means never being stuck using only standard controls available in the IDE or having to seek out and purchase third-party component solutions. The ability to incorporate your own custom components into your Delphi applications means that you have complete control over the application's user interface. Custom controls give you the final say in your application's look and feel.

Although Delphi 8 gives you the ability to create a variety of components, from WinForm to WebForm to VCL, this chapter focuses on WinForm components. Being a native .NET development tool, the WinForms components that you build in Delphi 8 can be easily used on other .NET IDEs with other .NET languages, such as Microsoft Visual Studio.NET with C# or Visual Basic .NET.

If your forte is component design, you will appreciate all the information this chapter has to offer. You will learn about all aspects of component design from concept to integration into the Delphi environment. You will also learn about the pitfalls of component design, as well as some tips and tricks to developing highly functional and extensible components.

Even if your primary interest is application development and not component design, you will get a great deal out of this chapter. Incorporating a custom component or two into your programs is an ideal way to spice up and enhance the productivity of your applications. Invariably, you will get caught in a situation while writing your application in which, of all the components at your disposal, none is quite right for some particular task. That's where component design comes in. You will be able to tailor a component to meet your exact needs, and hopefully design it smart enough to use again and again in subsequent applications.

Component Building Basics

The following sections teach you the basic skills required to get you started in writing components. Then, we show you how to apply those skills by demonstrating how we designed some useful components.

When to Write a Component

Why go through the trouble of writing a custom control in the first place when it's probably less work to make do with an existing component or hack together something quick and dirty that "will do"? There are a number of reasons to write your own custom control:

- You want to design a new user-interface element that can be used in more than one application.

- You want to make your application more robust by separating its elements into logical object-oriented classes.

- You cannot find an existing .NET WinForm component or ActiveX control that suits your needs for a particular situation.

- You recognize a market for a particular component, and you want to create a component to share with other .NET developers for fun or profit.

- You simply want to increase your knowledge of Delphi and the Microsoft .NET Framework.

TIP

One of the best ways to learn how to create custom components is by examining the source code of the framework's own components. This is certainly true of the VCL, as the VCL source is an invaluable resource for VCL developers. However, Microsoft does not make available the source code for the .NET Framework, making this rather difficult for .NET developers. However, it is possible to inspect portions of the source code using a utility that decompiles .NET assemblies back into source code. One such utility is Lutz Roeder's .NET Reflector, available on the Web at http://www.aisto.com/roeder/dotnet/. .NET Reflector allows you to peer into Microsoft's (or any other) assemblies, viewing all classes, types, methods, data, and resources. Using this tool, you can explore the FCL, using the built-in decompiler to see how the creators of .NET implemented the framework.

Writing custom components can seem like a pretty daunting task, but don't believe the hype. Writing a custom component is only as hard or as easy as you make it. Complex, highly functional components can be tough to write, of course, but you also can create very useful components fairly easily.

Component Writing Steps

Assuming that you have already defined a problem and have a component-based solution, the six basic steps to writing your WinForm component are as follows:

1. Deciding on an ancestor class.

2. Creating the Component Unit within a Package.

3. Adding properties, methods, and events to your new component.

4. Testing your component.

5. Adding your component to the IDE's ToolPalette.

6. Completing the component's documentation with the source code.

We will touch on each of these steps, in varying degrees of detail, throughout this chapter.

Deciding on an Ancestor Class

There are four basic superclasses from which your components will descend: existing FCL or third-party controls, user controls, custom controls, and nonvisual components. For instance, if you need to simply extend the behavior of an existing control such as TextBox, you'll be extending an existing FCL control. User controls work like forms, providing a design surface upon which you can manipulate the form-like control. If you need to define an entirely new visual component class, you'll be dealing with a custom control. Finally, if you want to create a component that can be edited from Delphi's Object Inspector but doesn't have a visual characteristic at runtime, you'll be creating a nonvisual component. Different .NET classes represent these diverse types of components, and Table 13.1 gives you a quick reference.

TABLE 13.1 Component Base Classes

.NET Class	Types of Custom Controls
TObject	Although classes descending directly from TObject aren't components, strictly speaking, they do merit mention. You will use TObject as a base class for reusable classes that you don't need to work with at design time. A good example is the System.IO.File object.
System.ComponentModel.Component	This is a starting point for many nonvisual components. Notably, this class implements the IComponent interface, enabling it to provide design-time functionality within the IDE.
System.Windows.Forms.Control	This is the base class for all components that render themselves visually on a form. It provides you with common properties and events specific to visual controls.
System.Windows.Forms.UserControl	The UserControl class operates like a form in the IDE, providing a design surface upon which you can drop other components. Use this as a base class when you want to create a compound component made up of two or more other components.

13

TABLE 13.1　Continued

.NET Class	Types of Custom Controls
ComponentName	This is an existing class such as TextBox, Button, or ListView. Use an already established component as a base class for your custom components when you want to extend them rather than creating a new one from scratch. Many of your custom components will fall into this category.

It is extremely important that you understand these various classes and also the capabilities of the existing components. The majority of the time, you'll find that an existing component already provides most of the functionality you require of your new component. Only by knowing the capabilities of existing components will you be able to decide from which component to derive your new component. We can't inject this knowledge into your brain from this book. What we can do is to tell you that you must make every effort to learn about the key FCL components and classes, and the only way to do that is to use it, even if only experimentally.

Creating a Component Unit

When you have decided on a component from which your new component will descend, you can go ahead and create a unit for your new component. We're going to go through the steps of designing a new component in the next several sections. Because we want to focus on the steps, and not on component functionality, this component will do nothing other than to illustrate these necessary steps.

The component is appropriately named JustWorthless. JustWorthless will descend from System. Windows.Forms.Control and will therefore have the capability to render itself on a form. This component will also inherit the many properties, methods, and events already belonging to Control.

The easiest way to get started is to create a new package in the IDE by selecting File, New, Package from the main menu. Next, use the New Items dialog box to provide you with a jumping off point for the component unit. Select File, New, Other from the main menu, and you will be presented with the New Items dialog box as shown in Figure 13.1.

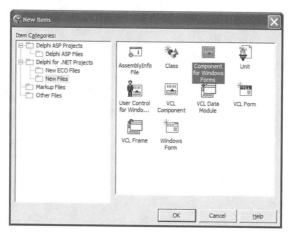

FIGURE 13.1　The New Items dialog box.

Select Component for Windows Forms from the Delphi from .NET\New Files, and a new unit will be created for you containing a class called TComponent descending from System.ComponentModel.Component. Because we want to demonstrate the creation of a visual control, we will modify the unit by adding System.Windows.Forms to the uses clause, changing the ancestor class to System.Windows.Forms.Control, and renaming the class to JustWorthless. Listing 13.1 shows this unit.

LISTING 13.1 d8dg.Worthless.pas—a Sample Delphi Component

```
1:   unit d8dg.Worthless;
2:
3:   interface
4:
5:   uses
6:     System.Drawing, System.Collections, System.ComponentModel,
7:     System.Windows.Forms;
8:
9:   type
10:    JustWorthless = class(System.Windows.Forms.Control)
11:    {$REGION 'Designer Managed Code'}
12:    strict private
13:      /// <summary>
14:      /// Required designer variable.
15:      /// </summary>
16:      Components: System.ComponentModel.Container;
17:      /// <summary>
18:      /// Required method for Designer support - do not modify
19:      /// the contents of this method with the code editor.
20:      /// </summary>
21:      procedure InitializeComponent;
22:    {$ENDREGION}
23:    strict protected
24:      /// <summary>
25:      /// Clean up any resources being used.
26:      /// </summary>
27:      procedure Dispose(Disposing: Boolean); override;
28:    private
29:      { Private Declarations }
30:    public
31:      constructor Create; overload;
32:      constructor Create(Container: System.ComponentModel.IContainer);
➥overload;
33:    end;
34:
35:   implementation
36:
37:   uses
38:     System.Globalization;
39:
40:   {$REGION 'Windows Form Designer generated code'}
41:   /// <summary>
42:   /// Required method for Designer support - do not modify
43:   /// the contents of this method with the code editor.
44:   /// </summary>
```

LISTING 13.1   Continued

```
45:  procedure JustWorthless.InitializeComponent;
46:  begin
47:    Self.Components := System.ComponentModel.Container.Create;
48:  end;
49:  {$ENDREGION}
50:
51:  constructor JustWorthless.Create;
52:  begin
53:    inherited Create;
54:    //
55:    // Required for Windows Form Designer support
56:    //
57:    InitializeComponent;
58:    //
59:    // TODO: Add any constructor code after InitializeComponent call
60:    //
61:  end;
62:
63:  constructor JustWorthless.Create(Container:
➥System.ComponentModel.IContainer);
64:  begin
65:    inherited Create;
66:    //
67:    // Required for Windows Form Designer support
68:    //
69:    Container.Add(Self);
70:    InitializeComponent;
71:    //
72:    // TODO: Add any constructor code after InitializeComponent call
73:    //
74:  end;
75:
76:  procedure JustWorthless.Dispose(Disposing: Boolean);
77:  begin
78:    if Disposing then
79:    begin
80:      if Components <> nil then
81:        Components.Dispose();
82:    end;
83:    inherited Dispose(Disposing);
84:  end;
85:
86:  end.
```

▶ Find the Code on the CD: \Code\Chapter 13

At this point, you can see that JustWorthless is nothing more than a skeleton component. In the following sections, you'll add properties, methods, and events to JustWorthless.

Creating Properties

This section shows you how to add the various types of properties to your components. We're going to add properties of each common type to the JustWorthless component to illustrate the differences between each type. Each type of property is edited a bit differently from the Object Inspector. You will examine each of these types and how they are edited.

Adding Simple Properties to Components

Simple properties refer to numbers, strings, characters, and DateTime types. They can be edited directly by the user from within the Object Inspector and require no special access method. Listing 13.2 shows the JustWorthless component with three simple properties.

LISTING 13.2 Simple Properties

```
 1:   type
 2:     JustWorthless = class(System.Windows.Forms.Control)
 3:     private
 4:       // Internal Data Storage
 5:       FIntegerProp: Integer;
 6:       FStringProp: String;
 7:       FCharProp: Char;
 8:     public
 9:       constructor Create; overload;
10:       constructor Create(Container: System.ComponentModel.IContainer);
11:         overload;
12:     published
13:       // Simple property types
14:       property IntegerProp: Integer read FIntegerProp write FIntegerProp;
15:       property StringProp: String read FStringProp write FStringProp;
16:       property CharProp: Char read FCharProp write FCharProp;
17:     end
```

▶ Find the code on the CD: \Code\Chapter 13.

Here, the internal data storage for the component is declared in a private section starting on line 3. The properties that refer to these storage fields are declared in the published section beginning on line 12, meaning that when you install the component in Delphi, you can edit the properties in the Object Inspector. Properties and events in the published portion of a class automatically receive the [Browsable(True)] attribute, causing them to appear in the Object Inspector.

> **NOTE**
>
> When writing components, the Object Pascal convention is to prefix private field names beginning with the letter *F*.
>
> Win32 Delphi also uses the convention of prefixing type names with the letter *T*, but this convention is generally not used in .NET Delphi as it does not conform with .NET conventions.

> **TIP**
>
> If want to ensure compatibility with all .NET conventions, including naming conventions, library design, localization, security, and performance, you should look into the FxCop utility (http://www.gotdotnet.com/team/fxcop/). FxCop analyzes your .NET assemblies and reports on a variety of convention conformance issues.

Adding Enumerated Properties to Components

You can edit user-defined enumerated properties and Boolean properties in the Object Inspector by double-clicking in the Value section or by selecting the property value from a drop-down list. An example of such a property is the FlatStyle property found on button-type controls. To create an enumerated property, you must first define the enumerated type as follows:

```
EnumType = (Zero, One, Two, Three);
```

You then define the internal storage field to hold the value specified by the user. Listing 13.3 shows new enumerated property types for the JustWorthless component along with a new Boolean property.

LISTING 13.3   Enumerated Properties

```
 1:    JustWorthless = class(System.Windows.Forms.Control)
 2:    private
 3:      // Internal Data Storage
 4:      FIntegerProp: Integer;
 5:      FStringProp: string;
 6:      FCharProp: Char;
 7:      FBooleanProp: Boolean;
 8:      FEnumProp: EnumType;
 9:    public
10:      constructor Create; overload;
11:      constructor Create(Container: System.ComponentModel.IContainer);
12:        overload;
13:    published
14:      // Simple property types
15:      property IntegerProp: Integer read FIntegerProp write FIntegerProp;
16:      property StringProp: string read FStringProp write FStringProp;
17:      property CharProp: Char read FCharProp write FCharProp;
18:      property BooleanProp: Boolean read FBooleanProp write FBooleanProp;
19:      // enum property
20:      property EnumProp: EnumType read FEnumProp write FEnumProp;
21:    end
```

▶ Find the code on the CD: \Code\Chapter 13.

If you were to install this component, its enumerated properties would appear in the Object Inspector as shown in Figure 13.2.

> **NOTE**
>
> Set-type properties are discouraged for WinForms components. Whereas the Object Inspector knows how to edit set properties for VCL applications, that is not the case for WinForms application, as it treats sets as simple enum properties. Sets are also, of course, not inherently supported in Microsoft Visual Studio .NET because they are not CLS compliant, so your set properties will not be properly recognized in that environment either.

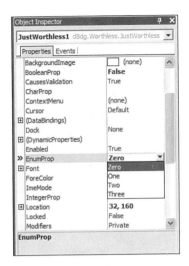

FIGURE 13.2   The Object Inspector showing enumerated property values for JustWorthless.

Adding Object Properties to Components

Properties can also be objects or other components. For example, the Font and Icon properties of a Form are themselves complex objects. When a property is an object, it is most helpful to users of the component to allow the property to be expanded in the Object Inspector so that its own properties can also be modified. This can be accomplished with a little bit of extra coding, as you will soon see.

The first step to adding an object property to the JustWorthless component is to define an object that will serve as this property's type. This object is shown in Listing 13.4.

LISTING 13.4   SomeObject Definition

```
type
  SomeObject = class(TObject)
  private
    FProp1: Integer;
    FProp2: string;
  public
    constructor Create;
  published
    property Prop1: Integer read FProp1 write FProp1;
    property Prop2: string read FProp2 write FProp2;
  end;
```

The SomeObject class descends directly from TObject, although it can descend from virtually any base class. We've given this class two properties of its own: Prop1 and Prop2, which are both simple property types. We've also added a constructor, which serves to initialize the fields to some slightly interesting value:

```
constructor SomeObject.Create;
begin
  inherited;
```

13

```
    FProp1 := 1971;
    FProp2 := 'hello';
end;
```

Now, you can add a field of the type SomeObject to the JustWorthless component. However, because this property is an object, it must be created. Otherwise, when the user places a JustWorthless component on the form, there won't be an instance of SomeObject that the user can edit. Therefore, it is necessary to modify the construction code for JustWorthless to create an instance of SomeObject. Listing 13.5 shows the declaration of JustWorthless with its new object property.

LISTING 13.5   Adding Object Properties

```
1:      JustWorthless = class(System.Windows.Forms.Control)
2:      private
3:        // Internal Data Storage
4:        FIntegerProp: Integer;
5:        FStringProp: string;
6:        FCharProp: Char;
7:        FBooleanProp: Boolean;
8:        FEnumProp: EnumType;
9:        FSomeObj: SomeObject;
10:     protected
11:       procedure Init; virtual;
12:     public
13:       constructor Create; overload;
14:       constructor Create(Container: System.ComponentModel.IContainer);
15:         overload;
16:     published
17:       // Simple property types
18:       property IntegerProp: Integer read FIntegerProp write FIntegerProp;
19:       property StringProp: string read FStringProp write FStringProp;
20:       property CharProp: Char read FCharProp write FCharProp;
21:       property BooleanProp: Boolean read FBooleanProp write FBooleanProp;
22:       // enum property
23:       property EnumProp: EnumType read FEnumProp write FEnumProp;
24:       // object property
25:       property SomeObj: SomeObject read FSomeObj write FSomeObj;
26:     end
```

▶ Find the code on the CD: \Code\Chapter 13.

Notice that we've added a method called Init() as shown on line 11. This method is called from the constructors to perform additional initialization—in our case, creating an instance of SomeObject, as shown here:

```
procedure JustWorthless.Init;
begin
  FSomeObj := SomeObject.Create;
end;
```

If we add this component to the IDE as it is currently written, the SomeObj property will show up in the IDE, but it will not be editable or expandable. This is because the Object

Inspector only knows how to represent and edit properties as strings. For simple property types, the Object Inspector already knows how to convert to and from strings in order to manipulate the properties. This is not the case, however, for complex types, such as SomeObject.

In order to provide proper edit and expand functionality for nested object properties, you must implement a TypeConverter. As the name implies, TypeConverters perform the task of converting an object from one type representation to another—for example, from native form to string form and back again. The base class for a TypeConverter is System.ComponentModel. TypeConverter, and the Object Inspector knows how to use one of these objects to represent nested objects on a component.

TypeConverters can be associated with either a class or a property using the TypeConverter attribute like this:

```
type
  [TypeConverter(TypeOf(SomeObjectConverter))]
  SomeObject = class(TObject)
```

System.Component.TypeConverter doesn't itself provide default behavior useful for nested object properties, but it does have a handy ancestor class called System.ComponentModel.ExpandableObjectConverter that exists for this very purpose. To make your object property editable and expandable in the Object Inspector, you need only use the ExpandableObjectConverter class or a descendent as the type converter. ExpandableObjectConverter provides the expandable behavior, but most implementations descend from this class in order to provide for the nifty editable string in the Object Inspector. This can be done by overriding three key methods: CanConvertFrom(), ConvertFrom(), and ConvertTo(). Respectively, these methods indicate whether conversion between types is possible, convert to native type, and convert from native type. Listing 13.6 shows the definition of SomeObject and its TypeConverter, SomeObjectConverter.

LISTING 13.6   A TypeConverter Implementation

```
1:   type
2:     SomeObjectConverter = class(ExpandableObjectConverter)
3:     public
4:       function CanConvertFrom(context: ITypeDescriptorContext;
5:         t: System.Type): Boolean; override;
6:       function ConvertFrom(context: ITypeDescriptorContext;
7:         info: CultureInfo; value: TObject): TObject; override;
8:       function ConvertTo(context: ITypeDescriptorContext;
9:         culture: CultureInfo; value: TObject;
10:        destType: System.Type): TObject; override;
11:    end;
12:
13:    [TypeConverter(TypeOf(SomeObjectConverter))]
14:    SomeObject = class(TObject)
15:    private
16:      FProp1: Integer;
17:      FProp2: string;
18:    public
19:      constructor Create;
```

LISTING 13.6   Continued

```
20:    published
21:      property Prop1: Integer read FProp1 write FProp1;
22:      property Prop2: string read FProp2 write FProp2;
23:    end;
24:
25:  { SomeObjectConverter }
26:
27:  function SomeObjectConverter.CanConvertFrom(context:
28:    ITypeDescriptorContext; t: System.Type): Boolean;
29:  begin
30:    if t = TypeOf(System.String) then
31:      Result := True
32:    else
33:      Result := inherited CanConvertFrom(context, t);
34:  end;
35:
36:  function SomeObjectConverter.ConvertFrom(context: ITypeDescriptorContext;
37:    info: CultureInfo; value: TObject): TObject;
38:  const
39:    Seps: array[0..0] of char = (',');
40:  var
41:    S: string;
42:    PropStrings: array of string;
43:    Obj: SomeObject;
44:  begin
45:    if value is System.String then
46:    begin
47:      S := value as System.String;
48:      if S = '' then
49:        Result := SomeObject.Create
50:      else begin
51:        // parse the format "Prop1, Prop2"
52:        PropStrings := S.Split(Seps);
53:        if Length(PropStrings) <> 2 then
54:          raise ArgumentException.Create(System.String.Format(
55:            'Cannot convert "{0}" to type SomeObject', S));
56:        Obj := SomeObject.Create;
57:        Obj.Prop1 := Convert.ToInt32(PropStrings[0].Trim);
58:        Obj.Prop2 := PropStrings[1].Trim;
59:        Result := Obj;
60:      end;
61:    end
62:    else
63:      Result := inherited ConvertFrom(context, info, value);
64:  end;
65:
66:  function SomeObjectConverter.ConvertTo(context: ITypeDescriptorContext;
67:    culture: CultureInfo; value: TObject; destType: System.Type): TObject;
68:  var
69:    Obj: SomeObject;
70:  begin
71:    if (destType = TypeOf(System.String)) and (value is SomeObject) then
72:    begin
```

LISTING 13.6 Continued

```
73:      Obj := value as SomeObject;
74:      // build the string as "Prop1, Prop2"
75:      Result := Obj.Prop1.ToString + ', ' + Obj.Prop2;
76:    end
77:    else
78:      Result := inherited ConvertTo(context, culture, value, destType);
79:  end;
80:
81:  { SomeObject }
82:
83:  constructor SomeObject.Create;
84:  begin
85:    inherited;
86:    FProp1 := 1971;
87:    FProp2 := 'hello';
88:  end
```

▶ Find the code on the CD: \Code\Chapter 13.

As Listing 13.6 shows, the `SomeObjectConverter` `TypeConverter` converts a `SomeObject` to and from a string representation in the form of *Prop1, Prop2*. The link between the component's property and the type converter is the attribute declaration found on line 13 of Listing 13.6. Figure 13.3 shows the view of this property in the IDE. Notice the string representation of the object as well as the expanded subproperties.

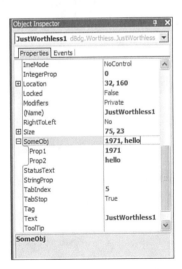

FIGURE 13.3 The JustWorthless.SomeObj property as viewed from the Object Inspector.

Adding Array Properties to Components   Some properties lend themselves to being accessed as though they were arrays. That is, they contain a list of items that can be referenced with an index value. The actual items referenced can be of any object type. `TextBox.Lines` is a good example of this type of property. We're going to put aside the `JustWorthless` component for a moment and instead look at the `Planets` component.

Planets contains two properties: `PlanetName` and `PlanetPosition`. `PlanetName` will be an array property that returns the name of the planet based on the value of an integer index. `PlanetPosition` won't use an integer index, but rather a string index. If this string is one of the planet names, the result will be the planet's position in the solar system.

For example, the following statement will display the string `"Neptune"` by using the `Planets.PlanetName` property:

```
P := Planets.Create;
ShowMessage(P.PlanetName[8]);
```

Compare the difference when the sentence `From the sun, Neptune is planet number: 8` is generated from the following statement:

```
P := Planets.Create;
MessageBox.Show('From the sun, Neptune is planet number: ' +
  P.PlanetPosition['Neptune']).ToString);
```

Before we show you this component, we'll list some key characteristics of array properties that differ from the other properties we've mentioned:

- Array properties are declared with one or more index parameters. These indexes can be of any simple type. For example, the index can be an integer or a string, but not a record or a class.

- Both the `read` and `write` property access directives must reference methods. They cannot reference one of the component's fields.

- If the array property is indexed by multiple index values—that is, the property represents a multidimensional array—the access method must include parameters for each index in the same order as defined by the property.

Note that array properties are not browseable in the Object Inspector.

Now, we'll get to the actual component shown in Listing 13.7.

LISTING 13.7   Using Planets to Illustrate Array Properties

```
1:   unit d8dg.SolarSystem;
2:
3:   interface
4:
5:   uses
6:     System.Drawing, System.Collections, System.ComponentModel;
7:
8:   type
9:     Planets = class(System.ComponentModel.Component)
10:    private
11:      // Array property access methods
12:      function GetPlanetName(AIndex: Integer): string;
13:      function GetPlanetPosition(APlanetName: string): Integer;
14:    public
15:      constructor Create; overload;
```

LISTING 13.7   Continued

```
16:      constructor Create(Container: System.ComponentModel.IContainer);
17:        overload;
18:      // Array property indexed by an integer value. This will be the
19:      // default array property.
20:      property PlanetName[AIndex: Integer]: string read GetPlanetName;
21:        default;
22:      // Array property indexed by a string value
23:      property PlanetPosition[APlantetName: string]: Integer
24:        read GetPlanetPosition;
25:    end;
26:
27:  implementation
28:
29:  uses
30:    System.Globalization;
31:
32:  const
33:    // Declare a constant array containing planet names
34:    PlanetNames: array[1..9] of string =
35:      ('Mercury', 'Venus', 'Earth', 'Mars', 'Jupiter', 'Saturn',
36:       'Uranus', 'Neptune', 'Pluto');
37:
38:  function Planets.GetPlanetName(AIndex: Integer): string;
39:  var
40:    LowP, HighP: Integer;
41:  begin
42:    LowP := Low(PlanetNames);
43:    HighP := High(PlanetNames);
44:    // Return the name of the planet specified by AIndex.
45:    // If AIndex is out of the range, then raise an exception
46:    if (AIndex < LowP) or (AIndex > HighP) then
47:      raise Exception.Create(System.String.Format(
48:        'Wrong Planet number, enter a number {0}-{1}',
49:        TObject(LowP), TObject(HighP)))
50:    else
51:      Result := PlanetNames[AIndex];
52:  end;
53:
54:  function Planets.GetPlanetPosition(APlanetName: string): Integer;
55:  var
56:    I: Integer;
57:  begin
58:    { Compare APlanetName to each planet name and return the index
59:      of the appropriate position where APlanetName appears in the
60:      constant array. Otherwise return zero. }
61:    Result := 0;
62:    for I := Low(PlanetNames) to High(PlanetNames) do
63:    begin
64:      if System.String.Compare(APlanetName, PlanetNames[I], True) = 0 then
65:      begin
66:        Result := I;
67:        Break;
68:      end;
```

13

LISTING 13.7 Continued

```
69:    end;
70:  end;
71:
72:  end.
```

▶ Find the code on the CD: \Code\Chapter 13.

This component gives you an idea of how you would create an array property with both an integer and string being used as an index. Notice how the value returned from reading the array property's value is based on the GetPlanetName() or GetPlanePosition() function return value and not a value from a storage field, as is the case with the other properties. The implementation of these methods is found on lines 38 and 54, respectively. Refer to the code's comments for additional explanation on this component.

Default Values   You can give a property a default value by assigning a value to the property in the component's constructor. Therefore, if we added the following statement to the constructor of the JustWorthless component, its FIntegerProp property would always default to 100 when the component is first placed on to the form:

```
FIntegerProp := 100;
```

This is probably the best place to mention the default and nodefault directives for property declarations. The default directive, for example, can be used to signal the default value for a property using code similar to the following:

```
property SomeProp: Integer read FSomeProp write FSomeProp default 0;
```

Don't confuse this statement with the default value specified in the component's constructor that actually sets the property value. For example, suppose that you were to change the declaration of the IntegerProp property for the JustWorthless component to read as follows:

```
property IntegerProp: Integer read FIntegerProp write FIntegerProp default 100;
```

This statement doesn't actually set the value of the property to 100. The default directive merely adds the .NET DefaultValue attribute to the property. The DefaultValue attribute is used by IDEs to reset a property to its default value or determine whether to generate code to set a property value.

Conversely, the nodefault directive is used to remove the DefaultValue attribute when used with a redeclared property. For example, you can redeclare your component to not specify a default value for the SomeProp property:

```
Sample = class(SomeComponent)
published
  property SomeProp nodefault;
```

Default Array Properties   You can declare an array property so that it is the default property for the component to which it belongs. This allows the component user to reference the object instance as though it were an array variable. For example, using the Planets component, we declared the Planets.PlanetName property with the default keyword. By doing this, the component user isn't required to use the property name, `PlanetName`, in order to retrieve a value. One simply has to place the index next to the object identifier. Therefore, the following lines of code will produce the same result:

```
P := Planets.Create;
MessageBox.Show(P.PlanetName[8]);
MessageBox.Show(P[8]);
```

Only one default array property can be declared for an object for any given array index type. This means that you might have, for example, a component with both an `Integer`- and a `string`-indexed default array property. Default array properties can also be overridden in descendants.

Creating Events

In Chapter 5, "The Delphi Language," we introduced events and told you that events were special properties linked to code that gets executed whenever a particular action occurs. In this section, we're going to discuss events in more detail. We'll show you how events are generated and how you can define your own event properties for your custom components.

Where Do Events Come From?

The general definition of an event is basically any type of occurrence that might result from user interaction, the system, or from code logic. The event is linked to some code that responds to that occurrence. The linkage of the event to code that responds to an event is called an event property and is provided in the form of a method pointer. The method or methods to which an event property points are called event handlers.

For example, when the user clicks the mouse button over a `Button` object, a message is sent to the Button window, which gets passed into the .NET system and eventually results in a method being called on the `Button` object. The button's response to this is to fire its `Click` event. When the event is fired, the event handler method of each of the listeners of this event are called, allowing them to perform actions in response to the click.

The `Click` event is just one of the standard event properties defined in FCL. `Click` and other event properties typically each have a corresponding event-dispatching method. This method is typically a protected virtual method of the component to which it belongs, and it is usually named `OnEventName`.

> **NOTE**
>
> The event/event-dispatching method naming convention for .NET is the opposite of the VCL convention. In .NET, an event called *EventName* will have an event-dispatching method called *OnEventName*, whereas in VCL an event called *OnEventName* will have an event-dispatching method called *EventName*.

The event-dispatching method often has only one or two lines of code—to check whether there is a listener for the event and then to fire the event. This method performs the logic to determine whether the event property refers to any code provided by the user of the component. For the `Jump` property, this would be the `OnJump()` method. The `Jump` property and the `OnJump()` method are shown in the following test class called `EventTest`:

```
type
  EventTest = class(Component)
  private
    FJump: System.EventHandler;
  protected
    procedure OnJump; virtual;
    property Jump: System.EventHandler add FJump remove FJump;
  end;
```

Here is the `EventTest.OnJump()` method:

```
procedure EventTest.OnJump;
begin
  if Assigned(FJump) then
    FJump(Self, EventArgs.Empty);
end;
```

Notice that the `FJump` property is defined to be a `System.EventHandler`. `EventHandler` is defined as follows:

```
EventHandler = procedure(Sender: TObject; e: EventArgs) of object;
```

This says that `EventHandler` is a procedural type that takes two parameters—`Sender`, which is of the type `TObject`, and `e`, of type `EventArgs`. The directive, `of object`, is what makes this procedure become a method. This means that an additional implicit parameter that you don't see in the parameter list also gets passed to this procedure. This is the `Self` parameter that refers to the object to which this method belongs.

In .NET terminology, `EventHandler` is referred to as a delegate.

When the `OnJump()` method of a component is called, it first checks to see if there are any listeners for `FJump`; and if so, calls that method.

> **NOTE**
>
> Note that this example uses multicast events. You should avoid using singleton events for WinForms components, as the event will not behave as expected in non-Delphi .NET environments. Singleton events exist primarily for backward compatibility with previous versions of Delphi.

As a component writer, you write all the code that defines your event, your event property, and your dispatching methods. The component user will provide the event handler when using your component. Your event-dispatching method will check to see whether there are any listeners for the event and then execute it when there are.

Defining Event Properties

Before you define an event property, you need to determine whether you need a special event type. It helps to be familiar with the common event properties that exist in FCL. Most of the time, you'll be able to have your component descend from one of the existing components and just use its event properties, or you might have to surface a protected event property. If you determine that none of the existing events meet your need, you can define your own.

As an example, consider the following scenario. Suppose you want a component that serves as an alarm, firing its alarm event at a date and time of your choosing. Although it probably wouldn't be difficult to simply write such logic into an application, componentizing the behavior provides a more clean division of labor within the source code as well as proving a reusable piece that can be leveraged in other applications.

The AlarmClock component shown in Listing 13.8 illustrates how you would design such a component. More importantly, it shows both how to create your own events as well as consume events from within the component.

LISTING 13.8   AlarmClock—Event Creation

```
1:   unit d8dg.Alarms;
2:
3:   interface
4:
5:   uses
6:     System.Drawing, System.Collections, System.ComponentModel,
7:     System.Windows.Forms;
8:
9:   type
10:     AlarmEventArgs = class(EventArgs)
11:     public
12:       FTime: DateTime;
13:     public
14:       property Time: DateTime read FTime write FTime;
15:     end;
16:
17:     AlarmHandler = procedure (Sender: TObject; e: AlarmEventArgs) of object;
18:
19:     AlarmClock = class(System.ComponentModel.Component)
20:     private
21:       FTimer: Timer;        // internal timer
22:       FAlarm: AlarmHandler; // alarm event
23:       FAlarmFired: Boolean;
24:       procedure TimerHandler(Sender: TObject; e: EventArgs); // tick handler
25:       function GetCurrentTime: DateTime;
26:       procedure SetEnabled(Value: Boolean);
27:       function GetEnabled: Boolean;
28:       procedure SetAlarmTime(const Value: DateTime);
29:     protected
30:       procedure OnAlarm(args: AlarmEventArgs); virtual;
31:       procedure Init; virtual;
32:     public
33:       FAlarmTime: DateTime;
34:       FEnabled: Boolean;
35:       constructor Create; overload;
36:       constructor Create(Container: System.ComponentModel.IContainer);
37:         overload;
38:       property CurrentTime: DateTime read GetCurrentTime;
39:     published
40:       property AlarmTime: DateTime read FAlarmTime write SetAlarmTime;
41:       property Enabled: Boolean read GetEnabled write SetEnabled;
42:       property Alarm: AlarmHandler add FAlarm remove FAlarm;
```

LISTING 13.8   Continued

```
43:    end;
44:
45:  implementation
46:
47:  uses
48:    System.Globalization;
49:
50:  procedure AlarmClock.TimerHandler(Sender: TObject; e: EventArgs);
51:  var
52:    Now: DateTime;
53:    Args: AlarmEventArgs;
54:  begin
55:    if not DesignMode then // don't fire in design mode
56:      begin
57:        Now := DateTime.Now;
58:        // compare Now to alarm time, ignoring milliseconds
59:        if (not FAlarmFired) and (Now >= FAlarmTime) then
60:        begin
61:          Args := AlarmEventArgs.Create;
62:          Args.Time := Now;
63:          OnAlarm(Args);
64:          FAlarmFired := True;
65:        end;
66:      end;
67:  end;
68:
69:  function AlarmClock.GetEnabled: Boolean;
70:  begin
71:    Result := FTimer.Enabled;
72:  end;
73:
74:  procedure AlarmClock.SetEnabled(Value: Boolean);
75:  begin
76:    FTimer.Enabled := Value;
77:    if Value then
78:      FAlarmFired := False;
79:  end;
80:
81:  function AlarmClock.GetCurrentTime: DateTime;
82:  begin
83:    Result := DateTime.Now;
84:  end;
85:
86:  procedure AlarmClock.Init;
87:  begin
88:    FTimer := Timer.Create;
89:    Self.Components.Add(FTimer);
90:    // tick every second
91:    FTimer.Interval := 1000;
92:    // listen to Timer's Tick event
93:    Include(FTimer.Tick, TimerHandler);
94:  end;
95:
```

LISTING 13.8   Continued

```
96:  procedure AlarmClock.OnAlarm(args: AlarmEventArgs);
97:  begin
98:    if Assigned(FAlarm) then
99:      FAlarm(Self, args);
100: end;
101:
102: procedure AlarmClock.SetAlarmTime(const Value: DateTime);
103: begin
104:   if FAlarmTime <> Value then
105:   begin
106:     FAlarmTime := Value;
107:     FAlarmFired := False;
108:   end;
109: end;
110:
111: end.
```

▶ Find the code on the CD: \Code\Chapter 13.

CAUTION

Never make an assignment to a property in a property's writer method. For example, examine the following property declaration:

```
property SomeProp: integer read FSomeProp write SetSomeProp;

  ....
  procedure SetSomeProp(Value: integer);
  begin
    SomeProp := Value;  // This causes infinite recursion
  end;
```

Because you are accessing the property itself (not the internal storage field), you cause the SetSomeProp() method to be called again, which results in a infinitely recursive loop. Eventually, the application will throw a stack overflow exception. Likewise, the same applies for reading a property value in its reader method. Always access the internal storage field in the reader and writer methods of properties.

When creating your own events, you must determine what information you want to provide to users of your component as a parameter in the event handler. For example, when you create an event handler for a Form's KeyPress event, your event handler looks like the following code:

```
procedure TWinForm.TWinForm_KeyPress(sender: System.Object;
  e: System.Windows.Forms.KeyPressEventArgs);
begin

end;
```

Not only do you get a reference to the object that caused the event, but you also get a KeyPressEventArgs parameter specifying additional information, such as what key was pressed. Deep in the FCL, this event occurred as a result of a WM_CHAR Win32 message that contains some additional information relating to the key pressed. FCL takes care of extracting the necessary data and making it available to component users as event handler parameters. One of the nice things about the whole scheme is that it enables component writers to take information that might be somewhat complex to understand and make it available to component users in a much more understandable and easy-to-use format.

Looking at Listing 13.8, you'll see that we've defined the delegate `AlarmHandler` as

```
AlarmHandler = procedure (Sender: TObject; e: AlarmEventArgs) of object;
```

This delegate defines the procedural type for the `Alarm` event handler. Here, we decided that we want the user to have a reference to the object causing the event to occur and the `AlarmEventArgs` value of when the event occurred.

TIP

You might notice that most events in .NET follow the same pattern of having sender object and event arguments object parameters, and you should strive to do the same. The event arguments object is typically an instance or descendant of `System.EventArgs`. If multiple pieces of information need to be passed to the event handler, these can be added as properties to the event arguments object. The advantage of using an event arguments object as opposed to separate event parameters for each bit of information is version resiliency: Properties can be added to the event arguments object without breaking backward compatibility, whereas backward compatibility would be violated if parameters were added in a newer version of a delegate definition.

The `FAlarm` storage field is the reference to the event handler and is surfaced to the Object Inspector at design time through the `Alarm` property.

The basic functionality of the component uses a `Timer` object to tick every second, checking the current time versus the `FAlarmTime` field with each tick. When they match, the `FAlarm` event is fired.

After installing this component to the Component Palette, you can place the component on the form and add the following event handler to the `Alarm` event:

```
procedure TWinForm.AlarmClock1_Alarm(Sender: System.Object;
  e: d8dg.Alarms.AlarmEventArgs);
begin
  MessageBox.Show(Convert.ToString(e.Time));
end;
```

This should illustrate how your newly defined delegate and event become an event handler.

Creating Methods

Adding methods to components is no different from adding methods to other objects. However, there are a few guidelines that you should always take into account when designing components.

No Interdependencies!

One of the key goals behind creating components is to simplify the use of the component for the end user. Therefore, you will want to avoid any method interdependencies as much as possible. For example, you never want to force the user to have to call a particular method in order to use the component, and methods shouldn't have to be called in any particular order. Also, methods called by the user shouldn't place the component in a state that makes other events or methods invalid. Finally, you will want to give your methods meaningful names that conform with the appropriate conventions so that the user doesn't have to try to guess what a method does.

Method Exposure

Part of designing a component is to know what methods to make private, public, or protected. You must take into account not only users of your component, but also those who might use your component as an ancestor for yet another custom component. Table 13.2 will help you decide what goes where in your custom component.

TABLE 13.2   Private, Protected, Public, Published, Oh My!

Directive	What Goes There?
private	Instance variables and methods that you don't want the descendant type to be able to access or modify. Typically, you will give access to some private instance variables through properties that have read and write directives set in such a way as to help prevent users from shooting themselves in the foot.
strict private	When a level of data hiding beyond private is necessary, and you want to prevent access to data or methods even to elements within the same unit.
protected	Instance variables, methods, overridable virtual methods, and properties that you want descendant classes to be able to access and modify—but not users of your class. It is a common practice to place properties in the protected section of a base class for descendant classes to publish at their discretion.
strict protected	Like strict private, strict protected members are not permitted access to items within the same unit.
public	Methods and properties that you want to have accessible to any user of your class. If you have properties that you want to be accessible at runtime, but not at design time, this is the place to put them.
published	Properties that you want to be placed on the Object Inspector at design time. The [Browsable(True)] attribute is applied to properties contained within this section, causing them to be displayed in the Object Inspector.

Constructors and Destructors

When creating a new component, you have the option of overriding the ancestor component's constructor and defining your own. You should keep a few precautions in mind when doing so.

Component Constructors

You might have noticed that the WinForm component wizard generated two overloaded constructors, as shown here:

```
type
  TComponent = class(System.ComponentModel.Component)
  strict private
```

```
    Components: System.ComponentModel.Container;
    procedure InitializeComponent;
  strict protected
    procedure Dispose(Disposing: Boolean); override;
  private
    { Private Declarations }
  public
    constructor Create; overload;
    constructor Create(Container: System.ComponentModel.IContainer); overload;
  end;
```

The implementation of each of these constructors calls the `InitializeComponent()` method, which is managed by the IDE's Form Designer. When you need to add to the constructor logic of a component, it's generally a better idea to use the `InitializeComponent()` pattern and create another method that is called by the constructors rather than adding a lot of special, similar code to each of the constructors. This is demonstrated in the `AlarmClock` component's `Init()` method.

Overriding Destructors

The code generated by the IDE automatically includes an override of the `Dispose()` method. This would be the best place to add any necessary resource cleanup code. Also, as you learned in Chapter 5, the `destuctor Destroy()` method, rather than being a true destructor, effectively implements the `IDisposable.Dispose()` method. Because all components implement `IDisposable`, `Destroy()` is also the legitimate place to release any resources necessary. Whether overriding `Dispose()` or `Destroy()`, the general guideline to follow is to make sure that you call the inherited destructor only after you free up resources allocated by your component, not before.

> **TIP**
>
> As a rule of thumb, when you override constructors, you usually call the inherited constructor first, and when you override destructors, you usually call the inherited destructor last. This ensures that the class has been set up before you modify it and that all dependent resources have been cleaned up before you dispose of a class.
>
> There are exceptions to this rule, but you generally should stick with it unless you have a good reason not to.

Design-Time Behavior

Consider the following bit of code from Listing 13.8:

```
procedure AlarmClock.TimerHandler(Sender: TObject; e: EventArgs);
var
  Now: DateTime;
  Args: AlarmEventArgs;
begin
  if not DesignMode then // don't fire in design mode
  begin
```

Note the use of the `DesignMode` property to prevent the `Alarm` event from firing while in design mode. `DesignMode` is a Boolean property of `System.ComponentModel.Component` that indicates whether the component is functioning in design mode in the IDE or live in a running application.

Testing the Component

Although it's very exciting when you finally write a component and are in the testing stages, don't get carried away by trying to add your component to the Component Palette before it has been debugged sufficiently. You should do all preliminary testing with your component by creating a project that creates and uses a dynamic instance of the component. The reason for this is that components are far more difficult to debug when running in the IDE than outside.

Keep in mind that even testing the component at design time doesn't mean that your component is foolproof. Some design-time behavior can still raise havoc with the Delphi IDE.

> **TIP**
>
> Sometimes a bug only manifests itself at design time—in which case, debugging within the IDE might be necessary. One technique you can employ to debug this scenario is to run one IDE instance within the debugger of another IDE instance. Do this by launching two IDE instances, and then using Run, Attach to Process from the main menu from one IDE instance to attach to the other as a debug process.

Providing a Component Icon

No custom component would be complete without its own icon for the Component Palette. To create one of these icons, use your favorite bitmap editor to create a 16×16 bitmap that will be the component's icon. The component bitmaps can then be placed in a .NET resource (`.resx`) file using a .NET resource editor program, which should be added to the project.

> **TIP**
>
> Lutz Roeder, of .NET Reflector fame, also makes a great freeware `.resx` file editor called *Resourcer*. You'll also find this tool on `http://www.aisto.com/roeder/DotNet/`.

The `ToolboxBitmap` attribute is used to relate a bitmap image to a specific component. The syntax for using this attribute is

```
[ToolboxBitmap(typeof(ComponentTypeName), "FileName.bmp")]
```

Sample Components

The remaining sections of this chapter give some real examples of component creation. The components created here serve two primary purposes. First, they illustrate the techniques explained in the first part of this chapter. Second, you can actually use these components in your applications. You might even decide to extend their functionality to meet your needs.

ExplorerViewer: A UserControl Example

As mentioned earlier, `UserControls` provide a means to design a component using a form-like design surface. The end result is very often a compound component, or a component that is made up of several other components into a single, atomic entity that can be used on any variety of forms.

The `ExplorerViewer` control is a great example of this type of control. Visually speaking, `ExplorerViewer` consists of three controls: `TreeView` on the left, `ListView` on the right, and `Splitter` in between. This control behaves much like a Windows Explorer window, and it is shown in the designer in Figure 13.4.

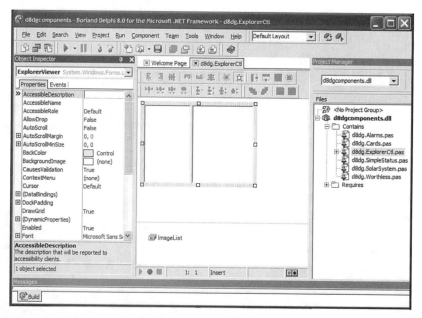

FIGURE 13.4   ExplorerViewer as seen in the designer.

The source code for ExplorerViewer is shown in Listing 13.9.

LISTING 13.9   ExplorerViewer Source Code

```
1:    unit d8dg.ExplorerCtl;
2:
3:    interface
4:
5:    uses
6:      System.Drawing, System.Collections, System.ComponentModel,
7:      System.Windows.Forms, System.IO, System.Runtime.InteropServices;
8:
9:    type
10:     ExplorerViewerEventArgs = class(System.EventArgs)
11:     private
12:       FActiveFile: string;
13:     public
```

LISTING 13.9   Continued

```
14:     /// <summary>
15:     /// Active file at time of event invocation.
16:     /// </summary>
17:     property ActiveFile: string read FActiveFile write FActiveFile;
18:  end;
19:
20:  ExplorerViewerEvent = procedure (Sender: System.Object;
21:    Args: ExplorerViewerEventArgs) of object;
22:
23:  ExplorerViewer = class(System.Windows.Forms.UserControl)
24:  private
25:    FIconList: ArrayList;
26:    FAutoActivate: Boolean;
27:    FFileActivated: ExplorerViewerEvent;
28:    function GetCurrentItem: string;
29:    procedure SetCurrentItem(const Value: string);
30:    procedure DisposeIcons;
31:    function IncludeBackslash(APath: string): string;
32:    function ExcludeBackslash(APath: string): string;
33:  protected
34:    /// <doc><desc>
35:    /// Adds a node to the TreeView with given parent.
36:    /// </desc></doc>
37:    procedure AddTreeNode(Parent: TreeNode; NodeName: string); virtual;
38:    /// <doc><desc>
39:    /// Fills ListView with files from given directory.
40:    /// </desc></doc>
41:    procedure FillListView(APath: string); virtual;
42:    /// <doc><desc>
43:    /// Initializes TreeView will logical drives.
44:    /// </desc></doc>
45:    procedure FillTreeView; virtual;
46:    /// <doc><desc>
47:    /// Gets list of subdirectories for a node and creates subnodes.
48:    /// </desc></doc>
49:    procedure RefreshNode(Node: TreeNode); virtual;
50:    /// <doc><desc>
51:    /// Fires FileActivated event.
52:    /// </desc></doc>
53:    procedure OnFileActivated(Args: ExplorerViewerEventArgs); virtual;
54:    /// <doc><desc>
55:    /// Activates the specified file by using the shell to execute.
56:    /// </desc></doc>
57:    procedure ActivateFile(FileName: string); virtual;
58:  public
59:    constructor Create;
60:  published
61:    /// <doc><desc>
62:    /// Specifies whether ActiveFile should be called when file is
63:    /// activated in the ListView.
64:    /// </desc></doc>
65:    property AutoActivate: Boolean read FAutoActivate
66:      write FAutoActivate default True;
```

LISTING 13.9   Continued

```
67:      /// <doc><desc>
68:      /// Full path name of currently selected file.
69:      /// </desc></doc>
70:      property CurrentItem: string read GetCurrentItem write SetCurrentItem;
71:      /// <doc><desc>
72:      /// Event that fires when item is activated in ListView.
73:      /// </desc></doc>
74:      property FileActivated: ExplorerViewerEvent add FFileActivated
75:        remove FFileActivated;
76:    end;
77:
78:    ExplorerViewerError = class(Exception)
79:    end;
80:
81:    [assembly: RuntimeRequiredAttribute(TypeOf(ExplorerViewer))]
82:
83:  function ExtractIcon(FileName: string): System.Drawing.Icon;
84:
85:  implementation
86:
87:  uses
88:    System.Globalization, System.Diagnostics;
89:
90:  { Icon extraction support }
91:
92:  type
93:    [StructLayout(LayoutKind.Sequential)]
94:    SHFILEINFO = record
95:      hIcon: IntPtr;
96:      iIcon: Integer;
97:      dwAttributes: Cardinal;
98:      [MarshalAs(UnmanagedType.ByValTStr, SizeConst=260)]
99:      szDisplayName: string;
100:     [MarshalAs(UnmanagedType.ByValTStr, SizeConst=80)]
101:     szTypeName: string;
102:   end;
103:
104:   SHGFI = (SmallIcon = $00000001, LargeIcon = $00000000,
105:     Icon = $00000100, DisplayName = $00000200, Typename = $00000400,
106:     SysIconIndex = $00004000, UseFileAttributes = $00000010);
107:
108: [DllImport('Shell32.dll')]
109: function SHGetFileInfo(pszPath: string; dwFileAttributes: Cardinal;
110:   out psfi: SHFILEINFO; cbfileInfo: Cardinal; uFlags: SHGFI): Integer;
111:   external;
112:
113: function ExtractIcon(FileName: string): System.Drawing.Icon;
114: var
115:   SHFI: SHFILEINFO;
116: begin
117:   if SHGetFileInfo(FileName, 0, SHFI, Marshal.SizeOf(SHFI),
118:     SHGFI.Icon or SHGFI.LargeIcon) <> 0 then
119:     Result := System.Drawing.Icon.FromHandle(SHFI.hIcon)
```

LISTING 13.9   Continued

```
120:   else
121:     Result := nil;
122: end;
123:
124: { Explorerview }
125:
126: constructor ExplorerViewer.Create;
127: begin
128:   inherited Create;
129:   //
130:   // Required for Windows Form Designer support
131:   //
132:   InitializeComponent;
133:   FAutoActivate := True;
134:   ListView.Dock := DockStyle.Right;
135:   Splitter.Dock := DockStyle.Right;
136:   TreeView.Dock := DockStyle.Fill;
137:   FIconList := ArrayList.Create;
138:   FillTreeView;
139: end;
140:
141: procedure ExplorerViewer.ListView_ItemActivate(sender: System.Object;
142:   e: System.EventArgs);
143: var
144:   I: Integer;
145:   FileName: string;
146:   Args: ExplorerViewerEventArgs;
147: begin
148:   for I := 0 to ListView.SelectedItems.Count - 1 do
149:   begin
150:     if TreeView.SelectedNode <> nil then
151:       FileName := IncludeBackslash(TreeView.SelectedNode.FullPath)
152:     else
153:       FileName := '';
154:     FileName := FileName + ListView.SelectedItems[I].Text;
155:     if FAutoActivate then
156:       ActivateFile(FileName);
157:     Args := ExplorerViewerEventArgs.Create;
158:     Args.ActiveFile := FileName;
159:     OnFileActivated(Args);
160:   end;
161: end;
162:
163: procedure ExplorerViewer.TreeView_BeforeExpand(sender: System.Object;
164:   e: System.Windows.Forms.TreeViewCancelEventArgs);
165: begin
166:   if e.Node.Tag = nil then
167:     RefreshNode(e.Node);
168: end;
169:
170: procedure ExplorerViewer.TreeView_AfterSelect(sender: System.Object;
171:   e: System.Windows.Forms.TreeViewEventArgs);
172: begin
```

LISTING 13.9   Continued

```
173:   FillListView(e.Node.FullPath);
174: end;
175:
176: procedure ExplorerViewer.Dispose(Disposing: Boolean);
177: begin
178:   if Disposing then
179:   begin
180:     DisposeIcons;
181:     if Components <> nil then
182:       Components.Dispose();
183:   end;
184:   inherited Dispose(Disposing);
185: end;
186:
187: function ExplorerViewer.GetCurrentItem: string;
188: var
189:   Selected: TreeNode;
190: begin
191:   Selected := TreeView.SelectedNode;
192:   if Selected <> nil then
193:     Result := Selected.FullPath
194:   else
195:     Result := '';
196: end;
197:
198: procedure ExplorerViewer.SetCurrentItem(const Value: string);
199: var
200:   I, J: Integer;
201:   Directories: array of string;
202:   Node: TreeNode;
203:   Nodes: TreeNodeCollection;
204: begin
205:   if Value <> '' then
206:   begin
207:     Node := nil;
208:     Nodes := TreeView.Nodes;
209:     // Split path string at backslashes to get all subdirs
210:     Directories := Value.Split(['\']);
211:     // Traverse tree, taking one subdir at a time
212:     for I := 0 to Length(Directories) - 1 do
213:     begin
214:       for J := 0 to Nodes.Count - 1 do
215:       begin
216:         if System.String.Compare(Nodes[J].Text, Directories[I], True) = 0
217:         then
218:         begin
219:           Node := Nodes[J];
220:           Nodes := Node.Nodes;
221:           Break;
222:         end;
223:       end;
224:     end;
225:     // select inner most node found
```

LISTING 13.9   Continued

```
226:     if Node <> nil then
227:     begin
228:       TreeView.SelectedNode := Node;
229:       Node.Expand;
230:     end;
231:   end;
232: end;
233:
234: procedure ExplorerViewer.FillListView(APath: string);
235: var
236:   DI: DirectoryInfo;
237:   FI: array of FileInfo;
238:   I: Integer;
239:   FileIcon: System.Drawing.Icon;
240:   Item: ListViewItem;
241: begin
242:   ListView.Items.Clear;
243:   ImageList.Images.Clear;
244:   DisposeIcons;
245:   DI := DirectoryInfo.Create(IncludeBackslash(APath));
246:   // Get array representing the files in the current directory.
247:   FI := DI.GetFiles;
248:   // add each file to the ListView
249:   for I := 0 to Length(FI) - 1 do
250:   begin
251:     Item := ListView.Items.Add(FI[I].Name);
252:     FileIcon := ExtractIcon(FI[I].FullName);
253:     if FileIcon <> nil then
254:     begin
255:       // Add icon to image list and save to ArrayList so it can be Disposed
256:       FIconList.Add(FileIcon);
257:       ImageList.Images.Add(FileIcon);
258:       Item.ImageIndex := ImageList.Images.Count - 1;
259:     end;
260:   end;
261: end;
262:
263: procedure ExplorerViewer.FillTreeView;
264: var
265:   LogDrives: array of string;
266:   I: Integer;
267: begin
268:   // Root nodes of tree are all logical drives
269:   TreeView.Nodes.Clear;
270:   DisposeIcons;
271:   LogDrives := Directory.GetLogicalDrives;
272:   for I := 0 to Length(LogDrives) - 1 do
273:     AddTreeNode(nil, LogDrives[I]);
274: end;
275:
276: procedure ExplorerViewer.RefreshNode(Node: TreeNode);
277: var
278:   SubDirs: array of string;
```

13

LISTING 13.9   Continued

```
279:    I: Integer;
280: begin
281:    // Node Tag indicates that directory has been processed
282:    Node.Tag := TObject(True);
283:    // Get list of subdirectories for this node
284:    SubDirs := Directory.GetDirectories(IncludeBackslash(Node.FullPath));
285:    // Prune tree at this point and add direct children
286:    Node.Nodes.Clear;
287:    // Add each subdir to tree
288:    for I := 0 to Length(SubDirs) - 1 do
289:      AddTreeNode(Node, Path.GetFileName(SubDirs[I]));
290: end;
291:
292: procedure ExplorerViewer.AddTreeNode(Parent: TreeNode; NodeName: string);
293: var
294:    Nodes: TreeNodeCollection;
295:    NewNode: TreeNode;
296: begin
297:    if Parent = nil then
298:      Nodes := TreeView.Nodes
299:    else
300:      Nodes := Parent.Nodes;
301:    NewNode := Nodes.Add(ExcludeBackslash(NodeName));
302:    NewNode.Nodes.Add('');  // add "fake" node to make plus sign appear
303: end;
304:
305: function ExplorerViewer.ExcludeBackslash(APath: string): string;
306: begin
307:    if APath.EndsWith('\') then
308:      Result := APath.SubString(0, APath.Length - 1)
309:    else
310:      Result := APath;
311: end;
312:
313: function ExplorerViewer.IncludeBackslash(APath: string): string;
314: begin
315:    if not APath.EndsWith('\') then
316:      Result := APath + '\'
317:    else
318:      Result := APath;
319: end;
320:
321: procedure ExplorerViewer.DisposeIcons;
322: var
323:    I: Integer;
324: begin
325:    for I := 0 to FIconList.Count - 1 do
326:    begin
327:      if FIconlist[I] <> nil then
328:        (FIconList[I] as System.Drawing.Icon).Dispose;
329:    end;
330:    FIconList.Clear;
331: end;
```

LISTING 13.9   Continued

```
332:
333: procedure ExplorerViewer.OnFileActivated(Args: ExplorerViewerEventArgs);
334: begin
335:   if Assigned(FFileActivated) then
336:     FFileActivated(Self, Args);
337: end;
338:
339: procedure ExplorerViewer.ActivateFile(FileName: string);
340: var
341:   Proc: System.Diagnostics.Process;
342: begin
343:   Proc := System.Diagnostics.Process.Create;
344:   try
345:     Proc.StartInfo.FileName := FileName;
346:     Proc.StartInfo.UseShellExecute := True;
347:     Proc.StartInfo.ErrorDialog := True;
348:     Proc.Start;
349:   finally
350:     Proc.Dispose;
351:   end;
352: end;
353:
354: end.
```

▶ Find the code on the CD: \Code\Chapter 13.

The basic logic of this component is that the left pane is filled with a directory view, whereas the right pane contains files within that directory. Because it would be potentially brutally time-consuming to traverse the entire hard disk for the directory structure for the left pane, the tree is only built one subdirectory at a time, as the user clicks on each successive node. The initial population of the TreeView is performed in the FillTreeView() method, shown in lines 263–274. The key to this method is the call to FCL's System.IO.Directory.GetLogicalDrives() method, which returns an array of strings—each representing a logical drive on the system. After the array is retrieved, the code iterates over that array, adding one element at a time as a root tree node.

When an attempt is made to expand a node in the TreeView, its BeforeExpand event fires, executing the listener found in lines 163–168 of Listing 13.9. This code checks to make sure that the directory hasn't already been processed and calls the RefreshNode() method to process the subdirectory, shown in lines 276–290.

Another handy method of System.IO.Directory, GetDirectories(), is used in RefreshNode() to get a list of subdirectories in the directory identified by the current tree node. Once the array is obtained, it is traversed to fill subnodes in the TreeView.

After the TreeView has been adjusted, the selection of a node also causes the FillListView() method (lines 234–261) to be called, filling the ListView with the files from the selected directory.

Note that the `FillListView()` method uses the local `ExtractIcon()` function, which wraps the Win32 API `SHGetFileInfo()` function in order to extract an icon from a file or the shell. It is necessary to call this Win32 API function because no wrapper for this functionality is available in FCL. This function and its supporting code is shown in lines 92–122 of Listing 13.9.

The `ExtractIcon()` function extracts a Win32 icon handle and converts it to a .NET `Icon` object, which is used in the ListView to represent the file. You'll note the `SHGetFielInfo()` function is imported directly from the Win32 API. To use this function, the `SHFILEINFO` structure and `SHGFI` enumeration are also added because these types are used by the function. The magic is done with the `DllImport` attribute, which links directly to the unmanaged Win32 API function.

To complete the control, we enable the user to execute the file by double-clicking on a file in the `ListView`. This causes the `ActivateFile()` method to be called, which uses the `System.Diagnosis.Process` object to launch a new process for the file:

```
procedure ExplorerViewer.ActivateFile(FileName: string);
var
  Proc: System.Diagnostics.Process;
begin
  Proc := System.Diagnostics.Process.Create;
  try
    Proc.StartInfo.FileName := FileName;
    Proc.StartInfo.UseShellExecute := True;
    Proc.StartInfo.ErrorDialog := True;
    Proc.Start;
  finally
    Proc.Dispose;
  end;
end;
```

Figure 13.5 shows the `ExplorerViewer` control in action at runtime.

FIGURE 13.5   ExplorerViewer as seen at runtime.

SimpleStatusBars: Using Extender Providers

One particularly cool and useful feature of WinForms components is extender providers. Extender providers enable one component to appear to add properties to other components. For example, consider the `System.Windows.Forms.ToolTip` component. When you drop this component on a form, it appears to add a `ToolTip` string property to all the controls on the form. The `ToolTip` property doesn't actually get added to other forms, however; instead, the `ToolTip` component manages a list of components with a `ToolTip` property and the corresponding property value.

With just a little work, it's possible to implement this type of feature in your own components. Key to doing this are two things: the `ProvideProperty` attribute and the `System.ComponentModel.IExtenderProvider` interface.

ProvidePropertyAttribute

You must use the `ProvideProperty` attribute on the class you want to extend other components by adding properties. The `ProvidePropertyAttribute` class has two constructors:

```
constructor Create(PropertyName, ReceiverTypeName: string); overload;
constructor Create(PropertyName: string; ReceiverType: System.Type); overload;
```

Both constructors take a property name as the first parameter. The second parameter allows either a string describing a type name in the first case or an actual type instance in the second. This parameter identifies the classes that should be extended with the property.

CAUTION

In early versions of Delphi 8, it is not possible to use the constructor that accepts a `System.Type` because of a bug in the compiler. Use the string constructor if you need to maintain compatibility with all versions of the Delphi 8 compiler. This bug was fixed in Delphi 8 Update 2.

The attribute code to add a property called `StatusText` to all other components would look something like this:

```
[ProvideProperty('StatusText', 'System.Object')]
```

The secret sauce that connects the property name string used in the attribute constructor with the actual code in your class is simple convention: Create methods in your class called `GetPropertyName()` and `SetPropertyName()`. These will be found by the FCL through Reflection and used to get and set the property.

TIP

Note that the string `'System.Object'` is passed as the class to be extended in the previous example. This is an artifact of the aforementioned compiler bug that prevents usage of the constructor that takes a `Type`. Classes other than `Object` require the use of the entire strong name string, which is both inconvenient and nonversion resilient. The only negative effect of passing `Object` is that `IExtenderProvider.CanExtend()` (described next) will get called a bit more often.

IExtenderProvider

IExtenderProvider is defined as

```
type
  IExtenderProvider = interface
    function CanExtend(extendee: TObject): Boolean;
  end;
```

You must also implement this simple interface in the component that you want to be the extender provider. When the ProvideProperty attribute is present, the FCL framework will look for IExtenderProvider and call CanExtend() for every class that meets the class specification provided in the second parameter to the ProvidePropertyAttribute constructor. For example, for the SimpleStatusBar control, which will be described shortly, the CanExtend() implementation looks like this:

```
function SimpleStatusBar.CanExtend(extendee: TObject): Boolean;
begin
  Result := (extendee is Control) and (not (extendee is SimpleStatusBar));
end;
```

This implementation of CanExtend() returns True for any Control that is not a SimpleStatusBar.

The SimpleStatusBar Control

SimpleStatusBar is a Control that descends from System.Windows.Forms.StatusBar, adding a twist: It adds a StatusText property to other controls on the form and monitors the focus change of the other control, setting its own text to be equal to the StatusText property of the focused control.

The source code for SimpleStatusBar is shown in Listing 13.10.

LISTING 13.10   SimpleStatusBar Source Code

```
1:   unit d8dg.SimpleStatus;
2:
3:   interface
4:
5:   uses System.Windows.Forms, System.ComponentModel, System.Collections,
6:     System.Windows.Forms.Design, System.ComponentModel.Design;
7:
8:   type
9:     [ProvideProperty('StatusText', 'System.Object')]
10:    SimpleStatusBar = class(System.Windows.Forms.StatusBar,
11:      IExtenderProvider)
12:    private
13:      FStatusTexts: HashTable;
14:      FActiveControl: Control;
15:      procedure HandleControlEnter(Sender: TObject; e: EventArgs);
16:      procedure HandleControlLeave(Sender: TObject; e: EventArgs);
17:    strict protected
18:      procedure Dispose(disposing: Boolean); override;
19:    public
```

LISTING 13.10   Continued

```
20:      constructor Create;
21:      function CanExtend(extendee: TObject): Boolean;
22:      function GetStatusText(Ctl: TObject): string;
23:      procedure SetStatusText(Ctl: TObject; Value: string);
24:    end;
25:
26:   implementation
27:
28:   { SimpleStatusBar }
29:
30:   function SimpleStatusBar.CanExtend(extendee: TObject): Boolean;
31:   begin
32:     Result := (extendee is Control) and (not (extendee is SimpleStatusBar));
33:   end;
34:
35:   constructor SimpleStatusBar.Create;
36:   begin
37:     inherited;
38:     FStatusTexts := HashTable.Create;
39:   end;
40:
41:   procedure SimpleStatusBar.Dispose(disposing: Boolean);
42:   var
43:     I, Size: Integer;
44:     A: array of TObject;
45:   begin
46:     if disposing then
47:     begin
48:       // make sure all event handlers are unhooked
49:       Size := FStatusTexts.Count;
50:       SetLength(A, Size);
51:       FStatusTexts.Keys.CopyTo(A, 0);
52:       for I := 0 to Size - 1 do
53:         SetStatusText(A[I] as Control, '');
54:     end;
55:     inherited;
56:   end;
57:
58:   function SimpleStatusBar.GetStatusText(Ctl: TObject): string;
59:   begin
60:     Result := string(FStatusTexts[Ctl as System.Windows.Forms.Control]);
61:     if Result = nil then
62:       Result := '';
63:   end;
64:
65:   procedure SimpleStatusBar.HandleControlEnter(Sender: TObject;
66:     e: EventArgs);
67:   begin
68:     FActiveControl := Sender as Control;
69:     Self.Text := GetStatusText(FActiveControl);
70:   end;
71:
```

13

LISTING 13.10   Continued

```
72: procedure SimpleStatusBar.HandleControlLeave(Sender: TObject;
73:   e: EventArgs);
74: begin
75:   if Sender = FActiveControl then
76:   begin
77:     FActiveControl := nil;
78:     Self.Text := '';
79:   end;
80: end;
81:
82: procedure SimpleStatusBar.SetStatusText(Ctl: TObject; Value: string);
83: var
84:   C: Control;
85: begin
86:   C := Ctl as System.Windows.Forms.Control;
87:   if Value = nil then
88:     Value := '';
89:   if Value.Length = 0 then
90:   begin
91:     FStatusTexts.Remove(C);
92:     Exclude(C.Enter, HandleControlEnter);
93:     Exclude(C.Leave, HandleControlLeave);
94:   end
95:   else begin
96:     FStatusTexts[Ctl] := Value;
97:     Include(C.Enter, HandleControlEnter);
98:     Include(C.Leave, HandleControlLeave);
99:   end;
100:   if C = FActiveControl then
101:     Text := Value;
102: end;
103:
104: end.
```

▶ Find the code on the CD: \Code\Chapter 13.

SimpleStatusBar uses a HashTable to store the individual component StatusText values, and the heavy lifting for the whole operation is done in the SetStatusText() method shown on lines 82–102. This method is responsible for adding and removing hash table class/value pairs as well as listeners for the control's Enter and Leave events. SimpleStatusBar uses these events to detect when focus changes from one control to another. When it does, it attempts to look up the control in the hash table, and, if found, sets the Text property appropriately.

Figure 13.6 shows the SimpleStatusBar control in action at design time, having added the StatusText property to a button. Figure 13.7 shows the SimpleStatusBar in operation at runtime.

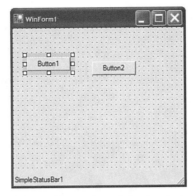

FIGURE 13.6   SimpleStatusBar doing its good work in the designer.

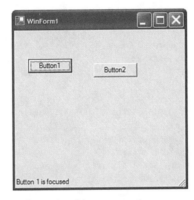

FIGURE 13.7   SimpleStatusBar doing its thing at runtime.

User Painting: The PlayingCard Control

We've discussed a number of controls that derive their look and feel from that of existing components. However, what if an existing control doesn't suit your user interface needs? That's where user painted controls come in. User painted controls allow you to have complete control over how the control is rendered onscreen.

To demonstrate, we'll walk through the implementation of a playing card WinForm control. The card will paint the suit and value on the face of the card and a color and image of the user's choice on the back.

To start, we'll define a couple of enums to represent suits and values:

```
type
  CardSuit = (CSClub, CSDiamond, CSHeart, CSSpade);
  CardValue = (CVAce, CVTwo, CVThree, CVFour, CVFive, CVSix, CVSeven,
    CVEight, CVNine, CVTen, CVJack, CVQueen, CVKing);
```

Let's now take a look at the class declaration:

```
  PlayingCard = class(System.Windows.Forms.Control)
  private
```

```
  class var
    FDrawBrush: SolidBrush;
    FBrushRef: Integer;
private
  FBackPen: Pen;
  FBorderPen: Pen;
  FSymbolFont: Font;
  FSansSerifFont: Font;
  FCardBackBrush: SolidBrush;
  FSuit: CardSuit;
  FValue: CardValue;
  FFaceUp: Boolean;
  FBorderWidth: Integer;
  procedure SetSuit(Value: CardSuit);
  procedure SetValue(Value: CardValue);
  procedure SetFaceUp(Value: Boolean);
  procedure SetBorderWidth(Value: Integer);
strict protected
  procedure InitComp;
  procedure OnPaint(e: PaintEventArgs); override;
  function get_DefaultSize: Size; override;
  property BorderWidth: Integer read FBorderWidth write SetBorderWidth;
public
  constructor Create; overload;
  constructor Create(Container: System.ComponentModel.IContainer); overload;
published
  [Description('The suit of the card'), Category('Appearance')]
  property Suit: CardSuit read FSuit write SetSuit;
  [Description('The face value of the card'), Category('Appearance')]
  property Value: CardValue read FValue write SetValue;
  [Description('Whether the card is face up or down'), Category('Appearance')]
  property FaceUp: Boolean read FFaceUp write SetFaceUp;
end;
```

This declaration shows the three published properties of the control—Suit, Value, and FaceUp—controlling the card's suite, value, and whether it is face up or down.

> **NOTE**
>
> The Description attribute, used for each property above, allows you to specify a description that will be displayed in the Object Inspector when the property is selected.
>
> The Category attribute allows you to specify to which Object Inspector category the property belongs.

Also of interest are the strict protected methods InitComp() and OnPaint(). InitComp() is called by the constructors to perform initialization of the control. OnPaint() performs all the painting of the control.

> **TIP**
>
> Override a control's get_DefaultSize() method to change the initial size of the control as it will be when initially created or dropped on a form in the designer.

The private section contains a number of GDI+ objects used for rendering as well as property accessors and private fields to hold property values.

The source code for PlayingCard is shown in Listing 13.11.

LISTING 13.11 PlayingCard Source Code

```
1:   unit d8dg.Cards;
2:
3:   interface
4:
5:   uses
6:     System.Drawing, System.Collections, System.ComponentModel,
7:     System.Windows.Forms, System.Threading;
8:
9:   type
10:    CardSuit = (CSClub, CSDiamond, CSHeart, CSSpade);
11:
12:    CardValue = (CVAce, CVTwo, CVThree, CVFour, CVFive, CVSix, CVSeven,
13:      CVEight, CVNine, CVTen, CVJack, CVQueen, CVKing);
14:
15:    /// <summary>
16:    /// Represents a single playing card, with  suit and value.
17:    /// </summary>
18:    [Serializable]
19:    Card = record
20:      cSuit: CardSuit;
21:      cValue: CardValue;
22:    end;
23:
24:    /// <summary>
25:    /// Card exception class
26:    /// </summary>
27:    [Serializable]
28:      ECardException = class(Exception)
29:    end;
30:
31:    [ToolboxItem(True)]
32:    PlayingCard = class(System.Windows.Forms.Control)
33:    strict protected
34:      /// <summary>
35:      /// Clean up any resources being used.
36:      /// </summary>
37:      procedure Dispose(Disposing: Boolean); override;
38:    private
39:      class var
40:        FDrawBrush: SolidBrush;
41:        FBrushRef: Integer;
42:    private
43:      FBackPen: Pen;
44:      FBorderPen: Pen;
45:      FSymbolFont: Font;
46:      FSansSerifFont: Font;
47:      FCardBackBrush: SolidBrush;
48:      FSuit: CardSuit;
```

LISTING 13.11   Continued

```
49:      FValue: CardValue;
50:      FFaceUp: Boolean;
51:      FBorderWidth: Integer;
52:      procedure SetSuit(Value: CardSuit);
53:      procedure SetValue(Value: CardValue);
54:      procedure SetFaceUp(Value: Boolean);
55:      procedure SetBorderWidth(Value: Integer);
56:    strict protected
57:      procedure InitComp;
58:      procedure OnPaint(e: PaintEventArgs); override;
59:      function get_DefaultSize: Size; override;
60:      property BorderWidth: Integer read FBorderWidth write SetBorderWidth;
61:    public
62:      constructor Create; overload;
63:      constructor Create(Container: System.ComponentModel.IContainer);
64:        overload;
65:    published
66:      [Description('The suit of the card'), Category('Appearance')]
67:      property Suit: CardSuit read FSuit write SetSuit;
68:      [Description('The face value of the card'), Category('Appearance')]
69:      property Value: CardValue read FValue write SetValue;
70:      [Description('Whether the card is face up or down'),
71:        Category('Appearance')]
72:      property FaceUp: Boolean read FFaceUp write SetFaceUp;
73:    end;
74:
75:  implementation
76:
77:  uses
78:    System.Globalization;
79:
80:  const
81:    SuitArray: array[0..3] of string = (Chr(167), Chr(168), Chr(169),
82:      Chr(170));
83:    ValueArray: array[0..12] of string = ('A', '2', '3', '4', '5', '6',
84:      '7', '8', '9', '10', 'J', 'Q', 'K');
85:
86:  procedure PlayingCard.Dispose(Disposing: Boolean);
87:  begin
88:    if Disposing then
89:    begin
90:      FBackPen.Dispose;
91:      FBorderPen.Dispose;
92:      FCardBackBrush.Dispose;
93:      FSymbolFont.Dispose;
94:      FSansSerifFont.Dispose;
95:      if System.Threading.Interlocked.Decrement(FBrushRef) = 0 then
96:      begin
97:        FDrawBrush.Dispose();
98:        FDrawBrush := nil;
99:      end;
100:     if Components <> nil then
101:       Components.Dispose();
```

LISTING 13.11   Continued

```
102:    end;
103:    inherited Dispose(Disposing);
104: end;
105:
106: procedure PlayingCard.InitComp;
107: begin
108:    FBorderWidth := 4;
109:    FFaceUp := True;
110:    SetStyle(ControlStyles.UserPaint, True);
111:    SetStyle(ControlStyles.AllPaintingInWmPaint, True);
112:    SetStyle(ControlStyles.DoubleBuffer, True);
113:    SetStyle(ControlStyles.ResizeRedraw, True);
114:    SetStyle(ControlStyles.StandardClick, True);
115:    SetStyle(ControlStyles.StandardDoubleClick, True);
116:    SetStyle(ControlStyles.Opaque, True);
117:    FBackPen := Pen.Create(BackColor, FBorderWidth);
118:    FBorderPen := Pen.Create(Color.FromKnownColor(KnownColor.Black), 1);
119:    FCardBackBrush := SolidBrush.Create(ForeColor);
120:    FSymbolFont := System.Drawing.Font.Create('Symbol', 36);
121:    FSansSerifFont := System.Drawing.Font.Create('Arial', 24);
122:    if System.Threading.Interlocked.Increment(FBrushRef) = 1 then
123:      FDrawBrush := SolidBrush.Create(Color.FromKnownColor(KnownColor.Red));
124:    System.Threading.Interlocked.Increment(FBrushRef);
125:    ForeColor := Color.FromKnownColor(KnownColor.White);
126:    BackColor := Color.FromKnownColor(KnownColor.Gray);
127: end;
128:
129: procedure PlayingCard.OnPaint(e: PaintEventArgs);
130: var
131:    penWidth: Double;
132:    rect: Rectangle;
133:    fmt: StringFormat;
134: begin
135:    rect := ClientRectangle;
136:    FDrawBrush.Color := Color.FromKnownColor(KnownColor.White);
137:    e.Graphics.FillRectangle(FDrawBrush, rect);
138:    rect.Inflate(FBorderWidth * -1, FBorderWidth * -1);
139:    if FFaceUp then  // card face up
140:    begin
141:      // get color from suit
142:      if (FSuit = CardSuit.CSDiamond) or (FSuit = CardSuit.CSHeart) then
143:        FDrawBrush.Color := Color.FromKnownColor(KnownColor.Red)
144:      else
145:        FDrawBrush.Color := Color.FromKnownColor(KnownColor.Black);
146:      fmt := StringFormat.Create;
147:      // Draw suit character
148:      fmt.Alignment := StringAlignment.Center;
149:      fmt.LineAlignment := StringAlignment.Center;
150:      e.Graphics.DrawString(SuitArray[Ord(FSuit)], FSymbolFont,
151:        FDrawBrush, rect, fmt);
152:      // Draw top/left value
153:      fmt.Alignment := StringAlignment.Near;
154:      fmt.LineAlignment := StringAlignment.Near;
```

LISTING 13.11   Continued

```
155:      e.Graphics.DrawString(ValueArray[Ord(FValue)], FSansSerifFont,
156:        FDrawBrush, rect, fmt);
157:      // Draw bottom/right value
158:      fmt.Alignment := StringAlignment.Far;
159:      fmt.LineAlignment := StringAlignment.Far;
160:      e.Graphics.DrawString(ValueArray[Ord(FValue)], FSansSerifFont,
161:        FDrawBrush, rect, fmt);
162:    end
163:    else begin // card face down
164:      // draw background image
165:      if BackgroundImage <> nil then
166:        e.Graphics.DrawImage(BackgroundImage,
167:          (Width - BackgroundImage.Width) div 2,
168:          (Height - BackgroundImage.Height) div 2);
169:      // draw inset border
170:      FBackPen.Color := BackColor;
171:      e.Graphics.DrawRectangle(FBackPen, rect);
172:      end;
173:    // draw outter border
174:    penWidth := FBorderPen.Width;
175:    e.Graphics.DrawRectangle(FBorderPen, 0, 0, Width - penWidth,
176:      Height - penWidth);
177: end;
178:
179: function PlayingCard.get_DefaultSize: Size;
180: begin
181:    Result := System.Drawing.Size.Create(90, 120);
182: end;
183:
184: procedure PlayingCard.SetBorderWidth(Value: Integer);
185: begin
186:    if FBorderWidth <> Value then
187:    begin
188:      FBorderWidth := Value;
189:      Invalidate();
190:    end;
191: end;
192:
193: procedure PlayingCard.SetSuit(Value: CardSuit);
194: begin
195:    if not Enum.IsDefined(TypeOf(CardSuit), Suit) then
196:      raise ArgumentOutOfRangeException.Create;
197:    if FSuit <> Value then
198:    begin
199:      FSuit := Value;
200:      Invalidate;
201:    end;
202: end;
203:
204: procedure PlayingCard.SetValue(Value: CardValue);
205: begin
206:    if not Enum.IsDefined(TypeOf(CardValue), Value) then
207:      raise ArgumentOutOfRangeException.Create;
208:    if FValue <> Value then
```

LISTING 13.11   Continued

```
209:    begin
210:      FValue := Value;
211:      Invalidate;
212:    end;
213: end;
214:
215: procedure PlayingCard.SetFaceUp(Value: Boolean);
216: begin
217:    if FFaceUp <> Value then
218:    begin
219:      FFaceUp := Value;
220:      Invalidate;
221:    end;
222: end;
223:
224: end.
```

▶ Find the code on the CD: \Code\Chapter 13.

InitComp() begins on line 106 of Listing 13.11. This method is called by the constructors and handles the construction-time housekeeping for the component. In particular, it uses the SetStyle() method inherited from Control to set a variety of control styles. This component sets the styles necessary to perform optimized user painting and handle mouse clicks. Table 13.3 details all the ControlStyles enumeration values that can be used with SetStyle().

TABLE 13.3   ControlStyles Enumeration Values

Name	Meaning
AllPaintingInWmPaint	The control will ignore the WM_ERASEBKGND Windows message, which might reduce flicker. This style can only be used in combination with the UserPaint style.
CacheText	For efficiency, the control keeps its own copy of its Text property value rather than getting it from the underlying window handle each time it is needed. You will need to take care to keep the property value synchronized with the underlying control when using this style.
ContainerControl	The control is a container-like control capable of containing child controls.
DoubleBuffer	To prevent flicker, drawing is performed in an in-memory buffer and output to the screen en masse when complete. To fully enable double-buffering, you must also include the UserPaint and AllPaintingInWmPaint style.
EnableNotifyMessage	The OnNotifyMessage method will be called for every message sent to the control's window procedure.
FixedHeight	The control has a fixed width when auto-scaled. For example, if a layout operation attempts to rescale the control to accommodate a new font, the control's width remains unchanged.
FixedHeight	The control has a fixed height when auto-scaled. For example, if a layout operation attempts to rescale the control to accommodate a new font, the control's height remains unchanged.
Opaque	The background of the control is not painted, making it opaque.
ResizeRedraw	The control will be redrawn when it is resized.
Selectable	The control can receive focus.

TABLE 13.3   Continued

Name	Meaning
StandardClick	The control implements the standard mouse click behavior.
StandardDoubleClick	The control implements the standard mouse double-click behavior. This style must be used in conjunction with the StandardClick style.
SupportsTransparentBackColor	The control accepts a BackColor with an alpha component of less than 255 to simulate transparency. Transparency will be simulated only if the UserPaint style is included and the parent control descends from System.Windows.Forms.Control.
UserMouse	The control does its own mouse processing, and mouse events will not be handled by the operating system.
UserPaint	The control paints itself rather than expecting the operating system to do so.

GDI+ pens, brushes, and fonts are also created in the InitComp() method. By creating these objects up front, the component doesn't have to take the efficiency hit that it might if it created each of these objects every time painting was necessary. Notice especially the thread protection around the creation of FDrawBrush. Because FDrawBrush is a class var variable, it is shared among all instances of this class, so we reference count this brush using FBrushRef and carefully thread-protect the creation and destruction.

The OnPaint() method is found starting at line 129 of Listing 13.11. The card rectangle is first painted white. If the card is face up, the suit character and value is drawn in the appropriate locations on the card. If the card is face dawn, the image provided by the BackgroundImage property is drawn on the card.

> **TIP**
>
> Rather than using a custom image, the suit symbols are drawn using the Windows Symbol font. Because the symbol font is available on all versions of Windows, its many images can provide for handy shortcuts when doing custom control painting.

Figure 13.8 shows an application containing face up and face down cards.

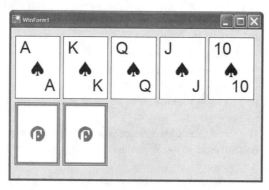

FIGURE 13.8   A great seven card draw hand.

CHAPTER 14

Threading in Delphi for .NET

By Rick Ross

IN THIS CHAPTER

- Processes
- Threading
- Threading .NET Style
- AppDomain
- The System.Threading Namespace
- Writing Thread-safe Code .NET Style
- User Interface Issues
- Threading Exceptions
- Garbage Collection and Threading

Applications that appear to be nonresponsive are seen as being poorly written. Whether it is waiting for a long-running report to finish, or printing a 100 page document, applications must respond to user input. Fortunately, writing responsive applications is not a difficult task as long as certain principles are understood.

This chapter provides the building blocks for writing applications that respond to user input during process-intensive tasks. In addition, these same concepts are applicable to other applications such as NT Services, Application Servers, and Internet applications.

Processes

A process is created when an application is started. This process contains an instruction pointer that keeps track of the location currently being executed. In addition to executable code, a process contains virtual address space, memory space, and numerous CPU registers.

The virtual address space contains a logical set of valid addresses in a process. Memory space contains the global process data—the stack where local variables are stored, the heap where memory is dynamically allocated, and the set of pages used for mapping virtual addresses to physical memory.

Processes have three unique states: running, stopped, or blocked. Stopped processes are those that are being debugged while blocked processes are waiting for the operating system to execute them. Each process is treated as an isolated entity that is scheduled by the operating system.

Because the operating system prevents processes from directly affecting each other, communication between two or more processes needs a predetermined protocol. Collectively, protocols used to communicate between multiple processes are called Interprocess Communications (IPC). Figure 14.1 illustrates multiple processes communicating with each other.

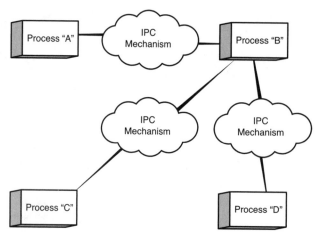

FIGURE 14.1   Multiple processes communicating.

The Windows (NT and above) operating system has several IPC mechanisms to choose from. These include

- Named Pipes
- Shared Memory
- Mutexes
- Events
- Semaphores
- TCP/IP Sockets

Heavyweight is a term associated with processes because they are resource intensive. Starting and stopping a process is relatively slower than other alternatives, which are discussed in the next section. Despite the hunger for increased resources, the level of protection offered by the operating system for processes is unmatched.

Threading

Threading overcomes many disadvantages of using processes to perform background processing. Threading allows for multiple independent paths within a process to be executed simultaneously. Each path of execution is referred to as a thread.

Technically, these independent paths can only run simultaneously on a machine with multiple processors. Single-processor machines switch between these independent paths rapidly, giving the illusion of simultaneous execution.

Most processes only have a single path of execution—a single threaded process. Processes containing multiple paths are called multithreaded. Figure 14.2 illustrates single-threaded and multithreaded processes.

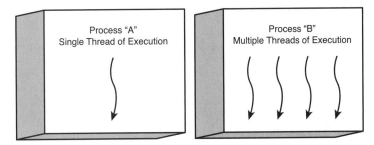

FIGURE 14.2   Single and multithreaded processes.

Each thread in a process has its own instruction pointer and CPU registers. All threads share the same virtual address space that is owned by the containing process. However, each thread receives its own stack space.

Because all threads within a process share the same address space, communication between threads is trivial. While easily accomplished, sharing address space requires diligent design. This topic is discussed later in this chapter.

The operating system gives each thread a time slice of the processor. Using a complex algorithm, the operating system looks at the thread's priority and whether it is waiting for something to occur. After a thread has either blocked or used up its time slice, the scheduler looks for another thread to execute.

Lightweight is a term associated with a thread because they require fewer resources than processes. Threads start and stop much more quickly than processes.

Threading .NET Style

As expected, the .NET Framework also has the concept of threading that is nicely wrapped in an object-oriented and platform-neutral fashion. By encapsulating and abstracting threading, the framework exposes a logical thread. These logical threads are managed by the framework and provide additional benefits not found in a physical Win32 thread. Using .NET Threads should make the code much more portable to other CLI platforms such as WinCE, Win64, and Mono. At the time of this writing, a logical thread maps to a physical thread, but this might change in future versions of .NET.

A logical thread is capable of doing things that a native thread cannot. For example, there is no simple method for a native thread to raise an exception in another thread. Logical threads, however, can raise an exception in another thread by calling the `Thread.Abort()` method. Exceptions are discussed in the "Threading Exceptions" section.

Logical .NET threads are scheduled by the CLR and run in the context of an AppDomain.

AppDomain

Similar to a process, an AppDomain provides a secure sandbox for .NET executables and assemblies. Just as multiple processes are protected, multiple .NET assemblies are protected if they reside in separate AppDomains. One important distinction is that AppDomains do not have to necessarily reside in separate processes. Multiple AppDomains can, and often do, occupy the same Win32 process.

When a .NET application is loaded, the CLR creates a process. In turn, this process creates the first AppDomain, which is called the default AppDomain. The default AppDomain cannot be unloaded and is destroyed when the process finishes. Additional AppDomains can be created dynamically at runtime. The relationship between processes and AppDomains is illustrated in Figure 14.3

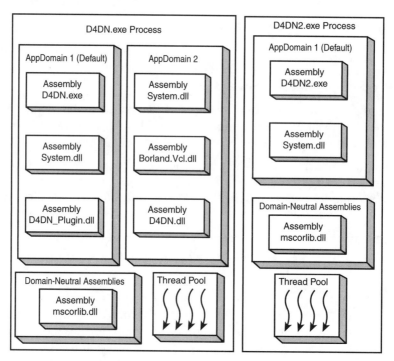

FIGURE 14.3   The Process/AppDomain relationship.

Like multiple processes, if an assembly needs to communicate with another assembly located in a different AppDomain, some IPC mechanism is required such as .NET Remoting. Unlike multiple processes, the major distinction between AppDomains and

Win32 processes is that AppDomains cannot currently share a common memory segment, whereas Win32 applications can.

AppDomains provide the capability to unloaded assemblies, as long as they are not located in the default AppDomain. All assemblies contained in an AppDomain are unloaded when the AppDomain is unloaded.

Configuration and security policies can be applied to an AppDomain to form either a more restrictive or relaxed environment.

The System.Threading Namespace

The .NET Framework has a rich collection of classes and enumerations that are needed for writing multithreaded applications, which are located in the System.Threading namespace.

The System.Threading.Thread Class

Directly inheriting from the System.Object class, the Thread class provides the necessary methods for creating, aborting, suspending, and resuming threads. In addition, several properties exist for controlling the priority and determining other useful information. Listing 14.1 contains a partial definition of the Thread class.

LISTING 14.1   Declaration of the System.Threading.Thread Class

```
System.Threading.Thread = class(System.Object)
public
  constructor Create(start: ThreadStart);
  procedure Start;
  // terminate a thread
  procedure Abort(stateInfo: System.Object); overload;
  procedure Abort; overload;
  // cancel an abort request
  class procedure ResetAbort; static;
  procedure Suspend;
  procedure Resume;

  // wakes a sleeping thread
  procedure Interrupt;

  // wait for a thread to finish
  procedure Join; overload;
  function Join(millisecondsTimeout: integer) : Boolean; overload;
  function Join(timeout: TimeSpan) : Boolean; overload;

  class procedure Sleep(millisecondsTimeout: Integer); overload; static;
  class procedure Sleep(timeout: TimeSpan); overload; static;

  // forces the thread to spin in a loop for a given number of iterations
  class procedure SpinWait(iterations: Integer); static;


  // thread local storage
  class function AllocateDataSlot: LocalDataStoreSlot; static;
```

LISTING 14.1   Continued

```
class function AllocateNamedDataSlot(name: String) : LocalDataStoreSlot;
➥static;
    class function GetNamedDataSlot(name: String) : LocalDataStoreSlot; static;
    class procedure FreeNamedDataSlot(name: String); static;
    class function GetData(slot: LocalDataStoreSlot) : System.Object; static;
    class procedure SetData(slot: LocalDataStoreSlot; data: System.Object); static;

    class function GetDomain: AppDomain; static;
    class function GetDomainID: integer; static;

    property Priority: System.Threading.ThreadPriority read; write;
    property IsAlive: Boolean read;
    property IsThreadPoolThread: Boolean read;
    class property CurrentThread: System.Threading.Thread read;
    property IsBackground: Boolean read; write;
    property ThreadState: System.Threading.ThreadState read;
    property ApartmentState: System.Threading.ApartmentState read; write;

    // culture information
    property CurrentUICulture: System.Globalization.CultureInfo read; write;
    property CurrentCulture: System.Globalization.CultureInfo read; write;

    // used with role based security
    property CurrentPrincipal: System.Security.Principal.IPrincipal read; write;

    property Name: System.String read; write;
end;
```

In particular, one property worth noting is the Name property. It can only be written to one time. Any attempt to write to the Name property more than once results in an exception.

> **NOTE**
>
> Notice that the Thread class contains methods to Suspend() and Resume() threads. Randomly suspending threads is not a good idea because it would be very easy to pause a thread during an inappropriate time. Imagine the results of suspending a thread when a lock is being held or in the middle of some file operation. The bottom line is that only the thread itself should call Suspend() because it knows the best places within the code to pause the thread. Calling Resume() on a suspended thread must be done from another thread.

Creating a thread using the Thread class is accomplished in one of two manners. The most frequent method is to use an instance method of a class. Another alternative is to use a static class method. These two methods of creating threads are referred to as manually created threads.

Regardless of the method used for manually created threads, both make use of delegates. A delegate is a .NET term for an object-oriented callback method that is type-safe. Similar to event handlers in Delphi, delegates provide a mechanism for multiple objects to be notified when called. Listings 14.2 and 14.3 demonstrate how delegates are used in Delphi when creating a thread.

LISTING 14.2   Creating Threads Using Instance Methods

```
1:    program instancethreads;
2:    {$APPTYPE CONSOLE}
3:
4:    //
5:    // This example demonstrates how to use native .NET methods to create a
6:    // thread on a class with an instance method.
7:    //
8:
9:    uses
10:      System.Threading;
11:
12:   type
13:     D4DNInstanceThread = class
14:     private
15:       FStartNumber : integer;
16:     public
17:       // ThreadMePlease will be executed on a different thread
18:       procedure ThreadMePlease;
19:       property StartNumber : integer write FStartNumber;
20:     end;
21:
22:   procedure D4DNInstanceThread.ThreadMePlease;
23:   var
24:     stop : integer;
25:     curNum : integer;
26:   begin
27:     curNum := FStartNumber;
28:     stop := FStartNumber + 10;
29:     while curNum < stop do
30:     begin
31:       writeln('Thread ', System.Threading.Thread.CurrentThread.Name ,
32:               ' current value is ',curNum);
33:       inc(curNum);
34:       Thread.Sleep(3);
35:     end;
36:   end;
37:
38:   var
39:     ThreadWork1 : D4DNInstanceThread;
40:     ThreadWork2 : D4DNInstanceThread;
41:     Thread1 : Thread;
42:     Thread2 : Thread;
43:   begin
44:     writeln('Starting threading instance method example...');
45:
46:     // Create D4DNInstanceThread instance
47:     ThreadWork1 := D4DNInstanceThread.Create;
48:     ThreadWork1.StartNumber := 10;
49:
50:     // Create the thread, specifying the instance method to execute
51:     Thread1 := Thread.Create(@ThreadWork1.ThreadMePlease);
52:     Thread1.Name := 'one';
53:
```

LISTING 14.2   Continued

```
54:    // Create another instance of D4DNInstanceThread
55:    ThreadWork2 := D4DNInstanceThread.Create;
56:    ThreadWork2.StartNumber := 100;
57:
58:    // Create the second thread, specifying the instance method to execute
59:    Thread2 := Thread.Create(@ThreadWork2.ThreadMePlease);
60:    Thread2.Name := 'two';
61:
62:    // Finally start the threads
63:    Thread1.Start;
64:    Thread2.Start;
65:
66:    // Wait for the two threads to finish
67:    Thread1.Join;
68:    Thread2.Join;
69:
70:    // Wait for the user to see the results
71:    writeln('Done');
72:    readln;
73:  end.
```

▶ Find the code on the CD: \Code\Chapter 14\Ex01\.

Listing 14.2 demonstrates how to create a thread using an instance method. Any instance method that does not have any parameters can be executed on a thread. Look at the Thread.Create() constructor call (shown in Listing 14.2 on line 51). The parameter to the Thread.Create constructor is the address of the ThreadMePlease method. Under the covers, the Delphi compiler is creating a ThreadStart delegate. Other languages, such as C#, require a few more lines of code to accomplish the same task.

> **NOTE**
>
> Although the ThreadStart delegate does not allow for passing parameters, using the instance method provides the opportunity to use either the constructor or properties to pass additional information needed by the thread. Listing 14.2 demonstrates this by setting the StartNumber.

LISTING 14.3   Creating Threads Using Static Methods

```
1:    program staticthreads;
2:    {$APPTYPE CONSOLE}
3:    uses
4:      System.Threading;
5:
6:  type
7:    D4DNStaticThread = class
8:    public
9:      class procedure ThreadMePlease; static;
10:   end;
11:
12:  class procedure D4DNStaticThread.ThreadMePlease;
13:  var
```

LISTING 14.3   Continued

```
14:    stop    : integer;
15:    curNum  : integer;
16:    rnd     : System.Random;
17:  begin
18:    rnd     := System.Random.Create;
19:    curNum := rnd.Next(1000);
20:    stop := curNum + 10;
21:    while curNum < stop do
22:    begin
23:      writeln('Thread ', System.Threading.Thread.CurrentThread.Name,
24: 'current value is ', curNum);
25:      inc(curNum);
26:      // Randomly give up time-slice to other thread
27:      if rnd.Next(100) < 50 then
28:        Thread.Sleep(0);
29:    end;
30:  end;
31:
32:  var
33:    thrd1 : Thread;
34:    thrd2 : Thread;
35:  begin
36:    Console.Writeline('Starting static method threading example...');
37:
38:    // create the thread passing the static method
39:    thrd1 := Thread.Create(@D4DNStaticThread.ThreadMePlease);
40:    thrd1.Name := 'one';
41:
42:    // create another identical thread
43:    thrd2 := Thread.create(@D4DNStaticThread.ThreadMePlease);
44:    thrd2.Name := 'two';
45:
46:    // start both threads
47:    thrd1.Start;
48:    thrd2.Start;
49:
50:    // wait until both threads have finished
51:    thrd1.Join;
52:    thrd2.Join;
53:
54:    Console.Writeline('Done');
55:    readln;
56:  end.
```

▶ Find the code on the CD: \Code\Chapter 14\Ex02\.

In Listing 14.3, a thread is created on a static class method. Similar to threading instance methods, any static class method without parameters can be executed on a thread.

Listings 14.2 and 14.3 contain a subtle bug. The output written to the console is performed in an unsynchronized manner. It is very likely that the output between two threads will be mixed together. This is caused by the implementation of the writeln procedure by the

Delphi compiler and the runtime library. Each parameter passed to the writeln procedure results in a separate call to either the Console.Write or Console.WriteLine method. Changing the writeln (on line 31 in Listing 14.2, and line 23 in Listing 14.3) to use Console.WriteLine instead or passing only one parameter to the writeln procedure (for example, using writeln(Format(..));) will produce the proper behavior.

System.Threading.ThreadPriority

All manually created threads have an associated priority. This priority allows for boosting or lowering the scheduling of the thread. Table 14.1 lists the enumeration values for ThreadPriority, from the highest to lowest.

TABLE 14.1   *System.Threading.ThreadPriority* Enumeration Values

Value	Description
Highest	Thread is scheduled before any other thread priority.
AboveNormal	Scheduled before any normal priority threads.
Normal	Default setting for threads. Scheduled before BelowNormal threads.
BelowNormal	Scheduled before any threads with lowest priority.
Lowest	Thread is scheduled after all other higher priority threads.

A thread's priority is set using its Priority property. Be careful when changing priorities arbitrarily because that can cause hard to debug conditions such as thread starvation, race conditions, and deadlocks. Never use a higher priority when a lower priority will work.

For GUI applications, most background threads should be set to BelowNormal or Lowest to ensure a responsive user interface no matter how much work the background threads are performing.

System.Threading.ThreadState

Once created, a thread has a state that indicates what the thread is doing. Table 14.2 contains the values of the ThreadState enumeration.

TABLE 14.2   System.Threading.ThreadState Enumeration

Value	Description
Running	The thread's start method has been called.
StopRequested	Used internally only, indicates that the thread has been requested to stop executing.
SuspendRequested	The thread has been requested to suspend itself
Background	Controlled by the Thread.IsBackground property, this value indicates that the thread is executing in the background. Background threads are automatically aborted when the main thread terminates. Only foreground threads will prevent an application from exiting as long as they are running.
Unstarted	A thread has been created but not started yet.
Stopped	The thread is no longer executing.
WaitSleepJoin	The thread is not running due to either being blocked, sleeping, or joining (waiting for another thread to finish executing).
Suspended	The thread is suspended.

TABLE 14.2   Continued

Value	Description
AbortRequested	The thread has been requested to abort, but has not received the ThreadAbortException yet.
Aborted	Indicates that the thread has been terminated because of Thread.Abort.

Because a thread can be in multiple states, the ThreadState enumeration is a set of bit flags. Not all combinations are valid, however. One valid combination is a thread in a WaitSleepJoin state and an AbortRequested state.

System.Threading.ApartmentState Enumeration

The .NET Framework creates an apartment when it interacts with COM objects. This apartment is specified in one of two ways. For manually created threads, the ApartmentState property can be set to the appropriate ApartmentState enumeration. These values are listed in Table 14.3.

14

TABLE 14.3   Values of the System.Threading.ApartmentState Enumeration

Value	Description
STA	Single-threaded apartment
MTA	Multi-threaded apartment
Unknown	Currently mapped to MTA

Once the ApartmentState property has been set, it cannot be changed again. No error or exception will result from attempting to set this property more than once.

An alternative method is to use either the [STAThread] or [MTAThread] attribute before the first line of code in the project's dpr file. Although it is possible to use the following code to set the apartment model,

```
Thread.CurrentThread.ApartmentState := ApartmentState.STA;
```

using the appropriate attribute guarantees that the apartment state will be set up before any startup code is executed.

The System.Threading.ThreadPool Class

One of the nicest features of threading in the .NET framework is the addition of a thread pooling class. Saving thousands of lines of code, this class provides the means necessary for using threads as easy as calling a single method.

Ideal for short-lived tasks, the ThreadPool class hides the underlying Thread class, taking away the flexibility and control that the Thread class provides.

Many features of the .NET platform use threads from the thread pool. Examples using the thread pool include asynchronous file I/O, timers, socket connections, and the asynchronous execution of delegates.

All AppDomains located within the same process share threads from the same thread pool. Figure 14.3 illustrates this relationship.

Applications request a thread by using one of the `QueueUserWorkItem()` methods of the ThreadPool class. These methods take a `WaitCallback` delegate that specifies which method to execute on a thread pool thread. This method is added to an internal queue and is executed when a thread is available.

Be careful when using any of the methods that begin with `Unsafe` because these methods bypass security checks in order to increase performance.

An example of using threads from the `ThreadPool` is shown in Listing 14.4.

LISTING 14.4   Using ThreadPool Threads

```
 1:   program threadpool;
 2:   {$APPTYPE CONSOLE}
 3:   uses
 4:     System.Threading;
 5:
 6:   type
 7:     TThreadPoolMe = class
 8:     public
 9:       // this method will be executed on a threadpool thread
10:       procedure ThreadMePlease(state : System.Object);
11:     end;
12:
13:   procedure TThreadPoolMe.ThreadMePlease(state : System.Object);
14:   var
15:     id : string;
16:   begin
17:     id := 'n/a';
18:     if assigned(state) then
19:       id := state.ToString;
20:
21:     writeln(id,') Hello from the thread pool. Thread ID is ',
22:       AppDomain.GetCurrentThreadID,' IsThreadPool = ',
23:       Thread.CurrentThread.IsThreadPoolThread);
24:
25:     Thread.Sleep(2000);
26:   end;
27:
28:   const
29:     MAX_THREADS = 10;
30:   var
31:     i : integer;
32:     thrd : array[1..MAX_THREADS] of TThreadPoolMe;
33:   begin
34:     writeln('The main thread''s id is ', AppDomain.GetCurrentThreadID);
35:     // queue up a bunch of threads to use the thread pool
36:     for i:=1 to MAX_THREADS do
37:     begin
38:       // create another instance of our class
39:       thrd[i] := TThreadPoolMe.Create;
40:       writeln('Queueing thread ', i);
41:       // now queue up the ThreadMePlease method, passing i in for the state
42:       System.Threading.ThreadPool.QueueUserWorkItem(
```

LISTING 14.4   Continued

```
43:                    @thrd[i].ThreadMePlease, System.Object(i));
44:    end;
45:    // watch the re-use of the thread id's when this application runs
46:    readln;
47:    writeln('Done');
48: end.
```

▶ Find the code on the CD: \Code\Chapter 14\Ex03\.

Listing 14.4 queues 10 threads to the thread pool for execution. Running this example will reveal how the CLR reuses existing threads by examining the reuse of thread IDs.

The System.Threading.Timer Class

The .NET Framework has three different Timer classes that are used for different purposes. System.Threading.Timer uses threads from the thread pool and instead of firing an event, it uses the specified callback method whose definition is shown below:

```
TimerCallback = procedure (state: System.Object) of object;
```

There are four overloaded constructors of the Timer class. All of the constructors are identical except for the type of the last two parameters. The callback parameter is the method to call when the timer fires. Use the state parameter to pass additional information in a System.Object parameter to the callback method. dueTime specifies how long to wait before the callback method is called. This value is specified in milliseconds. Finally, period, also specified in milliseconds, indicates how long to wait between successive calls to the callback method. Use one of the Change() methods to change dueTime or period after creating the Timer instance. Taken from timerthread.dpr, Listing 14.5 demonstrates how to use the Timer class.

LISTING 14.5   Declaration of the System.Threading.Timer Class Example

```
1:    program timerthread;
2:    {$APPTYPE CONSOLE}
3:    uses
4:      System.Threading;
5:
6:    type
7:    TD4DNTimerClass = class
8:    public
9:      // Alarm will be called when the Timer fires
10:      procedure Alarm(state : System.Object);
11:    end;
12:
```

LISTING 14.5   Continued

```
13:  procedure TD4DNTimerClass.Alarm(state : System.Object);
14:  begin
15:    writeln(AppDomain.GetCurrentThreadID,' Bzzzz. Time to wake up!');
16:    if assigned(state) then
17:      writeln('You passed me: ', state.ToString);
18:  end;
19:
20:  var
21:    tc : TD4DNTimerClass;
22:    t  : Timer;
23:  begin
24:    // create an instance of our class
25:    tc := TD4DNTimerClass.Create;
26:    // create the timer to call Alarm only once, after delaying 1 second
➡(1000 ms)
27:    t  := Timer.Create(tc.Alarm, System.Object('Some additional info'),
➡1000 , 0);
28:    writeln(AppDomain.GetCurrentThreadID,' Waiting for the timer to fire.');
29:    // give the timer a chance to fire
30:    Thread.Sleep(2000);
31:    writeln(AppDomain.GetCurrentThreadID,' Done!');
32:  end.
```

▶ Find the code on the CD: \Code\Chapter 14\Ex04\.

Delegates

A delegate is a type-safe callback mechanism inherited from System.Delegate. Delegates require a method that is called at the appropriate time. Delegates that descend from System.MulticastDelegate are capable of handling multiple methods. Although delegates are normally called in an synchronous manner using the Invoke() method, the BeginInvoke() method allows for calling delegate methods asynchronously. Only delegates that have one method to call are capable of using the BeginInvoke() method. Unfortunately, the Delphi 8 compiler does not recognize a method pointer as a delegate class instance. Fortunately, BeginInvoke() can still be called by using Reflection. Listing 14.6 demonstrates how to execute a delegate asynchronously.

LISTING 14.6   Executing Delegates Asynchronously

```
1:   program AsyncDelegate;
2:   {$APPTYPE CONSOLE}
3:   uses
4:     System.Reflection,
5:     System.Threading;
6:
7:   type
8:     TMyDelegate = procedure of object;
9:
10:    TMyClass = class
11:    private
12:      FOnDoSomething : TMyDelegate;
```

LISTING 14.5   Continued

```
13:    public
14:       procedure CallDelegate;
15:       property  OnDoSomething : TMyDelegate read FOnDoSomething write
➥FOnDoSomething;
16:    end;
17:
18:    TAnotherClass = class
19:    public
20:       procedure DoFoo;
21:    end;
22:
23:    procedure TMyClass.CallDelegate;
24:    var
25:       obj : System.Object;
26:       t : System.Type;
27:       m : MethodInfo;
28:       parms : array [0..1] of System.Object;
29:    begin
30:       writeln('CallDelegate');
31:       if Assigned(FOnDoSomething) then
32:       begin
33:         // writeln('call delegate');
34:         // Normally this would look similar to
35:         // @FOnDoSomething.BeginInvoke(nil, nil);
36:         // but the compiler doesn't support BeginInvoke, since
37:         // it thinks it's just a pointer to a method.
38:         //
39:         // the work around uses reflection to invoke the method
40:         // first cast the "method pointer" to an object
41:         obj := System.Object(@FOnDoSomething);
42:         // now get the type of the FOnDoSomething
43:         t := obj.GetType;
44:         // now we gat search for a method named BeginInvoke
45:         m := t.GetMethod('BeginInvoke');
46:         // build the parameter list
47:         parms[0] := nil;
48:         parms[1] := nil;
49:         // now we can call BeginInvoke with the parms
50:         m.Invoke(obj, parms);
51:       end;
52:    end;
53:
54:    procedure TAnotherClass.DoFoo;
55:    begin
56:       writeln(AppDomain.GetCurrentThreadID,' DoFoo');
67:    end;
58:
59:    var
60:       c : TMyClass;
61:       ac : TAnotherClass;
62:
63:    begin
64:       c := TMyClass.Create;
```

LISTING 14.5   Continued

```
65:    ac := TAnotherClass.Create;
66:    writeln(AppDomain.GetCurrentThreadID,' assigning the delegate');
67:    c.OnDoSomething := @ac.DoFoo;
68:    writeln(AppDomain.GetCurrentThreadID,' calling the delegate');
69:    c.CallDelegate;
70:    // give the delegate some time to call it...
71:    Thread.Sleep(2000);
72:    writeln(AppDomain.GetCurrentThreadID,' Done');
73:  end.
```

▶ Find the code on the CD: `\Code\Chapter 14\Ex05\`.

Writing Thread-safe Code .NET Style

Writing a multithreaded application is pointless if multiple threads cannot interact in a predictable and bug-free manner. A body of code is said to be thread-safe if multiple threads can safely execute it without any side effects. One way of making a method or function thread-safe is to serialize access to it, thereby allowing only one thread to execute the code at a time.

Thread-safe code can be accomplished by following a few guidelines:

- Avoid variables and objects shared between threads. If this is not feasible, use a locking mechanism to serialize access.

- Use variables declared on the stack (for example, local variables).

- Use stateless routines by passing in all parameters that are needed to do its work.

- Use stateless methods, performing work on the internal data of the object. (This assumes that each object instance is only accessible from one thread.) Any additional data should be passed as parameters. Make sure that parameters or fields do not refer to other global data or unprotected objects.

- Use thread local storage (`threadvar`), which is explained in a later section of this chapter.

Fortunately, the .NET Framework provides a rich collection of classes to help write thread-safe code. These classes are generalized as locking and event mechanisms. Locking performs serialization, whereas an event is used for communication between threads.

Locking Mechanisms

Serializing access to a resource is accomplished by using a locking mechanism. By only allowing one thread to enter into a protected region, other threads are locked out. When one thread exits a protected region of code, another thread is then allowed to enter it.

There are three locking mechanisms in the .NET Framework: mutexes, monitors, and Read-Write locks. In addition, the `Interlocked` class provides a basic set of operations that are atomic. Atomic operations are those that are guaranteed not to be interrupted once they begin.

The System.Threading.WaitHandle Class

Before discussing mutexes and monitors, it is necessary to begin with the WaitHandle class as these two locking mechanisms inherit common functionality from it. Listing 14.7 contains the definition of the WaitHandle class.

LISTING 14.7   Declaration of the System.Threading.WaitHandle Class

```
System.Threading.WaitHandle = class (System.MarshalByRefObject, IDisposable)
public
  constructor Create;
  procedure Close; virtual;
  function WaitOne: Boolean; overload; virtual;
  function WaitOne(timeout: TimeSpan;
                   exitContext: Boolean) : Boolean; overload; virtual;
  function WaitOne(millisecondsTimeout: Integer;
                   exitContext: Boolean) : Boolean; overload; virtual;
  class function WaitAll(waitHandles: array of WaitHandle;
                         millisecondsTimeout: Integer;
                         exitContext: Boolean) : Boolean; overload; static;
  class function WaitAll(waitHandles: array of WaitHandle;
                         timeout: TimeSpan;
                         exitContext: Boolean) : Boolean; overload; static;
  class function WaitAll(waitHandles: array of WaitHandle) : Boolean;
    overload; static;
  class function WaitAny(waitHandles: array of WaitHandle;
                         millisecondsTimeout: Integer;
                         exitContext: Boolean) : Integer; overload; static;
  class function WaitAny(waitHandles: array of WaitHandle;
                         timeout: TimeSpan;
                         exitContext: Boolean) : Integer; overload; static;
  class function WaitAny(waitHandles: array of WaitHandle) : Integer;
    overload; static;
  property Handle: System.IntPtr read; write;
end;
```

Similar to the Win32 API WaitForMultipleObjects(), the overloaded WaitAll() method accepts multiple WaitHandle objects and will only return if all handles are signaled. The WaitAny() method returns if any of the multiple WaitHandle objects are signaled. Both methods have optional timeout parameters that enable the methods to exit the wait prematurely and avoid deadlocks.

The System.Threading.Mutex Class

A mutex is a mutually exclusive object that acts similar to a lock. Locking the mutex is accomplished by calling one of the overloaded WaitOne() methods. Mutexes have the option of being named. Specifying a name allows for the mutex to be shared between AppDomains and processes. The mutex is unlocked by calling the ReleaseMutex() method. Listing 14.8 shows the methods declared in the Mutex class.

LISTING 14.8   Declaration of the System.Threading.Mutex Class

```
System.Threading.Mutex = class (System.Threading.WaitHandle)
public
```

LISTING 14.8   Continued

```
  constructor Create(initiallyOwned: Boolean; name: String;
    var createdNew: Boolean); overload;
  constructor Create(initiallyOwned: Boolean; name: String); overload;
  constructor Create(initiallyOwned: Boolean); overload;
  constructor Create; overload;
  procedure ReleaseMutex;
end;
```

In addition to the Wait methods inherited from WaitHandle, the Mutex class adds several constructors as well as the ReleaseMutex() method. These constructors provide the ability to create, optionally lock (own), and optionally name the mutex. A mutex is unlocked by using the ReleaseMutex() method.

The System.Threading.Monitor Class

The System.Threading.Monitor class has been designed to be more lightweight than the Mutex class. It should be used when a high-performance locking mechanism is needed.

Although the Monitor class looks similar to a mutex, there are some subtle differences. Take a look at Listing 14.9 for the definition of the Monitor class.

LISTING 14.9   Declaration of the System.Threading.Monitor Class

```
System.Threading.Monitor = class (System.Object)
public
  class procedure Enter(obj: System.Object); static;
  class function TryEnter(obj: System.Object) : Boolean; overload; static;
  class function TryEnter(obj: System.Object;
    millisecondsTimeout: Integer) : Boolean; overload; static;
  class function TryEnter(obj: System.Object;
    timeout: TimeSpan) : Boolean; overload; static;
  class function Wait(obj: System.Object; millisecondsTimeout: Integer;
    exitContext: Boolean) : Boolean; overload; static;
  class function Wait(obj: System.Object; timeout: TimeSpan;
    exitContext: Boolean) : Boolean; overload; static;
  class function Wait(obj: System.Object;
    millisecondsTimeout: Integer) : Boolean; overload; static;
  class function Wait(obj: System.Object;
    timeout: TimeSpan) : Boolean; overload; static;
  class function Wait(obj: System.Object) : Boolean; overload; static;
  class procedure Pulse(obj: System.Object); static;
  class procedure PulseAll(obj: System.Object); static;
  class procedure Exit(obj: System.Object); static;
end;
```

Using the Enter() and Exit() methods of the Monitor has the same effect as locking with a Mutex's WaitOne() and ReleaseMutex() methods. The Monitor class also has TryEnter() methods that attempt to acquire a lock without waiting. An optional timeout parameter specifies how long to wait on the lock before giving up.

Notice that all the methods of the Monitor class are class methods. This provides the flexibility to specify any object to lock upon.

Finally, the `Monitor` class allows for signaling and waiting for a signal with the `Wait()` and `Pulse()` methods. Both `Wait()` and `Pulse()` methods require the `Monitor` to be locked—that is, surround the `Wait()` and `Pulse()` methods with an `Enter()` / `Exit()` pair.

Find the code on the CD: \Code\Chapter 14\Ex06\prodcons.dpr for an example that demonstrates a thread-safe queue using the Mutex and Monitor classes.

The System.Threading.ReaderWriterLock Class

The `Mutex` and `Monitor` classes provide a locking mechanism that is useful for preventing a section of code from being executed simultaneously by multiple threads. However, there are times when a lock that can distinguish between a reader and a writer can increase performance. This is especially true when there are more readers than writers or if the writer is infrequent with its updates. Fortunately, the `ReaderWriterLock` class provides this functionality. Listing 14.10 contains the definition of the `ReaderWriterLock` class.

LISTING 14.10   Declaration of the System.Threading.ReaderWriterLock Class

```
System.Threading.ReaderWriterLock = class (System.Object)
  constructor Create;
  procedure AcquireReaderLock(millisecondsTimeout: Integer); overload;
  procedure AcquireReaderLock(timeout: TimeSpan); overload;
  procedure AcquireWriterLock(millisecondsTimeout: Integer); overload;
  procedure AcquireWriterLock(timeout: TimeSpan); overload;
  procedure ReleaseReaderLock;
  procedure ReleaseWriterLock;
  function UpgradeToWriterLock(millisecondsTimeout: Integer) :
    LockCookie; overload;
  function UpgradeToWriterLock(timeout: TimeSpan) :
    LockCookie; overload;
  procedure DowngradeFromWriterLock(var lockCookie: LockCookie);
  function ReleaseLock: LockCookie;
  procedure RestoreLock(var lockCookie: LockCookie);
  function AnyWritersSince(seqNum: Integer) : Boolean;
  property IsReaderLockHeld: Boolean read;
  property IsWriterLockHeld: Boolean read;
  property WriterSeqNum: integer read;
end;
```

As expected, two types of locks are available. These locks are referred to as a reader lock and a writer lock. Locks are acquired by using the `AcquireReaderLock()` and `AcquireWriterLock()` methods, respectively.

A reader lock is acquired only when no writer locks are being held. That way, multiple readers are allowed. However, all readers are blocked when a writer lock is obtained. Only one writer lock is allowed. Find the code on the CD: \Code\Chapter 14\Ex07\TestRWLock.dpr for an example of how to use the ReaderWriterLock class.

The System.Threading.Interlocked Class

Because of the random nature of the way the kernel schedules threads, there is no way to prevent a block of code from being interrupted to execute another thread. Code that needs to be executed atomically—that is, without interruption—requires the use of the

System.Threading.Interlocked class. Listing 14.11 contains the class definition of the Interlocked class.

LISTING 14.11   Declaration of the System.Threading.Interlocked Class

```
System.Threading.Interlocked = class (System.Object)
  class function Increment(var location: Integer) : Integer; overload; static;
  class function Increment(var location: Int64) : Int64; overload; static;

  class function Decrement(var location: Integer) : Integer; overload; static;
  class function Decrement(var location: Int64) : Int64; overload; static;
  class function Exchange(var location1: Integer; value: Integer)
                          : Integer; overload; static;
  class function Exchange(var location1: Single;
                          value: Single) : Single; overload; static;
  class function Exchange(var location1 : System.Object;
                          value : System.Object) : System.Object; overload;
                          ➥static;
  class function CompareExchange(var location1: Integer;
                                 value: Integer;
                                 comparand: Integer) : Integer; overload;
                                 ➥static;
  class function CompareExchange(var location1: Single;
                                 value: Single;
                                 comparand: Single) : Single; overload; static;
  class function CompareExchange(var location1 : System.Object;
                                 value : System.Object;
                                 comparand : System.Object) : System.Object;
                                 ➥overload; static;
end;
```

Notice that all methods are class methods, so an instance of this class is never needed. Each distinct operation is guaranteed to finish execution once it begins.

Events

Although preventing access to a critical block of code is an important task when writing multithreaded applications, there is also the need to be able to signal a waiting thread. It is common to have one or more threads produce work for other threads to manipulate. Threads that create work are referred to as producer threads. Consumer threads are those that do the actual work handed out by the producer threads.

The signal used by the .NET Framework is known as an event. Two types of events are available—AutoResetEvent and ManualResetEvent. When an event is set, it is signaled. Similarly, when an event is reset, the state of the event is not signaled. Events are automatically reset by the .NET Framework when exactly one thread is released when waiting on the event. Manually reset events must be cleared programmatically, and it is likely for multiple threads to be released. Listings 14.12 and 14.13 show the class definition of both types of events.

LISTING 14.12   Declaration of the System.Threading.ManualResetEvent Class

```
System.Threading.ManualResetEvent = class (System.Threading.WaitHandle)
public
  constructor Create(initialState: Boolean);
  procedure Close; virtual;
  function WaitOne: Boolean; virtual; overload;
  function WaitOne(timeout: TimeSpan; exitContext: Boolean) :
    Boolean; virtual; overload;
  function WaitOne(millisecondsTimeout: Integer; exitContext: Boolean) :
    Boolean; virtual; overload;
  function Reset: Boolean;
  function Set: Boolean;
  class function WaitAll(waitHandles: WaitHandle[];
    millisecondsTimeout: Integer; exitContext: Boolean) : Boolean; overload;
    ➥static;
  class function WaitAll(waitHandles: WaitHandle[]; timeout: TimeSpan;
    exitContext: Boolean) : Boolean; overload; static;
  class function WaitAll(waitHandles: WaitHandle[]) : Boolean; overload; static;
  class function WaitAny(waitHandles: WaitHandle[];
    millisecondsTimeout: Integer; exitContext: Boolean) : Integer; overload;
    ➥static;
  class function WaitAny(waitHandles: WaitHandle[]; timeout: TimeSpan;
    exitContext: Boolean) : Integer; overload;
  class function WaitAny(waitHandles: WaitHandle[]) : Integer; overload; static;
  property Handle: System.IntPtr read; write;
end;
```

LISTING 14.13   Declaration of the System.Threading.AutoResetEvent Class

```
System.Threading.AutoResetEvent = class (System.Threading.WaitHandle,
  IDisposable)
public
  constructor Create(initialState: Boolean);
  function Reset: Boolean;
  function Set: Boolean;
end;
```

Using either type of event is identical. Use the Set() method to signal an event and the Reset() method to clear the signal. Notice that several methods are used for waiting on an event. The overloaded WaitOne() method waits for only one event, whereas the WaitAll() method waits for every entity to be signaled, and the WaitAny() method allows for waiting for any one signal to be fired. Finally, both the WaitAll() and WaitAny() methods provide the capability of waiting for a Mutex or either type of event. Recall that the WaitAll() and WaitAny() methods are inherited from WaitHandle and are listed in the earlier section "The System.Threading.WaitHandle Class."

Find the code on the CD: \Code\Chapter 14\Ex06\prodcons.dpr for an example demonstrating how to use Events. Be sure to define the USE_EVENTS symbol.

Thread Local Storage

Using variables that are global in a multithreaded application is a surefire way to cause debugging nightmares. Unless these global variables are protected, sleepless nights are guaranteed.

Sometimes it is necessary to have a variable that is global to a thread. Thread Local Storage is the name given to variables that are global to a specific thread. The easiest way to create this kind of variable is to use the `threadvar` keyword. Although they are declared like a standard unit global variable, each thread is allocated a separate slot for storing the contents of the variable.

Initialization of `threadvars` is not allowed. Each thread needs to initialize the variable before using it. An example of a `threadvar` looks like

```
threadvar
  MyThreadVariable: integer; // remember, no initialization
```

In the .NET Framework, the `System.Threading.Thread` class has two methods for creating thread local storage. They are the `AllocateDataSlot()` and the `AllocateNamedDataSlot()` methods. Finally, use the `ThreadStaticAttribute` to create a static field unique for each thread. Delphi for .NET currently maps `threadvars` with the `[ThreadStatic]` attribute.

Take extra caution when using thread local storage with any mechanism that uses threads from the `ThreadPool`. Another thread might or might not have already initialized a thread local variable with an unexpected value.

Win32 Interprocess Communications

The Win32 API has more IPC mechanisms available that have not been ported to the managed world. Named pipes and semaphores can be leveraged by using Platform Invoke (PInvoke). This may be the best option when integration is needed with existing Win32 applications. Be wary of performance issues, however, because PInvoke has associated overhead costs. PInvoke is covered in Chapter 16, "Interoperability: COM Interop and the Platform Invocation Service."

Thread-safe .NET Framework Classes and Methods

Thread safety is a serious issue when writing multithreaded applications. So how can one determine if a particular method or class is thread-safe?

When it comes to thread safety in the .NET Framework, one thing is guaranteed: All methods that are `public class` (`static`) methods are thread-safe, as long as they only refer to their parameters. This makes sense because class methods cannot refer to any instance data. In general, all other methods are not thread-safe unless the SDK documentation clearly states otherwise.

The Synchronized() Method

Most collection classes have helper properties and methods. A thread-safe queue is obtained by using the following code:

```
myThreadSafeQueue = System.Collections.Queue.Synchronized(
    System.Collections.Queue.Create);
```

All access to the synchronized queue is now thread-safe. Be aware that a thread-safe collection will be approximately two times slower than an unsynchronized collection.

The IsSynchronized and SyncRoot Properties

Collections that support the Synchronized() method also have a property that indicates if the collection is in fact synchronized. Use the IsSynchronized property to determine if the collection is synchronized.

Another method of making a collection thread-safe is to use a System.Threading.Monitor. Recall that a Monitor requires an object to perform the locking. This object must be the object returned by collection's SyncRoot property.

Be sure to look for the IsSynchronized and SyncRoot properties on other classes within the .NET Framework—specifically, those classes that implement the ICollection interface. For example, the System.Array class is one class that implements these properties as well. Arrays are not thread-safe, and the IsSynchronized returns false. Serialize access to the array by locking on the SyncRoot property of the array.

> **CAUTION**
>
> Classes that contain the SyncRoot property require due diligence on the part of the developer to ensure that every access to the array is locked before iterating or indexing its members. Nothing within the .NET Framework prevents one thread from properly locking an instance and another from using the same instance, bypassing any locking mechanism. A better alternative is to write a thread-safe class that encapsulates the appropriate storage mechanism and guarantees that all accesses to the internal class are locked.

User Interface Issues

In order to optimize performance of the User Interface (UI), both WinForms and VCL applications have not implemented any thread-safety mechanisms. Any updates to a control must occur from the main user-interface thread.

For WinForm applications, most methods of the System.Windows.Forms.Control class are not thread-safe. There are, however, four methods that are safe to execute from any thread. These methods are identified in the following sections. Listing 14.14 contains the methods and properties of interest for this section.

LISTING 14.14   Thread-safe System.Windows.Forms.Control Methods

```
System.Windows.Forms.Control = class (
          System.ComponentModel.Component,
          ISynchronizeInvoke, …)
public
  …
  function Invoke(method: Delegate) : System.Object; overload;
  function Invoke(method: Delegate;
                  args: array of System.Object) :
              System.Object; overload;
  function EndInvoke(asyncResult: IAsyncResult) :
              System.Object;
```

LISTING 14.14   Continued

```
function BeginInvoke(method: Delegate;
                       args: array of System.Object) :
                     IAsyncResult; overload;
function BeginInvoke(method: Delegate) : IAsyncResult;
                     overload;
property InvokeRequired: Boolean read;
end;
```

The System.Windows.Forms.Control.Invoke() Method

The most common way of ensuring that a control is updated from the user interface thread is to use one of the overloaded `Invoke()` methods. `Invoke()` requires a delegate and an optional array of arguments. When `Invoke()` is called, it guarantees that the delegate method is executed on the same thread that the control was created on. In addition, `Invoke()` blocks until the method is executed, thereby causing the worker thread to pause. (Listing 14.15 shows an example of calling the `Invoke()` method.)

> **NOTE**
>
> Never call `Join()` from the main thread that uses the `Invoke()` method to update the UI thread. This causes the application to hang because the main thread is waiting for the worker thread and the worker thread is waiting for the UI thread.

The System.Windows.Forms.Control.InvokeRequired Property

Suppose that a method will be shared between a user-interface thread and a worker thread. As previously discussed, the worker thread will need to use the `Invoke()` method to ensure that the update occurs on the proper thread. However, the user-interface thread does not need to use the `Invoke()` method. Fortunately, the `InvokeRequired` property provides the flexibility to know if the method can be called directly or if the `Invoke()` method must be used. Listing 14.15 shows how to use the `InvokeRequired` property.

LISTING 14.15   Example of Invoke() and InvokeRequired

```
type
  TMyUpdateDelegate = procedure of object;

procedure TWinForm.UpdateControls;
var
  myDelegate: TMyUpdateDelegate;
  tmpStr     : string;
begin
  if progBar.InvokeRequired then
  begin
    tmpStr := System.String.Format('{0} invoke required!',
              System.Object(AppDomain.GetCurrentThreadID));
    UpdateTextBox(System.Object(tmpStr));
    myDelegate := @self.UpdateControls;
    progBar.Invoke(System.Delegate(@myDelegate));
  end
```

LISTING 14.15 Continued

```
  else
  begin
    progBar.Increment(1);
    trackBar.Value := trackBar.Value + 1;
  end;
end;
```

▶ Find the code on the CD: \Code\Chapter 14\Ex08\.

Taken from the ThreadingExamples project, the UpdateControls() method is called from the main user-interface thread and other worker threads. If it is called from the worker thread, a delegate is used to call the same method on the main user-interface thread. Notice that two controls are being updated: progBar and trackBar. The only InvokeRequired test is on the progress bar since both controls were created on the same thread.

The System.Windows.Forms.Control.BeginInvoke() Method

When it is not desirable to wait for the main thread to execute, use one of the overloaded BeginInvoke() methods. These methods do the same thing as Invoke() except that they execute the method asynchronously, without waiting. Make sure that the delegate method used is thread-safe. (Listing 14.16 shows an example of using BeginInvoke().)

The System.Windows.Forms.Control.EndInvoke() Method

Executing a method asynchronously is very powerful, especially if a return value is not needed. When a return value is needed from a method executed with BeginInvoke(), use the EndInvoke() method. EndInvoke() returns a System.Object, which represents the return value from the delegate executed asynchronously. Use EndInvoke() carefully because it will block if the method has not completed when EndInvoke() is called. Listing 14.16, which is also from the ThreadingExamples project, illustrates how to use the BeginInvoke() and EndInvoke() methods.

LISTING 14.16 BeginInvoke()/EndInvoke() Example

```
procedure TWinForm.UpdateControlsNoWaiting;
var
  myDelegate: TMyTextBoxDelegate;
  tmpStr    : string;
  parms     : array[0..0] of System.object;
  lastAsyncInvoke: IAsyncResult;

begin
  if textBox.InvokeRequired then
  begin
   tmpStr := System.String.Format(
               '{0} Invoke required in UpdateControlsNoWaiting',
               System.Object(AppDomain.GetCurrentThreadID));
   myDelegate := @self.LongRunningMethod;
   parms[0] := System.Object(tmpStr);
   lastAsyncInvoke := textBox.BeginInvoke(
                        System.Delegate(@myDelegate), parms );
```

LISTING 14.16   Continued

```
    tmpStr := System.String.Format(
        '{0} After BeginInvoke call in UpdateControlsNoWaiting',
               System.Object(AppDomain.GetCurrentThreadID)));
    UpdateTextBox(System.Object(tmpStr));
    // now let's wait for the async call to finish..
    textBox.EndInvoke(lastAsyncInvoke);
    tmpStr := System.String.Format(
          '{0} After EndInvoke call in UpdateControlsNoWaiting',
               System.Object(AppDomain.GetCurrentThreadID)));
    UpdateTextBox(System.Object(tmpStr));
  end
  else
    UpdateTextBox(
      'Invoke is not required in UpdateControlsNoWaiting');
end;
```

▶ Find the code on the CD: \Code\Chapter 14\Ex08\.

The System.Windows.Forms.Control.CreateGraphics() Method

Access to the GDI+ drawing subsystem is accomplished through the System.Drawing.Graphics
class. An instance of this class is available by calling a control's CreateGraphics() method.
The CreateGraphics() method is thread-safe, allowing multiple threads to update a GDI+
drawing surface without affecting each other. GDI+ resources are limited, so make sure to
use the Dispose() method when finished with the Graphics instance.

One word of caution when using CreateGraphics(). Make sure that any drawing is done
within a paint handler. Any updating of a control occurring outside of a paint handler will
be erased when the next paint message is processed. Listing 14.17, also from the
ThreadingExamples project, demonstrates how two threads can safely paint on a control at
the same time. The painting does not occur within a paint handler, so the drawing is easily
erased.

LISTING 14.17   CreateGraphics() Example

```
1:    procedure TWinForm.btnCreateGraphics_Click(sender: System.Object; e:
➥System.EventArgs);
2:    var
3:      inst : array[0..1] of TMyGraphicsClass;
4:      thrd : Thread;
5:      i    : integer;
6:    begin
7:      // this method creates a couple of TMyGraphicClass instances and executes
8:      // the draw method on different threads
9:      UpdateTextBox('Anything causing a repaint erase the graphics being
➥currently drawn');
10:     for i:=low(inst) to high(inst) do
11:     begin
12:       inst[i] := TMyGraphicsClass.Create;
13:       inst[i].Control := Self.Panel1;
14:       inst[i].DrawRectangle := (i = 0);
```

LISTING 14.17 Continued

```
15:
16:      thrd := Thread.Create(@inst[i].Draw);
17:      thrd.Start;
18:    end;
19:  end;
20:
21:  procedure TMyGraphicsClass.Draw;
22:  var
23:    gr : System.Drawing.Graphics;
24:    clr : Color;
25:    i   : integer;
26:    height : integer;
27:    width  : integer;
28:    rnd    : System.Random;
29:    curX   : integer;
30:    curY   : integer;
31:    curW   : integer;
32:    curH   : integer;
33:    thrdID : System.Object;
34:    tmpStr : string;
35:  begin
36:    // this method randomly draws either Red circles or Blue Rectangles
37:    thrdID := System.Object(AppDomain.GetCurrentThreadId);
38:    tmpStr := System.String.Format('{0} Graphics Class Thread
➥Started',thrdId);
39:    theWinFormInstance.UpdateTextBox(System.Object(tmpStr));
40:
41:    try
42:      clr := Color.Red;
43:      if FDrawRectangle then
44:        clr := Color.Blue;
45:
46:      gr := FControl.CreateGraphics;
47:      try
48:        rnd     := System.Random.Create;
49:
50:        height := System.Convert.ToInt32(gr.VisibleClipBounds.Height);
51:        width  := System.Convert.ToInt32(gr.VisibleClipBounds.Width);
52:
53:        for i:=1 to 10 do
54:        begin
55:          curX := rnd.Next(width);
56:          curY := rnd.Next(height);
57:          curW := rnd.Next(width div 3);
58:          curH := rnd.Next(height div 3);
59:
60:          if (curX + curW) > width then
61:            curX := width - curW;
62:
63:          if (curY + curH) > height then
64:            curY := height - curH;
65:
66:          if FDrawRectangle then
```

LISTING 14.17 Continued

```
67:              gr.FillRectangle(SolidBrush.Create(clr), curX, curY, curW, curH)
68:          else
69:              gr.FillEllipse(SolidBrush.Create(clr), curX, curY, curW, curH);
70:
71:          Thread.Sleep(2000);
72:        end;
73:      finally
74:        gr.Dispose;
75:      end;
76:    except
77:      on e : exception do
78:      begin
79:        thrdID := System.Object(AppDomain.GetCurrentThreadId);
80:        tmpStr := System.String.Format('{0} Graphics class thread
➥Exception {1}', thrdID,
81:                                        System.Object(e.message));
82:        theWinFormInstance.UpdateTextBox(System.Object(tmpStr));
83:      end;
84:    end;
85:
86:    thrdID := System.Object(AppDomain.GetCurrentThreadId);
87:    tmpStr := System.String.Format('{0} Graphics Class Thread
➥Finished',thrdId);
88:    theWinFormInstance.UpdateTextBox(System.Object(tmpStr));
89:  end;
```

▶ Find the code on the CD: \Code\Chapter 14\Ex08\.

Listing 14.17 creates two threads that draw either a rectangle or an ellipse. Before the Draw() method can paint on the control, it must first grab an instance to the Graphics class, which is illustrated on line 46. Once this instance is obtained, each thread is free to update the same control simultaneously.

Threading Exceptions

Exceptions need to be dealt with appropriately in order to avoid threads terminating prematurely. Any exception within a thread that is not handled will cause the thread to be terminated. Therefore, it is a good programming practice to at least report all exceptions and handle those exceptions that are expected.

System.Threading.ThreadAbortException

Calling the Thread.Abort() method will raise the ThreadAbortException on the target thread. Normally, this will cause the thread to terminate. However, a thread can catch the ThreadAbortException and choose to ignore it by using the Thread.ResetAbort() method.

There are two overloaded Abort() methods. One method does not take any parameters; the other takes a System.Object that provides state information to the thread. This parameter is examined by looking at the ExceptionState property of the ThreadAbortException. Listing 14.18 demonstrates how to handle the ThreadAbortException, taken from ThreadingExceptions.dpr.

LISTING 14.18   ThreadingExceptions Example

```
1:   program ThreadingExceptions;
2:   {$APPTYPE CONSOLE}
3:
4:   //
5:   // This example demonstrates ThreadingExceptions.
6:   //    - ThreadAbortException is handled, and reset
7:   //    - ThreadInterruptedException is handled
8:   //    - ThreadStateException is handled
9:   //    - SynchronizationLockException is handled
10:  //
11:
12:  uses
13:    System.Threading;
14:
15:  type
16:    D4DNThreadMe = class
17:    public
18:      procedure MyThreadMethod;
19:    end;
20:
21:  procedure D4DNThreadMe.MyThreadMethod;
22:  var
23:    numAborts : integer;
24:
25:  begin
26:    numAborts := 0;
27:    while true do
28:    begin
29:      try
30:        write('*');
31:        Thread.Sleep(1000);
32:      except
33:        on e : System.Threading.ThreadInterruptedException do
34:        begin
35:          writeln('Handled ThreadInterruptedException');
36:        end;
37:        on e : System.Threading.ThreadAbortException do
38:        begin
39:          writeln('Handled threadAbortException');
40:          inc(numAborts);
41:          if numAborts = 1 then
42:            Thread.ResetAbort;
43:        end;
44:        on e : exception do
45:        begin
46:          writeln('Unhandled exception ',e.message);
47:          raise;
48:        end;
49:      end;
50:    end;
51:  end;
52:
53:  var
```

LISTING 14.18   Continued

```
54:     thrdclass1 : D4DNThreadMe;
55:     thrd1 : Thread;
56:     cmd : string;
57:     bDone : boolean;
58:
59:   begin
60:     System.Console.WriteLine('Staring threading exceptions example...');
61:
62:     // create myDotNetThread instance
63:     thrdclass1 := D4DNThreadMe.create;
64:     thrd1 := Thread.Create(@thrdclass1.MyThreadMethod);
65:     thrd1.Start;
66:
67:     bDone := false;
68:     while not bDone do
69:     begin
70:       System.Console.WriteLine('Enter A = Abort, I = Interrupt, ' +
71:         'S = ThreadStateException, L = SyncLockException');
72:       cmd := System.Console.ReadLine.ToUpper;
73:       if (cmd = 'A') then
74:         thrd1.Abort // raise a ThreadAbortException
75:       else if (cmd = 'I') then
76:         thrd1.Interrupt // raise a ThreadInterruptedException
77:       else if (cmd = 'S') then
78:       begin
79:         try
80:           thrd1.Start
81:         except
82:           on e : System.Threading.ThreadStateException do
83:           begin
84:             System.Console.WriteLine('Handled ThreadStateException');
85:           end;
86:         end;
87:       end
88:       else if (cmd = 'L') then
89:       begin
90:         try
91:           // needs to be wrapped in an Enter/Exit() block
92:           System.Threading.Monitor.Wait(thrd1);
93:         except
94:           on e : System.Threading.SynchronizationLockException do
95:           begin
96:             System.Console.WriteLine('Handled SynchronizationLockException');
97:           end;
98:         end;
99:       end
100:      else
101:        bDone := true;
102:    end;
103:
104:    // ensure that the thread is terminated
105:    thrd1.Abort;
106:    Thread.Sleep(1000);
```

LISTING 14.18   Continued

```
107:    thrd1.Abort;
108:
109:    System.Console.WriteLine('Done - main');
110: end.
```

▶ Find the code on the CD: \Code\Chapter 14\Ex09\.

System.Threading.ThreadInterruptedException

Threads that are in a WaitSleepJoin state can be interrupted by using the Thread.Interrupt() method. If a thread is not in the WaitSleepJoin state, the exception will fire the next time that it goes into that state. Unhandled, this exception will terminate the thread. Listing 14.18 shows an example of the ThreadInterrupedException.

System.Threading.ThreadStateException

Suppose that an application has two threads—A and B. If thread A tries to coerce thread B into an invalid state, a ThreadStateException will be raised in thread A. Trying to transition from a running state to a restarted state or from a terminated state to a restarted state are both illegal state transitions that will trigger the ThreadStateException. Listing 14.18 contains an example of how the ThreadStateException is raised and handled.

System.Threading.SynchronizationLockException

Attempting to use certain methods of the Monitor class incorrectly will raise the SynchronizationLockException. For example, calling the Wait() method outside of a pair of Enter()/Exit() methods triggers this exception. Listing 14.18 illustrates an example.

Garbage Collection and Threading

Garbage collection can occur at any time. In order to perform its job, all threads are suspended. If any managed threads are currently executing unmanaged code, these threads are resumed. However, before resuming these threads, the CLR inserts code to suspend the thread when it returns to managed code. These threads are allowed to resume because memory is pinned (locked down) when it is referenced by unmanaged code.

IN THIS CHAPTER

- Reflecting an Assembly
- Reflecting a Module
- Reflecting Types
- Runtime Invocation of a Type's Members (Late Binding)
- Emitting MSIL Through Reflection

CHAPTER **15**

Reflection API

Reflection is the .NET way to obtain metadata information about classes and types. This is similar in nature to Delphi's runtime type information (RTTI), although the implementation is substantially different. Metadata is provided via the classes defined in the System.Reflection namespace.

Reflection offers more capabilities than just retrieving metadata information. Through Reflection, you can instantiate various classes, invoke their methods, get and set member values, define and create new classes, dynamically add types to an assembly, and more. Another powerful use of reflection is defining and checking for the presence of custom attributes. These can give additional information about properties, methods, classes, etc. that can be used for debugging, documentation, inspection, design time information, etc. This chapter covers the capabilities of the Reflection API.

> **WHAT HAPPENED TO RTTI?**
>
> RTTI is similar to Reflection and was the basis behind dynamically discovering information about Delphi VCL classes at runtime. RTTI has not disappeared: It can be found in the Borland.Vcl.TypInfo.pas file, is still used for class discovery of VCL classes, and is a means of portability between the Win32 and .NET versions of VCL.

Reflecting an Assembly

Chapter 8 discusses assemblies and how they contain metadata about the types contained in them. This section discusses reflecting the assembly itself. The following sections show how to drill down further into the assembly's modules, extracting detailed information about their structure and contents.

The Assembly class itself contains several properties and methods that you can use to reflect information about it. Listing 15.1 illustrates some of these methods.

LISTING 15.1   Example of Reflecting an Assembly

```
 1:   procedure TWinForm.ReflectAssembly(aAssembly: Assembly);
 2:   var
 3:     arModule: array of Module;
 4:     i: integer;
 5:     tn: TreeNode;
 6:     tni: TreeNode;
 7:     arAttrib: array of System.Object;
 8:     arAsmName: array of AssemblyName;
 9:     arType: array of System.Type;
10:   begin
11:     // Show key information
12:     tn := TreeView1.Nodes.Add(aAssembly.FullName);
13:     tn.Nodes.Add('Location: '+aAssembly.Location);
14:     if aAssembly.GlobalAssemblyCache then
15:       tn.Nodes.Add('Global Cache: Yes')
16:     else
17:       tn.Nodes.Add('Global Cache: No');
18:
19:     // Determine calling assembly
20:     tn.Nodes.Add('Calling Assembly: '+aAssembly.GetCallingAssembly.FullName);
21:
22:     // Examine custom attributes
23:     tni := tn.Nodes.Add('Custom Attributes');
24:     arAttrib := aAssembly.GetCustomAttributes(true);
25:     for i := Low(arAttrib) to High(arAttrib) do
26:       tni.Nodes.Add(arAttrib[i].ToString);
27:
28:     // Examine Referenced assemblies
29:     tni := tn.Nodes.Add('Referenced Assemblies');
30:     arAsmName := aAssembly.GetReferencedAssemblies;
31:     for i := Low(arAsmName) to High(arAsmName) do
32:       tni.Nodes.Add(arAsmName[i].FullName);
33:
34:     // Examine types defined in an assembly
35:     tni := tn.Nodes.Add('Assembly Types');
36:     arType := aAssembly.GetTypes;
37:     for i := Low(arType) to High(arType) do
38:       tni.Nodes.Add(arType[i].ToString);
39:
40:     // Examine and drill down into an assembly
41:     arModule := aAssembly.GetModules;
42:     tn := tn.Nodes.Add('Modules');
43:     for i := Low(arModule) to High(arModule) do
44:       ReflectModule(arModule[i], tn);
45:   end;
```

▶ Find the code on the CD: \Code\Chapter 15\Ex01\.

Listing 15.1 is actually part of a larger reflection application. It performs some of the same functions as the Reflection utility provided with Delphi for .NET.

NOTE

An excellent tool for reflecting metadata is Lutz Roeder's Reflector. This utility can not only reflect and display metadata, but it can also disassemble your code into IL or decompile it into other .NET languages. Currently, it supports C#, Visual Basic .NET, and Delphi. You can obtain this utility at

http://www.aisto.com/roeder/dotnet/

The `TWinForm.ReflectAssembly()` method shown here takes a reference to an `Assembly` class instance, which is really a reference to an `Assembly` class that was previously loaded using the following code:

```
if (OpenFileDialog1.ShowDialog = System.Windows.Forms.DialogResult.OK) then
begin
  Cursor.Current := Cursors.WaitCursor;
  try
    Assem := Assembly.LoadFrom(OpenFileDialog1.FileName);
    ReflectAssembly(Assem);
  finally
    Cursor.Current := Cursors.Default;
  end;
end;
```

This code loads an assembly specified by `OpenFileDialog1`. It is necessary to load the assembly in order to reflect its metadata.

This code simply populates a `TreeView` with information about the assembly. Table 15.1 describes the methods used in Listing 15.1.

TABLE 15.1   Assembly Class Members

Member	Description
FullName	Retrieves the display name of the assembly. The display name shows the major and minor versions, build and revision numbers, name, culture and public key or public key token.
Location	Retrieves the physical location of the assembly containing the manifest.
GlobalAssemblyCache	Indicates whether the assembly was loaded from the GAC by returning true. Otherwise, false is returned.
GetCallingAssembly()	Gets the assembly whose method invoked the currently executing method.
GetCustomAttributes()	Gets an array of custom attributes defined on this assembly.
GetReferencedAssemblies()	Gets an array of AssemblyName types for any assemblies referenced by this assembly.
GetTypes()	Gets all types that are defined in this assembly.
GetModules()	Gets the modules that make up this assembly.

Table 15.1 is a partial list of the methods and properties in the `Assembly` class. You can look in the .NET documentation for the complete reference to the `Assembly` class.

You can see that, in some cases, the metadata is directly obtained through a property or a method. Some methods return an array of items such as the `GetReferencedAssemblies()` and

`GetModules()` methods. In these cases, as Listing 15.1 illustrates, you assign the result of these methods to an appropriate array and then reflect the items in the array.

In lines 41–44, the array list of modules is obtained from the assembly object. Each module is then passed to a `ReflectModule()` method, which walks through the module's metadata. The following section discusses this topic.

Reflecting a Module

Listing 15.2 is an example of reflecting Module classes of an assembly.

LISTING 15.2   Reflecting a Module

```
1:   procedure TWinForm.ReflectModule(aModule: Module; aTn: TreeNode);
2:   var
3:     arType: array of System.Type;
4:     arAttrib: array of System.Object;
5:     arFields: array of FieldInfo;
6:     arMeth: array of MethodInfo;
7:     i: integer;
8:     tn: TreeNode;
9:     tni: TReeNode;
10:  begin
11:    tn := aTn.Nodes.Add(aModule.Name);
12:    tn.Nodes.Add('Fully Qualified Name: '+aModule.FullyQualifiedName);
13:    tn.Nodes.Add('Is Resource: '+ TObject(aModule.IsResource).ToString);
14:
15:    // Examine custom attributes
16:    tni := tn.Nodes.Add('Custom Attributes');
17:    arAttrib := aModule.GetCustomAttributes(true);
18:    for i := Low(arAttrib) to High(arAttrib) do
19:      tni.Nodes.Add(arAttrib[i].ToString);
20:
21:    // Examine fields
22:    tni := tn.Nodes.Add('Fields');
23:    arFields := aModule.GetFields;
24:    for i := Low(arFields) to High(arFields) do
25:      tni.Nodes.Add(arFields[i].ToString);
26:
27:    // Examine modules
28:    tni := tn.Nodes.Add('Methods');
29:    arMeth := aModule.GetMethods;
30:    for i := Low(arMeth) to High(arMeth) do
31:      tni.Nodes.Add(arMeth[i].ToString);
32:
33:    // Examine types
34:    arType := aModule.GetTypes;
35:    tn := tn.Nodes.Add('Types');
36:    for i := Low(arType) to High(arType) do
37:      ReflectType(arType[i], tn);
38:  end;
```

▶ Find the code on the CD: `\Code\Chapter 15\Ex01\`.

Listing 15.2 is called from the `ReflectAssembly()` method shown in Listing 15.1 for each module of an assembly. Similar to Listing 15.1, this method consists of calls to members of the module class that return information about itself. This information is then populated in the `TreeView`.

Table 15.2 describes the methods used in Listing 15.2.

TABLE 15.2   Module Class Members

Member	Description
`FullyQualifiedName`	Retrieves the fully qualified name including the path to this module.
`IsResource()`	Indicates whether the object is a resource.
`GetCustomAttributes()`	Retrieves an array of Custom Attributes for this module.
`GetFields()`	Returns an array of the type `FieldInfo` for fields defined for this module.
`GetMethods()`	Returns an array of the type `MethodInfo` for methods defined for this module.
`GetTypes()`	Returns an array of `System.Type` for types defined in this module.

Table 15.2 is a partial list of the methods and properties in the `Module` class. You can look in the .NET documentation for the complete reference to the `Module` class.

Listing 15.2 performs the same type of functions against `Module` class as for the `Assembly` class in Listing 15.1. Various methods and properties are invoked to obtain information about the module. In some cases, this is specific information about the module; whereas in others, an array of certain objects is obtained that must be enumerated and examined.

> **NOTE**
>
> It is possible to have flat global "methods" (or global routines and global fields defined in a module), but these are not CLS compliant and cannot be defined in either C#, Visual Basic .NET, or Delphi. Examining methods and fields is shown in Listing 15.2; however, it unlikely that you would ever encounter them.

Lines 34–37 in Listing 15.2 retrieve an array of types defined in the module. Each type from this list is then passed to the `ReflectType()` method, which, as the name implies, reflects the details of the specific type. This is discussed in greater detail in the following section.

Reflecting Types

This section shows you how to drill down further into the types defined in an assembly and how to reflect those types.

Listing 15.3 illustrates the processes of reflecting member information for types.

LISTING 15.3   Reflecting a Type's Member Information

```
1:    function GetDeclareString(st: System.Type): String;
2:    begin
3:      Result := '';
4:      if st.IsAbstract then Result := Result + 'abstract ';
```

LISTING 15.3 Continued

```
5:      if st.IsArray      then Result := Result + 'array ';
6:      if st.IsClass      then Result := Result + 'class ';
7:      if st.IsContextful then Result := Result + 'context ';
8:      if st.IsInterface  then Result := Result + 'interface ';
9:      if st.IsPointer    then Result := Result + 'pointer ';
10:     if st.IsPrimitive  then Result := Result + 'primitive ';
11:     if st.IsPublic     then Result := Result + 'public ';
12:     if st.IsSealed     then Result := Result + 'sealed ';
13:     if st.IsSerializable then Result := Result + 'serializable ';
14:     if st.IsValueType then Result := Result + 'record ';
15:   end;
16:
17:   procedure TWinForm.ReflectType(aType: System.Type; aTn: TreeNode);
18:   var
19:     arMembInfo: array of MemberInfo;
20:     arType: array of System.Type;
21:     i: integer;
22:     tn, fn: TreeNode;
23:   begin
24:     tn := aTn.Nodes.Add(aType.FullName);
25:     tn.Nodes.Add('Base Type: '+aType.BaseType.FullName);
26:     tn.Nodes.Add(GetDeclareString(aType));
27:     arMembInfo := aType.GetMembers;
28:
29:     for i := Low(arMembInfo) to High(arMembInfo) do
30:     begin
31:       fn := tn.Nodes.Add(System.String.Format('{0}: {1}',
32:         arMembInfo[i].MemberType, arMembInfo[i]));
33:     end;
34:
35:     arType := aType.GetNestedTypes;
36:     for i := Low(arType) to High(arType) do
37:       ReflectType(arType[i], tn);
38:   end;
```

▶ Find the code on the CD: \Code\Chapter 15\Ex01\.

Listings 15.1, 15.2, and 15.3 are all within the same application on the CD. Listing 15.3 consists of two methods, GetDeclareString() and ReflectType(). This listing shows a partial usage of the various methods and properties available for reflecting member information.

The first section of the ReflectType() method (lines 24–25) of Listing 15.3 adds each member's full name and base type to the Treeview. It then passes the member to the GetDeclareString() function. GetDeclareString() builds a string based on the member's access level and other declarative characteristics and adds the string to the TreeView.

The second section retrieves an array of MemberInfo references for the member of the specified type by calling the GetMembers() method. It then adds the type specification for the member and the name of the member to the TreeView (lines 35–36, Listing 15.3).

Figure 15.1 illustrates the output for this program used in Listings 15.1–15.3 in reflecting another assembly.

15

FIGURE 15.1   Output of Reflection application.

Runtime Invocation of a Type's Members (Late Binding)

Late binding is a process by which an application can invoke a member of a class (including creating that class) without knowing at compile time of that class or its methods. This is a useful technique, particularly when dealing with add-in functionality to applications. Consider the Delphi for .NET development environment. It must somehow have to determine information about the classes to allow you to visually design applications. It is reflection's capability to perform late binding that enables the IDE to work with classes it does not know about that exist in various assemblies.

To illustrate a simple add-in scheme, the following example consist of two assemblies—both of which define a class containing a single method. The method is given the same name for simplicity. An invoking application loads each assembly separately and invokes the methods on both classes. Listings 15.4 and 15.5 list the assemblies.

LISTING 15.4   First Assembly Example

```
1:    library asmRemInv1;
2:    type
3:      TClass1 = class
4:      public
5:        procedure WriteMessage(aMsg: String);
6:      end;
7:
8:    procedure TClass1.WriteMessage(aMsg: String);
9:    begin
10:       Console.WriteLine('In asmRemInv1.TClass1: '+aMsg);
11:   end;
```

LISTING 15.4 Continued

```
12:
13:  end.
```

▶ Find the code on the CD: \Code\Chapter 15\Ex02\.

LISTING 15.5 Second Assembly Example

```
1:   library asmRemInv2;
2:   type
3:     TClass1 = class
4:     public
5:       procedure WriteMessage(aMsg: String);
6:     end;
7:
8:   procedure TClass1.WriteMessage(aMsg: String);
9:   begin
10:    Console.WriteLine('In asmRemInv2.TClass1: '+aMsg);
11:  end;
12:
13:  end.
```

▶ Find the code on the CD: \Code\Chapter 15\Ex02\.

You will notice that both assemblies contain the same class, identically defined. The idea here is that the using application will be able to invoke either of these classes in the same manner. The implementation of these classes might differ. This is similar to using an Interface to define the signature of the class. Consider a class that performs a sorting scheme for instance. These classes could have been developed to perform two different types of sorting, such as a bubble and insertion sort. The calling application should not have to know about the implementation.

At this level, the calling application shown in Listing 15.6 must know something about the classes it is going to invoke, such as the class name and the method of the class. It is possible for the application to know nothing of the class and still be capable to query, through reflection, various methods, determine their parameters, and invoke those methods. The utility of this capability, although powerful, is difficult to determine. At some level, the invoking application should know what it is trying to do with the class it is dynamically invoking.

Listing 15.6 illustrates how these classes are invoked from the calling application.

LISTING 15.6 Invoking Application

```
1:   program InvProject;
2:
3:   {$APPTYPE CONSOLE}
4:
5:   uses
6:     System.Reflection,
7:     SysUtils;
8:
```

LISTING 15.6   Continued

```
9:    var
10:      Assem: Assembly;
11:      BFlags: BindingFlags;
12:
13:      procedure InvokeType(aNameSpace: String);
14:      var
15:        obj: System.Object;
16:        Meth: MethodInfo;
17:        t: System.Type;
18:        ParamTypes: array of System.Type;
19:      begin
20:        t := Assem.GetType(aNameSpace+'.TClass1');
21:        Console.WriteLine(t.ToString);
22:        obj := Activator.CreateInstance(t);
23:        Console.WriteLine(obj.ToString);
24:
25:        t.InvokeMember('WriteMessage', BFlags, nil, obj,
26:          ['This is the message']);
27:
28:        // An alternative method is shown below.
29:        SetLength(ParamTypes, 1);
30:        ParamTypes[0] := TypeOf(System.String);
31:        Meth := t.GetMethod('WriteMessage', ParamTypes);
32:        Console.WriteLine(Meth.ToString);
33:        Meth.Invoke(obj, ['This is the message']);
34:      end;
35:
36:    begin
37:      BFlags := BindingFlags.DeclaredOnly or BindingFlags.Public or
38:        BindingFlags.Instance or BindingFlags.InvokeMethod;
39:
40:      try
41:        Assem := Assembly.LoadFrom('asmRemInv1.dll');
42:        InvokeType('asmRemInv1');
43:
44:        Assem := Assembly.LoadFrom('asmRemInv2.dll');
45:        InvokeType('asmRemInv2');
46:      except
47:        on E: Exception do
48:        Console.WriteLine('Error: '+E.Message);
49:      end;
50:      Console.ReadLine();
51:    end.
```

▶ Find the code on the CD: \Code\Chapter 15\Ex02\.

Listing 15.6 first loads the assemblies and then calls the InvokeType() function, which creates the class from the assembly and then calls its WriteMessage() function. This code makes use of a few constructs, which I will explain.

The Activator class is used to create the instance of the class itself. Activator can be used to create instances of classes locally, remotely, or from a COM object using some of its alternate methods. For instance, Listing 15.6 could have used the `Activator.CreateInstanceFrom()` method to create the class without having to explicitly load the assembly. This method takes the classname, a named assembly file, and a constructor name. You might look at the documentation on the `Activator` class to examine its other methods.

Once an instance of the class is created, its method, `WriteMessage()`, is called by using the `InvokeMember()` function.

Table 15.3 describes the parameters required by the `InvokeMember()` function.

TABLE 15.3   InvokeMember's Parameters

Parameter	Description
name	A string parameter that specifies the name of the member to invoke.
invokeAttr	A `BindingFlags` type that specifies how members are to be searched for.
binder	A `Binder` type that specifies how to bind (match) members and their arguments.
target	The target type instance (`System.Object`) on which to invoke the member.
args	An array of arguments to pass to the member method.
modifiers	An array of `ParameterModifier` objects—each of which represents attributes associated with the corresponding item in the `args` array.
namedParameters	An array containing the names of the parameters that passed as values in the `args` array.
culture	A `CultureInfo` that is used to specify the globalization locale.

Note that the `InvokeMember()` method has three overloaded variants depending on which of these parameters are required. In Listing 15.6, only the method `name`, `invokeAttr`, `binder`, `target`, and `args` parameters are required.

The `invokeAttr` parameter is a `bitmask` that consists of one or more `BindingFlags` values that control binding and determine how the specified member is to be searched. Some of these flags specify the operation type, such as the `BindingFlags.InvokeMethod` flag, which indicates that a method is going to be called. Other flags specify the access to the member to search on. For instance, `BindingFlags.Public` specifies to include public members in the search. If nonpublic members are to be included in the search, you would include the `BindingFlags.NonPublic` flag. You will see more use of these flags in the following section. It would be a good idea to be familiar with the various flags that may be used with this parameter. You might look it over in the .NET documentation.

Invoking the Member's Types for Efficiency

Lines 29–33 in Listing 15.6 show an alternate way to invoke the method of the type by calling the type's `GetMethod()` function. This function returns a `MethodInfo` instance, which contains an `Invoke()` method that invokes the specified method.

This method is more efficient than calling `InvokeMember()` if you will be calling it repeatedly. The reason is that `InvokeMember()` must perform the search for the member and then bind to it when found every time it is called. By obtaining a reference to the member's type, you can directly access the member without the search/bind operation. Table 15.4 describes the various methods that return a reference to the member type and which of its methods to call to invoke that member.

TABLE 15.4   Accessing Members Through Their Types

Method	Returns	How to Access
GetConstructor()	ConstructorInfo	Invoke()
GetEvent()	EventInfo	AddEventHandler()
RemoveEventHandler()		
GetField()	FieldInfo	GetValue()
SetValue()		
GetMethod()	MethodInfo	Invoke()
GetProperty()	PropertyInfo	GetValue()
SetValue()		

Another Example of Member Invocation

Listing 15.7 illustrates another example of invoking the members of a type through reflection.

LISTING 15.7   Member Invocation

```
1:    program InvMemb;
2:    uses
3:      SysUtils,
4:      System.Reflection;
5:    {$APPTYPE CONSOLE}
6:
7:    type
8:      TOnWriteEvent = procedure of object;
9:
10:     TMyType = class(TObject)
11:     private
12:       FIntProp: Integer;
13:       FStrProp: String;
14:       FOnWriteEvent: TOnWriteEvent;
15:     public
16:       PublicStr: String;
17:       constructor Create(aStr: String; aInt: Integer;
18:         aStr2: String); override;
19:       procedure WriteSomething;
20:       procedure WriteProc;
21:       property IntProp: Integer read FIntProp write FIntProp;
22:       property StrProp: String read FStrProp write FStrProp;
23:       property OnWriteEvent: TOnWriteEvent read FOnWriteEvent
24:          write FOnWriteEvent;
25:     end;
26:
27:   constructor TMyType.Create(aStr: String; aInt: Integer; aStr2: String);
28:   begin
29:     inherited Create;
30:     PublicStr := aStr;
31:     FIntProp  := aInt;
32:     FStrProp  := aStr2;
```

LISTING 15.7   Continued

```
33:     OnWriteEvent := WriteProc;
34:   end;
35:
36:   procedure TMyType.WriteSomething;
37:   begin
38:     Console.WriteLine('PublicStr: '+PublicStr);
39:     Console.WriteLine('FIntProp: '+FIntProp.ToString);
40:     Console.WriteLine('FStrProp: '+FStrProp);
41:     if Assigned(FOnWriteEvent) then
42:       FOnWriteEvent;
43:   end;
44:
45:   procedure TMyType.WriteProc;
46:   begin
47:     Console.WriteLine('——In WriteProc');
48:   end;
49:
50:   var
51:     tp:  System.Type;
52:     obj: System.Object;
53:     BFlags: BindingFlags;
54:     parmAray: array[0..2] of System.Object;
55:     s: String;
56:     i: Integer;
57:   begin
58:     BFlags := BindingFlags.DeclaredOnly or BindingFlags.Public
59:       or BindingFlags.Instance;
60:
61:     tp  := TypeOf(TMyType);
62:     parmAray[0] := 'hello';
63:     parmAray[1] := System.Object(23);
64:     parmAray[2] := 'world';
65:
66:     try
67:       // create an instance of the type
68:
69:       obj := tp.InvokeMember('.ctor', BFlags or BindingFlags.CreateInstance,
70:         nil, nil,ParmAray);
71:       Console.WriteLine(obj.ToString);
72:
73:       // Call the type's method
74:       (obj as TMyType).WriteSomething;
75:       // or
76:       tp.InvokeMember('WriteSomething', BFlags or BindingFlags.InvokeMethod,
77:         nil, obj, nil);
78:
79:       // Set/Get a field
80:       tp.InvokeMember('PublicStr', BFlags or BindingFlags.SetField, nil, obj,
81:         ['67 Camaro']);
82:
83:       s := String(tp.InvokeMember('PublicStr', BFlags or
84:         BindingFlags.GetField, nil, obj, nil));
85:
```

LISTING 15.7   Continued

```
86:      Console.WriteLine(s);
87:
88:      // Set/Get a property
89:      tp.InvokeMember('IntProp', BFlags or BindingFlags.SetProperty, nil,
90:        obj, [23]);
91:      tp.InvokeMember('StrProp', BFlags or BindingFlags.SetProperty, nil,
92:        obj, ['Coffee']);
93:
94:      i := Integer(tp.InvokeMember('IntProp', BFlags or
95:        BindingFlags.GetProperty, nil, obj, nil));
96:      s := String(tp.InvokeMember('StrProp', BFlags or
97:        BindingFlags.GetProperty, nil, obj, nil));
98:
99:      Console.WriteLine('Get/Set Property: {0}, {1}', [i, s]);
100:
101:   except
102:     on E: Exception do
103:       Console.WriteLine(E.Message);
104:   end;
105:
106:   Console.ReadLine;
107: end.
```

▶ Find the code on the CD: \Code\Chapter 15\Ex03\.

In this example, the class is defined in the same application for simplicity. This example illustrates how through reflection, one can invoke various members of a given class, specifically the TMyType defined in lines 10–25.

TMyType declares various members such as a constructor, a procedure, a field, and a few properties.

TMyType.WriteSomething() simply writes the values contained in the various members to the console.

TMyType is created using a different technique than that previously illustrated in Listing 15.6. Instead of using the Activator class to create the class, we call the type's InvokeMember() function. This example passes as the member name, .ctor, which is the .NET name of the constructor. In fact, when you declare a constructor and name it Create(), the Delphi for .NET compiler will generate a constructor named ".ctor" with the appropriate parameters (See Figure 15.2).In reality, the first parameter is ignored. According to the .NET documentation, when you specify the BindingFlags.CreateInstance flag, it instructs Reflection to create an instance of the specified type and call the constructor that matches the arguments provided. It is included here for illustrative purposes.

Note also that BindingFlags.CreateInstance is included in the flags passed to InvokeMember(). By passing this flag, InvokeMember() will find the constructor that matches the arguments specified and will invoke that constructor and return an instance of the class. InvokeMember() also accepts the array of parameters required by TMyType's constructor.

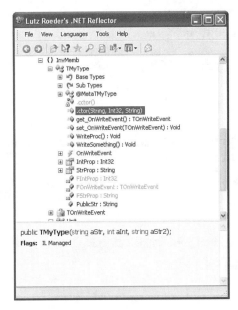

FIGURE 15.2 Definition of `TMyType`.

The remaining code simply illustrates how to access the various members of `TMyType` through the `InvokeMember()` function and by passing the appropriate flag along with the parameter containing the `BindingFlags`.

Emitting MSIL Through Reflection

The .NET framework provides you with the capability to create code on-the-fly through the `System.Reflection.Emit` namespace. The code that you create through `Emit` is MSIL code. Essentially, the functionality in this namespace gives you the ability to dynamically create an assembly and a module within that assembly. You can dynamically define any number of classes and methods within the assembly's module, and then invoke those methods at runtime (which will automatically be JIT compiled to very efficient machine code). You can even save the assembly to disk for later use.

> **NOTE**
>
> In addition to having the capability to generate MSIL code through `System.Reflection.Emit`, the .NET CodeDom technology provided by the `System.CodeDom` and `System.CodeDom.Compiler` namespaces supply the ability to generate code in languages such as C#, Visual Basic .NET, and Delphi (assuming that you have the proper licensed assemblies installed).

So why would anybody want to have the ability to generate code on-the-fly? There are several ideas thrown around for having this ability. First, visual design tools, such as Delphi for .NET and Microsoft Visual Studio.NET, generate code on-the-fly: Although this is in the form of a .NET language, the idea is the same. The possibility of an end user design tool that generates executable code is not unthinkable. This could also be used to generate more powerful "scripts" for your ASP.NET application. It will be interesting to see where and how far, practically, such a technology will go.

Tools/Classes for Emitting MSIL

Basically four types of tools exist that you will need to generate MSIL code. These are Info classes from the `System.Reflection` namespace, builder classes, and the `ILGenerator` and `OpCodes` classes.

Info classes are defined in the `System.Reflection` namespace. Examples of these are `MethodInfo`, `EventInfo`, `FieldInfo`, and so on.

Builder classes are defined in the `System.Reflection.Emit` namespace. These classes are used to define and create specific parts of the assembly, such as the assembly itself, the module, and a method. Table 15.5 describes the various builder classes.

TABLE 15.5   Builder Classes from System.Reflection.Emit

Builder Class	Description
AssemblyBuilder	Used to define and build a dynamic assembly.
ConstructorBuilder	Used to define and build a dynamic constructor for a class.
CustomAttributeBuilder	Used to define and build a dynamic custom attribute.
EnumBuilder	Used to define and build a dynamic enumeration type.
EventBuilder	Used to define and build a dynamic event for a class.
FieldBuilder	Used to define and build a dynamic field for a class.
LocalBuilder	Used to define and build a dynamic local variable for a method.
MethodBuilder	Used to define and build a dynamic method for a class.
ModuleBuilder	Used to define and build a dynamic module for an assembly.
ParameterBuilder	Used to define and associate parameters.
PropertyBuilder	Used to define and build dynamic properties for a class.
TypeBuilder	Used to define and build dynamic classes and records (value types).

The `ILGenerator` is a special class that is used to generate MSIL code. Recall that MSIL is the input to the JIT Compiler.

`OpCodes` are specific MSIL instructions and are represented by the `OpCodes` class in the `System.Reflection.Emit` namespace.

The Emitting Process

Emitting code is not that different from writing code in the sense that the tasks involved are somewhat sequential. For instance, you first create your assembly. You then create the module. Finally, you create your classes and define the specifics of those classes such as members, methods, and so on. This process will best be illustrated through an example.

A System.Reflection.Emit Example

Listing 15.8 illustrates the tasks involved in using the classes defined in `System.Reflection.Emit` to generate MSIL code.

LISTING 15.8   Example of Using System.Reflection.Emit

```
1:   program EmitDemo;
2:   {$APPTYPE CONSOLE}
3:
4:   uses
5:     System.Reflection,
6:     System.Reflection.Emit;
7:
8:   var
9:     appDmn:  AppDomain;
10:    asmName: AssemblyName;
11:    asmBuilder: AssemblyBuilder;
12:    modBuilder: ModuleBuilder;
13:    typBuilder: TypeBuilder;
14:    methBuilder: MethodBuilder;
15:    ilGen: ILGenerator;
16:    newType: System.Type;
17:
18:    procedure CreateWLCall;
19:    var
20:      parms: array of System.Type;
21:      methInfo: MethodInfo;
22:      wlTypes: array of System.Type;
23:      SysConsoleType : System.Type;
24:    begin
25:      SetLength(Parms, 1);
26:      Parms[0] := typeof(System.String);
27:
28:      methBuilder := typBuilder.DefineMethod('Main', MethodAttributes.Public
29:       or MethodAttributes.Static, typeof(integer), System.Type.EmptyTypes);
30:
31:      ilGen := methBuilder.GetILGenerator;
32:
33:      SetLength(wltypes, 1);
34:      wltypes[0] := typeof('System.String');
35:      methInfo := typeof(System.Console).GetMethod('WriteLine', wlTypes);
36:
37:      if methInfo = nil then
38:        raise Exception.Create('unable to find WriteLine');
39:
40:
41:      ilGen.Emit(Opcodes.Ldstr, 'Delphi for .NET');
42:      ilGen.Emit(OpCodes.Call, methInfo);
43:      ilGen.Emit(OpCodes.Ldc_I4_0);
44:      ilGen.Emit(OpCodes.Ret);
45:    end;
46:
47:   begin
48:     asmName := AssemblyName.Create;
49:     asmName.Name := 'D4DNeDevGuideAsm';
50:
51:     appDmn := AppDomain.CurrentDomain;
52:     asmBuilder := appDmn.DefineDynamicAssembly(AsmName,
53:       AssemblyBuilderAccess.Save);
```

LISTING 15.8   Continued

```
54:
55:    modBuilder := asmBuilder.DefineDynamicModule(asmName.Name,
56:      'd4dmasm.exe');
57:    typBuilder := ModBuilder.DefineType('Class1');
58:    CreateWLCall;
59:
60:    asmBuilder.SetEntryPoint(methBuilder, PEFileKinds.ConsoleApplication);
61:
62:    newType := typBuilder.CreateType();
63:    asmBuilder.Save('d4dmasm.exe');
64:    System.Console.Write('done');
65:  end.
```

▶ Find the code on the CD: \Code\Chapter 15\Ex04\.

Listing 15.8 generates the IL code for a simple assembly containing a class with a main method that writes a statement to the Console.

The main block of Listing 15.8 performs the functions of creating the dynamic assembly, the module, and the type for this class. As part of this process, the CreateWLCall () function is invoked (line 58), which performs the process of emitting the code for the method itself.

Dynamic entities are typically defined within the context of another entity. For instance, an assembly is created within the context of an AppDomain. A module is created within the context of an assembly. A type is created within the context of a module, and so on. Listing 15.8 reflects this structure.

As stated, a dynamic assembly must be created within the context of an AppDomain, so this example uses the current AppDomain (line 51). To create the assembly, the AppDomain.DefineDynamicAssembly() method is invoked. There are several overloaded versions of this method that return an AssemblyBuilder. The version used in this example takes AssemblyName and AssemblyBuilderAccess parameter types. AssemblyBuilderAccess is an enumeration type whose values dictate the access level for the dynamic assembly. Valid values are Run, RunAndSave, and Save, which represent an assembly that can be executed, executed and saved, or just saved, respectively. The example here will just save the assembly to disk, so the value passed is Save.

The next task is to build the module (lines 55–56). This is done by calling the AssemblyBuilder.DefineDynamicModule() method. This method also has overloaded variations, and it returns a ModuleBuilder class. The version used here passes the assembly name and the name of the file to which the assembly will be persisted. The method to actually save the assembly is called later, and it must use the same filename used here.

Once the ModuleBuilder is obtained, types can be defined within it. Line 57 creates a class named "Class1", and the next line calls the CreateWLCall() procedure, which creates a method for this class—more on this shortly.

Once the method is created and associated with a MethodBuilder class, it is set as the entry point for the assembly by calling the AssemblyBuilder.SetEntryPoint() method (line 60). This method takes the MethodBuilder class and a PEFileKinds type as a parameter. PEFileKinds is an enumeration type that specifies what type of PE file is generated from the dynamic assembly. Its values can be `ConsoleApplication`, `DLL`, and `WindowApplication`. This example generates a console application.

Finally, lines 62 and 63 create the type and save it to disk. At this point, one can actually execute the file.

The `MethodBuilder()` procedure is where the `ILGenerator` and `OpCodes` are used.

Lines 28–29 invoke the `TypeBuilder.DefineMethod()` method, which returns a `MethodBuilder` class. `DefineMethod()` takes the method name, method attributes, the return type, and an array of parameter types. When defining a method with no parameters, you can pass the `System.Type.EmptyTypes` type, which is a predefined empty array of type.

Given a `MethodBuilder` class, the code can now emit the code for the method. This is really just the process of writing out the IL code that you would type if you were coding in MSIL. In this case, you can use information from types through reflection to generate the IL code. Line 31 retrieves an `ILGenerator` instance. The first `OpCode` specified is `LdStr`, which loads a string reference onto the stack. It then uses reflection to find the method info for the `System.Console.WriteLine()` method—specifically, the version that takes a single string parameter. `System.Type.GetMethod()` is used to obtain the `MethodInfo` class for this method. With `MethodInfo`, `ILGenerator.Emit()` defines the `Call` OpCode for the `WriteLine()` method (line 42). Last, the method is returned by emitting the `Ret` OpCode (line 44) after placing its value of zero on the stack (line 43).

> **NOTE**
>
> The `IlGenerator` class has a helper method, `EmitWriteLine()`, that can be used to simplify emitting the MSIL for a `WriteLine()` method. Listing 15.8 takes the longer approach for illustrative purposes.

15

IN THIS CHAPTER

- Why Have Interoperability?
- Common Interoperability Issues
- Using COM Objects in .NET Code
- Using .NET Objects in COM Code
- Using Win32 DLL Exports in .NET Code
- Using .NET Routines in Win32 Code

CHAPTER **16**

Interoperability—COM Interop and the Platform Invocation Service

by Brian Long

Most of this book focuses on how to build code in Delphi 8 for .NET and how to use .NET code in other assemblies built with any .NET language. However, .NET also offers much support for mixing .NET code alongside regular Win32 code— both COM and plain DLL routines. This chapter explores the interoperability support offered by the .NET platform in all its guises after first gaining an understanding for why it is available at all.

Why Have Interoperability?

For most Delphi developers who have been coding in Delphi for Win32, the Microsoft .NET platform is a brand new programming environment and a reasonably new challenge. When considering moving a system to a new platform, it is usually impractical to consider re-implementing the whole system in one go. It would take far too long, and you would be hard-pressed to find organizations that can afford to halt the forward development of a system just to move it to a new platform. The VCL.NET layer provided in Delphi for .NET is intended to help move applications across from Win32 to .NET in one step, but things are never quite that straightforward; there are always hiccups that turn into big problems, which means that certain areas of the system prove tricky to port across.

There are other considerations such as all those third-party DLLs and COM objects you use in your system? How do those get ported across to .NET? Fortunately, Microsoft saw all these issues coming and worked solutions to them into the .NET Framework right from the start. Microsoft appreciates the fact that few people can afford to move entire systems across to a new platform in one fell swoop and that there is a massive Win32 code base existing in the form of applications, COM objects, and DLLs. Consequently, Microsoft ensured that interoperability between .NET code and Win32 code was well supported right from the initial release of .NET 1.0 in February 2002.

Interoperability between .NET and Win32 goes both ways. This means that you can make use of bits of .NET code in existing Win32 applications and that you can also make use of Win32 code in new .NET applications. So you can either test the water by moving small pieces of functionality in your system across to .NET, or you can start a .NET application and make use of portions of your Win32 code base.

Specifically, .NET offers four interoperability paths—all of which we will explore as we proceed through this chapter.

When developing a .NET application, you can

- use COM objects via Runtime Callable Wrappers (RCWs)

- use routines exported from Win32 DLLs using the Platform Invocation service (or P/Invoke)

When writing Win32 applications, you can

- consume .NET objects as if they were regular COM objects via COM Callable Wrappers (CCWs)

- use routines exposed from .NET assemblies using Inverse P/Invoke.

> **NOTE**
>
> When looking at Win32 code that is called from .NET or might call into .NET code, the examples will be presented using Delphi 7 as this will be familiar to most readers and is supplied in the Delphi 8 for .NET product box. Of course, the principles apply equally to all other Win32 languages as well.

Common Interoperability Issues

The primary issues that arise when using any of these interoperability mechanisms are twofold. First, you must make the code on one side of the managed/unmanaged boundary visible to code on the other; otherwise, it cannot be called. To one degree or another, .NET provides options for this in all cases.

Second, the parameters have to be marshaled back and forth across the managed/unmanaged boundary to cater for the difference between managed and unmanaged data types. After all, a Win32 PChar is markedly different from a .NET String or StringBuilder class. The Interop Marshaler does a fine job of providing default marshaling for most parameter types that we are likely to use.

One issue that isn't so obvious relates to the security of managed code calling into unmanaged code. Clearly unmanaged Win32 code is outside the scope of the security built into .NET and could do untold damage (for example, deleting files or formatting drives).

Consequently, to call into unmanaged code from managed code requires unmanaged code permission. On a default .NET installation, the My Computer zone (applications running on the local machine) has unmanaged code permission, but the Internet and Local intranet zones do not, so applications run from these zones would not be permitted to call into unmanaged code. You should be aware that the Local intranet zone includes applications run from network shares.

We'll start investigating the two COM/.NET interoperability mechanisms, usually referred to as the COM Interop support. In these cases, as well as parameter marshaling, we should also be aware that there needs to be reconciliation between the two lifetime management mechanisms used in the two programming platforms. COM uses reference counting, and .NET uses garbage collection. Again, COM Interop essentially brushes these differences aside by ensuring that the wrapper classes it produces for programs to use hide these issues from us.

Using COM Objects in .NET Code

First we'll look at .NET code using COM objects. Before we look at arbitrary COM objects that implement IUnknown and other custom interfaces, we will spend some time looking at using objects that support Automation—in other words, the special case of COM objects that implement IUnknown and IDispatch as well as other custom interfaces. Use of Automation is very common in Win32 code as Automation servers are widely available. The applications that make up Microsoft Office are prime examples of Automation servers that offer a rich hierarchy of objects supporting Automation.

Late Bound Automation

In Delphi for Win32, we orchestrate a late bound Automation session using a Variant. A Variant can be initialized with a call to CreateOleObject() (from the ComObj unit), which itself is passed an Automation object's class string or ProgID. For example, the entry point to the Microsoft Word Automation hierarchy is the ProgID 'Word.Application'. CreateOleObject() returns a reference to the IDispatch interface implementation in the instantiated Automation object and this is duly stored in the Variant variable.

You can treat the Variant as if it is the Automation object itself, calling methods on it and reading/writing its properties. When performing Automation through a Variant, you get to take advantage of nice things such as omitting optional parameters, using named parameters, and so on. All your instructions are compiled into special dispatch records and executed at runtime by a chunk of code in the ComObj unit, and thereby the Automation object is made to dance to your tune—that is, unless you got something wrong in one of your calls; in which case, you are treated to a runtime exception.

The reason for describing the Delphi for Win32 approach here is to contrast it with the approach required in Delphi for .NET. Although general support for Variants has been implemented in the Borland.Vcl.Variants unit, the special "magic" that lets you do late bound Automation through the Variant has not made it into the first .NET release of Delphi. Consequently, late bound Automation code must be written using reflection, so it will look different (and indeed a little more verbose) when you write it for .NET. And although we can still omit optional parameters, or parameters with default values, we don't get the luxury of using named parameters anymore.

Listing 16.1 is a simple example of automating Microsoft Word. This first snippet, from a WinForms application, simply instantiates the usual top-level Automation object in Microsoft Word.

LISTING 16.1   Creating an Instance of Microsoft Word through Automation

```
1:   var
2:     MSWordType: &Type;
3:     MSWord: TObject;
4:     ...
5:
6:   //Instantiate Microsoft Word
7:   MSWordType := &Type.GetTypeFromProgID('Word.Application', True);
8:   MSWord := Activator.CreateInstance(MSWordType);
```

> ▶ Find the code on the CD: Ch16\Ex01\.

The first statement on line 7 uses the static GetTypeFromProgID method in the System.Type class to create a new System.Type object that is associated with Word's ProgID. The returned object is the mechanism through which the members of any Word Automation objects will be invoked. The particular overloaded version of GetTypeFromProgID used here has a second parameter that specifies an exception should be raised if the ProgID is not registered on the system.

Line 8 uses the static CreateInstance() method of the System.Activator class to instantiate the CoClass represented by the MSWordType System.Type class. The result, stored in MSWord, represents the instance of the Automation object.

Having brought the Automation object to life, we can now use its methods and properties as we like. Listing 16.2 makes Word visible on lines 6 and 7. (It defaults to hiding when launched through Automation.) Then, it creates a new document in lines 10 to 13. (It starts with no documents under Automation.) Finally, it adds some text (lines 16 to 20), the date (lines 23 to 25), and a carriage return (lines 28 and 29).

LISTING 16.2.   Late Bound Automation against Microsoft Word

```
1:   var
2:     Documents, Selection: TObject;
3:     ...
4:   //Set the Visible property
5:   //MSWord.Visible := True;
6:   MSWordType.InvokeMember(
7:     'Visible', BindingFlags.SetProperty, nil, MSWord, [True]);
8:   //Create a document
9:   //MSWord.Documents.Add
10:  Documents := MSWordType.InvokeMember(
11:    'Documents', BindingFlags.GetProperty, nil, MSWord, nil);
12:  Documents.GetType.InvokeMember(
13:    'Add', BindingFlags.InvokeMethod, nil, Documents, nil);
14:  //Write some text
15:  //MSWord.Selection.TypeText('Hello world! Time is: ');
16:  Selection := MSWordType.InvokeMember(
17:    'Selection', BindingFlags.GetProperty, nil, MSWord, nil);
18:  Selection.GetType.InvokeMember(
```

LISTING 16.2.   Continued

```
19:    'TypeText', BindingFlags.InvokeMethod, nil, Selection,
20:    ['Hello world! Time is: ']);
21: //Insert date/time
22: //MSWord.Selection.InsertDateTime('dddd, dd MMMM yyyy', False);
23: Selection.GetType.InvokeMember(
24:    'InsertDateTime', BindingFlags.InvokeMethod, nil, Selection,
25:    ['dddd, dd MMMM yyyy', False]);
26: //Add CR/LF
27: //MSWord.Selection.TypeParagraph;
28: Selection.GetType.InvokeMember(
29:    'TypeParagraph', BindingFlags.InvokeMethod, nil, Selection, nil);
```

▶ Find the code on the CD: \Chapter 16\Ex01\.

In order to call a method or read/write a property, we must use the InvokeMember() method of our System.Type object. The first parameter specifies the method or property name that will be queried for at runtime, and the second parameter is a member of the BindingFlags enumeration and indicates whether a method is being called or a property is being read or written. This affects the way that the IDispatch.Invoke() method of the underlying Automation object is called at runtime.

The third parameter is not required here but specifies a Binder class, sometimes used when doing reflection. The final parameters provide the Automation object instance and any parameters that might be required (passed as an array).

Notice that a System.Type object for additional objects returned by Word properties can be accessed through the GetType() method, as used in lines 12, 18, 23, and 28.

Value, Reference, and Optional Parameters

Things are quite straightforward with value parameters as used so far. However, things get messier when the Automation server supports a method that takes reference parameters because you must use an overloaded version of InvokeMember that takes more parameters. One of these parameters is an array containing a single ParameterModifier structure. This object needs to be constructed with a value that indicates how many parameters the method takes whereupon it allocates a Boolean array with that many elements—one to represent each method parameter. The array is surfaced through the default Item array property, and, before calling InvokeMember(), you must populate each element with a value. If the corresponding parameter is a value parameter, pass False; if it's a reference parameter, pass True.

To show the idea, consider a COM object that implements the fictitious COM interface shown in Listing 16.3. The first method simply takes a value parameter, so it can be called using the same sort of code as in Listing 16.2. However, the second method has both a value parameter and a reference parameter—in this case, an output parameter. It also has a return value, so we should see some Delphi 7 code that shows how to use it.

LISTING 16.3   A Sample COM Interface in Delphi 7

```
1:  ICOMInterface = interface(IUnknown)
2:     ['{8E9B4AAE-5290-4360-AA38-97EA7E43375E}']
```

LISTING 16.3 Continued

```
3:    procedure One(const Msg: WideString); safecall;
4:    function Two(Input: Integer; out Output: Integer): WordBool; safecall;
5:    end;
```

▶ Find the code on the CD: \Chapter 16\Ex02\InProcCOMServer\.

Listing 16.4 shows the relevant code snippet to call the second interface method from the dotNetAppLateBound.bdsproj project.

CAUTION

Don't forget to register the COM server before testing this example. You can do this with the following command line:

regsvr32 ComServer.dll

You can also do this within the Delphi 7 IDE using the Run, Register ActiveX Server menu item.

LISTING 16.4 Late Bound Automation against a Custom COM Object

```
1:   var
2:     TwoArgs: array[0..1] of TObject;
3:     MethodResult: TObject;
4:     ParamModifiers: array[0..0] of ParameterModifier;
5:     RefParam: Integer;
6:   const
7:     ValParam = 45;
8:     ...
9:     //Set up a method call with a value parameter and a reference parameter
10:    TwoArgs[0] := TObject(Integer(ValParam)); //pass by value
11:    RefParam := 0;
12:    TwoArgs[1] := TObject(RefParam); //pass by reference
13:    //the modifier has items for each parameter
14:    ParamModifiers[0] := ParameterModifier.Create(2);
15:    ParamModifiers[0][0] := False; //1st arg is by value
16:    ParamModifiers[0][1] := True;  //2nd arg is by reference
17:    MethodResult := ComObjType.InvokeMember(
18:      'Two', BindingFlags.InvokeMethod, nil, ComObj,
19:      TwoArgs, ParamModifiers, nil, nil);
20:    if Boolean(MethodResult) then
21:      MessageBox.Show(System.String.Format('Twice {0} is {1}', TwoArgs));
```

▶ Find the code on the CD: \Chapter 16\Ex02\.

The code sets up a variable to hold the value for the reference parameter in line 11. Both the value and the reference parameters are then put in the arguments array in lines 10 and 12. Line 10 takes a literal value defined by the ValParam constant and casts it into an Integer before casting it to an object. This is to ensure that the compiler knows the type of the item before the TObject cast, whose effect is to box the integer value type into an object; the Integer cast is required to ensure that the correct value type (that matches the required method parameter) is boxed. The modified value of the reference parameter will be in TwoArgs[1] after the method call, not in the RefParam variable. Lines 14–16 set up the parameter modifier object, and then lines 17–19 make the late bound method call.

Some Automation methods offer parameters that can be omitted because they are marked as optional parameters or have a default value. In Delphi 7, you could use the EmptyParam variable in place of one of these parameters if it was required; however, this was rare with Automation code through Variants because of the support for named parameters in the Delphi Win32 compilers. In .NET, the equivalent to EmptyParam is System.Type.Missing.

Early Bound COM

In order to do early binding in COM, you need to have something in addition to the COM server and its type library. The compiler needs to bind directly to some representation of the interfaces. Because we are dealing with a .NET compiler, you will need to manufacture some form of assembly to help it out. Such an assembly is called an Interop Assembly and can be generated from the type library through some support classes provided in the Microsoft .NET Framework. Fortunately, this is automatically done by the Delphi IDE when you add a reference to the type library of the target COM server.

As an example, let's look at using the Microsoft Speech API (SAPI). SAPI version 5.0 or 5.1 is implemented as a number of COM objects in an in-proc COM server called sapi.dll. On Windows XP and later, SAPI 5 is pre-installed, but on earlier versions it must be installed separately. You can find the appropriate installation files for SAPI 5.1, including sample voices, from links available on http://www.microsoft.com/speech/download/sdk51.

To make a simple speech application in Delphi for .NET, you must add a reference to the SAPI type library to your project (the type library is bound into the COM server binary). Much like adding a reference to a regular .NET assembly to your project, you can also add a reference to a COM type library (either a standalone type library file or one that is contained within the COM server itself). In the Add Reference dialog box—obtained through Project, Add Reference or by right-clicking the References node in the Project Manager and choosing Add Reference—the COM Imports page is where we find a list of all the registered COM type libraries and from where we can also browse for unregistered type libraries. Locate the Microsoft Speech Object Library version 5.0 or 5.1 and click Add Reference to add it to the list of New References as shown in Figure 16.1.

When you press OK, the reference is added alongside the other references in the Project Manager, as illustrated in Figure 16.2. Notice that it is not added as a reference to sapi.dll, but to an Interop Assembly called Interop.SpeechLib.dll. With the reference added, we can now use the COM objects in .NET applications. The Interop Assembly defines a namespace, which in this case is SpeechLib. We'll look more at Interop Assemblies, including their naming scheme, namespace names, and contents after getting through this example.

Listing 16.5 shows some simple code that creates a COM object that implements the ISpVoice interface (see line 16) and then uses the basic Speak method to have it speak out loud the text written in the text box txtWords (line 22). Notice that the variable is actually defined as SpVoice, not ISpVoice, for reasons that will become clear shortly (although ISpVoice would also be valid). The SVSFDefault flag is part of the SpeechVoiceSpeakFlags enumeration from the original type library and causes the call to return only after the text has been spoken. It's a simple application, but you can have a lot of fun with it by making up interesting phrases, questions, and comments for the speech engine to say.

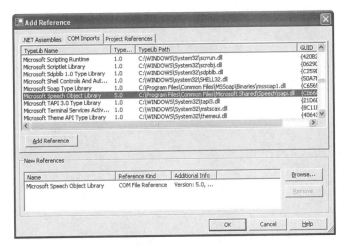

FIGURE 16.1   Importing a COM type library.

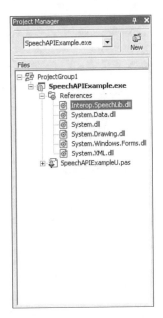

FIGURE 16.2   Project Manager with reference to a COM Interop Assembly.

LISTING 16.5   Simple Use of the Microsoft Speech API 5.x

```
1:   uses
2:     SpeechLib,
3:     ...
4:
5:   type
6:     TMainForm = class(System.Windows.Forms.Form)
7:     ...
8:     private
9:       Voice: SpVoice;
```

LISTING 16.5   Continued

```
10:    ...
11:    end;
12:  ...
13:  procedure TMainForm.TMainForm_Load(sender: System.Object;
14:    e: System.EventArgs);
15:  begin
16:    Voice := SpVoiceClass.Create;
17:  end;
18:
19:  procedure TMainForm.btnSay_Click(sender: System.Object;
20:    e: System.EventArgs);
21:  begin
22:    Voice.Speak(txtWords.Text, SpeechVoiceSpeakFlags.SVSFDefault);
23:  end;
```

▶ Find the code on the CD: Chapter 16\Ex03\.

Interop Assemblies

The act of adding a reference to a type library to a Delphi for .NET project (usually) causes the IDE to generate an Interop Assembly using the type library importing support in the .NET Framework. If you were using the command-line compiler, you would need to perform this step yourself, as discussed next.

The SAPI 5.x type library is linked into the in-proc COM server sapi.dll, but the type library specifies that the library name is actually SpeechLib. This can be verified by opening the file that contains the type library into Delphi for .NET; the library name shows as the top-level node in the type library hierarchy, as shown in Figure 16.3.

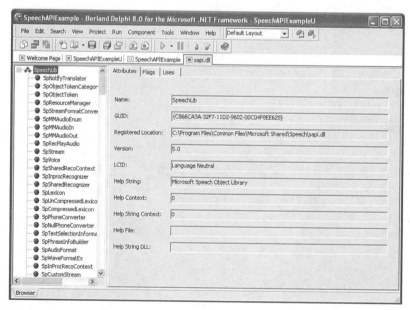

FIGURE 16.3   The Microsoft SAPI 5.x type library.

NOTE

COM servers created with Win32 versions of Delphi and C++Builder default to using the project name as the library name, so there is less confusion between the COM server name and the Interop Assembly name.

This library name is used as the basis of the Interop Assembly name and internal namespace. Convention dictates that Interop Assemblies are prefixed with Interop and a period, making the SAPI 5.x Interop Assembly called `Interop.SpeechLib.dll` containing items within a namespace of SpeechLib.

INTEROP ASSEMBLIES IN THE IDE

The IDE creates Interop Assemblies in a subdirectory of your project directory named `ComImports`. When the application is launched, the Interop Assembly would not normally be found in this location. (It isn't installed in the Global Assembly Cache and is not in a directory that would be found through probing the application base or culture directories.) Because of this, the reference to the Interop Assembly in the Project Manager has its Copy Local option set on its context menu, as shown in Figure 16.4, as well as displayed on the Object Inspector (see Figure 16.2).

FIGURE 16.4   Interop Assemblies use the Copy Local option.

The Copy Local option means that the Interop Assembly will be copied into the project's output directory to ensure that it compiles when run on the development machine.

However, consideration still needs to be given to what happens on machines the application is deployed to. You can deploy the Interop Assembly in the same directory as the application (or in a directory that will be found by probing), or you can install it in the Global Assembly Cache. Alternatively, you can set up an application configuration file that tells .NET where to find the assembly. A final option involves specifying a Primary Interop Assembly for the COM server, as we shall see a little later.

16

Creating an Interop Assembly

The IDE does a fine job of creating Interop Assemblies, as you saw previously. However, some developers need to know how to perform these operations by themselves—for example, in order to create batch building systems that use command-line tools.

The IDE accomplishes its goals by creating a `System.Runtime.InteropServices.TypeLibConverter` object and calling the `ConvertTypeLibToAssembly()` method. This operation is also performed by the command-line Type Library to Assembly Converter tool, `TlbImp.exe`, installed as part of the .NET Framework SDK (which, by default, resides in `C:\Program Files\Microsoft.NET\SDK\v1.1`). You can create the same resultant Interop Assembly as the IDE using this tool. For example, the Speech API Interop Assembly can be created with this command-line:

```
TlbImp "C:\Program Files\Common Files\Microsoft
➥Shared\Speech\sapi.dll" /sysarray /namespace:SpeechLib
➥/out:Interop.SpeechLib.dll
```

USING THE .NET FRAMEWORK SDK TOOLS

In order to use the Microsoft .NET Framework and Framework SDK command-line tools effectively, you must add both the Framework and the Framework SDK directory to your Windows search path. If you are planning on using the tools quite regularly, you can add these to the global PATH environment variable using the Environment Variables button on the Advanced page of the System Properties dialog box (accessible through Control Panel), by the Properties menu item on the context menu of My Computer, or more simply by pressing Windows logo key+Break.

An alternative approach is to set up a shortcut on the desktop or in the Framework SDK's Start menu program group that launches a command prompt that initially runs a batch file. The batch file can set up a local PATH, meaning the tools can all be used from within the command prompt. In fact, the Framework SDK comes equipped with a batch file fit for this purpose, called SDKVars.bat.

The shortcut can run a command prompt session that invokes the batch file by using this command line as a target, assuming the default installation directory

```
cmd /K "C:\Program Files\Microsoft.NET\SDK\v1.1\bin\SDKVars.bat"
```

What's in an Interop Assembly?

An Interop Assembly does not contain any real code but contains metadata describing all the types available through the COM server's type library. It is used by the CLR at runtime to construct suitable wrapper objects that enable .NET managed code to talk to the underlying COM objects. These wrapper objects are consequently called Runtime Callable Wrappers, or RCWs. Their creation is automatic, assuming that your code is compiled against a suitable Interop Assembly.

It is important to understand how items described in the original type library are made available in an Interop Assembly. Some of these can be deduced from the simple Speech API example from earlier. But just to give an overall picture, we will go through the details here. Consider an example in which you have a COM server that implements a CoClass (a COM object that can be created by a COM call) called Foo that happens to implement two interfaces called IFoo and IBar. The interfaces will be surfaced with the same names, IFoo and IBar; however, an additional interface will be created called Foo that is a combination of both IFoo and IBar. The CoClass itself will be exposed as a managed RCW class FooClass.

In the speech example earlier, the original COM CoClass being addressed was called SpVoice, which implements interfaces ISpeechVoice (intended for use through Automation and offering simple method signatures) and ISpVoice (targeted at lower-level COM languages and offering more cumbersome method signatures). The Interop Assembly combines the two interfaces into a new one called SpVoice, and makes the CoClass available though the RCW SpVoiceClass. So in Listing 16.5, the Voice variable in line 9 can be declared either using the manufactured interface SpVoice, as in the listing, or the original COM interface ISpeechVoice.

If a COM object has an outgoing interface (or events interface), all the event methods are exposed through delegate types with names that follow a pattern of SourceInterfaceName_MethodNameEventHandler. The Speech API voice object used in the previous example offers an outgoing interface called _ISpeechVoiceEvents. This offers a variety of event methods—OnWord that triggers each time a new word is encountered in the text being read aloud, OnSentence that fires each time a new sentence is encountered, and OnEndStream for when the whole speech stream has been processed. These events are available in .NET using the delegate types:

_ISpeechVoiceEvents_WordEventHandler, _ISpeechVoiceEvents_SentenceEventHandler, and _ISpeechVoiceEvents_EndStreamEventHandler, respectively.

Using COM Events

Listing 16.6 shows some code from a project that handles some speech events. This offers a simple UI that contains a multiline TextBox where you can write any text. In the form's Load event, the code creates a SAPI voice object (line 3) and requests the Word and EndStream events to be fired as appropriate (lines 4 and 5). Event handlers for these events are then set up using Include calls (lines 6 and 7).

LISTING 16.6   Using COM Events from the Microsoft Speech API

```
1:    procedure TMainForm.TMainForm_Load(sender: System.Object;
➥e: System.EventArgs);
2:    begin
3:      Voice := SpVoiceClass.Create;
4:      Voice.EventInterests :=
5:        SpeechVoiceEvents.SVEWordBoundary or
➥SpeechVoiceEvents.SVEEndInputStream;
6:      Include(Voice.Word, VoiceWord);
7:      Include(Voice.EndStream, VoiceEndStream);
8:    end;
9:
10:   procedure TMainForm.btnSay_Click(sender: System.Object;
➥e: System.EventArgs);
11:   begin
12:     //Speak asynchronously so the events can fire
13:     Voice.Speak(txtWords.Text, SpeechVoiceSpeakFlags.SVSFlagsAsync);
14:   end;
15:
16:   procedure TMainForm.VoiceEndStream(StreamNumber: Integer;
17:     StreamPosition: TObject);
18:   begin
19:     //When speech stream ends, remove the highlight from the text box
20:     txtWords.SelectionLength := 0;
```

LISTING 16.6   Continued

```
21:     txtWords.SelectionStart := Length(txtWords.Text);
22: end;
23:
24: procedure TMainForm.VoiceWord(StreamNumber: Integer;
25:     StreamPosition: TObject; CharacterPosition, Length: Integer);
26: begin
27:     //As each word is encountered, highlight it in the text box
28:     txtWords.SelectionStart := CharacterPosition;
29:     txtWords.SelectionLength := Length; //highlight word
30: end;
```

▶ Find the code on the CD: \Chapter 16\Ex04\.

IDENTIFYING REQUIRED COM EVENT HANDLER SIGNATURES

To find the required signature for the event handlers, you must look at the definition of the relevant delegate types. You can easily do this using Lutz Roeder's Reflector, available as a free download from http://www.aisto.com/roeder/dotnet. Reflector offers IL disassembly (although nicer and more feature-rich than the Framework SDK's ILDASM.exe), as well as the ability to view declarations in various languages and also decompile IL into those languages. It supports Microsoft's C# and Visual Basic .NET as well as Delphi 8 for .NET.

Open up the Interop Assembly into Reflector, select Language, Delphi, and then locate the delegate type you need from within the assembly. Figure 16.5 shows the declaration for the Word COM event managed delegate type being displayed. If you compare it with the event handler signature in Listing 16.6, you will see that it tells you all you need to know.

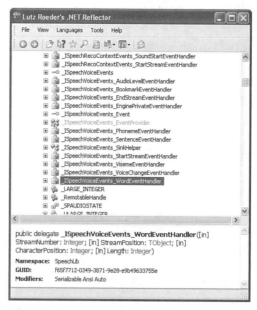

FIGURE 16.5   Lutz Roeder's Reflector.

The task of the event handlers in Listing 16.6 is to highlight individual words in the text box as they are spoken aloud and you can see the result in Figure 16.6. (Run the sample application and you can hear it too.)

FIGURE 16.6   Microsoft Speech API in action.

COM Lifetime Control

The lifetime of a COM object is controlled through reference counting, which is managed for you by the RCW. When a RCW gets garbage collected, the COM object reference count will drop to zero and will destroy itself. However, because you don't normally control when a garbage collection will occur, it is indeterminate when the COM object will be destroyed. Sometimes you need to deterministically dispense with a COM object, and this can be achieved by passing it to the static method `Marshal.ReleaseComObject()` from the `System.Runtime.InteropServices` namespace.

> **NOTE**
>
> Once `Marshal.ReleaseComObject` is called on an RCW instance, it becomes unusable for accessing any interfaces from that point on.

Error Handling

COM routines indicate errors by returning `HResult` status codes. However, you might recall from previous Delphi COM programming that Delphi offers the convenient `SafeCall` calling convention, which removes the `HResult` issue from the programmer's eyes and leaves it to the compiled code. Any `HResult` that is returned by a COM method that represents an error is transparently turned into an exception by the calling code. If the COM method sets extra error information through the `IErrorInfo` interface (as Delphi `SafeCall` methods do when an exception occurs in their implementation), the client-side exception will be more informative.

.NET uses this same model to hide `HResult`s from .NET code and silently turns them into managed exception objects. A wide variety of specific `HResult` error values are turned into specific exception types—for example, `COR_E_FILENOTFOUND` ($80070002), the `HResult` version of the Win32 error `ERROR_FILE_NOT_FOUND` (error 2), is transformed into `System.IO.FileNotFoundException`; however, custom `HResult` codes that are not recognized by the CLR are simply turned into `System.Runtime.InteropServices.COMException`.

Primary Interop Assemblies

If a particular COM server is in widespread use, you can appreciate the problem that might occur in which a variety of developers make their own Interop Assembly for it. As various applications are deployed to target machines, a given machine could end up with several Interop Assemblies for the same COM server installed in various locations. To avoid this situation, there is the notion of a Primary Interop Assembly or PIA.

The goal is for vendors of COM servers to create a PIA for their COM server and to make it available to .NET developers. As a .NET developer, you should check with the vendor of any COM servers you make use of to see whether they have a PIA available. Similarly, if you are the author of a COM server that is distributed to developers, you should build a PIA and make it available to them. PIAs can be created with the TlbImp.exe utility using the /primary command-line switch.

Microsoft Office XP predates the uptake of Microsoft .NET, so PIAs are available from http://msdn.microsoft.com/downloads/list/office.asp; however, Microsoft Office 2003 installs PIAs during a full product installation.

> **NOTE**
>
> These (and other) PIAs are customized after being manufactured to make the job of using the COM objects easier.

A PIA has certain requirements placed upon it to ensure that it works as designed. First, it must be given a strong name by the developer using a strong name key file. This is manufactured by the sn.exe .NET utility (using its /k option) and incorporated into the assembly through the AssemblyKeyFile attribute that is automatically placed in the project source file when making a new application. Second, if the COM server uses other COM objects, the PIA must only reference other PIAs (for the required COM servers) to resolve the references. A common location to install PIAs is C:\Program Files\Microsoft.NET\Primary Interop Assemblies; however, PIAs must be installed in the Global Assembly Cache when deployed so that they can be readily located, regardless of where they are physically deployed to on the machine.

PIAs must be registered with regasm.exe, which adds an entry describing the PIA in the registry in the original COM server type library subkey. This enables development environments such as Delphi for .NET to see that a PIA is available when you reference a type library and thereby avoids generating a regular Interop Assembly.

> **NOTE**
>
> The link to the PIA is found by the IDE calling the System.Runtime.InteropServices.TypeLibConverter object's GetPrimaryInteropAssembly() method when a type library reference is added to a project. If the method returns True, the reference is made to the identified PIA; otherwise, the IDE calls ConvertTypeLibToAssembly() to create an Interop Assembly as described earlier.

> **TIP**
>
> As an alternative to adding a reference to the type library for a COM server that you know has an associated PIA you can also link directly to the PIA. However, for the PIA to be physically located in the first place and added to the installed .NET assemblies, in the Add References dialog box, you will need to add the directory to the list of assembly search paths. This list can be customized

in the Assembly Search Paths page of the dialog invoked by the Installed .NET Components menu item on the Component menu.

There are guidelines for naming your PIA and the namespace within it. To help identify your PIA, it is recommended that you name it as `VendorName.LibraryName.dll`, where `LibraryName` is the name of the library as defined in the type library. This same convention of `VendorName.LibraryName` is recommended for naming the namespace within the PIA (specified by the namespace option to `TlbImp.exe`).

However, a secondary guideline suggests that the `VendorName.LibraryName` pattern be reserved for a future managed version of the COM server you might develop. If this can be seen as likely to happen, you should instead adopt the scheme `VendorName.LibraryName.Interop` for the PIA. When you move the COM library over to managed code, you can then use the `VendorName.LibraryName` pattern as the basis for your assembly name and namespace.

Customizing Interop Assemblies and PIAs

The principal issue you bump into with Interop Assemblies is parameter marshaling for "interesting" parameter types not being quite right. Marshaling involves translating data between unmanaged types, such as a C `char *` or a Delphi `PChar`, and a suitable managed type, such as the .NET `System.String` type. The .NET process of generating Interop Assemblies does a good job with marshaling many data types, but clearly with complex types there is great scope for it going wrong or at least not being as easy to work with as possible.

As a consequence, it might be desirable to tweak the types defined in an Interop Assembly to make the RCWs easier to work with. This is especially important when building a PIA that is to be used by numerous developers; it is desirable to make it as easy to use as possible. For example, the Office XP and Office 2003 PIAs are very much modified to make them as usable as possible by .NET application developers.

Unfortunately, there is little provision at this time for customizing Interop Assemblies in a sensible or maintainable way because they are simply generated by the `System.Runtime.InteropServices.TypeLibConverter` class with no hooks provided for intercepting the process. As a consequence, the only option is to use a process called creative round tripping, which is an extension of round tripping.

Round tripping is a term describing a two-step process that involves taking a managed .NET assembly and disassembling it to the corresponding IL source code and metadata (along with any managed or unmanaged resources), and then reassembling the IL code, metadata, and resources into a functionally equivalent .NET assembly. For example, given an assembly called `dotNetAssembly.dll`, these commands will disassemble and reassemble it to provide a functionally identical assembly:

```
ildasm dotNetAssembly.dll /linenum /nobar /out:dotNetAssembly.il
ilasm dotNetAssembly /dll /quiet /debug /resource:dotNetAssembly.res
```

Because of the rich, descriptive nature of the metadata in managed PE (Portable Executable, the Win32 file format) files this round-tripping process is very reliable. A few select things do not survive the process, but these are not things that are supported by the

Delphi for .NET compiler—for example, data on data (data that contains the address of another data constant) and embedded native, nonmanaged code. Also, local variable names will be lost if there is no debug symbol file (PDB file) available because they are only defined in the debug information and not in metadata.

Round tripping in itself is only useful to prove that you get a working executable back after a disassembly/reassembly process. The term creative round tripping is used to describe a round tripping job with an extra step. After disassembling the assembly into IL code, you modify the IL code before reassembly. Creative round tripping is used in scenarios in which you want to change the IL code generated by a compiler in a way not permitted by the compiler, such as using a feature of the CLR not supported by it or adding custom IL code to your classes.

> **NOTE**
>
> You can find information on creative round tripping in an article at `http://www.blong.com/Conferences/BorConUK2002/Interop1/Win32AndDotNetInterop.htm`. This article was written for the Delphi for .NET Preview compiler that shipped with Delphi 7, before Delphi for .NET had its full feature set; you will see in the section "Using .NET Routines in Win32 Code" that the reason for discussing creative round tripping in the article has gone away with the release of Delphi 8 for .NET, but the discussion of the subject is still interesting. At the very least, you get to see how Delphi 8 for .NET implements the `exports` directive (discussed at the end of the chapter).

In this case, to customize the marshaling of parameters, you will need to modify the IL generated by the type library importer to specify explicit marshaling options or to modify the parameter types. However, manipulating IL code is outside the scope of this chapter (and indeed the whole book). So that's left as an exercise for you to explore. We are able to look a bit more at marshaling data when exploring .NET objects being used in Win32 applications, as that is done at the Delphi level.

> **TIP**
>
> For more information on the default marshaling that will be applied in the Interop Assembly you can look up "default marshaling" in the Delphi for .NET help.

Using .NET Objects in COM Code

Having looked at .NET code that uses COM objects, let's now turn the tables and look at Win32 client applications using .NET objects as if they were COM objects. As you develop code in .NET, you might want to make use of it in existing COM client applications, and .NET supports this. With sufficient information in the registry, a COM client can request that an object be created by COM, and it will end up with a COM object being instantiated that represents your .NET object. The COM object will do the tricky stuff of marshaling parameter data back and forth across the managed/unmanaged boundary and reconciling the reference counted lifetime management of .NET with the garbage collected scheme in .NET. Because the COM object is a wrapper around a .NET object accessible by a Win32 COM client, it is called a COM Callable Wrapper or CCW.

Registering a .NET Assembly for Automation

Our first requirement in making .NET objects available to COM is to add the entries into the registry that COM uses to do its object creation work. This can be done using the `System.Runtime.InteropServices.RegistrationServices` class or more conveniently by the `regasm.exe` .NET Framework SDK command-line utility. For example, the .NET class in Listing 16.7 from project `dotNetAssembly.bdsproj` can be registered for use by Win32 applications with this command line:

```
regasm dotNetAssembly.dll
```

This command-line command sets up registry information for each class exposed from the assembly; in each case, a `ProgID` and a `ClassID` for a `CoClass` that represents the .NET class. The `ProgID` is the namespace qualified classname of the class, which, for the class in Listing 16.7, is `dotNetAssembly.DotNETClassForCOM`. (You can see the classname specified in line 2). The `ClassID` is manufactured by `regasm.exe` unless specified by the use of `GuidAttribute` on the class. Underneath the `ClassID` subkey, information can be found on the assembly that implements the .NET class and the version of the .NET runtime it is compiled against. However, the in-proc COM server for the `CoClass` is always specified as the .NET execution engine library, `mscoree.dll`. This DLL will manufacture a COM object at runtime (a CCW) that exposes methods and properties matching the underlying .NET class by using reflection to examine its class members. Figure 16.7 shows the registry information for our sample class.

LISTING 16.7   A Simple .NET Class to be Exposed to COM

```
1:   type
2:     DotNETClassForCOM = class
3:     public
4:       procedure ShowDotNetMessage(Msg, Caption: String);
5:       function DotNETVersion: String;
6:     end;
7:
8:   function DotNETClassForCOM.dotNETVersion: String;
9:   begin
10:    Result := System.String.Format('Running .NET {0} on {1}',
11:      Environment.Version, Environment.OSVersion);
12:  end;
13:
14:  procedure DotNETClassForCOM.ShowDotNetMessage(Msg, Caption: String);
15:  begin
16:    MessageBox.Show(Msg, Caption)
17:  end;
```

▶ Find the code on the CD: `\Chapter 16\Ex05\`.

Figure 16.7 shows the registry entries that enable a .NET class to be used by Win32 COM.

> **CAUTION**
>
> The assembly must be placed in a suitable directory to be found at runtime through natural DLL location mechanisms. Generally, it is wise to deploy the assembly in the GAC; however, during development, you typically leave it in the same directory as the application.

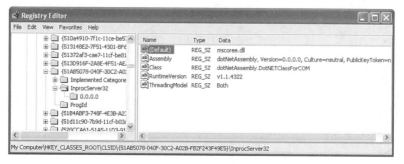

FIGURE 16.7 COM Interop Registry entries created by Regasm.

Late Bound Automation

Once your assembly has been registered in this way, the classes exposed are immediately available for access through late bound Automation. For example, it could be accessed in a Delphi 7 application using the code in Listing 16.8.

LISTING 16.8 Delphi 7 Code Using a .NET Object from Listing 16.7

```
1:   uses
2:     ComObj;
3:
4:   var
5:     dotNETObject: Variant;
6:
7:   procedure TfrmAutomation.FormCreate(Sender: TObject);
8:   begin
9:     dotNETObject := CreateOleObject('dotNetAssembly.DotNETClassForCOM')
10:  end;
11:
12:  procedure TfrmAutomation.btnAutomationClick(Sender: TObject);
13:  var
14:    Info: String;
15:  begin
16:    Info := dotNETObject.DotNETVersion;
17:    dotNETObject.ShowDotNetMessage(Info, 'Information')
18:  end;
```

▶ Find the code on the CD: \Chapter 16\Ex05\Delphi7AutomationClient.

> **CAUTION**
>
> Again, it is important to ensure that the .NET assembly is in a location where it can be found when testing out this application. The easiest thing to do is to put the application and the assembly into the same directory. You can help this process be automated by using the Output directory option in the project options for the assembly.

Because this Automation code relies on using the IDispatch interface exposed for the .NET class, this should work just fine as long as the data types used for the parameters of the exposed methods are limited to those that Windows automatically marshals on behalf of

Automation code. However, most production code will use early bound COM code, so that is what we will focus more attention on.

Interop Type Libraries

In order for a Win32 COM client to do early bound coding against a .NET class, we should create a type library so that your Win32 development tool can generate appropriate classes and interfaces to bind to at compiler time. A type library can be generated to describe the COM Callable Wrapper (CCW) that the CLR will build at runtime for exactly this purpose, and it is referred to as an Interop Type Library. You can create an Interop Type Library using the `System.Runtime.InteropServices.TypeLibConverter` class and its `ConvertAssemblyToTypeLib()` method, but the support is also offered through the `TlbExp.exe` Framework SDK utility.

`TlbExp.exe` will generate an Interop Type Library but will not do anything with it. This is not necessarily a problem, but the `RegAsm.exe` utility has a `/tlb` command-line switch that does the same job as `TlbExp.exe` and also registers the Interop Type Library for you so that it can be found in the registry by Win32 development tools.

What's in an Interop Type Library?

When you create an Interop Type Library, it will contain information on every visible class and interface in the assembly. In most cases, you will want to be selective about what is described in the Interop Type Library, and you can use `ComVisibleAttribute` to achieve this. When not specified, this attribute defaults to `True`, but you can apply it to items to keep them out of the type library. The attribute can be applied to a whole assembly, interfaces, classes, and records, as well as to fields, methods, properties, enumerations, and delegates. So you can mark the whole assembly as not exposed, and then pick and choose the items that you want to add to the type library.

For every .NET class `Foo` exposed to the type library, there will be a `CoClass Foo` and a corresponding interface `_Foo`. However, by default, the interface is actually a memberless `dispinterface`, which forces any Win32 client to use late bound Automation against the objects. This takes us no further forward than we were before discovering Interop Type Libraries. To control the situation, every class can have `ClassInterfaceAttribute` applied to it that dictates what type of interface will be generated for it in the Interop Type Library.

The default value for the attribute is `ClassInterfaceType.AutoDispatch`, which causes the behavior described previously. Note that when an interface is manufactured for a class, any public data fields will automatically be exposed as properties. You can specify a value of `ClassInterfaceType.AutoDual` to get an `IDispatch`-based dual interface to be generated, exposing all the public members of the class.

> **CAUTION**
>
> `ClassInterfaceType.AutoDual` might seem the most desirable option for `ClassInterfaceAttribute`, but you should be aware that it causes versioning problems. Each time you modify the class and rebuild the Interop Type Library, you will generate a modified version of the same interface, which of course is something we should avoid.

The other value we can give the attribute is `ClassInterfaceType.None`. This causes the type library to not contain any manufactured interface for the class. This attribute value is used when you have .NET classes that already implement an interface; there is no requirement to expose the whole of the class as code can access the important parts of it through the interface. The class itself will be exposed through a `CoClass` that implements the appropriate interface. If the class implements multiple interfaces, the `CoClass` will return the first COM-visible implemented interface as its default. If the class implements no interfaces, it will expose the first COM-visible interface implemented by its base class. If there are no implemented interfaces at all, it will return `_Object`, the interface that represents the `System.Object` public members.

The interface that you implement in the class can either be one solely defined in the .NET code, which is made visible to COM via the Interop Type Library, or it can be an existing COM interface. In the latter case, you would gain access to the COM interface by using an Interop Assembly generated by adding to your project a reference to the type library containing the interface definition. If the COM interface is not defined in a type library, you would need to write an equivalent interface definition in the .NET code.

> **NOTE**
>
> `ClassInterfaceType.None` is the preferred value for `ClassInterfaceAttribute` because it avoids unnecessary interface versioning problems.

Implementing Interfaces

Listing 16.9 shows a reworking of Listing 16.7, where the `DotNETClassForCOM` class implements the interface `IDotNETClassForCOM`. Line 7 hides all the RTL classes from the Interop Type Library (along with any of our own classes that might also be in a real-life assembly) by applying the `[ComVisible(False)]` attribute to the entire assembly. The interface is made visible to COM in line 10 and given an IID in line 11. Lines 17 and 18 make the class visible and expose a `CoClass` that returns the `IDotNetClassForCOM` interface.

LISTING 16.9   A Simple .NET Class Exposed to COM via an Interface

```
1:    library dotNetAssembly;
2:
3:    uses
4:      System.Runtime.InteropServices,
5:      System.Windows.Forms;
6:
7:    [assembly: ComVisible(False)]
8:
9:    type
10:     [ComVisible(True)]
11:     [Guid('3C32D881-43DA-40D2-A7F6-0AE830C2920F')]
12:     IDotNETClassForCOM = interface
13:       procedure ShowDotNetMessage(Msg, Caption: String);
14:       function DotNETVersion: String;
15:     end;
16:
17:     [ComVisible(True)]
```

LISTING 16.9   Continued

```
18:   [ClassInterface(ClassInterfaceType.None)]
19:   DotNETClassForCOM = class(TObject, IDotNETClassForCOM)
20:   public
21:     procedure ShowDotNetMessage(Msg, Caption: String);
22:     function DotNETVersion: String;
23:   end;
24:
25: function DotNETClassForCOM.dotNETVersion: String;
26: begin
27:   Result := System.String.Format('Running .NET {0} on {1}',
28:     Environment.Version, Environment.OSVersion);
29: end;
30:
31: procedure DotNETClassForCOM.ShowDotNetMessage(Msg, Caption: String);
32: begin
33:   MessageBox.Show(Msg, Caption)
34: end;
35:
36: begin
37: end.
```

▶ Find the code on the CD: `\Chapter 16\Ex06\`.

> **CAUTION**
>
> An IID was applied to the `IDotNETClassForCOM` interface in Listing 16.9 using `GuidAttribute` (line 11). This is different from how we achieved the same goal in Delphi 7, using the dedicated interface ID syntax:
>
> ```
> IDotNETClassForCOM = interface
> ['{3C32D881-43DA-40D2-A7F6-0AE830C2920F}']
>   ...
> end;
> ```
>
> This traditional Delphi syntax is still accepted by the Delphi for .NET compiler, but in the initial release is completely ignored. (The CLR is left to generate its own IID, which looks essentially random, but is made from a hashed value of the namespace, classname, and full assembly name, including version.) This oversight will hopefully be rectified in a subsequent update, but to avoid risk, you should use the .NET attribute instead.

An Interop Type Library can be created for this assembly using this command line:

```
RegAsm dotNetAssembly.dll /tlb
```

However, if you add on the `/verbose` command-line switch, `RegAsm.exe` will list out all the types it added into the type library. In this case, there are two: `IDotNETClassForCOM` and `DotNETClassForCOM`.

The resultant type library can then be imported into your favorite development tool and used as normal. A sample COM client written in Delphi 7 is provided on the CD in `Chapter 16\Ex06\Delphi7COMClient`. It calls the .NET class methods through its interface in a similar way to the Automation code in Listing 16.8. The application is shown running with the .NET message box on display in Figure 16.8.

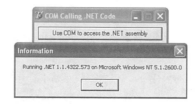

FIGURE 16.8   .NET Assembly being used by a Win32/COM client.

Parameter Types and Marshaling

Many managed method signatures will work correctly, having been exported through an Interop Type Library thanks to the default data mapping and marshaling rules used by the COM Interop system. Indeed, for many data types, no marshaling is required as they have a common representation in both managed and unmanaged code. These so-called blittable types include all the various Integer data types defined by the Delphi compiler (Byte, Smallint, Word, Shortint, Cardinal/LongWord, Integer/Longint, UInt64, Int64, NativeUInt, NativeInt) and their underlying types defined in the System namespace (System.Byte, System.SByte, System.UInt16, System.Int16, System.UInt32, System.Int32, System.UInt64, System.Int64), as well as any one-dimensional array of a blittable type.

Non-blittable types require marshaling because unmanaged types are ambiguous and can be represented in more than one way in managed code. The interop marshaler has certain rules as to what it will do for each type by default. For example, a .NET String will be marshaled to COM as a BSTR, which can be accessed in Delphi 7 as a WideString, and an array will be marshaled across as a safe array, which can be accessed through a Variant in Delphi 7. In some cases, these default marshaling rules differ for COM Interop and Platform Invoke simply because what is typically required in COM and non-COM differs.

When the default marshaling rules do not match the specific requirements of the function you are planning to call, you can modify the process using MarshalAsAttribute (in conjunction with the UnmanagedType enumeration) as well as the Marshal class. For example, to marshal a String to COM as a PWideChar instead of a WideString, you can apply this attribute to the parameter:

```
[MarshalAs(UnmanagedType.LPWStr)]
```

The unmanaged type enumeration has many values to give full control to the developer, and MarshalAsAttribute also has additional fields that can be used to help supply additional information—for example, when marshaling a managed array to a C style array (with UnmanagedType.LPArray), as opposed to a safe array, you can specify the element type and size of the array.

> **NOTE**
>
> You can apply an attribute, such as MarshalAsAttribute, to a function return value by using the special result attribute modifier, similar to the assembly modifier used in line 7 of Listing 16.9. For example,
>
> ```
> [result: MarshalAs(UnmanagedType.Bool)]
> function A(D: Double): Integer;
> ```

The requirement to customize the default marshaling might not always be because the marshaling is incorrect but can sometimes be because memory management needs to be specifically controlled. Generally, the interop marshaler has a well-intentioned habit to try and free up memory wherever it sees an opportunity to, but this is not always appropriate. For example, a pointer might be returned containing an address of a string compiled inside some unmanaged code, rather than of allocated memory. We'll look at an example like this when we move onto the P/Invoke system.

As a simple example, consider a .NET method that has two parameters, an Integer array, and a String. It might look like this to start with:

```
TSample = class
public
  procedure SomeMethod(Values: array of Integer; Msg: String);
end;
```

You might want to give COM access to this method but customize how it sees the parameters. Perhaps the Integer information needs to be passed across as Boolean values because the COM side only needs to know if the values are zero or non-zero. This matches the way C Boolean values operate, although it is different from regular Delphi Booleans, which use the least significant bit to decide if they represent True (the bit is set) or False (the bit is clear). And instead of the string going across as a WideString, you might want it to go across as a PWideChar. You could achieve this by extending the class as follows:

```
[ComVisible(True)]
ISample = interface
  procedure SomeMethod(
    [MarshalAs(UnmanagedType.SafeArray, SafeArraySubType=VarEnum.VT_BOOL)]
    Values: array of Integer;
    [MarshalAs(UnmanagedType.LPWStr)]
    Msg: String);
end;

[ComVisible(True)]
[ClassInterface(ClassInterfaceType.None)]
TSample = class(TObject, ISample)
public
  procedure SomeMethod(
    [MarshalAs(UnmanagedType.SafeArray, SafeArraySubType=VarEnum.VT_BOOL)]
    Values: array of Integer;
    [MarshalAs(UnmanagedType.LPWStr)]
    Msg: String);
end;
```

You customize the safe array data type using the VarEnum enumeration. When the assembly containing this class is run through the type library exporter, it generates type information that matches your attribute specifications, as pictured in the sample type library shown in Figure 16.9.

16

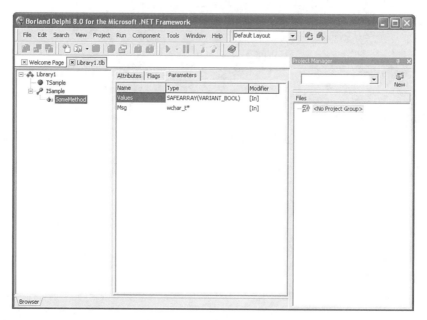

FIGURE 16.9   A customized Interop Type Library.

NOTE

If adding custom marshaling attributes onto a method, be sure to apply the same attributes everywhere the method is defined—that is, both in the defining class and also in the interface, assuming that the method is declared in one. Otherwise, COM clients could get different marshaling behavior based on how they access the method: directly through the defined interface or through the class `dispinterface`.

You can find more coverage of the .NET marshaling support in the section on using the Platform Invocation Service (P/Invoke) later in this chapter.

CAUTION

Parameters declared with the `const` modifier in COM interfaces and callbacks to unmanaged APIs (such as the Win32 API) are not passed by reference as they were in Delphi 7. To maintain the same parameter passing mechanics, change any `const` declarations to `[in]` `var`, as follows:

```
// VCL declaration
TFontEnumProc = function (const lplf: TLogFont;
  const lptm: TTextMetric; dwType: DWORD; lpData: LPARAM): Integer;

// VCL.NET declaration
TFontEnumProc = function ([in] var lplf: TLogFont;
  [in] var lptm: TTextMetric; dwType: DWORD; lpData: LPARAM): Integer;
```

Note that this only applies to COM Interop and is irrelevant for P/Invoke routines (discussed later).

Error Handling

When an exception occurs in a .NET method that is being called from COM, the CCW will perform the same helpful trick as Delphi Win32 developers are used to with safecall methods. The exception will be caught and turned into an error HResult code specific to the exception class that is silently returned from the routine to conform to COM error protocols. It is possible to map some HResult codes back to the originating exception type, but this is not a perfect science because HResult codes can be reused (and indeed are reused) by new exception classes.

However, the CCW will also set up a COM-rich error object with additional information (the exception message) for any COM client that is interested. If called from a Delphi Win32 COM client that understands all about rich error objects, the managed exception will be re-created on the client side, displaying the exception message.

> **TIP**
>
> You can alter this error handling behavior using PreserveSigAttribute on a per method basis. If you wanted to return various meaningful HResult success codes, you can specify an Integer return type and return the HResult codes yourself. To do this requires specifying the PreserveSigAttribute for that method so that the CLR doesn't modify the signature and return its own HResult code.

Using Win32 DLL Exports in .NET Code

Aside from using COM objects in .NET code, there is a common requirement to use regular Win32 DLL routines. These could be aspects of the Win32 API that are not already made available though the .NET Framework Class Library or could be routines from arbitrary DLLs written by yourself or a third party. Examples of the former might include the high performance timing APIs, QueryPerformanceCounter and QueryPerformanceFrequency. Another example is the simple API that makes a beep: Beep.

> **NOTE**
>
> Technically the .NET Framework does actually surface a routine that makes a beep, but this is part of the Visual Basic .NET runtime assembly Microsoft.VisualBasic.dll. Generally, only Visual Basic .NET applications have a dependency on this file, but if you wanted to you could add a reference to Microsoft.VisualBasic.dll to your project and add Microsoft.VisualBasic to your uses clause. Then a call to Interaction.Beep would make a beep.
>
> However, this is not implemented using the Beep API; rather it makes an unmanaged call to MessageBeep(MB_OK). So the result is in fact dependant on how the Default Beep Windows sound event is defined. Normally, it is not a beep at all but the ding.wav sound file.

The requirement to call unmanaged Win32 DLL exports is met by .NET's Platform Invocation Service, sometimes referred to as Platform Invoke, P/Invoke, or even PInvoke.

To use P/Invoke, you need to write a declaration of the unmanaged DLL routine in the managed code so that the CLR can locate it and work out how to call it. This is much the same task as writing a traditional DLL import declaration in the Win32 version of Delphi but requires additional support to cater for the marshaling of various parameter types across the managed/unmanaged boundary. Historically, the job of writing a DLL import declaration involved using Delphi data types that mapped directly onto the C data types used by the vast majority of DLLs. In .NET, fewer data types map directly across to unmanaged C types, so marshaling becomes very important.

> **NOTE**
>
> The Platform Invocation Service is defined as part of the CLI (Common Language Infrastructure) standard, so it should be present in some form in other conforming CLI implementations such as Ximian's Mono and dotGNU's Portable .NET. You can find details in section 14.5.2 of Partition II of the standards documents, which themselves are installed as part of the .NET Framework SDK. You can find all five Partitions as Microsoft Word documents in the Tool Developers Guide\docs subdirectory of the Framework SDK installation directory, which by default would be `C:\Program Files\Microsoft.NET\SDK\v1.1\Tool Developers Guide\docs`.

That said, Delphi for .NET does support the traditional Win32 DLL import declaration syntax, which will work for some DLL routines. Behind-the-scenes, this syntax is transposed into a form appropriate for .NET that uses the main DLL importing attribute (`DllImportAttribute`), which is flexible enough to cater for most requirements. We can also use `MarshalAsAttribute` against individual parameters, which save the day when `DllImportAttribute` reaches its limitation.

> **NOTE**
>
> Delphi for .NET comes with some import units containing P/Invoke import declarations for some portions of the Windows API. The primary example that will generally be useful is `Borland.Vcl.Windows.pas`, but you will also find `Borland.Vcl.Mapi.pas`, `Borland.Vcl.ShellAPI.pas`, `Borland.Vcl.SHFolder.pas`, and more.

Traditional Delphi Syntax

We'll look at a simple example to start with. Consider a DLL called `SomeDll.dll` that exports a routine you have used in a Win32 version of Delphi—a simple routine called `Some_Func()` that takes an `Integer`, returns an `Integer`, and uses the regular Win32 `StdCall` calling convention. To use this routine in Delphi 7, you would probably write an `import` declaration in an import unit like the one in lines 5, 9, and 10 of Listing 16.10.

LISTING 16.10   A Simple DLL Import Unit

```
1:   unit SomeDllImports;
2:
3:   interface
4:
5:   function SomeFunc(InputValue: Integer): Integer; stdcall;
6:
7:   implementation
8:
9:   function SomeFunc(InputValue: Integer): Integer; stdcall;
10:  external 'SomeDll.dll' name 'Some_Func';
11:
12:  end.
```

The great news is this will work just fine in Delphi for .NET. In fact, declarations for any routines that take and return simple parameter types such as integers, doubles, and Booleans will work just as before. The cases that require some work are routines with parameters that have more interesting data types, such as records and strings.

Custom Attribute Syntax

When compiling the code in Listing 16.10, the compiler will translate it to use DllImportAttribute (from the System.Runtime.InteropServices namespace), which is used to enable the P/Invoke system. So while you write code such as Listing 16.10, the compiler essentially compiles Listing 16.11. This shows DllImportAttribute being applied to the declaration in the implementation section. Line 12 constructs the attribute passing the DLL name as the constructor parameter, whereas lines 13–15 set up some field values (sometimes called named parameters) for the attribute.

LISTING 16.11 A Raw .NET Import Unit for a Simple DLL

```
1:   unit SomeDllImports;
2:
3:   interface
4:
5:   function SomeFunc(InputValue: Integer): Integer;
6:
7:   implementation
8:
9:   uses
10:    System.Runtime.InteropServices;
11:
12:  [DllImport('SomeDll.dll',
13:    EntryPoint = 'Some_Func',
14:    CharSet = CharSet.Auto,
15:    CallingConvention = CallingConvention.StdCall)]
16:  function SomeFunc(InputValue: Integer): Integer; external;
17:
18:  end.
```

DllImportAttribute supports a variety of fields to tailor its operation of which a few are specified by the compiler and shown in Listing 16.11. The EntryPoint field (line 13) specifies the true exported name of the routine in the DLL and is the same as the name modifier on an external clause; it is only required if the Delphi identifier for the routine differs from the real routine's exported name. The CallingConvention field (line 15) identifies the calling convention the DLL routine was compiled with; the primary values that work are CallingConvention.Cdecl and CallingConvention.StdCall. The value CallingConvention.FastCall might seem applicable to the Delphi for Win32 default register calling convention, but for two reasons. First, the internal support has not yet been implemented in the CLR. Second, the Microsoft implementation of the register calling convention is different from the Borland implementation.

The CharSet field (line 14) is irrelevant in this example as there are no textual parameters, but it nevertheless requires some coverage. The field instructs the CLR how to marshal string parameters across to the DLL, controlling whether .NET string values (which are implicitly Unicode strings) are marshaled across as ANSI or Unicode strings. It also affects the entry point name that is searched for when binding to the routine, assuming that you haven't set the DllImport field ExactSpelling to True. (It defaults to False, allowing this modified name matching to go ahead.)

The name matching behavior is more targeted at Win32 API routines that are routinely implemented twice when they take textual parameters. For example, the CreateProcess() API that is used to launch applications is implemented once as CreateProcessA() and once as CreateProcessW(). The version with the A suffix expects ANSI character strings (so uses PChar or PAnsiChar unmanaged types); the one with the W suffix expects Unicode characters (and takes PWideChar types). Normally, we would make a call to CreateProcess(), and this Delphi identifier is mapped through to CreateProcessA(). Since the Unicode implementations are typically stubbed out on Windows 95/98/Me there is a compelling reason to call the ANSI version by default. Table 16.1 describes the possible CharSet enumeration values.

TABLE 16.1   The CharSet Enumeration Values

CharSet enumeration value	Description
Ansi	This ensures that .NET String parameter values are marshaled across as ANSI strings. With regard to name matching, the CLR searches for the entry point you specify—for example, CreateProcess()—and if CLR cannot find it, it searches for CreateProcessA(). This is the default value if the CharSet field is not specified.
None	This is described as obsolete, even in .NET 1.0, and maps onto CharSet.Ansi.
Unicode	CharSet.Unicode marshals string values across as Unicode and searches first for CreateProcessW(), and then CreateProcess() if CreateProcessW() is not found.
Auto	This value is implicitly specified when you use traditional Delphi import syntax. It works like CharSet.Ansi on Windows 98 and Windows Me, but like CharSet.Unicode on Windows NT, Windows 2000, Windows XP, and Windows Server 2003.

> **CAUTION**
>
> The CharSet.Auto value should be used with care because the string marshaling works differently on the two main types of Windows platforms. This is often fine for Win32 APIs that have both an ANSI and a Unicode implementation, but typically custom DLL routines don't have this double implementation. Remember that the traditional Delphi import declaration syntax specifies this value, so routines that take string type parameters should generally not be declared using this syntax unless extra steps are taken. These extra steps would be applying MarshalAsAttribute to all textual parameters to specify the correct marshaling requirements.

You can browse through the implementation section of the Borland.Vcl.Windows unit to find plenty of examples of P/Invoke declarations that specify character sets. DllImport also supports other fields—some of which you will also see in that unit and some of which we will encounter as we explore P/Invoke further.

Parameter Types and Marshaling

The key ingredient for success in using P/Invoke is getting the marshaling of the parameters correct. Because you will generally be moving code that uses the DLL routines from

Win32 to .NET, you can often use the Win32 import declarations supplied with Delphi 7 for Win32 and Delphi for .NET as a guide to help you get the hang of translating the parameter lists across from Win32 to .NET.

So let's say that you have a routine in a C DLL that takes a certain type of parameter, a char * input parameter, that you declared as a PChar parameter in Delphi 7. You could look for a Win32 API that similarly takes an input char * parameter, such as SetWindowText(). In Delphi 7, the declaration of this import in the interface and implementation sections of the Windows.pas unit looks like this, where user32 is a constant defined to be 'user32.dll':

```
function SetWindowText(hWnd: HWND; lpString: PChar): BOOL; stdcall;
...
function SetWindowText; external user32 name 'SetWindowTextA';
```

The corresponding Delphi for .NET declarations look like this:

```
function SetWindowText(hWnd: HWND; lpString: string): BOOL;
...
[DllImport(user32, CharSet = CharSet.Auto, SetLastError = True,
  EntryPoint = 'SetWindowText')]
function SetWindowText; external;
```

As you can see, the PChar parameter is represented as a String in .NET. As a side note, you can see that the CharSet DllImport field has been set to CharSet.Auto, which will result in it being bound to SetWindowTextA() on Windows 98/Me and SetWindowTextW() on NT-based Windows platforms. Ignore the SetLastError field for now; we will come back to it later.

Now let's try a char * output parameter where the program sets up a character buffer of a certain length and passes it to the DLL routine to be filled in. The GetUserName() Win32 API uses this type of parameter. Again, here is the Delphi 7 declarations, where advapi32 is a constant defined as 'advapi32.dll':

```
function GetUserName(lpBuffer: PChar; var nSize: DWORD): BOOL; stdcall;
...
function GetUserName; external advapi32 name 'GetUserNameA';
```

And here are the Delphi for .NET equivalents:

```
function GetUserName(lpBuffer: StringBuilder; var nSize: DWORD): BOOL;
...
[DllImport(advapi32, CharSet = CharSet.Auto, SetLastError = True,
  EntryPoint = 'GetUserName')]
function GetUserName; external;
```

Because the .NET String type is immutable, you use a StringBuilder object for an output textual parameter; it has to be set up to have the appropriate capacity as specified by the nSize parameter.

The provided P/Invoke import declarations can help you get familiar with the parameter equivalents. You can also see how to set up record parameters to be marshaled correctly by examining the definitions of some API parameter types. Going back to CreateProcess(), this API takes a number of different record types. You need to take care with records because .NET is generally at liberty to lay out the fields in whichever order it chooses. Clearly, we weren't used to this in unmanaged code, and we need to specify that records being marshaled across as P/Invoke routine parameters maintain their sequential layout. Borland supplies declarations such as this for CreateProcess():

```
function CreateProcess(lpApplicationName: string; lpCommandLine: StringBuilder;
  const lpProcessAttributes: TSecurityAttributes; lpThreadAttributes: IntPtr;
  bInheritHandles: BOOL; dwCreationFlags: DWORD; lpEnvironment: string;
  lpCurrentDirectory: string; const lpStartupInfo: TStartupInfo;
  out lpProcessInformation: TProcessInformation): BOOL; overload;
...
[DllImport(kernel32, CharSet = CharSet.Auto, SetLastError = True,
  EntryPoint = 'CreateProcess')]
function CreateProcess(lpApplicationName: string; lpCommandLine: StringBuilder;
  const lpProcessAttributes: TSecurityAttributes; lpThreadAttributes: IntPtr;
  bInheritHandles: BOOL; dwCreationFlags: DWORD; lpEnvironment: string;
  lpCurrentDirectory: string; const lpStartupInfo: TStartupInfo;
  out lpProcessInformation: TProcessInformation): BOOL; external;
```

Various record types are used in the parameter list: TSecurityAttributes (defined to be the same as _SECURITY_ATTRIBUTES), TStartupInfo (or _STARTUPINFO), and TProcessInformation (or _PROCESS_INFORMATION). Looking at any of these shows the use of another attribute, StructLayoutAttribute, for example:

```
[StructLayout(LayoutKind.Sequential)]
_SECURITY_ATTRIBUTES = record
  nLength: DWORD;
  lpSecurityDescriptor: IntPtr; { PSecurityDescriptor }
  bInheritHandle: BOOL;
end;
```

If the record type comes from a custom DLL, some specific field alignment might need to be matched by the marshaler. You can use StructLayoutAttribute with a parameter of Explicit to accommodate this. Each field has its byte offset specified with a second custom attribute: FieldOffsetAttribute. And, of course, if the record fields need to be marshaled across as specific data types, you can continue to use MarshalAsAttribute on those individual fields.

As mentioned in the discussion of COM Interop, the interop marshaler has some default rules for marshaling, but some of these rules change between P/Invoke and COM Interop. For example, with P/Invoke a String will be marshaled by default to an unmanaged PChar (PAnsiChar), whereas with COM Interop it will be marshaled to a WideString. A managed array will be marshaled to a C-style array with P/Invoke, whereas with COM Interop it is marshaled as a safe array. You should become familiar with the interop marshaler's defaults; otherwise, you can end up littering your code with unrequired marshaling attributes, needlessly decreasing the readability of your code.

Sometimes a DLL routine takes a parameter that is a pointer type, or perhaps is a record that takes a pointer type. In cases in which it is tricky to represent the data type with something suitable on the managed side, you can specify it as an IntPtr type. IntPtr is designed to represent a native integer sized pointer and is CLS compliant. The System.Runtime.InteropServices.Marshal class can be used in .NET code to copy data in or out of the unmanaged buffer represented by the IntPtr parameter, as well as to allocate unmanaged memory.

You can also use IntPtr to represent a parameter of which you will control the memory management, in order to avoid problems with the default behavior. A prime example of this is with the GetCommandLine() API. This routine returns a pointer to the command line used to start the process and, like many other APIs, is unlikely to be called in practice as the .NET Environment.CommandLine static property does it for you. However, it allows us to look at a particular problem that might crop up with custom DLL routines in that it returns a pointer to some memory in the Windows kernel that must not be freed. If you declare the routine in the most obvious way, it would look like this:

```
function GetCommandLine: String;
...
[DllImport(kernel32, CharSet = CharSet.Auto]
function GetCommandLine; external;
```

However, with this declaration, the marshaler would step in and try to free the unmanaged memory represented by the String object, and that would not be right. Instead, we can avoid the problem by declaring the return type as an IntPtr:

```
function GetCommandLine: IntPtr;
...
[DllImport(kernel32, CharSet = CharSet.Auto]
function GetCommandLine; external;
```

To use the routine, you assign the return value to an IntPtr variable and then use an appropriate member of the Marshal class to obtain the information behind it:

```
var
  CmdLinePtr: IntPtr;
  CmdLineStr: String;
...
  CmdLinePtr := GetCommandLine;
  CmdLineStr := Marshal.PtrToStringAuto(CmdLinePtr);
```

Error Handling

As has been mentioned, many of the regular Win32 APIs already have P/Invoke import declarations in import units such as Borland.Vcl.Windows. These are set up appropriately for you to use, but occasionally you might require an API that is not covered by the provided import units. Clearly, you can write your own import declaration, but there are one or two issues with regard to error handling with Win32 routines that need to be addressed.

The Windows API is not consistently organized with regard to error handling. Many routines use an approach of returning either a Bool value indicating success or failure, or an Integer value that can be treated as Boolean (zero means False, nonzero means True). If your call returns False, you follow it up with a call to GetLastError() to retrieve an error code that was set by the routine with SetLastError. To translate this into a textual error message means jumping through several metaphorical hoops with the Win32 FormatMessage() API or, for Delphi programmers, a simple call to SysErrorMessage().

However, there is a family of API routines related to COM that follows a different error model. They return HResult status codes that indicate success or failure, the category (or facility) of result, and an actual code number. The P/Invoke mechanism has specific support of different kinds for each of these error handling approaches.

Win32 Error Codes

APIs that require a call to GetLastError() need special treatment to work correctly. If you call such an API through a P/Invoke declaration and then try calling the GetLastError() API through another P/Invoke declaration, you can get inconsistent results. The CLR might actually make other API calls of its own in between your first call returning and the call through to GetLastError(). As a result of this, the error code returned by GetLastError() might have actually been set by a completely different API routine, and thereby give thoroughly misleading information. Because of this, it is considered bad practice to call the GetLastError() API directly.

The DllImportAttribute field SetLastError is provided to help with this situation. It defaults to False, but if set to True, it means that the P/Invoke mechanism will call GetLastError() for you after the routine exits and will store the result value. When you need it, you can get it with a call to Marshal.GetLastWin32Error(). The Borland.Delphi.System unit that is implicitly in the uses clause of all Delphi for .NET source files has a wrapper function called GetLastError() that calls this routine. Additionally, to avoid any ambiguity in the case in which you are calling Win32 routines and have Borland.Vcl.Windows (or simply Windows) in your uses clause, that unit does not define a P/Invoke import declaration for GetLastError(). Instead, it contains a simple implementation of GetLastError() that calls the wrapper routine in Borland.Delphi.System.

> **NOTE**
>
> All the P/Invoke import declarations provided in the Borland import units for Win32 APIs that use this error code model have the SetLastError field set to True. However, if you know you do not need the error code, it is a pointless exercise having the CLR make the GetLastError() call. You can make a very minor performance improvement by redeclaring the API import and omitting the SetLastError field.

If you were accustomed to using the Win32 API helper routines supplied in the Delphi RTL, you will be relieved to know that they are still there:

- SysErrorMessage() will turn a Win32 error code into a descriptive string.

- RaiseLastWin32Error() is deprecated as in Delphi 7 and 6 in favor of RaiseLastOSError().

- RaiseLastOSError() calls GetLastError() (the Borland.Delphi.System wrapper); if it is a nonzero error code, an EOSError exception is raised with the error description (from SysErrorMessage) as its message.

- Win32Check() takes a Boolean API return value; if it is False, it calls RaiseLastOSError().

As an example to show the principle, we can call the GetUserName() API. This is not required in normal programming scenarios because the logged on user can be identified through the `System.Windows.Forms.SystemInformation.UserName` static property, but it will serve as an example. `GetUserName` is defined in the `Borland.Vcl.Windows` P/Invoke import unit like this:

```
function GetUserName(lpBuffer: StringBuilder; var nSize: DWORD): BOOL;
...
[DllImport(advapi32, CharSet = CharSet.Auto, SetLastError = True,
  EntryPoint = 'GetUserName')]
function GetUserName; external;
```

If the buffer passed in is too small, the function sets an error code and returns `False`. We can avoid writing code to check the return value and branch by using `Win32Check()` as in Listing 16.12.

LISTING 16.12   Using Win32Check() to Generate Exceptions

```
1:   uses
2:     Windows, SysUtils, System.Text;
3:
4:   procedure frmWin32Example.frmWin32Example_Load(sender: System.Object;
5:     e: System.EventArgs);
6:   var
7:     UserName: StringBuilder;
8:     UserNameLen: DWord;
9:   begin
10:    UserName := StringBuilder.Create;
11:    //Make room for 5 characters, not including a null terminator
12:    UserName.Capacity := 5;
13:    //Pass in the buffer size including the null terminator
14:    UserNameLen := Succ(UserName.Capacity);
15:    Win32Check(GetUserName(UserName, UserNameLen));
16:    lblUserName.Text := System.String.Format(
17:      'Logged on user is: {0}', UserName)
18:  end;
```

▶ Find the code on the CD: `\Chapter 16\Ex07`.

Lines 10 and 12 set up a `StringBuilder` object with enough room for five characters (deliberately small, so some usernames won't fit). Line 14 initializes the length variable with the buffer size; in the case of this API, the size value must include the space for the `null` terminator. Line 15 makes use of the `Win32Check()` helper routine. If all goes well (if you have a short username), it is displayed on a label on the form. If not, an exception is raised describing the problem.

HResult Error Codes

The Win32 routines that revolve around the COM subsystem report errors through `HResult` return values. For example, `CLSIDFromProgID()` is an API defined in the Delphi 7 `ActiveX` unit that takes the `ProgID` of a COM object and returns the `ClassID`.

It is declared in Delphi 7 like this, where `ole32` is a constant defined as `'ole32.dll'`:

```
function CLSIDFromProgID(pszProgID: POleStr;
  out clsid: TCLSID): HResult; stdcall;
...
function CLSIDFromProgID; external ole32 name 'CLSIDFromProgID';
```

In Delphi for .NET, it is defined thus, where TCLSID is defined to be the same as the System.Guid value type:

```
function CLSIDFromProgID(pszProgID: IntPtr; out clsid: TCLSID): HResult;
...
[DllImport(Ole32, CharSet = CharSet.Ansi, SetLastError = True,
  EntryPoint = 'CLSIDFromProgID')]
function CLSIDFromProgID; external;
```

The definition constructed by Borland has the ProgID defined as an unmanaged integer-sized pointer, but we can redefine these imports with different parameters as we see fit. There is not necessarily a *right* way to define a P/Invoke import; as long as it works, you can use whatever parameter types are most appropriate.

AVOIDING UNWANTED VCL SIDE EFFECTS

In this case, there is little real need to redefine this API as the Borland.Vcl.ComObj unit provides a wrapper routine called ClassIDToProgID() that calls the underlying API after marshaling a string into the IntPtr parameter. However, you should be aware that when building a WinForms application, any use of many of the old Delphi RTL/VCL units will have possibly undesirable side effects. First, you will pull in quite a bit of overhead—for example, you might want to use the Borland.Vcl.ComObj unit just to get access to the helpful wrapper routine, but this will pull in Borland.Vcl.SysUtils and perhaps even more. Inadvertently using these extra units will increase the size of your executable by varying amounts, and you might prefer to avoid all the heritage VCL support when building fresh WinForms applications in Delphi for .NET.

The second side effect is more important—any application that uses Borland.Vcl.SysUtils will not run from a network drive. The reason for this is that the unit initialization code causes a Win32 API routine to be called through P/Invoke. P/Invoke calls require certain privileges that are not granted for the Local Intranet zone; this causes the application to promptly terminate with a security exception. The bottom line is that VCL.NET applications will not run from network drives and neither will any WinForms application that implicitly or explicitly uses Borland.Vcl.SysUtils.

We could avoid using the wrapper routine in this instance either by copying the implementation of it to our own source files or by simply redefining the P/Invoke import declaration. For example, this declaration uses DllImportAttribute to specify that string parameters should be marshaled as Unicode strings:

```
[DllImport(ole32, CharSet = CharSet.Unicode)]
function CLSIDFromProgID(ppsz: String; out rclsid: Guid): Integer; external;
```

An alternative declaration might use traditional import syntax, but with an inline specification of the required marshaling on the first parameter with MarshalAsAttribute to override the default CharSet.Auto value that Delphi will set up for the implied DllImportAttribute field CharSet:

```
function CLSIDFromProgID([MarshalAs(UnmanagedType.LPWStr)] ppsz: String;
  out rclsid: Guid): Integer; stdcall;
external ole32;]
```

It is easy enough to detect success or failure of this type of routine by passing the HResult returned into either the Succeeded or Failed helper routines in the Borland.Vcl.Windows unit, for example:

```
if Failed(CLSIDFromProgID('Word.Application', Guid)) then
  //do something about the failure
```

There is also still support for the old `OleCheck()` helper routine in the `Borland.Vcl.ComObj` unit. This takes a `HResult` code as a parameter, and if it indicates failure, it will raise an `EOleSysError` exception with the `HResult` exposed through the `ErrorCode` property. But again, this might increase the size of your executable more than you would like by pulling in various other units:

```
OleCheck(CLSIDFromProgID('Word.Applicatio', Guid));
```

When using COM objects in .NET, the default behavior of the RCW is to hide the `HResult` codes and represent failure `HResults` through exceptions. It is essentially the same as a call to `OleCheck()`, but is automatically performed without programmer intervention rather like the Win32 Delphi safecall calling convention. This same mechanism is also supported by P/Invoke, although in this case it is optional because only a subset of potential DLL routines use `HResults` to convey error information. You control it with the `PreserveSig` field of `DllImportAttribute`, which defaults to `True`. Setting it to `False` tells .NET that you will be altering the import signature to hide the `HResult` and expect .NET to fill in the gaps. So we could rewrite the P/Invoke import declaration like this:

```
[DllImport(ole32, CharSet = CharSet.Unicode, PreserveSig = False)]
procedure CLSIDFromProgID(ppsz: String; out rclsid: Guid); external;
```

It could also be written like this:

```
[DllImport(ole32, PreserveSig = False)]
procedure CLSIDFromProgID([MarshalAs(UnmanagedType.LPWStr)] ppsz: String;
  out rclsid: Guid); external;
```

Now any failures will immediately be transformed into an exception describing the error. Figure 16.10 shows the error produced when the API is passed an invalid `ProgID`. The error `HResult` is $800401F3 and the description of the problem is displayed as *Invalid class string*. This implies that an unrecognized `ProgID` was passed in.

Performance Issues

Any P/Invoke call carries with it a certain cost. Making the transition from managed to unmanaged code is clearly going to take some time. A basic P/Invoke call on an x86 processor will always incur an overhead of around 10 machine instructions, but this might increase because of other factors. The amount of time depends on how much marshaling is to be done, whether `GetLastError()` is to be called on your behalf, whether a `HResult` return value is to be examined in case an exception is to be raised, and so on. In addition to all this is the fact that on the first call of a P/Invoke routine, the implementing DLL has to be loaded into memory and the routine located within it. And of course there are also the security checks. When you make a P/Invoke call, all functions on the call stack are checked to see if they have unmanaged code permissions. Unmanaged code can do anything on a machine, so unmanaged code permission has to be granted for it to run. Code running in the Internet or intranet zone won't have this permission by default.

There will be cases in which it is important to optimize the time taken by P/Invoke calls—for example, if you call one or more of them in a tight loop. Or if you are trying to accurately time some operations by using the Win32 high performance timing APIs (these have not yet been surfaced in the .NET Framework), clearly you will require as little overhead as possible involved in calling the timing routines themselves.

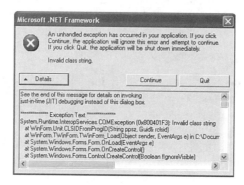

FIGURE 16.10 Exception from an HResult.

Things to take into consideration for optimizing a P/Invoke call include the following:

- Put some work into making the marshaling as efficient or as limited as possible. In particular, try to avoid marshaling .NET Unicode strings to or from unmanaged ANSI strings as this is costly.

- Selectively use InAttribute and OutAttribute (from System.Runtime.InteropServices) where possible to help the marshaler know when it does not need to copy data in a given direction.

- Avoid setting the SetLastError field to True unless you really need to get at the Win32 error code. Remember that all the Borland P/Invoke imports do set this to True, so you might need to copy the declaration and modify it.

- If the resources accessed by the API cannot be used maliciously, or the API is defined internally in your assembly in a way that is not callable from external code (in the implementation section of a unit), you can consider turning off the usual runtime Code Access Security checks. This should only be done after careful consideration of the possible impact, but if you are sure, you can use SuppressUnmanagedCodeSecurityAttribute (from System.Security) to disable the checks when the P/Invoke routine is called.

- To avoid the delay of loading the DLL the first time you call a P/Invoke routine, you can instruct the CLR to do the runtime linking in advance with a call to Marshal.Prelink(). You can also tell it to pre-link all the P/Invoke routines in a given unit with Marshal.PrelinkAll(). However, in the case of Win32 APIs, this won't necessarily do much as the core Win32 DLLs will already be loaded into your process address space. After all, much of the current implementation of the .NET Framework involves using the existing Win32 API to do its job through its own P/Invoke calls.

Let's look at some of these in the context of a couple of examples. The first one would be the GetUserName() API from earlier. Again, this is an unrealistic example as .NET does offer a way of finding the logged on user's name, but it suffices to demonstrate the principles. As it stands, the Delphi for .NET Windows P/Invoke import unit offers these declarations:

```
function GetUserName(lpBuffer: StringBuilder; var nSize: DWORD): BOOL;
...
[DllImport(advapi32, CharSet = CharSet.Auto, SetLastError = True,
  EntryPoint = 'GetUserName')]
function GetUserName; external;
```

From a performance standpoint, there are a couple of things we can do to improve this. First, we can remove the SetLastError field; there is no need to get the error code if the API returns False because we know it almost certainly means the buffer was too small.

The CharSet field can stay as it is so that on NT platforms the Unicode version for the API will be found and used. On Windows 98 type platforms, there is no Unicode implementation, so we rely on the unmanaged ANSI string to .NET Unicode String marshaling.

The second thing we can change concerns the StringBuilder object. It is only used to pass information from the API back to the calling code; there is no information being passed in. To that end, we can use OutAttribute to instruct the marshaler that there is no need to copy the StringBuilder contents across when calling the routine. Note that changing the parameter definition to be an out parameter would not be appropriate because an out parameter adds an extra level of indirection, as does a var parameter. The new definitions would look like this:

```
function GetUserName([Out]lpBuffer: StringBuilder; var nSize: DWORD): BOOL;
...
[DllImport(advapi32, CharSet = CharSet.Auto, EntryPoint = 'GetUserName')]
function GetUserName; external;
```

Now let's try another example using the high performance timing routines. These are currently defined in Delphi 8 like this:

```
function QueryPerformanceCounter(out lpPerformanceCount: TLargeInteger): BOOL;
function QueryPerformanceFrequency(out lpFrequency: TLargeInteger): BOOL;
...
[DllImport(kernel32, CharSet = CharSet.Ansi, SetLastError = True,
  EntryPoint = 'QueryPerformanceCounter')]
function QueryPerformanceCounter; external;
[DllImport(kernel32, CharSet = CharSet.Ansi, SetLastError = True,
  EntryPoint = 'QueryPerformanceFrequency')]
function QueryPerformanceFrequency; external;
```

If no high performance counter hardware is present, these APIs return False; there is no need for the SetLastError field. Because there are no string parameters, there is no need for the CharSet field; this is not a performance optimization, just the removal of a redundant field. A similar thing can be said for the EntryPoint field, which is also redundant.

Because these routines simply do timing and cannot be used maliciously, it would be safe to disable the normal CAS unmanaged code permission check. Again, the same could be done for GetUserName(), but as mentioned, that is essentially an academic example. The timing APIs represent a more realistic example. Here are their modified declarations:

16

```
function QueryPerformanceCounter(out lpPerformanceCount: TLargeInteger): BOOL;
function QueryPerformanceFrequency(out lpFrequency: TLargeInteger): BOOL;
...
[DllImport(kernel32), SuppressUnmanagedCodeSecurity]
function QueryPerformanceCounter; external;
[DllImport(kernel32), SuppressUnmanagedCodeSecurity]
function QueryPerformanceFrequency; external;
```

> **NOTE**
>
> Several VCL.NET units do declare their own private imports of key Win32 API routines (such as
> `SendMessage`, `DefWindowProc`, and `CallWindowProc`) in a similar way to improve performance.
> These set `SetLastError` to `False` and also specify the `SuppressUnmanagedCodeSecurity`
> attribute. You can see examples of this in the source for `Borland.Vcl.Controls`,
> `Borland.Vcl.Forms`, and other units. These imports are in the implementation section of the
> units and thus cannot be used by external code. This makes sense as the
> `SuppressUnmanagedCodeSecurity` attribute asserts that the use of the API functions are safe, and
> Borland cannot assert that for other people's code.

The other thing we can do is to have the CLR pre-link to the P/Invoke routines before they
are called. This can be done on a routine-by-routine basis or en masse for all the routines
declared in a given Delphi unit. Listing 16.13 shows part of a simple form unit called
`PInvokeExampleU.pas` that times how long 50 million square root calculations take to
perform using `QueryPerformanceCounter` and `QueryPerformanceFrequency`. To avoid any unnecessary delay linking to the routines on their first call, the form's `Load` event requests they get
pre-linked. Lines 6 and 7 pre-link one routine, and lines 8 and 9 do the other.

LISTING 16.13   Removing the First-call Delay on P/Invoke Calls

```
1:    unit PInvokeExampleU;
2:    ...
3:    procedure frmPInvoke.frmPInvoke_Load(sender: System.Object;
4:      e: System.EventArgs);
5:    begin
6:      Marshal.Prelink(GetType.Module.GetType('PInvokeExampleU.Unit').GetMethod(
7:        'QueryPerformanceFrequency'));
8:      Marshal.Prelink(GetType.Module.GetType('PInvokeExampleU.Unit').GetMethod(
9:        'QueryPerformanceCounter'));
10:   end;
11:
12:   procedure frmPInvoke.btnDoPInvoke_Click(sender: System.Object;
13:     e: System.EventArgs);
14:   var
15:     StartTime, EndTime, TimerFrequency: Int64;
16:     TimeDiff, SqrRoot: Double;
17:     I: Integer;
18:   const
19:     NumIterations = 50000000;
20:
21:     procedure TimerError;
22:     begin
23:       raise Exception.Create('High accuracy timing not supported')
24:     end;
```

LISTING 16.13   Continued

```
25:
26:  begin
27:    if not QueryPerformanceFrequency(TimerFrequency) then
28:      TimerError;
29:    if not QueryPerformanceCounter(StartTime) then
30:      TimerError;
31:    for I := 1 to NumIterations do
32:      SqrRoot := Sqrt(2);
33:    if not QueryPerformanceCounter(EndTime) then
34:      TimerError;
35:    TimeDiff := (EndTime - StartTime) / TimerFrequency;
36:    MessageBox.Show(System.String.Format(
37:      '{0} square roots takes {1:f02} seconds', [NumIterations, TimeDiff]),
38:      'Timing Results', MessageBoxButtons.OK, MessageBoxIcon.Information)
39:  end;
40:
41:  end.
```

▶ Find the code on the CD: \Chapter 16\Ex08.

The `Prelink()` method takes a `MethodInfo` parameter to describe the P/Invoke routine to pre-link. We can get this by getting a `System.Type` object that represents the form class and using its `Module()` method to get a `Module` object describing the binary module it resides in. Then a `System.Type` object is extracted from the `Module` for a specified class in the module. Here, we take advantage of the fact that Delphi generates a class to represent the entire unit behind-the-scenes, which is used to implement what we see as global routines; they are not actually global but part of the manufactured unit class. From the unit class's `System.Type` object, we can request a `MethodInfo` object describing any of that class's methods, such as the P/Invoke routines.

In order to pre-link all global P/Invoke routines declared in the unit, you can replace lines 6–9 with this call:

```
Marshal.PrelinkAll(GetType.Module.GetType('PInvokeExampleU.Unit'));
```

Using .NET Routines in Win32 Code

The CLR offers support for the opposite of what Platform Invoke offers, which is to expose .NET static methods to the unmanaged Win32 world. These are often referred to as unmanaged exports. Unmanaged exports are implemented by the CLR using the exact inverse of its P/Invoke mechanism which is why the support is sometimes referred to as Inverse P/Invoke.

A Win32 application can import these exposed routines in the same way as with any regular DLL exported routines. The support for this CLR feature is not taken advantage of by many languages; only Managed C++ and Delphi for .NET support it directly as a language feature. In Delphi's case, it is limited to exporting global functions, which internally are implemented as static methods of a class wrapper generated by the compiler to represent the unit.

> **NOTE**
>
> This aspect of .NET interoperability, calling managed routines from unmanaged Win32 code, receives very little coverage in textbooks and on the World Wide Web presumably because neither C# nor Visual Basic .NET support the Inverse P/Invoke mechanism.

Code written in other languages can actually be exported with Inverse P/Invoke, but doing so relies on a creative round tripping, as described earlier. This involves disassembling the assembly to IL source, modifying it in several places to achieve the Inverse P/Invoke effect, and then reassembling it. As you can probably imagine, this process is rather unfriendly toward the normal goals of code maintenance.

Because C# and Visual Basic .NET do not readily support this feature, you can use Delphi for .NET to effectively enhance these languages. If you have codevelopers using these or other languages that do not support unmanaged exports and who have assemblies with code that needs to be accessed from Win32 applications, you can write a simple assembly in Delphi for .NET that acts as a wrapper around the target assembly. You add in some global routines that call into the target assembly static methods, and these global routines can then be exported from the Delphi assembly. This provides a simple way of overcoming the shortcomings of other .NET languages in this area.

Traditional Delphi Syntax

Unmanaged exports are supported in Delphi for .NET as a simple part of the language via the exports clause we used when writing Win32 DLLs. As a result of this, there are only a few things to say about them. You can add exports clauses in the project source file or in the interface or implementation sections of your units.

You can see the principles demonstrated by the trivial example assembly in Listing 16.14 that exports two procedures called DoSomething() and DoSomethingElse(). The global routines you export will be available to unmanaged code as routines using the stdcall calling convention.

LISTING 16.14   Simple .NET Routines Exported to Win32

```
1:    library dotNetAssembly;
2:
3:    {$UNSAFECODE ON}
4:
5:    uses
6:      System.Windows.Forms;
7:
8:    procedure DoSomething(I: Integer);
9:    begin
10:     MessageBox.Show(Convert.ToString(I))
11:   end;
12:
13:   procedure DoSomethingElse(const Msg: String);
14:   begin
15:     MessageBox.Show(Msg)
16:   end;
17:
18:   exports
19:     DoSomething,
```

LISTING 16.14   Continued

```
20:    DoSomethingElse;
21:
22:  begin
23:  end.
```

▶ Find the code on the CD: \Chapter 16\Ex09\.

An important aspect of producing unmanaged exports is that it generates unsafe code—PEVerify.exe will complain about the resultant assembly having an unverifiable PE Header/native stub. Because of this, you must enable unsafe code compilation by inserting the {$UNSAFECODE ON} compiler directive in the source file containing the exports clause as done in line 3. Alternatively, if you are compiling with the command-line compiler, you can use the --unsafe+ compiler switch.

Parameter Types and Marshaling

Parameter marshaling will work the same as with P/Invoke. So for example, the .NET String data type will default to being marshaled as an ANSI string. This means that these two routines could be accessed from Delphi Win32 code using the import declarations displayed in the import unit in Listing 16.15.

LISTING 16.15   Delphi 7 Import Declarations for Unmanaged Exports in Listing 16.14

```
1:    unit dotNetAssemblyImport;
2:
3:    interface
4:
5:    procedure DoSomething(I: Integer); stdcall;
6:    procedure DoSomethingElse(Msg: PChar); stdcall;
7:
8:    implementation
9:
10:   const
11:     dotNETAssembly = 'dotNETAssembly.dll';
12:
13:   procedure DoSomething(I: Integer); stdcall; external dotNETAssembly;
14:   procedure DoSomethingElse(Msg: PChar); stdcall; external dotNETAssembly;
15:
16:   end.
```

▶ Find the code on the CD: \Chapter 16\Ex09\.

That example is quite straightforward, so let's look at one that's a little more interesting. Let's use an assembly that offers a function to Win32 code that supplies some textual information. The normal practice, as we have seen earlier, is for Win32 code to allocate a character buffer and pass it into a routine along with its size. The called routine then populates the buffer (in this example, with a string describing the .NET version) and returns. That way, the caller is responsible for allocating and freeing the buffer. Often, such routines will return the number of characters required for the string. This enables the calling code to identify if it passed a buffer that was too small and perhaps make a bigger one and try again. We'll follow this common Win32 API model in our sample routine; however, in this case, it will be a Unicode character buffer.

The assembly will also export another routine that displays a message box, and for consistency with the first routine, it will be exported to take a Unicode string. This requirement forces us to do some custom marshaling (.NET Strings to ANSI strings) as the default P/Invoke marshaling—that is, PChar or PAnsiChar in Delphi for Win32.

The result can be found in the assembly project shown in Listing 16.16. Because the assembly has to be marked unsafe anyway, we can readily use an unsafe pointer type in the parameter list of the first routine, GetDotNETVersion(). Line 13 defines a PWideChar parameter, which could equally have been defined a PChar parameter given the platform we are compiling to. The use of an appropriate character pointer type saves us from having to worry about marshaling issues.

> **CAUTION**
>
> Borland has told developers for many years not to rely on Char being the same as AnsiChar forever. In Delphi for .NET, this warning comes to fruition as all text information is dealt with as Unicode text. So Char is now synonymous with WideChar, String is the same as WideString, and PChar is the same as a PWideChar.
>
> Of course, we generally work on the understanding that pointers and .NET do not mix very well, but in unsafe code, you can use pointer types such as PWideChar. Just be careful what you do with them if you do!

LISTING 16.16   More Interesting Unmanaged Exports

```
1:    library dotNetAssembly;
2:
3:    {$UNSAFECODE ON}
4:
5:    uses
6:      System.Text,
7:      System.Runtime.InteropServices,
8:      System.Windows.Forms;
9:
10:   //BufferLen is the length of the unmanaged buffer,
11:   //not counting the null terminator, i.e. the number of characters
12:   function GetDotNETVersion(
13:     Buffer: PWideChar; BufferLen: Integer): Integer; unsafe;
14:   var
15:     I: Integer;
16:     VersionStr: String;
17:     MinLen: Integer;
18:   begin
19:     VersionStr := System.String.Format(
20:       '.NET version {0}', Environment.Version.ToString);
21:     MinLen := Math.Min(VersionStr.Length, BufferLen);
22:     for I := 0 to MinLen-1 do
23:       Buffer[I] := VersionStr.Chars[I];
24:     Buffer[MinLen] := #0;
25:     Result := VersionStr.Length
26:   end;
```

LISTING 16.16   Continued

```
27:
28:  //With P/Invoke, String defaults to marshalling as UnmanagedType.LPStr
29:  //So In D7 we would need to use a PChar. However, for consistency with the
30:  //other routine exported from here we'll make it go out as PWideChar
31:  procedure ShowAMessage([MarshalAs(UnmanagedType.LPWStr)]Msg: String);
32:  begin
33:    MessageBox.Show(Msg)
34:  end;
35:
36:  exports
37:    GetDotNETVersion,
38:    ShowAMessage;
39:
40:  begin
41:  end.
```

▶ Find the code on the CD: Ch16\Ex10\.

> **CAUTION**
>
> Notice that the StringBuilder class was not used in this example. This is because of a limitation of .NET 1.x, where only the first 32 bytes of string data from an unmanaged buffer will be marshaled into the StringBuilder, giving it a capacity of just 16 Unicode characters no matter how large the unmanaged buffer was. This represents an unfortunate problem that needs to be understood and avoided.

After lines 19 and 20 build up the string to return, the code in lines 22 and 23 loops through its characters copying them into the buffer. Care is taken to ensure that we don't go past the end of the buffer by taking note of the buffer length passed in. Once the characters have all been copied, the all important null terminator is added at the end of the string in the buffer and the return value is set up to be the length of the string.

> **CAUTION**
>
> You should take care when extracting characters from strings. Line 23 in Listing 16.16 explicitly uses the Chars array property available from the System.String type, which operates on the basis that the first character is at position 0. Historically though, Delphi strings have operated on the basis that the first character is at offset 1. If you want to avoid the Chars array property you can rewrite the line like this
>
>   Buffer[I] := VersionStr[I+1];
>
> You can consider the Chars array property to have a similar effect on Delphi for .NET String character indexing as you get in Delphi 7 when typecasting a String to a PChar.

Line 31 of Listing 16.16 contains the marshaling attribute that ensures the default ANSI character marshaling is replaced by Unicode character marshaling. Listing 16.17 shows the corresponding Win32 import declarations in Delphi syntax; you can see the use of the PWideChar type as both unmanaged exports deal in Unicode strings. Finally, Listing 16.18 shows some Delphi 7 code using both the unmanaged exports to display the .NET platform version in a .NET message box. The managed message box is pictured being displayed from a Win32 application in Figure 16.11.

16

LISTING 16.17   Import Declarations for Unmanaged Exports in Listing 16.16

```
 1:  unit DotNetAssemblyImports;
 2:
 3:  interface
 4:
 5:  procedure ShowAMessage(Msg: PWideChar); stdcall;
 6:  function GetDotNETVersion(
 7:    Buffer: PWideChar; BufferLen: Integer): Integer; stdcall;
 8:
 9:  implementation
10:
11:  procedure ShowAMessage(Msg: PWideChar); stdcall;
12:  external 'dotNetAssembly.dll';
13:
14:  function GetDotNETVersion(
15:    Buffer: PWideChar; BufferLen: Integer): Integer; stdcall;
16:  external 'dotNetAssembly.dll';
17:
18:  end.
```

▶ Find the code on the CD: \Chapter 16\Ex10\.

LISTING 16.18   Delphi 7 Code Using Delphi 8 for .NET Unmanaged Exports

```
 1:  procedure TfrmUseUnmanagedExports.btnCallUnmanagedExportsClick(
 2:    Sender: TObject);
 3:  const
 4:    NumChars = 32;
 5:  var
 6:    Buf: array[0..NumChars] of WideChar;
 7:    CharsRequired: Integer;
 8:  begin
 9:    CharsRequired := GetDotNETVersion(Buf, NumChars);
10:    if CharsRequired <= NumChars then
11:      ShowAMessage(Buf)
12:    else
13:      raise Exception.CreateFmt(
14:        'Buffer too small. Should be %d characters', [CharsRequired])
15:  end;
```

▶ Find the code on the CD: \Chapter 16\Ex10\.

FIGURE 16.11   A .NET message box from a Win32 application.

Overview of ADO.NET

**PART IV:
DATABASE
DEVELOPMENT WITH
ADO.NET**

CHAPTER 17   Overview of
ADO.NET

CHAPTER 18   Using the
Connection
Object

CHAPTER 19   Using Command
and DataReader
Objects

CHAPTER 20   DataAdapters and
DataSets

CHAPTER 21   Working with
WinForms:
DataViews and
Data Binding

CHAPTER 22   Saving Data to
the Data Source

CHAPTER 23   Working with
Transactions and
Strongly Typed
Datasets

CHAPTER 24   The Borland Data
Provider

ADO.NET is the .NET technology that allows developers to create applications against a variety of data sources using a modern approach to distributed development. While similar to its predecessor ADO, the differences are significant. ADO.NET was designed around different goals—many of which were prompted by the limitations of prior technologies.

Design Principles

According to Microsoft, the design goals of ADO.NET are

- Disconnected data architecture that supports n-tier programming

- Tight integration with XML

- Common data representation

- Built upon the .NET Framework

- Leverage past technologies

These goals are a result of both the need to address the current trend in distributed development and the limitations of the existing technologies.

Disconnected Data Architecture

Modern distributed system architectures have evolved to being based on decoupled or disconnected components. This approach has been triggered by the increased demand for Web applications. Systems built on this architecture often use XML as the data transport between components and rely on protocols such as HTTP, requiring stateless management between requests. Prior technologies such as ADO, ODBC, DAO, and RDO fall short or simply cannot meet the needs of developers to create such systems. For instance, while the original Recordsets in ADO 2.x were disconnected, they relied on COM. This requirement existed on both sides of the connection. Therefore, a server could not be written using recordsets that fed a non-Windows client.

IN THIS CHAPTER

- Design Principles
- ADO.NET Objects
- .NET Data Providers

Integration with XML

XML has become exceedingly popular not only for transporting data between distributed systems, but also as a common format for data manipulation. Microsoft's past attempts to incorporate XML into its data management technologies has been useful; however, they do not provide the capabilities that developers require today. For instance, ADO was capable of streaming XML representations of data to a file. This capability fell short in giving the developer control over the format of such files.

ADO.NET not only embraces XML, but also XML is the base format on which data is manipulated. For instance, you can retrieve data from SQL Server in XML. Streaming data in XML to disk or to remote services is also made easy. Developers also have complete control over the XSD schema. ADO.NET is fully XML capable.

Common Data Representation

An ongoing problem with database applications is that different data stores or formats required different mechanisms to manipulate their data. The ADO.NET classes abstract the data format to a level that allows developers to work with data in a uniform manner, regardless of the originating format.

Built on .NET Framework

In order to achieve uniformity in data, it made sense to build ADO.NET on the .NET Framework. This enabled Microsoft to take advantage of a common type system and the rich object-oriented model in .NET. This enables developers to leverage both previous ADO and .NET knowledge to easily and quickly build robust distributed systems. For example, the combination of ADO.NET and ASP.NET is a powerful duo for developing full-fledged business Web Services.

Leverage Existing Technologies

I already stated how developers will be able to capitalize on their existing ADO knowledge. Most developers who have done any ADO development will feel comfortable working with ADO.NET. Although there are differences, many concepts have transferred into ADO.NET.

ADO.NET Objects

ADO.NET supports two types of development environments: connected and disconnected (see Figure 17.1). Each environment includes its own set of classes to support the intended functionality.

The connected environment classes provide read-only data retrieval from data sources. It also enables developers to execute commands against the data source to make changes to it—provided that such functionality is supported by the data source. The connected environment basically works with a physical data store to which a connection is maintained.

The disconnected environment classes enable developers to fully manipulate an abstract or generic data source. You can think of this data source as an in-memory cache.

These two environments work together using a bridging class named the `DataAdaptor`. For instance, you can retrieve data from a specific data source such as SQL Server or Oracle using the connected classes. Using `DataAdaptor`, you can transfer that data to the disconnected class objects where you can manipulate the data. While working within the disconnected environment, you need not maintain any connection to the data store. Finally, you can reconcile your changes back to the data store through `DataAdaptor`.

Figure 17.1 depicts these classes in their respective environments. This chapter provides a brief overview of each object. The remaining chapters on ADO.NET cover each in greater detail.

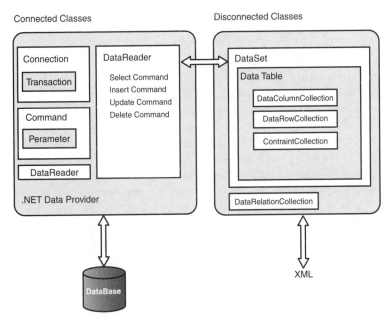

FIGURE 17.1   Connected and disconnected classes in ADO.NET.

DISCONNECTED DATA—A FAMILIAR FACE

The idea of disconnected and connected data is old news for Delphi developers. Years ago, Delphi's MIDAS technology (now called DataSnap) introduced the concept to Delphi in Delphi 3. Later in Delphi 6, it was renamed DataSnap. `TClientDataSet` is the Delphi Win32 component for manipulating disconnected datasets, and `TDataSetProvider` is the bridging component between Delphi client and server applications. Many of the ADO.NET concepts will not be a new idea if you have developed using MIDAS/Datasnap before, so you should have no problem jumping right in to ADO.NET development.

Connected Classes

Table 17.1 lists and describes the classes you would use when developing within the connected environment for ADO.NET.

TABLE 17.1   ADO.NET Connected Classes

Class	Description
Connection	The Connection class maintains information about a data source including location, name, authorization credentials, and other settings specific to the type of data store. The Connection is the channel through which other classes gain access to a data store. Connection also defines the methods for opening and closing and transaction processing.
Command	The Command class enables you to execute SQL commands against a data source. For instance, you can execute a SELECT statement or a stored procedure using Command. Command has methods that you use based on the type of command you intend to execute against the data source. In essence, Command is the class that gives you the ability to manipulate the data source in the disconnected environment.
DataReader	DataReader provides uni-directional (forward only) read-only access to data from a data source. This class is used in conjunction with a Command class. DataReader is efficient because it is limited in functionality.
DataAdapter	The DataAdapter class is a new concept to ADO developers and an old concept to Delphi MIDAS/DataSnap developers. DataAdapter serves as a communications bridge between connected classes and disconnected classes. For instance, you would use the connected objects to retrieve data. Then using DataAdapter, you move that data to disconnected objects where you manipulate that data. In fact, you can go offline completely and still maintain that data in a disconnected state. Finally, DataAdapter is used to reconcile your changes back to the data source.
Parameter	The Parameter class enables you to use parameterized queries and stored procedures in the Command class. Parameter is accessed through the ParameterCollection of the Command class.
Transaction	Transaction enables functions performed against the database to be treated as an atomic unit. This enables the capability to revert back to the original state of the database if an error were to occur or to accept all changes made to the database. In database terms, these common functions are called roll back and commit, respectively.

Disconnected Classes

Table 17.2 lists and describes the classes you would use when developing within the disconnected environment for ADO.NET.

TABLE 17.2   ADO.NET Disconnected Classes

Class	Description
DataSet	DataSet enables you to work with data independent of any data source specific format. DataSet can serialize data based on the XML format. DataSet maintains a collection of DataTables, which themselves maintain collections of other objects. DataSet basically represents an in-memory relational database that you can manipulate completely disconnected from its physical data store and from which you can reconcile your changes back to the originating source. Although the names are similar, a DataSet does not correspond directly to a Delphi Win32 TClientDataSet (see description on DataTable). A DataSet is more like a DataModule with multiple TClientDataSets, but without the underlying event-driven coding logic.

TABLE 17.2 Continued

Class	Description
DataTableCollection	DataTableCollection is the collection of DataTables maintained by a DataSet. Through this class, you obtain access to a specific DataTable.
DataTable	A DataTable, as the name implies, maintains data in a collection of columns. Using database terminology, a DataTable is synonymous with a table, and a row and column with a record and field, respectively. The DataTable most directly corresponds to a Delphi Win32 TClientDataSet.
DataRelation	DataRelation encapsulates relationships between DataTables. A DataSet contains a DataRelationCollection that contains a collection of DataRelations.
DataColumn	DataColumn stores information about the structure of a DataTable's column. Such information includes type, accessibility, and calculation expressions, just to name a few. DataColumn is maintained by the DataColumnCollection collection.
DataRow	DataRow exposes the properties and methods that enable editing of data in the DataTable. DataRow is maintained by the DataRowCollection collection.
Constraint	Constraint enables you to place constraints such as foreign keys on the disconnected data. Constraint is maintained by the ConstraintCollection collection.
DataView	DataView enables you to view data stored in a DataSet in various ways by sorting, filtering, and so on.

.NET Data Providers

.NET data providers provide access to specific types of data stores. These providers are also called managed providers. Data providers can be developed to provide access to any type of data source. Four data providers ship with the .NET Framework version 1.1. Several third parties have also developed and are developing providers for additional data sources.

The .NET Framework version 1.1 ships with the four .NET data providers listed in Table 17.3.

TABLE 17.3 ADO.NET Data Providers

.NET Data Provider	Description
SQL Server	Support for Microsoft SQL Server, version 7.0 or later. SQL Server classes exist in the System.Data.SqlClient namespace.
OLE DB	Support for data sources that are exposed via the OLE DB provider. OLE DB data provider classes exist in the System.Data.OleDb namespace.
ODBC	Support for data sources exposed via ODBC. Note: This provider does not ship with the .NET Framework 1.0, but is available as an add-in. These provider classes exist in the Microsoft.Data.Odbc namespace.
Oracle	Support for Oracle using the Oracle Call Interface (OCI). This provider supports Oracle 8i release 3, version 8.1.7. These provider classes exist in the Microsoft.Data.OracleClient namespace.

17

IN THIS CHAPTER

- Connection Functionality
- Setting up the ConnectionString Property
- Opening and Closing Connections
- Connection Events
- Connection Pooling

CHAPTER **18**

Using the Connection Object

Connections are the classes that deal with the actual communication of your .NET application with the data store. The connection classes are part of the Data Provider layer and therefore, a separate connection class is provided for each type of Data Provider.

Connection Functionality

Connections handle low-level tasks such as user authentication, networking, database identification, connection pooling, and transaction processing. Each connection object implements the IDbConnection interface defined in the System.Data namespace.

Tables 18.1 and 18.2 list the various properties and methods of the IDbConnection interface, respectively.

TABLE 18.1   IDbConnection Properties

Property	Description
ConnectionString	Contains connection settings in the name-value pair format. This information might include user authentication information, database identification and data provider specific settings.
ConnectionTimeout	The amount of time that must elapse when connecting before raising a data provider specific exception.
Database	Contains the current database or name that will be used when the database is opened.
State	Contains the current state of the connection. Currently, valid states are Open and Closed.

Table 18.2 lists the IDbConnection methods.

TABLE 18.2   IDbConnection Methods

Method	Description
BeginTransaction()	Initiates a database transaction and returns an IDbTransaction instance.
ChangeDatabase()	Changes the current data store name.
Close()	Closes the connection to the data store.
CreateCommand()	Create a command object (an object that implements the IDbCommand interface) associated with this connection.
Open()	Opens the connection to the data store.

Note that Data Provider specific connections might contain additional methods or properties not listed in these tables.

Setting Up the ConnectionString Property

When setting up a connection, you must specify certain information about the connection in the ConnectionString property. Typically, this would be user authentication information, the database name, and its location. The ConnectionString for the OLE DB provider also requires a provider parameter. Likewise, if you are using an ODBC connection, you must specify an ODBC driver name. Other settings are specific to the Data Provider being used.

Specifying a SqlConnection.ConnectionString

Table 18.3 lists the various parameters for the connection string. These parameters, although specific to SQL Server, are similar to the parameters for other data providers. The table shows the parameter name and alternates names. Consult the documentation for specific parameters settings for the data provider you would be using.

TABLE 18.3   SqlConnection.ConnectionString Parameters

Parameter	Description
AttachDBFilename, Initial File Name	Full path and filename of an attachable database file.
Connect Timeout, Connection Timeout	Number of seconds to elapse before aborting a connection attempt and raising an error.
Data Source, Server, Address, Addr, Network Address	The name of the server that hosts the SQL Server on the network.
Database, Initial Catalog	The name of the database within the SQL Server specified by Data Source.
Integrated Security, Trusted Connection	When True, uses Windows Authentication. Otherwise, uses SQL Server authentication.
User ID	The database user ID.
Packet Size	The size of packet that communicates with SQL Server across the network. This defaults to 8192.
Password, Pwd	The password of the user.

When configuring a connection to SQL Server using the SqlConnection class, you must specify at least the Data Source, the Initial Catalog, and authentication information. An example of assigning a connection string is shown here:

```
sqlcn := SqlConnection.Create('Data Source=XWING;Initial
➥Catalog=ugly_bug;Trusted_Connection=Yes');
```

Note the use of the `Trusted Connection` setting tells SQL Server to use the Windows security settings for user authentication.

Specifying an OleDbConnection.ConnectionString

The `ConnectionString` for an `OleDbConnection` targeting a SQL Server 7 (or higher) database looks like

```
oledbcn := OleDbConnection.Create('Data Source=XWING;
➥Database=ugly_bug;User id=sa;Password=mypw;Provider=SQLOLEDB');
```

In this setting, notice that you must provide the specific OLE DB provider needed, which will vary depending on the OLE DB provider. The following example illustrates what this connection string might look like when connecting to a Microsoft Access database:

```
oledbcn := OleDbConnection.Create('Data Source=XWING;
➥Database=c:\data\UglyBug.mdb;Provider=Microsoft.Jet.OLEDB.4.0');
```

Similarly to the previous example, you must provide the OLE DB provider specific to the Microsoft Jet engine.

Specifying an OdbcConnection.ConnectionString

The ODBC connection is similar to the previously mentioned connections; however, the required parameters will depend on the specific ODBC driver being used. For example, the following setting illustrates a connection provided by a MySQL ODBC driver:

```
odbccn := OdbcConnection.Create('Driver={MySQL ODBC 3.51
➥Driver};Database=ACMEDB;UID=user1;PWD=MyPwd;Options=3');
```

Note the differences in the specific parameter name/value pairs used and the format of the driver parameter when specifying the driver string. This will differ even more between ODBC drivers. It is necessary to consult the specific driver information for connection strings settings.

Specifying an OracleConnection.ConnectionString

Oracle connection settings are similar to the previously discussed setting with a small subset of parameters. A typical `ConnectionString` is illustrated here:

```
oraclecn := OracleConnection.Create('Data Source=Oracle8i;
➥Integrated Security=true');
```

Opening and Closing Connections

To open a connection to the data store, you simply invoke the `SqlConnection.Open()` method. Likewise, to close the connection, invoke the `SqlConnection.Close()` method.

> **NOTE**
>
> If connection pooling is supported, opening a connection will try to use a connection from the pool; otherwise, a new connection is established to the data store. Also, closing a pooled connection adds the connection to the pool instead of actually closing it. Connection pooling is discussed later in this chapter.

Listing 18.1 illustrates the opening and closing of a SQL Server connection.

LISTING 18.1   Opening and Closing a Connection

```
1:   program test;
2:    {$APPTYPE CONSOLE}
3:   uses
4:      System.Data.SQLClient;
5:   const
6:      CNSTR = 'server=localhost;database=Northwind;Trusted_Connection=Yes';
7:   var
8:      sqlcn: SqlConnection;
9:   begin
10:     sqlcn := SqlConnection.Create(CNSTR);
11:     sqlcn.Open();
12:     try
13:       Console.WriteLine(System.String.Format('Connected to: {0}',
14:         sqlcn.ConnectionString));
15:     finally
16:       sqlcn.Close();
17:     end;
18:   end.
```

▶ Find the code on the CD: \Code\Chapter 18\Ex01\.

Note the use of the `try..finally` construct. The `finally` block will execute whether an error occurs between lines 12 and 15, which will ensure that the `Connection` is closed and database resources are freed.

Connection Events

This section illustrates how you can use the events that belong to the `SqlConnection` class. There are two events that `SqlConnection` exposes. These are shown in Table 18.4.

TABLE 18.4   Connection Object Events

Connection Event	Description
InfoMessage	Fires when a warning or informational message is sent by the database server.
StateChange	Fires whenever the state changes from open to closed or visa versa.

Listing 18.2 illustrates how to process the information contained in the `SQLConnection` class events.

LISTING 18.2   Events in the SQLConnection Object

```
1:   program events;
2:
3:    {$APPTYPE CONSOLE}
4:
5:    {%DotNetAssemblyCompiler 'c:\windows\microsoft.net\framework\v1.1.4322\
➥System.Data.dll'}
6:   uses
7:      SysUtils,
```

LISTING 18.2   Continued

```
8:     System.Data,
9:     System.Data.SQLClient,
10:    System.Collections,
11:    System.Reflection;
12:
13:  procedure OnStateChangeEvent(sender: System.Object;
14:    args: StateChangeEventArgs);
15:  begin
16:    Console.WriteLine(System.String.Format(
17:      'State changed from {0} to {1}.', args.CurrentState,
18:      args.OriginalState));
19:  end;
20:
21:  procedure OnInfoMessageEvent(sender: System.Object;
22:    args: SqlInfoMessageEventArgs);
23:  var
24:    se: System.Data.SqlClient.SqlError;
25:    erEnum: IEnumerator;
26:  begin
27:    erEnum := args.Errors.GetEnumerator;
28:    while erEnum.MoveNext do
29:    begin
30:      se := erEnum.Current as SqlError;
31:      Console.WriteLine('Server:  '+se.Server);
32:      Console.WriteLine('Source:  '+se.Source);
33:      Console.WriteLine('Class:  '+se.&Class.ToString);
34:      Console.WriteLine('State:  '+se.State.ToString);
35:      Console.WriteLine('Number:  '+se.Number.ToString);
36:      Console.WriteLine('LineNumber:  '+se.LineNumber.ToString);
37:      Console.WriteLine('Procedure:  '+se.&Procedure);
38:      Console.WriteLine('Message: '+se.Message);
39:    end;
40:  end;
41:
42:  const
43:    CNSTR = 'server=XWING;database=Northwind;Trusted_Connection=Yes';
44:  var
45:    sqlcn: SqlConnection;
46:    cmd: SqlCommand;
47:  begin
48:    sqlcn := SqlConnection.Create(CNSTR);
49:    Include(sqlcn.InfoMessage, OnInfoMessageEvent);
50:    Include(sqlcn.StateChange, OnStateChangeEvent);
51:    sqlcn.Open();
52:    try
53:      System.Console.WriteLine(System.String.Format('Connected to: {0}',
54:        sqlcn.ConnectionString));
55:      cmd := sqlcn.CreateCommand;
56:      cmd.CommandText := 'PRINT ''hello''';
57:      cmd.ExecuteNonQuery;
58:    finally
59:      sqlcn.Close;
60:    end;
```

LISTING 18.2 Continued

```
61:    Console.ReadLine;
62:  end.
```

▶ Find the code on the CD: \Code\Chapter 18\Ex02\.

The InfoMessage event is invoked when a nonerror event occurs. This event can be used to obtain and display information to the user as shown in Listing 18.2 and in Figure 18.1. This event is not used to process errors. When an error occurs, an exception is raised instead.

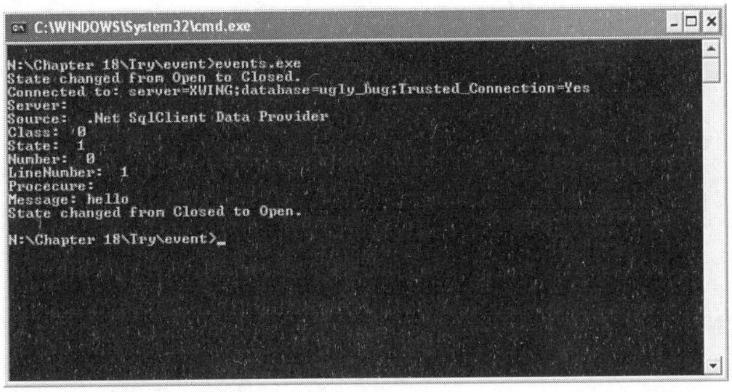

FIGURE 18.1 SqlConnection events.

The StateChange event fires whenever SqlConnection is opened. It also fires when SqlConnection is closed. Listing 18.2 and Figure 18.1 illustrate how to write information to the console when SqlConnection is opened/closed.

Connection Pooling

When building data-driven applications, particularly distributed applications, connection pooling can be valuable. Consider distributed applications based on services that host database connections which get created and destroyed frequently. Having to reestablish a connection could drastically impact the scalability and performance. Although it might be fine for a few users executing many transactions, it would not be sufficient for many users executing few transactions.

Connection pooling is not a function of the .NET Framework, but rather made available by the .NET provider.

The function of connection pooling is to recycle previously opened connections, thus saving time when a new connection is requested. The reason for this savings is that a connection request will not invoke low-level actions such as authentication of credentials.

Connection pooling is not provided natively by ADO.NET. However, both Oracle and SQL Server provide their own connection pooling mechanisms, which are enabled by default.

IN THIS CHAPTER

- Executing Commands
- Non-Query Commands
- Retrieving Single Values
- Executing Data Definition Language (DDL) Commands
- Specifying Parameters Using IDbParameter
- Executing Stored Procedures
- Deriving Parameters
- Querying for Resultsets Using DataReaders
- Querying a Resultset
- Querying Multiple Resultsets Using DataReaders
- Using DataReader to Retrieve BLOB Data
- Using DataReader to Retrieve Schema Information

CHAPTER **19**

Using Command and DataReader Objects

The previous chapter covers how to get connected to a database. This chapter discusses how to query database data in a read-only, high-performance manner. Specifically, it covers the Command and DataReader classes. This chapter uses the Microsoft SQL Provider classes SqlCommand and SqlDataReader, which implement the IDbCommand and IDataReader interfaces, respectively. Keep in mind that other providers such as the OLE DB and Borland Data Providers (BDP) will have slight differences in usage.

Executing Commands

Executing commands against a database is done using an implementation of the IDbCommand interface, such as the SqlCommand, OleDBCommand, and BdpCommand objects. Typically, this object sends SQL statements to the database to execute through the IDbCommand.CommandText property. This could be a SELECT, INSERT, UPDATE, DELETE, or other similar SQL commands. When using the IDbCommand object against a non-SQL data provider, CommandText can hold non-SQL statements, as long as the information being sent can be represented as a String.

The IDbCommand Interface

The IDbCommand interface properties and methods are discussed in Tables 19.1 and 19.2, respectively.

TABLE 19.1   IDbCommand Properties

Property	Description
CommandText	Contains the command text that will be run against the data store. For SQL data stores, this is typically SQL commands. For non-SQL data stores, this might be proprietary text formatted as a String.

TABLE 19.1   Continued

Property	Description
CommandTimeout	Specifies the wait time that must elapse prior to terminating an unexecuted command and raising an error. The default is 30 seconds.
CommandType	Specifies the type of command contained in the CommandText property. This type may be set to one of three types: StoredProcedure, TableDirect, or Text. These types represent a stored procedure call, a table name, and an SQL statement, respectively. Note that the TableDirect option is not recommended as it might result in poor performance because it retrieves all columns of the specified table. TableDirect is basically turned into a SELECT * FROM TableName statement. Additionally, it is only supported by the OLE DB Provider according to Microsoft documentation.
Connection	Reference to an IDbConnection object.
Parameters	Retrieves the IDataParameterCollection.
Transaction	Maintains the transaction in which the command will be executed.
UpdateRowSource	Specifies how command results are applied to the DataRow when used by the DbDataAdaptor.Update() method. This is discussed in a later chapter.

TABLE 19.2   IDbCommand Methods

Method	Description
Cancel()	Attempts to cancel the execution of the IDbCommand object.
CreateParameter()	Creates an instance of an IDbParameter class.
ExecuteNonQuery()	Executes an SQL command against the data store and returns the number of rows affected by the command.
ExecuteReader()	Executes the SQL command text against the database and returns an IDataReader instance.
ExecuteScalar()	Executes a query and returns the first column of the first row.
Prepare()	Prepares the call to a stored procedure by precompiling the command in the data store. This is beneficial only when you will be invoking the command multiple times. In this case, you would call Prepare() once prior to invoking multiple commands. Because it causes a hit on the database, it is not used when invoking the command once, or infrequently.

You can execute a command using an IDbCommand object by calling one of three different methods—ExecuteNonQuery(), ExecuteScalar(), and ExecuteReader(). Specific IDbCommand implementations can extend the number of methods that may be invoked for executing commands. For instance, the SqlCommand object has an ExecuteXMLReader() method that returns the query result into an XML document.

Non-Query Commands

To execute SQL statements that do not return any resultset, you would use the ExecuteNonQuery() method to invoke the command. SQL statements that fall into this category are, for instance, INSERT, UPDATE, and DELETE. Additionally, you can execute stored procedures, which also do not return a resultset, by using ExecuteNonQuery. Listing 19.1 illustrates the use of this method to insert a record into a database table.

LISTING 19.1   Use of the IDbCommand.ExecuteNonQuery() Method

```
 1:   program nonquery;
 2:
 3:   {$APPTYPE CONSOLE}
 4:
 5:   {%DotNetAssemblyCompiler 'c:\windows\microsoft.net\framework\
➥v1.1.4322\System.Data.dll'}
 6:
 7:   uses
 8:     SysUtils,
 9:     System.Data,
10:     System.Data.SqlClient;
11:
12:   const
13:     c_string = 'server=XWING;database=ugly_bug;Trusted_Connection=Yes';
14:     c_ins = 'insert into dg_user (user_id, user_name, password) values '+
15:             '(2, ''xpacheco'', ''password'')';
16:   var
17:     cmd: SqlCommand;
18:     rowsChanged: Integer;
19:     sqlcon: SqlConnection;
20:   begin
21:     sqlcon := SqlConnection.Create(c_string);
22:     sqlcon.Open;
23:     try
24:       cmd := SqlCommand.Create(c_ins, sqlcon);
25:       rowsChanged := cmd.ExecuteNonQuery;
26:       System.Console.WriteLine('Rows Changed: '+rowsChanged.ToString);
27:     finally
28:       sqlcon.Close;
29:     end;
30:     Console.ReadLine;
31:   end.
```

▶ Find the code on the CD: \Code\Chapter 19\Ex01\.

Lines 14 and 15 are the declaration of the constant c_ins, which contains the command that gets executed against the database. This example shows an INSERT statement into the dg_user table of the ugly_bug database.

Line 24 shows one way to construct the SqlCommand object. It takes two parameters. The first parameter is the SQL statement that will be executed. In this example, the constant c_ins is passed. The second parameter is the SqlConnection class to be associated with this SqlCommand.

This example simply executes the command and displays the number of rows that are affected, which in this case should be one.

The specific Command class may have additional constructors with different parameters. For example, the SqlCommand class defines the following constructors:

To create a SqlCommand object without specifying additional properties, use
SqlCommand.Create;

To create a `SqlCommand` object and only specify the command text to execute, use

```
SqlCommand.Create(cmdText: String);
```

To create a `SqlCommand` object and specify the command text to execute and the associated `SqlConnection` object, use

```
SqlCommand.Create(cmdText: String, connection: SqlConnection);
```

To create a `SqlCommand` object and specify the command text to execute, the associated `SqlConnection`, and Transact-SQL transaction, `SqlTransaction`, use

```
SqlCommand.Create(cmdText: String, connection: SqlConnection,
➥transaction: SqlTransaction);
```

Retrieving Single Values

Oftentimes, you'll need to retrieve a single value from a query, particularly when returning an aggregate value. `SqlCommand` implements the `ExecuteScalar()` method, which returns such a value.

Examine the following SQL statement:

```
SELECT Count(*) AS CanCust FROM customers WHERE country = 'Canada'
```

This particular statement will retrieve the total number of records in a table named customers, indicating customers who reside in Canada. The value returned will be returned as a single field named CanCust. Listing 19.2 illustrates using the `ExecuteScalar()` method to retrieve this value.

LISTING 19.2   Use of IDbCommand.ExecuteScalar() Method

```
1:    program ExScalar;
2:
3:    {$APPTYPE CONSOLE}
4:
5:    {%DotNetAssemblyCompiler 'C:\windows\microsoft.net\framework\
➥v1.1.4322\System.Data.dll'}
6:
7:    uses
8:      SysUtils,
9:      System.Data,
10:     System.Data.SqlClient;
11:
12:   const
13:     c_string = 'server=XWING;database=Northwind;Trusted_Connection=Yes';
14:     c_cmd = 'select Count(*) as CanCust from customers '+
15:       'where country = ''Canada''';
16:   var
17:     sqlCon: SqlConnection;
18:     sqlCmd: SqlCommand;
19:     CanCust: Integer;
20:   begin
21:     sqlCon := SqlConnection.Create(c_string);
22:     sqlCon.Open;
```

LISTING 19.2   Continued

```
23:    try
24:      sqlCmd := SqlCommand.Create(c_cmd, sqlCon);
25:      CanCust := Integer(sqlCmd.ExecuteScalar);
26:      Console.WriteLine(System.String.Format('Canadian Customers: {0}',
27:        CanCust.ToString));
28:    finally
29:      sqlCon.Close;
30:    end;
31:    Console.ReadLine;
32:  end.
```

▶ Find the code on the CD: \Code\Chapter 19\Ex02\.

The Listing 19.2 example connects to the Northwind database that is installed with Microsoft SQL Server when you install the example databases. This SQL statement is executed against the customers table.

Much of this example is very similar to that of Listing 19.1. Line 27 is where the ExecuteScalar() method is called, which returns the value retrieved. In this example, the value is of the Integer type; therefore, it is typecast to an Integer and assigned to the CanCust variable.

In this example, the SQL statement explicitly returns a single value. In a general query that possibly returns multiple rows, the ExecuteScalar() method will return the value contained in the first row, first column.

Executing Data Definition Language (DDL) Commands

The majority of commands that are invoked against a database are data retrieval and manipulation commands. Occasionally, however, one must do something dynamically to the structure of the database itself. This might be adding or modifying a table, stored procedure, or other such operations.

There are no dedicated .NET classes that perform these operations explicitly. However, you can still execute DDL commands using the IDbCommand.ExecuteNonQuery() method. Listing 19.3 illustrates this technique.

LISTING 19.3   Executing DDL Commands

```
1:    program ddlquery;
2:
3:    {$APPTYPE CONSOLE}
4:
5:    {%DotNetAssemblyCompiler 'c:\windows\microsoft.net\framework\
➥v1.1.4322\System.Data.dll'}
6:
7:    uses
8:      SysUtils,
9:      System.Data.SqlClient;
10:
11:   const
```

LISTING 19.3   Continued

```
12:    ub_proc = 'CREATE PROCEDURE ub_select_defect AS select '+
13:        'd.*, dt.title AS defect_type, ds.title AS defect_severity, '+
14:        'dst.title AS defect_status '+
15:        'FROM defect d left OUTER JOIN lu_defect_type dt '+
16:        'ON d.defect_type_id = dt.defect_type_id '+
17:        'LEFT OUTER JOIN lu_defect_severity ds '+
18:        'ON d.defect_severity_id = ds.defect_severity_id '+
19:        'LEFT OUTER JOIN lu_defect_status dst '+
20:        'ON d.defect_status_id = dst.defect_status_id';
21:
22:    const
23:        c_string = 'server=XWING;database=ugly_bug; Trusted_Connection=Yes';
24:
25:    var
26:        sqlcon: SqlConnection;
27:        cmd:    SqlCommand;
28:        rowsChanged: Integer;
29:    begin
30:        sqlcon := SqlConnection.Create;
31:        sqlcon.ConnectionString := c_string;
32:        sqlcon.Open;
33:        try
34:          cmd := SqlCommand.Create(ub_proc, sqlcon);
35:          rowsChanged := cmd.ExecuteNonQuery;
36:          sqlcon.Close;
37:          Console.WriteLine(System.String.Format('Rows Changed: {0}',
38:            rowsChanged.ToString));
39:        finally
40:          sqlcon.Close;
41:        end;
42:        Console.ReadLine;
43:    end.
```

▶ Find the code on the CD: \Code\Chapter 19\Ex03\.

Admittedly, the example in Listing 19.3 is not the ideal way to create a stored procedure in the database. However, the intent of this example is to illustrate how to execute DDL against a database and not to dazzle you with elegant coding style.

You'll notice the stored procedure that is assigned to the string constant ub_proc. This statement is nothing more than that same statement you might execute through Query Analyzer. Here, we run it through the SqlCommand object in line 32. The value returned will actually be -1.

Specifying Parameters Using IDbParameter

When executing SQL code, it's highly unlikely that the SQL statement values will be hard-coded as in Listing 19.2, which searched on Canadian customers. What if we wanted to search on German or Mexican customers? The query would have to somehow support dynamic specification of the search criteria. This is done through parameterized queries. In a parameterized query, a placeholder is put in the query statement where the hard-coded search criteria initially resided. Consider the following SQL statement:

```
c_cmd = 'SELECT * FROM customers WHERE country = @country
```

In this SQL statement, instead of hard-coding a country name, a parameter is specified using the at symbol (@) prefix to the parameter name (@country). To actually insert a value in place of the parameter, an IDbParameter implementing class is required.

For the Microsoft SQL Data Provider, SqlParameter class implements the IDbParameter interface. Other providers have their own classes, such as the OleDbParameter and BdpParameter for the OLE DB Data Provider and Borland Data Provider, respectively.

To use a parameter, you must first create and then associate it with the specific SqlCommand object that will execute the command. When creating a SqlParameter, you will likely want to specify the parameter name, data type, and size in the constructor. Six possible constructors exist that you can use, which allow you to specify less or more information such as the source column, parameter direction, and so on. Refer to the documentation on SqlParameter for more information on these additional constructors.

Listing 19.4 illustrates using the SqlParameter object to specify a parameter value in a parameterized query statement.

LISTING 19.4   Using SqlParameter in a Parameterized Query

```
1:    program Params;
2:
3:    {$APPTYPE CONSOLE}
4:
5:    {%DotNetAssemblyCompiler 'C:\windows\microsoft.net\framework\
➡v1.1.4322\System.Data.dll'}
6:
7:    uses
8:      SysUtils,
9:      System.Data,
10:     System.Data.SqlClient;
11:   const
12:     c_cmd = 'select * from customers where country = @country';
13:
14:   var
15:     sqlcon: SqlConnection;
16:     cmd:    SqlCommand;
17:     param:  SqlParameter;
18:     rowsChanged: Integer;
19:   begin
20:     sqlcon := SqlConnection.Create;
21:     sqlcon.ConnectionString := 'server=XWING;database=Northwind;'+
22:     'Trusted_Connection=Yes';
23:     cmd := SqlCommand.Create(c_cmd, sqlcon);
24:     param := cmd.Parameters.Add('@country', SqlDbType.NVarChar, 15);
25:     param.Value := 'USA';
26:
27:     sqlcon.Open;
28:     try
```

LISTING 19.4   Continued

```
29:     rowsChanged := cmd.ExecuteNonQuery;
30:   finally
31:     sqlcon.Close;
32:   end;
33:
34:   Console.WriteLine(System.String.Format('Rows Changed: {0}',
35:     rowsChanged.ToString));
36:   Console.ReadLine;
37: end.
```

▶ Find the code on the CD: \Code\Chapter 19\Ex04\.

In this example, one parameter is required. Line 24 invokes the `SqlCommand.Parameters.Add()` method, which creates, adds, and returns an `IDbParameter` instance. The `Parameters` property is a collection class (`SqlParameterCollection`) of `IDbParameter` instances that gets used internally when the query is invoked. The `Add()` method takes the parameter name, the data type of the parameter, and the column width. After adding and getting a reference to the parameter, a value is assigned to the parameter; in this case, we are assigning the string `'USA'` to indicate a search on U.S. customers. Normally, some other dynamic means would be used to specify the search criteria such as a drop down combo or similar.

When specifying data types for the parameter, you must use the database types specific to the data provider. For the SQL Server data provider, you must use the types defined by the `System.Data.SqlDbType` enumeration. For the OLE DB data provider, you would use data types defined by the `System.Data.OleDB.OleDbType` enumeration. The same is true for other data providers.

Executing Stored Procedures

The steps to executing a stored procedure is just as straightforward as executing other non-query commands. Listing 19.5 illustrates these steps.

LISTING 19.5   Stored Procedure Example

```
1:  program sp_addco;
2:
3:  {$APPTYPE CONSOLE}
4:
5:  {%DotNetAssemblyCompiler 'C:\windows\microsoft.net\framework\
➥v1.1.4322\System.Data.dll'}
6:
7:  uses
8:    SysUtils,
9:    System.Data,
10:    System.Data.SqlClient;
11:
12: const
13:   c_cnstr = 'server=XWING;database=ddn_company;Trusted_Connection=Yes';
14:   c_ddn_add_company = 'ddn_add_company';
15: var
```

LISTING 19.5 Continued

```
16:    sqlcon: SqlConnection;
17:    cmd:    SqlCommand;
18:    param:  SqlParameter;
19:  begin
20:    sqlcon := SqlConnection.Create(c_cnstr);
21:    cmd := SqlCommand.Create(c_ddn_add_company, sqlcon);
22:    cmd.CommandType := CommandType.StoredProcedure;
23:
24:    param := cmd.Parameters.Add('@company_name', SqlDbType.VarChar, 100);
25:    param.Value := 'Xapware Technologies Inc.';
26:
27:    param := cmd.Parameters.Add('@address_1', SqlDbType.VarChar, 100);
28:    param.Value := '4164 Austin Bluffs Parkway';
29:
30:    param := cmd.Parameters.Add('@address_2', SqlDbType.VarChar, 100);
31:    param.Value := 'Ste 363';
32:
33:    param := cmd.Parameters.Add('@city', SqlDbType.VarChar, 50);
34:    param.Value := 'Colorado Springs';
35:
36:    param := cmd.Parameters.Add('@state_abbr', SqlDbType.Char, 2);
37:    param.Value := 'CO';
38:
39:    param := cmd.Parameters.Add('@zip', SqlDbType.VarChar, 20);
40:    param.Value := '80918';
41:
42:    param := cmd.Parameters.Add('@company_id', SqlDbType.Int);
43:    param.Direction := ParameterDirection.Output;
44:
45:    sqlcon.Open;
46:    try
47:      cmd.ExecuteNonQuery;
48:      param := cmd.Parameters['@company_id'];
49:    finally
50:      sqlcon.Close;
51:    end;
52:
53:    Console.WriteLine(System.String.Format('New company id: {0}',
54:      param.Value));
55:
56:    Console.ReadLine;
57:  end.
```

▶ Find the code on the CD: \Code\Chapter 19\Ex05\.

This example executes a simple stored procedure that inserts a record into a table of companies. The stored procedure is shown in Listing 19.6. From examining Listing 19.6, you will see that this procedure declares both input and output parameters.

LISTING 19.6 Stored Procedure for Adding a Company

```
1.   CREATE PROCEDURE ddn_add_company
2.   (
```

LISTING 19.6   Continued

```
3.    @company_name varchar(100),
4.    @address_1 varchar(100),
5.    @address_2 varchar(100),
6.    @city varchar(50),
7.    @state_abbr char(2),
8.    @zip varchar(20),
9.    @company_id int output
10.   )
11.   AS
12.     INSERT INTO company (company_name, address_1, address_2, city, state_abbr,
13.     zip)
14.   VALUES (@company_name, @address_1, @address_2, @city, @state_abbr, @zip)
15.   SELECT @company_id = @@Identity
16.   GO
```

Looking back at Listing 19.5, line 21, you notice that instead of specifying the SQL statement to execute, you specify the name of the stored procedure. In this example, the name of the stored procedure is contained in the string constant c_ddn_add_company. Additionally, the value CommandType.StoredProcedure is assigned to the SqlCommand.CommandType property specifying that the command text contains a stored procedure and not an SQL statement.

The remaining lines, 24–40, simply add parameters and assign their respective values expected by the stored procedure. Lines 42–43 are dealing with the outbound parameter. Instead of specifying a value, a parameter direction is indicated by assigning ParameterDirection.Output to the Direction property of SqlParameter.

After executing the command, the output parameter can be retrieved (line 51) and its value accessed. The example here returns the value of the record's auto incrementing field.

Deriving Parameters

Listing 19.5 shows how to invoke a call that requires multiple parameters. This type of code, however, can be unmanageable because database specifics such as the parameters' names and data types are hard-coded into your source code.

You can use the CommandBuilder class, which essentially queries the database for metadata about the parameters and populates the SqlCommand object with that information. Therefore, you only have to specify the values. Listing 19.7 shows the alternative code from Listing 19.5.

LISTING 19.7   Specifying Parameters Using CommandBuilder

```
1:    program storedproc_cb;
2:
3:    {$APPTYPE CONSOLE}
4:
5:    {%DotNetAssemblyCompiler 'c:\windows\microsoft.net\framework\
➥v1.1.4322\System.Data.dll'}
6:
7:    uses
8:      SysUtils,
9:      System.Data,
```

LISTING 19.7 Continued

```
10:    System.Data.SqlClient;
11:
12:  const
13:    c_cnstr = 'server=XWING;database=ddn_company;Trusted_Connection=Yes';
14:    c_ddn_add_company = 'ddn_add_company';
15:  var
16:    sqlcon: SqlConnection;
17:    cmd:    SqlCommand;
18:  begin
19:    sqlcon := SqlConnection.Create(c_cnstr);
20:    cmd := SqlCommand.Create(c_ddn_add_company, sqlcon);
21:    cmd.CommandType := CommandType.StoredProcedure;
22:
23:    sqlcon.Open;
24:    try
25:
26:      SqlCommandBuilder.DeriveParameters(cmd);
27:      cmd.Parameters[1].Value := 'Xapware Technologies Inc.';
28:      cmd.Parameters[2].Value := '4164 Austin Bluffs Parkway';
29:      cmd.Parameters[3].Value := 'Ste 363';
30:      cmd.Parameters[4].Value := 'Colorado Springs';
31:      cmd.Parameters[5].Value := 'CO';
32:      cmd.Parameters[6].Value := '80918';
33:      cmd.Parameters[7].Value := DBNull.Value;
34:      cmd.ExecuteNonQuery;
35:    finally
36:      sqlcon.Close;
37:    end;
38:
39:    Console.WriteLine(System.String.Format('New company id: {0}',
40:      cmd.Parameters[7].Value));
41:    Console.ReadLine;
42:
43:  end.
```

▶ Find the code on the CD: \Code\Chapter 19\Ex06\.

Line 26 is where the CommandBuilder.DeriveParameters() call is made to retrieve parameter metadata, which gets injected into the SqlCommand class passed as a parameter.

> **CAUTION**
>
> Use of the CommandBuilder object might not be the best option because it adds the overhead of an additional call to the database. Although convenient from a coding standpoint, when you know the metadata information, use it instead and avoid performance pitfalls.

Querying for Resultsets Using DataReaders

Up to this point, this chapter has only covered invoking SQL commands that return one or no values from the database. When needing to return a resultset of multiple records, you would use the data provider–specific object that implements the IDataReader interface.

The IDataReader Interface

The IDataReader interface defines the ability to read streams of resultsets in a forward-only manner. The significance of this is one of performance.

DataReaders do not retrieve the entire resultset into memory immediately. Instead, the results are cached in a network buffer on the client. When needed, records are fetched and loaded into memory via the IDataReader.Read() method. One record is fetched at a time, thus reducing system overhead.

You cannot create a DataReader explicitly. An IDataReader instance is returned from the SqlCommand.ExecuteReader() method.

Like other classes, DataReaders exist for each specific data provider.

Querying a Resultset

The SQLDataReader class can be used to query a single or multiple resultsets. Listing 19.8 illustrates the single resultset technique.

LISTING 19.8   Using SqlDataReader on a Single Resultset

```
1:   program rsltset;
2:
3:   {$APPTYPE CONSOLE}
4:
5:   {%DotNetAssemblyCompiler 'C:\windows\microsoft.net\framework\
➥v1.1.4322\System.Data.dll'}
6:
7:   uses
8:     SysUtils,
9:     System.Data,
10:    System.Data.SqlClient;
11:
12:  const
13:    c_cnstr = 'server=XWING;database=ddn_company;Trusted_Connection=Yes';
14:    c_select_company = 'select company_id, company_name from company';
15:  var
16:    sqlcon: SqlConnection;
17:    cmd:    SqlCommand;
18:    rdr:    SqlDataReader;
19:  begin
20:    sqlcon := SqlConnection.Create(c_cnstr);
21:    cmd := SqlCommand.Create(c_select_company, sqlcon);
22:    sqlcon.Open;
23:    try
24:      rdr := cmd.ExecuteReader;
25:      while rdr.Read do
26:        Console.WriteLine(System.String.Format('{0}-{1}',
27:          rdr['company_id'], rdr['company_name']));
28:    finally
29:      sqlcon.Close;
30:    end;
```

19

LISTING 19.8   Continued

```
31:    Console.ReadLine;
32:  end.
```

▶ Find the code on the CD: \Code\Chapter 19\Ex07\.

Lines 24–27 illustrate the use of the SqlDataReader class. First, the ExecuteReader() method is invoked to return the SqlDataReader instance into the variable rdr. Then, Read() is invoked to iterate through the resultset. Read() returns a boolean indicating whether a record has been retrieved.

Querying Multiple Resultsets Using DataReaders

You can use data readers to iterate through multiple resultsets, as shown in Listing 19.9.

LISTING 19.9   Querying Multiple Resultsets

```
 1:   program multrsltset;
 2:
 3:   {$APPTYPE CONSOLE}
 4:
 5:   {%DotNetAssemblyCompiler 'C:\windows\microsoft.net\framework\
➥v1.1.4322\System.Data.dll'}
 6:
 7:   uses
 8:     SysUtils,
 9:     System.Data,
10:     System.Data.SqlClient;
11:
12:   const
13:     c_cnstr = 'server=XWING;database=ddn_company;Trusted_Connection=Yes';
14:     c_select_company = 'select company_id, company_name from company;'+
15:                        'select state_abbr, state_name from lu_state;';
16:   var
17:     sqlcon: SqlConnection;
18:     cmd:    SqlCommand;
19:     rdr:    SqlDataReader;
20:   begin
21:     sqlcon := SqlConnection.Create(c_cnstr);
22:     cmd := SqlCommand.Create(c_select_company, sqlcon);
23:     sqlcon.Open;
24:     try
25:       rdr := cmd.ExecuteReader;
26:       repeat
27:         while rdr.Read do
28:           Console.WriteLine(System.String.Format('{0}-{1}',rdr[0], rdr[1]));
29:       until not rdr.NextResult;
30:     finally
31:       sqlcon.Close;
32:     end;
33:     Console.ReadLine;
34:   end.
35:
```

▶ Find the code on the CD: \Code\Chapter 19\Ex08\.

In this example, the command text contains multiple SELECT statements, thus retrieving multiple resultsets. Additionally, the SqlDataReader is used differently from the previous listing. Here, the SqlDataReader.NextResult() method is used to advance to the next resultset.

Using DataReader to Retrieve BLOB Data

Occasionally, you will need to retrieve a BLOB from a database. A BLOB is a mass from outer space that grows proportionally to the number of people it devours. It is also a block of data that, as far as the database is concerned, contains no structure. The acronym BLOB stands for Binary Large OBject. Typically, images, files, and other such data is stored in BLOBS. DataReaders can be used to retrieve BLOBS as Listing 19.10 illustrates.

LISTING 19.10   Retrieving BLOB Data from a Database

```
1:    program readblob;
2:
3:    {$APPTYPE CONSOLE}
4:
5:    {%DotNetAssemblyCompiler 'c:\windows\microsoft.net\framework\
➥v1.1.4322\System.Data.dll'}
6:
7:    uses
8:      SysUtils,
9:      System.Data,
10:     System.Data.SqlClient,
11:     System.IO;
12:
13:   const
14:     c_cnstr = 'server=XWING;database=Northwind;Trusted_Connection=Yes';
15:     c_sel   = 'select employeeID, Photo from employees';
16:     c_bufferSize = 100;
17:   var
18:     sqlcon: SqlConnection;
19:     cmd:    SqlCommand;
20:     rdr:    SqlDataReader;
21:
22:     barray: array[0..c_bufferSize-1] of byte;
23:     bytesRead: Integer;
24:     idx: Integer;
25:
26:     fName: String;
27:     fStream: FileStream;
28:     bWriter: BinaryWriter;
29:
30:   begin
31:     sqlcon := SqlConnection.Create(c_cnstr);
32:     cmd := SqlCommand.Create(c_sel, sqlcon);
33:     sqlcon.Open;
34:     try
35:       rdr := cmd.ExecuteReader(CommandBehavior.SequentialAccess);
36:       rdr.Read;
37:       fName := 'emp_'+rdr.GetSqlInt32(0).ToString+'.bmp';
```

LISTING 19.10   Continued

```
38:      fStream := FileStream.Create(fName, FileMode.OpenOrCreate,
39:        FileAccess.Write);
40:      try
41:        bWriter := BinaryWriter.Create(fStream);
42:        try
43:          idx := 0;
44:          repeat
45:            bytesRead := Integer(rdr.GetBytes(1, idx, barray, 0,
46:              c_bufferSize));
47:            bWriter.Write(barray, 0, bytesRead);
48:            idx := idx+c_bufferSize;
49:          until bytesRead < c_buffersize;
50:        finally
51:          bWriter.Close;
52:        end;
53:      finally
54:        fStream.Close;
55:      end;
56:    finally
57:      sqlcon.Close;
58:    end;
59:  end.
```

▶ Find the code on the CD: \Code\Chapter 19\Ex09\.

This example makes use of the `FileStream` and `BinaryWriter` classes and illustrates how to incrementally read from the BLOB field based on a buffer size. The process is the standard approach of reading sections of the BLOB one at a time and placing them into a file buffer that is eventually saved to a file.

Line 35 is worthy of further mention. When executing the `SqlCommand.ExecuteReader()` method, the `CommandBehavior` parameter is `SequentialAccess`. This value is specific to BLOB formatted data as it causes the reader to load data as a stream rather than loading the entire resultset. You can then use the `GetBytes()` or `GetChars()` methods to retrieve data in chunks. A requirement of using `SequentialAccess` is that columns must be read in the order that they are retrieved. You can skip columns; however, you will not be able to go back and read a skipped column.

Using DataReader to Retrieve Schema Information

The DataReader can be used to retrieve schema information using the `SqlDataReader.GetSchemaTable()` method. This method returns a `DataTable` that is populated with information about a resultset's columns. Therefore, each row in this schema resultset represents a column in the actual resultset. The schema row contains information about the column, such as its name, uniqueness, data type, and more. Listing 19.11 illustrates using this method.

LISTING 19.11   Retrieving Schema Information

```
1:   program schemaquery;
2:
3:   {$APPTYPE CONSOLE}
4:
5:   {%DotNetAssemblyCompiler 'C:\windows\microsoft.net\framework\
➡v1.1.4322\System.Data.dll'}
6:
7:   uses
8:     SysUtils,
9:     System.Data,
10:    System.Data.SqlClient,
11:    System.Collections;
12:  const
13:    c_cnstr = 'server=XWING;database=Northwind;Trusted_Connection=Yes';
14:    c_select_employees = 'select * from Employees';
15:  var
16:    sqlcon: SqlConnection;
17:    cmd:    SqlCommand;
18:    rdr:    SqlDataReader;
19:    schema: DataTable;
20:    row:    DataRow;
21:    col:    DataColumn;
22:    enRow: IEnumerator;
23:    enCol: IEnumerator;
24:  begin
25:    sqlcon := SqlConnection.Create(c_cnstr);
26:    cmd := SqlCommand.Create(c_select_employees, sqlcon);
27:    sqlcon.Open;
28:    try
29:      rdr := cmd.ExecuteReader(CommandBehavior.SequentialAccess);
30:      schema := rdr.GetSchemaTable;
31:    finally
32:      sqlcon.Close;
33:    end;
34:
35:    enRow := schema.Rows.GetEnumerator;
36:    while enRow.MoveNext do
37:    begin
38:      row := enRow.Current as DataRow;
39:      enCol := schema.Columns.GetEnumerator;
40:      while enCol.MoveNext do
41:      begin
42:        col := enCol.Current as DataColumn;
43:        Console.WriteLine(col.ColumnName+'='+row[col].ToString);
44:      end;
45:      Console.WriteLine;
46:    end;
47:    Console.ReadLine;
48:  end.
```

▶ Find the code on the CD: \Code\Chapter 19\Ex10\.

Listing 19.11 uses the `CommandBehavior.SequentialAccess` enumeration in the constructor of `SqlCommand.ExecuteReader()` so that we read only a field at a time. The `while` statement in lines 40–44 retrieves the schema information from the result and produces the following output for each column.

```
ColumnName=EmployeeID
ColumnOrdinal=0
ColumnSize=4
NumericPrecision=10
NumericScale=255
IsUnique=False
IsKey=
BaseServerName=
BaseCatalogName=
BaseColumnName=EmployeeID
BaseSchemaName=
BaseTableName=
DataType=System.Int32
AllowDBNull=False
ProviderType=8
IsAliased=
IsExpression=
IsIdentity=True
IsAutoIncrement=True
IsRowVersion=False
IsHidden=
IsLong=False
IsReadOnly=True
```

CHAPTER 20

DataAdapters and DataSets

IN THIS CHAPTER

- DataAdapters
- Working with DataSets
- Working with DataTables

This chapter talks about the classes that allow you to work with in-memory data which you might have retrieved from a data source or are simply using in your application logic. The primary disconnected classes within the .NET Framework are DataAdapters, DataSets, DataColumns, and DataRows.

DataAdapters

The DataAdapter class is a bridge between the data source and the disconnected objects that allow you to manipulate data. DataAdapters retrieve information from the data store and populate disconnected DataSets with that data. Also, DataAdapters store any updates, which are cached back to the data store. The DataAdapter class implements the IDBDataAdapter interface. Like other database classes, each data provider contains its own DataAdapter class. Therefore, the SQL Data Provider uses a SQLDataAdapter, and the Borland Data Provider uses a BDPDataAdapter. Each data provider's specific DataAdapter descends from the DBDataAdapter class, which descends from the DataAdapter class. This chapter demonstrates the use of the SQLDataAdapter class, but the same concepts can be applied to DataAdapters from other data providers.

DataAdapter Composition

Figure 20.1 illustrates how the DataAdapter class is composed.

The various objects in the DataAdapter class are used to populate the contents of a DataSet class. The DataAdapter class consists of four Command objects: *Select*Command, *Insert*Command, *Update*Command, and *Delete*Command. As implied by their names, these Command objects contain the SQL statement that you would use to perform the specified operation against the data store. Additionally, the DataAdapter contains a collection to map names between the source tables and DataSet tables. Figure 20.2 depicts the structure of the TableMappings collection.

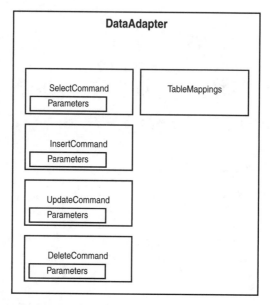

FIGURE 20.1   DataAdapter composition.

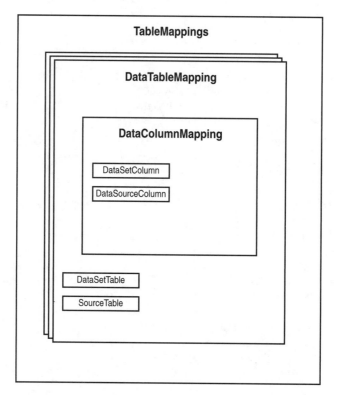

FIGURE 20.2   TableMappings collection.

Given that a DataSet class is entirely disconnected from the originating data source, it knows nothing about how the tables it contains map to the data source. The DataAdapter class handles this through the TableMappings collection member.

As shown in Figure 20.2, the TableMappings collection contains a collection of DataTableMapping objects. Each DataTableMapping object maps a single DataTable to the data source table. Its DataSetTable property gets and sets the name of the table in a DataSet. The SourceTable refers to the case-sensitive table name in the originating data source. The number of such objects depends on how many data source tables were retrieved from the data source. In most cases, this would be a single table. Each DataTableMapping object contains a collection of DataColumnMapping objects. The DataColumnMapping object contains two members. The DataSetColumn is not a case-sensitive name for a column name within the DataSet. The SourceColumn is a case sensitive name of the column as it exists in the data source.

Creating a DataAdapter

The DataAdapter class has four constructors—each with a different combination of parameters to specify a select command or connection. For instance, given the following connection and select command strings

```
c_cnstr = 'server=XWING;database=Northwind;Trusted_Connection=Yes';
c_sel_emp = 'select * from Employees';
```

A DataAdapter can be created without specifying any parameter—in which case, the appropriate command property must be specified:

```
var
  sqlDA: SqlDataAdapter;
  sqlCMD: SQLCommand;
  sqlCN: SQLConnection;
begin
  sqlCN := SQLConnection.Create(c_cnstr);
  sqlCmd := SQLCommand.Create(c_sel_emp, sqlCN);
  sqlDA := SQLDataAdapter.Create;
  sqlDA.SelectCommand := sqlCmd;
end.
```

Otherwise, the select command can be passed as a parameter to the DataAdapter's constructor:

```
sqlDA := SQLDataAdapter.Create(sqlCmd);
```

You can also pass a select command string and a Connection object to the DataAdapter's constructor:

```
  c_sel_emp = 'select * from Employees';
var
  sqlDA: SqlDataAdapter;
  sqlCN: SQLConnection;
begin
  sqlCN := SQLConnection.Create(c_cnstr);
  sqlDA := SQLDataAdapter.Create(c_sel_emp, sqlCN);
```

Finally, you can construct a DataAdapter by specifying the select command string and connection string:

```
const
  c_cnstr = 'server=XWING;database=Northwind;Trusted_Connection=Yes';
  c_sel_emp = 'select * from Employees';
var
  sqlDA: SqlDataAdapter;
begin
  sqlDA := SQLDataAdapter.Create(c_sel_emp, c_cnstr);
end.
```

When passing a Connection to the DataAdapter's constructor, the DataAdapter will open the Connection if it is not already open. In a typical scenario, you will be using multiple DataAdapters to retrieve and perform updates on different tables in the data source. When passing a connection string as opposed to a Connection object to the DataAdapter constructor, the DataAdapter internally creates and connects to the data source. It is better to pass a Connection object because multiple DataAdapters can share the same Connection.

Retrieving Query Results

The DataAdapter.SelectCommand object is used to retrieve results of a query. These results can then be used to fill either a DataSet or a DataTable object. Also, DataAdapter can be used to execute parameterized queries or stored procedures for retrieving resultsets from a data store.

Populating a DataSet

Listing 20.1 illustrates how to use DataAdapter to fill a DataSet object.

LISTING 20.1   Filling a DataSet Object

```
1:    program FillDataSet;
2:
3:    {$APPTYPE CONSOLE}
4:
5:    {%DelphiDotNetAssemblyCompiler 'c:\windows\microsoft.net\framework\
➥v1.1.4322\System.Data.dll'}
6:
7:    uses
8:      System.Data,
9:      System.Data.SqlClient;
10:
11:   const
12:     c_cnstr = 'server=XWING;database=Northwind;Trusted_Connection=Yes';
13:     c_sel_emp = 'select * from Employees; select * from Customers;';
14:   var
15:     sqlDA: SqlDataAdapter;
16:     nwDS: DataSet;
17:   begin
18:     sqlDA := SQLDataAdapter.Create(c_sel_emp, c_cnstr);
19:     nwDS  := DataSet.Create;
20:
21:     sqlDA.Fill(nwDS);
22:   end.
```

▶ Find the code on the CD: \Code\Chapter 20\Ex01\.

The `DataAdapter` class in Listing 20.1 retrieves two tables from the data source: Employees and Customers (line 13). The method used to take the results from this query and to populate a `DataSet` is through the `Fill()` method as shown in line 21.

In this example, the `Fill()` method internally performs several steps. First, it creates a `Connection` object and connects to the data source specified in the `c_cnstr` constant. Then, it executes the query statement contained in the `SelectCommand` object against the data source. The command is the `c_sel_emp` constant that was passed to the constructor in line 19. Finally, it retrieves both data and the column names and types, which it uses to populate the `DataSet` object.

Populating a DataTable

When retrieving a single table, the `DataAdapter` class can be used to populate a `DataTable` object. For example, given a `SelectCommand` with the following select statement

```
c_sel_emp = 'select * from Employees';
```

You could pass the `DataTable` to the `DataAdapter.Fill()` method instead of a `DataSet`.

```
empDT  := DataTable.Create;
sqlDA.Fill(empDT);
```

▶ Find the code on the CD: \Code\Chapter 20\Ex02\.

Retrieving Data from a Parameterized Query

Listing 20.2 illustrates how to retrieve data from a parameterized query.

LISTING 20.2   Using DataAdapter with a Parameterized Query

```
1:    program FillFromParamQry;
2:
3:    {$APPTYPE CONSOLE}
4:
5:    {%DelphiDotNetAssemblyCompiler 'c:\windows\microsoft.net\framework\
➥v1.1.4322\System.Data.dll'}
6:
7:    uses
8:      SysUtils,
9:      System.Data,
10:     System.Data.SqlClient;
11:
12:   const
13:     c_cnstr = 'server=XWING;database=Northwind;Trusted_Connection=Yes';
14:     c_sel_cst = 'select * from customers where country = @Country';
15:   var
16:     sqlCn: SqlConnection;
17:     sqlDA: SqlDataAdapter;
18:     sqlCmd: SqlCommand;
19:     nwDS: DataSet;
20:   begin
21:     sqlCn := SqlConnection.Create(c_cnstr);
22:     sqlCmd := SqlCommand.Create(c_sel_cst, sqlCn);
23:     sqlCmd.Parameters.Add('@Country', SqlDBType.NChar, 15);
```

20

LISTING 20.2   Continued

```
24:    sqlCmd.Parameters['@Country'].Value := 'Germany';
25:
26:    sqlDA := SqlDataAdapter.Create(sqlCmd);
27:    nwDS := DataSet.Create;
28:
29:    sqlDA.Fill(nwDS);
30: end.
```

▶ Find the code on the CD: \Code\Chapter 20\Ex03\.

Chapter 19, "Using Command and DataReader Objects," illustrates how to use the SQLCommand object with parameters. This is no different. As shown in Listing 20.2, you simply add the parameters, assign their values, and then create the DataAdapter class with the Command object containing the parameters.

Mapping Query Results

When populating a DataSet from a DataAdapter, the table names in the DataSet do not correspond to the table names in the DataSource by default. Instead, they are named Table, Table1, Table2, and so on, by default. The column names, however, do correspond to the originating data source column names. This can be confusing when working the table; therefore, you'll want to remedy this. First, you may want to name the table in the DataSet to something more meaningful. Most likely, you will give it the same name that it has in the data source. Also, you want to remove any obscurity in the field names. For instance, if you have a field in the data source named FName or SCode, you can name the same fields in the DataSet to FirstName or StateCode. The DataAdapter will retain the relationship in the TableMappings collection. Listing 20.3 illustrates this concept.

LISTING 20.3   DataMapping Example

```
1:     program mappings;
2:
3:     {$APPTYPE CONSOLE}
4:
5:     {%DelphiDotNetAssemblyCompiler 'c:\windows\microsoft.net\framework\v1.1.4322\
➥System.Data.dll'}
6:
7:     uses
8:       System.Data,
9:       System.Data.SqlClient,
10:      System.Data.Common,
11:      System.Collections;
12:
13:    const
14:      c_cnstr = 'server=XWING;database=Northwind;Trusted_Connection=Yes';
15:      c_sel_emp = 'select * from Employees; select * from Customers;';
16:    var
17:      sqlDA: SqlDataAdapter;
18:      nwDS: DataSet;
19:      dt: DataTable;
20:      dtEnum: IEnumerator;
```

LISTING 20.3   Continued

```
21:     coEnum: IEnumerator;
22:     dc: DataColumn;
23:
24:     tmEnum: IEnumerator;
25:     dtm: DataTableMapping;
26:
27:     cmEnum: IEnumerator;
28:     dcm: DataColumnMapping;
29:   begin
30:     sqlDA := SQLDataAdapter.Create(c_sel_emp, c_cnstr);
31:     nwDS := DataSet.Create;
32:
33:     // Map the tables
34:
35:     // Uncommment here to perform mapping
36:     dtm := sqlDA.TableMappings.Add('Table', 'Employees');
37:     dtm.ColumnMappings.Add('EmployeeID', 'EmpID');
38:     dtm := sqlDA.TableMappings.Add('Table1', 'Customers');
39:     dtm.ColumnMappings.Add('CustomerID', 'CustID');
40:
41:     sqlDA.Fill(nwDS);
42:
43:     tmEnum := sqlDA.TableMappings.GetEnumerator;
44:
45:     while tmEnum.MoveNext do
46:     begin
47:       dtm := tmEnum.Current as DataTableMapping;
48:       Console.WriteLine('DataSet Table: {0}, Data source table: {1}',
49:        [dtm.DataSetTable, dtm.SourceTable]);
50:
51:       cmEnum := dtm.ColumnMappings.GetEnumerator;
52:       while cmEnum.MoveNext do
53:       begin
54:         dcm := cmEnum.Current as DataColumnMapping;
55:         Console.WriteLine('  DataSet Column: {0}, Data source column: {1}',
56:           dcm.DataSetColumn, dcm.SourceColumn);
57:       end;
58:     end;
59:
60:     // Write out the tables.
61:     dtEnum := nwDS.Tables.GetEnumerator;
62:     while dtEnum.MoveNext do
63:     begin
64:       dt := dtEnum.Current as DataTable;
65:       Console.WriteLine(dt.TableName);
66:
67:       coEnum := dt.Columns.GetEnumerator;
68:
69:       while coEnum.MoveNext do
70:       begin
71:         dc := coEnum.Current as DataColumn;
72:         Console.WriteLine('   '+dc.ColumnName);
73:       end;
```

LISTING 20.3   Continued

```
74:     Console.WriteLine('=================');
75:   end;
76:
77:   Console.ReadLine;
78: end.
```

▶ Find the code on the CD: \Code\Chapter 20\Ex04\.

In Listing 20.3, when lines 36–39 are commented out, there are no mapping objects contained in the `DataAdapter.TableMappings` collection. Therefore, the output is that shown here:

```
[n:\chapter 20\mappings]mappings.exe
Table
  EmployeeID
  LastName
...
Table1
  CustomerID
  CompanyName
...
```

Note that the names of the tables have nothing to do with the actual table names retrieved, whereas the column names do. By uncommenting lines 36–39, the output changes to

```
[n:\chapter 20\mappings]mappings.exe
DataSet Table: Employees, Data source table: Table
  DataSet Column: EmpID, Data source column: EmployeeID
DataSet Table: Customers, Data source table: Table1
  DataSet Column: CustID, Data source column: CustomerID
Employees
  EmpID
  LastName
Customers
  CustID
  CompanyName
```

Now, you will see that mapping information gets printed and the table names are those specified in the call to the `TableMappings.Add()` function. This function returns a `DataTableMapping` object. Lines 37 and 39 then use this object to map different column names to the `EmployeeID` and `CustomerID` columns by calling its `ColumnMappings.Add()` function. In a sense, the `Add()` function for the `TableMappings` and `ColumnMappings` objects creates alias names for those that are retained in the `DataSet` object.

Working with DataSets

The `DataSet` is an in-memory representation of data structured in the form of tables, relationships, and constraints such as unique and foreign keys.

The DataSet is disconnected from the data source. It typically gets its data from the DataAdapter and never communicates directly with a Connection. When manipulating data in the DataSet, it maintains versions of each row changed. This enables changes to either be stored back to the data source through a DataAdapter or cancelled. DataSets are not provider specific. They are capable of retrieving and storing data through any provider specific DataAdapter.

You will work with two types of DataSets—untyped and strongly typed. An untyped DataSet refers to the base class, DataSet, whereas a strongly typed DataSet is a descendant of DataSet whose internal classes, such as DataTable and DataRow, are named and contain additional properties according to the schema within the DataSet. This chapter focuses on untyped DataSets. A later chapter discusses how to create strongly typed DataSets. The operations discussed here will apply to both types of DataSets.

DataSet Composition

Some might say that the only native Delphi object that resembles the DataSet is the ClientDataSet. The TClientDataSet, however, only appears similar to the DataSet in that it is an in-memory, disconnected object that can manipulate a resultset. The DataSet, in contrast, is capable of containing multiple resultsets, their relations, and constraints. In other words, the DataSet might contain multiple elements from a relational database.

Figure 20.3 illustrates the composition of a DataSet.

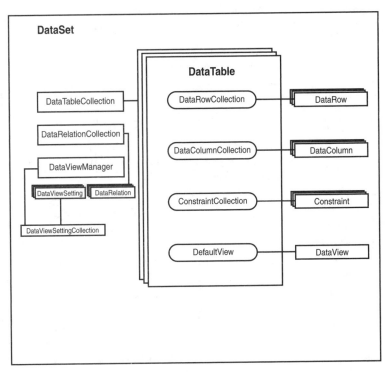

FIGURE 20.3   Classes that make up a DataSet.

20

The DataTableCollection and DataTables

The DataSet contains a collection of DataTables, which is accessed through the DataSet.Tables property. DataSet.Tables is of the type DataTableCollection. Earlier, it was mentioned that a DataSet is similar to the TClientDataSet. In fact, the DataTable is most similar to the TClientDataSet.

The DataTable contains DataColumn objects that encapsulate columns and Constraint objects that encapsulate constraints such as uniqueness, cascading deletes, and so on. These objects are accessed through the Columns and Constraints properties of the types DataColumnCollection and ConstraintCollection, respectively.

The DataSet.Rows property enables you to access a row within the DataTable. The Rows property is of the type DataRowCollection and contains a collection of DataRow objects.

Every DataTable contains a DataView object, DefaultDataView. Chapter 21, "Working with WinForms: DataViews and Data Binding," gets into more detail on DataViews; therefore, they will not be covered here except to say that these objects provide the mechanism for interactive data display and manipulation.

DataTables are similar to DataReaders, but they differ in that a DataReader is a connected object with forward, read-only access to data. A DataTable is an in-memory container for data with few restrictions on modifying, navigating, searching, and filtering data.

The DataRelationCollection

The DataSet is capable of maintaining links between parent and child tables. These links or relationships are maintained by DataRelation objects. These objects are accessible through a DataRelationCollection property, DataSet.Relations.

The DataRelation object is useful in maintaining data integrity within the DataSet and for navigating parent and child tables. This can be used to logically connect a customer table to the order table, for instance.

The DataViewManager

Displaying data contained in DataSets requires that the user interface objects be connected somehow with the actual DataSet objects. This concept is called data binding. The object that sits between the display objects and DataTable objects is a DataView. Therefore, a DataView represents the display of DataTable data. The DataViewManager manages default view settings for all the tables in a DataSet. Chapter 21 discusses data binding in greater detail.

DataSet Operations

You have already seen various operations on the DataSet class in the illustrations regarding the DataAdapter. Specifically, you have seen how a DataSet may be populated with both schema and data from a data source. This is the typical scenario that you will likely need to use the DataSet. However, it is possible to both construct and manipulate a DataSet having never populated it from a data source. In both scenarios, the operations are the same. This chapter focuses primarily on standalone DataSet usage. Chapter 22, "Saving Data to the Data Source," discusses how to create applications that retrieve, manipulate, and save data back to a data store.

Creating DataSets

There are two constructors to the DataSet class. One takes no parameters and is used as

```
MyDataSet := DataSet.Create();
```

This constructor creates the DataSet instance with a default name of NewDataSet. A second constructor takes the name as a parameter and is invoked as shown here:

```
MyDataSet := DataSet.Create('DataSetName');
```

Some other methods used to create a DataSet are

- Copy()—Creates a DataSet from another, copying both schema and data.
- Clone()—Creates a DataSet from another, copying only the schema information.
- GetChanges()—Creates a DataSet from another, copying only rows that have been modified.

Adding, Removing, and Indexing Tables

You have already seen how DataTables can be added to a DataSet through the DataAdapter.Fill() method. You can also add a table directly to the DataSet by calling the Add() method of the DataTableCollection object.

```
dsNW := DataSet.Create('BusinessApp');
dsNW.Tables.Add('Employee');
```

You can also add several tables in one call by passing an array of tables to the AddRange() method.

```
dsNW := DataSet.Create('BusinessApp');
dtEmp  := DataTable.Create('Employee');
dtCust := DataTable.Create('Customer');
dsNW.Tables.AddRange([dtEmp, dtCust]);
```

To remove a table from the DataSet, call the Remove() or RemoveAt() method. Remove() removes the specified DataTable:

```
var
  dsNW: DataSet;
  dtTemp: DataTable;
begin
  dtTemp := dsNW.Tables.Add('TempTable');
  // use dtTemp
  dsNW.Tables.Remove(dtTemp);
```

The RemoteAt() method removes a table from the specified index:

```
dsNW.Tables.RemoveAt(2);
```

To remove all tables from the DataSet, use the Clear() method:

```
dsNW.Tables.Clear;
```

20

You can determine if a DataSet contains a table by using the Contains() method, which returns a Boolean value, the IndexOf() method, which returns the table's index, or -1 if the table does not exist.

Working with DataTables

One of the most versatile components that Delphi contained is the TClientDataSet. While originally included for use in Delphi's DataSnap technology, TClientDataSet turned out to be a useful object for manipulating in-memory tables.

Likewise, the typical usage of DataSet is to work on data from a data source that was retrieved through a DataAdapter. However, DataSet and DataTables are also in-memory structures that give you the same level of versatility offered by TClientDataSet. In fact, the DataTable most closely resembles the TClientDataSet. This section focuses on how to use the DataTable.

Defining Columns

To define columns in a DataTable, you can use either the Add() or AddRange() methods of the DataColumnCollection. The following code illustrates using the Add() method:

```
dtEmp   := DataTable.Create('Employee');
dtEmp.Columns.Add('FirstName', TypeOf(String));
dtEmp.Columns.Add('LastName', TypeOf(String));
dtEmp.Columns.Add('Age', TypeOf(Integer));
```

In the preceding examples, you specify the column name and type. Notice that column attributes, such as field length, allow null, read-only, and so on, are not specified. You would have to refer to each column instance to set those values. Another approach would be to create DataColumn instances directly, which would allow you to specify these various attributes and then pass each DataColumn to the Add() method as shown here:

```
dtEmp := DataTable.Create('Employee');
dcFName := DataColumn.Create('FirstName', TypeOf(String));
dcFName.MaxLength := 30;
dcFName.AllowDBNull := False;
dcLName := DataColumn.Create('LastName', TypeOf(String));
dcLName.MaxLength := 30;
dcFName.AllowDBNull := False;

dcAge    := DataColumn.Create('Age', TypeOf(Integer));
dcAge.AllowDBNull := True;
dtEmp.Columns.Add(dcFName);
dtEmp.Columns.Add(dcLName);
dtEmp.Columns.Add(dcAge);
```

Using the AddRange() method, you can pass an array of Columns, which accomplishes the same as the last three lines shown previously:

```
dtEmp.Columns.AddRange([dcFName, dcLName, dcAge]);
```

Some of the more common attributes for a DataColumn are listed in Table 20.1.

TABLE 20.1   DataColumn Attributes

DataColumn Property	Description
AllowDBNull	Specifies whether null values are allowed for this column.
AutoIncrement	Specifies if the column is an auto-incrementing field that occurs when new rows are added to the table.
AutoIncrementSeed	Specifies the initial value for auto-incrementing fields.
AutoIncrementStep	Specifies the value at which auto-incrementing fields are increased.
Caption	Specifies the name of the field as it will appear in data bound controls.
DataType	Specifies the data type for the column.
DefaultValue	Specifies a default value for the column when a new row is added to the table.
MaxLength	Specifies a maximum length for the column.
ReadOnly	Specifies whether the column is read-only.
Unique	Specifies if the values in the column must be unique.

To find whether a column exists in a DataTable, you can use the Contains() method of the DataColumnsCollection. The following code illustrates how to obtain a reference to a DataColumn and then to remove the DataColumn from the DataTable:

```
if dtEmp.Columns.Contains('Age') then
begin
  dcAge := dtEmp.Columns['Age'];
  dtEmp.Columns.Remove(dcAge);
end;
```

An alternative way to write this statement would be

```
dcAge := dtEmp.Columns['Age'];
if Assigned(dcAge ) then
  dtEmp.Columns.Remove(dcAge);
```

You can also specify the name of the column to remove it:

```
dtEmp.Columns.Remove('Age');
```

Defining Primary Keys

A primary key is made up of one or more columns that define a unique row in the DataTable. If a single column is defined as a primary key, that row contains a unique constraint. If multiple rows are defined as primary keys, the combination of such columns must be unique among rows in the DataTable.

The DataTable.PrimaryKey property is defined as an array of DataColumns. To create a primary key on a table, simply assign such an array to this property. This array might contain a single or multiple DataColumn references. The following code illustrates the assignment of a single-column primary key:

```
var
  pkAry: array[0..0] of DataColumn;
...
begin
  dtEmp := DataTable.Create('Employee')
  dcEmpNo := DataColumn.Create('EmpNo', TypeOf(Integer));
```

20

```
dcFName := DataColumn.Create('FirstName', TypeOf(String));
dtEmp.Columns.AddRange([dcFName, dcLName, dcAge]);
pkAry[0] := dcEmpNo;
dtEmp.PrimaryKey := pkAry;
```

Working with Constraints

Constraints enable you to maintain data integrity within the DataSet. As the name implies, constraints impose a restriction on what can be added to a data table. Certain constraints, such as uniqueness and cascading deletes, have been discussed earlier in this chapter, as well as constraints such as disabling a null value or making a column unique. ADO.NET also has the Constraint class from which two derived classes descend: UniqueConstraint and ForeignKeyConstraint.

> UniqueConstraint—Prevents multiple rows within a DataTable from having identical values in the specific columns that make up the unique constraint.

> ForeignKeyConstraint—Establishes a rule on a DataSet based on a parent/child relationship of two DataTables.

Adding a UniqueConstraint Object

The UniqueConstraint object enforces integrity by preventing duplicate values in a single or multiple columns of a DataTable. The following code snippets illustrate how to create a UniqueConstraint on a DataTable:

```
uc := UniqueConstraint.Create('EmpNo', dtEmp.Columns['EmpNo'], True);
dtEmp.Constraints.Add(uc);
```

The first parameter to the UniqueConstraint constructor is the name of the constraint. The second parameter is a reference to the column on which the constraint is to be applied. The final parameter indicates whether this is a primary key constraint. Once the constraint is created, it is added to the DataTable.Constraints collection. To add a unique constraint on multiple columns, simply pass an array of DataColumns as the second parameter to the UniqueConstraint constructor:

```
dcAry[0] := dtEmp.Columns['EmpNo'];
dcAry[1] := dtEmp.Columns['FirstName'];

uc := UniqueConstraint.Create('EmpNo', dcAry, True);
dtEmp.Constraints.Add(uc);
```

Using the ForeignKeyConstraint Object

A ForeignKeyConstraint object enables you to impose referential integrity rules on DataTables within a DataSet. Additionally, it enables you to specify an action to take when the parent of a parent/child relationship has been deleted, updated, or accepted. The following code illustrates how to create and add a ForeignKeyConstraint to a DataTable within a DataSet. For illustrative purposes, this code assumes a parent table, Employee, with a child table, Address.

```
fc := ForeignKeyConstraint.Create('EmpAddress',
  dsCompany.Tables['Employee'].Columns['EmpNo'],
```

```
  dsCompany.Tables['Address'].Columns['EmpNo']);
dsCompany.Tables['Employee'].Constraints.Add(fc);
```

By placing this constraint upon the Employee table, columns within the child table must refer to a valid row in the parent table.

Three properties of the ForeignKeyConstraint each allow you to specify what should happen when changes are made to the parent row. These properties are

- AcceptRejectRule—Specifies an action to take on the constraint when AcceptChanges() is called.

- DeleteRule—Specifies an action to take on the constraint when the parent row is deleted.

- UpdateRule—Specifies the action that occurs when the parent row is updated.

Tables 20.2, 20.3, and 20.4 describe the valid values for the AcceptRejectRule, DeleteRule, and UpdateRule properties, respectively.

TABLE 20.2   AcceptRejectRule Values

Value	Description	Default
none	No action is taken on child rows.	Yes
Cascade	Causes the AcceptChanges() method to be called on the child rows when AcceptChanges() is called on the parent row. This might cause undesirable results, such as setting the RowState flag on child rows to Unchanged and therefore preventing updates to the data source.	

TABLE 20.3   DeleteRule Values

Value	Description	Default
Cascade	Causes child rows to be deleted.	Yes
None	No action is taken. If referential integrity is violated, an exception is raised.	
SetDefault	Sets the child row value to the specified default.	
SetNull	Sets the child row value to NULL if allowed.	

TABLE 20.4   UpdateRule Values

Value	Description	Default
Cascade	When a change is made to the parent linked value, the same change is made to children.	Yes
None	No action is taken on child rows. An exception is raised if referential integrity is violated.	
SetDefault	Sets the child row value to a specified default.	
SetNull	Sets the child row value to NULL if allowed.	

Retrieving Constraints from a Data Source

By using the FillSchema() method to populate a DataSet, UniqueConstraints are automatically created for the DataSet. This is not true when simply using the Fill() method. Listing 20.4 illustrates this point.

LISTING 20.4   Using FillSchema() to Get UniqueContraints

```
1:   program FillConstraints;
2:
3:   {$APPTYPE CONSOLE}
4:
5:   {%DelphiDotNetAssemblyCompiler 'c:\windows\microsoft.net\framework\
➥v1.1.4322\System.Data.dll'}
6:
7:   uses
8:     System.Data,
9:     System.Data.SqlClient,
10:    System.Collections;
11:
12:  const
13:    c_cnstr = 'server=XWING;database=Northwind;Trusted_Connection=Yes';
14:    c_sel_ord = 'select * from orders';
15:
16:  var
17:    cnNW: SqlConnection;
18:    dsNW: DataSet;
19:    daNW: SqlDataAdapter;
20:    cmdOrd: SqlCommand;
21:
22:    enumConst: IEnumerator;
23:    uc: UniqueConstraint;
24:
25:  begin
26:    cnNW := SqlConnection.Create(c_cnstr);
27:    dsNW := DataSet.Create;
28:    cmdOrd := SqlCommand.Create(c_sel_ord, cnNW);
29:    daNW := SqlDataAdapter.Create(cmdOrd);
30:
31:    cnNW.Open;
32:    try
33:      daNW.FillSchema(dsNW, SchemaType.Mapped, 'Orders');
34:      daNW.Fill(dsNW, 'Orders');
35:    finally
36:      cnNW.Close;
37:    end;
38:
39:    enumConst := dsNW.Tables['Orders'].Constraints.GetEnumerator;
40:    while enumConst.MoveNext do
41:    begin
42:      uc := enumConst.Current as UniqueConstraint;
43:      Console.WriteLine('{0}, PrimaryKey: {1}', [uc.Columns[0].ColumnName,
44:        uc.IsPrimaryKey.ToString]);
45:    end;
46:    Console.ReadLine;
47:  end.
```

▶ Find the code on the CD: \Code\Chapter 20\Ex05\.

Note that only UniqueConstraints are created using FillSchema() (line 33).
ForeignKeyConstraints are not automatically created.

Working with DataRelations

DataRelations are similar to ForeignContraints in that they form a link between a parent table and a child table through which referential integrity can be enforced. In fact, when creating DataRelations, they implicitly create the ForeignConstraint instance in the Constraints collection. DataRelations go beyond the capabilities of ForeignConstraints in that they also support navigability between parent and child tables. This is particularly useful with data-bound controls. Through DataRelations, you can also create additional calculated columns from expressions.

Listing 20.5 shows the Create() method of a WinForm application. The form in this application contains the SqlConnection, SqlAdapter, SqlCommand, and DataSet components. This listing illustrates how to create and use DataRelations by retrieving two tables from the Northwind database that are related and by programmatically creating the DataRelation objects for both the parent table (Suppliers) and the child table (Products). Lines 19–25 perform the setup of the data components. The rest of the example deals with creating and using the DataRelation objects.

LISTING 20.5   DataRelations Example

```
1:    constructor TWinForm.Create;
2:    const
3:      c_cnstr = 'server=XWING;database=Northwind;Trusted_Connection=Yes';
4:      c_sel = 'select * from suppliers; select * from products;';
5:    var
6:      pEnum: IEnumerator;
7:      pDr: DataRow;
8:      pCol: DataColumn;
9:      cCol: DataColumn;
10:     dr: DataRelation;
11:     tn: TreeNode;
12:     drAry: array of DataRow;
13:     i: integer;
14:
15:   begin
16:     inherited Create;
17:     InitializeComponent;
18:
19:     SqlConnection1.ConnectionString := c_cnstr;
20:     SqlCommand1.CommandText := c_sel;
21:     SqlCommand1.Connection := SqlConnection1;
22:     SqlDataAdapter1.SelectCommand := SqlCommand1;
23:     SqlDataAdapter1.TableMappings.Add('Table', 'Suppliers');
24:     SqlDataAdapter1.TableMappings.Add('Table1', 'Products');
25:     SqlDataAdapter1.Fill(DataSet1);
26:
27:     pCol := DataSet1.Tables['Suppliers'].Columns['SupplierID'];
28:     cCol := DataSet1.Tables['Products'].Columns['SupplierID'];
29:
30:     dr := DataRelation.Create('Sup_Prod', pCol, cCol);
31:     DataSet1.Relations.Add(dr);
32:
33:     // Create expression columns.
34:     DataSet1.Tables['Products'].Columns.Add('ContactName', TypeOf(String),
35:       'Parent(Sup_Prod).ContactName');
```

20

LISTING 20.5   Continued

```
36:
37:    DataSet1.Tables['Suppliers'].Columns.Add('AvgPrice', TypeOf(Decimal),
38:      'AVG(Child(Sup_Prod).UnitPrice)');
39:
40:    pEnum := DataSet1.Tables['Suppliers'].Rows.GetEnumerator;
41:    while pEnum.MoveNext do
42:    begin
43:      pDr := pEnum.Current as DataRow;
44:      tn := TreeView1.Nodes.Add(pDr['CompanyName'].ToString);
45:      drAry := pDr.GetChildRows(dr);
46:      for i := Low(drAry) to High(drAry) do
47:        tn.Nodes.Add(drAry[i]['ProductName'].ToString)
48:    end;
49:  end;
```

▶ Find the code on the CD: \Code\Chapter 20\Ex06\.

The constructor for the DataRelation class shown in this listing (line 30) takes a string name for the relation, a DataColumn reference to the parent table, and a DataColumn reference to the child table. There are other overloaded constructors that take arrays of columns and an additional Boolean parameter to specify whether to create constraints.

Lines 40–48 enumerate through the parent/child rows and populate a TreeView control. This application shown in Figure 20.4 also has a data-bound grid connected to this dataset. Lines 40–48 are provided to show you how to iterate through the rows based on the DataRelation object. In Line 45, the child rows are retrieved from the parent row. This is done by calling the DataRow.GetChildRow() method, which takes DataRelation as the parameter.

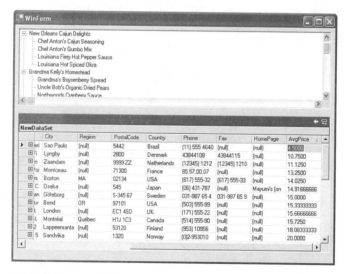

FIGURE 20.4   DataRelation example.

Lines 34–38 illustrate how to create expression-based columns on both the parent and the child DataTables by using the DataRelation. This is done by passing an expression as the third parameter to the `DataColumns.Add()` method. The syntax for this expression is either `Parent(RelationName).ColumnName` or `Child(RelationName).ColumnName`. In lines 34–35, a new column, `'ContactName'`, is added to the child table rows. In Lines 37–38, a new column, `'AvgPrice'`, is added to the parent table. Notice how we are able to pass the expression to an aggregate function (AVG in this case), which will operate on all the child rows.

Manipulating Data—Working with DataRow

Modifications to data contained in a `DataTable` are performed at the row level. The `DataRow` class contains the methods that you would use to perform updates, deletions, and additions to a `DataTable`.

Adding Rows

To add a row to a `DataTable`, first call the `DataTable.NewRow()` method, which returns a `DataRow` instance containing the schema information for that row. Then, assign column values using the retrieved `DataRow` instance. The following code illustrates the use of this function:

```
drCust := dtCust.NewRow;
drCust['CustomerID'] := 'XAWPA';
drCust['CompanyName'] := 'Xapware';
drCust['ContactName'] := 'Xavier Pacheco';
drCust['ContactTitle'] := 'Author';
dtCust.Rows.Add(drCust);
```

In the preceding code, `dtCust` is a `DataTable` instance. `drCust` is a `DataRow` instance. Once the `DataRow` columns have been assigned values, add the `DataRow` instance to the `DataTable` by passing it to the `Rows.Add()` method. Note that when `NewRow()` is invoked, the `DataRow` columns will be populated with NULL or default values, depending on the `DataTable` schema.

▶ Find the code on the CD: `\Code\Chapter 20\Ex07\`.

Modifying Rows

To modify a row, you can simply modify the column values directly as shown here:

```
drCust := dtCust.Rows[0];
drCust['ContactName'] := 'Mickey Mouse';
```

Another way to modify a row is to buffer the changes. Do this by calling `DataRow.BeginEdit()` and `DataRow.EndEdit()`, as shown here:

```
drCust := dtCust.Rows[0];
drCust.BeginEdit;
drCust['ContactName'] := 'Mickey Mouse';
drCust.EndEdit;
```

By calling `BeginEdit()`, constraints and validation rules are prevented from occurring until `EndEdit()` is invoked. Once `EndEdit()` is called, all validation rules are checked against the proposed changes. `BeginEdit()` is implicitly called whenever the contents of a data-bound control are modified. `EndEdit()` is called by the `DataRow.AcceptChanges()` method.

▶ Find the code on the CD: `\Code\Chapter 20\Ex07\`.

20

Deleting Rows

To delete a row, simply call the `DataRow.Delete()` method as shown here:

```
dtCust.Rows[0].Delete;
```

▶ Find the code on the CD: `\Code\Chapter 20\Ex07\`.

Canceling Changes

When `DataRow.BeginEdit()` has been called, you can invoke `DataRow.CancelEdit()`, which discards any buffered modifications.

Examining RowState

`DataSets`, `DataTables`, and `DataRows` are all disconnected objects that are operating on in-memory data. The common case is one in which you will retrieve data from a data source, modify it offline, and then save those changes back to the data store. In order for this to work, it is necessary for the `DataSet` to cache both the type of change and the changes made so that it can know what needs to be sent back to the data source. These changes are cached in the `DataRow`. The type of changes is kept in the `DataRow.RowState` property. Actual changes are handled through row versioning, which is discussed momentarily.

Table 20.5 shows the various `RowState` values.

TABLE 20.5   DataRow.RowState Values

RowState Value	Description
Unchanged	The row has not been modified.
Detached	The row has not been assigned to the `DataTable`.
Added	The row has been added to the `DataTable`, but has not been saved to the data source.
Modified	The row has been modified, and changes have not been posted to the data source.
Deleted	The row has been deleted, and changes have not been posted to the data source.

At any point, you can evaluate the `RowState` property.

Row Versions

Just as ADO.NET needs to know of the type of changes, it also needs to have both the original and changed data. `DataRow` keeps a copy of the original and current data for a row. Column values from each version can be read from the row by specifying one of the `DataRowVersion` enumerations shown in Table 20.6.

TABLE 20.6   DataRowVersion Enumerations

DataRowVersion	Description
Current	The value currently in the column including latest changes but not buffered changes.
Original	The original value of the column when retrieved from the data source.
Proposed	The buffered change in the column.
Default	The `Current` column value if not being edited. The `Proposed` column value if the row is being edited.

The following code illustrates how to check for the existence of a row version and then how to retrieve the specific version in the column index specifier:

```
if drCust.HasVersion(DataRowVersion.Proposed) then
begin
  Console.WriteLine('Proposed Row--');
  Console.WriteLine('    {0} : {1} : {2} : {3}',
    [drCust['CustomerID', DataRowVersion.Proposed],
     drCust['CompanyName', DataRowVersion.Proposed],
     drCust['ContactName', DataRowVersion.Proposed],
     drCust['ContactTitle', DataRowVersion.Proposed]]);
end;
```

▶ Find the code on the CD: \Code\Chapter 20\Ex08\.

Searching, Sorting, and Filtering Data

Being able to manipulate in-memory DataSets is only partially useful. One must be able to also sort, search, and filter data to really add utility to these objects. This section demonstrates the various means by which to accomplish these tasks.

Search by Using the Find() Method

Often, you will need to search for a single record. The DataRowCollection class contains a Find() method that searches on a column or columns that make up a primary key. The following code illustrates how to use the Find() method to retrieve a row-based primary key made up of one column:

```
dt := dsNW.Tables['Customers'];
pkAry[0] := dt.Columns['CustomerID'];
dt.PrimaryKey := pkAry;

dr := dt.Rows.Find('THEBI');
if dr <> nil then
  Console.WriteLine(dr['CompanyName'])
else
  Console.WriteLine('Record not found');
```

In this example, dt is the DataTable for the Customers table in the Northwind database. pkAry is a single dimension array of DataColumn declared as

```
pkAry: array[0..0] of DataColumn;
```

It is used to set up the primary key in the DataTable. Finally, the DataTable.Rows.Find() method is invoked passing a value on which to search.

The Find() method can also be used on a primary key composed of two or more columns. The following code illustrates this:

```
dt := dsNW.Tables['Order Details'];
pkAry2[0] := dt.Columns['OrderID'];
pkAry2[1] := dt.Columns['ProductID'];

dt.PrimaryKey := pkAry2;

dr := dt.Rows.Find([10251, 22]);
if dr <> nil then
  Console.WriteLine('Quantity: {0} : Unit Price {1}',
```

20

```
    [dr['Quantity'], dr['UnitPrice']])
else
  Console.WriteLine('Record not found');
```

▶ Find the code on the CD: \Code\Chapter 20\Ex09\.

In this example, the only difference is that an array is used with more than one item. Also an array of integers is passed to the Find() method. Note that the array parameter for the Find() method might contain heterogeneous data—that is, data of mixed types (a string, an integer, and so on).

Search by Using Select Statements

You might also want to filter information based on some filter criteria. This is possible by using the DataTable.Select() method. This method returns an array of DataRow objects based on the criteria passed to the Select() method. The following code illustrates this by selecting only customers in Germany:

```
dt := dsNW.Tables['Customers'];
drAry := dt.Select('Country = ''Germany''');
for i := Low(drAry) to High(drAry) do
  Console.WriteLine('{0} : {1} : {2} : {3}', drAry[i]['ContactName'],
  drAry[i]['City'], drAry[i]['Region'], drAry[i]['Country']);
```

▶ Find the code on the CD: \Code\Chapter 20\Ex10\.

Adding Sort Criteria

You can add sort criteria to the Select() method similar to how you would sort using SQL. The following code shows how this is done by using an overloaded version of the Select() method. The Select() method takes an additional string parameter that specifies what to sort on and in which order to perform the sort.

```
drAry := dt.Select('Country = ''USA''', 'ContactName DESC');
for i := Low(drAry) to High(drAry) do
  Console.WriteLine('{0} : {1} : {2} : {3}', drAry[i]['ContactName'],
  drAry[i]['City'], drAry[i]['Region'], drAry[i]['Country']);
```

▶ Find the code on the CD: \Code\Chapter 20\Ex10\.

Filtering RowState Using DataViewRowState

In a previous section, the concept of RowState was discussed. That is, as a row is modified, deleted, or added, its state and version is maintained by the DataRow. Another overloaded version of the Select() method takes an additional parameter, which is a DataViewRowState enumeration. The following code shows how this would be used to filter only those records that have been deleted:

```
dt.Rows[0].Delete;
dt.Rows[1].Delete;

dvrs := DataViewRowState.Deleted;
drAry := dt.Select('', '', dvrs);
for i := Low(drAry) to High(drAry) do
  Console.WriteLine(drAry[i]['CompanyName', DataRowVersion.Original]);
```

▶ Find the code on the CD: \Code\Chapter 20\Ex10\.

CHAPTER 21

Working with WinForms—DataViews and Data Binding

IN THIS CHAPTER

- Displaying Data Using DataView and DataViewManager
- Data Binding

Many of the examples around ADO.NET thus far have been focused on working with the ADO.NET classes and therefore have not gone into how you would design user interfaces around such classes. Obviously, it wouldn't be very useful to have this great data manipulation technology without the ability to expose it through a GUI. To effectively build practical user interfaces, you must present the user with the ability to not only view the data, but also to manipulate it easily. ADO.NET relies on two techniques to accomplish this. The first is provided through the DataView and DataViewManager classes. These classes provide a layer between the underlying data and the consumer of that data—be it custom code or data bound controls. They also provide the ability to modify how the data is displayed through sorting, filtering, and searching. The second technique is the method by which data is represented in the various user interface controls. This technique is called data binding. Several components come into play when dealing with data binding. This chapter covers these concepts in detail.

Displaying Data Using DataView and DataViewManager

DataView and DataViewManager are the two classes that enable data binding for visual controls.

> DataView can be used to create customized filters that provide a subset of the underlying DataTable.
>
> DataViewManager maintains default DataView settings for each DataTable.

The DataView Class

A DataView class represents the view of a single DataTable. A good way is to think of DataView as being similar to a VIEW in an SQL database. The DataView allows users to not only sort, filter, and search rows, but also to manipulate them. Therefore, the DataView allows you to specify criteria that determine how the underlying DataTable is represented to the end user. You can also have multiple DataViews applied to a single DataTable. Therefore, one DataView can present the data by sort order, for instance, whereas another can present the data with certain rows filtered out. Both DataViews would be presenting data from the same underlying table.

COMPARING THE DATAVIEW AND DATASOURCE CLASSES

DataView might appear to be similar in nature to the TDataSource component from classic Delphi. The DataView, however, is entirely different. For instance, in classic Delphi, the TDataSet class is most synonymous with the .NET DataTable class. A classic Delphi TDataSet maintained its own cursor. When linking multiple TDataSource objects to a single TDataSet object, scrolling one TDataSource would cause the cursor to change at the TDataSet level. This, in turn, would cause the second TDataSource to also display the scroll. DataViews do not behave this way. You can link two DataView classes to a single DataTable. Because the DataTable does not maintain a cursor (this is handled by the binding classes—more on these later), scrolling one DataView has no impact on the second DataView. This is just one example of many differences between the classic Delphi database architecture and the .NET architecture.

DataViews are a powerful way to customize how data is displayed to the end user without having to go through the SQL layer to retrieve multiple representations of the data.

Table 21.1 lists some key properties of the DataView class.

TABLE 21.1   DataView Properties

Property	Description
AllowDelete	Specifies whether to allow deletion of rows within the DataView.
AllowEdit	Specifies whether to allow editing of values in the DataView.
AllowNew	Specifies whether to allow insertion of rows within the DataView.
AllowDefaultSort	Specifies whether to use the default sort for the DataView.
Count	Returns the number of rows contained by the DataView after filtering has been applied.
DataViewManager	Returns the DataViewManager associated with this DataView. A DataViewManager would be nil for manually created DataSets.
Item	Returns a DataRowView from the underlying table for a specified row index.
RowFilter	Holds the expression used to filter rows against the underlying table.
RowStateFilter	Holds a set of DataViewRowState enumerations to filter against.
Sort	Holds the column and sort order. It also supports sorting on multiple tables by separating sort order statements with commas.
Table	Refers to the DataTable being represented by the DataView.

Table 21.2 lists key methods of the DataView class.

TABLE 21.2   DataView Methods

Method	Description
AddNew()	Adds a DataRowView to the DataView.
CopyTo()	Copies the items contained in the DataView to an Array.
Delete()	Deletes a row from the DataView.
Find()	Finds a row according to a specified sort key value.
FindRows()	Returns an Array of DataRowView objects according to a specified sort key value.

The DataViewManager Class

The DataViewManager class is basically the same in function as the DataView class except that it provides these capabilities across the entire DataSet. You can also use DataViewManager to create a DataView class for a table within the DataSet contained by the DataViewManager. Table 21.3 lists the key properties of the DataViewManager class.

TABLE 21.3   DataViewManager Properties

Property	Description
DataSet	Gets or sets the DataSet that the DataViewManager represents.
DataViewSettings	Returns a DataViewSettingCollection containing the DataViewSetting for each DataTable in the underlying DataSet.

The DataViewManager class contains the CreateDataView() method, which creates an instance of a DataView for a specified table in the DataSet.

Example Projects Using DataView and DataViewManager

The following sections illustrate some techniques using the DataView and DataViewManager classes. You will use many of these techniques in designing your own applications.

Simple DataView Binding

Listing 21.1 illustrates how to bind a user-interface component to a DataView and DataViewManager.

LISTING 21.1   Simple DataView Example

```
1:   const
2:     c_cnstr = 'server=XWING;database=Northwind;Trusted_Connection=Yes';
3:     c_sel = 'SELECT * FROM customers; SELECT * FROM employees; '+
4:              ' SELECT * FROM suppliers';
5:
6:   constructor TWinForm.Create;
7:   begin
8:     inherited Create;
9:     InitializeComponent;
10:    SqlConnection1.ConnectionString := c_cnstr;
11:    SqlCommand1.Connection := SqlConnection1;
12:    SqlCommand1.CommandText := c_sel;
13:    SqlConnection1.Open;
14:    try
```

LISTING 21.1   Continued

```
15:        SqlDataAdapter1.SelectCommand := SqlCommand1;
16:        SqlDataAdapter1.TableMappings.Add('Table', 'Customers');
17:        SqlDataAdapter1.TableMappings.Add('Table1', 'Employees');
18:        SqlDataAdapter1.TableMappings.Add('Table2', 'Suppliers');
19:
20:        SqlDataAdapter1.Fill(DataSet1);
21:        DataGrid1.DataSource := DataSet1;
22:        DataGrid2.DataSource := DataSet1.Tables['Employees'].DefaultView;
23:     finally
24:        SqlConnection1.Close;
25:     end;
26:   end;
27:
28:   procedure TWinForm.RadioButton3_Click(sender: System.Object;
➥e: System.EventArgs);
29:   begin
30:     DataGrid2.DataSource := DataSet1.Tables['Suppliers'].DefaultView;
31:   end;
32:
33:   procedure TWinForm.RadioButton2_Click(sender: System.Object;
➥e: System.EventArgs);
34:   begin
35:     DataGrid2.DataSource := DataSet1.Tables['Customers'].DefaultView;
36:   end;
37:
38:   procedure TWinForm.RadioButton1_Click(sender: System.Object;
➥e: System.EventArgs);
39:   begin
40:     DataGrid2.DataSource := DataSet1.Tables['Employees'].DefaultView;
41:   end;
```

▶ Find the code on the CD: \Code\Chapter 21\Ex01\.

Listing 21.1 is a partial code block from one of the example projects. The purpose of this example is to illustrate how a DataGrid can be bound to both a DataSet and to a DataTable through the DefaultView of a DataTable.

> **NOTE**
>
> Although many of the property assignments shown in this listing can be made at design time in the IDE, they are shown here in code for illustrative purposes.

Much of the code in this constructor (lines 10–20) performs the setup of the DataSet through the DataAdapter. In line 21, DataGrid1 is linked to the DataSet; and in line 22, DataGrid2 is linked to the DefaultView of the Employees table in the DataSet. The DataTable.DefaultView property returns the default DataView for that DataTable. The various event handlers illustrate how DataGrid2 can be linked to different DataViews within the DataSet through a simple assignment. Even though the code to accomplish this is simple as the name of this section would imply, this binding technique is referred to as a complex data bind. This seeming contradiction in terms is discussed later in this chapter.

Figure 21.1 illustrates the resulting form of this application. Note how the first `DataGrid` allows you to examine multiple tables within the `DataSet`, whereas the second `DataGrid` views only a single `DataTable` at a time.

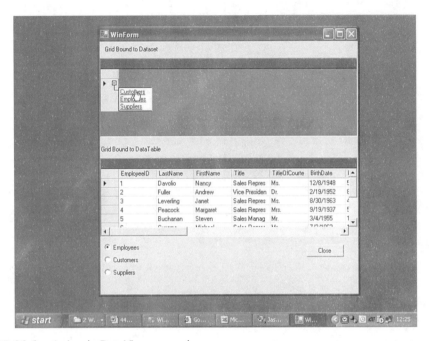

FIGURE 21.1   A simple DataView example.

Filtering a DataView

Filtering a `DataView` to display only a certain set of rows is done by specifying a filter expression to the `DataView.RowFilter` property.

Listing 21.2 shows the setup for the example code used in this section.

LISTING 21.2   Example Showing DataView Filtering

```
1:   const
2:     c_cnstr = 'server=XWING;database=Northwind;Trusted_Connection=Yes';
3:     c_sel = 'SELECT * FROM Customers; SELECT * FROM Employees; '+
4:             'SELECT * FROM Products;';
5:
6:   constructor TWinForm.Create;
7:   begin
8:     inherited Create;
9:     InitializeComponent;
10:    SqlConnection1.ConnectionString := c_cnstr;
11:    SqlCommand1.Connection := SqlConnection1;
12:    SqlCommand1.CommandText := c_sel;
13:    SqlConnection1.Open;
14:    try
15:      SqlDataAdapter1.SelectCommand := SqlCommand1;
```

LISTING 21.2 Continued

```
16:       SqlDataAdapter1.TableMappings.Add('Table', 'Customers');
17:       SqlDataAdapter1.TableMappings.Add('Table1', 'Employees');
18:       SqlDataAdapter1.TableMappings.Add('Table2', 'Products');
19:       SqlDataAdapter1.Fill(DataSet1);
20:       DataGrid1.DataSource := DataSet1.Tables['Customers'];
21:    finally
22:       SqlConnection1.Close;
23:    end;
24:  end;
```

▶ Find the code on the CD: \Code\Chapter 21\Ex02\.

Basically, this code sets up a DataSet with the data from three tables in the Northwind database. In the example project, the WinForm contains a DataGrid to display the data and a Label to display the filter. Several buttons enable the user to select a different filter. Upon doing so, the filter is applied and displayed in the Label with the code similar to the following:

```
lblFilter.Text := System.String.Format('Table: {0}, Filter = {1}',
  ['Customers', DataSet1.Tables['Customers'].DefaultView.RowFilter]);
```

Filtering by Column Values It is possible to perform a column filter similar to that of the WHERE clause in an SQL statement, as shown here:

```
DataSet1.Tables['Customers'].DefaultView.RowFilter := 'Country = ''Mexico'''+
' OR Country = ''Spain''';
```

Filtering Using Comparison Operators Several filter operators can be used against the DataView. Some of the common operators are presented in Table 21.4.

TABLE 21.4 Filter Operators

Operator	Description
+	Performs a numeric addition or a string concatenation.
-	Performs a numeric subtraction.
*	Performs a numeric multiplication.
/	Performs a numeric division.
%	Returns the modulus of a division operation.
AND	Performs AND logic to combine two filter clauses. Example:
	`Filter Country = 'USA' AND State = 'Colorado'`
IN	Short form for the OR logic operator. Example:
	`Column IN ('Spain', 'France', 'China')`
LIKE	Performs pattern matching.
NOT	Reverse logic expression. Example:
	`NOT (Country = 'Canada')`
OR	Logic OR operation. Example:
	`Country = 'USA' OR Country = 'Canada'`

Table 21.5 presents the complete list of comparison operators.

TABLE 21.5   Comparison Operators Using DataViews Filtering

Comparison Operator	Description
=	Performs an equality evaluation.
<	Performs a less than evaluation.
>	Performs a greater than evaluation.
<>	Performs an inequality evaluation.
<=	Performs a less than or equality evaluation.
>=	Performs a greater than or equality evaluation.

An example of row filtering would resemble the following code:

```
DataSet1.Tables['Customers'].DefaultView.RowFilter :=
  'Country = ''Mexico'' OR Country = ''Spain''';
```

This example illustrates the equality operator as well as the OR operator to combine two conditions.

The following code illustrates the use of the IN operator:

```
DataSet1.Tables['Customers'].DefaultView.RowFilter := 'Country IN '+
  '(''Spain'', ''China'', ''France'', ''Mexico'')';
```

To negate the filter, you would use the NOT operator as such:

```
DataSet1.Tables['Customers'].DefaultView.RowFilter :=
'Country NOT IN (''Spain'', ''China'', ''France'', ''Mexico'')';
```

To filter records that contain a column value less than the amount in another column, use the less than (<) operator as illustrated here:

```
DataSet1.Tables['Products'].DefaultView.RowFilter :=
  'UnitsInStock < UnitsOnOrder';
```

The following code snippet illustrates how to filter on items between certain values by using the greater than (>), less than (<), and the logical AND operators:

```
DataSet1.Tables['Products'].DefaultView.RowFilter :=
  'UnitPrice > 50 AND UnitPrice < 100';
```

The following code illustrates how to use the mathematical operators within the filter expression:

```
DataSet1.Tables['Products'].DefaultView.RowFilter :=
  'UnitsOnOrder * UnitPrice > 500';
```

To clear a filter, simply assign an empty string to the RowFilter property:

```
DataSet1.Tables['Customers'].DefaultView.RowFilter := '';
```

Filtering Using the LIKE Pattern Operator   The pattern matching filter in ADO.NET supports using the (%) and (*) characters as a wildcard for one or more characters at the beginning or ending of a pattern of characters. The following two code examples illustrate how it is used. The code

```
DataSet1.Tables['Customers'].DefaultView.RowFilter :=
 'Country LIKE ''F%''';
```

filters on all countries that begin with the character 'F'. This, for example, would return the countries France and Finland. The following example searches on the specified characters within a string:

```
DataSet1.Tables['Customers'].DefaultView.RowFilter :=
 'ContactName LIKE ''%ta%''';
```

Unlike the SQL "LIKE" keyword, the ADO.NET LIKE keyword does not support the single variable character or range searching.

▶ Find the code on the CD: \Code\Chapter 21\Ex03\.

Functions in Filtering   ADO.NET also supports certain SQL functions in the filter expression. For instance, to filter based on the length of a column value, you can use the LEN() function as shown here:

```
DataSet1.Tables['Employees'].DefaultView.RowFilter := 'Len(PhotoPath) <= 35';
```

The SubString() function returns the substring of a specified string, whereas the second parameter is a 1-based starting index and the third parameter is the length of the string to return. The following code illustrates this technique:

```
DataSet1.Tables['Customers'].DefaultView.RowFilter :=
 'SubString(Country, 1, 2) = ''fr''';
```

The IFF() function is a boolean evaluator that can return one of two results. This is illustrated in the following code:

```
DataSet1.Tables['Products'].DefaultView.RowFilter :=
  'IIF(UnitPrice <= 50, UnitsInStock < 10, UnitsInStock >=10)';
```

The preceding code will result in rows with less than 10 units in stock being displayed if the UnitPrice is less than or equal to 50. Otherwise, the rows with 10 or more UnitsInStock are returned.

▶ See the example on the CD: \Code\Chapter 21\Ex04\.

Filtering Based on DataViewRowState   The DataView.RowStateFilter property can hold one or a combination of the enumeration values presented in Table 21.6. These values enable you to filter rows based on their state.

TABLE 21.6   DataViewRowState Enumeration Values

Value	Description
Added	Displays newly added rows.
CurrentRows	Displays current rows, including those that are unchanged, new, and modified.
Deleted	Displays deleted rows.
ModifiedCurrent	A currently modified row with the original row existing in the DataSet.
ModifiedOriginal	The original row that has since been modified and therefore is available as ModifiedCurrent.

TABLE 21.6   Continued

Value	Description
None	No DataViewRowState filter is applied.
OriginalRows	Displays unchanged and deleted rows.
Unchanged	Displays unchanged rows.

The following code illustrates how you would set a filter on the DataView.RowStateFilter property:

```
DataSet1.Tables['Customers'].DefaultView.RowStateFilter := DataSet1.Tables['Customers'].Default-
View.RowStateFilter or
DataViewRowState.Added;
```

▶ See the example on the CD: \Code\Chapter 21\Ex05\.

Note how the DataViewRowState.Added enumeration is logically ored with the value currently assigned to this property.

To illustrate further how you might use the RowStateFilter, examine Listing 21.3, which shows how you would use a DataView to remove records from a DataTable.

LISTING 21.3   RowStateFilter Example

```
1:   const
2:     c_cnstr = 'server=XWING;database=Northwind;Trusted_Connection=Yes';
3:     c_sel = 'SELECT * FROM Customers';
4:
5:   constructor TWinForm.Create;
6:   begin
7:     inherited Create;
8:     InitializeComponent;
9:     SqlConnection1.ConnectionString := c_cnstr;
10:    SqlCommand1.Connection := SqlConnection1;
11:    SqlCommand1.CommandText := c_sel;
12:    SqlConnection1.Open;
13:    try
14:      SqlDataAdapter1.SelectCommand := SqlCommand1;
15:
16:      SqlDataAdapter1.TableMappings.Add('Table', 'Customers');
17:      SqlDataAdapter1.Fill(DataSet1);
18:      DataGrid1.DataSource := DataSet1.Tables['Customers'].DefaultView;
19:    finally
20:      SqlConnection1.Close;
21:    end;
22:  end;
23:
24:  procedure TWinForm.Button1_Click(sender: System.Object;
25:    e: System.EventArgs);
26:  var
27:    dvEnum: IEnumerator;
28:    drvCustomers: DataRowView;
29:  begin
30:    DataView1.Table := DataSet1.Tables['Customers'];
```

LISTING 21.3   Continued

```
31:    DataView1.RowFilter := 'Country = ''USA''';
32:    // Must set RowStateFilter to view deleted rows also.
33:    DataView1.RowStateFilter := DataViewRowState.Deleted or
34:      DataViewRowState.CurrentRows;
35:    dvEnum := DataView1.GetEnumerator;
36:
37:    while dvEnum.MoveNext do
38:    begin
39:      drvCustomers := dvEnum.Current as DataRowView;
40:      drvCustomers.Delete;
41:    end;
42:  end;
```

▶ See the example on the CD: \Code\Chapter 21\Ex06\.

Listing 21.3 is a partial listing of the application that demonstrates this technique. The setup in the constructor is similar to that of previous examples. Notice in line 18 that that DataGrid1 is linked to the default DataView for the Customers table in the DataSet.

The Button1_Click() event handler obtains a separate DataView to the Customer table from the DataSet. This DataView is not linked to any user interface control like a DataGrid. Instead, a filter is applied to list only those customers in the country, 'USA' (line 31). The purpose of this event handler is to use this DataView to remove its records from the DataTable. A DataGrid linked to the default DataView will display only current rows or those rows with the DataViewRowState of CurrentRows. Therefore, when the second DataView removes its records, the DataGrid1 will no longer display any records whose Country column contains 'USA'. This illustrates how two views can both have separate visibility into a single DataTable, yet modifications to the DataTable are realized by both DataViews.

Support for Aggregate Functions   The DataView.RowFilter property also supports aggregate functions, allowing you to filter rows based on criteria from child rows. To accomplish this, the DataSet must have a DataRelation object defining the parent/child relationship. Listing 21.4 illustrates this technique.

LISTING 21.4   Aggregate Function Example

```
1:    const
2:      c_cnstr = 'server=XWING;database=Northwind;Trusted_Connection=Yes';
3:      c_sel = 'SELECT * FROM Suppliers; SELECT * FROM Products;';
4:
5:    constructor TWinForm.Create;
6:    begin
7:      inherited Create;
8:      InitializeComponent;
9:      SqlConnection1.ConnectionString := c_cnstr;
10:     SqlCommand1.Connection := SqlConnection1;
11:     SqlCommand1.CommandText := c_sel;
12:     SqlConnection1.Open;
13:     try
14:       SqlDataAdapter1.SelectCommand := SqlCommand1;
15:
```

LISTING 21.4   Continued

```
16:     SqlDataAdapter1.TableMappings.Add('Table', 'Suppliers');
17:     SqlDataAdapter1.TableMappings.Add('Table1', 'Products');
18:     SqlDataAdapter1.Fill(DataSet1);
19:
20:     DataSet1.Relations.Add('SupProd',
21:       DataSet1.Tables['Suppliers'].Columns['SupplierID'],
22:       DataSet1.Tables['Products'].Columns['SupplierID']);
23:
24:     DataSet1.Tables['Suppliers'].DefaultView.RowFilter :=
25:       'Count(Child(SupProd).SupplierID) <= 10';
26:
27:     DataGrid1.DataSource := DataSet1.Tables['Products'];
28:   finally
29:     SqlConnection1.Close;
30:   end;
31: end;
```

▶ See the example on the CD: \Code\Chapter 21\Ex07\.

Listing 21.4 is partial code from the CD example. This example retrieves data from two tables of the Northwind database. The Suppliers table is the parent table to the Products table. In this example, we use the Count() function to retrieve a list of suppliers who have 10 or fewer supplies in the Products table.

Lines 20–22 create and add the DataRelation between the Suppliers and Products table. This DataRelation is named SupProd. Lines 24–25 assign the filter expression to the DataView.RowFilter property.

When using aggregate functions, their syntax within the filter expression is Child(RelationName).ChildColumnName. In addition, in simple filters (with no aggregation function being used), expressions of the form Parent(RelationName).ParentColumnName can be used to filter on child tables with specific constraints on the parent's column values.

DataView Sorting

To sort a DataView, simply assign the ColumnName SortOrder pair to the DataView.Sort property. For example, the following code specifies to sort the Customers table from the Northwind database by the ContactName in ascending order:

```
FdvContactName := DataView.Create(DataSet1.Tables['Customers']);
FdvContactName.Sort := 'ContactName ASC';
```

▶ See the entire example on the CD: \Code\Chapter 21\Ex08\.

Also, multiple columns are supported for the Sort property.

DataView Searching

To search on a DataView, you must first establish a sort order. You can then use either the DataView.Find() or DataView.FindRows() methods to conduct your search.

The Find() function returns an index of the row if located. Otherwise, it returns -1. FindRows() returns an Array of DataRowView objects or an empty array.

The following code is a partial listing of the CD example, which uses the `Find()` function to search for the contents of a `TextBox` control:

```
var
  RowIdx: Integer;
  RowBinding: System.Windows.Forms.BindingContext;
begin
  RowIdx := DataSet1.Tables['Customers'].DefaultView.Find(TextBox1.Text);
  if RowIdx = -1 then
    MessageBox.Show('Not found')
  else begin
    RowBinding := Self.BindingContext;
    RowBinding[DataSet1.Tables['Customers']].Position := RowIdx;
  end;
```

▶ See the entire example on the CD: \Code\Chapter 21\Ex09\.

In this example if the row is found, the `DataView`'s current row is positioned to that row. This is done through the form's `BindingContext` object, which is discussed later in this chapter.

The following code illustrates how to use the `FindRows()` method on the same `DataView`:

```
var
  drvArray: Array of DataRowView;
  i: integer;
begin
  drvArray := DataSet1.Tables['Customers'].DefaultView.FindRows(TextBox1.Text);
  if High(drvArray) = 0 then
    MessageBox.Show('Not found')
  else
    for i := Low(drvArray) to High(drvArray) do
      MessageBox.Show(drvArray[i]['ContactName'].ToString);
```

In this example, the `FindRows()` method will return the array of `DataRowView` objects. If the array is not empty, the `ContactName` column value for each matching row is displayed.

▶ See the entire example on the CD: \Code\Chapter 21\Ex09\.

Simulating a Join

By using the `DataRelation` class, it is possible to simulate an SQL join. Listing 21.5 illustrates how this is done.

LISTING 21.5   Join Example

```
1:   const
2:     c_cnstr = 'server=XWING;database=Northwind;Trusted_Connection=Yes';
3:     c_sel = 'SELECT * FROM EmployeeTerritories; SELECT * FROM Employees;';
4:
5:   constructor TWinForm.Create;
6:   begin
7:     inherited Create;
8:     InitializeComponent;
9:     SqlConnection1.ConnectionString := c_cnstr;
```

LISTING 21.5   Continued

```
10:    SqlCommand1.Connection := SqlConnection1;
11:    SqlCommand1.CommandText := c_sel;
12:    SqlConnection1.Open;
13:    try
14:      SqlDataAdapter1.SelectCommand := SqlCommand1;
15:
16:      SqlDataAdapter1.TableMappings.Add('Table', 'EmployeeTerritories');
17:      SqlDataAdapter1.TableMappings.Add('Table1', 'Employees');
18:      SqlDataAdapter1.Fill(DataSet1);
19:
20:      DataSet1.Relations.Add('TerritoryEmp',
21:        DataSet1.Tables['Employees'].Columns['EmployeeID'],
22:        DataSet1.Tables['EmployeeTerritories'].Columns['EmployeeID']);
23:
24:      DataSet1.Tables['EmployeeTerritories'].Columns.Add('EmployeeName',
25:        TypeOf(System.String),
26:        'Parent(TerritoryEmp).FirstName + '' ''+
➥Parent(TerritoryEmp).LastName');
27:
28:      DataGrid1.DataSource := DataSet1.Tables['EmployeeTerritories'];
29:    finally
30:      SqlConnection1.Close;
31:    end;
32:  end;
```

▶ See the entire example on the CD: \Code\Chapter 21\Ex10\.

Using the same Northwind database, we retrieve the Employees and EmployeeTerritories tables into the DataSet. Then, we establish a DataRelation with the Employees table being the parent to the EmployeeTerritories table linked by the EmployeeID column (lines 20–22). This DataRelation is named TerritoryEmp.

Finally, to simulate the JOIN, we create a column in the child table (EmployeeTerritories). This example uses the overloaded Add() method of the DataTable.Columns property, which takes an expression as the last parameter. This expression is similar in syntax to the aggregate expression syntax (Parent(RelationName).ParentColumnName). In this example, the expression is a concatenation of the FirstName and LastName columns in the parent Employees table.

Data Binding

Data binding is having the ability to synchronize user interface controls with the underlying data. Data binding is not only for database related classes. Developers can bind controls to any data source whether it is a DataSet or some other data container such as a Collection or an Array. This chapter focuses on WinForm's binding with Delphi for .NET. WebForms are covered in Part V, "Internet Development with ASP.NET."

The Data Binding Interfaces

In previous versions of Delphi, the data binding equivalent technology was called "data aware," and under this scheme you had data aware controls. Often, component vendors would provide two versions of their controls—one that was data aware and one that was not. Additionally, the data awareness of a control was linked to only database-related classes, for the most part.

In .NET, data awareness happens as a result of the control being bound to a data source in a decoupled manner. For instance, classic Delphi data aware controls had DataSource and Field properties that connected them to a data source and the specific field within that data source. In .NET, controls are bound with data sources through classes that sit between them and establish the data connection and synchronization. For a control to be bindable, it must implement the interfaces that enable this capability. These interfaces are listed in Table 21.7.

TABLE 21.7   Data Binding Interfaces

Interface	Description
Ilist	IList is implemented by classes such as the Array and Collection. It provides support to bind a control's property to a list of homogeneous data.
IbindingList	Provides notification support. Notifications occur when the list content or a list element value changes. This is implemented by classes such as the DataView and DataViewManager.
IEditableObject	Provides a simple, transaction-like update control to the underlying data. Changes within the bound control can be rolled back or committed to the object representing the data.
IDataErrorInfo	Provides support to offer custom error information to which the user interface can bind.

WinForms also contain their own set of classes specifically designed to work within this binding scheme. Examples throughout this chapter illustrate the WinForm binding classes.

Simple Versus Complex Binding

There are basically two types of binding—simple and complex.

With simple binding, a control that contains a single value, such as the TextBox control, can be bound to a single value from the data source. For instance, you can bind the Text property of the TextBox control to a column value from a DataSet.

With complex binding, the control contains multiple values. The DataGrid is the typical control you will see using this scheme. Other examples are ListBox and ComboBox.

WinForm Data Binding Classes

Several classes interact to provide this binding capability. These classes are depicted in Figure 21.2.

Every WinForm (and Control descendant) has a BindingContext object. The BindingContext object manages a collection of BindingManagerBase objects. The BindingManagerBase class (not shown in the figure) is actually an abstract class. It has two descendants, which are the CurrencyManager and PropertyManager. Figure 21.2 shows only the CurrencyManager because that is the class we will be dealing with in this chapter.

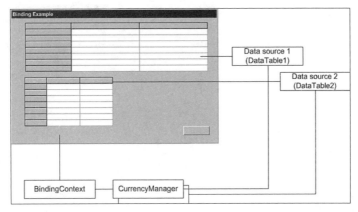

FIGURE 21.2   Binding classes.

There is one CurrencyManager per data source on a Windows Form. The CurrencyManager is what manages the position (current row) within the data source list. This is similar to the curser concept with classic Delphi TDataSet classes. In ADO.NET, the DataSet does not maintain cursors, and, therefore, the current row position is handled by the CurrencyManager.

When multiple controls are bound to a single data source, there will be one CurrencyManager. If some controls are bound to a data source and other controls are bound to a separate data source (as is the case with a master detail setup), there will be two CurrencyManagers present.

You use the BindingContext to create a new CurrencyManager or to retrieve one of the existing CurrencyManagers.

> **NOTE**
>
> Typically, you will be using the Windows Form's BindingContext. However, every control that can be a container (a descendant of Control) has its own BindingContext object. Therefore, it is possible to create a Windows Form with BindingContext objects specific to container controls on the form.

Building Data Bound Windows Forms

The following examples illustrate the various techniques you can use with the capabilities of data binding.

Binding Lists

Certain list controls (descendants of the ListControl class), such as the ListBox and ComboBox, have the capability to bind to a single column from a DataView and to display the list of values in that column. These controls provide read-only display of these values. Listing 21.6 illustrates how you would bind the contents of a column in the Customers table to a ListBox control.

LISTING 21.6   ListBox Binding

```
1:    const
2:      c_cnstr = 'server=XWING;database=Northwind;Trusted_Connection=Yes';
3:      c_sel = 'SELECT * FROM Customers';
4:
5:    constructor TWinForm.Create;
6:    begin
7:      inherited Create;
8:      InitializeComponent;
9:      SqlConnection1.ConnectionString := c_cnstr;
10:     SqlCommand1.Connection := SqlConnection1;
11:     SqlCommand1.CommandText := c_sel;
12:     SqlConnection1.Open;
13:     try
14:       SqlDataAdapter1.SelectCommand := SqlCommand1;
15:
16:       SqlDataAdapter1.TableMappings.Add('Table', 'Customers');
17:       SqlDataAdapter1.Fill(DataSet1);
18:       ListBox1.DataSource    := DataSet1.Tables['Customers'].DefaultView;
19:       ListBox1.DisplayMember := 'ContactName';
20:       ListBox1.ValueMember   := 'CustomerID';
21:
22:       DataGrid1.DataSource := DataSet1.Tables['Customers'].DefaultView;
23:     finally
24:       SqlConnection1.Close;
25:     end;
26:   end;
```

▶ See the entire example on the CD: \Code\Chapter 21\Ex11\.

Lines 18–20 are where the binding actually occurs. First, the DataSource property of the ListBox is assigned a DataView—in this case, the DefaultView from the Customers DataTable. The DisplayMember property is than assigned the name of the column it is to display. ListControls can also store an additional value from the data source that can be used as the selected value. This is established through the ValueMember property. In Listing 21.6, ValueMember is assigned the CustomerID column. If the control being used were a ComboBox, it could be used to establish a lookup list.

Simple, Single Value Binding

User interface controls descend from the Control class. Control contains a ControlBindingsCollection property called DataBindings. The DataBindings collection contains a list of Binding objects. The Binding class is that which maintains the link of a Control's property to a value from a data source.

It is possible to bind several properties of a single Control to different values from the data source. For instance, you can bind the Text property of a TextBox control to a value such as a CustomerName field from a DataView. At the same time, you can bind the same TextBox's Tag property to the CustomerID field. Given this scenario, the TextBox.DataBindings collection would contain two Binding objects.

To add a binding to a Control, you would create an instance of the Binding class and pass that to the Control's DataBindings.Add() method as shown here:

```
bnding := Binding.Create('Text', DataSet1.Tables['Customers'].DefaultView,
  'CompanyName');
txtbxCompanyName.DataBindings.Add(bnding);
```

The first parameter of the `Binding.Create()` constructor is the name of the property to
which you want the value to appear. The second parameter is the data source, and the
third parameter is the name of the data source value to be assigned to the property value.
Alternatively, you can simply pass the same parameters to the overloaded
`DataBindings.Add()` method, which will internally create the `Binding` object instance:

```
txtbxCompanyName.DataBindings.Add('Text',
  DataSet1.Tables['Customers'].DefaultView, 'CompanyName');
```

▶ See the entire example on the CD: \Code\Chapter 21\Ex12\.

Binding Navigation and Event Handling

The previous section discusses simple, single value control binding. This section extends
this example and provides the capability to programmatically navigate through the `DataView`
using the `CurrencyManager` class. Recall that the `CurrencyManager`, a `BindingManagerBase` descendant, is what manages the position of the `DataView`. Basically, this is the cursor position.
Listing 21.7 demonstrates how to programmatically reposition the current row of a `DataView`.
It also illustrates how to add one of four event handlers of the `CurrencyManager` object.

LISTING 21.7 Navigation and Event Handling Example

```
1:   const
2:     c_cnstr = 'server=XWING;database=Northwind;Trusted_Connection=Yes';
3:     c_sel = 'SELECT * FROM Customers';
4:
5:   constructor TWinForm.Create;
6:   var
7:     dv: DataView;
8:   begin
9:     inherited Create;
10:    InitializeComponent;
11:    SqlConnection1.ConnectionString := c_cnstr;
12:    SqlCommand1.Connection := SqlConnection1;
13:    SqlCommand1.CommandText := c_sel;
14:    SqlConnection1.Open;
15:    try
16:      SqlDataAdapter1.SelectCommand := SqlCommand1;
17:
18:      SqlDataAdapter1.TableMappings.Add('Table', 'Customers');
19:      SqlDataAdapter1.Fill(DataSet1);
20:      DataGrid1.DataSource := DataSet1.Tables['Customers'].DefaultView;
21:      dv := DataSet1.Tables['Customers'].DefaultView;
22:
23:      // Bind the individual controls
24:      lblCustomerID.DataBindings.Add('Text', dv, 'CustomerID');
25:      txtbxCompanyName.DataBindings.Add('Text', dv, 'CompanyName');
26:      txtbxContactName.DataBindings.Add('Text', dv, 'ContactName');
27:      txtbxContactTitle.DataBindings.Add('Text', dv, 'ContactTitle');
28:      txtbxAddress.DataBindings.Add('Text', dv, 'Address');
```

LISTING 21.7   Continued

```
29:       txtbxCity.DataBindings.Add('Text', dv, 'City');
30:       txtbxCountry.DataBindings.Add('Text', dv, 'Country');
31:
32:       FCurrencyMgr := BindingContext[DataGrid1.DataSource] as
33:         CurrencyManager;
34:       Include(FCurrencyMgr.PositionChanged, FCurrency_PositionChanged);
35:
36:     finally
37:       SqlConnection1.Close;
38:     end;
39:  end;
40:
41:  procedure TWinForm.btnPrior_Click(sender: System.Object;
42:     e: System.EventArgs);
43:  begin
44:     FCurrencyMgr.Position := FCurrencyMgr.Position - 1;
45:  end;
46:
47:  procedure TWinForm.btnNext_Click(sender: System.Object;
48:     e: System.EventArgs);
49:  begin
50:     FCurrencyMgr.Position := FCurrencyMgr.Position + 1;
51:  end;
52:
53:  procedure TWinForm.btnLast_Click(sender: System.Object;
54:     e: System.EventArgs);
55:  begin
56:     FCurrencyMgr.Position := FCurrencyMgr.Count - 1;
57:  end;
58:
59:  procedure TWinForm.btnFirst_Click(sender: System.Object;
60:     e: System.EventArgs);
61:  begin
62:     FCurrencyMgr.Position := 0;
63:  end;
64:
65:  procedure TWinForm.Button1_Click(sender: System.Object;
66:     e: System.EventArgs);
67:  begin
68:     Close;
69:  end;
70:
71:  procedure TWinForm.FCurrency_PositionChanged(sender: TObject;
72:     e: System.EventArgs);
73:  begin
74:     btnFirst.Enabled := FCurrencyMgr.Position > 0;
75:     btnPrior.Enabled := FCurrencyMgr.Position > 0;
76:     btnLast.Enabled  := FCurrencyMgr.Position < FCurrencyMgr.Count - 1;
77:     btnNext.Enabled  := FCurrencyMgr.Position < FCurrencyMgr.Count - 1;
78:  end;
```

▶ See the entire example on the CD: \Code\Chapter 21\Ex13\.

Figure 21.3 is the form for this application. It contains a number of `TextBox` controls and some buttons whose events will handle navigation.

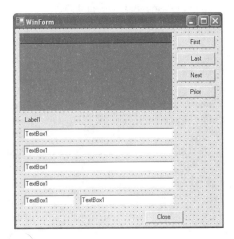

FIGURE 21.3   Navigation example form.

The `Create()` constructor, similar to previous examples, sets up the connection and populates the `DataSet`. It also establishes the binding with the individual controls. The form defines a field, `FCurrencyMgr`, which is of the type `CurrencyManager`. The `CurrencyManager` for this form is obtained from the form's `BindingContext` in line 32. Note how this can be obtained from the `DataSource` property of one of the controls. Line 34 assigns an event handler to the `FCurrencyMgr.PositionChanged` event.

Each of the `Button` event handlers changes the `FCurrencyMgr.Position` property accordingly. Each time this occurs, the `PositionChanged` event handler is invoked. The code in this event handler (lines 74–77) enables/disables the buttons based on the `FCurrencyMgr.Position` value.

The `CurrencyManager` has four events, all listed in Table 21.8.

TABLE 21.8   CurrencyManager Events

Event	Description
CurrentChanged	Invoked when the value of a bound control has changed.
ItemChanged	Invoked when the current item has been modified.
MetaDataChanged	Invoked when the metadata has been modified.
PositionChanged	Invoked when the position of the `CurrencyManager` is moved.

Modifying Data

Although not typical, you can modify data through the `CurrencyManager` and then have that data committed to the underlying `DataSet`. Normally, modifications are handled through the `DataTable` or `DataRowView` classes. Nevertheless, a technique illustrating modifications handled through the `CurrencyManager` is shown here. Table 21.9 lists the various methods of the `CurrencyManager` class.

TABLE 21.9   CurrencyManager Methods

Method	Description
AddNew()	Adds an item to the underlying list.
CancelCurrentEdit()	Cancels an edit operation and aborts any modifications.
EndCurrentEdit()	Ends an edit operation and commits modifications to the underlying list.
Refresh()	Repopulates bound controls.
RemoveAt()	Removes the item from the specified parameter index.
ResumeBinding()	Resumes binding and validation previously suspended from the SuspendBinding() call.
SuspendBinding()	Suspends binding and validation until ResumeBinding() re-enables it.

When modifying data through the CurrencyManager class, you must make sure that the user performs the proper sequential steps. For instance, once a user starts typing data into a control, EndCurrentEdit() or CancelCurrentEdit() must be called to either commit or cancel the changes made. This is not handled automatically. Therefore, a way to do this is to explicitly force the user to put the form into "edit mode" before changes can be made within the controls. Likewise, the user must save or cancel these changes for them to be committed to the underlying list. Listing 21.8 is partial code from the CD example that illustrates this technique.

LISTING 21.8   Modification Example

```
1:   const
2:     c_cnstr = 'server=XWING;database=Northwind;Trusted_Connection=Yes';
3:     c_sel = 'SELECT * FROM Customers';
4:
5:   constructor TWinForm.Create;
6:   var
7:     dv: DataView;
8:   begin
9:     inherited Create;
10:    InitializeComponent;
11:    SqlConnection1.ConnectionString := c_cnstr;
12:    SqlCommand1.Connection := SqlConnection1;
13:    SqlCommand1.CommandText := c_sel;
14:    SqlConnection1.Open;
15:    try
16:      SqlDataAdapter1.SelectCommand := SqlCommand1;
17:      SqlDataAdapter1.TableMappings.Add('Table', 'Customers');
18:      SqlDataAdapter1.Fill(DataSet1);
19:      DataGrid1.DataSource := DataSet1.Tables['Customers'].DefaultView;
20:      dv := DataSet1.Tables['Customers'].DefaultView;
21:
22:      // Bind the individual controls
23:      lblCustomerID.DataBindings.Add('Text', dv, 'CustomerID');
24:      txtbxCompanyName.DataBindings.Add('Text', dv, 'CompanyName');
25:      txtbxContactName.DataBindings.Add('Text', dv, 'ContactName');
26:      txtbxContactTitle.DataBindings.Add('Text', dv, 'ContactTitle');
27:      txtbxAddress.DataBindings.Add('Text', dv, 'Address');
28:      txtbxCity.DataBindings.Add('Text', dv, 'City');
29:      txtbxCountry.DataBindings.Add('Text', dv, 'Country');
```

LISTING 21.8   Continued

```
30:
31:       FCurrencyMgr := BindingContext[DataGrid1.DataSource] as
32:         CurrencyManager;
33:       Include(FCurrencyMgr.PositionChanged, FCurrency_PositionChanged);
34:       SetMode(dmBrowse);
35:
36:    finally
37:      SqlConnection1.Close;
38:    end;
39:  end;
40:
41:  procedure TWinForm.btnDelete_Click(sender: System.Object;
42:    e: System.EventArgs);
43:  begin
44:    FCurrencyMgr.RemoveAt(FCurrencyMgr.Position);
45:  end;
46:
47:  procedure TWinForm.btnSave_Click(sender: System.Object;
48:    e: System.EventArgs);
49:  begin
50:    if FDataMode = dmEdit then
51:      FCurrencyMgr.EndCurrentEdit;
52:
53:    SetMode(dmBrowse);
54:  end;
55:
56:  procedure TWinForm.btnEdit_Click(sender: System.Object;
57:    e: System.EventArgs);
58:  begin
59:    SetMode(dmEdit);
60:  end;
61:
62:  procedure TWinForm.btnCancel_Click(sender: System.Object;
63:    e: System.EventArgs);
64:  begin
65:    if FDataMode = dmAdd then
66:      FCurrencyMgr.RemoveAt(FCurrencyMgr.Position)
67:    else
68:      FCurrencyMgr.CancelCurrentEdit;
69:
70:    SetMode(dmBrowse);
71:  end;
72:
73:  procedure TWinForm.btnAdd_Click(sender: System.Object;
74:    e: System.EventArgs);
75:  begin
76:    FCurrencyMgr.AddNew;
77:    SetMode(dmAdd);
78:  end;
79:
80:  procedure TWinForm.SetMode(aDataMode: TDataMode);
81:  var
82:    i: integer;
```

LISTING 21.8   Continued

```
83:  begin
84:    FDataMode := aDataMode;
85:    btnAdd.Enabled    := aDataMode = dmBrowse;
86:    btnEdit.Enabled   := aDataMode = dmBrowse;
87:    btnDelete.Enabled := aDataMode = dmBrowse;
88:    btnCancel.Enabled := aDataMode <> dmBrowse;
89:    btnSave.Enabled   := aDataMode <> dmBrowse;
90:
91:    for i := 0 to Controls.Count - 1 do
92:      if Controls.Item[i] is System.Windows.Forms.TextBox then
93:         (Controls[i] as TextBox).Readonly := aDataMode = dmBrowse;
94:
95:    DataGrid1.ReadOnly := aDataMode = dmBrowse;
96:  end;
97:
98:  procedure TWinForm.FCurrency_PositionChanged(sender: TObject;
99:    e: System.EventArgs);
100: begin
101:   if (FDataMode = dmAdd) or (FDataMode = dmEdit) then
102:     SetMode(dmBrowse);
103: end;
```

▶ See the entire example on the CD: `\Code\Chapter 21\Ex14\`.

The key to this example is the SetMode() method (lines 80–96). This method first enables or disables buttons on the form based on the value of a TDataMode parameter. TDataMode is defined as

```
TDataMode = (dmBrowse, dmEdit, dmAdd);
```

Next, SetMode() iterates through the various TextBox controls and sets their ReadOnly property to True if the form is in browse mode, indicating that the user has not explicitly set the form into add or edit mode. Therefore, the user will not be able to type in to the controls until explicitly setting the appropriate mode.

The other event handlers simply invoke the respective methods of the CurrencyManager member.

Admittedly, this approach, although used in many applications, is not the most efficient for the end user. Alternatively, you could provide a way to automatically set the form into edit mode by providing an event handler for the CurrentChanged event. This event could force the form into edit mode. Then, you will only have to ensure that the user either commits or aborts his modifications.

Formatting and Parsing Through the Binding Class

Recall that the Binding class is that which holds the binding between a control's property and a data source value. This class also contains two events—Format and Parse.

Consider that data in the originating data source might not be the friendliest format to display to the end user. Likewise, the way that the end users enter data in to a control might be formatted incorrectly for the data source. These two events enable you to convert the data to the format required at both ends of the binding.

> The Format event gives you the opportunity to format the data from the data source before it is displayed in the bound control.

> The Parse event gives you the opportunity to modify the data as entered by the end user before it gets stored in the data source.

Listing 21.9 illustrates this technique used for a typical case. Monetary values are stored in the data source as the Decimal type. However, the display and even entry of the data might take the form of a Currency string.

LISTING 21.9   Format and Parse Example

```
1:  const
2:    c_cnstr = 'server=XWING;database=Northwind;Trusted_Connection=Yes';
3:    c_sel = 'SELECT ProductName, UnitPrice FROM Products';
4:
5:  constructor TWinForm.Create;
6:  var
7:    bndUnitPrice: Binding;
8:  begin
9:    inherited Create;
10:   InitializeComponent;
11:   SqlConnection1.ConnectionString := c_cnstr;
12:   SqlCommand1.Connection := SqlConnection1;
13:   SqlCommand1.CommandText := c_sel;
14:   SqlConnection1.Open;
15:   try
16:     SqlDataAdapter1.SelectCommand := SqlCommand1;
17:
18:     SqlDataAdapter1.TableMappings.Add('Table', 'Products');
19:     SqlDataAdapter1.Fill(DataSet1);
20:     DataGrid1.DataSource := DataSet1.Tables['Products'].DefaultView;
21:
22:     // Create the Binding Object
23:     bndUnitPrice := Binding.Create('Text',
24:       DataSet1.Tables['Products'].DefaultView, 'UnitPrice');
25:     // Assign the two event handlers.
26:     Include(bndUnitPrice.Format, Self.DecimalToCurrencyString);
27:     Include(bndUnitPrice.Parse, Self.CurrencyStringToDecimal);
28:     // Add the Binding to the TextBox control's DataBindings property
29:     txbxUnitPrice.DataBindings.Add(bndUnitPrice);
30:
31:   finally
32:     SqlConnection1.Close;
33:   end;
34: end;
35:
36: procedure TWinForm.DecimalToCurrencyString(sender: TObject;
37:   e: ConvertEventArgs);
38: begin
39:   if e.Value = DBNull.Value then
```

LISTING 21.9   Continued

```
40:        e.Value := Decimal(0.00).ToString('c')
41:     else
42:        e.Value := Decimal(e.Value).ToString('c');
43:     end;
44:
45:     procedure TWinForm.CurrencyStringToDecimal(sender: TObject;
46:       e: ConvertEventArgs);
47:     begin
48:       if e.DesiredType <> typeof(Decimal) then
49:         Exit
50:       else
51:         e.Value := Decimal.Parse(e.Value.ToString,
52:           System.Globalization.NumberStyles.Currency, nil)
53:     end;
```

▶ See the entire example on the CD: \Code\Chapter 21\Ex15\.

Two methods to serve as the Format and Parse event handlers are defined at DecimalToCurrencyString() and CurrencyStringToDecimal(), respectively. DecimalToCurrencyString() takes the decimal value from the data source and converts it to the string representation of its Currency type. The CurrencyStringToDecimal() method does the reverse by using the System.Globalization.NumberStyles enumeration to parse the string to retrieve its Decimal equivalent.

> ### MONETARY FIELDS AND LOCALES BY HALLVARD
>
> With regard to database design and monetary fields, all too often, the assumed currency of the values is just that, assumed. Sample databases typically assume that amounts are in U.S. Dollars, whereas sample programs that format the values using a currency style will show them in the current locale's currency. In a real application, it might not be a bad idea to specify the currency type and adjust their display accordingly.

Lines 22–29 in the Create() constructor handle creating the Binding object and making the event handler assignments.

Establishing Master Detail with Binding

By using the PositionChanged event of the CurrencyManager, you can establish a master detail configuration. This is very similar to adding an event handler to the TDataSource.OnChange event in classic Delphi.

When the master PositionChanged event is invoked, simply use the primary key value from the master to filter the detail table based on this key (which is a foreign key value in the detail). Listing 21.10 illustrates this technique.

LISTING 21.10   Master Detail Example

```
1:    const
2:      c_cnstr = 'server=XWING;database=Northwind;Trusted_Connection=Yes';
3:      c_sel = 'SELECT * FROM Customers; select * from Orders';
4:
```

LISTING 21.10   Continued

```
5:    constructor TWinForm.Create;
6:    begin
7:      inherited Create;
8:      InitializeComponent;
9:      SqlConnection1.ConnectionString := c_cnstr;
10:     SqlCommand1.Connection := SqlConnection1;
11:     SqlCommand1.CommandText := c_sel;
12:     SqlConnection1.Open;
13:     try
14:       SqlDataAdapter1.SelectCommand := SqlCommand1;
15:
16:       SqlDataAdapter1.TableMappings.Add('Table', 'Customers');
17:       SqlDataAdapter1.TableMappings.Add('Table1', 'Orders');
18:
19:       SqlDataAdapter1.Fill(DataSet1);
20:       dgrdCustomers.DataSource := DataSet1.Tables['Customers'].DefaultView;
21:       dgrdOrders.DataSource := DataSet1.Tables['Orders'].DefaultView;
22:       Include(BindingContext[dgrdCustomers.DataSource].PositionChanged,
23:         Currency_PositionChanged);
24:     finally
25:       SqlConnection1.Close;
26:     end;
27:   end;
28:
29:   procedure TWinForm.Currency_PositionChanged(sender: TObject;
30:     e: System.EventArgs);
31:   var
32:     MastRow: DataRowView;
33:   begin
34:     MastRow := BindingContext[dgrdCustomers.DataSource].Current as
35:       DataRowView;
36:     lblFilter.Text := System.String.Format('CustomerID = ''{0}''',
37:       [MastRow['CustomerID'].ToString]);
38:     DataSet1.Tables['Orders'].DefaultView.RowFilter := lblFilter.Text;
39:   end;
```

▶ See the entire example on the CD: \Code\Chapter 21\Ex16\.

In this example, we are again using tables from the Northwind database. The master table is the Customers table, and the detail table is the Orders table. When the PositionChanged event (line 29) is invoked, its handler, Currency_PositionChanged, uses the CustomerID field from the master to create a filter expression that is assigned to the RowFilter property of the detail tables DefaultView (lines 36–38). This is a very simple, yet effective means to display the master detail relationship within a Windows Form.

IN THIS CHAPTER

- Updating the Data Source Using SQLCommandBuilder

- Updating the Data Source Using Custom Updating Logic

CHAPTER **22**

Saving Data to the Data Source

Up to this point, discussion on ADO.NET has been restricted to working with data apart from the originating data source. This is true at least as it relates to data persistence. This chapter discusses how you save data changes back to the originating data source. It also discusses how to group related updates into a single operation called a transaction in order to ensure that the grouping succeeds or fails collectively. In the chapter, I discuss the SQLDataAdapter, SQLCommandBuilder, and SQLCommand classes. However, the content here also applies, for the most part, to the equivalent classes in other data providers.

From the standpoint of using ADO.NET classes, there are basically two ways to update a data source with your changes. One way involves using a SQLCommandBuilder class. This method is very easy from a coding standpoint, but there are limitations. A more powerful technique is to use custom logic, which gives you greater control over the updating process. Both techniques are illustrated in this chapter.

Updating the Data Source Using SQLCommandBuilder

SQLDataAdapter does not automatically create the SQL statements to reconcile changes back to the data source. The SQLCommandBuilder class will perform this task for you. SQLCommandBuilder is easy to use and requires little coding.

The SQLCommandBuilder class uses the SelectCommand property of SQLDataAdapter to retrieve metadata about the data set. From this information, SQLCommandBuilder builds the appropriate InsertCommand, UpdateCommand, and DeleteCommand classes. These classes contain the appropriate SQL statements needed to perform their functions against the data source. There are, however, limitations with SQLCommandBuilder, which are listed here:

- `SQLCommandBuilder` works with only a single table.

- `SQLCommandBuilder` requires a primary key column to be included in the originating resultset.

- `SQLCommandBuilder` does not provide optimum performance at runtime in that it must retrieve and process metadata prior to being able to perform updates.

- You cannot control the updating logic by modifying the SQL that `SQLCommandBuilder` uses to perform updates.

- You cannot use `SQLCommandBuilder` with stored procedures.

- You cannot specify a type of optimistic concurrency using `SQLCommandBuilder`.

For simple updates that do not require customization, and in which optimum performance is not an issue, `SQLCommandBuilder` is a good option.

To illustrate how `SQLCommandBuilder` works, consider the following code that associates a `SQLCommandBuilder` object with a `SqlDataAdapater` object.

```
sqlCn := SqlConnection.Create(c_cnstr);
sqlDA := SqlDataAdapter.Create(c_sel_cst, sqlCn);
sqlCB := SqlCommandBuilder.Create(sqlDA);
```

The `SqlCommandBuilder` class registers itself as a *handler* of the `SqlDataAdapter.RowUpdating` event. `SqlCommandBuilder` constructs INSERT, UPDATE, and DELETE SQL statements by using the `SelectCommand` property of `SqlDataAdapter` to retrieve metadata about the table it is working with.

> **CAUTION**
>
> If you make any changes to the `SelectCommand` or to the `Connection` properties of the DataAdapter with which `SqlCommandBuilder` is associated, you must call the `SqlCommandBuilder.RefreshSchema()` method so that `SqlCommandBuilder` can reconstruct its commands.

When the `Update()` method of a `SqlDataAdapter` class is invoked, `SqlCommandBuilder` generates the various SQL statements required to update the data source. Given the `SelectCommand` property of

```
select ProductID, ProductName, UnitPrice, ReorderLevel from Products;
```

The `InsertCommand` command generated by `SqlCommandBuilder` would be

```
INSERT INTO products(ProductName, UnitPrice, ReorderLevel)
VALUES (@p1, @p2, @p3)
```

You'll see that the statement is based on a parameterized command. The `UpdateCommand` and `DeleteCommand` statements are similarly constructed.

Listing 22.1 is an example that demonstrates updating a row in the Northwind database using the `SqlCommandBuilder` class. Note that some lines have been removed from the actual example in this listing.

LISTING 22.1   Saving Updates Using SqlCommandBuilder

```
1:    program CmdBldr;
2:
3:    {$APPTYPE CONSOLE}
4:    {%DelphiDotNetAssemblyCompiler 'c:\windows\microsoft.net\
➥framework\v1.1.4322\System.Data.dll'}
5:
6:    uses
7:      System.Data,
8:      System.Data.SqlClient;
9:    var
10:     sqlCn: SqlConnection;
11:     sqlDA: SqlDataAdapter;
12:     sqlCB: SqlCommandBuilder;
13:     dsNorthWind: DataSet;
14:     tblProduct: DataTable;
15:
16:   const
17:     c_cnstr = 'server=XWING;database=Northwind;Trusted_Connection=Yes';
18:     c_sel_cst = 'SELECT * FROM Products';
19:
20:   begin
21:     sqlCn := SqlConnection.Create(c_cnstr);
22:     sqlDA := SqlDataAdapter.Create(c_sel_cst, sqlCn);
23:     sqlCB := SqlCommandBuilder.Create(sqlDA);
24:     dsNorthWind := DataSet.Create('NorthWind');
25:     sqlDA.TableMappings.Add('Table', 'Products');
26:     sqlDA.Fill(dsNorthWind);
27:
28:     tblProduct := dsNorthWind.Tables['Products'];
29:
30:     tblProduct.Rows[0]['ReorderLevel'] := TObject(10);
31:     sqlDA.Update(dsNorthWind);
32:
33:     Console.WriteLine(sqlCB.GetUpdateCommand.CommandText);
34:     Console.ReadLine;
35:   end.
```

▶ Find the code on the CD: \Code\Chapter 22\Ex01.

Most of the code in this listing is similar to previous examples you have seen. The first part of this listing basically sets up the connection and retrieves data into a DataSet. Line 30 changes the value of the ReorderLevel column and then saves that change to the data source in line 31.

Although this is a very simple example, most updates you perform using the SqlCommandBuilder class will appear along these lines.

You should understand another point about SqlCommandBuilder. Even though you provide a primary key, SqlCommandBuilder, when performing an UPDATE or DELETE operation, searches on the record containing an exact match of all columns in the record or at least all columns that had been retrieved form the data source because it is possible to retrieve a subset of columns. SqlCommandBuilder uses both the current and original values of the row in performing the update. So, the SQL generated requires a matching record to be found on all original column values; then the record is updated using the current column values. It does this to prevent an overwrite of another user's update. When you consider this, you can see how using `SqlCommandBuilder` can add significant overhead. In many cases, this is fine. However, when you require more optimum performance, you will have to provide your own custom logic.

Updating the Data Source Using Custom Updating Logic

Using custom updating logic simply means that you provide your own INSERT, UPDATE, or DELETE SQL statements as opposed to letting `SqlCommandBuilder` do this for you. By using custom logic, you can write SQL statements to address scenarios in which `SqlCommandBuilder` is limited. For instance, you can write logic that updates the data source through a stored procedure. You can also write logic that updates the data source in which the original query was a joined table. In this scenario, you want to update only a subset of the columns. Using `SqlCommandBuilder`, you have no way of specifying this. Finally, using custom logic, you can handle concurrency in a more optimized fashion than what `SqlCommandBuilder` can handle.

The `SqlDataAdapter` class has the capability to submit pending changes to your data source based on SQL statements that it contains. This section explains how to manually configure `SqlDataAdapter`'s `InsertCommand`, `UpdateCommand`, and `DeleteCommand` properties. First, to understand how `SqlDataAdapter` works with these various `Command` classes, let's examine how updates would occur using only a `Command` class.

Using a Command Class

One way that you can update the data source and have complete control over your update logic would be to simply use the `SqlCommand` class (or other data provider equivalent). To illustrate this technique, consider Listing 22.2, which is an excerpt from the complete example on the accompanying CD.

LISTING 22.2   Command Class Excerpt

```
1:  var
2:    sqlCn: SqlConnection;
3:    sqlDA: SqlDataAdapter;
4:    dsNorthWind: DataSet;
5:    tblProduct: DataTable;
6:    dr: DataRow;
7:  const
8:    c_cnstr = 'server=XWING;database=Northwind;Trusted_Connection=Yes';
9:    c_sel_cst = 'SELECT * FROM Products';
10: ...
11: begin
12:   sqlCn := SqlConnection.Create(c_cnstr);
13:   sqlDA := SqlDataAdapter.Create(c_sel_cst, sqlCn);
14:   dsNorthWind := DataSet.Create('NorthWind');
15:   sqlDA.TableMappings.Add('Table', 'Products');
16:   sqlDA.Fill(dsNorthWind);
17:   tblProduct := dsNorthWind.Tables['Products'];
18:
```

LISTING 22.2   Continued

```
19:    // Insert a Row
20:    dr := tblProduct.NewRow;
21:    dr['ProductName'] := 'Second Burn Hot Sauce';
22:    dr['SupplierID']  := System.Object(2);
23:    dr['CategoryID']  := System.Object(2);
24:    dr['QuantityPerUnit'] := '48 - 6 oz jars';
25:    dr['UnitPrice'] := System.Object(23.00);
26:    dr['UnitsInStock'] := System.Object(50);
27:    dr['UnitsOnOrder'] := System.Object(0);
28:    dr['ReorderLevel'] := System.Object(15);
29:    dr['Discontinued'] := System.Object(0);
30:    tblProduct.Rows.Add(dr);
31:
32:    //Modify a Row
33:    dr := tblProduct.Rows[5];
34:    dr['UnitsInStock'] := System.Object(10);
35:
36:    tblPrduct.Rows[0].Delete;
37:    SubmitUpdates;
38:  end.
```

▶ Find the code on the CD: \Code\Chapter 22\Ex02.

In this example, you see that I set up a DataSet that contains a single table from the NorthWind Database. Specifically, this is the Products table. Lines 20–30 add a new row to the table and lines 33–34 update an existing row. Line 36 deletes the first row from in the table. Line 37 calls a SubmitUpdates() procedure, which is listed in Listing 22.3.

LISTING 22.3   SubmitUpdates() Procedure

```
1:   procedure SubmitUpdates;
2:   var
3:     rowEnum: IEnumerator;
4:     CurrRow: DataRow;
5:   begin
6:     sqlCn.Open;
7:     try
8:       rowEnum := tblProduct.Rows.GetEnumerator;
9:       while rowEnum.MoveNext do
10:      begin
11:        CurrRow := (rowEnum.Current as DataRow);
12:        case CurrRow.RowState of
13:          DataRowState.Modified:  SubmitModifiedRow(CurrRow);
14:          DataRowState.Added:     SubmitAddedRow(CurrRow);
15:          DataRowState.Deleted:   SubmitDeletedRow(CurrRow);
16:        end; // case
17:      end;
18:    finally
19:      sqlCn.Close;
20:    end;
21:  end;
```

▶ Find the code on the CD: \Code\Chapter 22\Ex02.

This procedure is fairly straightforward. It ensures that the connection to the database is open and then iterates through each row in the table checking for the type of update that was performed on that row. When a row is found that has been modified, added, or deleted as indicated by its RowState property (line 12), the respective procedure is invoked to handle that update to the database (lines 13–15). Each of the three procedures contains its own update logic. These three procedures are discussed individually in more detail shortly.

Listing 22.4 is the INSERT Transact-SQL statement that is used in the SubmitAddedRow() procedure. Note that this listing does not contain line numbers to avoid confusion.

LISTING 22.4   INSERT Transact-SQL Statement

```
INSERT INTO Products (
  ProductName,
  SupplierID,
  CategoryID,
  QuantityPerUnit,
  UnitPrice,
  UnitsInStock,
  UnitsOnOrder,
  ReorderLevel,
  Discontinued)
VALUES (
  @ProductName,
  @SupplierID,
  @CategoryID,
  @QuantityPerUnit,
  @UnitPrice,
  @UnitsInStock,
  @UnitsOnOrder,
  @ReorderLevel,
  @Discontinued);
```

▶ Find the code on the CD: \Code\Chapter 22\Ex02.

Listing 22.4 is actually the contents of a c_ins.sql file that is used in the SubmitAddedRow() method. SubmitAddedRow() is shown in Listing 22.5.

LISTING 22.5   Custom INSERT Using the SqlCommand Class

```
1:   procedure SubmitAddedRow(aRow: DataRow);
2:   var
3:     sqlCmd: SqlCommand;
4:   begin
5:     // Create the Command
6:     sqlCmd := SqlCommand.Create(GetCommand('c_ins.sql'), sqlCn);
7:     sqlCmd.Parameters.Add('@ProductName', SqlDbType.NVarChar, 40);
8:     sqlCmd.Parameters.Add('@SupplierID', SqlDbType.Int);
9:     SqlCmd.Parameters.Add('@CategoryID', SqlDbType.Int);
10:    SqlCmd.Parameters.Add('@QuantityPerUnit', SqlDbType.NVarChar, 20);
11:    SqlCmd.Parameters.Add('@UnitPrice', SqlDbType.Money);
12:    SqlCmd.Parameters.Add('@UnitsInStock', SqlDbType.SmallInt);
```

LISTING 22.5   Continued

```
13:     SqlCmd.Parameters.Add('@UnitsOnOrder', SqlDbType.SmallInt);
14:     SqlCmd.Parameters.Add('@ReorderLevel', SqlDbType.SmallInt);
15:     SqlCmd.Parameters.Add('@Discontinued', SqlDbType.Bit);
16:
17:     // Add Values to the Command
18:
19:     sqlCmd.Parameters['@ProductName'].Value := aRow['ProductName'];
20:     sqlCmd.Parameters['@SupplierID'].Value := aRow['SupplierID'];
21:     sqlCmd.Parameters['@CategoryID'].Value := aRow['CategoryID'];
22:     sqlCmd.Parameters['@QuantityPerUnit'].Value := aRow['QuantityPerUnit'];
23:     sqlCmd.Parameters['@UnitPrice'].Value := aRow['UnitPrice'];
24:     sqlCmd.Parameters['@UnitsInStock'].Value := aRow['UnitsInStock'];
25:     sqlCmd.Parameters['@UnitsOnOrder'].Value := aRow['UnitsOnOrder'];
26:     sqlCmd.Parameters['@ReorderLevel'].Value := aRow['ReorderLevel'];
27:     sqlCmd.Parameters['@Discontinued'].Value := aRow['Discontinued'];
28:
29:     sqlCmd.ExecuteNonQuery;
30: end;
```

▶ Find the code on the CD: \Code\Chapter 22\Ex02.

Line 6 in Listing 22.5 creates the SqlCommand instance. The first parameter is a call to a function, GetCommand(), which simply loads the specified file and returns its contents—in this case, the contents that are shown in Listing 22.4. Lines 7–15 create the parameter objects for the SqlCommand object. Lines 19–27 assign values from the DataRow passed in to this procedure to these parameters. Note that the values assigned to each parameter are the default DataRowVersion of DataRowVersion.Default, which is the case when the DataRowVersion is not specified in the indexer. Recall from Chapter 20, "DataAdapters and DataSets," that each DataRow contains a version of the data it contains. The DataRowVersions we'll be dealing with here are Original and Current. When line 29 is executed, the contents of this DataRow are added to the underlying data source.

You can see how by providing your own INSERT SQL statement: You can use a SqlCommand class to perform the persistence to the underlying data source.

This INSERT operation is fairly simple. Listing 22.6 shows the UPDATE operation, which is slightly more complex.

LISTING 22.6   Custom UPDATE Using the SqlCommand Class

```
1:     procedure SubmitModifiedRow(aRow: DataRow);
2:     var
3:       sqlCmd: SqlCommand;
4:     begin
5:       sqlCmd := sqlCommand.Create(GetCommand('c_upd.sql'), sqlCn);
6:       sqlCmd.Parameters.Add('@C_ProductName', SqlDbType.NVarChar, 40);
7:       sqlCmd.Parameters.Add('@C_SupplierID', SqlDbType.Int);
8:       sqlCmd.Parameters.Add('@C_CategoryID', SqlDbType.Int);
9:       sqlCmd.Parameters.Add('@C_QuantityPerUnit', SqlDbType.NVarChar, 20);
10:      sqlCmd.Parameters.Add('@C_UnitPrice', SqlDbType.Money);
11:      sqlCmd.Parameters.Add('@C_UnitsInStock', SqlDbType.SmallInt);
```

LISTING 22.6   Continued

```
12:    sqlCmd.Parameters.Add('@C_UnitsOnOrder', SqlDbType.SmallInt);
13:    sqlCmd.Parameters.Add('@C_ReorderLevel', SqlDbType.SmallInt);
14:    sqlCmd.Parameters.Add('@C_Discontinued', SqlDbType.Bit);
15:
16:    sqlCmd.Parameters.Add('@O_ProductID', SqlDbType.Int);
17:    sqlCmd.Parameters.Add('@O_ProductName', SqlDbType.NVarChar, 40);
18:    sqlCmd.Parameters.Add('@O_SupplierID', SqlDbType.Int);
19:    sqlCmd.Parameters.Add('@O_CategoryID', SqlDbType.Int);
20:    sqlCmd.Parameters.Add('@O_QuantityPerUnit', SqlDbType.NVarChar, 20);
21:    sqlCmd.Parameters.Add('@O_UnitPrice', SqlDbType.Money);
22:    sqlCmd.Parameters.Add('@O_UnitsInStock', SqlDbType.SmallInt);
23:    sqlCmd.Parameters.Add('@O_UnitsOnOrder', SqlDbType.SmallInt);
24:    sqlCmd.Parameters.Add('@O_ReorderLevel', SqlDbType.SmallInt);
25:    sqlCmd.Parameters.Add('@O_Discontinued', SqlDbType.Bit);
26:
27:    // Add Values to the Command
28:
29:    sqlCmd.Parameters['@C_ProductName'].Value := aRow['ProductName'];
30:    sqlCmd.Parameters['@C_SupplierID'].Value := aRow['SupplierID'];
31:    sqlCmd.Parameters['@C_CategoryID'].Value := aRow['CategoryID'];
32:    sqlCmd.Parameters['@C_QuantityPerUnit'].Value := aRow['QuantityPerUnit'];
33:    sqlCmd.Parameters['@C_UnitPrice'].Value := aRow['UnitPrice'];
34:    sqlCmd.Parameters['@C_UnitsInStock'].Value := aRow['UnitsInStock'];
35:    sqlCmd.Parameters['@C_UnitsOnOrder'].Value := aRow['UnitsOnOrder'];
36:    sqlCmd.Parameters['@C_ReorderLevel'].Value := aRow['ReorderLevel'];
37:    sqlCmd.Parameters['@C_Discontinued'].Value := aRow['Discontinued'];
38:
39:    sqlCmd.Parameters['@O_ProductID'].Value :=
40:      aRow['ProductID', DataRowVersion.Original];
41:    sqlCmd.Parameters['@O_ProductName'].Value :=
42:      aRow['ProductName', DataRowVersion.Original];
43:    sqlCmd.Parameters['@O_SupplierID'].Value :=
44:      aRow['SupplierID', DataRowVersion.Original];
45:    sqlCmd.Parameters['@O_CategoryID'].Value :=
46:      aRow['CategoryID', DataRowVersion.Original];
47:    sqlCmd.Parameters['@O_QuantityPerUnit'].Value :=
48:      aRow['QuantityPerUnit', DataRowVersion.Original];
49:    sqlCmd.Parameters['@O_UnitPrice'].Value :=
50:      aRow['UnitPrice', DataRowVersion.Original];
51:    sqlCmd.Parameters['@O_UnitsInStock'].Value :=
52:      aRow['UnitsInStock', DataRowVersion.Original];
53:    sqlCmd.Parameters['@O_UnitsOnOrder'].Value :=
54:      aRow['UnitsOnOrder', DataRowVersion.Original];
55:    sqlCmd.Parameters['@O_ReorderLevel'].Value :=
56:      aRow['ReorderLevel', DataRowVersion.Original];
57:    sqlCmd.Parameters['@O_Discontinued'].Value :=
58:      aRow['Discontinued', DataRowVersion.Original];
59:
60:    sqlCmd.ExecuteNonQuery;
61:  end;
```

▶ Find the code on the CD: \Code\Chapter 22\Ex02.

Unlike Listing 22.5, Listing 22.6 makes use of both the Original and Current DataRowVersions (lines 39–58). To see why, consider the Transact-SQL statement that is used (see Listing 22.7). This statement is loaded in line 5 in Listing 27.6 by the GetCommand() method.

LISTING 22.7   UPDATE Transact-SQL Statement

```
UPDATE Products
SET
  ProductName     = @C_ProductName,
  SupplierID      = @C_SupplierID,
  CategoryID      = @C_CategoryID,
  QuantityPerUnit = @C_QuantityPerUnit,
  UnitPrice       = @C_UnitPrice,
  UnitsInStock    = @C_UnitsInStock,
  UnitsOnOrder    = @C_UnitsOnOrder,
  ReorderLevel    = @C_ReorderLevel,
  Discontinued    = @C_Discontinued
WHERE
  ProductID       = @O_ProductID       AND
  ProductName     = @O_ProductName      AND
  SupplierID      = @O_SupplierID       AND
  CategoryID      = @O_CategoryID       AND
  QuantityPerUnit = @O_QuantityPerUnit AND
  UnitPrice       = @O_UnitPrice       AND
  UnitsInStock    = @O_UnitsInStock    AND
  UnitsOnOrder    = @O_UnitsOnOrder    AND
  ReorderLevel    = @O_ReorderLevel    AND
  Discontinued    = @O_Discontinued;
```

▶ Find the code on the CD: \Code\Chapter 22\Ex02.

The UPDATE SQL statement contains both the SET and WHERE clauses. The SET portion determines which values to assign to the specified columns. The WHERE portion specifies the search criteria that the data source uses to find the specific record to update. The SET clause assigns all the new or DataRowVersion.Current values. The WHERE clause searches on the records using the old or DataRowVersion.Original values.

Therefore, in lines 29–37 of Listing 22.6, when values are assigned to the parameters used in the SET clause, DataRowVersion does not need to be specified in the indexer because the default is the DataRowVersion.Current value. However, in lines 39–58 of Listing 22.6, DataRowVersion.Original must be specified for the values being assigned to parameters in the WHERE clause.

One aspect about this code is worth mentioning. You'll note that the WHERE clause uses all the fields in the table. This is certainly one way to handle concurrency. If the values in any of the rows change, the update will fail because the record will not be located. This is not the most efficient way to handle concurrency. Different concurrency handling options are discussed later in this chapter. Listing 22.8 shows the Transact SQL statement used to delete a record.

LISTING 22.8   DELETE Transact-SQL Statement

```
DELETE FROM Products
WHERE
  ProductID       = @ProductID       AND
  ProductName     = @ProductName      AND
  SupplierID      = @SupplierID       AND
  CategoryID      = @CategoryID       AND
  QuantityPerUnit = @QuantityPerUnit  AND
  UnitPrice       = @UnitPrice        AND
  UnitsInStock    = @UnitsInStock     AND
  UnitsOnOrder    = @UnitsOnOrder     AND
  ReorderLevel    = @Discontinued;
```

▶ Find the code on the CD: \Code\Chapter 22\Ex02.

This is the simplest of the three Transact-SQL statements. Listing 22.9 shows the SubmitDeletedRow() method that makes use of the DELETE Transact-SQL.

LISTING 22.9   Custom DELETE Using the SqlCommand Class

```
1:  procedure SubmitDeletedRow(aRow: DataRow);
2:  var
3:    sqlCmd: SqlCommand;
4:  begin
5:    // Create the Command
6:    sqlCmd := SqlCommand.Create(GetCommand('c_del.sql'), sqlCn);
7:    sqlCmd.Parameters.Add('@ProductID', SqlDbType.Int);
8:    sqlCmd.Parameters.Add('@ProductName', SqlDbType.NVarChar, 40);
9:    sqlCmd.Parameters.Add('@SupplierID', SqlDbType.Int);
10:   sqlCmd.Parameters.Add('@CategoryID', SqlDbType.Int);
11:   sqlCmd.Parameters.Add('@QuantityPerUnit', SqlDbType.NVarChar, 20);
12:   sqlCmd.Parameters.Add('@UnitPrice', SqlDbType.Money);
13:   sqlCmd.Parameters.Add('@UnitsInStock', SqlDbType.SmallInt);
14:   sqlCmd.Parameters.Add('@UnitsOnOrder', SqlDbType.SmallInt);
15:   sqlCmd.Parameters.Add('@ReorderLevel', SqlDbType.SmallInt);
16:   sqlCmd.Parameters.Add('@Discontinued', SqlDbType.Bit);
17:
18:    // Add Values to the Command
19:
20:    sqlCmd.Parameters['@ProductID'].Value :=
21:      aRow['ProductID', DataRowVersion.Original];
22:    sqlCmd.Parameters['@ProductName'].Value :=
23:      aRow['ProductName', DataRowVersion.Original];
24:    sqlCmd.Parameters['@SupplierID'].Value :=
25:      aRow['SupplierID', DataRowVersion.Original];
26:    sqlCmd.Parameters['@CategoryID'].Value :=
27:      aRow['CategoryID', DataRowVersion.Original];
28:    sqlCmd.Parameters['@QuantityPerUnit'].Value :=
29:      aRow['QuantityPerUnit', DataRowVersion.Original];
30:    sqlCmd.Parameters['@UnitPrice'].Value :=
31:      aRow['UnitPrice', DataRowVersion.Original];
32:    sqlCmd.Parameters['@UnitsInStock'].Value :=
33:      aRow['UnitsInStock', DataRowVersion.Original];
34:    sqlCmd.Parameters['@UnitsOnOrder'].Value :=
```

LISTING 22.9   Continued

```
35:      aRow['UnitsOnOrder', DataRowVersion.Original];
36:    sqlCmd.Parameters['@ReorderLevel'].Value :=
37:      aRow['ReorderLevel', DataRowVersion.Original];
38:    sqlCmd.Parameters['@Discontinued'].Value :=
39:      aRow['Discontinued', DataRowVersion.Original];
40:
41:    sqlCmd.ExecuteNonQuery;
42:  end;
```

▶ Find the code on the CD: \Code\Chapter 22\Ex02.

Listing 22.9 makes use of only the DataRowVersion.Original values in lines 20–39 because it is only passing the search criteria to the data source to specify which record to delete.

In any of these three operations, INSERT, UPDATE, DELETE, you can customize the Transact-SQL statements to handle your specialized needs. For instance, you can have specialized searching criteria or more efficient concurrency handling. The idea is that you can write customized code, which you could not do using the SqlCommandBuilder class. The next section illustrates how to do the same using the properties of the SqlDataAdapter class.

Using the SqlDataAdapter Class

The SqlDataAdapter class contains three SqlCommand properties in addition to the SelectCommand property—InsertCommand, UpdateCommand, and DeleteCommand.

When you invoke SqlDataAdapter's Update() method to save changes to the data source, SqlDataAdapter determines which of the three SqlCommand properties it will use to update the data source. To illustrate how SqlDataAdapter works, I'll use the same Transact-SQL statements that were used to demonstrate using the SqlCommand classes to update the data source (refer to Listings 22.4, 22.7, and 22.8).

Listing 22.10 shows an excerpt from the main block of an application that uses SqlDataAdapter to make updates to the data source.

LISTING 22.10   DataAdapter Main Block Example

```
1:    program SqlDADemo;
2:
3:    {$APPTYPE CONSOLE}
4:
5:    uses
6:      System.Data,
7:      System.Data.SqlClient,
8:      System.IO,
9:      System.Collections;
10:
11:   var
12:      sqlCn: SqlConnection;
13:      sqlDA: SqlDataAdapter;
14:      dsNorthWind: DataSet;
15:      tblProduct: DataTable;
16:      dr: DataRow;
```

LISTING 22.10   Continued

```
17:  ...
18:  const
19:    c_cnstr = 'server=XWING;database=Northwind;Trusted_Connection=Yes';
20:    c_sel_cst = 'SELECT * FROM Products';
21:  begin
22:    sqlCn := SqlConnection.Create(c_cnstr);
23:    sqlDA := SqlDataAdapter.Create(c_sel_cst, sqlCn);
24:    dsNorthWind := DataSet.Create('NorthWind');
25:    sqlDA.TableMappings.Add('Table', 'Products');
26:    sqlDA.Fill(dsNorthWind);
27:    tblProduct := dsNorthWind.Tables['Products'];
28:
29:    sqlDA.InsertCommand := GetDataAdapterInsertCommand;
30:    sqlDA.UpdateCommand := GetDataAdapterUpdateCommand;
31:    sqlDA.DeleteCommand := GetDataAdapterDeleteCommand;
32:
33:    // Insert a Row
34:    dr := tblProduct.NewRow;
35:    dr['ProductName'] := 'Second Burn Hot Sauce';
36:    dr['SupplierID']  := System.Object(2);
37:    dr['CategoryID']  := System.Object(2);
38:    dr['QuantityPerUnit'] := '48 - 6 oz jars';
39:    dr['UnitPrice']   := System.Object(23.00);
40:    dr['UnitsInStock'] := System.Object(50);
41:    dr['UnitsOnOrder'] := System.Object(0);
42:    dr['ReorderLevel'] := System.Object(15);
43:    dr['Discontinued'] := System.Object(0);
44:    tblProduct.Rows.Add(dr);
45:
46:    //Modify a Row
47:    dr := tblProduct.Rows[5];
48:    dr['UnitsInStock'] := System.Object(10);
49:
50:     tblProduct.Rows[0].Delete;
51:
52:    sqlDA.Update(tblProduct);
53:  end.
```

▶ Find the code on the CD: \Code\Chapter 22\Ex03.

You might have noticed that this does not differ too much from the previous example in Listing 22.2. Lines 29–31 are different. These three lines call the functions `GetDataAdapterInsertCommand()`, `GetDataAdapterUpdateCommand()`, and `GetDataAdapterDeleteCommand()` and assign the resulting `SqlCommand` to the properties `InsertCommand`, `UpdateCommand`, and `DeleteCommand`, respectively. Also, line 52 shows the call to the `SqlDataAdapter.Update()` method. The version of the heavily overloaded method used here takes the table that we want to update as the parameter. As previously mentioned, the three `SqlCommand` properties are used by `SqlDataAdapter` to actually perform the updates to the data source similarly to how the straight `SqlCommand` technique handled this. Let's look at the content of the three functions that return the `SqlCommand` class instances. Listing 22.11 shows how the `SqlCommand` is constructed for the INSERT operation.

LISTING 22.11   GetDataAdapterInsertCommand() Function

```
 1:   function GetDataAdapterInsertCommand: SqlCommand;
 2:   var
 3:     sqlCmd: SqlCommand;
 4:   begin
 5:     // Create the Command
 6:     sqlCmd := SqlCommand.Create(GetCommand('c_ins.sql'), sqlCn);
 7:     sqlCmd.Parameters.Add('@ProductName', SqlDbType.NVarChar, 40);
 8:     sqlCmd.Parameters.Add('@SupplierID', SqlDbType.Int);
 9:     sqlCmd.Parameters.Add('@CategoryID', SqlDbType.Int);
10:     sqlCmd.Parameters.Add('@QuantityPerUnit', SqlDbType.NVarChar, 20);
11:     sqlCmd.Parameters.Add('@UnitPrice', SqlDbType.Money);
12:     sqlCmd.Parameters.Add('@UnitsInStock', SqlDbType.SmallInt);
13:     sqlCmd.Parameters.Add('@UnitsOnOrder', SqlDbType.SmallInt);
14:     sqlCmd.Parameters.Add('@ReorderLevel', SqlDbType.SmallInt);
15:     sqlCmd.Parameters.Add('@Discontinued', SqlDbType.Bit);
16:
17:     Result := sqlCmd;
18:   end;
```

▶ Find the code on the CD: \Code\Chapter 22\Ex03.

Again, we make use of a utility function, GetCommand(), to load the contents of a text file containing the actual Transact-SQL statement shown in Listing 22.4. This function simply sets up the parameters for the SqlCommand class. Also, nothing has to be done to specify which DataRowVersion to use because this is an INSERT command and DataRowVersion.Current is the default when none is specified. The UPDATE operation requires both the Current and Original DataRowVersions, as shown in Listing 22.12.

LISTING 22.12   GetDataAdapterUpdateCommand() Function

```
 1:   function GetDataAdapterUpdateCommand: SqlCommand;
 2:   var
 3:     sqlCmd: SqlCommand;
 4:   begin
 5:     sqlCmd := sqlCommand.Create(GetCommand('c_upd.sql'), sqlCn);
 6:     sqlCmd.Parameters.Add('@C_ProductName', SqlDbType.NVarChar, 40);
 7:     sqlCmd.Parameters.Add('@C_SupplierID', SqlDbType.Int);
 8:     sqlCmd.Parameters.Add('@C_CategoryID', SqlDbType.Int);
 9:     sqlCmd.Parameters.Add('@C_QuantityPerUnit', SqlDbType.NVarChar, 20);
10:     sqlCmd.Parameters.Add('@C_UnitPrice', SqlDbType.Money);
11:     sqlCmd.Parameters.Add('@C_UnitsInStock', SqlDbType.SmallInt);
12:     sqlCmd.Parameters.Add('@C_UnitsOnOrder', SqlDbType.SmallInt);
13:     sqlCmd.Parameters.Add('@C_ReorderLevel', SqlDbType.SmallInt);
14:     sqlCmd.Parameters.Add('@C_Discontinued', SqlDbType.Bit);
15:
16:     sqlCmd.Parameters.Add('@O_ProductID', SqlDbType.Int);
17:     sqlCmd.Parameters.Add('@O_ProductName', SqlDbType.NVarChar, 40);
18:     sqlCmd.Parameters.Add('@O_SupplierID', SqlDbType.Int);
19:     sqlCmd.Parameters.Add('@O_CategoryID', SqlDbType.Int);
20:     sqlCmd.Parameters.Add('@O_QuantityPerUnit', SqlDbType.NVarChar, 20);
21:     sqlCmd.Parameters.Add('@O_UnitPrice', SqlDbType.Money);
22:     sqlCmd.Parameters.Add('@O_UnitsInStock', SqlDbType.SmallInt);
```

LISTING 22.12   Continued

```
23:    sqlCmd.Parameters.Add('@O_UnitsOnOrder', SqlDbType.SmallInt);
24:    sqlCmd.Parameters.Add('@O_ReorderLevel', SqlDbType.SmallInt);
25:    sqlCmd.Parameters.Add('@O_Discontinued', SqlDbType.Bit);
26:
27:    sqlCmd.Parameters['@O_ProductID'].SourceVersion :=
28:      DataRowVersion.Original;
29:    sqlCmd.Parameters['@O_ProductName'].SourceVersion :=
30:      DataRowVersion.Original;
31:    sqlCmd.Parameters['@O_SupplierID'].SourceVersion :=
32:      DataRowVersion.Original;
33:    sqlCmd.Parameters['@O_CategoryID'].SourceVersion :=
34:      DataRowVersion.Original;
35:    sqlCmd.Parameters['@O_QuantityPerUnit'].SourceVersion :=
36:      DataRowVersion.Original;
37:    sqlCmd.Parameters['@O_UnitPrice'].SourceVersion :=
38:      DataRowVersion.Original;
39:    sqlCmd.Parameters['@O_UnitsInStock'].SourceVersion :=
40:      DataRowVersion.Original;
41:    sqlCmd.Parameters['@O_UnitsOnOrder'].SourceVersion :=
42:      DataRowVersion.Original;
43:    sqlCmd.Parameters['@O_ReorderLevel'].SourceVersion :=
44:      DataRowVersion.Original;
45:    sqlCmd.Parameters['@O_Discontinued'].SourceVersion :=
46:      DataRowVersion.Original;
47:
48:    Result := sqlCmd;
49:  end;
```

▶ Find the code on the CD: \Code\Chapter 22\Ex03.

Again, using the Transact-SQL statement shown in Listing 22.7, this function first creates the parameters for the SET clause of the SQL statement. These parameters require the Current version of row values (lines 5–14). Then, lines 16–25 create the parameters required for the WHERE clause of the SQL statement. The WHERE clause requires the Original row values; therefore, lines 27–46 specify so by assigning DataRowVersion.Original to the SourceVersion property of the parameters for the WHERE clause.

Listing 22.13 illustrates how the DeleteCommand is set up.

LISTING 22.13   GetDataAdapterDeleteCommand() Function

```
function GetDataAdapterDeleteCommand: SqlCommand;
var
  sqlCmd: SqlCommand;
begin
  sqlCmd := SqlCommand.Create(GetCommand('c_del.sql'), sqlCn);
  sqlCmd.Parameters.Add('@ProductID', SqlDbType.Int);
  sqlCmd.Parameters.Add('@ProductName', SqlDbType.NVarChar, 40);
  sqlCmd.Parameters.Add('@SupplierID', SqlDbType.Int);
  SqlCmd.Parameters.Add('@CategoryID', SqlDbType.Int);
  SqlCmd.Parameters.Add('@QuantityPerUnit', SqlDbType.NVarChar, 20);
  SqlCmd.Parameters.Add('@UnitPrice', SqlDbType.Money);
```

22

LISTING 22.13   Continued

```
SqlCmd.Parameters.Add('@UnitsInStock', SqlDbType.SmallInt);
SqlCmd.Parameters.Add('@UnitsOnOrder', SqlDbType.SmallInt);
SqlCmd.Parameters.Add('@ReorderLevel', SqlDbType.SmallInt);
SqlCmd.Parameters.Add('@Discontinued', SqlDbType.Bit);

sqlCmd.Parameters['@ProductID'].SourceVersion :=
  DataRowVersion.Original;
sqlCmd.Parameters['@ProductName'].SourceVersion :=
  DataRowVersion.Original;
sqlCmd.Parameters['@SupplierID'].SourceVersion :=
  DataRowVersion.Original;
sqlCmd.Parameters['@CategoryID'].SourceVersion :=
  DataRowVersion.Original;
sqlCmd.Parameters['@QuantityPerUnit'].SourceVersion :=
  DataRowVersion.Original;
sqlCmd.Parameters['@UnitPrice'].SourceVersion :=
  DataRowVersion.Original;
sqlCmd.Parameters['@UnitsInStock'].SourceVersion :=
  DataRowVersion.Original;
sqlCmd.Parameters['@UnitsOnOrder'].SourceVersion :=
  DataRowVersion.Original;
sqlCmd.Parameters['@ReorderLevel'].SourceVersion :=
  DataRowVersion.Original;
sqlCmd.Parameters['@Discontinued'].SourceVersion :=
  DataRowVersion.Original;

Result := sqlCmd;
end;
```

▶ Find the code on the CD: \Code\Chapter 22\Ex03.

Similar to the GetDataAdapterUpdateCommand(), this setup function for DeleteCommand also requires the Original version of row data.

You can see that by using the SqlDataAdapter, you can set up the various SqlCommand properties once and the SqlDataAdapter will take care of mapping the columns to the appropriate parameters. Basically, when adding a parameter, the parameter name is assigned to the SourceColumn property of the Parameter object. SourceColumn refers to a column in the DataTable to which the DataAdapter refers. This is a name by name reference. Additionally, when you invoke the SqlDataAdapter.Update() method, SqlDataAdapter determines which SqlCommand to use in the update on a row by row basis.

Using straight SqlCommand classes or the SqlCommand properties of the SqlDataAdapter class requires more code than using the CommandBuilder class. However, because you are writing the update code, more options are at your disposal for optimization and customization. One option would be in using a stored procedure in performing your updates, which the next section discusses.

Updating Using a Stored Procedure

The SqlDataAdapter allows you to execute your update statements through stored procedures. The following examples illustrate this process. Listing 22.14 is an excerpt from the example on the CD that shows the main code block illustrating the use of the SqlDataAdapter.

LISTING 22.14   SqlDataAdapter Using a Stored Procedure

```
1:    program SqlDAProc;
2:    {$APPTYPE CONSOLE}
3:    uses
4:      System.Data,
5:      System.Data.SqlClient,
6:      System.IO,
7:      System.Collections;
8:    var
9:      sqlCn: SqlConnection;
10:     sqlDA: SqlDataAdapter;
11:     dsNorthWind: DataSet;
12:     tblProduct: DataTable;
13:     dr: DataRow;
14:   const
15:     c_cnstr = 'server=XWING;database=Northwind;Trusted_Connection=Yes';
16:     c_sel_cst = 'SELECT * FROM Products';
17:
18:     ...
19:   begin
20:     sqlCn := SqlConnection.Create(c_cnstr);
21:     sqlDA := SqlDataAdapter.Create('SelectProduct', sqlCn);
22:     sqlDA.SelectCommand.CommandType := CommandType.StoredProcedure;
23:     sqlDA.InsertCommand := GetDataAdapterInsertCommand;
24:     sqlDA.UpdateCommand := GetDataAdapterUpdateCommand;
25:     sqlDA.DeleteCommand := GetDataAdapterDeleteCommand;
26:
27:     dsNorthWind := DataSet.Create('NorthWind');
28:     sqlDA.Fill(dsNorthWind, 'Products');
29:     sqlDA.TableMappings.Add('Table', 'Products');
30:     tblProduct := dsNorthWind.Tables['Products'];
31:
32:     // Insert a Row
33:     dr := tblProduct.NewRow;
34:     dr['ProductName'] := 'Second Burn Hot Sauce';
35:     dr['SupplierID']   := System.Object(2);
36:     dr['CategoryID']   := System.Object(2);
37:     dr['QuantityPerUnit'] := '48 - 6 oz jars';
38:     dr['UnitPrice'] := System.Object(23.00);
39:     dr['UnitsInStock'] := System.Object(50);
40:     dr['UnitsOnOrder'] := System.Object(0);
41:     dr['ReorderLevel'] := System.Object(15);
42:     dr['Discontinued'] := System.Object(0);
43:     tblProduct.Rows.Add(dr);
44:
45:     //Modify a Row
46:     dr := tblProduct.Rows[5];
```

LISTING 22.14   Continued

```
47:     dr['UnitsInStock'] := System.Object(10);
48:
49:     // Delete a row
50:     dr := tblProduct.Rows[tblProduct.Rows.Count-1];
51:     dr.Delete;
52:
53:     sqlDA.Update(tblProduct);
54:  end.
```

▶ Find the code on the CD: \Code\Chapter 22\Ex04.

Again, this is not very different from the previous examples. Notice in line 21 that the name of the stored procedure SelectProduct is passed to the constructor of the SqlDataAdapter instead of a Transact-SQL statement. The SelectProduct stored procedure is shown in Listing 22.15.

LISTING 22.15   SelectProduct Stored Procedure

```
CREATE PROCEDURE SelectProduct
AS
  SET NOCOUNT ON

  SELECT
    ProductId,
    ProductName,
    SupplierID,
    CategoryID,
    QuantityPerUnit,
    UnitPrice,
    UnitsInStock,
    UnitsOnOrder,
    ReorderLevel,
    Discontinued
  FROM
    Products

  return

GO
```

▶ Find the code on the CD: \Code\Chapter 22\Ex04.

Also notice in line 22 of Listing 22.14 that I indicate that SelectCommand is a stored procedure by assigning CommandType.StoredProcedure to its CommandType property. Like the previous examples, this example contains three functions that return a SqlCommand for each operation to be performed. Each of these SqlCommands will be associated with a stored procedure in the database. Listing 22.16 illustrates the function that retrieves a SqlCommand instance for inserting a record.

LISTING 22.16   GetDataAdapterInsertCommand()

```
1:   function GetDataAdapterInsertCommand: SqlCommand;
2:   var
3:     sqlCmd: SqlCommand;
4:   begin
5:     sqlCmd := SqlCommand.Create('InsertProduct', sqlCn);
6:     sqlCmd.CommandType := CommandType.StoredProcedure;
7:
8:     sqlCmd.Parameters.Add('@ProductID',     SqlDbType.Int, 0,
9:       'ProductID');
10:    sqlCmd.Parameters.Add('@ProductName',   SqlDbType.NVarChar, 40,
11:      'ProductName');
12:    sqlCmd.Parameters.Add('@SupplierID',    SqlDbType.Int, 0,
13:      'SupplierID');
14:    sqlCmd.Parameters.Add('@CategoryID',     SqlDbType.Int, 0,
15:      'CategoryID');
16:    sqlCmd.Parameters.Add('@QuantityPerUnit', SqlDbType.NVarChar, 20,
17:      'QuantityPerUnit');
18:    sqlCmd.Parameters.Add('@UnitPrice',      SqlDbType.Money, 0,
19:      'UnitPrice');
20:    sqlCmd.Parameters.Add('@UnitsInStock',   SqlDbType.SmallInt, 0,
21:      'UnitsInStock');
22:    sqlCmd.Parameters.Add('@UnitsOnOrder',   SqlDbType.SmallInt, 0,
23:      'UnitsOnOrder');
24:    sqlCmd.Parameters.Add('@ReorderLevel',   SqlDbType.SmallInt, 0,
25:      'ReorderLevel');
26:    sqlCmd.Parameters.Add('@Discontinued',   SqlDbType.Bit, 0,
27:      'Discontinued');
28:
29:    sqlCmd.Parameters['@ProductID'].Direction :=
30:      ParameterDirection.Output;
31:    sqlCmd.Parameters['@ProductID'].SourceVersion :=
32:      DataRowVersion.Original;
33:
34:    Result := sqlCmd;
35:  end;
```

▶ Find the code on the CD: \Code\Chapter 22\Ex04.

As with the SelectCommand, line 6 specifies that this SqlCommand class is dealing with a stored procedure. Note that in creating the parameters for the stored procedure, I use the over-loaded Add() method, which takes the field name as the last parameter. Not doing this causes an exception to be raised because the SqlDataAdapter will not have mapped the DataTable column to a parameter in the stored procedure. Lines 29–30 show how to indicate one of the stored procedure parameters as an output parameter. This means that the value will be returned back to the calling application. In this case, I am returning the ProductID, which is the primary key for the Products table. The INSERT stored procedure is shown in Listing 22.17.

LISTING 22.17 InsertProduct Stored Procedure

```
CREATE PROCEDURE InsertProduct
  @ProductID        int output,
  @ProductName        nvarchar(40),
  @SupplierID       int,
  @CategoryID       int,
  @QuantityPerUnit    nvarchar(20),
  @UnitPrice        money,
  @UnitsInStock       smallint,
  @UnitsOnOrder       smallint,
  @ReorderLevel       smallint,
  @Discontinued       bit
AS
  SET NOCOUNT ON
  INSERT INTO Products (
    ProductName,
    SupplierID,
    CategoryID,
    QuantityPerUnit,
    UnitPrice,
    UnitsInStock,
    UnitsOnOrder,
    ReorderLevel,
    Discontinued)
  VALUES (
    @ProductName,
    @SupplierID,
    @CategoryID,
    @QuantityPerUnit,
    @UnitPrice,
    @UnitsInStock,
    @UnitsOnOrder,
    @ReorderLevel,
    @Discontinued)

  IF @@rowcount = 0
    return 0

  SET @ProductID = Scope_Identity()

  SELECT @ProductID ProductID

  return

GO
```

▶ Find the code on the CD: \Code\Chapter 22\Ex04.

Listing 22.18 is the GetDataAdapterUpdateCommand(), which shows the creating of the SqlCommand instance associated with the UPDATE stored procedure.

LISTING 22.18   GetDataAdapterUpdateCommand()

```
1:   function GetDataAdapterUpdateCommand: SqlCommand;
2:   var
3:     sqlCmd: SqlCommand;
4:   begin
5:     sqlCmd := SqlCommand.Create('UpdateProduct', sqlCn);
6:     sqlCmd.CommandType := CommandType.StoredProcedure;
7:
8:     sqlCmd.Parameters.Add('@ProductID', SqlDbType.Int, 0,
9:       'ProductID');
10:    sqlCmd.Parameters.Add('@ProductName', SqlDbType.NVarChar, 40,
11:      'ProductName');
12:    sqlCmd.Parameters.Add('@SupplierID', SqlDbType.Int, 0,
13:      'SupplierID');
14:    sqlCmd.Parameters.Add('@CategoryID', SqlDbType.Int, 0,
15:      'CategoryID');
16:    sqlCmd.Parameters.Add('@QuantityPerUnit', SqlDbType.NVarChar, 20,
17:      'QuantityPerUnit');
18:    sqlCmd.Parameters.Add('@UnitPrice', SqlDbType.Money, 0,
19:      'UnitPrice');
20:    sqlCmd.Parameters.Add('@UnitsInStock', SqlDbType.SmallInt, 0,
21:      'UnitsInStock');
22:    sqlCmd.Parameters.Add('@UnitsOnOrder', SqlDbType.SmallInt, 0,
23:      'UnitsOnOrder');
24:    sqlCmd.Parameters.Add('@ReorderLevel', SqlDbType.SmallInt, 0,
25:      'ReorderLevel');
26:    sqlCmd.Parameters.Add('@Discontinued', SqlDbType.Bit, 0,
27:      'Discontinued');
28:
29:    sqlCmd.Parameters['@ProductID'].SourceVersion :=
30:      DataRowVersion.Original;
31:
32:    Result := sqlCmd;
33:  end;
```

▶ Find the code on the CD: \Code\Chapter 22\Ex04.

This function is similar to that in Listing 22.16 dealing with the INSERT stored procedure. The GetDataAdapterUpdateCommand() function, however, does not deal with an output parameter. This might not always be the case. You might have UPDATE stored procedures that must return values that get assigned by the system. To keep the calling application in sync with the data store, you'll need to return any system generated values. This would be handled in the same manner as shown in Listing 22.16. Listing 22.19 shows the UPDATE stored procedure associated with the SqlCommand class in line 5 of Listing 22.18.

LISTING 22.19   UpdateProduct Stored Procedure

```
CREATE PROCEDURE UpdateProduct
  @ProductID          int,
  @ProductName        nvarchar(40),
  @SupplierID         int,
  @CategoryID         int,
  @QuantityPerUnit    nvarchar(20),
```

LISTING 22.19   Continued

```
    @UnitPrice              money,
    @UnitsInStock            smallint,
    @UnitsOnOrder            smallint,
    @ReorderLevel            smallint,
    @Discontinued            bit
AS
  SET NOCOUNT ON
  UPDATE Products
  SET
    ProductName     = @ProductName,
    SupplierID      = @SupplierID,
    CategoryID      = @CategoryID,
    QuantityPerUnit = @QuantityPerUnit,
    UnitPrice       = @UnitPrice,
    UnitsInStock    = @UnitsInStock,
    UnitsOnOrder    = @UnitsOnOrder,
    ReorderLevel    = @ReorderLevel,
    Discontinued    = @Discontinued
  WHERE
    ProductID       = @ProductID

  IF @@rowcount = 0
    return 0

  return

GO
```

▶ Find the code on the CD: \Code\Chapter 22\Ex04.

Finally, Listing 22.20 shows the function that creates a SqlCommand instance that deals with the DELETE stored procedures for the Products table.

LISTING 22.20   GetDataAdapterDeleteCommand()

```
1:    function GetDataAdapterDeleteCommand: SqlCommand;
2:    var
3:      sqlCmd: SqlCommand;
4:    begin
5:      sqlCmd := SqlCommand.Create('DeleteProduct', sqlCn);
6:      sqlCmd.CommandType := CommandType.StoredProcedure;
7:
8:      sqlCmd.Parameters.Add('@ProductID', SqlDbType.Int, 0, 'ProductID');
9:
10:     sqlCmd.Parameters['@ProductID'].SourceVersion :=
11:        DataRowVersion.Original;
12:
13:     Result := sqlCmd;
14:   end;
```

▶ Find the code on the CD: \Code\Chapter 22\Ex04.

You'll note that the `GetDataAdapterDeleteCommand()` is quite a bit smaller than the other two functions. The reason here is because the stored procedure for deleting a record uses only the primary key field, `ProductID`, for locating the record to be deleted in the database. This is shown in Listing 22.21.

LISTING 22.21   DeleteProduct Stored Procedure

```
CREATE PROCEDURE DeleteProduct
  @ProductID  int
AS
  SET NOCOUNT ON

  DELETE FROM Products
  WHERE
    ProductID      = @ProductID

  return
GO
```

▶ Find the code on the CD: `\Code\Chapter 22\Ex04`.

Handling Concurrency

If you are developing a multiuser application, you will inevitably run in to a situation in which two users retrieve a record and try to modify it at the same time. In few cases, the "last in wins" approach is acceptable especially if users are unaware that this occurs.

For most cases, there are two primary ways that concurrency can be managed. You have seen the first with the `CommandBuilder` class. This approach requires that the user saving the record must pass the `Original` values of all columns for a modified row so that the server can ensure that each row matches that which exists in the database before updating the database row. If there is no match, it means that the record has been modified by another user. An exception should be raised, and the second user should be given an opportunity to do something about the exception.

Although effective, this approach is highly inefficient. A better approach would be to use time stamp fields, or something equivalent to time stamps, for data sources that do not support timestamps.

A time stamp is not, as the name implies, a `DateTime` value. It is a binary value that is unique within the database. When a record containing a time stamp has been modified, the time stamp is also changed. This works because the database uses a time stamp as part of the search on a record when it is updated. Therefore, only the primary key and the time stamp are used to locate the record instead of every column in the row.

To illustrate this, I've created a database based on that shown in Figure 22.1. The scripts to create and populate this database can be found on the CD in the directory `\Code\Databases`.

You'll notice that the two tables, company and contact, both contain a time stamp field, `row_version`. The following example illustrates how to use the time stamp column; it also illustrates how you can use `SqlDataAdapter.RowUpdatedEvent` to possibly handle errors.

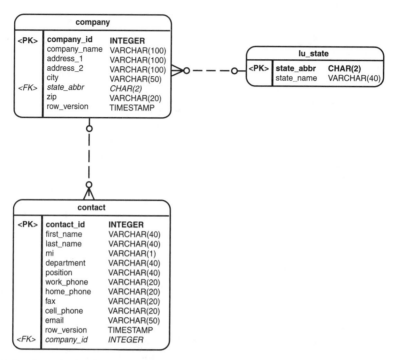

FIGURE 22.1   Sample database diagram.

Listing 22.22 shows the main code block for this example. This is a partial listing of the example on the CD.

LISTING 22.22   Concurrency Example

```
1:     program ConcurrencyDemo;
2:
3:     uses
4:        System.Data,
5:        System.Data.SqlClient,
6:        System.IO;
7:     var
8:        sqlCn: SqlConnection;
9:       sqlDA: SqlDataAdapter;
10:       dsCompany: DataSet;
11:       tblcontact: DataTable;
12:       dr: DataRow;
13:
14:    const
15:       c_cnstr = 'server=XWING;database=ddn_company;Trusted_Connection=Yes';
16:       c_sel_cst = 'SELECT * FROM company; SELECT * FROM contact';
17:
18:    begin
19:       sqlCn := SqlConnection.Create(c_cnstr);
20:       sqlDA := SqlDataAdapter.Create(c_sel_cst, sqlCn);
21:       dsCompany := DataSet.Create('ddn_company');
```

LISTING 22.22   Continued

```
22:
23:     sqlDA.TableMappings.Add('Table', 'company');
24:     sqlDA.TableMappings.Add('Table1', 'contact');
25:     sqlDA.Fill(dsCompany);
26:     sqlDA.ContinueUpdateOnError := True;
27:     Include(sqlDA.RowUpdated, OnRowUpdated);
28:     sqlDA.UpdateCommand := GetDAUpdateCommand;2929:
30:     tblcontact := dsCompany.Tables['contact'];
31:     //Modify two rows
32:     dr := tblcontact.Rows[0];
33:     dr['cell_phone'] := '111-111-1122';
34:     dr := tblcontact.Rows[1];
35:     dr['cell_phone'] := '555-555-5556';
36:
37:     Console.WriteLine('Press enter when you are ready to update.');
38:     Console.ReadLine;
39:
40:     sqlDA.Update(tblcontact);
41: end.
```

▶ Find the code on the CD: \Code\Chapter 22\Ex05.

Line 26 sets the SqlDataAdapter.ContinueUpdateOnError property to True in order to allow all updates to occur—even if one of the updates results in an error. By not setting this to True, a DBConcurrencyException is raised upon the first error. Line 27 provides an event handler that is invoked after a row is updated. Within this event handler, you have the opportunity to provide some special handling when an error occurs.

Listing 22.23 shows the OnRowUpdated event handler that is added to the SqlDataAdapter.RowUpdatedEvent in line 27 of Listing 22.22.

LISTING 22.23   OnRowUpdated() Event Handler

```
1:  procedure OnRowUpdated(sender: System.Object; e: SqlRowUpdatedEventArgs);
2:  begin
3:    Console.WriteLine('Command: '+e.Command.ToString);
4:    Console.WriteLine('CommandType: '+Enum(e.StatementType).ToString);
5:    Console.WriteLine('RecordsAffected: '+e.RecordsAffected.ToString);
6:    Console.WriteLine('Status: '+Enum(e.Status).ToString);
7:
8:    if e.Status = UpdateStatus.ErrorsOccurred then
9:    begin
10:     Console.WriteLine('Error Type: '+e.Errors.GetType.ToString);
11:     Console.WriteLine('On contact_id: '+E.Row['contact_id'].ToString);
12:    end;
13:
14:   Console.WriteLine('—');
15: end;
```

▶ Find the code on the CD: \Code\Chapter 22\Ex05.

One of the parameters to the `OnRowUpdated` event handler is a `SqlRowUpdateEventArgs` class (line 1). This class contains information about the row and the update status. This example simply writes information back to the console about each row update. If an error occurs, the row identifier, `contact_id` (line 11), is also displayed.

> **CAUTION**
>
> When processing errors in the `RowUpdated` event, the application has a live connection to the data source. It is important not to do any lengthy processing in this event. This would include any processing that would require user interaction. If an error exists that requires user interaction, it is best to asynchronously invoke some action that would enable this event to finish but still allow the user to perform her task.

> **TIP**
>
> A way to handle the asynchronous invocation mentioned in the preceding caution would be to use the asynch call model of a delegate through the `BeginInvoke()` and `EndInvoke()` methods. Delphi hides these methods, so you would have to use Reflection to do this. Although this is not something specifically covered in this book, numerous examples are available at various locations on the Internet.

The setting up of the `UpdateCommand` property is where you specify to use the `Original` version of the time stamp parameter. I will not list the entire procedure here. The specific lines that do this within the `GetDAUpdateCommand()` function are

```
sqlCmd.Parameters.Add('@row_version', SqlDbType.TimeStamp, 0,
  'row_version');
sqlCmd.Parameters['@row_version'].SourceVersion :=
  DataRowVersion.Original;
```

The remaining lines of the `GetDAUpdateCommand()` function look very similar to those shown in previous examples.

To demonstrate the concurrency handling, I added the `ReadLine()` method prior to actually sending the updated data to the data source (refer to Listing 22.22, line 38). This allowed me to use the SQL Analyzer tool to modify the first row in the contact table, thus simulating a concurrent write. The modification I made was

```
update contact set first_name = 'Robert' where contact_id = 1
```

After submitting this update and then pressing the Enter key within the application's console window, the following output is displayed showing that one record update succeeded, whereas another failed:

```
[n:\chapter 22\Ex05]ConcurrencyDemo.exe
Press enter when you are ready to update.

Command: System.Data.SqlClient.SqlCommand
CommandType: Update
RecordsAffected: 0
Status: ErrorsOccurred
Error Type: System.Data.DBConcurrencyException
```

```
On contact_id: 1
—
Command: System.Data.SqlClient.SqlCommand
CommandType: Update
RecordsAffected: 1
Status: Continue
—
```

You can see that the first record update failed because another user had made modifications to that record prior to it being posted within this application.

Refreshing Data After It Is Updated

For the most part, when you are updating or adding data to a data source, you have most of the information already in your DataSet. However, you will be lacking data generated by the data source, such as auto-incrementing fields that are used as identifiers and perhaps timestamps that you'll need for further updates so that concurrency is handled correctly.

There are a few ways in which you can get this information back into the DataSet, which are discussed here.

The SqlCommand class' UpdatedRowSource property determines how data is passed back to the DataRow whenever an update is made through the SqlDataAdapter.Update() method. This property can hold one of four values shown in Table 22.1.

TABLE 22.1   UpdatedRowSource Values

Value	Description
Both	Both output parameters and the first returned row are passed back to the modified DataRow.
FirstReturnedRecord	Only the values in the first returned row are passed back to the modified DataRow.
None	Returned row values and parameters are ignored.
OutputParameters	Only output parameters are passed back to the modified DataRow.

One of the ways to return values back to the modified DataRow involves performing a batch query as part of the INSERT or UPDATE Transact-SQL statements. This requires that the underlying data source support batch queries.

Using the database from the last example, Listings 22.24 and 22.25 show the Transact-SQL statements for an INSERT and UPDATE operation, respectively.

LISTING 22.24   INSERT Transact-SQL Statement

```
INSERT INTO contact (
  first_name,
  last_name,
  mi,
  department,
  position,
  work_phone,
  home_phone,
```

LISTING 22.24   Continued

```
  fax,
  cell_phone,
  email,
  company_id)
VALUES (
  @first_name,
  @last_name,
  @mi,
  @department,
  @position,
  @work_phone,
  @home_phone,
  @fax,
  @cell_phone,
  @email,
  @company_id);

SET @contact_id = Scope_Identity();
SELECT row_version, @contact_id contact_id
FROM contact
WHERE  (contact_id = @contact_id)
```

▶ Find the code on the CD: \Code\Chapter 22\Ex06.

LISTING 22.25   UPDATE Transact-SQL Statement

```
UPDATE contact
SET
  first_name     = @first_name,
  last_name      = @last_name,
  mi             = @mi,
  department     = @department,
  position       = @position,
  work_phone     = @work_phone,
  home_phone     = @home_phone,
  fax            = @fax,
  cell_phone     = @cell_phone,
  email          = @email
WHERE
  contact_id     = @contact_id AND
  row_version    = @row_version;

SELECT row_version FROM contact WHERE (contact_id = @contact_id)
```

▶ Find the code on the CD: \Code\Chapter 22\Ex06.

You'll notice that both of these statements contain a SELECT statement following the UPDATE statement. In the case of the INSERT statement (see Listing 22.24), the SELECT statement retrieves both the new contact_id and row_version. In the case of the UPDATE statement (see Listing 22.25), only the row_version is retrieved.

Another technique to retrieve the identity of a newly added record is to use the RowUpdated event of SqlDataAdapter. Recall that the RowUpdated event occurs when the connection is still live and the scope of the transaction is still valid. Therefore, Listing 22.26 shows how you can retrieve the last identifier and add it to the DataRow.

LISTING 22.26   RowUpdated Event Used to Retrieve Last Identifier

```
// handler for RowUpdated event
procedure OnRowUpdated(sender: System.Object; e: SqlRowUpdatedEventArgs);
var
  sqlCmdID: SqlCommand;
  contact_id: Integer;
begin
  if (e.Status = UpdateStatus.Continue) and
     (e.StatementType = StatementType.Insert) then
  begin
    sqlCmdID := SqlCommand.Create('SELECT @@IDENTITY', sqlCn);
    e.Row['contact_id'] := sqlCmdID.ExecuteScalar;
    e.Row.AcceptChanges;
  end;
end;
```

▶ Find the code on the CD: \Code\Chapter 22\Ex07.

IN THIS CHAPTER

- Transaction Processing
- Strongly-Typed DataSets

CHAPTER **23**

Working with Transactions and Strongly-Typed DataSets

This chapter will provide you with an understanding of a data source capability that you can use to enforce data integrity with your database applications. This capability is called transaction processing. Additionally, this chapter also covers strongly-typed DataSets. This feature, supported by the IDE, can greatly increase your development productivity.

Transaction Processing

Often, updates to tables must occur as a grouped operation. For instance, suppose that within an operation you must update multiple tables. If the update operation on any of the tables fails, the entire operation must fail. This includes previous updates to other tables within the same operation.

This type of protection can be achieved using transaction processing. Transactions are statements that define the beginning and ending of operation boundaries. Transactions are represented by the SqlTransaction class. This class is returned as the result of the SqlConnection.BeginTransaction() method.

When a transaction is invoked, all operations through the specified connection occur within the transaction's boundaries. When the operations are complete, changes are posted by invoking the SqlTransaction.Commit() method. If, however, an error occurs as a result of one of the operations, it might be necessary to abort the transaction. This is done through the SqlTransaction.Rollback() method.

The typical skeleton code of a transaction operation, therefore, looks like this:

```
MyTransaction := MysqlConnection.BeginTransaction;
try
  // Do operations
  MyTransaction.Commit;
except
  MyTransaction.Rollback;
  raise; // or do some other error processing as needed
end;
```

Any updates made to the data source after the `try` statement will succeed upon invoking the `MyTransaction.Commit()` method. However, if an exception occurs at anytime prior to calling `MyTransaction.Commit()`, the `except` block is executed and the `MyTransaction.Rollback()` method is invoked, thus aborting all data source updates. What you do within the `except` block really depends on the circumstances. At a minimum, you would reraise the exception. You could also log the error without causing the exception to be reraised, but spawn some other process that the user must respond to.

A Simple Transaction Processing Example

Using the company database from Chapter 22, "Saving Data to the Data Source," the following example illustrates how a transaction can contain a save operation to two tables. The program will first add a record to the company table. Then, using the company_id obtained from that operation, it will add a record to the contact table. Listing 23.1 shows this example program.

LISTING 23.1   Simple Transaction Processing Example

```
1:    program TransEx;
2:    uses
3:      System.Data,
4:      System.Data.SqlClient,
5:      System.IO;
6:
7:    const
8:      c_cnstr = 'server=XWING;database=ddn_company;Trusted_Connection=Yes';
9:      c_sel_cst = 'SELECT * FROM company; SELECT * FROM contact';
10:
11:   var
12:     sqlCn: SqlConnection;
13:     sqlDA: SqlDataAdapter;
14:     dsCompany: DataSet;
15:     sqlTrans: sqlTransaction;
16:
17:     cmdInsCompany: SqlCommand;
18:     cmdInsContact: SqlCommand;
19:     drCompany: DataRow;
20:     drContact: DataRow;
21:
22:   function GetInsertContactCmd: SqlCommand;
23:   begin
24:     ...
25:   end;
26:
```

LISTING 23.1   Continued

```
27: function GetInsertCompanyCmd: SqlCommand;
28: begin
29: ...
30: end;
31:
32: function InsertCompany: DataRow;
33: begin
34:    // add a company
35:    Result := dsCompany.Tables['company'].NewRow;
36:    Result['company_name'] := 'Xapware Technologies Inc.';
37:    Result['address_1']    := '4164 Austin Bluffs Pkwy, #363';
38:    Result['city']         := 'Colorado Springs';
39:    Result['state_abbr']   := 'CO';
40:    Result['zip']          := '80918';
41:
42:    // populate the SqlCommand parameters
43:    cmdInsCompany.Parameters['@company_name'].Value :=
44:      Result['company_name'];
45:    cmdInsCompany.Parameters['@address_1'].Value := Result['address_1'];
46:    cmdInsCompany.Parameters['@address_2'].Value := Result['address_2'];
47:    cmdInsCompany.Parameters['@city'].Value := Result['city'];
48:    cmdInsCompany.Parameters['@state_abbr'].Value := Result['state_abbr'];
49:    cmdInsCompany.Parameters['@zip'].Value := Result['zip'];
50:    cmdInsCompany.Transaction := sqlTrans;
51:    cmdInsCompany.ExecuteNonQuery;
52:
53:    // assign the system generated id to the data row
54:    Result['company_id'] := cmdInsCompany.Parameters['@company_id'].Value;
55: end;
56:
57: function InsertContact(acompany_id: Integer): DataRow;
58: begin
59:    Result := dsCompany.Tables['contact'].NewRow;
60:    Result['first_name'] := 'Xavier';
61:    Result['last_name']  := 'Pacheco';
62:    Result['mi']         := 'G';
63:    Result['department'] := 'Dept 1';
64:    Result['position']   := 'Worker bee';
65:    Result['work_phone'] := '123-123-1234';
66:    Result['home_phone'] := '234-234-2344';
67:    Result['fax']        := '456-456-4566';
68:    Result['cell_phone'] := '345-345-3654';
69:    Result['email']      := 'xavier@somewhere.com';
70:    Result['company_id'] := System.Object(acompany_id);
71:
72:    // populate the SqlCommand parameters
73:    cmdInsContact.Parameters['@first_name'].Value := Result['first_name'];
74:    cmdInsContact.Parameters['@last_name'].Value := Result['last_name'];
75:    cmdInsContact.Parameters['@mi'].Value := Result['mi'];
76:    cmdInsContact.Parameters['@department'].Value := Result['department'];
77:    cmdInsContact.Parameters['@position'].Value := Result['position'];
78:    cmdInsContact.Parameters['@work_phone'].Value := Result['work_phone'];
79:    cmdInsContact.Parameters['@home_phone'].Value := Result['home_phone'];
```

LISTING 23.1   Continued

```
80:    cmdInsContact.Parameters['@fax'].Value := Result['fax'];
81:    cmdInsContact.Parameters['@cell_phone'].Value := Result['cell_phone'];
82:    cmdInsContact.Parameters['@email'].Value := Result['email'];
83:    cmdInsContact.Parameters['@company_id'].Value :=
84:      System.Object(acompany_id);
85:    cmdInsContact.Transaction := sqlTrans;
86:    cmdInsContact.ExecuteNonQuery;
87:
88:    // assign the system generated id to the data row
89:    Result['contact_id'] := cmdInsContact.Parameters['@contact_id'].Value;
90:
91:  end;
92:
93:  begin
94:    sqlCn := SqlConnection.Create(c_cnstr);
95:    sqlDA := SqlDataAdapter.Create(c_sel_cst, sqlCn);
96:    dsCompany := DataSet.Create('ddn_company');
97:
98:    sqlDA.TableMappings.Add('Table', 'company');
99:    sqlDA.TableMappings.Add('Table1', 'contact');
100:   sqlDA.Fill(dsCompany);
101:
102:   cmdInsCompany := GetInsertCompanyCmd;
103:   cmdInsContact := GetInsertContactCmd;
104:
105:   sqlcn.Open;
106:   try
107:     sqlTrans := sqlcn.BeginTransaction;
108:     try
109:       drCompany := InsertCompany;
110:       drContact := InsertContact(Integer(drCompany['company_id']));
111:       sqlTrans.Commit;
112:     except
113:       sqlTrans.Rollback;
114:       raise;
115:     end;
116:     // Add the rows to the dataset
117:     dsCompany.Tables['company'].Rows.Add(drCompany);
118:     dsCompany.Tables['contact'].Rows.Add(drContact);
119:   finally
120:     sqlcn.Close;
121:   end;
122: end.
```

▶ Find the code on the CD: \Code\Chapter 23\Ex01.

Listing 23.1 is an excerpt of an application that illustrates using a SqlTransaction class to insert rows to two tables within a SQL Server database. The updates are done using SqlCommand classes.

The functions GetInsertCompanyCmd() and GetInsertContactCmd() (both of which are excluded from the listing) simply load the Transact-SQL statements for inserting records into the company and contact tables, respectively. They return the resulting SqlCommand class instances (lines 102, 103).

The main idea is to add the record to the master table first (company), and then use the resulting primary key as the foreign key to the detail table insert (contact). System generated values, such as the primary keys, are retrieved from output parameters and assigned to their respective column in the DataRow. If both insertions are successful, the DataRows are added to the DataSet to keep the DataSet in sync with the data source.

The two functions InsertCompany() and InsertContact() perform the insertion operations. First, each function creates a new DataRow from the DataSet for its respective table. It adds the column values—except for the primary keys as these are generated by the data source. They then assign these values to the parameters in their respective SqlCommand objects and invoke the update by calling the SqlCommand.ExecuteNonQuery() function. The output parameters of the SqlCommand objects are the primary keys for each record insert. The primary keys are assigned to the DataRow, which is the result of the insertion function.

Lines 107–115 show the transaction code. The transaction is initiated in line 107. Within the try block, the InsertCompany() function is called and returns the inserted DataRow. The primary key column from this DataRow is used as the parameter to the InsertContact() function. InsertContact() also returns the inserted DataRow. If all succeeds without error, the transaction's Commit() method is called (line 111). Otherwise, if an exception is raised, the function is rolled back and the exception is reraised. Lines 117–118 show how the rows are added to the DataSet to keep it in sync with the DataSource. These lines would not be called if an exception occurs.

Transactions When Using a DataAdapter

You can do transaction processing when using a DataAdapter by assigning the transaction class to each of the DataAdapter's command objects. Then, you simply enclose the DataAdapter's Update() function within the transaction as illustrated in the following code:

```
sqlTrans := sqlcn.BeginTransaction;
try
  sqlDA.InsertCommand.Transaction := sqlTrans;
  sqlDA.UpdateCommand.Transaction := sqlTrans;
  sqlDA.DeleteCommand.Transaction := sqlTrans;
  // do updates, insertions, deletions
  sqlDA.Update(dsCompany);
  sqlTrans.Commit;
except
  sqlTrans.Rollback;
  raise;
end;
```

Isolation Levels

In a multiuser environment, simultaneous operations will likely be performed on the data source, such as reads, updates, insertions, and deletions. The extent to which outside operations can see changes being made within a transaction prior to committal is controlled using isolation levels. Isolation levels enforce a locking mode on the data source that, when properly used, can avoid concurrency problems and data corruption. In ADO.NET, there are two locking modes—Shared and Exclusive. In the Shared locking mode, a concurrent transaction can read, but not modify, a locked resource. In the Exclusive locking mode, no access is allowed on the locked resource.

Isolations levels establish a degree of privacy that exists between simultaneously running transactions. Depending on the desired isolation level, reads performed within a transaction might fall in to one of several categories. These are shown in Table 23.1.

TABLE 23.1   Transaction Reads

Name	Description
Dirty Read	A transaction reads uncommitted data from a previous transaction. Because update is uncommitted, the data might be invalid. For instance, suppose that transaction A writes some rows to a table but does not commit them. Now suppose that transaction B reads them. This is called a dirty read because it is possible for transaction A to roll back the changes, resulting in transaction B having invalid data.
Nonrepeatable read	A transaction reads uncommitted data from a previous transaction. If subsequent reads by this transaction are performed, the data might be inconsistent as the prior transaction commits its updates. This is a condition in which transaction A reads a row or rows; after which, transaction B modifies some of the data that transaction A has. It is not possible for transaction A to read the same data; thus the read is nonrepeatable.
Phantom read	A transaction deletes and inserts rows that are part of a range of rows selected by another transaction. For instance, transaction A reads a set of rows based on a query. Transaction B writes some rows to the table that would have met that query. These are phantom rows.

Transaction can control the level concurrency through one of five levels of isolation that are listed in Table 23.2.

TABLE 23.2   Isolation Levels

Isolation Level	Description
ReadUncommitted	Outside transactions are able to perform a dirty read. Share locks are established, and exclusive locks are honored.
ReadCommitted	Dirty reads are prevented. Shared locks are held while a transaction reads the data. Because the data might be updated, phantom reads or nonrepeatable reads might occur.
RepeatableRead	Shared locks are placed on all data in a query preventing subsequent transactions from performing updates. Phantom reads might still occur.
Serializable	Range locks are placed on data reads, preventing subsequent transactions from updating data until the transaction is committed. This isolation level prevents phantom reads.
Chaos	Pending changes from higher isolation levels cannot be overwritten. This is not supported in SQL Server.
Unspecified	An isolation different from the others listed but not determinable.

Different data sources dictate a default isolation level. For example, the default isolation level for SQL Server is ReadCommitted. To change the isolation level of a transaction, pass the desired isolation level to the constructor when the transaction is constructed:

```
sqlTrans := sqlCN.BeginTransaction(IsolationLevel.Serializable);
```

Savepoints

In some cases, you might need to roll back only a portion of a transaction. Assuming that the data source supports this, you can use savepoints. A savepoint is equivalent to the following Transact-SQL statement:

```
SAVE TRANSACTION
```

To create a savepoint, you use the transaction's Save() method, passing a name of the savepoint. To roll back a savepoint, call the Rollback() function passing the same name used in the Save() method as shown here:

```
sqlTrans := sqlcn.BeginTransaction;
try
  // do updates 1
  sqlTrans.Save('mysave');
  try
    // do update 2
  except
    sqlTrans.Rollback('mysave');
  end;
  sqlDA.Update(dsCompany);
except
  sqlTrans.Rollback;
  raise;
end;
```

Note that the exception should not be reraised after the rollback of the savepoint, which would cause the outertransaction to fail. However, there should be a reraise of the outer rollback.

Nested Transactions

For data providers that support them, nested transactions are an alternative to savepoints. A nested transaction is created by invoking the Begin() method of the transaction object as shown in the following skeleton code:

```
oledbTransOuter := oleDBConn.BeginTransaction;
try
  oledbTransInner := oledbTransOuter.Begin;
  // outer updates
  try
    // inner updates
    oledbTransInner.Commit;
  except
    oledbTransInner.Rollback;
  end;
  oledbTransOuter.Commit;
```

```
except
  oledbTransOuter.RollBack;
end;
```

Note that nested transactions are not supported by the SqlTransaction but are potentially with the OleDBTransaction. Support for transaction nesting is contingent on the underlying driver's support for this capability.

Nested transactions can be emulated using savepoints. Although they can't individually be committed, even with nested transaction, the outer transaction determines whether the entire operation is committed.

Strongly-Typed DataSets

Up to this point, all examples using a DataSet class have used the untyped DataSet. This section discusses the strongly-typed DataSet. A strongly-typed DataSet is a DataSet class that descends from DataSet. It contains descendant DataTables and DataRows for the tables it contains. It extends the DataSet by providing properties, events, and methods that are named and strongly typed according to the tables it holds.

Strongly-typed DataSets are normally generated by the IDE or by using the xsd command-line tool included within the .NET SDK.

Advantages/Disadvantages

There are several advantages for using strongly-typed DataSets over untyped DataSets. They are

- Writing code is easier to understand because strong names make sense, and with code completion, it is further simplified.

- Developers write less code overall because named members are accessed directly rather than using indexer properties.

- Strongly-typed DataSets already contain schema information improving performance.

- The strong typing can prevent runtime errors that would occur because they will be caught at compile time.

- There could be some performance increases as lookups from strings to table and column instances is done only once instead of for each and every table and column access.

There may also be some disadvantages to using strongly-typed DataSets. These are

- There might be some performance drawbacks. This could be because of code-bloat caused by having a large number of classes and methods if you have many tables. This requires more JIT time and disk space.

- They will be difficult to maintain if the underlying schema is likely to change. The strongly-typed DataSet will need to be re-created.

- Even maintaining an untyped DataSet needs to be done when there are changes. This is likely to be more error prone, as you must manually identify and perform updates to the code to make it match the new database structure. With untyped DataSets, you lose compile-time errors, and many mistakes will not be identified until runtime. With the auto-generated typed datasets, you just have to remember to regenerate it— you are then guaranteed that the class matches the database. And changing the code that uses the typed dataset should be easier.

Creating Strongly-Typed DataSets

This section walks you through the process of creating a strongly-typed DataSet within the IDE. It assumes that you have the Northwind example database installed for a SQL Server database. If not, the steps are the same for any database.

1. Create a new Windows Forms Application and save it somewhere.

2. Add a SqlConnection component to the form. It will be named SqlConnection1.

3. Set the SqlConnection1.ConnectionString property to "server=XWING;database=Northwind; Trusted_Connection=Yes".

4. Add a SqlDataAdapter to the form. Assign to its SelectCommand.CommandText property the following string: "SELECT * FROM customers; SELECT * FROM employees". Also, set the SelectCommand.Connection property to SqlConnection1.

5. Press the ellipsis (...) button in the TableMappings property editor in the Object Inspector. This will launch the Table Mappings dialog box (see Figure 23.1).

FIGURE 23.1   Table Mappings dialog box.

Figure 23.1 shows the mapping of the Source table, Table, to Customers . Do the same for the Employees table by mapping the Source Table Table1 to Employees. Press OK to close the dialog box.

6. Right-click over the `SqlDataAdapter` to invoke the local menu and select Generate `DataSet`. The Generate Dataset dialog box will appear and should look like that shown in Figure 23.2.

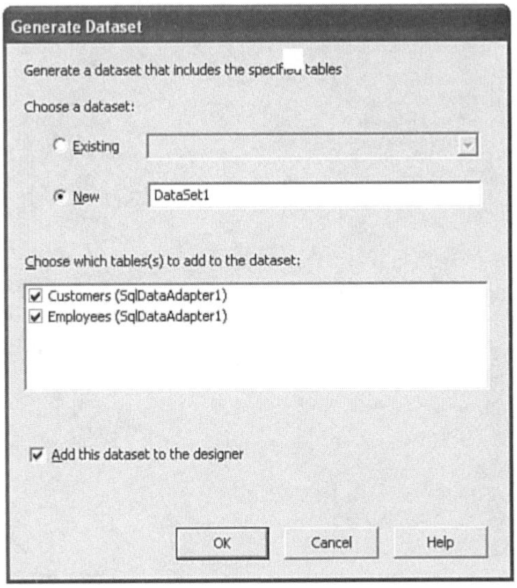

FIGURE 23.2   Generate Dataset dialog box.

7. Press OK to add the `DataSet`, named `DataSet1`, to the forms designer. This will generate the `DataSet1.xsd` and `DataSet1Unit.pas` files when you press OK.

> **NOTE**
>
> The default name given to the typed `DataSet` of `"DataSet1"` is not only dull, but also entirely nondescriptive of the data it represents. You should change it accordingly. For instance, `NorthWindDataSet` could have been used in the preceding example.

Examining the Strongly-Typed DataSet .pas File

After creating the strongly-typed DataSet, two files are added to your project. One is a `.xsd` file, and the other is a `.pas` file with a matching filename. The `.xsd` file contains the schema definition for the DataSet that is used in the construction of the source code defining the strongly-typed DataSet. The source code is contained in the `.pas` file.

Listing 23.2 is an excerpt from a project that contains the strongly-typed DataSet generated when performing the aforementioned steps.

LISTING 23.2   Strongly-typed DataSet

```
1:    DataSet1 = class(DataSet)
2:    strict private
3:    public
4:    type
```

LISTING 23.2   Continued

```
 5:       CustomerRowChangeEvent = class;
 6:       CustomerRowChangeEventHandler = procedure(sender: System.Object;
 7:         e: CustomerRowChangeEvent) of object;
 8:      CustomerRow = class;
 9:    strict private
10:     public
11:    type
12:      EmployeeRowChangeEvent = class;
13:      EmployeeRowChangeEventHandler = procedure(sender: System.Object;
14:         e: EmployeeRowChangeEvent) of object;
15:      EmployeeRow = class;
16:    strict private
17:    type
18:      [System.Diagnostics.DebuggerStepThrough]
19:      CustomerDataTable = class(DataTable,
➥System.Collections.IEnumerable) ...
20:
21:      [System.Diagnostics.DebuggerStepThrough]
22:      CustomerRow = class(DataRow) ...
23:
24:      [System.Diagnostics.DebuggerStepThrough]
25:      CustomerRowChangeEvent = class(EventArgs) ...
26:
27:      [System.Diagnostics.DebuggerStepThrough]
28:      EmployeeDataTable = class(DataTable,
➥System.Collections.IEnumerable) ...
29:
30:      TArrayOfByte = array of Byte;
31:      [System.Diagnostics.DebuggerStepThrough]
32:      EmployeeRow = class(DataRow)...
33:
34:      [System.Diagnostics.DebuggerStepThrough]
35:      EmployeeRowChangeEvent = class(EventArgs) ...
36:
37:    strict private
38:      tableCustomer: CustomerDataTable;
39:      tableEmployee: EmployeeDataTable;
40:    public
41:      constructor Create; overload;
42:    strict protected
43:      constructor Create(info: SerializationInfo;
44:         context: StreamingContext); overload;
45:    public
46:      function get_Customer: CustomerDataTable;
47:      function get_Employee: EmployeeDataTable;
48:      [System.ComponentModel.Browsable(False)]
49:      [System.ComponentModel.DesignerSerializationVisibilityAttribute(
50:        System.ComponentModel.DesignerSerializationVisibility.Content)]
51:      property Customer: CustomerDataTable read get_Customer;
52:      [System.ComponentModel.Browsable(False)]
53:      [System.ComponentModel.DesignerSerializationVisibilityAttribute(
54:        System.ComponentModel.DesignerSerializationVisibility.Content)]
55:      property Employee: EmployeeDataTable read get_Employee;
```

LISTING 23.2   Continued

```
56:       function Clone: DataSet; override;
57:    strict protected
58:       function ShouldSerializeTables: Boolean; override;
59:       function ShouldSerializeRelations: Boolean; override;
60:       procedure ReadXmlSerializable(reader: XmlReader); override;
61:       function GetSchemaSerializable: System.Xml.Schema.XmlSchema; override;
62:    private
63:       procedure InitVars;
64:    strict private
65:       procedure InitClass;
66:       function ShouldSerializeCustomer: Boolean;
67:       function ShouldSerializeEmployee: Boolean;
68:       procedure SchemaChanged(sender: System.Object;
69:          e: System.ComponentModel.CollectionChangeEventArgs);
70:    end;
```

▶ Find the code on the CD: \Code\Chapter 23\Ex02.

Listing 23.2 shows the Dataset1 class as it appears in the IDE. Dataset1 descends directly from DataSet and contains nested classes, which are descendants of DataTable and DataRow and EventArgs. The listing shows any nested classes as folded in the IDE. The various internal properties, classes, and events contained in Dataset1 are type specific according to the two tables that were included in the SELECT statement used to build the DataSet. Lines 5–7, for instance, declare the event handler that will be used for the RowChanged, RowChanging, RowDeleted, and RowDeleting events of the customer DataTable. Lines 12–14 do the same for the employee DataTable.

A CustomerDataTable class is declared on line 19. CustomerDataTable descends from DataTable. A CustomerRow class is declared on line 22, and it descends for DataRow. The matching DataTable and DataRow descendants for the employee table are declared on lines 28 and 32, respectively. The instance members of the CustomDataTable and EmployeeDataTable are declared in lines 38–39.

Two key properties of Dataset1 are shown in lines 51 and 55. These properties refer to the DataTable instances for CustomerDataTable and EmployeeDataTable.

By examining this listing, you should get a feel for how strongly-typed DataSet are constructed of three strongly-typed and nested DataTable, DataRow, and DataRowChangeEvent classes for each table contained in the Dataset. Already, you should see that just referring to a specific table is cleaner. Instead of the following code,

```
Dataset1.Tables['customer']
```

You would use the following:

```
Dataset1.Customer
```

Momentarily, you'll see how much easier it is to deal with column values.

Listing 23.3 shows the definition of one of the nested DataTables, specifically the EmployeeDataTable. The CustomerDataTable is similar in structure.

LISTING 23.3   The EmployeeDataTable Definition

```
 1:   EmployeeDataTable = class(DataTable, System.Collections.IEnumerable)
 2:   strict private
 3:     columnEmployeeID: DataColumn;
 4:     columnLastName: DataColumn;
 5:     columnFirstName: DataColumn;
 6:     columnTitle: DataColumn;
 7:     columnTitleOfCourtesy: DataColumn;
 8:     columnBirthDate: DataColumn;
 9:     columnHireDate: DataColumn;
10:     columnAddress: DataColumn;
11:     columnCity: DataColumn;
12:     columnRegion: DataColumn;
13:     columnPostalCode: DataColumn;
14:     columnCountry: DataColumn;
15:     columnHomePhone: DataColumn;
16:     columnExtension: DataColumn;
17:     columnPhoto: DataColumn;
18:     columnNotes: DataColumn;
19:     columnReportsTo: DataColumn;
20:     columnPhotoPath: DataColumn;
21:   public
22:     EmployeeRowChanged: EmployeeRowChangeEventHandler;
23:     EmployeeRowChanging: EmployeeRowChangeEventHandler;
24:     EmployeeRowDeleted: EmployeeRowChangeEventHandler;
25:     EmployeeRowDeleting: EmployeeRowChangeEventHandler;
26:   private
27:     constructor Create; overload;
28:     constructor Create(table: DataTable); overload;
29:   public
30:     function get_Count: Integer;
31:   private
32:     function get_EmployeeIDColumn: DataColumn;
33:     function get_LastNameColumn: DataColumn;
34:     function get_FirstNameColumn: DataColumn;
35:     function get_TitleColumn: DataColumn;
36:     function get_TitleOfCourtesyColumn: DataColumn;
37:     function get_BirthDateColumn: DataColumn;
38:     function get_HireDateColumn: DataColumn;
39:     function get_AddressColumn: DataColumn;
40:     function get_CityColumn: DataColumn;
41:     function get_RegionColumn: DataColumn;
42:     function get_PostalCodeColumn: DataColumn;
43:     function get_CountryColumn: DataColumn;
44:     function get_HomePhoneColumn: DataColumn;
45:     function get_ExtensionColumn: DataColumn;
46:     function get_PhotoColumn: DataColumn;
47:     function get_NotesColumn: DataColumn;
48:     function get_ReportsToColumn: DataColumn;
49:     function get_PhotoPathColumn: DataColumn;
50:   public
51:     function get_Item(index: Integer): EmployeeRow;
52:     [System.ComponentModel.Browsable(False)]
53:     property Count: Integer read get_Count;
```

LISTING 23.3   Continued

```
54: private
55:    property EmployeeIDColumn: DataColumn read get_EmployeeIDColumn;
56:    property LastNameColumn: DataColumn read get_LastNameColumn;
57:    property FirstNameColumn: DataColumn read get_FirstNameColumn;
58:    property TitleColumn: DataColumn read get_TitleColumn;
59:    property TitleOfCourtesyColumn: DataColumn
60:       read get_TitleOfCourtesyColumn;
61:    property BirthDateColumn: DataColumn read get_BirthDateColumn;
62:    property HireDateColumn: DataColumn read get_HireDateColumn;
63:    property AddressColumn: DataColumn read get_AddressColumn;
64:    property CityColumn: DataColumn read get_CityColumn;
65:    property RegionColumn: DataColumn read get_RegionColumn;
66:    property PostalCodeColumn: DataColumn read get_PostalCodeColumn;
67:    property CountryColumn: DataColumn read get_CountryColumn;
68:    property HomePhoneColumn: DataColumn read get_HomePhoneColumn;
69:    property ExtensionColumn: DataColumn read get_ExtensionColumn;
70:    property PhotoColumn: DataColumn read get_PhotoColumn;
71:    property NotesColumn: DataColumn read get_NotesColumn;
72:    property ReportsToColumn: DataColumn read get_ReportsToColumn;
73:    property PhotoPathColumn: DataColumn read get_PhotoPathColumn;
74: public
75:    property Item[index: Integer]: EmployeeRow read get_Item;
76:    procedure AddEmployeeRow(row: EmployeeRow); overload;
77:    function AddEmployeeRow(LastName: string; FirstName: string;
78:       Title: string; TitleOfCourtesy: string; BirthDate: System.DateTime;
79:       HireDate: System.DateTime; Address: string; City: string;
80:       Region: string; PostalCode: string; Country: string;
81:       HomePhone: string; Extension: string; Photo: array of Byte;
82:       Notes: string; ReportsTo: Integer; PhotoPath: string):
83:        EmployeeRow; overload;
84:    function FindByEmployeeID(EmployeeID: Integer): EmployeeRow;
85:    function GetEnumerator: System.Collections.IEnumerator;
86:    function Clone: DataTable; override;
87: strict protected
88:    function CreateInstance: DataTable; override;
89: private
90:    procedure InitVars;
91: strict private
92:    procedure InitClass;
93: public
94:    function NewEmployeeRow: EmployeeRow;
95: strict protected
96:    function NewRowFromBuilder(builder: DataRowBuilder): DataRow; override;
97:    function GetRowType: System.Type; override;
98:    procedure OnRowChanged(e: DataRowChangeEventArgs); override;
99:    procedure OnRowChanging(e: DataRowChangeEventArgs); override;
100:    procedure OnRowDeleted(e: DataRowChangeEventArgs); override;
101:    procedure OnRowDeleting(e: DataRowChangeEventArgs); override;
102: public
103:    procedure RemoveEmployeeRow(row: EmployeeRow);
104: end;
```

▶ Find the code on the CD: \Code\Chapter 23\Ex02.

Like the strongly-typed DataSet, the internal DataTable is another class containing strongly-typed members that directly correspond to the schema of the table it represents. Some key public properties and methods are contained in the descendant DataTables, and these are described in Table 23.3.

TABLE 23.3   Descendant DataTable Properties/Methods

Method/Property	Description
Item	This indexer property returns the EmployeeRow for the specified index (line 75)
AddEmployeeRow()	There are two overloaded versions of this method (lines 76 and 77). The procedure takes an EmployeeRow as a parameter and adds it to the underlying DataTable. The function takes as parameters the values for each column and performs the insertion. It also returns the EmployeeRow instance of the newly added row.
Count	This property returns the number of rows contained by the EmployeeDataTable. It is declared in line 53.
FindByEmployeeID()	This function returns the EmployeeRow for the specified EmployeeID. It is declared in line 84.
NewEmployeeRow()	This function returns a new instance of an EmployeeRow class. It is declared on line 94.
RemoveEmployeeRow()	This procedure removes the row specified by the EmployeeRow parameter. It is declared on line 103.

The properties and methods described in Table 23.3 are created for every table contained within the DataSet. The names would correspond to each table.

For each table, a strongly-typed DataRow is also created. Listing 23.4 shows the definition of the EmployeeRow descendant.

LISTING 23.4   The EmployeeRow Definition

```
1:   EmployeeRow = class(DataRow)
2:   strict private
3:     tableEmployee: EmployeeDataTable;
4:   private
5:     constructor Create(rb: DataRowBuilder);
6:   public
7:     function get_EmployeeID: Integer;
8:     function get_LastName: string;
9:     function get_FirstName: string;
10:    function get_Title: string;
11:    function get_TitleOfCourtesy: string;
12:    function get_BirthDate: System.DateTime;
13:    function get_HireDate: System.DateTime;
14:    function get_Address: string;
15:    function get_City: string;
16:    function get_Region: string;
17:    function get_PostalCode: string;
18:    function get_Country: string;
```

LISTING 23.4   Continued

```
19:     function get_HomePhone: string;
20:     function get_Extension: string;
21:     function get_Photo: TArrayOfByte;
22:     function get_Notes: string;
23:     function get_ReportsTo: Integer;
24:     function get_PhotoPath: string;
25:     procedure set_EmployeeID(Value: Integer);
26:     procedure set_LastName(Value: string);
27:     procedure set_FirstName(Value: string);
28:     procedure set_Title(Value: string);
29:     procedure set_TitleOfCourtesy(Value: string);
30:     procedure set_BirthDate(Value: System.DateTime);
31:     procedure set_HireDate(Value: System.DateTime);
32:     procedure set_Address(Value: string);
33:     procedure set_City(Value: string);
34:     procedure set_Region(Value: string);
35:     procedure set_PostalCode(Value: string);
36:     procedure set_Country(Value: string);
37:     procedure set_HomePhone(Value: string);
38:     procedure set_Extension(Value: string);
39:     procedure set_Photo(Value: TArrayOfByte);
40:     procedure set_Notes(Value: string);
41:     procedure set_ReportsTo(Value: Integer);
42:     procedure set_PhotoPath(Value: string);
43:     property EmployeeID: Integer read get_EmployeeID write set_EmployeeID;
44:     property LastName: string read get_LastName write set_LastName;
45:     property FirstName: string read get_FirstName write set_FirstName;
46:     property Title: string read get_Title write set_Title;
47:     property TitleOfCourtesy: string read get_TitleOfCourtesy
➥write set_TitleOfCourtesy;
48:     property BirthDate: System.DateTime read get_BirthDate
➥write set_BirthDate;
49:     property HireDate: System.DateTime read get_HireDate write set_HireDate;
50:     property Address: string read get_Address write set_Address;
51:     property City: string read get_City write set_City;
52:     property Region: string read get_Region write set_Region;
53:     property PostalCode: string read get_PostalCode write set_PostalCode;
54:     property Country: string read get_Country write set_Country;
55:     property HomePhone: string read get_HomePhone write set_HomePhone;
56:     property Extension: string read get_Extension write set_Extension;
57:     property Photo: TArrayOfByte read get_Photo write set_Photo;
58:     property Notes: string read get_Notes write set_Notes;
59:     property ReportsTo: Integer read get_ReportsTo write set_ReportsTo;
60:     property PhotoPath: string read get_PhotoPath write set_PhotoPath;
61:     function IsTitleNull: Boolean;
62:     procedure SetTitleNull;
63:     function IsTitleOfCourtesyNull: Boolean;
64:     procedure SetTitleOfCourtesyNull;
65:     function IsBirthDateNull: Boolean;
66:     procedure SetBirthDateNull;
67:     function IsHireDateNull: Boolean;
```

23

LISTING 23.4   Continued

```
68:     procedure SetHireDateNull;
69:     function IsAddressNull: Boolean;
70:     procedure SetAddressNull;
71:     function IsCityNull: Boolean;
72:     procedure SetCityNull;
73:     function IsRegionNull: Boolean;
74:     procedure SetRegionNull;
75:     function IsPostalCodeNull: Boolean;
76:     procedure SetPostalCodeNull;
77:     function IsCountryNull: Boolean;
78:     procedure SetCountryNull;
79:     function IsHomePhoneNull: Boolean;
80:     procedure SetHomePhoneNull;
81:     function IsExtensionNull: Boolean;
82:     procedure SetExtensionNull;
83:     function IsPhotoNull: Boolean;
84:     procedure SetPhotoNull;
85:     function IsNotesNull: Boolean;
86:     procedure SetNotesNull;
87:     function IsReportsToNull: Boolean;
88:     procedure SetReportsToNull;
89:     function IsPhotoPathNull: Boolean;
90:     procedure SetPhotoPathNull;
91:   end;
```

▶ Find the code on the CD: \Code\Chapter 23\Ex02.

The descendant `DataRow` declares a typed accessor property for each column contained in the row. Lines 7–42 are the `getter/setter` methods for the various column properties. The accessor properties are defined in lines 43–60. For each property, a function to determine whether the row is `Null` is created. A procedure to set the column value to `Null` is also created for each column.

Using the Strongly-Typed DataSet

Using a strongly-typed DataSet is rather simple. One of the real advantages of dealing with them is within the IDE because the IDE's code-completion feature recognizes the typed names. These are the types of productivity enhancers that developers appreciate.

Adding a Row

To add a row, you can retrieve a new `DataRow` from a `DataTable`, set its column values, and then pass it to the `AddEmployeeRow()` procedure as shown here:

```
var
  er: Dataset1.EmployeeRow;
```

```
begin
  er := Dataset11.Employee.NewEmployeeRow;
  er.LastName         := 'Pacheco';
  er.FirstName        := 'Xavier';
  er.Title            := 'Programmer';
...
  Dataset11.Employee.AddEmployeeRow(er);
end;
```

Alternatively, you can call the `AddEmployeeRow()` function, which takes each column value as a parameter and returns an instance of the newly added `EmployeeRow`.

> **NOTE**
>
> At the time of this writing, I had to move the declaration of the `EmployeeRow` and `CustomerRow` types to a public section within the strongly-typed `DataSet`. This was based on the released version of Delphi for .NET. This has been reported as a defect and should be patched.

Editing a Row

Editing a row is fairly straightforward, as shown in the following code:

```
var
  er: Dataset1.EmployeeRow;
begin
  er := DataSet11.Employee.Item[0];
  er.FirstName := 'Bob';
  er.LastName  := 'The Builder';
```

All the methods, such as `BeginEdit()`, `EndEdit()`, and `CancelEdit()`, are available as a consequence of having inherited them from the `DataSet` parent class.

Deleting a Row

Deleting a row involves using the `RemoveTableNameRow()` procedure, which takes a `DataRow` as a parameter as shown here:

```
DataSet11.Employee.RemoveEmployeeRow(DataSet11.Employee.Item[0]);
```

Finding a Row

Finding a row involves using the `FindTableNameByID()` function, as shown next. This function returns the located `DataRow`.

```
er := Dataset11.Employee.FindByEmployeeID(Convert.ToInt32(TextBox1.Text));
```

In the preceding example, if the primary key value cannot be found, `nil` is returned.

Hierarchical Data

If the `DataSet` contains relational data in the form of `DataRelation` classes, the `DataRow` descendant classes will contain two additional methods. These methods are provided to allow you to navigate through the hierarchical relationships. The methods are `GetChildTableNameRows()` and `GetParentTableNameRow()`.

The Get*ChildTableName*Rows() function returns an array of *ChildTableName*Row objects.

The Get*ParentTableName*Row() function returns the *ParentTableName*Row of the child row.

> **TIP**
>
> It is recommended that you examine the implementation of the generated methods within a strongly-typed DataSet, which will give you a better understanding of what is happening under the hood, so to speak.

CHAPTER 24

The Borland Data Provider

IN THIS CHAPTER

- Architecture Overview
- Borland Data Provider Classes
- Designers within the IDE

As part of the Delphi for .NET and C# Builder toolsets, Borland has included its own implementation of the core Data Provider interfaces. This chapter discusses the Borland Data Provider (BDP) and the components that make up the BDP. It demonstrates the use of these components in developing your own .NET applications.

Architecture Overview

The Borland Data Provider Architecture is best described as an open architecture that provides the necessary interfaces for third-party integration. This architecture is depicted in Figure 24.1.

By implementing the core interfaces, data sources of any type can be integrated into the BDP architecture. The provider that the BDP components will be working with is determined by its entry in the CommandText of the BdpConnection component. Implementation details are completely hidden from users of the BDP components.

Hiding implementation details has the following key advantages:

- Users can code to a unified model.

- Code written for one data source will work for another data source.

- Data types are mapped by the BDP to specific .NET data types.

- There is no COM Interop layer.

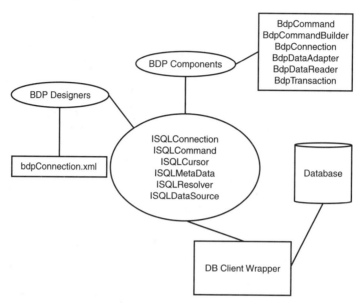

FIGURE 24.1   The Borland Data Provider architecture.

Whereas the .NET Framework ships with multiple data providers for accessing different data sources, the Borland Data Provider is a single unified provider through which multiple data sources are accessed. Currently, the following databases are supported by the BDP:

- Interbase

- Oracle

- IBM DB2

- Microsoft SQL

The following sections demonstrate using the various BDP classes.

Borland Data Provider Classes

The BDP classes correspond to other data provider classes directly. BDP classes are defined in the Borland.Data.Provider namespace. In fact, much of what you have read in the chapters covering ADO.NET used the classes from the System.Data.SQLClient namespace only. This coverage pertained to other Data Providers classes as well, and the same goes for the BDP classes. You should already know how to use these classes for the most part. Therefore, this chapter introduces each class and provides an example on its usage. The details of using these classes are not repeated. Table 24.1 shows the corresponding classes from the Borland, SqlClient, and OleDB data providers.

TABLE 24.1   Data Provider Classes

BDP Class	SqlClient Class	OleDB Class
BdpCommand	SqlCommand	OleDBCommand
BdpCommandBuilder	SqlCommandBuilder	OleDbCommandBuilder
BdpConnection	SqlConnection	OleDbConnection
BdpDataAdapter	SqlDataAdapter	OleDBDataAdapter
BdpDataReader	SqlDataReader	OleDbDataReader
BdpTransaction	SqlTransaction	OleDbTransaction

> **NOTE**
>
> In demonstrating the following components, I will mostly use a runtime assignment to properties so that the various property assignments are clear. These properties can be set at design-time and in doing so will use the various design-time editors, which can make developing with these components much easier.

BdpConnection

The BdpConnection class is used to connect to databases. Prior to opening a connection using the BdpConnection class, you must specify a valid entry to its ConnectionString property. Use the Open() method to open a database connection. Likewise, use the Close() method to close a database connection. Listing 24.1 illustrates opening and closing a BdpConnection class.

LISTING 24.1   Establishing a Connection with BdpConnection

```
1:   const
2:     cnStr = 'assembly=Borland.Data.Interbase, Version=1.5.0.0, '+
3:       'Culture=neutral,PublicKeyToken=91d62ebb5b0d1b1b;
➥vendorclient=gds32.dll;'+
4:       'database=C:\Program Files\Common Files\Borland
➥Shared\Data\EMPLOYEE.GDB;'+
5:       'provider=Interbase;username=sysdba;password=masterkey';
6:   procedure TWinForm.btnOpen_Click(sender: System.Object;
7:     e: System.EventArgs);
8:   var
9:     bdpCn: BdpConnection;
10:  begin
11:    bdpCn := BdpConnection.Create(cnStr);
12:    Include(bdpCn.StateChange, Self.BdpCn_StateChange);
13:    bdpCn.Open;
14:    bdpCn.Close;
15:  end;
```

▶ Find the code on the CD: \Code\Chapter 24\Ex01.

Lines 2–5 represent the connection string to an Interbase database. The ConnectionString assignment is handled implicitly by the BdpConnection.Create() constructor call (line 11). Line 12 creates and also demonstrates adding an event handler to the StateChange event. Both the assignment to ConnectionString and to the StateChange event could have been done at design time through the Object Inspector. The last section of this chapter demonstrates using the Connections Editor to create a connection for the BdpConnection at design time.

When using the BdpConnection, you must always match a call to Open() with a call to Close() as this is not done implicitly. The bdpCn_StateChange() event handler performs one line of code:

```
ListBox1.Items.Add(e.CurrentState)
```

This code writes out one of the two states in which the BdpConnection can be. This is either Open or Closed.

General use of the BdpConnection class is similar to the SqlConnection class discussed in previous chapters.

BdpCommand

The BdpCommand class is used to execute SQL statements against the underlying data source. This includes the execution of stored procedures. Listing 24.2 illustrates using the BdpCommand class.

LISTING 24.2   Using the BdpCommand Class

```
1:   const
2:     cnStr = 'assembly=Borland.Data.Interbase, Version=1.5.0.0, '+
3:       'Culture=neutral,PublicKeyToken=91d62ebb5b0d1b1b;
➥vendorclient=gds32.dll;'+
4:       'database=C:\Program Files\Common Files\Borland
➥Shared\Data\EMPLOYEE.GDB;'+
5:       'provider=Interbase;username=sysdba;password=masterkey';
6:   procedure TWinForm.btnOpen_Click(sender: System.Object;
7:     e: System.EventArgs);
8:   var
9:     bdpCn: BdpConnection;
10:    bdpCmd: BdpCommand;
11:    bdpRdr: BdpDataReader;
12:  begin
13:    bdpCn := BdpConnection.Create(cnStr);
14:    Include(bdpCn.StateChange, Self.BdpCn_StateChange);
15:
16:    bdpCn.Open;
17:    try
18:      bdpCmd := bdpCn.CreateCommand;
19:      bdpCmd.CommandText := 'SELECT * FROM customer';
20:      bdpRdr := bdpCmd.ExecuteReader;
21:    finally
22:      bdpCn.Close;
23:    end;
24:  end;
```

▶ Find the code on the CD: \Code\Chapter 24\Ex02.

The BdpConnection must be opened before you can execute any of the BdpCommand methods that access the database. In this example, the BdpCommand.ExecuteReader() method is called, which returns a BdpDataReader. The next section discusses the BdpDataReader class. The additional commands that can be executed against the underlying data source are

- `ExecuteNonQuery()`—Executes statements that do not return a resultset. Instead, this method returns the number of records affected by the statement.

- `ExecuteReader()`—Executes statements that return a resultset that is returned in a `BdpDataReader`.

- `ExecuteScalar()`—Executes a query and returns the value from the first column of the first row of the resultset.

- `Prepare()`—Creates (prepares) a compiled version of the command in the data source.

General use of the `BdpCommand` class is similar to that of the `SqlCommand` class, which is discussed in Chapter 23, "Working with Transactions and Strongly Typed DataSets."

BdpDataReader

The `BdpDataReader` class is a read-only, forward-only cursor representation of a resultset returned from the `BdpCommand.ExecuteReader()` method. `BdpDataReader` is not created explicitly with a constructor. Listing 24.3 shows how to loop through the `BdpDataReader` rows and add their values to a `ListBox` control.

LISTING 24.3 Using the BdpDataReader Class

```
1:  const
2:    cnStr = 'assembly=Borland.Data.Interbase, Version=1.5.0.0, '+
3:      'Culture=neutral,PublicKeyToken=91d62ebb5b0d1b1b;
➥vendorclient=gds32.dll;'+
4:      'database=C:\Program Files\Common Files\Borland
➥Shared\Data\EMPLOYEE.GDB;'+
5:      'provider=Interbase;username=sysdba;password=masterkey';
6:  procedure TWinForm.btnOpen_Click(sender: System.Object;
7:    e: System.EventArgs);
8:  var
9:    bdpCn: BdpConnection;
10:   bdpCmd: BdpCommand;
11:   bdpRdr: BdpDataReader;
12:   s: String;
13: begin
14:   bdpCn := BdpConnection.Create(cnStr);
15:   Include(bdpCn.StateChange, Self.BdpCn_StateChange);
16:
17:   bdpCn.Open;
18:   try
19:     bdpCmd := bdpCn.CreateCommand;
20:     bdpCmd.CommandText := 'SELECT * FROM country';
21:     bdpRdr := bdpCmd.ExecuteReader;
22:
23:     while bdpRdr.Read do
24:     begin
25:       s := bdpRdr['country'].ToString+' '+bdpRdr['currency'].ToString;
26:       ListBox2.Items.Add(s);
27:     end;
28:
29:     finally
```

24

LISTING 24.3   Continued

```
30:      bdpCn.Close;
31:    end;
32:  end;
```

▶ Find the code on the CD: \Code\Chapter 24\Ex03.

This example reads the records from the country table of the Employes.gdb database. Line 21 invokes the ExecuteReader() function, which assigns the resulting BdpDataReader to the bdpRdr variable. Lines 23–27 loop through bdpRdr and assign the column values from each row to ListBox2. General use of the BdpDataReader class is similar to using the SqlDataReader class, which is discussed in the chapters prior to this.

BdpDataAdapter

The BdpDataAdapter class is the conduit between the in-memory DataSet and the underlying data source. It contains all the methods required for manipulating the data it contains and for posting changes to the data source. BdpDataAdapter must have a valid statement in its SelectCommand property before it can be used to fill a DataSet. Listing 24.4 illustrates using BdpDataAdapter to retrieve the Customer table from the Employee.gdb Interbase database.

LISTING 24.4   Using the BdpDataAdapter Class

```
1:   const
2:     cmdStr = 'SELECT * FROM customer';
3:
4:   procedure TWinForm.btnOpen_Click(sender: System.Object;
5:     e: System.EventArgs);
6:   var
7:     bdpCn: BdpConnection;
8:     bdpDA: BdpDataAdapter;
9:     ds: DataSet;
10:  begin
11:    bdpCn := BdpConnection.Create(cnStr);
12:    bdpDA := BdpDataAdapter.Create(cmdStr, bdpCn);
13:    ds := DataSet.Create;
14:    bdpDA.Fill(ds);
15:    try
16:      DataGrid1.DataSource := ds.Tables['Table'];
17:    finally
18:      bdpCn.Close;
19:    end;
20:  end;
```

▶ Find the code on the CD: \Code\Chapter 24\Ex04.

This example uses the same connection string as from the previous examples. Line 12 shows where the BdpDataAdapter is created using the cmdStr constant as the SelectCommand parameter. It also passes the BdpConnection object, bdpCn. Line 14 fills a DataSet with the values queried from the database and binds the resulting table to DataGrid1. General use of the BdpDataAdapter class follows closely to the SqlDataAdapter discussed in the previous chapters of Part IV, "Database Development with ADO.NET."

BdpParameter/BpdParameterCollection

The `BdpCommand.Parameters` property is of the type `BdpParameterCollection`. This type is defined in the `Borland.Data.Common` namespace. The `Parameters` collection maintains instances of `BdpParameter` objects. Each `BdpParameter` instance refers to a parameter in the SQL statement that the `BdpComamand` represents. For instance, consider the following stored procedure:

```
CREATE PROCEDURE CustOrdersOrders @CustomerID nchar(5)
AS
  SELECT OrderID, OrderDate,RequiredDate,ShippedDate
  FROM Orders
  WHERE CustomerID = @CustomerID
  ORDER BY OrderID
GO
```

This stored procedure accepts a single parameter `@CustomerID`. Listing 24.5 shows how to use the `BdpParameter` class to provide a value for this parameter when executing this stored procedure using a `BdpCommand` object.

LISTING 24.5   Using the BdpParameter Class

```
 1:   const
 2:     cnStr = 'assembly=Borland.Data.Mssql, Version=1.5.0.0, Culture=neutral,'+
 3:       'PublicKeyToken=91d62ebb5b0d1b1b;vendorclient=sqloledb.dll;'+
 4:       'osauthentication=True;database=Northwind;username=;'+
 5:       'hostname=localhost;password=sa;provider=MSSQL';
 6:
 7:   procedure TWinForm1.Button1_Click(sender: System.Object;
 8:     e: System.EventArgs);
 9:   var
10:     bdpCn: BdpConnection;
11:     bdpCmd: BdpCommand;
12:     bdpParm: BdpParameter;
13:     bdpDA: BdpDataAdapter;
14:     ds: DataSet;
15:   begin
16:     bdpCn := BdpConnection.Create(cnStr);
17:     bdpCmd := BdpCommand.Create;
18:     bdpCmd.Connection := bdpCn;
19:     bdpCmd.CommandText := 'CustOrdersOrders';
20:     bdpCmd.ParameterCount := 1;
21:     bdpCmd.CommandType := CommandType.StoredProcedure;
22:     bdpCn.Open;
23:     try
24:       bdpCmd.Prepare;
25:       bdpParm := BdpParameter.Create('@CustomerID', dbType.StringFixedLength,
26:         5);
27:       bdpParm.Value := 'ANTON';
28:       bdpCmd.Parameters.Add(bdpParm);
29:       bdpDA := BdpDataAdapter.Create(bdpCmd);
30:       ds := DataSet.Create;
31:       bdpDA.Fill(ds);
32:       DataGrid1.DataSource := ds;
33:     finally
34:       bdpCn.Close;
```

24

LISTING 24.5   Continued

```
35:    end;
36:  end;
```

▶ Find the code on the CD: \Code\Chapter 24\Ex05.

In Listing 24.5, lines 17–21 set up the BdpCommand object. Line 25–26 create a BdpParameter instance. Its Create() constructor takes the parameter name, as well as the parameter's type and the size if required. The parameter value is set on line 27 and added to the BdpCommand's Parameters collection on line 28. The remaining code shows how the BdpDataAdapter instance invokes the stored procedure through the BdpCommand class. Using the BpdParmeter class is similar to using the SqlParameter and other data provider classes as illustrated in earlier chapters.

BdpTransaction

The BdpTransaction class is that which establishes a boundary within which a group of database operations occur. The BeginTransaction() method of the BdpConnection class returns an instance of the BdpTransaction class. Transactions are finalized by either calling BdpTransaction.Commit() or BdpTranaction.RollBack(). The former is called when the set of transactions are successful. The latter is called when there has been a failure in processing the operation. Listing 24.6 shows a template for executing transactions.

LISTING 24.6   Transaction Example

```
1:    procedure TWinForm.Button1_Click(sender: System.Object;
2:      e: System.EventArgs);
3:    var
4:      bdpCn: BdpConnection;
5:      bdpTrans: BdpTransaction;
6:    begin
7:      bdpCn := BdpConnection.Create(cnStr);
8:      bdpCn.Open;
9:      try
10:       bdpTrans := bdpCn.BeginTransaction;
11:       try
12:         // Do your stuff
13:         bdpTrans.Commit;
14:       except
15:         bdpTrans.Rollback;
16:         raise;
17:       end;
18:     finally
19:       bdpCn.Close;
20:     end;
21:   end;
```

▶ Find the code on the CD: \Code\Chapter 24\Ex06.

On line 10, a transaction is created. Any database activities that occur between line 10 and line 13 would occur within the context of the transaction and would be committed on line 13. If a failure occurs (an exception is raised), the except block will get invoked and the transaction will roll back all pending actions.

Designers within the IDE

Now that you've seen how to programmatically assign various properties to the Borland Data Provider components, this section demonstrates the various designers that are available within the IDE.

The Connections Editor

The Connections Editor dialog box is where you manage connections to various data sources that are accessed by Borland Data Provider components. The Connections Editor dialog box is shown in Figure 24.2.

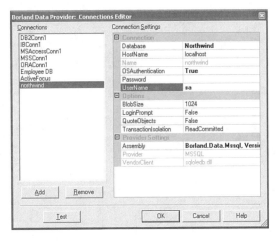

FIGURE 24.2   The Connections Editor dialog box.

From the Connections Editor dialog box, you can add, edit, and remove connections to data sources. You can also test the connection once you've created it. Connections created from within this dialog box are stored in the `BdpConnection.xml` file, which resides in the `\Bin` directory where Delphi for .NET was installed.

The Command Text Editor

The Command Text Editor is used to build the command text for the `BdpCommand.CommandText` property. This dialog box is shown in Figure 24.3.

Looking at Figure 24.3, the Tables list is where you select the table on which you want to perform a query. The Columns list is where you select the columns that you want returned for the `DataSet`. When you click the Generate SQL button, the SQL statement will be generated based on the radio button selected in the Command Type selection list. The Preview Data tab allows you to preview the results of your SQL statement.

Parameter Collection Editor

The Parameter Collection Editor dialog box allows you to define `BdpParameter` objects for a parameterized query. This dialog box is shown in Figure 24.4.

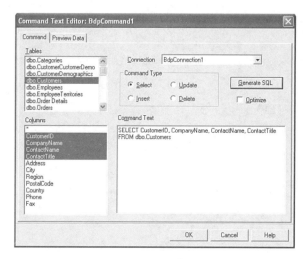

FIGURE 24.3   The Command Text Editor dialog box.

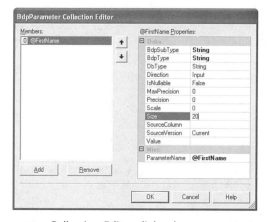

FIGURE 24.4   The Parameter Collection Editor dialog box.

Through this dialog box, you can create new parameters and set the properties that you would normally do programmatically as shown in Listing 24.5.

Data Adapter Configuration Dialog Box

The Data Adapter Configuration dialog box is used to generate the SELECT, UPDATE, INSERT, and DELETE statements for the SelectCommand, UpdateCommand, InsertCommand, and DeleteCommand properties of the BdpDataAdapter class. This dialog box is shown in Figure 24.5.

You can see from Figure 24.5 that this dialog box is similar to the Command Text Editor except that the Data Adapter Configuration dialog box contains a tab for each SQL statement generated. Additionally, the Data Adapter Configuration dialog box has a DataSet Table where you can specify a DataSet control that will be populated by the BdpDataAdapter (see Figure 24.6).

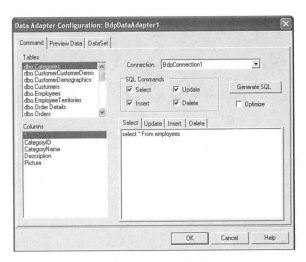

FIGURE 24.5   The Data Adapter Configuration dialog box.

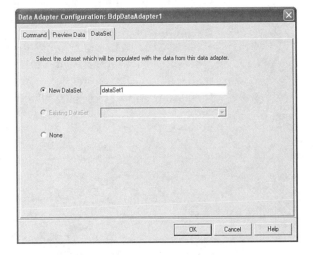

FIGURE 24.6   DataSet options in the BdpDataAdapter dialog box.

There are three options that you can select from the DataSet tab. These are

- New DataSet—Specifies that a new DataSet object will be added to the form that will contain the data retrieved by the DataAdapter.

- Existing DataSet—Specifies that an existing DataSet (which you select in the DropDownList) will be populated by the BdpDataAdapter.

- None—No DataSet is specified.

PART V: INTERNET DEVELOPMENT WITH ASP.NET

CHAPTER 25	ASP.NET Fundamentals
CHAPTER 26	Building ASP.NET Web Pages
CHAPTER 27	Building Database Driven ASP.NET Applications
CHAPTER 28	Building Web Services
CHAPTER 29	.NET Remoting and Delphi
CHAPTER 30	.NET Remoting in Action
CHAPTER 31	Securing ASP.NET Applications
CHAPTER 32	ASP.NET Deployment and Configuration
CHAPTER 33	Caching and Managing State in ASP.NET Applications
CHAPTER 34	Developing Custom ASP.NET Server Controls

IN THIS CHAPTER

- Web Technologies—How They Work
- ASP.NET—How It Works
- ASP.NET Classes

CHAPTER **25**

ASP.NET Fundamentals

When it comes to developing Web-based enterprise solutions, ASP.NET is hands down the most robust and easiest to use technology on developers' desks today. Not only is ASP.NET simple to work with from a development standpoint, but it also enables developers to create highly complex, functionally rich, interactive, and secure Internet applications that no other tool can accomplish with such ease. Its power, robustness, and ease of development and deployment make it a developer's dream come true. People who understand Rapid Application Development (RAD) understand that the end user/customer ultimately benefits from RAD. ASP.NET is all about RAD of Web applications. It is extremely easy to develop Web applications, and this translates to faster release cycles, more features, and less expensive software. On top of that, the deployment and configuration of .NET is child's play compared to other Web development solutions. The chapters in this book's section will guide you in taking advantage of this enabling technology using Delphi for .NET. ASP.NET is likely the most exciting feature of the Microsoft .NET strategy.

Web Technologies—How They Work

Generally speaking, the Web works on a client-server and stateless model. Communication occurs between a client and a server over the HTTP protocol.

HTTP Protocol Overview

HTTP stands for "Hypertext Transfer Protocol." It is packet/text-based, and it defines how communication occurs between Web browsers such as Internet Explorer and Opera and Web Servers such as Microsoft Internet Information Server (IIS) and Apache. Details about HTTP can be obtained from RFC 2616 at ftp://ftp.isi.edu/in-notes/rfc2616.txt.

Under HTTP, browsers communicate with servers using a request/response model. The client, or browser, sends a request for a Web page to a Web server, which finds or dynamically creates the Web page and sends a Response back to the browser, which then displays the page to the end user. This simple communication model is depicted in Figure 25.1.

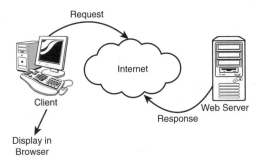

FIGURE 25.1   ASP.NET Browser/Web Server communication.

HTTP is stateless protocol. This means that each request/response exchange, or transaction, is independent of prior or subsequent transactions. Unlike the two-tier models in distributed applications, no constant connections maintain state information.

This description is probably the simplest form of Internet communication and is likely the most popular. It is a static form of Internet communication, which in many cases is very appropriate. Innumerable Web pages on the Internet only provide content, and users do not need to interact with them. However, where dynamic processing and interactivity is required, such a model simply does not suffice.

ASP.NET (and some other technologies) makes use of how HTTP operates to enable highly interactive Web sites. Before we delve into how ASP.NET does this, let's look at the content of the HTTP request and response packets. By the way, the term packet is synonymous with the term message when discussing HTTP transactions.

The HTTP Request Packet

The HTTP request package consists of three pieces, which are

- Request line
- HTTP header consisting of 0-n header lines
- HTTP body

The Request line has three parts. These are a method, a path to a resource on the server that the client is requesting, and the HTTP version number. Such a line would look like this:

```
GET /web/index.htm HTTP/1.1
```

In this example, GET is the method indicating that the client wants to get something from the server. The path/file is the requested file the client desires. Finally, the HTTP version is included in every request.

There is more to the GET method when used in conjunction with the <form> tag. This tag enables the client to send additional information to the server. This information is appended to the URL by the browser. Therefore, the URL might look like this:

www.DelphiGuru.com/form.aspx?topic=Programming

The portion following the question mark is called a query string and might be used by the server to execute a search on a specified topic.

Another method that you should know about is the POST method. Unlike the GET method, the POST method embeds the information it sends to the server in the HTTP body. Many developers prefer not having the additional content contained in the URL. This might be important because of limitations on the length of the URL that can be sent to some servers. In that case, it is possible to send more information using the POST command. Additionally, using the POST method hides ugly parameters and values that developers might not want to be shown in the browser's address field.

The HTTP Response Packet

The HTTP response packet also consists of three parts, which are

- Status line

- HTTP header consisting of 0-n header lines

- HTTP body

The Status line consists of three parts. These are the HTTP version, a status code, and a text string describing the status code. An example Status line would look like this:

HTTP/1.1 200 OK

In this example, the version is HTTP/1.1. 200 is the status code, which is described as OK, meaning successful. Other status codes are classified by their numbers. These codes with their classifications are listed here:

- 1xx—Information

- 2xx—Successful

- 3xx—Redirection

- 4xx—Client Error

- 5xx—Server Error

The HTTP header lines contain information about the request or the response. They appear as one header per line in the name: value format. At this point, we won't get into the various types of headers other than to say that there are basically four forms of headers: general, request, response, and entity. General headers contain information about the server or client. Response headers contain information about the server that might be useful. Entity sends information about the data being transferred. For more information on the various types of headers, visit www.w3c.org and see the document RFC 2068 section 4 and 7.

Finally, the HTTP body of the Response packet typically contains the HTML code that the browser is to translate and display to the end user. Therefore, an example of an HTTP Response package might look something like this:

```
HTTP/1.1 200 OK
Date: Fri, 19 Dec 2000 15:12:00 GMT
Content-Type: text/html
Content-Length: 420

<html>
<body>
<h1>Welcome to DelphiGuru.com</h1>
  .
  .
  .
</body>
</html>
```

There's a simple explanation of the HTTP protocol. Now let's see how ASP.NET works.

ASP.NET—How It Works

Figure 25.1 depicts the static model for how a browser and Web server communicate. In ASP.NET, some extra steps occur on the server side. Figure 25.2 illustrates this process.

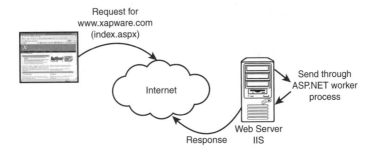

FIGURE 25.2   ASP.NET Browser/Web Server communication.

To the client, the process is the same: The client, or browser, makes a request to the server. Upon receiving the request, the server—IIS in this case—determines that the client is requesting an ASP.NET page by its (.aspx) extension. IIS then sends the Web page to a separate ISAPI server, aspnet_isapi.dll. This server sends the page to an ASP.NET Worker Process, aspnet_wp.exe. The Worker Process invokes the Common Language Runtime, which takes care of compiling and executing the page's code. The result of the Worker Process is HTML, which is then sent back to the client in the response body. In simple terms, you can view the Worker Process as a black box whose input is an .aspx file and output is HTML text.

At this point, we need a simple example to discuss further how all this works. So without further ado, we'll launch Delphi for .NET and create an ASP.NET application.

A Simple Web Application

In this section, we'll create a simple ASP.NET application using Delphi for .NET.

NOTE

It is assumed that you have installed the required components for developing and running ASP.NET applications. If you haven't done this, read through the README file that ships with Delphi for .NET instruction on these installation requirements.

To create a new ASP.NET application, simply select File, New, ASP.NET Web Application from the main menu. This launches a dialog box that asks for a name of the new application and the location. Note that the location is a subdirectory of the IIS Web root directory. I have entered d4dnEx01 as the name of this application as shown in Figure 25.3.

FIGURE 25.3   A new ASP.NET application dialog box.

After pressing OK, I am given three pages within the Designer. These are WebForm1.aspx, WebForm1.pas, and Design. At this point, after selecting the Design tab, I select three controls from the Web Controls category in the Component Palette and place them on the Designer surface. These controls are a Label, a Button, and a TextBox. Figure 25.4 shows my resulting WebForm.

The following is the event handler that I have created for the Button Click event:

```
procedure TWebForm1.Button1_Click(sender: System.Object;
  e: System.EventArgs);
begin
  Label1.Text := TextBox1.Text;
end;
```

Upon compiling and running the application, my form will appear in my browser. After typing text into the TextEdit control and pressing the button, my browser displays the content in Figure 25.5.

Now, that's about as easy as it gets. A lot is going on here that needs explaining, so I'll move on.

ASP.NET Page Structure

The WebForm1.aspx file is shown in Listing 25.1. This file holds the text of the Web page, similar to an HTML page.

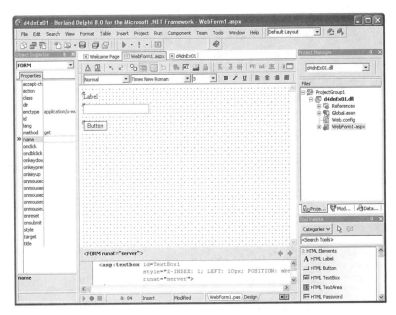

FIGURE 25.4 A simple WebForm example.

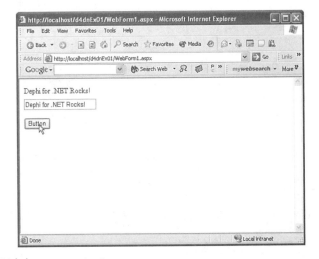

FIGURE 25.5 Web browser output.

LISTING 25.1 WebForm1.aspx Content

```
1:   <%@ Page language="c#" Debug="true" Codebehind="WebForm1.pas"
➥AutoEventWireup="true" Inherits="WebForm1.TWebForm1" %>
2:   <!DOCTYPE HTML PUBLIC "-//W3C//DTD HTML 4.0 Transitional//EN">
3:
4:   <script runat="server">
5:     void Page_Load(Object obj, EventArgs e) {
6:       Label1.Text = "Tell me about Delphi for .NET";
```

LISTING 25.1   Continued

```
 7:    }
 8:  </script>
 9:
10:  <html>
11:    <head>
12:      <title></title>
13:      <meta name="GENERATOR" content="Borland Package Library 7.1">
14:    </head>
15:
16:    <body ms_positioning="GridLayout">
17:    <form runat="server">
18:      <asp:textbox id=TextBox1
19:        style="Z-INDEX: 1; LEFT: 10px; POSITION: absolute; TOP: 42px"
20:                     runat="server">
21:      </asp:textbox>
22:      <asp:button id=Button1 style="LEFT: 10px; POSITION: absolute;
23:         TOP: 81px" runat="server" text="Button">
24:      </asp:button>
25:      <asp:label id=Label1 style="LEFT: 10px; TOP: 15px"
➥runat="server">Label</asp:label>
26:    </form>
27:  </body>
28:  </html>
```

In Listing 25.1, lines 4–8 were not in the original file generated by Delphi for .NET. I added these lines manually.

All ASP.NET pages have the .aspx extension, which is required for the Web Server to know that they are ASP.NET pages. I could have typed this page in Notepad, placed it in a subdirectory to my Web server, and run it just as well.

The first element of the .aspx file is the @ Page directive (line 1). This directive contains attributes that are used by ASP.NET during compile. These attributes have to do with compile instructions, behavior, or output of the page. There are too many attributes that can be covered in this chapter, but I'll discuss those shown here so that you can get an idea of the type of information that goes here.

> **NOTE**
>
> Visit http://msdn.microsoft.com/library/default.asp?url=/library/en-us/ cpgenref/html/cpconPage.asp for complete documentation on the @ Page directive.

The language attribute specifies the language to use when compiling inline code blocks and code that appears in the <script> tag. In this example, C# is the default language. This only applies to script tags with the runat="Server" attributes. Normal script tags execute at the client and typically contain JavaScript code.

> **NOTE**
>
> There were plans to include support for Delphi scripting with Delphi for .NET; however, it was held back from this version. It might be included in a later release of Delphi.

The `Debug` attributes specifies whether to compile the page with symbol information.

The `CodeBehind` attribute indicates the source file that has the page class associated with this page. This attribute tells the IDE which source file to associate with this ASP.NET page. I will discuss this in more detail later in this chapter.

`AutoEventWireup` specifies whether events are automatically wired to event handlers. This is set to `False` by default when creating a new ASP.NET application in Delphi. You must manually set this to `True` so that the `Page_Load` event handler gets automatically wired up.

`Inherits` specifies a class from which this page inherits. Such a class must directly or indirectly inherit from the `System.Web.UI.Page` class.

The next primary section is the `<script>` block (lines 4–8). This block contains code that gets executed on the server when this page is processed. Note the tag `runat="server"`. This tag instructs ASP.NET to process the code on the server. The code itself is actually C# code. `Page_Load` is an event handler that is automatically associated with the `Page` class. Therefore, when this page is loaded by ASP.NET, you can place code here to initialize various elements on the Web page as shown in Listing 25.1.

The HTML block (lines 10–28) contains HTML code that ASP.NET will use to formulate the final HTML content. Notice that in the `form` tag, you see the `runat="server"` tag again. This directive renders this form as a WebForm. The various elements within this Web form are used by ASP.NET in generating the HTML that ultimately gets to the client. These controls are those that can interact with the server to invoke server processing known as code-behind. I'll discuss more on code-behind in a section later in this chapter.

Event-Driven Communication

The following listing should help you understand how ASP.NET works as an event-driven model between the client and server.

In the previous example, when the user types the URL for the Web page from Listing 25.1, Listing 25.2 is the actual HTML source returned to the client.

LISTING 25.2 WebForm1.aspx Resulting HTML

```
 1:   <!DOCTYPE HTML PUBLIC "-//W3C//DTD HTML 4.0 Transitional//EN">
 2:
 3:   <html>
 4:     <head>
 5:      <title></title>
 6:      <meta name="GENERATOR" content="Borland Package Library 7.1">
 7:     </head>
 8:     <body ms_positioning="GridLayout">
 9:       <form name="_ctl0" method="post" action="WebForm1.aspx" id="_ctl0">
10:   <input type="hidden" name="__VIEWSTATE"
➥value="dDwtNzA2MDcxNTQ5O3Q8O2w8TwyPjs+O2w8dDw7bDxpPDU+Oz47bDx0PHA8cDxsPFR
➥leHQ7PjtsPFRlbGwgbWUgYWJvdXQgRGVscGhpIGZvciAuTkVUOz4+Oz47O47Pj47Pj47
➥j47PriouWT0tSYLFvbR51o1q3beLGLB" />
11:       <input name="TextBox1" type="text" id="TextBox1" style="Z-INDEX: 1;
12:          LEFT: 10px; POSITION: absolute; TOP: 42px" />
13:       <input type="submit" name="Button1" value="Button" id="Button1"
```

LISTING 25.2   Continued

```
14:        style="LEFT: 10px; POSITION: absolute; TOP: 81px" />
15:      <span id="Label1" style="LEFT: 10px;
16:        TOP: 15px">Tell me about Delphi for .NET</span>
17:    </form>
18:  </body>
19:  </html>
```

Notice that this is very different from the originating `WebForm1.aspx` file. In fact, this looks like a regular old HTML file, which is because it is. ASP.NET took the `WebForm1.aspx` file and processed it to generate this HTML script. Notice that lines 5 and 6 from Listing 25.1

```
void Page_Load(Object obj, EventArgs e) {
  Label1.Text = "Tell me about Delphi for .NET";
```

resulted in lines 15–16 in Listing 25.2. This is an example of the event processing model in ASP.NET. When ASP.NET loaded the `WebForm1.aspx` file, it executed this code, which resulted in setting `Label1`'s text. Now recall that we added an event handler to `Button1`'s `Click` event. If you were to type something into the `TextBox` and press `Button1`, the HTML would become slightly different because `Label1`'s text would contain the text you typed into the `TextBox`. This probably raises the question of how the server knew to associate the event handler in the `WinForm1.pas` file with `Button1` of the `WinForm.aspx` file. In simple terms, by pressing the button, a round-trip is made to the server and back. On the server end, the code for `Button1`'s `Click` event gets executed and a new page is returned to the client. I'll get to that, but first, there's one additional piece of information of importance: the __VIEWSTATE hidden field.

VIEWSTATE and State Maintenance

In Listing 25.2, a rather cryptic stream of characters exist for a hidden field named __VIEWSTATE. This field enables ASP.NET to maintain state between client/server transactions. For instance, if you were to run this page, enter text into the `TextBox`, and press `Button1`, the result would show what you would expect—`Label1` would display the text you entered. However, if you were to press the Back button on your browser, experience might have you believe that you'll return to the original page with an empty `TextBox`. This is not the case: In fact, `TextBox1` seems to have retained the text you entered.

This is a significant departure from traditional Web development in which state maintenance has been cumbersome or nonexistent. This is also the mechanism by which developers will be able to create powerful, interactive applications.

The VIEWSTATE field you see in the resulting HTML code is a hidden field in which ASP.NET places state information about each control. This information is transferred between client/server transactions.

CodeBehind

Consider once again Listing 25.1. You can change line 1 to

```
<%@ Page language="c#" %>
```

and rename the page to something different, such as demo.aspx. By entering the page in your browser, it would still run. However, you will notice that pressing the button does not perform the function it originally performed.

ASP.NET introduced a concept termed code-behind. There are two distinctions between runtime and design-time code-behind.

In Delphi for .NET, when you create an ASP.NET application, you are given two files. The first file is the ASP.NET page with an .aspx extension. The second is a source file with a .pas extension. This file contains the specific Page class for the ASP.NET page. When you compile the application, the resulting assembly will contain the definition of this specific Page class. The design-time association between the .aspx and .pas file is determined by the CodeBehind attribute of the @Page directive. The runtime association between the .aspx file and the Page class is determined by the inherits attribute of the @Page directive in the .aspx file.

When requesting an .aspx file that has no inherits attribute (such as the case with our demo.aspx file), ASP.NET instantiates a generic class that directly inherits from the System.Web.UI.Page class. In this case, the descendant Page class inherits the standard functionality of the base Page class. Put another way, System.Web.UI.Page is the base class to the dynamically created class. When a more specific class is provided, this new class now becomes the base class for the dynamically created class. It will include any customizations that the developer might have programmed into the various events and methods of this new base class, such as our Button_Click event handler.

When running the demo.aspx page, the Page class created on the ASP.NET side contained no specialized code. Therefore, pressing the button didn't accomplish anything. However, when running the original WebForm1.aspx class containing Inherits="PageWebForm1.TWebForm1", pressing the button causes its event handler to be invoked. This attribute refers to the class defined in the WebForm1.pas file where we created a Click event handler that changed the text of Label1 to that contained in the TextBox.

This rather loose association between the ASP.NET page and the code behind it (thus the term) creates at least two primary advantages to developing in ASP.NET. The first is the separation of Web design and Web programming. The second has to do with page inheritance.

Design/Programming Separation

The two distinct files enable both developers and Web designers to work on the same project without having to share the same file. Web designers can focus on the look and feel of the page by working on the .aspx file, whereas the programmers can focus on the functionality provided by the page.

Page Inheritance

A much greater advantage is likely that of page inheritance. It is possible to create a Page class (named BasePage) that descends from the System.Web.UI.Page class and from which all other Page classes in your application will descend. This enables a concept similar to visual form inheritance. All final Page classes will inherit the functionality of the BasePage. Additionally, BasePage can be used to establish a common look and behavior for an entire site. At this point, we can examine some fundamental objects within ASP.NET.

ASP.NET Classes

The following examples will examine some of the core objects that you will likely use in developing your own ASP.NET applications. There are several objects within the ASP.NET framework, and it would be impossible to cover them all in this book. Instead, this section covers some of the key classes and their methods.

The HTTPResponse Class

The HTTPResponse class is used when the server needs to return a response back to the browser. This section covers key aspects of this class.

Writing Text to the Client

When the Page object is created on the server, one of its property is an HTTPResponse object called Response. You can reference this object in your code to send information back to the client. A common use is to write text to the client browser. The following code produces the output in the browser shown in Figure 25.6.

```
for i := 1 to 7 do
  Response.Write(
    System.String.Format('<font size={0}>Delphi for .NET<br></font>', [i]));
```

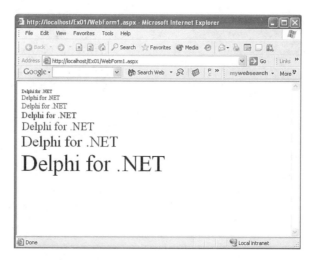

FIGURE 25.6   Response.Write() output.

> ▶ **SEE** the entire example on the CD: \Code\Chapter 25\Ex01\.

The following code demonstrates how to write information from the HTTP Response packet:

```
Response.Write(Response.StatusCode.ToString);
Response.Write(Response.StatusDescription);
Response.Write(Response.Status);
```

> ▶ **SEE** the entire example on the CD: \Code\Chapter 25\Ex02\.

TIP

If you look at the HTML code for the previous example, you will see that the Resonse.Write() output "2000K2000K" precedes the dummy HTML output:

```
" 2000K200 OK
<!DOCTYPE HTML PUBLIC "-//W3C//DTD HTML 4.0 Transitional//EN">
<html>
  <head>
    <title></title>
    <meta name="GENERATOR" content="Borland Package Library 7.1">
  </head>
  <body ms_positioning="GridLayout">
    <form name="_ctl0" method="post" action="WebForm1.aspx" id="_ctl0">
<input type="hidden" name="__VIEWSTATE" value=
➥"dDwtMTI3OTMzNDM4NDs7PktG25iT1NcUAmnlzewNqw6xHn/f" />
    </form>
  </body>
</html>"
```

To avoid the unused HTML part, you could add one line:

```
Response.&End;
```

The End() method "sends all currently buffered output to the client, stops execution of the page, and raises the Application_EndRequest event." Note that it must be escaped using & because End is a Delphi keyword.

Filtering Output

Another use for the HTTPResponse class is to filter output before it goes to the client. This is done by assigning a filter, which is a class that descends from the Stream class or a derivative thereof. HTTPResponse class passes any text that goes to the client through the filter before actually sending it to the client. Listing 25.3 shows partial code to an example that demonstrates this technique.

LISTING 25.3   Filter Output Demo

```
1:    type
2:      TWebForm1 = class(System.Web.UI.Page)
3:      strict private
4:        procedure Page_Load(sender: System.Object; e: System.EventArgs);
5:      end;
6:
7:      TChangeCaseFilter = class(MemoryStream)
8:      private
9:        mStream: Stream;
10:     public
11:       constructor Create(aStream: Stream); override;
12:       procedure Write(bfr: array of byte; offset: integer;
13:         count: Integer); override;
14:     end;
15:
16:  implementation
17:
```

LISTING 25.3   Continued

```
18:  procedure TWebForm1.Page_Load(sender: System.Object; e: System.EventArgs);
19:  begin
20:    Response.Filter := TChangeCaseFilter.Create(Response.Filter);
21:    Response.Write('Hello Delphi for .NET');
22:  end;
23:
24:  { TChangeCaseFilter }
25:
26:  constructor TChangeCaseFilter.Create(aStream: Stream);
27:  begin
28:    inherited Create;
29:    mStream := aStream;
30:  end;
31:
32:  procedure TChangeCaseFilter.Write(bfr: array of byte; offset,
33:    count: Integer);
34:  var
35:    data: array of byte;
36:    i: integer;
37:    diff: Integer;
38:  begin
39:    inherited;
40:    Borland.Delphi.System.SetLength(data, count);
41:    Buffer.BlockCopy(bfr, offset, data, 0, count);
42:    diff := ord('a')-ord('A');
43:
44:    for i := 0 to count-1 do
45:    begin
46:      if (data[i] >= ord('a')) and (data[i] <= ord('z')) then
47:        data[i] := data[i] - diff
48:      else if (data[i] >= ord('A')) and (data[i] <= ord('Z')) then
49:        data[i] := data[i] + diff;
50:    end;
51:
52:    mStream.Write(data, 0, count);
53:  end;
54:
55:  end.
```

▶ **SEE** the entire example on the CD: \Code\Chapter 25\Ex03\.

The TChangeCaseFilter class is derived from MemoryStream (line 7). This could have been derived from Stream; however, this would have required additional methods to be overridden. In the Page_Load() event handler, an instance of this filter is created and assigned to the HTTPResponse.Filter property (line 20). This newly created stream filter takes the existing filter as a parameter and forwards the modified output to it (in a chain of filters). Prior to sending the HTTP body to the client, the HTTPResponse class sends the HTTP body through the filter's Write() method. It is within this method that you have the opportunity to filter the HTTP body content. In this simple example, the TChangeCaseFilter.Write() method reverses the case of characters in the text stream.

Redirecting the Browser

Another use of the HTTPResponse class is to redirect the user's browser to another URL. This is very simple to do from within the Page_Load() event handler as shown here:

```
procedure TWebForm1.Page_Load(sender: System.Object; e: System.EventArgs);
begin
  Response.Redirect('http://www.xapware.com');
end;
```

▶ **SEE** the entire example on the CD: \Code\Chapter 25\Ex04\.

The HTTPRequest Class

The HTTPRequest class is the converse of the HTTPResponse class. It enables the client to send information back to the server. Additionally, through the HTTPRequest class, the server can elect to use it to give information to the client and it holds detailed information about the client's request. Listing 25.4 illustrates this technique.

LISTING 25.4 HTTPRequest Example

```
 1:    procedure TWebForm1.Page_Load(sender: System.Object; e: System.EventArgs);
 2:    var
 3:      NameValCol: NameValueCollection;
 4:      StrArray: array of String;
 5:      i: integer;
 6:    begin
 7:      // Client can request server information through the Request
 8:      Response.Write(System.String.Format('Application Path: {0} <br>',
 9:        [Request.ApplicationPath]));
10:      Response.Write(System.String.Format('File Path: {0} <br>',
11:        [Request.FilePath]));
12:      Response.Write(System.String.Format('Path Info: {0} <br>',
13:        [Request.PathInfo]));
14:      Response.Write(System.String.Format('Physical Path: {0} <br>',
15:        [Request.PhysicalPath]));
16:      Response.Write(System.String.Format('Physical Application Path: {0} <br>',
17:        [Request.PhysicalApplicationPath]));
18:      Response.Write(System.String.Format('User Host Address: {0} <br>',
19:        [Request.UserHostAddress]));
20:      Response.Write(System.String.Format('User Host Name: {0} <br>',
21:        [Request.UserHostName]));
22:
23:
24:      // Write HTTP Request information
25:      Response.Write(System.String.Format('HTTP Method: {0} <br>',
26:        [Request.HTTPMethod]));
27:      Response.Write('Headers<br>');
28:
29:      NameValCol := Request.Headers;
30:      StrArray := NameValCol.AllKeys;
31:      for i := Low(StrArray) to High(StrArray) do
32:        Response.Write(System.String.Format('    {0} : {1} <br>',
33:          [StrArray[i], Request.Headers.Item[StrArray[i]]]));
34:      // Write browser information
```

25

LISTING 25.4   Continued

```
35:     Response.Write('<br>');
36:     Response.Write('Browser Information<br>');
37:     Response.Write(System.String.Format('Type: {0}<br>',
38:       [Request.Browser.&Type.ToString]));
39:     Response.Write(System.String.Format('Version: {0}<br>',
40:       [Request.Browser.Version]));
41:     Response.Write(System.String.Format('ClrVersion: {0}<br>',
42:       [Request.Browser.ClrVersion.ToString]));
43:     Response.Write(System.String.Format('PlatForm: {0}<br>',
44:       [Request.Browser.Platform]));
45:     Response.Write(System.String.Format('Supports Frames: {0}<br>',
46:       [Request.Browser.Frames.ToString]));
47:
48:     // Write query information
49:
50:     Response.Write('<br>');
51:     Response.Write(System.String.Format('Query String: {0}<br>',
52:       [Request.QueryString]));
53:     Response.Write(System.String.Format('Query String ''Name'': {0}<br>',
54:       [Request.QueryString['Name']]));
55:     Response.Write(System.String.Format('Query String ''State'': {0}<br>',
56:       [Request.QueryString['State']]));
57:  end;
```

▶ **SEE** the entire example on the CD: `\Code\Chapter 25\Ex05\`.

The first portion of Listing 25.4 illustrates how the server can return information to the client about itself (lines 8–21). Then, in lines 25–27, the clients looks at the HTTP request packet. Lines 29–46 illustrate how to print out information about the client's browser. Finally, lines 50–56 illustrate how to extract and print information from the querystring portion of the URL. Therefore, if the following URL were entered in your browser,

```
http://localhost/Ex05/WebForm1.aspx?Name=XaviePacheco&State=Colorado
```

the output of lines 50–56 would be

```
Query String: Name=XaviePacheco&State=Colorado
Query String 'Name': XaviePacheco
Query String 'State': Colorado
```

The HTTPCookie Class

The HTTPResponse and HTTPRequest classes have a Cookies property, which is a collection of cookies. Through this property, you would save and manage cookies on the client's computer.

The following code demonstrates how to create a cookie in the Cookies collection:

```
var
  hc: HttpCookie;
begin
  hc := HttpCookie.Create('Name', TextBox1.Text);
  hc.Expires := DateTime.Now.AddMonths(1);
```

```
  Response.Cookies.Add(hc);
  Label1.Text := System.String.Format('Hello {0}', TextBox1.Text);
end
```

▶ **SEE** the entire example on the CD: \Code\Chapter 25\Ex06\.

In this example, an instance of the HTTPCookie class is created. Cookies are stored as a name/value pair. In this example, the cookie name is 'Name' and the value is the contents of a TextBox control. You can specify a date for the cookie to expire by assigning that date to the HTTPCookie.Expires property. Cookies can store simple data types such as strings, integers, floats, and so on. Also, a single cookie can store a list of string values (see the HttpCookie.Values property).

To evaluate the contents of a cookie, you simply access the Cookies property as you would any other collection, as illustrated here:

```
if Request.Cookies['Name'] = nil then
  Label1.Visible := False
else
  Label1.Text := System.String.Format('Hello {0}',
    Request.Cookies['Name'].Value);
```

To delete a cookie, you can clear the HTTPCookie class as shown here:

```
var
  emptyCookie: HttpCookie;
begin
  EmptyCookie := Request.Cookies['Name'];
  EmptyCookie.Values.Clear;
  Response.Cookies.Add(emptyCookie);
end;
```

By doing this, the cookie will be removed from the users cookie directory.

Handling Postback Events

The Page class contains a Boolean property named IsPostBack. When a user first requests a URL, the Page.IsPostBack value is false. This property value is true with any subsequent postings of the page back to the client.

Consider the code in Listing 25.5, which demonstrates the use of the IsPostBack property.

LISTING 25.5   IsPostBack Property Usage

```
1:    procedure TWebForm1.Page_Load(sender: System.Object;
2:      e: System.EventArgs);
3:    begin
4:      if IsPostback and (TextBox1.Text <> '') then
5:      begin
6:        Label1.Visible := True;
7:        Label1.Text := System.String.Format('Hello {0}', TextBox1.Text);
8:      end
9:      else begin // is not a postback - initial visit
10:       if Request.Cookies['Name'] = nil then
```

LISTING 25.5   Continued

```
11:          Label1.Visible := False
12:       else
13:          Label1.Text := System.String.Format('Hello {0}',
14:             Request.Cookies['Name'].Value);
15:       end;
16:    end;
17:
18:    procedure TWebForm1.btnDeleteCookie_Click(sender: System.Object;
19:       e: System.EventArgs);
20:    var
21:       emptyCookie: HttpCookie;
22:    begin
23:       EmptyCookie := Request.Cookies['Name'];
24:       EmptyCookie.Values.Clear;
25:       Response.Cookies.Add(emptyCookie);
26:       Label1.Visible := False;
27:    end;
28:
29:    procedure TWebForm1.btnAddCookie_Click(sender: System.Object;
30:       e: System.EventArgs);
31:    var
32:       hc: HttpCookie;
33:    begin
34:       hc := HttpCookie.Create('Name', TextBox1.Text);
35:       hc.Expires := DateTime.Now.AddMonths(1);
36:       Response.Cookies.Add(hc);
37:    end;
```

▶ **SEE** the entire example on the CD: `\Code\Chapter 25\Ex07\`.

This is an example of a page with two buttons. The `Button1_Click()` event handler adds a cookie. The `Button2_Click()` event handler deletes a cookie. When the page is first loaded, the `Page_Load()` event handler fires. If this is the first time the page is loaded, the `else` clause is processed (lines 9–15). This section of code simply determines if the cookie already exists and sets a `Label` to show that cookie value. If this is a subsequent rendering of the page (`IsPostBack=true`), the `then` clause is processed only if the user typed text in to the `TextBox`. If so, the `TextBox` contents are displayed back to the user. You will see the `IsPostBack` used often in performing validation as well.

CHAPTER 26

Building ASP.NET Web Pages

IN THIS CHAPTER

- Building Web Pages Using ASP.NET Controls
- Pre-populating List Controls
- Performing Web Form Validation
- Web Form Formatting
- Navigating Between Web Forms
- Tips and Techniques

This chapter gets down to the nitty-gritty of building interactive Web pages using ASP.NET Web Forms. In this chapter, you will see how various controls are used within WebForms. You will learn how to perform validation on the data users enter into your forms and how to format your forms for display. This chapter shows you how to navigate between pages within your ASP.NET application. You will also see other very useful techniques for building Web applications.

> **NOTE**
>
> When developing interactive Web pages, there are primarily two participants. One is the developer/programmer. The other is the creative designer. Both skills are necessary to build world-class Web sites/applications. This chapter focuses on the development/programming aspect of Web application. Admittedly, I couldn't even draw a straight line, much less discuss the creative aspect of Web site development. This topic I will leave to those gifted with this talent.

Building Web Pages Using ASP.NET Controls

Generally speaking, a purely HTML Web page is static. The controls that are placed on an HTML page exist and function on the client. HTML pages might have script for performing some level of interaction, but this is a far cry from highly functional Web pages.

ASP.NET works with server controls. Server controls function on the server and are rendered on the client in HTML. Through client-side script in the HTML page, the server is notified of user interactivity and has the opportunity to respond. The user really doesn't see all this happening—the result of which is a highly interactive Web application.

Five different types of controls exist that you can use to develop WebForms. These are described briefly here:

- HTML Controls—HTML controls map to the HTML elements that you are used to if you have performed any sort of Web site development. When you add the runat="server" attribute to an HTML control, you enable ASP.NET to manipulate various properties of that control from the server. HTML controls exists in the System.Web.UI.HtmlControls namespace.

- Web Server Controls—Web controls are similar to HTML controls, but they are typically more functional and do not map to the standard HTML elements. Web controls require the runat="server" attribute. For the most part, they can be used as a replacement to HTML controls. Web controls derive from ASP.NET classes, giving them greater functional capabilities than you would have from HTML controls.

- Validation Controls—Validation controls are nonvisible controls that you use to validate user input. Five different validation controls can be used to validate everything from the existence of an entry to the exact format of that entry. When a standard validation control does not meet the need, you can even perform custom validation on either the client or the server.

- User Controls—User controls are controls that you or some third party provides with specialized functionality. They are really Web Server controls, but they are not part of the standard Web Server control package. Chapter 34, "Developing Custom ASP.NET Server Controls," discusses developing your own Web Server controls.

- Data-Bound Controls—Data-bound controls are Web Server controls that have automatic data-binding capabilities. By automatic, I mean that their properties support the capability to extract and display data from a data source. Obviously, you can programmatically extract and assign the same data to any control. Data-bound controls are simply more supportive of the data-binding technique through their properties.

To illustrate the use of controls, this chapter builds a sample Web application. This application contains a form that a user would fill out to request to download a product.

Sample Download Request Form

This typical WebForm is one that an organization might use to obtain information from people interested in its product(s). The idea is that before a user can download demo software, he must provide at least some information about himself. Preferably, you obtain his email address to which you send the download URL. When doing so, it is wise to obtain permission to send additional information about your company's products. Usually, the information needed is the person's name, email, and perhaps some additional information as to how the prospect found out about your product. The following sections illustrate how to build such a page.

The Page Layout

One of the initial considerations in developing a Web page is how it is going to look to the end user. This is not referring to what sort of "look and feel" from an artistic standpoint, but more from the standpoint of where controls are positioned—in what order, and so forth. One must consider that various browsers might render your page differently; therefore, you might want to be sure that you use the method that addresses most browsers. There are really three primary approaches to how you lay out controls on your page. Each is discussed here:

- Use of Tables—This is possibly the most popular method of positioning controls within a Web page. You simply use tables to design the layout of your forms. The positioning of controls within the form is dictated by the cell positions of the tables. Because you can nest tables within cells, you can design your entire Web page using this technique.

- Use of Cascading Style SheCSS (Cascading Style Sheet (CSS)ets—The Cascading Style Sheet (CSS) specification adds support for absolute positioning of controls within HTML pages. The drawback of course is whether the target browser supports CSS. Most modern browsers do support CSS, but it is really your call whether to use them. Cascading Style Sheets provide a wealth of capabilities not available through pure HTML.

- Use of ASP.NET Absolute Positioning—With ASP.NET, you can specify how a control is positioned as you drop it on your page. This causes the definition of the control to have the `absolute` tag placed in the `.aspx` file as shown here:

```
<asp:textbox id=TextBox1
style="LEFT: 38px; POSITION: absolute; TOP: 46px"
runat="server">
```

This is syntactically identical to CSS. To enable absolute positioning in a control, you simply check the absolute position tool button in the HTML Design Toolbar. Although this technique simplifies the page layout from a design standpoint, it also requires that the browser support CSS. Therefore, this technique has the same requirement as the preceding CSS method.

> **NOTE**
>
> Ideally, it would be great if ASP.NET could reformat the output to use tables if the browser does not support CSS. It does not at this point; I tried it. Nevertheless, the majority of browsers do support CSS, and one can safely assume that their Web pages will be readable by practically everyone who visits.

Creating a Form

For the download request form in this sample application, I will opt for the table-based formatting. Figure 26.1 shows the form I created in the Delphi IDE. This is the default form that was set up during the creation of an ASP.NET Web application. I renamed this form `DwnLdForm.aspx`. This form uses Web control `Labels`, `TextBoxes`, `DropDownLists`, and

CheckBoxes. You will find that selecting these controls and manipulating their properties is not any different than dealing with Windows Form's controls.

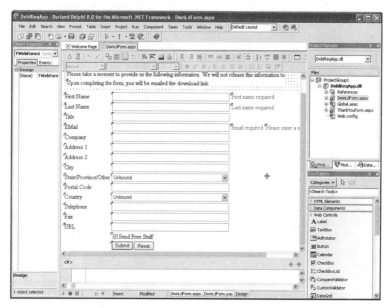

FIGURE 26.1 Download Request form.

▶ **SEE** the full example on the CD under \Code\Ex01.

This form also uses a standard HTML Control for the Reset button and a Web control for the Submit button. The Submit button does as it says and submits the user's response back to the server. For validation to work, the Submit button must be a Web control. The Reset button, on the other hand, is capable of doing this on the client; using the standard HTML Control prevents a trip to the server just to clear the controls.

Processing the Load Event

At this point, the demo application doesn't do anything. Certainly, you can run it, fill out the form, and press submit, but you'll find that the form returns back where you left it. Normally, you'll want to take the information provided by the user, process it, and then return the user to a page indicating a successful submission. To demonstrate this, I have added an additional form to the application, ThankYouForm.aspx, which simply contains a Label, thanking the user for his request.

When the user presses the Submit button, the default behavior of ASP.NET is to resend the form back to the client. This is called a post-back. You can capture this event on the server and redirect the user to another page, for instance. The Page_Load() event handler performs the following for this application:

```
procedure TWebForm1.Page_Load(sender: System.Object; e: System.EventArgs);
begin
```

```
  if IsPostBack then
    Response.Redirect('ThankYouForm.aspx');
end;
```

When the server loads this page a second time as a result of a post-back, the `IsPostBack` property will be `True`. In this event, the `Response.Redirect()` method is invoked, so the user is redirected to the Thank You page.

Saving Files from within an ASP.NET Application

Although it's great that we can have a user fill out our form and that we can even thank him for doing so, we didn't do anything with the data he provided. Therefore, a `SaveUserInfo()` procedure is added to the form. This procedure takes the data that the user entered into the form and saves it to a file on the local drive. Listing 26.1 shows this procedure.

LISTING 26.1   SaveUserInfo() Procedure

```
 1:  procedure TWebForm1.SaveUserInfo;
 2:  const
 3:    fname = '.\files\dld_{0}.txt';
 4:  var
 5:    fs: FileStream;
 6:    sw: StreamWriter;
 7:  begin
 8:    fs := FileStream.Create(Server.MapPath(System.String.Format(fname,
 9:      [System.Guid.NewGuid.ToString])), FileMode.Append,
10:      FileAccess.Write);
11:    try
12:      sw := StreamWriter.Create(fs);
13:      try
14:        sw.WriteLine(System.String.Format('{0}={1}', [tbxFirstName.ID,
15:          tbxFirstName.Text]));
16:        sw.WriteLine(System.String.Format('{0}={1}', [tbxLastName.ID,
17:          tbxLastName.Text]));
18:        sw.WriteLine(System.String.Format('{0}={1}', [tbxTitle.ID,
19:          tbxTitle.Text]));
20:        sw.WriteLine(System.String.Format('{0}={1}', [tbxEmail.ID,
21:          tbxEmail.Text]));
22:        sw.WriteLine(System.String.Format('{0}={1}', [tbxCompany.ID,
23:          tbxCompany.Text]));
24:        sw.WriteLine(System.String.Format('{0}={1}', [tbxAddress1.ID,
25:          tbxAddress1.Text]));
26:        sw.WriteLine(System.String.Format('{0}={1}', [tbxAddress2.ID,
27:          tbxAddress2.Text]));
28:        sw.WriteLine(System.String.Format('{0}={1}', [tbxCity.ID,
29:          tbxCity.Text]));
30:        sw.WriteLine(System.String.Format('{0}={1}', [tbxPostalCode.ID,
31:          tbxPostalCode.Text]));
32:        sw.WriteLine(System.String.Format('{0}={1}', [tbxTelephone.ID,
33:          tbxTelephone.Text]));
34:        sw.WriteLine(System.String.Format('{0}={1}', [tbxFax.ID,
35:          tbxFax.Text]));
36:        sw.WriteLine(System.String.Format('{0}={1}', [tbxURL.ID,
```

26

LISTING 26.1 Continued

```
37:              tbxURL.Text]));
38:          if ddlCountry.SelectedIndex >= 0 then
39:            sw.WriteLine(System.String.Format('{0}={1}', [ddlCountry.ID,
40:              ddlCountry.Items[ddlCountry.SelectedIndex]]));
41:          if ddlState.SelectedIndex >= 0 then
42:            sw.WriteLine(System.String.Format('{0}={1}', [ddlState.ID,
43:              ddlState.Items[ddlState.SelectedIndex]]));
44:          sw.WriteLine(System.String.Format('{0}={1}', [cbxFreeStuff.ID,
45:            cbxFreeStuff.Checked.ToString]));
46:      finally
47:        sw.Close;
48:      end;
49:    finally
50:      fs.Close;
51:    end;
52:  end;
```

▶ **SEE** the full example on the CD under \Code\Ex01.

This procedure uses a stream to save the user's information into a text file. To make sure that the filename being generated is unique, the procedure creates a filename by using the System.Guid.NewGuid() function (line 9). Note the use of the Server.MapPath() function on line 8. The Server object is an HTTPServerUtility class that provides various helper functions for processing Web requests. The constant

```
const
  fname = '.\files\dld_{0}.txt';
```

is used to format the proper filename. The resulting name must be a virtual directory that ASP.NET will convert to a physical directory. The rest of the code is fairly straightforward. It relies on the FileStream and StreamWriter classes covered in Chapter 12, "File and Streaming Operations," to save the user's data. This also demonstrates how various controls are accessible from within the code-behind code.

> **NOTE**
>
> In order for an ASP.NET application to save a file, the proper IIS and NTFS rights must be set up. Chapter 31, "Securing ASP.NET Applications," covers ASP.NET Security.

At this point, the program must invoke the SaveUserInfo procedure, which is handled in the Page_Load() event handler as shown here:

```
procedure TWebForm1.Page_Load(sender: System.Object; e: System.EventArgs);
begin
  if IsPostBack then
  begin
    SaveUserInfo;
    Response.Redirect('ThankYouForm.aspx');
  end;
end;
```

It is important that the procedure is first invoked prior to executing the `Redirect()` statement to ensure that it actually gets executed. In fact, this is why we don't just place the code in the `SaveUserInfo()` procedure into the `Click` event for the Submit button.

Event Processing Order for a Web Form

Consider the following sequence of event processing for a Web form:

1. Page (.aspx) is requested.

2. Control's `ViewState` is restored.

3. The `Page`'s `Load` event fires.

4. Other control events fire.

5. The `Page`'s `Unload` event fires.

Had we placed the code to save user info into the Submit button's `Click` event, the `Page`'s `Load` event fires first and redirects the user to another page, circumventing the `Click` event altogether. It is common that you will evaluate a particular state within the `Load` event to determine what should be processed.

Pre-populating List Controls

Two of the controls on the download request form are `DropDownList` controls to allow the user to select his country and state/province. Obviously, we'll need to populate these controls. The method by which this is currently done is to read these values from a file containing name/value pairs. So, for instance, a `states.txt` file contains data such as

```
AL=Alabama
AK=Alaska
AB=Alberta
AS=American Samoa
AZ=Arizona
AR=Arkansas
BC=British Columbia
CA=California
CO=Colorado
```

Likewise, a file, `countries.txt`, contains similar data but with countries. Listing 26.2 is a function that reads these files and populates the `DropDownList` that is passed as a parameter with the contents of the file whose name is also passed as a parameter.

LISTING 26.2 PopulateDdlFromFile() Procedure

```
1:   procedure TWebForm1.PopulateDdlFromFile(aDDL: DropDownList;
2:   aFileName: String);
3:   var
4:     sr: StreamReader;
5:     FileLine: array of String;
6:     NameStr: String;
7:     ValueStr: String;
```

26

LISTING 26.2   Continued

```
8:   begin
9:     if System.IO.File.Exists(aFileName) then
10:    begin
11:      sr := StreamReader.Create(System.IO.File.OpenRead(aFileName));
12:      try
13:        while sr.Peek > -1 do
14:        begin
15:          FileLine := sr.ReadLine.Split(['=']);
16:          NameStr   := FileLine[0];
17:          ValueStr  := FileLine[1];
18:          aDDL.Items.Add(ListItem.Create(ValueStr, NameStr));
19:        end;
20:      finally
21:        sr.Close;
22:      end;
23:    end;
24:  end;
```

Listing 26.2 uses the System.String.Split() function (line 15) to separate the name/value entries, which are then used to populate the DropDownList (lines 13–18). This function is called in the Page's Init event as shown in Listing 26.3.

LISTING 26.3   Init Event Handler

```
1:   procedure TWebForm1.OnInit(e: EventArgs);
2:   begin
3:     InitializeComponent;
4:     inherited OnInit(e);
5:     PopulateDdlFromFile(ddlCountry,
6:       Request.PhysicalApplicationPath+'countries.txt');
7:     ddlCountry.Items.FindByText('United States').Selected := True;
8:     PopulateDdlFromFile(ddlState,
9:       Request.PhysicalApplicationPath+'states.txt');
10:  end;
```

Performing Web Form Validation

If you want to collect garbage from your users, avoid validating their data. On the other hand, proper use of the validation controls can help your users enter the correct information. The validations controls provided by ASP.NET should cover most needs. When they fall short, you can provide your own custom validation logic.

Validation controls allow you to specify the type of validation to occur and the error message that occurs when the user enters faulty data. Validation controls work just like Server controls in that you place them on the form and set their properties. When the form is rendered in HTML, the validation routines can be handled on the client side, thus preventing a round-trip to the server and back.

Client Versus Server-side Validation

Validation can occur either on the client through script, or on the server through code-behind. The advantage of performing client-side validation is that it does not require a trip to the server. The disadvantage to client-side validation is that not all browsers support the script that performs the validation, or users have disabled this capability. Fortunately, ASP.NET takes care of this matter by performing the validation where it makes sense. If it can be done on the client because the browser supports it, the validation script will be rendered on the client. If, however, the client browser does not support scripting, the validation will occur on the server. You can, through the common EnableClientScript property, disable client-side scripting if you desire. This is not recommended, however.

BaseValidator Class

All validation controls descend from the BaseValidator class. This class defines the common members and methods of each validation control. Table 26.1 lists some key properties of the BaseValidator class.

TABLE 26.1   Key Properties of the BaseValidator Class

Property	Description
ControlToValidate	References the input control to validate.
Display	Refers to a ValidatorDisplay enumeration that determines display behavior of validation error messages (Text property). There are three types of display behavior—none (Text displayed in ValidationSummary control only), static (Text displayed as part of the Page), and dynamic (Text added dynamically to the Page).
EnableClientScript	Specifies whether to enable client-side validation script.
Enabled	Specifies whether validation control is enabled.
ErrorMessage	Specifies the text of the error message that is displayed inline or in a ValidationSummary control when validation fails.
IsValid	Specifies whether the content entered into the input control is valid.
Page	Refers to the Page on which the server control resides.
Text	Specifies the text that is displayed when validation fails.

Other properties related to display attributes exist that are not listed in Table 26.1.

I will mention one key method of the BaseValidator class, which is the Validate() method. This method, when invoked, performs the validation against the specified input control (ControlToValidate) and updates the IsValid property accordingly.

RequiredFieldValidator

The RequiredFieldValidator control checks whether the input control contains a value. The Download Request Form presented in this chapter contains three RequiredFieldValidator controls to ensure that the user enters a first, a last name, and his email into the form. The following code shows the declaration of one of these controls in the .aspx file:

```
<asp:requiredfieldvalidator id=RequiredFieldValidator1
    runat="server"
```

26

```
    errormessage="First name required"
    controltovalidate="tbxFirstName">
</asp:requiredfieldvalidator>
```

What you see in the .aspx file are the property settings made in the Object Inspector. You might explore some of the display settings, such as font and color, to achieve the look you desire for your error messages.

When the user does not enter a value into the control specified by the ControlToValidate property, the message entered in the ErrorMessage property is displayed when the user attempts to submit the form. Figure 26.2 shows the form that has been submitted when the user has not entered a last name.

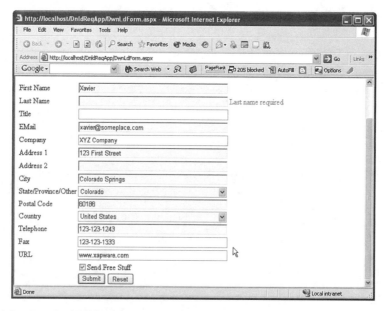

FIGURE 26.2   RequiredFieldValidator error message.

The InitialValue property of the RequiredFieldValidator enables you to test against a value with which you initialize the ControlToValidate. This allows you to prevent the user from submitting the form with initialized values—in other words, the user will have to modify the original value. Basically, the InitialValue property must match the initial value contained in the ControlToValidate.

CompareValidator

CompareValidator allows you to compare a value entered into a control with a constant or with a value from another control. CompareValidator has some additional key properties not inherited from BaseValidator, as shown in Table 26.2.

TABLE 26.2 CompareValidator Properties

Property	Description
ControlToCompare	Refers to the control whose content will be used in the comparison.
Operator	Specifies a comparison operator enumeration, which might be DataTypeCheck, Equal, GreaterThan, GreaterThanEqual, LessThan, LessThanEqual, or NotEqual.
Type	Specifies the data type to which values being compared are converted prior to performing the comparison. Possible values are Currency, Date, Double, Integer, and String.
ValueToCompare	Specifies a value to be used in the comparison.

Listing 26.4 illustrates the use of several CompareValidator controls that are used in a sample application. This is partial code from an .aspx file.

LISTING 26.4 CompareValidator Control Usage

```
1.  <asp:comparevalidator id=CompareValidator1
2.    style="Z-INDEX: 8; LEFT: 182px; POSITION: absolute; TOP: 86px"
3.    runat="server" operator="GreaterThan"
4.    controltovalidate="txbxEndDate"
5.    controltocompare="txbxBeginDate"
6.    errormessage="End date must follow begin date"
7.    type="Date">
8.  </asp:comparevalidator>
9.  <asp:comparevalidator id=CompareValidator2
10.   style="Z-INDEX: 9; LEFT: 182px; POSITION: absolute; TOP: 142px"
11.   runat="server" operator="LessThanEqual"
12.   controltovalidate="txbxValue"
13.   errormessage="Value must be less than or equal to 10"
14.   type="Integer" valuetocompare="10">
15. </asp:comparevalidator>
16. <asp:comparevalidator id=CompareValidator3
17.   style="Z-INDEX: 12; LEFT: 190px; POSITION: absolute; TOP: 206px"
18.   runat="server" operator="DataTypeCheck"
19.   controltovalidate="txbxDateType"
20.   errormessage="Value must be a date" type="Date">
21. </asp:comparevalidator>
```

Listing 26.4 is a portion from an .aspx file for the Web Form shown in Figure 26.3.

The first two text fields in Figure 26.3 demonstrate using CompareValidator to compare values from two separate form controls—in this case, two TextBox controls containing a begin and an end date. CompareValidator1 for these controls ensures that the end date is greater or less than the begin date.

CompareValidator2 performs a check against a static value. It ensures that the value entered into txbxValue is less than or equal to the value 10. Finally, CompareValidator3 checks that the entry into txbxDateType is date.

▶ **SEE** the example from this section on the CD: \Code\Ex02.

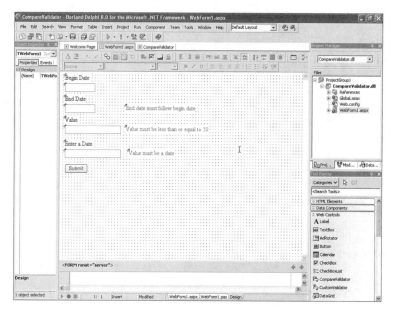

FIGURE 26.3   CompareValidator WebForm.

RegularExpressionValidator

Regular expressions are string patterns that specify the entry that users can enter into your input controls. Regular expressions are covered in Chapter 11, "Working with the `String` and `StringBuilder` Classes." The `RegularExpressionValidator` control lets you validate user input based on a regular expression. For instance, you can specify a valid string pattern for a phone number, ZIP Code, email address, and so forth. Listing 26.5 shows a partial `.aspx` file for a demo project that accepts a valid phone number, SSN, ZIP Code, nine-character password, email, and a URL.

LISTING 26.5   RegularExpressionValidator Example

```
1:  <asp:regularexpressionvalidator id=regexPhoneNo
2:    runat="server" width="222px"
3:    height="15px"
4:    controltovalidate="txbxPhoneNo"
5:    validationexpression="((\(\d{3}\) ?)¦(\d{3}-))?\d{3}-\d{4}"
6:    errormessage="Invalid phone number">
7:  </asp:regularexpressionvalidator>
8:  <asp:regularexpressionvalidator id=regexSSN
9:    runat="server"
10:   controltovalidate="txbxSSN"
11:   validationexpression="\d{3}-\d{2}-\d{4}"
12:   errormessage="Invalid SSN">
13: </asp:regularexpressionvalidator>
14: <asp:regularexpressionvalidator id=regexZipCode
15:   runat="server"
16:   controltovalidate="txbxZip"
17:   validationexpression="\d{5}(-\d{4})?"
```

LISTING 26.5   Continued

```
18:     errormessage="Invalid zip code">
19:   </asp:regularexpressionvalidator>
20:   <asp:regularexpressionvalidator id=regexPassword
21:     runat="server"
22:     controltovalidate="txbxPassword"
23:     validationexpression="\w{6,9}"
24:     errormessage="Invalid password (6-9 chars)">
25:   </asp:regularexpressionvalidator>
26:   <asp:regularexpressionvalidator id=regexEmail
27:     runat="server"
28:     controltovalidate="txbxEmail"
29:     validationexpression="\w+([-+.]\w+)*@\w+([-.]\w+)*\.\w+([-.]\w+)*"
30:     errormessage="Invalid email address"
31:     display="Dynamic">
32:   </asp:regularexpressionvalidator>
33:   <asp:requiredfieldvalidator id=reqFldEmail
34:     runat="server"
35:     controltovalidate="txbxEmail"
36:     errormessage="Email required"
37:     display="Dynamic">
38:   </asp:requiredfieldvalidator>
39:   <asp:regularexpressionvalidator id=regexURL
40:     runat="server"
41:     controltovalidate="txbxURL"
42:     validationexpression="http://([\w-]+\.)+[\w-]+(/[\w- ./?%&amp;=]*)?"
43:     errormessage="Invalid URL">
44:   </asp:regularexpressionvalidator>
```

The `ValidationExpression` property for each `RegularExpressionValidator` control contains the specific regular expression. The other properties are the same as with the other `BaseValidator` descendant controls.

Note that the `txbxEmail` control is associated with two different validation controls (lines 26, 33). The `reqFldEmail` control is a `RequiredFieldValidator` to make sure that the user enters an email. The `regexEmail` control ensures that the email entered is a valid email address.

▶ **SEE** the example from this section on the CD: `\Code\Ex03`.

RangeValidator

The `RangeValidator` control lets you specify a minimum and maximum value that the user can enter. Strictly speaking, the values in the min/max properties are always strings, but as with all validators, the inherited `Type` determines what type the input value and the min/max value is converted to before checking. These can be dates, numbers strings, or currency values. The `RangeValidator` control adds two key properties: `MinimumValue` and `MaximumValue`.

The following code declares a `RangeValidator` control that specifies a date range for a `TextBox` control:

```
<asp:rangevalidator id=RangeValidator1
  style="Z-INDEX: 3; LEFT: 182px; POSITION: absolute; TOP: 38px"
  runat="server"
```

```
errormessage="Date must be between Jan 1, 2003 and Dec 31, 2003"
controltovalidate="TextBox1" type="Date">
</asp:rangevalidator>
```

The Load event for this page contains the following code to specify the short date format for user entry:

```
RangeValidator1.MinimumValue :=
  DateTime(EncodeDate(2003, 1, 1)).ToShortDateString;
RangeValidator1.MaximumValue :=
  DateTime(EncodeDate(2003, 12, 31)).ToShortDateString;
```

Given these specification, the user will not be able to submit a date outside of the year 2003.

▶ **SEE** the example from this section on the CD: \Code\Ex04.

CustomValidator

Occasionally, the standard validation controls do not provide the sort of validation you require. In this event, you can use custom validation. The CustomValidator control allows you to perform custom validation on either the client or on the server. The following code illustrates the declaration of a CustomValidator control in the .aspx file:

```
<asp:customvalidator id=CustomValidator1
  style="Z-INDEX: 3; LEFT: 166px; POSITION: absolute; TOP: 30px"
  runat="server"
  errormessage="Please enter an even number"
  controltovalidate="TextBox1"
  clientvalidationfunction="ClientValidate">
</asp:customvalidator>
```

The clientvalidationfunction property is assigned the name of the client-side function. This function exists in the .aspx file and can be VBScript or JavaScript. The following code illustrates the client-side function for this example in VBScript:

```
<script Language="VBScript">
  Sub ClientValidate(source, args)
    args.IsValid = (args.Value mod 2) == 0
  End Sub
</script>
```

This function checks to make sure that the user enters an even number. This same validation routine should also be performed on the server, which will always occur anyway. The client-side check is just to reduce the round-trips. The server-side validation always takes place to verify the input values—the server can never be sure that the client-side checks have not been sidestepped. You simply attach an event handler to the ServerValidate event. The following code illustrates such an event handler:

```
procedure TWebForm1.CustomValidator1_ServerValidate(source: System.Object;
  args: System.Web.UI.WebControls.ServerValidateEventArgs);
begin
  args.IsValid := Convert.ToInt32(TextBox1.Text) mod 2 = 0;
end;
```

▶ **SEE** the example from this section on the CD: \Code\Ex05.

ValidationSummary

In larger WebForms, it can become difficult for users to see various errors without having to scroll through the entire form. The ValidationSummary control allows you to summarize all errors on a particular location on the page, such as at the top of the page. The ValidationSummary control properties are listed in Table 26.3.

TABLE 26.3   ValidationSummary Properties

Member	Description
DisplayMode	Determines the display format for errors. This enumeration value can be BulletList, List, or SingleParagraph.
EnableClientScript	Determines whether the ValidationSummary control updates itself from the client-side validation script.
HeaderText	Specifies the header text displayed at the top of the summary.
ShowMessageBox	Specifies whether error text is displayed in a message box.
ShowSummary	Specifies whether the error text is displayed inline.

When setting up a Validator control, it is important to note that the ErrorText property is used to hold the text to be displayed by the ValidationSummary control and not the Text property. Also, if you want to prohibit other validation controls from also displaying their error text, you must set their Display property to ValidationDisplay.None. Figure 26.4 shows the results of using a ValidationSummary control.

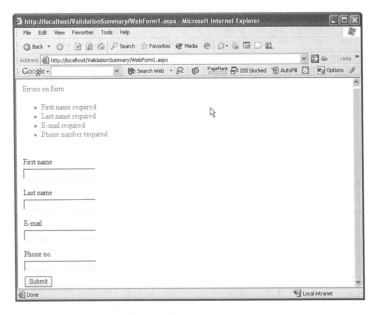

FIGURE 26.4   Validation summary example.

▶ **SEE** the example from this section on the CD: \Code\Ex06.

Web Form Formatting

When designing Web pages, you will need to consider how to give them a more pleasant and attractive look without eliminating their readability. There are two ways to do this in ASP.NET Forms—through formatting properties of the WebControl base class and through Cascading Style Sheets (CSS).

WebControl Strongly-Typed Properties

Web controls descend from the WebControl class, which contains various properties for display formatting. These properties are listed in Table 26.4.

TABLE 26.4 WebControl Strongly-typed Formatting Properties

Property	Description
AccessKey	Specifies a keyboard shortcut key to set focus to the WebControl.
BackColor	Background color of the WebControl.
BorderColor	Border color of the WebControl.
BorderStyle	Border style of the WebControl.
BorderWidth	Border width for the WebControl.
CssClass	Specifies a CSS class that UWebControl will be rendered with on the client.
Font	Specifies Font properties for the WebControl.
ForeColor	Specifies the foreground color for the WebControl.
Height	Specifies the WebControl's height.
Style	A collection of HTML style attributes that are rendered in the outer tag of the WebControl. Note that strongly-typed styles such as BackColor will override styles in this collection.
TabIndex	Specifies the Web server control's tab index.
ToolTip	Specifies balloon text that appears when hovering the mouse cursor over the WebControl.
Width	Specifies the height for the WebControl.

Listing 26.6 shows the declaration for controls in an .aspx file with strongly-typed style settings.

LISTING 26.6 Strongly-Typed Styles on WebControls

```
1:   <asp:textbox id=TextBox1
2:     style="Z-INDEX: 2; LEFT: 14px; POSITION: absolute; TOP: 6px"
3:     runat="server" borderstyle="Ridge" width="307px"
4:     font-names="Bradley Hand ITC" height="37"
5:     bordercolor="Yellow" backcolor="#C0FFFF" font-size="Large"
6:     forecolor="#000040" font-bold="True">Strongly Typed Settings</asp:textbox>
7:   <asp:label id=Label1
8:     style="Z-INDEX: 1; LEFT: 14px; POSITION: absolute; TOP: 54px"
9:     runat="server" borderstyle="Solid" font-names="Comic Sans MS"
10:    height="35px" bordercolor="Magenta" backcolor="#0000C0"
11:    font-size="Large" forecolor="White">Strongly Typed Settings</asp:label>
```

> **NOTE**
>
> Figure 26.5, shown later in the chapter, illustrates the results of these settings in a Web page.

Cascading Style Sheets

A Cascading Style Sheet (CSS) is a special file that contains definitions for styles that you can use on your Web pages. CSS files are great because they allow you to store the definition of styles in a single location. Changes to styles in the CSS affect all controls that refer to the modified style. This occurs in all pages that refer to that CSS file. Listing 26.7 shows an example CSS file containing two such styles definitions.

LISTING 26.7   Sample .css File

```
1:   BODY {
2:   }
3:   .MyBodyText {
4:       font-family: Verdana, Arial, Helvetica, sans-serif;
5:       font-size: 9px;
6:       font-style: normal;
7:       color: #333300;
8:   }
9:   .MyHeader {
10:      font-family: Verdana, Arial, Helvetica, sans-serif;
11:      font-size: 12px;
12:      font-style: normal;
13:      font-weight: bold;
14:      text-transform: capitalize;
15:      color: #000000;
16:  }
```

Lines 3–7 define one style class, .MyBodyText. Lines 9–15 define a second style class, .MyHeader. To attach this .css file to an .aspx file, you can use the link attribute as shown here within the Head block of the .aspx file:

```
<head>
  <title></title>
  <meta name="GENERATOR" content="Borland Package Library 7.1">
  <link href="FormFormat.css" rel="stylesheet" type="text/css">
</head>
```

In this example, the file, FormFormat.css, is linked to this .aspx file. At this point, you can add any of the two classes defined in FormFormat.css to the CssClass property of any WebControl. The following .aspx code illustrates such a class:

```
<asp:textbox id=TextBox2
  style="Z-INDEX: 3; LEFT: 14px; POSITION: absolute; TOP: 102px"
  runat="server" cssclass="MyHeader" borderstyle="None"
  width="259px" height="24">cssclass style setting</asp:textbox>
```

> **NOTE**
>
> Figure 26.5, shown later in the chapter, illustrates the results of these settings in a Web page.

26

Using the Style Class

You can use a Style class to apply formatting attributes to WebControls on the server side that are rendered as HTML on the client. Listing 26.8 shows how to use this class and how to apply it to a WebControl through the ApplyStyle() method.

LISTING 26.8   Using the Style Class

```
 1:   procedure TWebForm1.Page_Load(sender: System.Object;
 2:     e: System.EventArgs);
 3:   var
 4:     MyStyle: Style;
 5:   begin
 6:     MyStyle := Style.Create;
 7:     MyStyle.BackColor := Color.Aqua;
 8:     MyStyle.ForeColor := Color.Yellow;
 9:     MyStyle.BorderColor := Color.BlueViolet;
10:     MyStyle.BorderWidth := &Unit.Create(3);
11:     MyStyle.Font.Name := 'Comic Sans MS';
12:     Label2.ApplyStyle(MyStyle);
13:   end;
```

Figure 26.5 illustrates the results of these settings in a Web page.

FIGURE 26.5   Form formatting example.

> ▶ **SEE** the example from this section on the CD: \Code\Ex07.

Navigating between Web Forms

In developing ASP.NET applications, consider that your users will still need to navigate through various pages of the application, and in some cases they will need to carry data from a previous form. There are several ways to accomplish this, which are covered in this section.

Passing Data via POST

With server-side processing of Web Forms, the POST mechanism no longer works as it used to in classic ASP development. You can still POST to another Web Form by specifying the target Web Form in the Action attribute. However, you cannot send data along with that action—at least not automatically. Still, you can resort to classic POST processing to achieve this technique. For example, given two Web Forms, TWebForm1 might contain the following form tag to send the user to TWebForm2 when the form is submitted:

```
<form method="Post" Action="WebForm2.aspx">
```

Note that this form does not contain the runat="server" attribute. Therefore, under this scheme, you cannot use any server controls. In other words, you must use only HTML controls. Considering that TWebForm1 contains two input controls, FirstName and LastName, TWebForm2 would be capable of accessing these controls through the HttpRequest.Params property. A Load method for TWebForm2 might resemble

```
procedure TWebForm2.Page_Load(sender: System.Object;
  e: System.EventArgs);
begin
  Response.Write(System.String.Format(c_ty, [Request.Params['FirstName'],
    Request.Params['LastName']]));
end;
```

▶ SEE the example from this section on the CD: \Code\Ex08.

Using the Response.Redirect() Method and QueryString

The preceding technique might be simple; however, it defeats the advantages to using server controls with code-behind and so forth. Another way to send data to a different form is to invoke the URL for that form using the HttpResponse.Redirect() method. The Redirect() method redirects the client to a specified URL. Along with that URL, you would also send QueryString parameters that can be retrieved on the target form. For instance, suppose that you have a Web app with two Web Forms. TWebForm1 has the following code in its Load event to build a QueryString based on the content of its controls:

```
const
  UrlStr = 'WebForm2.aspx?FirstName={0}&LastName={1}';
procedure TWebForm1.Page_Load(sender: System.Object; e: System.EventArgs);
begin
  if IsPostBack then
    Response.Redirect(System.String.Format(UrlStr, [txbxFirstName.Text,
      txbxLastName.Text]));
end;
```

The URL that this would form when the user presses the submit button would be

```
http://localhost/QueryString/WebForm2.aspx?FirstName="Xavier"&LastName="Pacheco"
```

Within the Load event of TWebForm2, you can have the following code write a greeting to the user by retrieving the parameters from the Request.QueryString property:

```
const
  c_hello = 'hello {0} {1}!';
```

26

```
procedure TWebForm2.Page_Load(sender: System.Object; e: System.EventArgs);
begin
  Response.Write(System.String.Format(c_hello,
    Request.QueryString['FirstName'], Request.QueryString['LastName']));
end;
```

▶ **SEE** the example from this section on the CD: \Code\Ex09.

Using the Server.Transfer() Method

The Response.Redirect() method, although simple, has drawbacks. First, the parameters are passed in the URL where they are visible in the browser's address field. Second, there might be limitations as to the size of text some browsers can handle in the URL string. Third, you can only pass primitive values such as strings and numbers. You cannot pass objects to different pages. Finally, the Redirect() method is a request to the browser on the client. It's as if the server is telling the client to take a look at the suggested URL.

A Server.Transfer() method happens on the server, and therefore the client doesn't know it is happening. Basically, the client requests a URL and is sent to another URL. Using the Server.Transfer() method is more complicated than the Redirect() method, but it has more capabilities such as being able to pass objects. Consider the same two page examples from the previous sections. TWebForm1 cannot contain the following code in its Load event:

```
procedure TWebForm1.Page_Load(sender: System.Object; e: System.EventArgs);
begin
  if IsPostBack then
  begin
    Context.Items.Add('FirstName', txbxFirstName.Text);
    Context.Items.Add('LastName', txbxLastName.Text);
    Server.Transfer('WebForm2.aspx');
  end;
end;
```

Here, we access the Context property and add the two name/value items to its Items property. Then, the call to Transfer() is invoked, sending the user requesting the URL to WebForm2.aspx. On TWebForm2, the following code might appear in its Load event:

```
const
  c_hello = 'hello {0} {1}!';
procedure TWebForm2.Page_Load(sender: System.Object; e: System.EventArgs);
begin
  Response.Write(System.String.Format(c_hello, [
    Context.Items['FirstName'], Context.Items['LastName']]));
end;
```

Although it requires a bit more work, it is a much cleaner approach. Another way to accomplish this in a more OOP-like fashion is to add public properties that return the required values on the invoking form—in this case, TWebForm1. The target form, TWebForm2, can then get a reference to TWebForm1 through the Context dictionary.

So, for instance, TWebForm1 might contain the following properties:

```
property FirstName: String read get_FirstName;
property LastName: String read get_LastName;
```

The getter methods for these properties would resemble the following:

```
function TWebForm1.get_FirstName: String;
begin
  Result := txbxFirstName.Text;
end;
function TWebForm1.get_LastName: String;
begin
  Result := txbxLastName.Text;
end;
```

TWebForm2's Load event would now contain the following code:

```
const
  c_hello = 'hello {0} {1}!';
procedure TWebForm2.Page_Load(sender: System.Object; e: System.EventArgs);
var
  wf1: TWebForm1;
begin
  wf1 := TWebForm1(Context.Handler);
  Response.Write(System.String.Format(c_hello, [wf1.FirstName,
    wf1.LastName]));
end;
```

▶ **SEE** the example from this section on the CD: \Code\Ex10.

Using Session Variables

Another way to transfer the user to another Web page along with data is to use session variables. This technique is covered in greater detail in Chapter 33, "Caching and Managing State in ASP.NET Applications," which deals with state management. The example here is provided to illustrate how to transfer data from one page to another using this technique. Again, using the same application as in the previous examples, TWebForm1's Load event handler would have the following code to load the contents of two TextBox controls into session variables:

```
procedure TWebForm1.Page_Load(sender: System.Object; e: System.EventArgs);
begin
  if IsPostBack then
  begin
    Session.Add('FirstName', txbxFirstName.Text);
    Session.Add('LastName', txbxLastName.Text);
    Server.Transfer('WebForm2.aspx');
  end;
end;
```

TWebForm2's Load event would contain the following to extract these values from the Session object and to write out a greeting using these values:

```
const
  c_hello = 'Hello {0} {1}!';
```

```
procedure TWebForm2.Page_Load(sender: System.Object; e: System.EventArgs);
begin
  Response.Write(System.String.Format(c_hello, [Session['FirstName'],
    Session['LastName']]));
end;
```

▶ **SEE** the example from this section on the CD: \Code\Ex11.

Tips and Techniques

The following sections present some of the common techniques used by Web developers. Although these examples are specific, each demonstrates different techniques that you'll likely use under various circumstances, such as creating files on the server machine, generating in-memory images, and so forth.

Using the Panel Control for Multiform Simulation

Occasionally, you must create forms that request a lot of data from users, such as a survey. One might be inclined to use multiple .aspx Web forms in order to avoid forcing the user to scroll through a single lengthy form. This might be impractical given that not only must you manage multiple forms, but you must also store all the data the user is entering between forms for later use. An easier approach would be to use sections of a single form, which are toggled between visible and invisible depending on which section of the form the user happens to be filling out. This can be done using the Panel Web control.

Listing 26.9 is partial code to an example that illustrates this technique using three Panel controls.

LISTING 26.9   Multipage Simulation with Panels

```
1:    unit WebForm1;
2:
3:    interface
4:
5:    type
6:      TWebForm1 = class(System.Web.UI.Page)
7:      strict private
8:        procedure btnPrev_Click(sender: System.Object; e: System.EventArgs);
9:        procedure btnNext_Click(sender: System.Object; e: System.EventArgs);
10:     strict private
11:       procedure Page_Load(sender: System.Object; e: System.EventArgs);
12:     private
13:       procedure SetPanel(aOp: Integer);
14:     end;
15:
16:   implementation
17:
18:   procedure TWebForm1.Page_Load(sender: System.Object;
19:     e: System.EventArgs);
20:   begin
21:     if not IsPostBack then
22:     begin
```

LISTING 26.9   Continued

```
23:        ViewState['CurrentPanel'] := Convert.ToString(1);
24:        btnPrev.Enabled := False;
25:     end;
26:  end;
27:
28:  procedure TWebForm1.btnNext_Click(sender: System.Object;
29:     e: System.EventArgs);
30:  begin
31:     SetPanel(1);
32:  end;
33:
34:  procedure TWebForm1.btnPrev_Click(sender: System.Object;
35:     e: System.EventArgs);
36:  begin
37:     SetPanel(-1);
38:  end;
39:
40:  procedure TWebForm1.SetPanel(aOp: Integer);
41:  var
42:     pnl: Panel;
43:     pnlInt: Integer;
44:  begin
45:     // disable the current panel
46:     pnlInt := Convert.ToInt32(ViewState['CurrentPanel']);
47:     pnl := (FindControl('Panel'+pnlInt.ToString) as Panel);
48:     pnl.Visible := False;
49:     // Save the new current panel and make it visible
50:     pnlInt := pnlInt + aOp;
51:     ViewState['CurrentPanel'] := pnlInt.ToString;
52:     pnl := (FindControl('Panel'+pnlInt.ToString) as Panel);
53:     pnl.Visible := True;
54:
55:     btnPrev.Enabled := pnlInt <> 1;
56:     btnNext.Enabled := pnlInt <> 3;
57:  end;
58:
59:  end.
```

▶ **SEE** the example from this section on the CD: \Code\Ex12.

In this example, the idea is that we use the ViewState to store the current panel being displayed. When the user presses either the btnNext or btnPrev button, the SetPanel() method is invoked, which sets the current panel to invisible (lines 46–48) and then makes visible the new panel as determined by the aOp parameter. This parameter will either be a value of -1 or 1 depending on whether the user has pressed the btnPrev or btnNext button. After the appropriate Panel is made visible, its integer position is stored in the ViewState under the CurrentPanel key. Finally, the btnPrev and btnNext buttons are enabled/disabled based on the CurrentPanel.

26

Uploading a File from the Client

Allowing the user to upload files from a Web page has often been an arduous task. Under ASP.NET, the `HtmlInputFile` control encapsulates this process.

You must declare the `HtmlInputFile` control on the actual `.aspx` page as it is not a control that exists in design mode. Listing 26.10 shows the `.aspx` file that demonstrates the use of this control.

LISTING 26.10   Using the HtmlInputFile Control

```
1:    <%@ Page language="c#" Debug="true" Codebehind="WebForm1.pas"
➥AutoEventWireup="True" Inherits="WebForm1.TWebForm1" %>
2:    <!DOCTYPE HTML PUBLIC "-//W3C//DTD HTML 4.0 Transitional//EN">
3:    <script runat="server">
4:        void btnSubmit_Click(Object sender, EventArgs e){
5:        String fName =
6:          System.IO.Path.GetFileName(UpFile.PostedFile.FileName);
7:        String pName =
8:          Server.MapPath(System.String.Format(".\\Files\\{0}", fName));
9:        UpFile.PostedFile.SaveAs(pName);
10:       Response.Write(pName);
11:      }
12:   </script>
13:
14:   <html>
15:     <head>
16:       <title></title>
17:       <meta name="GENERATOR" content="Borland Package Library 7.1">
18:     </head>
19:
20:     <body ms_positioning="GridLayout">
21:     <form enctype="multipart/form-data" runat="server">
22:       <input id=UpFile type=file name=UpFile runat="server">
23:       <asp:button id=Button1
24:          style="Z-INDEX: 1; LEFT: 6px; POSITION: absolute; TOP: 62px"
25:          onclick=btnSubmit_Click runat="server" text="Upload File">
26:       </asp:button>
27:     </form>
28:   </body>
29:   </html>
```

▶ **SEE** the example from this section on the CD: `\Code\Ex13`.

The `HTMLInputFile` control is declared in line 22. This renders a `TextBox`/`Button` combination as shown in Figure 26.6. This control corresponds to a `HTMLInputFile` object on the server. It is the combination of the `"<input ...>"` control with the `"type=file"` and `"runat=server"` that causes the ASP.NET server to create an `HTMLInputFile` control to represent it at runtime on the server.

Another required step is to change the default encoding format for the Web Form. Line 21 does this by specifying the `enctype` attribute in the `form` tag. When the user presses the Browse button, a File Open dialog box is displayed from which the user can select the file to upload. When a file is selected, the `TextBox` control is assigned the full path to the file on the user's machine. The Upload File button invokes the `btn_SubmitClick` event handler defined in the C# server-side script block. This event handler performs the process of uploading the file by invoking the `HttpInputFile.PostedFile.SaveAs()` method against the file chosen by the user. The `UpFile` control is this `HTMLInputFile` instance that represents the uploaded file. There are other properties of the `HttpPostedFile` from which you can examine information about the file that you might want to research.

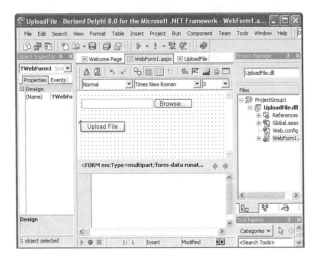

FIGURE 26.6   Uploading a file.

Sending an Email Response from a Form

Having the ability to send email from a Web application is critical if you want to be able to provide timely feedback to users who visit your Web site. Consider the Download Request Form from earlier in this chapter. When users request the product, the application saves the information that they entered into a text file for later retrieval. Their email addresses are included in that information. At some point, they need to be emailed the download link for the product. You wouldn't want to be manually processing these requests provided that your site is generating many requests per day. Ideally, the user is sent an email immediately after having submitted his request.

The `System.Web.Mail` namespace contains two classes that allow you to send email through your Web site. These are the `MailMessage` and `SmtpMail` classes.

Table 26.5 lists the various properties of the `MailMessage` class.

TABLE 26.5   MailMessage Properties

Property	Description
Attachments	Contains a collection of attachments.
Bcc	A semicolon delimited list of email addresses that will receive a blind carbon copy of the email.

TABLE 26.5   Continued

Property	Description
Body	The body of the email message.
BodyEncoding	Specifies the encoding type for the body of the email message.
BodyFormat	Specifies the format of the email message. This can be Text or HTML.
Cc	A semicolon delimited list of email addresses that will receive a carbon copy of the email.
From	Sender's email address.
Headers	Custom headers that are transmitted with the email address.
Priority	Priority of the email address.
Subject	Subject of the email address.
To	A semicolon delimited list of email recipients.

The SmtpMail class is a static class that encapsulates the SMTP protocol. It handles sending MailMessage through a standard SMTP Server as specified through its SmtpServer property.

Revisiting the Product Download Application, the main WebForm now has an additional procedure named SendEMail() as shown in Listing 26.11.

LISTING 26.11   SendEMail() Method for Product Download Request App

```
 1:    procedure TWebForm1.SendEmail(aEmail: &String);
 2:    var
 3:      MailMsg: MailMessage;
 4:      sr: StreamReader;
 5:    begin
 6:      MailMsg := MailMessage.Create;
 7:      MailMsg.From     := 'info@xapware.com';
 8:      MailMsg.&To      := aEmail;
 9:      MailMsg.Bcc      := 'sales@somehwere.com';
10:      MailMsg.Subject := 'Your request to download XYZ Product';
11:      MailMsg.BodyFormat := MailFormat.HTML;
12:
13:      sr := StreamReader.Create(System.IO.File.OpenRead(
14:        Request.PhysicalApplicationPath+'dnloadmail.htm'));
15:      try
16:        MailMsg.Body := sr.ReadToEnd;
17:      finally
18:        sr.Close;
19:      end;
20:
21:      SmtpMail.SmtpServer := 'localhost';
22:      SmtpMail.Send(MailMsg);
23:    end;
```

> ▶ **SEE** the example from this section on the CD: \Code\Ex01.

Most of this code is simply making the proper assignments to the MailMessage class properties. Lines 13–19 load an HTML template that gets sent as the body of the email. Last, the SmtpMail.SmtpServer property is assigned the value of 'localhost', indicating that it should refer to the locally installed SMTP server. SmtpMail.Send() is invoked passing the MailMessage instance.

Displaying Images

Surely at some point, you will either need to display or generate images if you are creating Web applications. This section demonstrates how to dynamically generate a thumbnail image from a larger image in a directory. The technique demonstrated here uses two Web forms. A main form contains an `ImageButton` whose `ImageUrl` property points to another Web form (`ImageForm.aspx` file). `ImageForm.aspx` contains code that dynamically generates a thumbnail image that gets displayed in the `ImageButton` on the main form. This technique makes use of classes defined in the `System.Drawing` and `System.Drawing.Imaging` namespaces. Listing 26.12 shows the `Load` event handler for the `ImageForm`.

LISTING 26.12   ImageForm Load Event—Creating a Thumbnail

```
1:   procedure TImageForm.Page_Load(sender: System.Object;
2:     e: System.EventArgs);
3:   var
4:     bm: Bitmap;
5:     im: System.Drawing.Image;
6:     tni: System.Drawing.Image;
7:   begin
8:     // Grab the image from disk
9:     im := System.Drawing.Image.FromFile(
10:       Request.PhysicalApplicationPath+'z.jpg');
11:     // Create the thumbnail image
12:     tni := im.GetThumbNailImage(96, 112, nil, IntPtr.Zero);
13:     // Create a bitmap from the thumbnail image
14:     bm := Bitmap.Create(tni);
15:     // Save the image in the Response output stream.
16:     bm.Save(Response.OutputStream, ImageFormat.jpeg);
17:   end;
```

> ▶ **SEE** the example from this section on the CD: `\Code\Ex14`.

This code makes use of various classes defined in the `System.Drawing` namespace. First, an image is loaded from disk (line 9–10). It is converted to a thumbnail image by invoking the `GetThumbNailImage()` method of the `Image` class (line 12). Finally, a `Bitmap` is created from the thumbnail image and drawn to the `OutputStream` of the `HttpResponse` class (line 16). The `MainForm` contains no special code. It merely contains an `ImageButton` component that has an `ImageUrl` property pointing to the `ImageForm`. You can attach a `Click` event to the `ImageForm` to redirect the user's browser to the actual larger image such as

```
Response.Redirect('j.jpg');
```

The result of this code is shown in Figure 26.7.

Dynamically Adding Controls—A Thumbnail Based Image Viewer

This example illustrates how you might programmatically add controls to a Web page. The idea behind this application is to have an image view that automatically creates thumbnail images based on the images that exist within the site directory. Thumbnail images are kept in a separate directory. From the thumbnail images, individual `ImageButtons` are added to the page, and when clicked, they redirect the client browser to display the actual image.

Listing 26.13 illustrates the method from the Web form that performs the process of looping though all images in the site directory, creating the thumbnails and creating the ImageButtons for each thumbnail. Also demonstrated is how an event is dynamically assigned to the ImageButton.

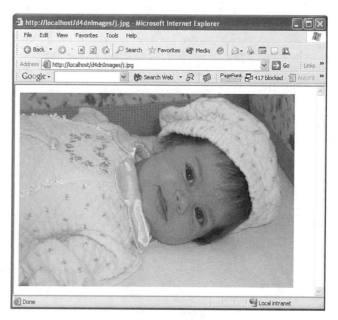

FIGURE 26.7   Larger image.

LISTING 26.13   GenerateThumbs() Method

```
1:    procedure TWebForm1.GenerateThumbs;
2:    var
3:      fArray: array of String;
4:      i: integer;
5:      bm: Bitmap;
6:      tni: System.Drawing.Image;
7:      im: System.Drawing.Image;
8:      fName: String;
9:      fs: FileStream;
10:     ib: ImageButton;
11:   begin
12:     fArray := Directory.GetFiles(Request.PhysicalApplicationPath, '*.jpg');
13:     for i := Low(fArray) to High(fArray) do
14:     begin
15:       fName := System.IO.Path.GetFileName(fArray[i]);
16:       fName := 'tn_'+fName;
17:       fName := Request.PhysicalApplicationPath+'thumbs\'+fName;
18:       if not System.IO.File.Exists(fName) then
19:       begin
20:         im := System.Drawing.Image.FromFile(fArray[i]);
21:         tni := im.GetThumbNailImage(96, 112, nil, IntPtr.Zero);
```

LISTING 26.13   Continued

```
22:       bm := Bitmap.Create(tni);
23:       fs := FileStream.Create(fName, FileMode.OpenOrCreate,
24:         FileAccess.Write);
25:       try
26:         bm.Save(fs, ImageFormat.Jpeg);
27:       finally
28:         fs.Close;
29:       end;
30:     end;
31:     ib := ImageButton.Create;
32:     ib.ImageUrl := fName;
33:     ib.Attributes['runat'] := '"server"';
34:     Include(ib.Click, ImageButton1_Click);
35:     Panel1.Controls.Add(ib);
36:   end;
37: end;
```

▶ **SEE** the example from this section on the CD: \Code\Ex15.

This example only works with JPEG files. The `for` loop (line 13) iterates through all files in the Web site directory that have a `.jpg` extension. The filename used for the thumbnail is the same as with the image with the characters `"tn_"` prepended to the filename (line 16). If the thumbnail file does not exist, it is created (line 20–30). Finally, an `ImageButton` is created, linked to the thumbnail file, and added to the page. Figure 26.8 shows the resulting Web page with thumbnail images.

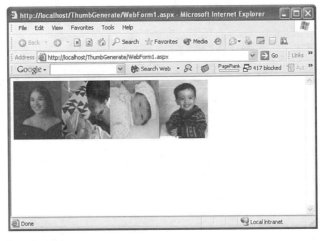

FIGURE 26.8   Thumbnail image page.

A few things need to be pointed out here. First, line 34 adds the `ImageButton1_Click()` event handler to each `ImageButton` created. This event handler contains the code shown in Listing 26.14.

LISTING 26.14   ImageButton1_Click() Event Handler

```
1:    procedure TWebForm1.ImageButton1_Click(sender: System.Object;
2:      e: System.Web.UI.ImageClickEventArgs);
3:    var
4:      fName: String;
5:    begin
6:      with sender as ImageButton do
7:      begin
8:        fName := ImageUrl;
9:        fName := System.IO.Path.GetFileName(fName);
10:       fName := fName.Remove(0, 3);
11:       Response.Redirect(fName);
12:     end;
13:   end;
```

This event handler reconstructs the original filename and redirects the user's browser to the JPEG file, which displays the full image.

Additionally, note that the image is actually added to a Panel control container. The reason for this is that when adding WebControl's to the Page, they must exist within the Form tag containing the runat="server" attribute. Otherwise, an error will be generated. By adding the controls to a Panel, this assures that the control will be added within the Form tag.

CHAPTER 27

Building Database Driven ASP.NET Applications

IN THIS CHAPTER

- Data Binding
- Data Bound List Controls
- Data Bound Iterative Controls
- Working with the DataGrid
- Database-Driven Download Request Form and Administrator

Today's modern Web sites are no longer simple static pages of information. They are highly interactive Web applications that allow end users to view and manipulate data. What was once only available to the desktop platform is now also available through modern Web browsers. In fact, software vendors know that it is not unusual for customers to desire a Web version of an application.

Internet enabled applications create a much different paradigm to how we develop software. ASP.NET combined with ADO.NET or BDP offers powerful capabilities to work with data sources. This chapter delves into developing database-driven Web applications using these capabilities.

Data Binding

In Chapter 21, "Working with WinForms: DataViews and Data Binding," you learned about data binding when working with Windows Forms. Data binding for Web Forms is similar. You might recall that data binding is the process of associating data from a data source to a property of a control. Some of the Web Controls are specifically designed to be data bound controls. These are discussed later in this chapter.

There are two forms of data binding that you'll use when developing Web applications. The first is property based, or simple, data binding. The second is data source based, or complex, data binding.

Simple Data Binding

In ASP.NET, simple data binding refers to the process of associating a Web Control with database data or any data held directly or indirectly by the Web Form—fields, properties, methods, and so on—with a property of a Web Control. To accomplish this, you must include a data binding expression. The expression follows the syntax shown here:

```
<%# data binding expression %>
```

This expression can be part of the value portion of the attribute-value pair in the server control's opening tag as shown here:

```
<asp:textbox id=TextBox1 style="Z-INDEX: 2; LEFT: 46px; POSITION:
  absolute; TOP: 326px" runat="server" text="<%# MyName %>">
```

It can also be placed anywhere with the page body using the following syntax:

```
Literal text <%# data binding expression %>
```

For instance, given a Web Form with a public string field of MyName as shown here:

```
TWebForm1 = class(System.Web.UI.Page)
public
  { Public Declarations }
  MyName: String;
end;
```

You can use the previous expression with TextBox1 to bind the TextBox to the contents of the String field.

You can also bind to the result of a function. For example, the following shows the opening tag for a TextBox control that binds its Text property to the result of the GetMyName() function, which returns a String:

```
<asp:textbox id=TextBox1
    style="Z-INDEX: 2; LEFT: 22px; POSITION: absolute; TOP: 422px"
    runat="server" text="<%# GetMyName() %>">
</asp:textbox>
```

Note that although parenthesis is not required when writing Delphi code, you must include the parenthesis when referring to a function in the binding expression. Additionally, the method to which you refer must be declared as public or protected, or strict protected. The reason for this is because the expression is really script code and the script code is declared as C#. There is currently no official support for using Delphi as the script language in this release of Delphi.

Data binding actually occurs when you invoke the Page's DataBind() function. You can do this in the Load event for a page after establishing the data to which the control will be bound. In other words, call DataBind() after populating an array, filling a DataSet, setting the value of a field, and so on. The DataBind() method resolves data binding expressions with the server controls.

▶ Find the code on the CD: \Code\Chapter 27\Ex01.

Probably the most common use of simple data binding is to bind to a database field. In reality, you don't actually bind a control to a database field, but rather to a function or property that provides the database field value. The reason for this is to simulate the concept of a cursor (or current record) within the form. An example will illustrate this concept.

Listing 27.1 contains an excerpt from an example on the CD, which illustrates how to write a page that can navigate a database table. This example displays three fields from the current record. This pseudo-current record is accomplished by maintaining a reference to a record number in the Session. This record number gets incremented or decremented based on the direction that the user selects and is used in retrieving the record to display.

LISTING 27.1   Table Navigation in a Web Page

```
1:  type
2:
3:    TRowMove = (rmFirst, rmPrev, rmNext, rmLast);
4:
5:    TWebForm1 = class(System.Web.UI.Page)
6:    strict private
7:      procedure Page_Load(sender: System.Object; e: System.EventArgs);
8:    private
9:      procedure ReBind;
10:     function GetField(aFieldName: String): String;
11:     procedure SetRowNum(aRowMove: TRowMove);
12:   public
13:     function GetFirstName: String;
14:     function GetLastName: String;
15:     function GetTitle: String;
16:   end;
17:
18:  implementation
19:
20:  procedure TWebForm1.Page_Load(sender: System.Object;
21:    e: System.EventArgs);
22:  begin
23:    ReBind;
24:  end;
25:
26:  function TWebForm1.GetFirstName: String;
27:  begin
28:    Result := GetField('FirstName');
29:  end;
30:
31:  function TWebForm1.GetLastName: String;
32:  begin
33:    Result := GetField('LastName');
34:  end;
35:
36:  function TWebForm1.GetTitle: String;
37:  begin
38:    Result := GetField('Title');
39:  end;
40:
41:  procedure TWebForm1.btnLast_Click(sender: System.Object;
42:    e: System.EventArgs);
43:  begin
44:    SetRowNum(rmLast);
45:  end;
46:
```

LISTING 27.1   Continued

```
47:   procedure TWebForm1.btnNext_Click(sender: System.Object;
48:     e: System.EventArgs);
49:   begin
50:     SetRowNum(rmNext);
51:   end;
52:
53:   procedure TWebForm1.btnPrev_Click(sender: System.Object;
54:     e: System.EventArgs);
55:   begin
56:     SetRowNum(rmPrev);
57:   end;
58:
59:   procedure TWebForm1.btnFirst_Click(sender: System.Object;
60:     e: System.EventArgs);
61:   begin
62:     SetRowNum(rmFirst);
63:   end;
64:
65:   function TWebForm1.GetField(aFieldName: &String): String;
66:   var
67:     dt: DataTable;
68:     rowNum: System.Int32;
69:   begin
70:     dt := Session['Employees'] as DataTable;
71:     rowNum := Session['RowNum'] as System.Int32;
72:     result := dt.Rows[RowNum][aFieldName].ToString;
73:   end;
74:
75:   procedure TWebForm1.ReBind;
76:   var
77:     rowNum:  System.Int32;
78:     numRows: System.Int32;
79:   begin
80:     txbxFirstName.DataBind;
81:     txbxLastName.DataBind;
82:     txbxTitle.DataBind;
83:
84:     rowNum := Session['RowNum'] as System.Int32;
85:     numRows := Session['NumRows'] as System.Int32;
86:
87:     btnPrev.Enabled  := rowNum > 1;
88:     btnFirst.Enabled := rowNum > 1;
89:     btnNext.Enabled  := rowNum < numRows;
90:     btnLast.Enabled  := rowNum < numRows;
91:
92:     Label4.Text := 'Number of rows: '+numRows.ToString;
93:     Label5.Text := 'Row number: '+rowNum.ToString;
94:
95:   end;
96:
97:   procedure TWebForm1.SetRowNum(aRowMove: TRowMove);
98:   var
99:     rowNum: System.Int32;
```

LISTING 27.1 Continued

```
100:    numRows: System.Int32;
101: begin
102:    rowNum  := Session['RowNum'] as System.Int32;
103:    numRows := Session['NumRows'] as System.Int32;
104:
105:    case aRowMove of
106:      rmFirst : rowNum := 1;
107:      rmPrev  : rowNum := rowNum - 1;
108:      rmNext  : rowNum := rowNum + 1;
109:      rmLast  : rowNum := numRows;
110:    end; // case
111:
112:    Session.Add('RowNum', System.Object(RowNum));
113:    ReBind;
114: end;
115:
116: end.
```

▶ Find the code on the CD: \Code\Chapter 27\Ex02.

First, there are three functions that return a string corresponding to one of the three database fields. These are GetFirstName(), GetLastName(), and GetTitle() (lines 26–39). These are the functions that are referenced in the data binding expression in the .aspx file. An example follows:

```
<asp:textbox id=txbxLastName
      style="Z-INDEX: 1; LEFT: 134px; POSITION: absolute;
      TOP: 118px" runat="server" height="24" width="180px"
      text="<%# GetLastName()%>">
</asp:textbox>
```

Each function calls the GetField() function, which is implemented in lines 65–73.

> **NOTE**
>
> Before I explain any further, I must add that you can assume that a DataTable, its row count, and an integer representing a current row number are all stored in the Session object. I haven't discussed the Session object yet; this is a topic for Chapter 33 "Caching and Managing State in ASP.NET Applications." For now, just assume that it is a holding place for objects that survive during the entire session. In other words, the data is not lost in between requests.

GetField() takes a single String parameter representing the field name to get. GetField() first retrieves the DataTable object from the Session object. It also retrieves the RowNum integer value. From these values, it returns the value of the field represented by the aFieldName parameter. This is basically how the control is bound to the control.

The demo has some additional functionality not specific to data binding but worthy of mention nonetheless. The form contains four navigation buttons (btnFirst, btnPrev, btnNext, and btnLast). The Click event for each button calls a SetRowNum() procedure (lines 97–114), which takes a TRowMove parameter telling it how to navigate. This function simply sets the value of the RowNum entry in the Session object accordingly.

27

The ReBind() function (lines 75–76), which is called by the Page_Load() event handler and the SetRowNum() procedure, invokes the DataBind() method for each of the bound controls and enables/disables the buttons based on whether the current row is at the beginning or end of the DataTable.

Complex Data Binding

Complex data binding involves binding list or iterative controls to data in a list or in a column. In ASP.NET, the list controls are the CheckBoxList, DropDownList, ListBox, and RadioButtonList. The iterative controls are the Repeater, DataList, and DataGrid.

Data Bound List Controls

Typically, list controls are bound to a collection (an implementer of ICollection) through its DataSource property.

CheckBoxList Control

The CheckBoxList control represents a multiselect check box group that can be associated with a data source. CheckBoxList descends from the ListControl defined in the System.Web.UI.WebControls namespace. Other list controls discussed in this chapter also descend from ListControl. ListControl contains some key properties that its descendants, such as CheckBoxList, inherit. These are listed in Table 27.1.

TABLE 27.1   Key Properties of the ListControl

Property	Description
Items	Returns a collection of items contained in the CheckBoxList.
DataSource	Sets the data source that populates the controls.
DataMember	Sets the table in a data source to bind to the control.
DataTextField	Sets the field of a data source that provides the text for each list item.
DataValueField	Sets the field of a data source that provides the value for each item.
DataTextFormatString	A formatting string that determines how text is formatted in bound controls.
SelectedIndex	Index of the selected item or lowest index in a multiselected list.
SelectedItem	Selected item or item with the lowest index in a multiselected listing.
SelectedValue	Value of the selected item in the control.

The CheckBoxList control contains two additional key properties—RepeatLayout and RepeatDirection. RepeatLayout enables you to set the layout of the check boxes as either in a table (RepeatLayout.Table) or without a table structure (RepeatLayout.Flow). RepeatDirection specifies whether the CheckBoxList items display vertically or horizontally.

Binding to an Array

The following Page_Load() event handler illustrates the populating of an array of String and binding that array to a CheckBoxList instance:

```
procedure TWebForm1.Page_Load(sender: System.Object; e: System.EventArgs);
var
```

```
  i: integer;
begin
  for i := 0 to 9 do
    MyArray[i] := 'Item '+i.ToString;
  DataBind;
end;
```

▶ Find the code on the CD: \Code\Chapter 27\Ex03.

This example assumes that the CheckBoxList control's opening tag in the .aspx file appears as

```
<asp:checkboxlist id=CheckBoxList1
  style="Z-INDEX: 1; LEFT: 38px; POSITION: absolute; TOP: 62px"
  runat="server" repeatdirection="Horizontal"
  repeatlayout="Flow" datasource="<%# MyArray %>"
  width="331px" height="26">
</asp:checkboxlist>
```

This example would generate the output shown in Figure 27.1. Note how setting the RepeatDirection property to Horizontal affects the layout of the control.

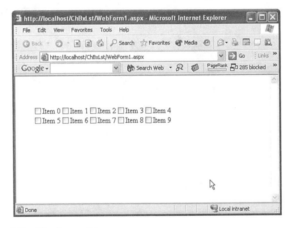

FIGURE 27.1 CheckBoxList bound to an array.

Binding to a Database Table

When binding a CheckBoxList to a Table within a DataSet, you'll likely want to make use of the DataTextFields and DataValueField properties as well. Listing 27.2 illustrates what the code to set up these bindings looks like.

LISTING 27.2   Binding a CheckBoxList to a Table

```
1:    procedure TWebForm1.Page_Load(sender: System.Object; e: System.EventArgs);
2:    const
3:      c_cnstr = 'server=XWING;database=Northwind;Trusted_Connection=Yes';
4:      c_sel   = 'SELECT * FROM categories';
5:    var
6:      sqlcn: SqlConnection;
```

LISTING 27.2   Continued

```
 7:    sqlDA: SqlDataAdapter;
 8:    ds: DataSet;
 9:    dt: DataTable;
10:  begin
11:    sqlcn := SqlConnection.Create(c_cnstr);
12:    sqlDA := SqlDataAdapter.Create(c_sel, sqlcn);
13:    ds := DataSet.Create;
14:    sqlDA.Fill(ds, 'Categories');
15:    dt := ds.Tables['Categories'];
16:    CheckBoxList1.DataSource := dt.DefaultView;
17:    CheckBoxList1.DataTextField  := 'CategoryName';
18:    CheckBoxList1.DataValueField := 'CategoryID';
19:    DataBind;
20:    sqlcn.Close;
21:  end;
```

▶ Find the code on the CD: `\Code\Chapter 27\Ex04`.

Lines 16–18 perform the assignment to the properties of the `CheckBoxList` control. Line 17 determines which field of the categories table is displayed in the browser (see Figure 27.2). Line 18 determines which field represents the value returned by the checked items

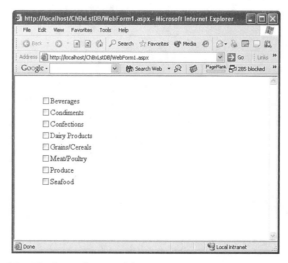

FIGURE 27.2   CheckBoxList bound to a table.

DropDownList Control

The `DropDownList` control is similar to the Windows Form `ComboBox`. It allows users to select a single value from a list of items. The `DropDownList` descends from the `ListControl` and therefore inherits its properties as listed in Table 27.1.

Binding to an Array

The following Page_Load() event handler illustrates the populating of an array of String and binding that array to a DropDownList instance:

```
procedure TWebForm1.Page_Load(sender: System.Object; e: System.EventArgs);
var
  i: integer;
begin
  for i := 0 to 9 do
    MyArray[i] := 'Item '+i.ToString;
  DataBind;
end;
```

▶ Find the code on the CD: \Code\Chapter 27\Ex05.

This example assumes that the DropDownList control's opening tag in the .aspx file appears as

```
<asp:dropdownlist id=DropDownList1
  style="Z-INDEX: 1; LEFT: 62px; POSITION: absolute; TOP: 78px"
  runat="server" datasource="<%# MyArray %>" height="22"
  width="195px">
</asp:dropdownlist>
```

This example would generate the output shown in Figure 27.3.

FIGURE 27.3   DropDownList bound to an array.

Binding to a Database Table

When binding a DropDownList to a Table within a DataSet, you will make use of the DataTextFields and DataValueField properties. Listing 27.3 illustrates what the code to set up these bindings looks like.

LISTING 27.3   Binding a DropDownList to a Table

```
 1:  procedure TWebForm1.Page_Load(sender: System.Object; e: System.EventArgs);
 2:  const
 3:    c_cnstr = 'server=XWING;database=Northwind;Trusted_Connection=Yes';
 4:    c_sel   = 'SELECT * FROM categories';
 5:  var
 6:    sqlcn: SqlConnection;
 7:    sqlDA: SqlDataAdapter;
 8:    ds: DataSet;
 9:    dt: DataTable;
10:  begin
11:    sqlcn := SqlConnection.Create(c_cnstr);
12:    sqlDA := SqlDataAdapter.Create(c_sel, sqlcn);
13:    ds := DataSet.Create;
14:    sqlDA.Fill(ds, 'Categories');
15:    dt := ds.Tables['Categories'];
16:    DropDownList1.DataSource := dt.DefaultView;
17:    DropDownList1.DataTextField  := 'CategoryName';
18:    DropDownList1.DataValueField := 'CategoryID';
19:    DataBind;
20:    sqlcn.Close;
21:  end;
```

▶ Find the code on the CD: \Code\Chapter 27\Ex06.

You'll note that this code is almost identical to Listing 27.2 with the exception of lines 16–18, which operate on a DropDownList control rather than a CheckBoxList control. Figure 27.4 shows the output of this listing.

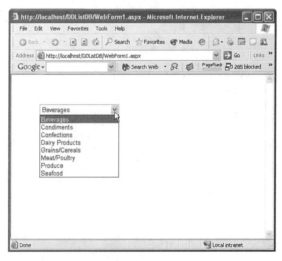

FIGURE 27.4   DropDownList bound to a table.

ListBox Control

The ListBox control is a vertical list of items that supports single or multiple item selection. When the list exceeds the bounds of the control, it is scrollable. ListBox descends from the ListControl and therefore inherits its properties as listed in Table 27.1. ListControl has the additional properties of RepeatDirection and RepeatLayout. These properties serve the same purpose as the properties of the same name for the CheckBoxList control.

Binding to an Array

The following Page_Load() event handler illustrates the populating of an array of String and binding that array to a ListBox instance:

```
procedure TWebForm1.Page_Load(sender: System.Object; e: System.EventArgs);
var
  i: integer;
begin
  for i := 0 to 9 do
    MyArray[i] := 'Item '+i.ToString;
  DataBind;
end;
```

▶ Find the code on the CD: \Code\Chapter 27\Ex07.

This example assumes that the ListBox control's opening tag in the .aspx file appears as

```
<asp:listbox id=ListBox1
             style="Z-INDEX: 1; LEFT: 46px; POSITION: absolute; TOP: 38px"
             runat="server" height="123px" width="171px"
             datasource="<%# MyArray %>" selectionmode="Multiple">
</asp:listbox>
```

Note that the selectionmode attribute is set to Multiple to allow for multiselect.

This example would generate the output shown in Figure 27.5.

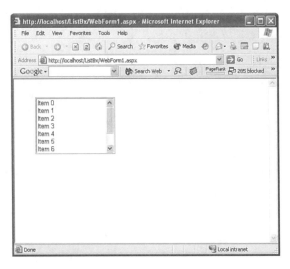

FIGURE 27.5   ListBox bound to an array.

Binding to a Database Table

When binding a ListBox to a Table within a DataSet, you will make use of the DataTextFields and DataValueField properties as with the previous controls. Listing 27.4 illustrates what the code to set up these bindings looks like.

LISTING 27.4   Binding a ListBox to a Table

```
 1:   procedure TWebForm1.Page_Load(sender: System.Object; e: System.EventArgs);
 2:   const
 3:     c_cnstr = 'server=XWING;database=Northwind;Trusted_Connection=Yes';
 4:     c_sel   = 'SELECT * FROM categories';
 5:   var
 6:     sqlcn: SqlConnection;
 7:     sqlDA: SqlDataAdapter;
 8:     ds: DataSet;
 9:     dt: DataTable;
10:   begin
11:     sqlcn := SqlConnection.Create(c_cnstr);
12:     sqlDA := SqlDataAdapter.Create(c_sel, sqlcn);
13:     ds := DataSet.Create;
14:     sqlDA.Fill(ds, 'Categories');
15:     dt := ds.Tables['Categories'];
16:     ListBox1.DataSource := dt.DefaultView;
17:     ListBox1.DataTextField  := 'CategoryName';
18:     ListBox1.DataValueField := 'CategoryID';
19:     DataBind;
20:     sqlcn.Close;
21:   end;
```

▶ Find the code on the CD: \Code\Chapter 27\Ex08.

Again, this code is practically the same as in Listings 27.2 and 27.3 except that the control is now a ListBox control. Figure 27.6 shows the output of this listing.

FIGURE 27.6   ListBox bound to a table.

RadioButtonList Control

The RadioButtonList control encapsulates a group of RadioButton. RadioButtonList descends from ListControl and inherits its properties as shown in Table 27.1.

Binding to an Array

The following Page_Load() event handler illustrates the populating of an array of String and binding that array to a RadioButtonList instance:

```
procedure TWebForm1.Page_Load(sender: System.Object; e: System.EventArgs);
var
  i: integer;
begin
  for i := 0 to 9 do
    MyArray[i] := 'Item '+i.ToString;
  DataBind;
end;
```

▶ Find the code on the CD: \Code\Chapter 27\Ex09.

This example assumes that the RadioButtonList control's opening tag in the .aspx file appears as

```
<asp:radiobuttonlist id=RadioButtonList1
  style="Z-INDEX: 1; LEFT: 38px; POSITION: absolute; TOP: 14px"
  runat="server" datasource="<%# MyArray %>" height="26"
  width="211px" repeatlayout="Flow"
  repeatdirection="Horizontal" repeatcolumns="3">
</asp:radiobuttonlist>
```

This example sets the repeatdirection attribute to Horizontal and the repeatcolumns attribute to 3, resulting in the output shown in Figure 27.7.

FIGURE 27.7   RadioButtonList bound to an array.

Binding to a Database Table

When binding a RadioButtonList to a Table within a DataSet, you will make use of the DataTextFields and DataValueField properties as with the previous controls. Listing 27.5 illustrates what the code to set up these bindings looks like.

LISTING 27.5   Binding a RadioButtonList to a Table

```
1:   procedure TWebForm1.Page_Load(sender: System.Object; e: System.EventArgs);
2:   const
3:     c_cnstr = 'server=XWING;database=Northwind;Trusted_Connection=Yes';
4:     c_sel   = 'SELECT * FROM categories';
5:   var
6:     sqlcn: SqlConnection;
7:     sqlDA: SqlDataAdapter;
8:     ds: DataSet;
9:     dt: DataTable;
10:  begin
11:    sqlcn := SqlConnection.Create(c_cnstr);
12:    sqlDA := SqlDataAdapter.Create(c_sel, sqlcn);
13:    ds := DataSet.Create;
14:    sqlDA.Fill(ds, 'Categories');
15:    dt := ds.Tables['Categories'];
16:    RadioButtonList1.DataSource := dt.DefaultView;
17:    RadioButtonList1.DataTextField  := 'CategoryName';
18:    RadioButtonList1.DataValueField := 'CategoryID';
19:    DataBind;
20:    sqlcn.Close;
21:  end;
```

▶ Find the code on the CD: \Code\Chapter 27\Ex10.

Figure 27.8 shows the output of this listing.

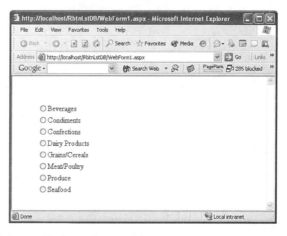

FIGURE 27.8   RadioButtonList bound to a table.

Data Bound Iterative Controls

Iterative controls are also bound through their Datasource property. Iterative controls apply templated HTML to each item within the collection, giving you more customizable options for data presentation.

Repeater Control

The Repeater control iterates through a collection of data and uses templates to determine how each item in the collection will be rendered. Templates are constructs that enable you to apply formatting to items that the Repeater control displays. There are five types of templates, which are listed in Table 27.2.

TABLE 27.2   Repeater Control Templates

Template	Description
HeaderTemplate	Formatting specified in this template is rendered prior to any of the items. This template does not contain data bindings.
ItemTemplate	Formatting specified in this template is rendered for each item, or row, of the data source. This template might contain data binding expressions.
AlternatingItemTemplate	Formatting specified in this optional template is rendered for each alternate item or row. It functions the same as ItemTemplate but for oddly numbered rows.
SeparatorTemplate	Formatting specified in this template specifies the HTML between each row.
FooterTemplate	Opposite of the HeaderTemplate. It is rendered once after all rows have been rendered. It cannot contain data binding expressions.

Table 27.3 lists some key properties and events of the Repeater class.

TABLE 27.3   Repeater Properties and Events

Property/Event	Description
DataMember	A property that refers to the specific table in the DataSource property that the Repeater will bind to
DataSource	A property that refers to the data source that provides the list of bindable data
Items	A property that returns the collection of RepeaterItem objects
ItemCommand	An event that fires when a command button is pressed in the Repeater
ItemCreated	An event that fires when an item is created in the Repeater
ItemDataBound	An event that fires after an item is bound, but before it is rendered in HTML

A simple example bound to the employees table of the Northwind database will illustrate the use of the Repeater control and the various headers. Listing 27.6 shows the Load event for a Web Form containing a Repeater control.

LISTING 27.6   Repeater Control Example

```
1:    procedure TWebForm1.Page_Load(sender: System.Object; e: System.EventArgs);
2:    const
3:      c_cnstr = 'server=XWING;database=Northwind;Trusted_Connection=Yes';
4:      c_sel   = 'SELECT * FROM employees';
5:    var
6:      sqlcn: SqlConnection;
```

27

LISTING 27.6   Continued

```
7:      sqlDA: SqlDataAdapter;
8:      ds: DataSet;
9:      dt: DataTable;
10:  begin
11:      sqlcn := SqlConnection.Create(c_cnstr);
12:      sqlDA := SqlDataAdapter.Create(c_sel, sqlcn);
13:      ds := DataSet.Create;
14:      sqlDA.Fill(ds, 'Employees');
15:      dt := ds.Tables['Employees'];
16:
17:      Repeater1.DataSource := dt.DefaultView;
18:      DataBind;
19:      sqlcn.Close;
20:  end;
```

▶ Find the code on the CD: \Code\Chapter 27\Ex11.

Listing 27.6 is not too different from the previous example. Similar to other Web controls, the Repeater has a Datasource property to which you can assign the data source that it will be bound to (line 17). In this case, we are binding to the DataTable representing the employees table. The declaration of the Repeater control within the .aspx file is where most of the information about how it will render is specified. Listing 27.7 shows this declaration.

LISTING 27.7   Repeater Control Declaration (.aspx)

```
1:   <asp:repeater id=Repeater1 runat="server">
2:     <headertemplate>
3:     <table>
4:       <tr height=12>
5:         <td bgcolor="#e0e0e0" width=100>
6:           <b>First Name</b>
7:         </td>
8:         <td bgcolor="#e0e0e0" width=100>
9:           <b>Last Name</b>
10:        </td>
11:      </tr>
12:    </headertemplate>
13:      <itemtemplate>
14:      <tr>
15:        <td><%# ((System.Data.DataRowView)Container.DataItem)["FirstName"]%>
16:        </td>
17:        <td><%# DataBinder.Eval(Container.DataItem, "LastName")%>
18:        </td>
19:      </tr>
20:    </itemtemplate>
21:    <separatortemplate>
22:      <tr>
23:        <td colspan="2" align="center">— — — — — — — — — — — —
24:        </td>
25:      </tr>
26:    </separatortemplate>
27:    <footertemplate>
28:          </table>
```

LISTING 27.7   Continued

```
29:    </footertemplate>
30:  </asp:repeater>
```

▶ Find the code on the CD: \Code\Chapter 27\Ex11.

Lines 2–12 contain the HeaderTemplate. This example specifies a table row with two columns to represent a header. The FooterTemplate (lines 27–29) complete this table. The ItemTemplate (lines 13–20) specify the formatting for each item in the Repeater.

A Repeater control contains a collection of RepeaterItem objects. A RepeaterItem object is bound to an item of the data source. In this example, each item is a DataRowView. Lines 15 and 17 make use of the Container.DataItem property, which returns the class to which the RepeaterItem is bound. You'll notice that lines 15 and 17 are different. I did this intentionally to illustrate a point (see the sidebar for this point).

EVALUATING BINDING EXPRESSIONS

The data binding expression <%# data-binding expression %> is evaluated by the CLR based on the language specified in the <%@ Page %> directive. Therefore, the syntax you use within the expression should conform to whatever the language expects. For example, in many examples of the Container.DataItem usage that you might see online or in other publications, you will see the following syntax:

```
<td><%# Container.DataItem("LastName")%>
```

This will work if the language used by the page is VB. If, however, the language is C#, it will result in an error. In C#, you must cast the expression to the appropriate type as shown in line 15 of Listing 27.6. How you cast this, of course, depends on the class to which Container.DataItem refers.

The following lines illustrate some differences between VB and C# expressions when the Repeater is bound to a DataView object.

```
// VB:
<%# Container.DataItem("FirstName") %>

// C#:
<%# ((DataRowView)Container.DataItem)["FirstName"] %>
```

When the Repeater is bound to a DataTable

```
// VB:
<%# Container.DataItem("FirstName") %>

// C#:
<%# ((DataRow)Container.DataItem)["FirstName"] %>
```

To alleviate having to remember how to typecast the DataItem, Microsoft provided the DataBinder.Eval() helper function. This function figures out the proper typecast and formats the resulting string for you. However, exercise caution because this function relies on reflection to determine this information. This can be costly performance-wise. The better option is to figure out the proper typecast and use it. Another option would be to expose a method on the WebForm that returns the current DataRow or DataRowView, alleviating the need for a scripting typecast.

Lines 21–26 illustrate the SeparatorTemplate. This template provides the HTML, a set of dashes that will appear between each row. Figure 27.9 shows the output of this program.

27

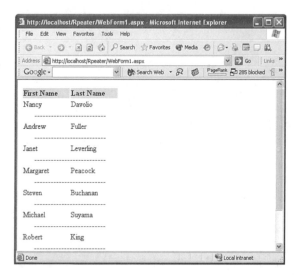

FIGURE 27.9   Repeater control output.

Alternatively, to separate rows, you can use the `AlternatingItemTemplate` by replacing the `SeparatorTemplate` with the following code:

```
<alternatingitemtemplate>
  <tr>
    <td bgcolor="#fff7d7"><%# DataBinder.Eval(Container.DataItem, "FirstName")%>
    </td>
    <td bgcolor="#fff7d7"><%# DataBinder.Eval(Container.DataItem, "LastName")%>
    </td>
    </tr>
</alternatingitemtemplate>
```

The output changes to that shown in Figure 27.10.

DataList Control

The `DataList` control is basically the `Repeater` control but extended in functionality, particularly around the graphical layout capabilities. For instance, `DataList` adds the `SelectedItemTemplate` and `EditItemTemplate`. Therefore, it supports the idea of selecting and editing an item. You can change the directional layout of items—either vertical or horizontal. It has more events than the `Repeater` class. In addition to the templates listed in Table 27.2, `DataList` has the templates shown in Table 27.4.

TABLE 27.4   Additional DataList Control Templates

Template	Description
SelectedItemTemplate	Formatting specified in this template is rendered for the item, or row, of the data source when an item is selected.
EditItemTemplate	Formatting specified in this template is rendered for the item, or row, of the data source when an item is edited.

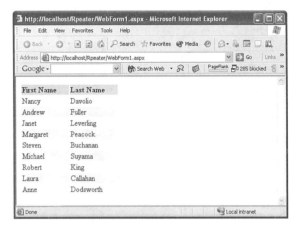

FIGURE 27.10 Repeater control output, alternating items.

Table 27.5 lists some key properties and events of the DataList class.

TABLE 27.5 DataList Properties and Events

Property/Event	Description
AlternatingItemStyle	Property that refers to the alternating item's styles
EditItemIndex	Property that refers to the index of the item currently being edited
EditItemStyle	Property that refers to the style properties of the item currently being edited
FooterStyle	Property that refers to the style properties of the DataList's footer
GridLines	Property referring to the grid line style properties
HeaderStyle	Property referring to the header style properties
Items	Property that refers to a collection of DataListItem objects—each of which refer to individual items in the DataList object
ItemStyle	Property referring to the style properties for the DataListItem
RepeatColumns	Property that specifies the number of columns to display
RepeatDirection	Property that determines vertical or horizontal display of the DataList
RepeatLayout	Property that determines either table or flow layout
SelectedIndex	Property referring to the index of the selected item in the DataList
SelectedItem	Property referring to the selected DataListItem
SelectedItemStyle	Property referring to the style attributes for the selected DataListItem
SeparatorStyle	Property referring to the style attributes for the separator
CancelCommand	Event that fires when the Cancel command is invoked for the DataList
DeleteCommand	Event that fires when the Delete command is invoked for the DataList
EditCommand	Event that fires when the Edit command is invoked for the DataList
ItemCommand	Event that fires when any command button is clicked in the DataList control
ItemCreated	Event that fires when a DataListItem is created
ItemDataBound	Event that fires when a DataListItem is bound but before it is rendered
UpdateCommand	Event that fires when the Update command is invoked for the DataList

To illustrate the use of the DataList class, I'll use the employee table in the Northwind database. This example performs formatting of the SelectedItem. It also shows how to respond to the user selecting an item where it retrieves additional information about each employee and displays this information on the Page. Listing 27.8 shows the DataList declaration of the .aspx file for this example.

LISTING 27.8   DataList Control Declaration (.aspx)

```
1:    <asp:datalist id="DataList1" style="Z-INDEX: 1" runat="server"
2:      horizontalalign="Left" height="70px" datakeyfield="EmployeeID">
3:      <selecteditemstyle font-bold="True" forecolor="LightGray"
4:        backcolor="Black"></selecteditemstyle>
5:      <headertemplate>
6:          <b>Employees</b>
7:      </headertemplate>
8:      <itemtemplate>
9:          <asp:linkbutton commandname="select"
10:            text='<%# ((System.Data.DataRowView)Container.DataItem)
➥["FirstName"].ToString()+" "+
11:            ((System.Data.DataRowView)Container.DataItem)
➥["LastName"].ToString()%>'
12:            runat="Server" />
13:      </itemtemplate>
14:    </asp:datalist>
```

▶ Find the code on the CD: \Code\Chapter 27\Ex12.

First, notice the SelectedItemStyle tag (lines 3–4). Within this tag, the display properties for the selected item are set. The ItemTemplate declares the item as a LinkButton that will invoke an event in the Page.

Listing 27.9 is an excerpt from the source file of the WebForm for this application.

LISTING 27.9   DataList Example

```
1:    procedure TWebForm1.Page_Load(sender: System.Object; e: System.EventArgs);
2:    const
3:      c_cnstr = 'server=XWING;database=Northwind;Trusted_Connection=Yes';
4:      c_sel   = 'SELECT * FROM employees';
5:    var
6:      sqlcn: SqlConnection;
7:      sqlDA: SqlDataAdapter;
8:      ds: DataSet;
9:      dt: DataTable;
10:   begin
11:     Session.Add('EmpID', System.Object(-1));
12:     Image1.Visible := False;
13:     sqlcn := SqlConnection.Create(c_cnstr);
14:     sqlDA := SqlDataAdapter.Create(c_sel, sqlcn);
15:     ds := DataSet.Create;
16:     sqlDA.Fill(ds, 'Employees');
17:     dt := ds.Tables['Employees'];
18:
19:     DataList1.DataSource := dt.DefaultView;
20:     DataBind;
21:     sqlcn.Close;
```

LISTING 27.9   Continued

```
22:  end;
23:
24:  procedure TWebForm1.btnUnSelect_Click(sender: System.Object;
25:    e: System.EventArgs);
26:  begin
27:    DataList1.SelectedIndex := -1;
28:    Label1.Text := '';
29:  end;
30:
31:  procedure TWebForm1.DataList1_SelectedIndexChanged(sender: System.Object;
32:    e: System.EventArgs);
33:  const
34:    c_cnstr = 'server=XWING;database=Northwind;Trusted_Connection=Yes';
35:    c_sel   = 'SELECT FirstName, LastName, Title, TitleOfCourtesy, Notes '+
36:    ' FROM employees WHERE employeeid = {0}';
37:  var
38:    sqlcn: SqlConnection;
39:    sqlCmd: SqlCommand;
40:    sqlRdr: SqlDataReader;
41:    dt: DataTable;
42:    selStr: String;
43:    EmpID: Integer;
44:    Line: String;
45:  begin
46:    Label1.Text := '';
47:    Image1.Visible := True;
48:    EmpID := Integer(DataList1.DataKeys[DataList1.SelectedIndex]);
49:    sqlcn := SqlConnection.Create(c_cnstr);
50:    selStr := System.String.Format(c_sel, [EmpID]);
51:    sqlCmd := SqlCommand.Create(selStr, sqlcn);
52:
53:    sqlcn.Open;
54:    try
55:      sqlRdr := sqlCmd.ExecuteReader;
56:      sqlRdr.Read;
57:      Line := System.String.Format('<b>{0} {1} {2}</b><br>',
58:        [sqlRdr['TitleOfCourtesy'], sqlRdr['FirstName'],
➥sqlRdr['LastName']]);
59:      Label1.Text := Label1.Text+Line;
60:      Label1.Text := Label1.Text + sqlRdr['Title'].ToString+'<hr>';
61:      Label1.Text := Label1.Text + sqlRdr['Notes'].ToString;
62:      Session.Add('EmpID', System.Object(EmpID));
63:    finally
64:      sqlcn.Close;;
65:    end;
66:  end;
```

▶ Find the code on the CD: \Code\Chapter 27\Ex12.

The Page_Load() event handler is similar to the others you've already seen in this chapter. Of note are lines 11 and 12, where I place a -1 in the Session object, which will be used by another page. I'll discuss this momentarily.

When an item is selected within the DataList, the SelectedIndex property is set to the items index. The btnUnSelect_Click() (lines 24–29) event handler is a response to a button on the Page. This handler sets the SelectedIndex to -1, which effectively deselects any items.

When an item is selected, the DataList1_SelectedIndexChanged() event handler is invoked. This event handler retrieves additional information about the employee and displays this information in a Label control. Another page handles displaying the employee's picture in an Image control. The Image rendering uses the technique shown in Chapter 26, "Building ASP.NET Web Pages," for rendering images; simply put, this technique illustrates how to refer the Image control to another .aspx page that handles the rendering. Line 62 shows that the EmployeeID is added to the Session object. This value will be used by the image rendering page.

Listing 27.10 lists the Page_Load() event for the Web Form that renders the employee's picture.

LISTING 27.10   Image Rendering from a Database

```
 1:    procedure TImageForm.Page_Load(sender: System.Object;
 2:      e: System.EventArgs);
 3:    const
 4:      c_cnstr = 'server=XWING;database=Northwind;Trusted_Connection=Yes';
 5:      c_selphoto = 'SELECT Photo FROM employees WHERE employeeid = {0}';
 6:    var
 7:      sqlcn: SqlConnection;
 8:      sqlCmd: SqlCommand;
 9:      selStr: String;
10:      EmpID: Integer;
11:      photo: TByteArray;
12:    begin
13:      EmpID := Integer(Session['EmpID']);
14:      if EmpID > -1 then
15:      begin
16:        sqlcn := SqlConnection.Create(c_cnstr);
17:        selStr := System.String.Format(c_selphoto, [EmpID]);
18:        sqlcn.Open;
19:        try
20:          sqlCmd := SqlCommand.Create(selStr, sqlcn);
21:          photo := TByteArray(sqlCmd.ExecuteScalar);
22:        finally
23:          sqlcn.Close;
24:        end;
25:        Response.ContentType := 'image/jpeg';
26:        Response.OutputStream.Write(photo, 78, System.Array(photo).Length);
27:      end;
28:    end;
```

▶ Find the code on the CD: \Code\Chapter 27\Ex12.

First, line 13 retrieves the employee's ID from the Session into the EmpID variable. It then uses this to retrieve the BLOB field containing the employee's picture.

> **NOTE**
>
> Normally, a BLOB field in a database contains only the image. This is not the case for the images contained in the Northwind database. These images were initially stored as an OLE object and therefore contain 78 bytes of header information about this object. The image follows the header. In Listing 27.10 code, it is necessary to specify the offset as that of 78 bytes from the beginning of the BLOB.

The remaining code renders the picture within the Page. Because the Image control on the main Page refers to this page, it is displayed with the other information as shown in Figure 27.11.

FIGURE 27.11   DataList and Image controls.

Working with the DataGrid

The DataGrid has the most functionality of the iterative controls. The DataGrid represents data in a table format in which every item is represented in a row and fields are represented in columns. The DataGrid supports full template capabilities. Within the DataGrid, you can provide the capability to select, sort, and edit deleting and paging items.

Five column types are supported in the DataGrid—one of which allows you to create custom templated columns. This makes the possibilities with the DataGrid columns unlimited.

Table 27.6 lists the various column types supported by the DataGrid.

TABLE 27.6   Data Grid Column Types

Column Type	Description
BoundColumn	Renders a column that is bound to a data source field.
ButtonColumn	Renders a command button in each item in this column, giving you the ability to add functionality as a response to button commands.
EditCommandColumn	Renders a column that adds buttons for editing items in the DataGrid.
HyperLinkColumn	Renders the column item as a hyperlink. This value might be bound to a data source field, or it might contain static text.
TemplateColumn	Renders the column according to the specified template. You would use this column type to add custom controls to the DataGrid.

You can also set various display styles for the following elements:

AlternatingItemStyle	Style of alternating rows in the DataGrid
EditItemStyle	The row being edited
FooterStyle	Style of the DataGrid's footer
HeaderStyle	Style of the DataGrid's header
ItemStyle	Style of each item within the DataGrid (unless an AlternatingItemStyle is provided)
PagerStyle	Styles of the page selection section of the DataGrid
SelectedItemStyle	Style of the DataGrid's selected item

The property list of the DataGrid is extensive, and therefore I won't discuss each of them. Instead, I will discuss some of the key properties within the context of the examples provided here.

> **NOTE**
>
> For further information on the DataGrid, I would recommend looking at the documentation online at www.msdn.microsoft.com or in the .NET SDK docs provided in the Delphi for .NET help.

Paging the DataGrid

One of the nice features of the DataGrid is its capability to display and navigate through divided chunks of large resultsets. The DataGrid itself handles the rendering of each chunk and adds a Pager bar, a row at the bottom of the DataGrid with links to allow the user to move forward or backward through the data chunks. Of course, you have the option of customizing how the DataGrid retrieves chunks to display, and you can also change the look and behavior of the Pager bar.

It should be noted, however, that the DataGrid handles the rendering in usability of paging. It does not handle the management of the data within the data source. If you think of how ASP.NET operates, each time a page is requested, the data obtained from the last request is no longer present. This new request is a new page; therefore, all actions that are required to display the new page must occur, which includes retrieving data, reassigning the data source to the data grid, and rebinding. With paging, you add the step to tell the DataGrid which item should be displayed as the top item in the DataGrid. Considering this, it is possible to retrieve thousands of records from the data source into a data set each time the user pages through the DataGrid. This is not typically a problem. But if it were to be problematic, you do have the option of smarter data retrieval to reduce the number of records obtained from the DataSet, or you have caching options that will be discussed in Chapter 33. For this discussion, we'll stay simple.

This first example illustrates the paging capabilities of the DataGrid. Additionally, it demonstrates the use of the AlternatingItemStyle.

Listing 27.11 shows the declaration of the DataGrid within the .aspx file.

LISTING 27.11   DataGrid Declaration (.aspx)

```
1:    <%@ Page language="c#" Debug="true" Codebehind="WebForm1.pas"
2:    AutoEventWireup="false" Inherits="WebForm1.TWebForm1" %>
3:    <!DOCTYPE HTML PUBLIC "-//W3C//DTD HTML 4.0 Transitional//EN">
4:
5:    <html>
6:      <head>
7:        <title></title>
8:        <meta name="GENERATOR" content="Borland Package Library 7.1">
9:      </head>
10:
11:    <body ms_positioning="GridLayout">
12:    <form runat="server">
13:      <asp:datagrid id=DataGrid1
14:            style="Z-INDEX: 1; LEFT: 6px; POSITION: absolute; TOP: 6px"
15:            runat="server" height="243" width="523px" font-names="Arial"
16:            font-size="X-Small" borderwidth="1px" bordercolor="Gray"
17:            borderstyle="Solid" cellspacing="2" cellpadding="2"
18:            pagesize="5" allowpaging="True">
19:        <alternatingitemstyle borderstyle="Solid" backcolor="#FFFFC0">
20:        </alternatingitemstyle>
21:        <itemstyle borderstyle="Solid" backcolor="#C0FFFF">
22:        </itemstyle>
23:      </asp:datagrid>
24:    </form>
25:  </body>
26:  </html>
```

▶ Find the code on the CD: \Code\Chapter 27\Ex13.

Line 18 shows the setting of the two attributes that enable paging within the DataGrid. Lines 19 and 20 set the AlternateItemStyle and line 21 sets the ItemStyle attribute. The code-behind source for this Page is shown in Listing 27.12.

LISTING 27.12   DataGrid Page

```
1:    TWebForm1 = class(System.Web.UI.Page)
2:      procedure DataGrid1_PageIndexChanged(source: System.Object; e:
3:      System.Web.UI.WebControls.DataGridPageChangedEventArgs);
```

LISTING 27.12   Continued

```
 4:    strict private
 5:      procedure Page_Load(sender: System.Object; e: System.EventArgs);
 6:    private
 7:      { Private Declarations }
 8:      procedure GetData;
 9:    end;
10:
11:  implementation
12:
13:  procedure TWebForm1.Page_Load(sender: System.Object; e: System.EventArgs);
14:  begin
15:    if not IsPostBack then
16:      GetData;
17:  end;
18:
19:  procedure TWebForm1.DataGrid1_PageIndexChanged(source: System.Object;
20:    e: System.Web.UI.WebControls.DataGridPageChangedEventArgs);
21:  begin
22:    DataGrid1.CurrentPageIndex := e.NewPageIndex;
23:    GetData;
24:  end;
25:
26:  procedure TWebForm1.GetData;
27:  const
28:    c_cnstr = 'server=XWING;database=Northwind;Trusted_Connection=Yes';
29:    c_sel   = 'select * from customers';
30:  var
31:    sqlcn: SqlConnection;
32:    sqlDA: SqlDataAdapter;
33:    ds: DataSet;
34:    dt: DataTable;
35:  begin
36:    sqlcn := SqlConnection.Create(c_cnstr);
37:    sqlDA := SqlDataAdapter.Create(c_sel, sqlcn);
38:    ds := DataSet.Create;
39:    sqlDA.Fill(ds, 'customers');
40:    dt := ds.Tables['customers'];
41:
42:    DataGrid1.DataSource := dt.DefaultView;
43:    DataBind;
44:    sqlcn.Close;
45:  end;
46:
47:  end.
```

▶ Find the code on the CD: \Code\Chapter 27\Ex13.

Listing 27.12 contains portions of the actual code. The GetData() method retrieves information from the data source. You'll note that this method is invoked both from the Page_Load() event handler and from the DataGrid_1_PageIndexChanged() event handler. This illustrates how you are required to retrieve the data whenever you are going to generate a new page. Line 22 shows how to set the index of the item for the DataGrid prior to rebinding the DataGrid. The result of this code is shown in Figure 27.12.

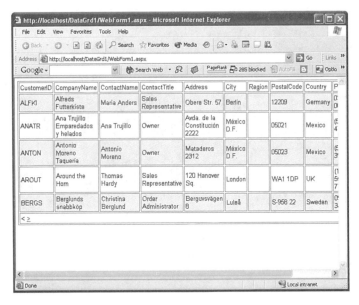

FIGURE 27.12   DataGrid control.

Editing the DataGrid

The DataGrid has a special column of the type EditCommandColumn of which you supply a single instance if you want in-place editing in the DataGrid. The declaration of this column would look like that shown here:

```
<asp:editcommandcolumn edittext="Edit" updatetext="Update"
    canceltext="Cancel" headertext="Edit"
    itemstyle-wrap="False">
</asp:editcommandcolumn>
```

When this column is present, a column with a link will appear on the DataGrid. When this link is clicked, the editable controls on the grid become text controls with the exception of those that are based on a templated column. The EditCommandColumn will then contain two links referring to the Cancel and Update commands.

When the user clicks the Edit command, the EditCommand event is invoked. When the user clicks the Update and Cancel commands, the UpdateCommand and CancelCommand events are invoked, respectively.

The DataGrid handles all the work to convert the columns to editable TextBoxes. It also handles converting the EditCommandColumn to contain the proper text. It doesn't include the code to actually perform the data source update.

I'll get into these event handlers momentarily. I've already shown the declaration of the EditComandColumn for the upcoming example. Consider the following declaration of a standard column for the DataGrid:

```
<asp:boundcolumn datafield="QuantityPerUnit"
  headertext="Qty Per Unit" itemstyle-wrap="False"
  sortexpression="ORDER BY QuantityPerUnit">
</asp:boundcolumn>
```

This column will correspond to the QuantityPerUnit fields of the Products database in the Northwind database. When the DataGrid is placed into edit mode, this column is converted to a TextBox. Take note of the sortexpression attribute. This will come into play later. The remaining columns appear similar to this.

Consider the declaration of the TemplateColumn in Listing 27.13.

LISTING 27.13   Declaration of a TemplateColumn

```
1. <asp:templatecolumn runat="server" headertext="Discontinued">
2.      <itemtemplate>
3.          <asp:checkbox id="CheckBox1" runat="server" enabled="False"
4.          checked='<%# Convert.ToBoolean(((System.Data.DataRowView)
➥Container.DataItem)["Discontinued"])%>'/>
5.      </itemtemplate>
6.      <edititemtemplate>
7.          <asp:checkbox id="CheckBox1" runat="server" enabled="True"
8.              checked='<%# Convert.ToBoolean(((System.Data.DataRowView)
➥Container.DataItem)["Discontinued"])%>'/>
9.      </edititemtemplate>
10. </asp:templatecolumn>
```

▶ Find the code on the CD: \Code\Chapter 27\Ex14.

A TemplateColumn typically consists of two pieces. The first represents the read rendering of a control. In this case, this is a CheckBox control that appears within the itemtemplate tag (lines 2–5). The second represents the control that will be present when the grid is in edit mode. This control appears within the edititemtemplate tag (lines 6–9). The only difference between the two controls in this example is the enabled attribute of the CheckBox.

The TemplateColumn in Listing 12.14 demonstrates how two separate controls are used for display/editing.

> **NOTE**
>
> The BoundColumn also uses two different controls for display/edit. You just don't see them declared as such. When displaying a column, the control is a Label. When editing it, it is a TextBox.

LISTING 27.14   Declaration of Another TemplateColumn

```
<asp:templatecolumn runat="Server" headertext="Suppliers"
        itemstyle-wrap="False">
  <itemtemplate>
```

LISTING 27.14   Continued

```
    <asp:label id="lblSupplier" runat="server"
     text='<%# GetSupplierName(Convert.ToInt32(((System.Data.DataRowView)
►Container.DataItem)["SupplierID"])) %>'>  </asp:label>
  </itemtemplate>
  <edititemtemplate>
      <asp:dropdownlist id="DropDownList1" runat="server"
       datasource='<%# htSupplierNames.Values %>' />
      </asp:dropdownlist>
  </edititemtemplate>
</asp:templatecolumn>
```

▶ Find the code on the CD: \Code\Chapter 27\Ex14.

In this example, the itemtemplate is label control, and the editable control is a DropDownList. The ID attribute of these controls has relevance, as you will see momentarily.

Listing 27.15 lists an excerpt of the example program that contains the Page_Load() event handler and the GetData() method.

LISTING 27.15   Page_Load() and GetData()

```
1:    type
2:      TWebForm1 = class(System.Web.UI.Page)
3:      strict private
4:        procedure Page_Load(sender: System.Object; e: System.EventArgs);
5:      private
6:        procedure GetData;
7:      public
8:        htSupplierNames: HashTable;
9:        htSupplierIDs: HashTable;
10:       function GetSupplierName(aSupplierID: Integer): String;
11:     end;
12:
13:   implementation
14:
15:   const
16:     c_cnstr = 'server=XWING;database=Northwind;Trusted_Connection=Yes';
17:     c_sel_prod  = 'SELECT * FROM products';
18:     c_sel_sup   = 'SELECT companyname, supplierid FROM suppliers';
19:
20:   procedure TWebForm1.Page_Load(sender: System.Object; e: System.EventArgs);
21:   var
22:     SelStr: String;
23:   begin
24:     if not IsPostBack then
25:     begin
26:       SelStr := c_sel_prod;
27:       Session.Add('SelStr', SelStr);
28:       GetData;
29:     end;
30:   end;
31:
32:   procedure TWebForm1.GetData;
```

LISTING 27.15   Continued

```
33:  var
34:    sqlcn: SqlConnection;
35:    sqlDA: SqlDataAdapter;
36:    sqlCmd: SqlCommand;
37:    sqlRdr: SqlDataReader;
38:    ds: DataSet;
39:    dt: DataTable;
40:    SelStr: String;
41:  begin
42:
43:    SelStr := Session['SelStr'] as System.String;
44:    sqlcn := SqlConnection.Create(c_cnstr);
45:    sqlDA := SqlDataAdapter.Create(SelStr, sqlcn);
46:    ds := DataSet.Create;
47:    sqlDA.Fill(ds, 'Products');
48:
49:    htSupplierNames := HashTable.Create;
50:    htSupplierIDs   := HashTable.Create;
51:
52:    sqlCmd := SqlCommand.Create(c_sel_sup, sqlcn);
53:    sqlcn.Open;
54:    try
55:      sqlRdr := sqlCmd.ExecuteReader;
56:      while sqlRdr.Read do
57:      begin
58:        htSupplierIDs.Add(sqlRdr['CompanyName'].ToString,
59:          sqlRdr['SupplierID'].ToString);
60:        htSupplierNames.Add(sqlRdr['SupplierID'].ToString,
61:          sqlRdr['CompanyName']);
62:      end;
63:    finally
64:      sqlcn.Close;
65:    end;
66:
67:    DataGrid1.DataKeyField := 'ProductID';
68:    dt := ds.Tables['products'];
69:    DataGrid1.DataSource := dt.DefaultView;
70:    DataBind;
71:
72:  end;
```

▶ Find the code on the CD: \Code\Chapter 27\Ex14.

The GetData() method is responsible for retrieving the data from the data source. This method should be familiar to you by now, as it is very similar to previous examples. One difference is between lines 49–65. In this portion of the code, the method retrieves supplier information (SupplierID and CompanyName). It then adds this information to two HashTables. htSupplierNames will be used for populating a DropDownList. htSupplierIDs will be used to retrieve the ID for a given supplier. This information is needed to update the data source. Admittedly, this is a rather crude way to maintain this data. This is for illustration purposes only. In Chapter 33, I will illustrate a more efficient means of dealing with this kind of information.

The `Page_Load()` event handler initializes the selection string that is used in `GetData()` and then calls `GetData()`. You'll notice that `Page_Load()` stores the selection string in the `Session` object. (Again, I haven't talked about the `Session` object; it is a topic of Chapter 33.) However, for this example, consider it to be a store that maintains data placed within it across page requests. In the section "Sorting the DataGrid," you'll see why it is important to save the selection string.

CAUTION

When using the example application in Listing 27.15, you might occasionally get an error stating that `CommandText` had not been initialized when line 47 was executed. Yet, nothing in the code reveals why the `CommandText` has no value. What's happening has to do with the `Session` object losing data when the ASP.NET worker process (`aspnet_wp.exe`) is restarted. Basically, when the `Session` exists within the context of the worker process, shutting down the worker process also kills any `Session` stored data. Therefore, I suggest that you develop your applications having your `Session` exist within a State Client Manager (`aspnet_state.exe`). Do this by starting the manager on the command prompt as

`c:\net start aspnet_state`

Then, change the `<sessionState>` tag in the `web.config` file to use the `StateServer` as

```
<sessionState mode="StateServer"
stateConnectionString="tcpip=127.0.0.1:42424" />
```

Session management is further discussed in Chapter 33.

So far, we've only populated the `DataGrid`. The following code shows what happens when the `Edit` command is clicked:

```
procedure TWebForm1.DataGrid1_EditCommand(source: System.Object;
  e: System.Web.UI.WebControls.DataGridCommandEventArgs);
begin
  DataGrid1.EditItemIndex := e.Item.ItemIndex;
  GetData;
end;
```

First, the `EditItemIndex` property is set, which specifies the index of the item that the `DataGrid` is to place into edit mode. Then, `GetData()` is invoked again. This goes back to what I said earlier that you have to retrieve data each time a new page is rendered. When the `DataGrid` is in edit mode, it appears as shown in Figure 27.13.

At this point, there is one of two actions that the user can take. He can click the `Update` or the `Cancel` commands. The event handler for the `Cancel` command looks similar to that of the `Edit` command, except that `-1` is assigned instead of `e.Item.ItemIndex` as shown here:

```
procedure TWebForm1.DataGrid1_CancelCommand(source: System.Object;
  e: System.Web.UI.WebControls.DataGridCommandEventArgs);
begin
  DataGrid1.EditItemIndex := -1;
  GetData;
end;
```

The `Update` command is more interesting, and is shown in Listing 27.16.

27

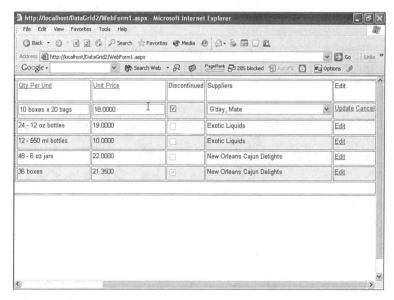

FIGURE 27.13   DataGrid control in edit mode.

LISTING 27.16   Update Command Event Handler

```
1:    procedure TWebForm1.DataGrid1_UpdateCommand(source: System.Object;
2:      e: System.Web.UI.WebControls.DataGridCommandEventArgs);
3:    var
4:      tb: TextBox;
5:      cb: CheckBox;
6:      ddl: DropDownList;
7:      ddlStr: String;
8:    begin
9:      GetData;
10:
11:     tb := e.Item.Cells[1].Controls[0] as TextBox;
12:     Label1.Text := tb.Text+'<br>';
13:     tb := e.Item.Cells[2].Controls[0] as TextBox;
14:     Label1.Text := Label1.Text + tb.Text+'<br>';
15:     tb := e.Item.Cells[3].Controls[0] as TextBox;
16:     Label1.Text := Label1.Text + tb.Text+'<br>';
17:     cb := e.Item.FindControl('CheckBox1') as CheckBox;
18:     Label1.Text := Label1.Text + Convert.ToString(cb.Checked)+'<br>';
19:     ddl := e.Item.FindControl('DropDownList1') as DropDownList;
20:     ddlStr := ddl.Items[ddl.SelectedIndex].Value;
21:     Label1.Text := Label1.Text + ddlStr +
22:       ': '+ htSupplierIDs[ddlStr].ToString;
23:
24:     // Write Updates to the Data source
25:     DataGrid1.EditItemIndex := -1;
26:     DataGrid1.DataBind;
27:   end;
```

▶ Find the code on the CD: \Code\Chapter 27\Ex14.

The idea behind this method is that you extract the data from the controls within the DataGrid, use those values to update the underlying data source, re-query, and re-bind. Lines 11–22 illustrate how to extract the modified data from the DataGrid. For BoundColumns, the underlying control in the DataGrid is a TextBox. You can get to the specific column through the Item.Cells property of the DataGridCommandEventArgs parameter. For TemplateColumns, you must use the Item.FindControl() method to retrieve the reference to the control. This method takes the control's ID as the parameter. Earlier, I said that the ID of a control in a TemplateColumn was relevant—this is why.

I didn't demonstrate issuing the update to the data store because this is no different from any of the examples shown for doing this in the ADO chapters. You simply use the appropriate components and perform the update before retrieving the data.

Also, you'll notice that I call GetData() prior to extracting the values from the controls. I do this because otherwise the HashTables would be invalid. However, after updating the data, I would have to do yet another GetData() call. An optional, and better, approach would be to retrieve the data that is to go into the HashTable, once on application startup and to persist that information into a session or cache, as was done with the select string. This is covered in Chapter 33.

Adding Items to the DataGrid

The DataGrid does not support adding items. I've read reasons having to do with this making the DataGrid too complex, but I have trouble understanding this reason. Frankly, the DataGrid is already quite complex; what's wrong with a little more complexity?

There is a way to achieve this effect, however. Basically, it involves adding a new row to the DataSet with empty and default values, positioning the Grid to that item, and setting it into edit mode. This scenario works best when working with disconnected and cached data.

Sorting the DataGrid

In the section "Editing the DataGrid," I pointed out the sortexpression attribute of a column tag. This expression is a holder for information that you would need to programmatically sort the DataGrid. The DataGrid provides the SortCommand event to which you can provide an event handler as shown here:

```
procedure TWebForm1.DataGrid1_SortCommand(source: System.Object;
  e: System.Web.UI.WebControls.DataGridSortCommandEventArgs);
begin
  selStr := c_sel_prod + ' ' + e.SortExpression;
  GetData;
end;
```

This event handler is fired when a user clicks on the header of a column of a DataGrid with the allowsorting attribute for the column set to True.

In this example, the sortexpression for the various columns contain an ORDER BY expression that is appended to the selection string used to retrieve the products table. The following column declaration demonstrates this:

```
<asp:boundcolumn datafield="ProductName"
    headertext="Product Name" itemstyle-wrap="False"
    sortexpression="ORDER BY ProductName">
</asp:boundcolumn>
```

In line 45 of Listing 27.15, you already saw that the SelStr item stored in the Session object is used as the SelectCommand for the DataAdapter in that method. When the SortCommand event is invoked, the appropriate ORDER BY clause is appended to SelStr and it is re-added to the Session object. The next GetData() call will retrieve the data in the specified sort order. When the DataGrid is bound, it shows the elements in the order specified.

The example with which we have been working demonstrates this technique.

Database-Driven Download Request Form and Administrator

To illustrate a real-world ASP.NET application, we'll revisit the download request application that was introduced in Chapter 26. In Chapter 26, this application performed a few functions that we will change. First, if you recall, the application retrieved the lookup values for the state and country from a text file. Additionally, the application saved the information that the user entered into a text file, which the application then persisted to disk.

This example will retrieve the lookup values for the state and country from database tables. Additionally, the application will save the user's information to a table in a database. Figure 27.14 depicts the download request database diagram. You'll note that the download table contains two foreign keys, which are from the lu_state and lu_country tables.

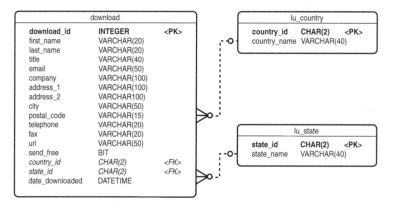

FIGURE 27.14   Download Request database.

Listing 27.17 shows the source for the download application. Portions of the code that are not relevant have been left out.

LISTING 27.17   Download Request Application—Database Enabled

```
1:   unit DwnLdForm;
2:
3:   interface
4:
5:   uses
6:     System.Collections, System.ComponentModel,
7:     System.Data, System.Drawing, System.Web, System.Web.SessionState,
8:     System.Web.UI, System.Web.UI.WebControls, System.Web.UI.HtmlControls,
9:     System.IO, System.Web.Mail, System.Data.SqlClient, Borland.Vcl.Classes;
10:
11:  type
12:    TWebForm1 = class(System.Web.UI.Page)
13:    strict private
14:      procedure Page_Load(sender: System.Object; e: System.EventArgs);
15:    strict protected
16:      procedure SendEmail(aEmail: String);
17:    private
18:      { Private Declarations }
19:      procedure GetData;
20:      procedure SaveUserInfo;
21:    public
22:      aryCountryName: array of String;
23:      aryCountryAbbr: array of String;
24:      aryStateName: array of String;
25:      aryStateAbbr: array of String;
26:    end;
27:
28:  implementation
29:
30:  const
31:    c_cnstr = 'server=XWING;database=ddg_download;Trusted_Connection=Yes';
32:
33:  procedure TWebForm1.Page_Load(sender: System.Object; e: System.EventArgs);
34:  begin
35:    if IsPostBack then
36:    begin
37:      SaveUserInfo;
38:      SendEMail(tbxEmail.Text);
39:      Response.Redirect('ThankYouForm.aspx');
40:    end
41:    else GetData;
42:  end;
43:
44:  function GetCommand(aFileName: String): String;
45:  var
46:    sr: StreamReader;
47:  begin
48:    if System.IO.File.Exists(aFileName) then
49:    begin
50:      sr := StreamReader.Create(System.IO.File.OpenRead(aFileName));
51:      try
52:        Result := sr.ReadToEnd;
53:      finally
```

LISTING 27.17   Continued

```
54:        sr.Close;
55:      end;
56:    end;
57:  end;
58:
59:  procedure TWebForm1.SaveUserInfo;
60:  var
61:    sqlCmd: SqlCommand;
62:    sqlcn: SqlConnection;
63:    idx: Integer;
64:  begin
65:    GetData;
66:    sqlcn := SqlConnection.Create(c_cnstr);
67:    sqlCmd := SqlCommand.Create(GetCommand(
68:      Request.PhysicalApplicationPath+'c_ins.sql'), sqlCn);
69:
70:    sqlcn.Open;
71:    try
72:      sqlCmd.Parameters.Add('@first_name',   SqlDbType.NVarChar, 20);
73:      sqlCmd.Parameters.Add('@last_name',    SqlDbType.NVarChar, 20);
74:      SqlCmd.Parameters.Add('@title',        SqlDbType.NVarChar, 40);
75:      SqlCmd.Parameters.Add('@email',        SqlDbType.NVarChar, 50);
76:      SqlCmd.Parameters.Add('@company',      SqlDbType.NVarChar, 100);
77:      SqlCmd.Parameters.Add('@address_1',    SqlDbType.NVarChar, 100);
78:      SqlCmd.Parameters.Add('@address_2',    SqlDbType.NVarChar, 100);
79:      SqlCmd.Parameters.Add('@city',         SqlDbType.NVarChar, 50);
80:      SqlCmd.Parameters.Add('@postal_code', SqlDbType.NVarChar, 15);
81:      SqlCmd.Parameters.Add('@telephone',    SqlDbType.NVarChar, 20);
82:      SqlCmd.Parameters.Add('@fax',          SqlDbType.NVarChar, 20);
83:      SqlCmd.Parameters.Add('@url',          SqlDbType.NVarChar, 50);
84:      SqlCmd.Parameters.Add('@send_free',   SqlDbType.Bit);
85:      SqlCmd.Parameters.Add('@country_id',  SqlDbType.Char, 2);
86:      SqlCmd.Parameters.Add('@state_id',    SqlDbType.Char, 2);
87:      SqlCmd.Parameters.Add('@date_downloaded', SqlDbType.DateTime);
88:
89:      // Add Values to the Command
90:
91:      sqlCmd.Parameters['@first_name'].Value  := tbxFirstName.Text;
92:      sqlCmd.Parameters['@last_name'].Value   := tbxLastName.Text;
93:      sqlCmd.Parameters['@title'].Value       := tbxTitle.Text;
94:      sqlCmd.Parameters['@email'].Value       := tbxEmail.Text;
95:      sqlCmd.Parameters['@company'].Value     := tbxCompany.Text;
96:      sqlCmd.Parameters['@address_1'].Value   := tbxAddress1.Text;
97:      sqlCmd.Parameters['@address_2'].Value   := tbxAddress2.Text;
98:      sqlCmd.Parameters['@city'].Value        := tbxCity.Text;
99:      sqlCmd.Parameters['@postal_code'].Value := tbxPostalCode.Text;
100:     sqlCmd.Parameters['@telephone'].Value   := tbxTelephone.Text;
101:     sqlCmd.Parameters['@fax'].Value         := tbxFax.Text;
102:     sqlCmd.Parameters['@url'].Value         := tbxUrl.Text;
103:     sqlCmd.Parameters['@send_free'].Value   :=
104:       System.Object(cbxFreeStuff.Checked);
105:
106:     idx := System.Array.IndexOf(aryCountryName,
```

LISTING 27.17   Continued

```
107:      ddlCountry.Items[ddlCountry.SelectedIndex].Text);
108:    sqlCmd.Parameters['@country_id'].Value   := aryCountryAbbr[idx];
109:
110:    idx := System.Array.IndexOf(aryStateName,
111:      ddlState.Items[ddlState.SelectedIndex].Text);
112:    sqlCmd.Parameters['@state_id'].Value     := aryStateAbbr[idx];
113:
114:    sqlCmd.Parameters['@date_downloaded'].Value := System.DateTime.Now;
115:    sqlCmd.ExecuteNonQuery;
116:  finally
117:    sqlcn.Close;
118:  end;
119: end;
120:
121: procedure TWebForm1.GetData;
122: const
123:   c_sel_ccount = 'SELECT count(*) AS count FROM lu_country';
124:   c_sel_scount = 'SELECT count(*) AS count FROM lu_state';
125:   c_sel_country = 'SELECT * FROM lu_country';
126:   c_sel_state = 'SELECT * FROM lu_state;';
127: var
128:   sqlcn: SqlConnection;
129:   sqlCmd: SqlCommand;
130:   sqlRdr: SqlDataReader;
131:   count: integer;
132:   idx: Integer;
133: begin
134:   sqlcn := SqlConnection.Create(c_cnstr);
135:
136:   sqlcn.Open;
137:   try
138:     sqlCmd := SqlCommand.Create(c_sel_ccount, sqlcn);
139:     count := Integer(sqlCmd.ExecuteScalar);
140:     SetLength(aryCountryName, count);
141:     SetLength(aryCountryAbbr, count);
142:
143:     sqlCmd := SqlCommand.Create(c_sel_scount, sqlcn);
144:     count := Integer(sqlCmd.ExecuteScalar);
145:     SetLength(aryStateName, count);
146:     SetLength(aryStateAbbr, count);
147:   finally
148:     sqlcn.Close;
149:   end;
150:
151:   sqlcn.Open;
152:   try
153:     sqlCmd := SqlCommand.Create(c_sel_country, sqlcn);
154:     sqlRdr := sqlCmd.ExecuteReader;
155:     idx := 0;
156:     while sqlRdr.Read do
157:     begin
158:       aryCountryAbbr[idx] := sqlRdr['country_id'].ToString;
159:       aryCountryName[idx] := sqlRdr['country_name'].ToString;
```

27

LISTING 27.17   Continued

```
160:        inc(idx);
161:      end;
162:    finally
163:      sqlcn.Close;
164:    end;
165:
166:    sqlcn.Open;
167:    try
168:      sqlCmd := SqlCommand.Create(c_sel_state, sqlcn);
169:      sqlRdr := sqlCmd.ExecuteReader;
170:      idx := 0;
171:      while sqlRdr.Read do
172:      begin
173:        aryStateAbbr[idx] := sqlRdr['state_id'].ToString;
174:        aryStateName[idx] := sqlRdr['state_name'].ToString;
175:        inc(idx);
176:      end;
177:    finally
178:      sqlcn.Close;
179:    end;
180:
181:    DataBind;
182:  end;
183:
184: end.
```

▶ Find the code on the CD: \Code\Chapter 27\Ex15.

First, examine the Page_Load() event handler. You'll notice that on the post-back, the methods SaveUserInfo() and SendEmail() are invoked before redirecting the user to a Thank You page. SaveUserInfo() is the method that has been modified from the example in Chapter 26. I discuss this method momentarily. SendEmail() was not changed; therefore, it is not shown here. If this is the first time the page is loaded, the GetData() method is invoked.

GetData() performs the retrieval of data from a data source that is needed by the download page. Two tables are required, and both are actually required in two arrangements. First, we want to display the full name of both countries and states in the DropDownList controls on the page. Therefore, we declare two array members, aryCountryName and aryStateName (lines 22 and 24), in which these values will be stored and to which the DropDownLists will be bound. Second, when saving data back to the database, we want to save the keys, which are the abbreviations of both lists. Therefore, we save these values in two additional arrays, aryCountryAbbr and aryStateAbbr (lines 23 and 25). These additional arrays correspond to the previously mentioned arrays. In other words, the index of an item in the aryCountryName array will be the same index in the aryCountryAbbr array. We'll use this to retrieve the abbreviation (or key) for the item that the user selected. The GetData() method in Listing 27.17 involves retrieving and setting up these arrays.

The SaveUserInfo() method should look familiar to you if you read the chapters covering ADO.NET. Basically, the function creates a SqlCommand object with the command's text to insert a record into the download table of this database. The INSERT Transact-SQL statement resides in a file, c_ins.sql, which gets loaded and the contents are assigned to the CommandText property (lines 67–68). The rest of the SaveUserInfo() method creates parameters and assigns values to them. Notice how we had to call the GetData() method at the beginning of the SaveUserInfo() method. Recall that each time a page is going to be rendered, any data that it requires needs to be reloaded. Information such as this is not retained between page requests. In Chapter 33, I'll show you some other methods for managing this information so that you will not have to re-query the database upon each page request.

Finally, at the end of the SaveUserInfo() method, the user's data is saved to the database.

This should give you an idea of how database Web apps are developed under ASP.NET.

27

IN THIS CHAPTER

- Terms Related to Web Services
- Web Service Construction
- Consuming Web Services
- Securing Web Services

CHAPTER **28**

Building Web Services

There are several reasons why it is important to understand how to develop Web Services. One reason has to do with keeping current on development trends and leading edge technologies. Chapter 1, "Introduction to .NET," gives an overview of Web Services. Another reason is that Web Services enable you to expose your service (or application) in a standard way to any client, implemented on any platform, potentially accessed from anywhere in the world. This chapter delves right into using Delphi for .NET and .NET to create and consume Web Services.

Terms Related to Web Services

The following terms were introduced in Chapter 1. I'm repeating them here for quick reference. These are terms that you will encounter frequently when working with Web Services.

- XML—Extensible Markup Language. XML is a flexible text-based format originally derived from SGML for the purpose of electronic publishing. XML's richness and self-defining format make it ideal for use in passing messages between Web Service consumers and servers.

- SOAP—Simple Object Access Protocol. SOAP is the protocol for Web Services based on the XML standard for invoking remote procedure calls over the Internet/intranet. SOAP specifies the format of the request/response and the format of parameters passed in the request/response. SOAP is only specific to the message. It only imposes adherence to the SOAP specifications but is otherwise platform and language agnostic.

- WSDL—Web Service Description Language. WSDL is an XML-based language used to describe the facilities of a Web Service. This includes all the various methods and their parameters as well as the location of the Web Service. Web Service consumers can understand WSDL and can determine the functionality provided by the

Web Service. WSDL is typically used by tools and IDEs to automatically create proxy classes used to access the service.

- UDDI—Universal Description, Discovery, and Integration. UDDI is a standard for public registries for storing information about publishing Web Services. You can visit UDDI at www.uddi.org for information on the UDDI standard. Examples of UDDI registries are www.xmethods.net and uddi.microsoft.com.

Web Service Construction

In this section, I will demonstrate the process of creating three types of Web Services. One will be a simple Web Service that returns the sum of two numbers. The second one will return a DataSet containing a table from the Northwind database. A third will demonstrate the use of the [WebMethod] attribute.

For the most part, creating the initial files for the Web Service is a step-by-step process when using the wizard from Delphi for .NET.

1. Select File, New, Other from the main menu to launch the New Items dialog box.

2. Select the Item Category, Delphi ASP Projects.

3. Select the ASP.NET Web Service Application icon (see Figure 28.1). Click OK.

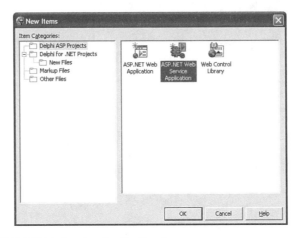

FIGURE 28.1   ASP.NET Web Service Application icon.

4. In the Application Name dialog box (see Figure 28.2), enter the name of your Web Service, such as MyFirstWebService, and click OK.

That's it! You will now have the files WebService1.asmx and WebService1.pas. Let's examine the WebService1.pas file. Listing 28.1 shows the contents of the file. (Lines irrelevant to this discussion are removed.) Listing 28.1 also contains some additional code, which I've added. This code appears in bold.

28

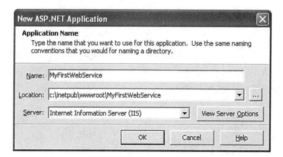

FIGURE 28.2   Naming the ASP.NET Web Service application.

LISTING 28.1   First Web Service Example

```
 1:   unit WebService1;
 2:
 3:   interface
 4:
 5:   uses
 6:     System.Collections, System.ComponentModel,
 7:     System.Data, System.Diagnostics, System.Web,
 8:     System.Web.Services;
 9:
10:   type
11:     TWebService1 = class(System.Web.Services.WebService)
12:     strict private
13:       components: IContainer;
14:       procedure InitializeComponent;
15:     strict protected
16:       procedure Dispose(disposing: boolean); override;
17:     public
18:       constructor Create;
19:       // Sample Web Service Method
20:       [WebMethod]
21:       function HelloWorld: string;
22:       [WebMethod]
23:       function Add(A, B: Integer): Integer;
24:     end;
25:
26:   implementation
27:
28:   constructor TWebService1.Create;
29:   begin
30:     inherited;
31:     InitializeComponent;
32:   end;
33:
34:   procedure TWebService1.Dispose(disposing: boolean);
35:   begin
36:     if disposing and (components <> nil) then
37:       components.Dispose;
38:     inherited Dispose(disposing);
39:   end;
```

LISTING 28.1   Continued

```
40:
41:  function TWebService1.HelloWorld: string;
42:  begin
43:    Result := 'Hello World';
44:  end;
45:
46:  function TWebService1.Add(A, B: Integer): Integer;
47:  begin
48:    Result := A + B;
49:  end;
50:
51:  end.
```

▶ Find the code on the CD: \Code\Chapter 28\Ex01.

You'll also notice that I've uncommented the HelloWorld() method (lines 41–44). At this point, you have a valid Web Service that can be deployed and consumed externally.

First, you'll see that TWebService1 descends from System.Web.Services.WebService (line 11). It is actually not required that you descend from this class to create a Web Service. However, by doing so, you obtain easy access to common ASP.NET objects such as Application, Context, Session, and so on.

The TWebService1 class looks similar to any other Delphi class. One difference is that the method declarations are preceded by the [WebMethod] attribute. This attribute is the one responsible for specifying which method of the Web Service is exposed externally. Certain properties of this attribute can also enable developers to extend or change the behavior of the method. I'll discuss the [WebMethod] attribute in more detail momentarily.

> **NOTE**
>
> You'll notice that the [WebMethod] attribute is added by the IDE for the implementation of the HelloWorld() example but commented out with the example. This is incorrect. The [WebMethod] is only needed in the interface section. Adding it to the implementation will result in it being duplicated in the metadata.

At this point, you can test the Web Service by running it.

> **TIP**
>
> An easy way to run the application without debugging it within the Delphi IDE is to Select Run, Run Without Debugging from the main menu. I take it a step further and add the tool button to my toolbar because I frequently use this option. You can do this by right-clicking on the toolbar and selecting the Customize option. From the Commands tab of the Custom dialog box, you can drag the command buttons you want to the toolbar.

Figure 28.3 is HMTL Interface showing the Web Service.

28

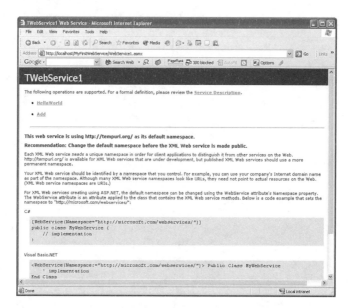

FIGURE 28.3   Output from MyFirstWebSerice.

When a Web Service's base URI is requested without any parameters, ASP.NET returns the service description in the form shown in Figure 28.3. You can see that the name of the class that implements the Web Service is shown at the top of the browser. Also, it shows the names of the methods that are available to the user of the Web Service. It then shows some descriptive developer related information about changing the namespace for the Web Service. When you click on the Service Description link, you are taken to the page shown in Figure 28.4.

Figure 28.4 shows the Service Description in XML, also known as the WDSL of the Web Service. This is for those of you who would rather examine the service description in XML form. It is also for tools that can automatically generate classes, test user interfaces, and so on. Going back to the previous page (refer to Figure 28.3), you can actually test the methods. In fact, click on the Add link, and you will be taken to the page shown in Figure 28.5.

You can now enter two integer values in to the TextBox controls and press the Invoke button, which will return the following result:

```
<?xml version="1.0" encoding="utf-8" ?>
  <int xmlns="http://tempuri.org/">5</int>
```

You can also invoke the Web Service using the HTTP-GET protocol through the following URL:

```
http://localhost/MyFirstWebService/WebService1.asmx/Add?A=3&B=4
```

You can also invoke the Web Service using the HTTP-POST protocol using the following .html document:

```
<html>
<form method="post" action="http://localhost/MyFirstWebService
➥/WebService1.asmx/Add">
<input name="A" value ="2">
```

```
<input name="B" value ="4">
<input type="submit" value="Add!">
</form>
</html>
```

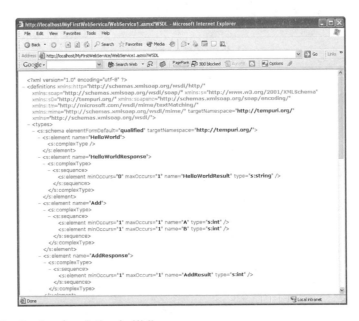

FIGURE 28.4   Service description in XML.

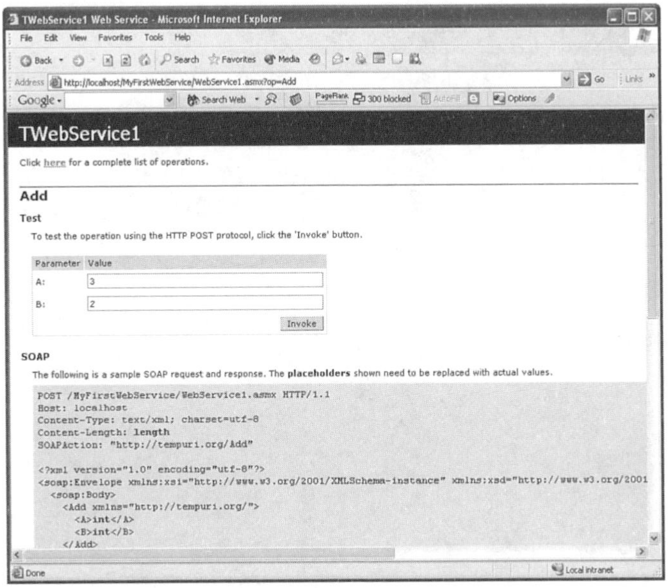

FIGURE 28.5   Testing the Web Service.

This is all there is to creating a Web Service—a simple one anyway. Later, we'll look at consuming this Web Service into a client application. In the next example, I'll create a Web Service that serves a DataSet to the consumer. First, I need to discuss the [WebService] attribute briefly.

The [WebService] Attribute

When you create a Web Service, three properties of a Web Service get default values. You should change these values prior to publishing your Web Service. These properties are the description, the name, and the namespace. In Figure 28.3, you'll see that the Web Service name is WebService1 and the namespace is the default of http://tempuri.org/. You should especially change the default namespace before releasing your Web Service to production. A convention to use is to form the namespace using a company domain combined with your specific Web Service. For example,

www.xapware.com/MyFirstWebService

There need not be any physical file or directory behind the namespace name; it is used only as a logical unique identifier.

You can change these properties through the [WebService] attribute. This attribute is placed above the Web Service class declaration, as shown here:

```
[WebService(
  Namespace='www.xapware.com/MyFirstWebService',
  Name='My First Web Service',
  Description='This is My First Web Service which demonstrates two methods.')]
TWebService1 = class(System.Web.Services.WebService)
```

By doing this, the output of the Web Service now becomes as shown in Figure 28.6.

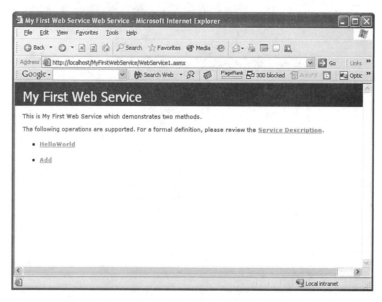

FIGURE 28.6 MyFirstWebService output after changing the [WebService] attribute.

You'll notice that the Web Service name and description now show what was specified in the [WebService] attribute properties. Additionally, you'll also notice that the descriptions and code example are also removed. This developer information is removed because having a different namespace deems the Web Service as production ready.

Returning Data from a Web Service

To create this Web Service, I followed the same steps as the previous except I called this one MySecondWebService. I also renamed the implementing class to WebService2. In this Web Service, I created the function shown in Listing 28.2.

LISTING 28.2   Web Service Demonstrating a DataSet Result

```
 1:   function TWebService2.GetEmployees: DataSet;
 2:   const
 3:     c_cnstr = 'server=XWING;database=Northwind;Trusted_Connection=Yes';
 4:     c_sel   = 'Select * From employees';
 5:   var
 6:     sqlcn: SqlConnection;
 7:     sqlDA: SqlDataAdapter;
 8:     ds: DataSet;
 9:   begin
10:     try
11:       sqlcn := SqlConnection.Create(c_cnstr);
12:       sqlDA := SqlDataAdapter.Create(c_sel, sqlcn);
13:       ds := DataSet.Create;
14:       sqlDA.Fill(ds, 'employees');
15:       sqlcn.Close;
16:       Result := ds;
17:     except
18:       Result := nil;
19:       Ralse;
20:     end;
21:   end;
```

▶ Find the code on the CD: \Code\Chapter 28\Ex02.

You should recognize this process of retrieving a DataSet from Northwind. Line 17 is the significant line that returns the DataSet class, which will get marshaled as XML, as you will see. When you run the Web Service, you are shown the page in Figure 28.7.

First, notice the addition of a description underneath the method name. I'll address this in a moment. When you test the Web Service, you'll see the page with XML as shown in Figure 28.8.

You should recognize this data from the employee table in the Northwind database. Later, I'll demonstrate how you would consume this DataSet in both an ASP.NET and a Windows Forms application.

The [WebMethod] Attribute Explained

In the previous example, you might have noticed the following line above the GetEmployees() method:

```
[WebMethod(Description='Gets the employees table')]
```

28

FIGURE 28.7   MySecondWebService output.

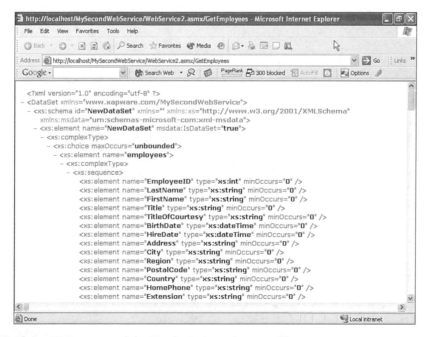

FIGURE 28.8   XML output of the Northwind employees table.

It was already mentioned that the [WebMethod] attribute is the one responsible for exposing a method externally. This attribute contains additional properties that you can set such as description, which was demonstrated in the previous example. Table 28.1 lists the various properties of [WebMethod].

TABLE 28.1   [WebMethod] Properties

Property	Description
BufferResponse	Determines if the response for the request is buffered to memory before sending it back to the client. When True (the default), the response is buffered to memory until complete or until the buffer is full. Then, it is sent to the client. When False, the response is sent in 16Kb chunks. Keep in mind that this size is an implementation detail of the MS CLR v1.1, which could change in the future. You would only set this to False if you know the response will be excessive, which could improve performance, keeping in mind that it could also reduce memory usage and improve (lower) latency.
CacheDuration	This property is useful if you will be invoking a method several times using the same parameter set. It causes the server to cache the response for the specified number of seconds. When a subsequent request is made within the time window, the response is obtained from the cache, thus potentially improving performance.
Description	This property provides a String description of the method.
EnableSession	This property enables/disables session state. When enabled, the Web Service method might make use of the Session object.
MessageName	This property allows you to specify an alias for the method name. This is useful to distinguish between overloaded methods of the same name.
TransactionOption	This property allows the code within a Web Service to work similar to a database transaction. The transaction support is provided through a COM+ level of transactional support.

To demonstrate the use of the [WebMethod] attribute, consider the declaration of the following methods:

```
[WebMethod]
function Add(A, B: Integer): Integer; overload;
[WebMethod]
function Add(A, B: Double): Double; overload;
```

When using a class directly, just having the overload directive would be sufficient to use both methods. This is because the compiler would be capable of resolving the methods by their parameters. However, attempting to run a Web Service containing these methods would result in a server error because the SOAP standard does not support overloaded methods; it relies on the method name for method resolution.

To correct this, you would use the MessageName property as shown here:

```
[WebMethod (
MessageName='AddInt')]
function Add(A, B: Integer): Integer; overload;
[WebMethod(
MessageName='AddDouble')]
function Add(A, B: Double): Double; overload;
```

Consumers of the Web Service would see and invoke the method according to the names specified as the MessageName property.

▶ Find the code on the CD: \Code\Chapter 28\Ex03.

28

Consuming Web Services

This section discusses the process of Web Service consumption. Applications that make use of Web Services are said to consume the Web Service and are therefore known as consumers. A Web Service consumer must perform at least three steps in order to use the Web Service. These are discovery (a process of extracting information about a Web Service), generating a proxy class, and using the proxy class to invoke the Web Service methods. The first two steps can be done manually; however, the Delphi IDE provides the integrated tools to make the process much easier. I will walk through the step-by-step process.

The Discovery Process

Before you can use a Web Service, you have to know how to use it. You must discover available methods, properties, parameters, types, and so on. Recall that the WSDL document is how Web Services describe themselves to consumers. Therefore, for each Web Service you intend to use, you'll have to examine this document. It's true that you can examine the WSDL and manually hard-code the Delphi class needed to use the service. However, this is unnecessary because the Delphi IDE will examine the WSDL of the Web Service for you and will perform the necessary steps to allow you to use the Web Service; specifically, it will create a proxy class. The following examples assume that you know the location of the Web Service you intend to use.

Constructing a Proxy Class

In this section, I discuss how to create a client application that consumes the latter two Web Services created earlier in this chapter. The steps are

1. Create the application and save it to a directory.

2. Add a Web Reference; this will create the proxy class.

3. Use the proxy class.

Assuming that step 1 is completed, adding the Web Reference is simple. Simply select the project within the Project Manager in the IDE and invoke the local menu by right-clicking. One of the options is Add Web Reference (see Figure 28.9).

This launches the Add Web Reference dialog box. Through this dialog box, you can enter the URL of known Web Service URLs or you can also select from one of the UDDI directories presented in the dialog box. For now, we'll use the URL from one of the Web Services we created. The URL we need is

```
http://localhost/MyFirstWebService/WebService1.asmx?WSDL
```

Specifying the ?WSDL parameter will return the WSDL document that we need to generate a proxy class. When you click the blue arrow button on the Add Web Reference dialog box, you will see the WSDL in the dialog box as shown in Figure 28.10.

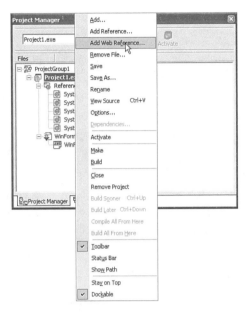

FIGURE 28.9   Add Web Reference menu from the Project Manager.

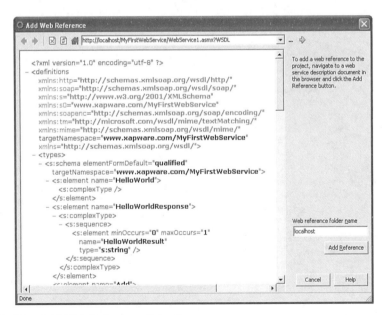

FIGURE 28.10   Add Web Reference dialog box.

At this point, you can click the Add Reference button to generate the proxy class. Looking at the Project Manager, you will see that some files have been generated and added to your project. These files are

- WebService1.map—The .map file is an XML file that contains information about the WDSL references for the Web Service.

- WebService1.wsdl—The .wsdl file is the Service Description file. It contains XML that describes the Web Service interface.

- WebService1.pas—The .pas file is the source file that contains the proxy class.

The next section discusses exactly what this proxy class is and how to use it in order to consume the Web Service.

Using the Proxy Class

A proxy class is a class that hides the implementation internals of invoking a Web Service. Put another way, the proxy class is a class layer between the HTTP SOAP requests to the Web Server and the code that you will be writing to make those requests. It allows you to work with a Delphi class as you are used to. As you just saw in the previous section, the creation of the proxy class is simple using the IDE. Certainly, you can manually create this class, although it is entirely unnecessary because the IDE performs this task perfectly.

Listing 28.3 shows the class proxy created for the Web Service that we consumed.

LISTING 28.3   WebService1 Proxy Class

```
1:    unit localhost.WebService1;
2:
3:    interface
4:
5:    uses System.Diagnostics,
6:      System.Xml.Serialization,
7:      System.Web.Services.Protocols,
8:      System.ComponentModel,
9:      System.Web.Services, System.Web.Services.Description;
10:
11:   type
12:     [System.Diagnostics.DebuggerStepThroughAttribute]
13:     [System.ComponentModel.DesignerCategoryAttribute('code')]
14:     [System.Web.Services.WebServiceBindingAttribute(
15:       Name='My First Web ServiceSoap',
16:       Namespace='www.xapware.com/MyFirstWebService')]
17:     MyFirstWebService = class(System.Web.Services.Protocols.
➥SoapHttpClientProtocol)
18:     public
19:       constructor Create;
20:       [System.Web.Services.Protocols.SoapDocumentMethodAttribute(
21:         'www.xapware.com/MyFirstWebService/HelloWorld',
22:         RequestNamespace='www.xapware.com/MyFirstWebService',
23:         ResponseNamespace='www.xapware.com/MyFirstWebService',
24:         Use=System.Web.Services.Description.SoapBindingUse.Literal,
25:         ParameterStyle=System.Web.Services.Protocols.SoapParameterStyle.
➥Wrapped)]
26:       function HelloWorld: string;
27:       function BeginHelloWorld(callback: System.AsyncCallback;
```

LISTING 28.3   Continued

```
28:        asyncState: System.Object): System.IAsyncResult;
29:      function EndHelloWorld(asyncResult: System.IAsyncResult): string;
30:      [System.Web.Services.Protocols.SoapDocumentMethodAttribute(
31:       'www.xapware.com/MyFirstWebService/Add',
32:        RequestNamespace='www.xapware.com/MyFirstWebService',
33:        ResponseNamespace='www.xapware.com/MyFirstWebService',
34:        Use=System.Web.Services.Description.SoapBindingUse.Literal,
35:        ParameterStyle=System.Web.Services.Protocols.SoapParameterStyle.
➥Wrapped)]
36:      function Add(A: Integer; B: Integer): Integer;
37:      function BeginAdd(A: Integer; B: Integer; callback:
➥System.AsyncCallback;
38:        asyncState: System.Object): System.IAsyncResult;
39:      function EndAdd(asyncResult: System.IAsyncResult): Integer;
40:    end;
41:
42:  implementation
43:
44:  {$AUTOBOX ON}
45:  {$HINTS OFF}
46:  {$WARNINGS OFF}
47:
48:  constructor MyFirstWebService.Create;
49:  begin
50:    inherited Create;
51:    Self.Url := 'http://localhost/MyFirstWebService/WebService1.asmx';
52:  end;
53:
54:  function MyFirstWebService.HelloWorld: string;
55:  type
56:    TSystem_ObjectArray = array of System.Object;
57:    TArrayOfSystem_Object = array of System.Object;
58:  var
59:    results: TArrayOfSystem_Object;
60:  begin
61:    results := Self.Invoke('HelloWorld', new(TSystem_ObjectArray, 0));
62:    Result := (string(results[0]));
63:  end;
64:
65:  function MyFirstWebService.BeginHelloWorld(callback: System.AsyncCallback;
66:    asyncState: System.Object): System.IAsyncResult;
67:  type
68:    TSystem_ObjectArray = array of System.Object;
69:  begin
70:    Result := Self.BeginInvoke('HelloWorld', new(TSystem_ObjectArray, 0),
71:      callback,asyncState);
72:  end;
73:
74:  function MyFirstWebService.EndHelloWorld(
75:    asyncResult: System.IAsyncResult): string;
76:  type
77:    TArrayOfSystem_Object = array of System.Object;
78:  var
```

28

LISTING 28.3 Continued

```
79:     results: TArrayOfSystem_Object;
80:  begin
81:     results := Self.EndInvoke(asyncResult);
82:     Result := (string(results[0]));
83:  end;
84:
85:  function MyFirstWebService.Add(A: Integer; B: Integer): Integer;
86:  type
87:     TSystem_ObjectArray = array of System.Object;
88:     TArrayOfSystem_Object = array of System.Object;
89:  var
90:     results: TArrayOfSystem_Object;
91:  begin
92:     results := Self.Invoke('Add', TSystem_ObjectArray.Create(A, B));
93:     Result := (Integer(results[0]));
94:  end;
95:
96:  function MyFirstWebService.BeginAdd(A: Integer; B: Integer;
97:     callback: System.AsyncCallback;
98:     asyncState: System.Object):  System.IAsyncResult;
99:  type
100:    TSystem_ObjectArray = array of System.Object;
101: begin
102:    Result := Self.BeginInvoke('Add', TSystem_ObjectArray.Create(A, B),
103:        callback, asyncState);
104: end;
105:
106: function MyFirstWebService.EndAdd(asyncResult: System.IAsyncResult):
➡ Integer;
107: type
108:    TArrayOfSystem_Object = array of System.Object;
109: var
110:    results: TArrayOfSystem_Object;
111: begin
112:    results := Self.EndInvoke(asyncResult);
113:    Result := (Integer(results[0]));
114: end;
115:
116: end.
```

▶ Find the code on the CD: \Code\Chapter 28\Ex04.

The proxy class serves as a surrogate object for the Web Service and declares methods that can be invoked by the consuming application, which themselves invoke the methods of the Web Service. In fact, it defines two ways that you can invoke the Web Service methods. You can do so synchronously or asynchronously. The synchronous methods are given the same name as they had in the Web Service (or as the MessageName in the [WebMethod] attribute). For instance, lines 26 and 36 show the method declarations for the HelloWorld() and Add() methods from the Web Service. The asynchronous method invocation requires two methods per Web Service method. These are defined using the form

Begin*FunctionName*() End*FunctionName*(). You'll see these method declarations on lines 27–29 for the `HelloWorld()` method and on lines 37–39 for the `Add()` method.

NOTE

You might have noticed the following included as a parameter to `Self.Invoke()` (line 92):

```
TSystem_ObjectArray.Create(A, B)
```

This is new Delphi syntax for creating a dynamic array. Given the dynamic array type declared as,

```
TSystem_ObjectArray = Array of System.Object;
```

You can create an instance of this type using the forms

```
TSystem_ObjectArray.Create('hello', 'world');
```

or

```
new(TSystem_ObjectArray, 2);
```

The first form creates and adds two elements to the array. The second simply creates the `Array` with space for two elements.

Notice that the proxy class descends from the `SoapHttpClientProtocol` protocol class, which is defined in the `System.Web.Services.Protocols` namespace. If you wanted to use the HTTP-GET or HTTP-POST protocols, you would descend from the appropriate classes (`HttpGetClientProtocol` or `HttpPostClientProtocol`). Additionally, you would have to specify the corresponding attribute, which is the `HTTPMethodAttribute`.

Using the Web Service is simply too easy. The following code illustrates how you would use this Web Service to add two numbers entered from two `TextBox` controls:

```
procedure TWinForm1.Button1_Click(sender: System.Object; e: System.EventArgs);
var
  mfws: MyFirstWebService;
  result: Integer;
begin
  mfws := MyFirstWebService.Create;
  Result := mfws.Add(Convert.ToInt32(TextBox1.Text),
    Convert.ToInt32(TextBox2.Text));
  Label1.Text := Label1.Text + Result.ToString;
end;
```

▶ Find the code on the CD: \Code\Chapter 28\Ex04.

Consuming a DataSet from a Web Service

In this next example, I consumed the following Web Service through the Add Web Reference dialog:

```
http://localhost/MySecondWebService/WebService2.asmx
```

This resulted in the proxy class shown in Listing 28.4.

LISTING 28.4 WebService2 Proxy Class

```
 1:  unit localhost.WebService2;
 2:
 3:  interface
 4:
 5:  uses System.Diagnostics,
 6:    System.Xml.Serialization,
 7:    System.Web.Services.Protocols,
 8:    System.ComponentModel,
 9:    System.Web.Services, System.Web.Services.Description, System.Data;
10:
11:  type
12:    [System.Diagnostics.DebuggerStepThroughAttribute]
13:    [System.ComponentModel.DesignerCategoryAttribute('code')]
14:    [System.Web.Services.WebServiceBindingAttribute(
15:      Name='My Second Web ServiceSoap',
16:      Namespace='www.xapware.com/MySecondWebService')]
17:    MySecondWebService = class(System.Web.Services.Protocols.
➥SoapHttpClientProtocol)
18:    public
19:      constructor Create;
20:      [System.Web.Services.Protocols.SoapDocumentMethodAttribute(
21:        'www.xapware.com/MySecondWebService/GetEmployees',
22:         RequestNamespace='www.xapware.com/MySecondWebService',
23:         ResponseNamespace='www.xapware.com/MySecondWebService',
24:         Use=System.Web.Services.Description.SoapBindingUse.Literal,
25:         ParameterStyle=System.Web.Services.Protocols.
➥SoapParameterStyle.Wrapped)]
26:      function GetEmployees: System.Data.DataSet;
27:      function BeginGetEmployees(callback: System.AsyncCallback;
28:        asyncState: System.Object): System.IAsyncResult;
29:      function EndGetEmployees(asyncResult: System.IAsyncResult):
30:        System.Data.DataSet;
31:    end;
32:
33:  implementation
34:
35:  {$AUTOBOX ON}
36:  {$HINTS OFF}
37:  {$WARNINGS OFF}
38:
39:  constructor MySecondWebService.Create;
40:  begin
41:    inherited Create;
42:    Self.Url := 'http://localhost/MySecondWebService/WebService2.asmx';
43:  end;
44:
45:  function MySecondWebService.GetEmployees: System.Data.DataSet;
46:  type
47:    TSystem_ObjectArray = array of System.Object;
48:    TArrayOfSystem_Object = array of System.Object;
49:  var
50:    results: TArrayOfSystem_Object;
51:  begin
```

LISTING 28.4   Continued

```
52:     results := Self.Invoke('GetEmployees', new(TSystem_ObjectArray, 0));
53:     Result := (System.Data.DataSet(results[0]));
54:   end;
55:
56:   function MySecondWebService.BeginGetEmployees(callback:
➥System.AsyncCallback;
57:     asyncState: System.Object): System.IAsyncResult;
58:   type
59:     TSystem_ObjectArray = array of System.Object;
60:   begin
61:     Result := Self.BeginInvoke('GetEmployees', new(TSystem_ObjectArray, 0),
62:       callback, asyncState);
63:   end;
64:
65:   function MySecondWebService.EndGetEmployees(asyncResult:
66:     System.IAsyncResult): System.Data.DataSet;
67:   type
68:     TArrayOfSystem_Object = array of System.Object;
69:   var
70:     results: TArrayOfSystem_Object;
71:   begin
72:     results := Self.EndInvoke(asyncResult);
73:     Result := (System.Data.DataSet(results[0]));
74:   end;
75:
76: end.
```

▶ Find the code on the CD: \Code\Chapter 28\Ex05.

In Listing 28.4, you'll see the declaration of the methods GetEmployees(),
BeginGetEmployees(), and EndGetEmployees()—each of which returns a DataSet instance. Using
this Web Service is no different from the previous in terms of its simplicity. The following
code invokes the synchronous method, GetEmployees() and assigns the results to its own
DataSet instance. This instance, which is bound to a DataGrid, results in the output shown
in Figure 28.11.

```
procedure TWinForm.Button1_Click(sender: System.Object; e: System.EventArgs);
var
  ds: DataSet;
  msws: MySecondWebService;
begin
  msws := MySecondWebService.Create;
  ds := msws.GetEmployees;
  DataGrid1.DataSource := ds.Tables['Employees'];
end;
```

▶ Find the code on the CD: \Code\Chapter 28\Ex05.

NOTE

When returning a DataSet from a method, it makes the method .NET specific because another
type of client would not understand how to use the resultset.

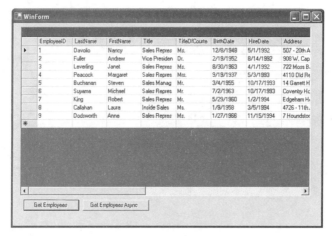

FIGURE 28.11   Output of a DataSet from a Web Service.

Invoking an Asynchronous Web Service Method

The proxy class creates a pair of methods that you use to invoke a Web Service method asynchronously. Listing 28.5 illustrates how to do this using the same example from Listing 28.4.

LISTING 28.5   WebService2 Method Invoked Asynchronously

```
1:    procedure TWinForm.Button2_Click(sender: System.Object;
2:      e: System.EventArgs);
3:    var
4:      ds: DataSet;
5:      msws: MySecondWebService;
6:      ar: IAsyncResult;
7:    begin
8:      msws := MySecondWebService.Create;
9:      ar := msws.BeginGetEmployees(nil, nil);
10:
11:      // Do other local processing
12:      ar.AsyncWaitHandle.WaitOne;
13:
14:      ds := msws.EndGetEmployees(ar);
15:      DataGrid1.DataSource := ds.Tables['Employees'];
16:    end;
```

▶ Find the code on the CD: \Code\Chapter 28\Ex05.

Most asynchronous usage will likely be more complex than that shown here. The purpose of this example is to show you how these methods are invoked. Line 9 calls the BeginGetEmployees() method, which returns an IAsyncResult instance. IAsyncResult is an interface that represents the status of an asynchronous operation. It has a few properties—one of which is the AsyncWaitHandle. You use this handle to wait for an asynchronous operation to complete. Optionally, you could provide your own AsyncCallBack method to the BeginGetEmployees() method.

On line 12, the `AsyncWaitHandle.WaitOne()` method is invoked. This method blocks the current thread until a signal is received by the `AsyncWaitHandle`. When a signal is received, the operation is complete and the `EndGetEmployees()` method is invoked. This method returns the `DataSet` instance that is then bound to the `DataGrid`.

Securing Web Services

There are likely several ways to secure a Web Service. One involves general security of IIS. Another involves user access to the Web Service through authentication. I'll discuss the latter here. General security will be discussed in Chapter 31, "Securing ASP.NET Applications."

The typical way one might secure a resource is through a username/password combination. In database applications, for instance, you might store an encrypted form of the user's password in the database. When the user attempts to log in to the application, the application requests the friendly name of the password, encrypts it, and compares it with what resides in the database. This approach is more secure using a one-way hashing algorithm such as MD5-hashing. Otherwise, perpetrators would be able to derive the password from its hashed form.

This same approach can be used in securing a Web Service. As long as you have stored the encrypted form of the user's credentials, you will be able to authenticate the user.

One way to accomplish this would be to pass the username and password to the methods; however, as you can probably imagine, this would become quite cumbersome having to define and expect the consumers of your Web Services to pass a username, password pair with every method invocation.

A better way is to pass the authentication information in the SOAP header. A SOAP header is XML information that is attached to the SOAP request sent to the Web Service. It is a convenient way to pass along additional information with the request that is not part of the parameter list.

For this to work, your Web Service must declare a class that descends from the `SoapHeader` class. `SoapHeader` is defined in the `System.Web.Services.Protocols` namespace. This class contains the properties that the Web Service needs to authenticate the user. The Web Service class also contains a public instance of the `SoapHeader` descendant that will be accessible to both the Web Service and the consumer. Listing 28.6 shows a Web Service that makes use of a `SoapHeader` descendant class.

LISTING 28.6   SoapHeader Descendant Class for User Authentication

```
1:    unit WebService1;
2:
3:    interface
4:
5:    uses
6:      System.Collections, System.ComponentModel,
7:      System.Data, System.Diagnostics, System.Web,
8:      System.Web.Services, System.Web.Services.Protocols,
```

28

LISTING 28.6   Continued

```
 9:     System.Security.Cryptography, System.Text;
10:
11:   type
12:
13:     TAuth = class(SoapHeader)
14:       UserName: String;
15:       Password: String;
16:     end;
17:
18:     TWebService1 = class(System.Web.Services.WebService)
19:     strict protected
20:       procedure Dispose(disposing: boolean); override;
21:     private
22:       function Authenticate(aUserName, aPassword: String): Boolean;
23:     public
24:       Auth: TAuth;
25:       constructor Create;
26:       [WebMethod(), SoapHeader('Auth')]
27:       function HelloWorld: string;
28:     end;
29:
30:   implementation
31:
32:   constructor TWebService1.Create;
33:   begin
34:     inherited;
35:     InitializeComponent;
36:   end;
37:
38:   procedure TWebService1.Dispose(disposing: boolean);
39:   begin
40:     if disposing and (components <> nil) then
41:       components.Dispose;
42:     inherited Dispose(disposing);
43:   end;
44:
45:   function TWebService1.HelloWorld: string;
46:   begin
47:     if Auth = nil then
48:       raise Exception.Create('Invalid Login');
49:
50:     if Authenticate(Auth.UserName, Auth.Password)  then
51:       Result := ' You are logged in.'
52:     else
53:       Result := 'Incorrect username/password combo';
54:   end;
55:
56:   function TWebService1.Authenticate(aUserName, aPassword: String): Boolean;
57:   var
58:     PasswordInDB: array of byte;
59:     encoder: UTF8Encoding;
60:     md5Hasher: MD5CryptoServiceProvider;
61:     HashedBytes: array of byte;
```

LISTING 28.6   Continued

```
62:    dbPWStr: String;
63:    aPWStr: String;
64:    i: integer;
65:  begin
66:    try
67:      encoder := UTF8Encoding.Create;
68:      md5Hasher := MD5CryptoServiceProvider.Create;
69:      // Pretend you've gotten the hashed password from the Database
70:      PasswordInDB := md5Hasher.ComputeHash(encoder.GetBytes(
➥'ZacharyCamaro'));
71:
72:      aPWStr := aUserName + APassword;
73:      // Hash the password passed in.
74:      HashedBytes := md5Hasher.ComputeHash(encoder.GetBytes(aPWStr));
75:      aPWStr := '';
76:
77:      // Convert to regular strings
78:      for i := Low(PasswordInDB) to High(PasswordInDB) do7979:        dbPWStr :=    dbPWStr +
Convert.ToString(PasswordInDB[i], 16);
80:
81:      for i := Low(HashedBytes) to High(HashedBytes) do
82:        aPWStr :=    aPWStr + Convert.ToString(HashedBytes[i], 16);
83:
84:      // Compare
85:      Result := System.String.Compare(dbPWStr, aPWStr) = 0;
86:
87:    except
88:      Result := False;
89:    end;
90:  end;
91:
92:  end.
```

▶ Find the code on the CD: \Code\Chapter 28\Ex06.

Lines 13–16 show the declaration of the SoapHeader descendant class, TAuth. This class contains two fields, UserName and Password. If you wanted to pass additional information to this Web Service, this is where you would declare those fields.

Notice also that the Web Service declares an instance of the TAuth class (line 24). Another modification to the Web Service is to add the SoapHeader attribute to the Web Service's methods, which enables the Web Service to receive the header, create the TAuth instance, and set the corresponding fields. This attribute takes the name of the SoapHeader instance—in this case, 'Auth'—as a parameter.

You will also see the declaration of an Authenticate() method, which I will discuss in a minute.

In examining the HelloWorld() method (lines 45–54), you see that if Auth is not provided, the Web Service raises an exception. The consumer must provide an instance of this class, or there is the possibility of unauthorized access. Line 50 invokes the Authenticate()

28

method, passing the `Auth.UserName` and `Auth.Password` members as parameters. Later, you'll see how these get initialized by the consuming application. `Authenticate()` will return `True` or `False` depending on whether valid user credentials were provided.

The `Authenticate()` method is where the meat is. This method uses the class for computing the MD5 hash on the user's credentials, which it then compares to fictional, database derived credentials to see if there is a match. If there is, the user is authorized; otherwise, access to the Web Service is rejected.

On the client side, the method that uses this Web Service is shown in the following code:

```
procedure TWinForm.Button1_Click(sender: System.Object; e: System.EventArgs);
var
  ws: TWebService1;
begin
  ws := TWebService1.Create;
  ws.TAuthValue := TAuth.Create;
  ws.TAuthValue.UserName := tbxUserName.Text;
  ws.TAuthValue.Password := tbxPassword.Text;
  TextBox1.Text := ws.HelloWorld;
end;
```

▶ Find the code on the CD: `\Code\Chapter 28\Ex07`.

In this code, you'll see that the client is responsible for creating the instance of the `TAuth` instance. The Delphi IDE generated this member as `TAuthValue` within the proxy class. In this example, the `UserName` and `Password` strings are retrieved from two `TextBox` controls. `TextBox1` will be populated with the result of the function, which will indicate authorization or rejection.

There is a drawback to the scheme provided here. That is, the information you are passing to the Web Service is in plain text format. Obviously, somebody curious would be able to examine the XML packet if he really wanted to. You could, however, use a similar encryption scheme prior to sending information to the Web Service.

CHAPTER 29

.NET Remoting and Delphi

IN THIS CHAPTER

- Remoting Technologies Available Today
- Distributed Architectures
- Benefits of Multitier Application Development
- .NET Remoting Basics
- Your First .NET Remoting Application

Remoting is the process through which applications communicate across certain boundaries. The simplest form of boundary is a process, whereas a more complex one (and more common) is a network.

COM, DCOM, CORBA are all remoting technologies that, despite the different names and the incompatibles, work following a similar pattern: A client packages the name and parameters of a request, sends it over the boundary to a predefined location, and waits for a response.

Remoting technologies allow you to enter the world of "distributed systems" and achieve a level of flexibility and scalability not possible otherwise.

Remoting Technologies Available Today

Forms of Remoting have been usable from Delphi for a long time.

You could have used the COM/DCOM or CORBA frameworks included since version 3, the support for SOAP WebServices introduced in version 6, or even just simple TCP/IP components such as Indy.

The following section lists some of the most common remoting technologies available in the IT industry.

Sockets

Sockets are the basis of all network communication and allow developers to access network resources as if they were streams.

Sockets give full control to developers when it comes to low-level features. Unfortunately, sockets are difficult to program and add unnecessary complexity to the development of distributed applications.

All the other technologies listed in this section are built on top of sockets and provide developers with abstraction layers that simplify communication.

RPC

RPC is both an abbreviation for Remote Procedure Call and a specification designed by the the Open Group (www.opengroup.org/).

RPC outlined many of the architectural pillars used in Remoting technologies such as DCOM, SOAP, and CORBA.

These include

- proxies and stubs: code present on clients and servers whose purpose is to make remote calls look as if they were local

- data marshalling: the process of packaging a stream of data containing a request name and its parameters

- interface definition language (IDL): a type of document that lists the name and parameters of the procedures that remote clients can invoke

Refer to www.opengroup.org/ for more information.

Java RMI

Java RMI enables programmers to create distributed Java to Java applications in which the methods of remote Java objects can be invoked from other Java virtual machines on the same or different computer.

It is the equivalent of .NET Remoting for the Java platform, but it is only accessible from Java environments.

Refer to http://java.sun.com/products/jdk/rmi/ for more information.

CORBA

CORBA is the abbreviation for Common Object Request Broker Architecture, and it is an open, vendor-independent specification defined by the Object Management Group (www.omg.org).

Companies such as Borland, Iona, PrismTech, and 2AB provide products that implement the specification.

CORBA is based on the IIOP protocol to transmit messages.

Read more about CORBA at www.omg.com and about IIOP at http://www.omg.org/gettingstarted/corbafaq.htm#RemoteInvoke.

XML-RPC

XML-RPC is a specification for an XML-based messaging protocol designed to work over HTTP.

The XML-RPC encoding is very simple to understand and use and provides support for most simple data types (integers, strings, and so on) and complex structures (objects).

Many XML-RPC implementations are available for the Linux, Unix, and Windows platforms.

Refer to `http://www.xmlrpc.com` for more information.

DCOM

The Distributed Component Object Model (DCOM) was the technology recommended by Microsoft for building distributed applications and, simply put, allows to access COM automation servers from remote computers.

DCOM was designed to work using different network transports (that is, TCP/IP and HTTP), to be cross platform, and it was based on the Open Group DCE-RPC specification.

Although the framework provides support for non-x86 architectures and has been ported to some Unix platforms, it has never been successful on non-Microsoft platforms.

Delphi supported DCOM, starting from version 3, with a framework that greatly simplified the development of DCOM servers and clients.

COM-Interop

COM-Interop is a technology that enables .NET and COM/DCOM applications to interoperate with each other. COM-Interop was covered in Chapter 16.

SOAP

SOAP is the acronym for Simple Object Access Protocol.

The official definition found in the recent 1.2 specification says

> SOAP is a lightweight protocol intended for exchanging structured information in a decentralized, distributed environment. SOAP uses XML technologies to define an extensible messaging framework, which provides a message construct that can be exchanged over a variety of underlying protocols. The framework has been designed to be independent of any particular programming model and other implementation specific semantics.

SOAP is the foundation of Web Services (applications programmatically accessible by remote clients via HTTP) and is a de facto standard supported by many vendors including Microsoft, IBM, Borland, and Sun.

While relatively new, SOAP is the most accepted protocol for cross-platform communication. It is one of the best candidates to write systems accessible by applications written in any language, from any platform. Figure 29.1 illustrates this relationship.

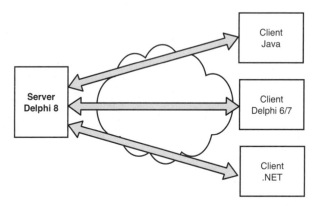

FIGURE 29.1   SOAP cross-platform communication.

Microsoft .NET SDK provides a lot of infrastructure and prebuilt classes to create and consume Web Services that are fully accessible from Delphi.

You can build SOAP servers and clients in both Delphi 7 and Delphi for .NET, although the approach you have to use is very different.

.NET Remoting

.NET technologies use the term .NET Remoting to indicate two different things:

- A form of remoting that uses binary messaging and is native to .NET

- The foundation of classes that allow for *any* kind of remoting in .NET (either SOAP, binary, or user defined)

Throughout this chapter and Chapter 30, we will use the second definition.

The binary messaging protocol available in the .NET Remoting framework is Microsoft's official replacement for COM/DCOM. It is the most efficient way to make .NET applications communicate with each other, but, differently from SOAP, it is not meant for cross-platform communication because it only works between .NET applications.

We'll see how to create applications that use this form of remoting later in this chapter and in Chapter 30.

Distributed Architectures

A system divided in two or more executable modules running on different machines, processes, or AppDomains is said to use a distributed architecture. Processes and AppDomains are mentioned because marshalling would still be required.

Although it could be argued that a single executable divided in several units also represents an example of a distributed architecture, we'll stick to examples in which some form of marshaling is required.

Distributed architecture had existed for a long time before .NET Remoting was created. These systems and the technologies used to build them have been the foundation for the design and implementation of what is now available in Delphi for .NET and the Microsoft .NET Framework. Each of these architectures makes use of one or multiple remoting technologies to perform remote communication.

Client/Server

This is the earliest and most well-known distributed architecture. Delphi applications using technologies such as dbGo, Interbase Express, or the Borland Database Engine/SQL Links are client/server.

This type of architecture is usually referred to as two-tier in which a client is responsible for the presentation of the data (that is, using data-aware controls such as TDBGrid) and a server for the retrieval and storage of it.

Although this architecture is simpler to understand and use than others, it has several problems that are critical in today's Internet enabled world:

- It usually only works in local area network(s).

- It cannot efficiently serve thousands of concurrent users.

- It is not easy to update and maintain: Because each client requires a permanent connection to the database and most business logic is contained in the clients themselves, whenever a change is due, all clients need to be redeployed.

Figure 29.2 illustrates a client/server model.

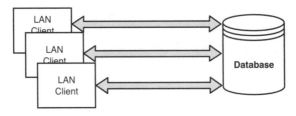

FIGURE 29.2   Client-server model.

29

Peer-to-peer

Peer-to-peer indicates networks without a central server in which each computer acts as a client and a server at the same time. A Windows workgroup without a domain server is a peer-to-peer network, for instance.

This type of architecture generally only works in local area networks and depends on frequent UDP broadcasts to make each node aware of the status of the others. These broadcasts are normally not possible over the Internet. Figure 29.3 depicts the peer-to-peer network.

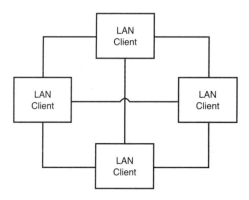

FIGURE 29.3   A peer-to-peer network.

Gnutella or Napster are forms of hybrid peer-to-peer systems in which each node communicates with a server to find out about the existence of other nodes and then initiates direct communication with each.

Although convenient for file sharing and chat programs, this architecture fails to provide benefits to regular, data-oriented applications.

Multitier

Multitier is the preferred type of distributed architecture today. Delphi applications built using technologies such as DataSnap or Windows DNA are multitier. You will use .NET Remoting to develop multitier systems in Delphi for .NET.

This type of architecture is commonly referred to as three-tier, where a client communicates to a process on a remote server and this, in turn, communicates with an RDBMS located on a different server. This is shown in Figure 29.4.

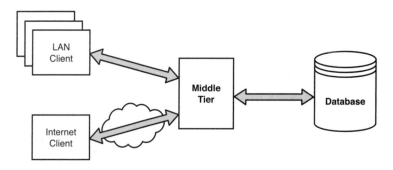

FIGURE 29.4   Multitier distributed model.

The key aspect of this type of architecture is the presence of the middle tier. Middle tiers are usually composed of two layers:

- Data access—Responsible for querying and updating the underlying data source. It can perform data caching to improve performance and minimize access to the database. It can abstract the RDBMS engine dialect and provide a simple object-oriented API for the business layer.

- Business—Normally composed by objects accessible from the clients through Remoting. These objects perform data validation, transformation, in-memory calculations, and so on.

Data access and business layers could reside in different application domains or simply be placed in one. In general, using one application domain makes things easier, although you might opt for a more marked division in a few cases.

An example could be providing a hot-swappable data access layer that works as a plug-in and can be replaced at runtime or during installation without the need to recompile the business layer.

The next section lists some of the most evident advantages of multitier systems.

Benefits of Multitier Application Development

A multitier design offers several advantages over two-tier client/server designs, although it is probably more complex to understand and implement.

Scalability and Fault Tolerance

The first and most prominent advantage of multitier architectures is scalability.

Client/server systems depend on a central database server and require permanent connections to be present. The more clients, the worse the server will perform because of the increased resource consumption (that is, network connections constantly open, frequent access to tables, cursors, and so on). Client/server systems aren't usually capable of handling more than a couple of hundred concurrent users in an efficient manner.

By having a middle tier composed of multiple servers (cluster), you will be able to divide the workload between them and only hit the database server when really needed. By implementing caching techniques, you could also minimize access to what is strictly necessary, increasing overall performance.

Figure 29.5 shows two (or more) clients accessing a cluster of two (or more) servers, which, in turn, are connected to a single database server.

In order to benefit from clustering, your clients will need to operate in a disconnected fashion and only connect to the middle-tier when they need to read data or send some updates. Regardless of the status of the remote machine—which could have become irresponsive or have been shut down for maintenance—this ensures that the client will continue to function by using another server.

From a server perspective, this approach is called stateless. The server only has a means to communicate with clients when they initiate a call. Once this is completed, the client ceases to exist for the server.

If you are familiar with Web development, you will find many analogies: Stateless design is almost mandatory when you need high scalability and have large numbers of concurrent clients.

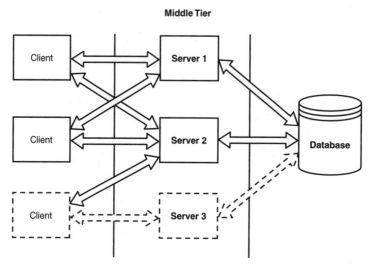

FIGURE 29.5   Multitier cluster model.

We will explain how remote objects are instantiated later in the sections "Server Activation" and "Client Activation." In order to ensure that your system is highly scalable, you'll have to use one of the two Server Activation models (SingleCall or Singleton). If you need a more coupled, but less scalable and certainly not clusterable approach, you could instead decide to tie a client to a specific instance of an object residing on one server, using Client activation.

> **NOTE**
>
> You can find .NET specific articles on distributed architectures at:
>
> `http://msdn.microsoft.com/architecture/`

Development and Deployment

In client/server systems, business processing is mostly done on the client applications—sometimes with the help of stored procedures running on the database server.

Unfortunately, because stored procedures are more complex to write and debug than Delphi code, they are not used extensively—especially in companies that don't have a dedicated database administration staff.

If the number of clients is large, updating each desktop with a new copy of the client executable might be laborious and error prone.

In multitier systems, a big part (if not all) of business processing happens in the middle tier. The applications running on the middle tier are simple to write (Delphi code), and, once updated, all clients automatically benefit from fixes or enhancements without the need for redeployment.

Somebody might argue that having an executable placed on a shared network drive could be just as easy to update, but consider what would happen if a workstation is keeping the file locked or if you needed to access it from an office in another city.

Security

Because clients don't directly communicate with the database, it becomes much easier for administrators to enforce programmatic security into their applications and protect the database from unauthorized access.

The request made by clients can travel, encrypted, over SSL connections. Methods of business objects can return less data to clients based on session information: This would be transparent to the caller and changeable over time without the need to redeploy the clients.

.NET Remoting Basics

The following sections provide an overview of the .NET remoting technology.

Architectural Overview

The .NET Remoting architecture is extremely flexible and provides developers with a framework that is easy to customize and extend.

This section provides you with a brief description of the most important elements of the framework and introduces a few concepts only present in .NET Remoting.

Application Domains

Application Domains are at the core of the remoting infrastructure and represent the boundaries for Interprocess Communication (IPC).

In classical Win32, Windows creates a new process when an executable is launched. Processes are the lowest level of isolation and cannot directly share memory between each other. Memory addresses are process relative: Pointers to memory in one process are meaningless to another.

Application Domains, or AppDomains, are to .NET what processes are to Win32. AppDomains provide a more granular level of separation and better security than Win32 processes.

You can run several application domains in a single process with the same level of isolation that would exist in separate processes, but without incurring the additional overhead of making cross-process calls or switching between processes. Figure 29.6 illustrates this concept.

.NET Remoting is necessary to make objects in one domain communicate with those hosted in another, regardless of the domains being in the same process or in processes running on different machines.

The System.Runtime.Remoting Namespace

In order to develop applications that use .NET Remoting, you will need to reference the namespace System.Runtime.Remoting in both your clients and servers.

29

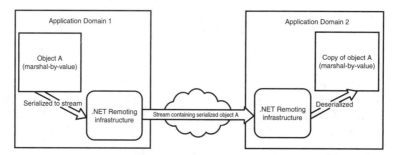

FIGURE 29.6   Cross AppDomain communication using .NET Remoting.

The `System.Runtime.Remoting` namespace and those depending on it provide classes and interfaces that allow developers to create and configure distributed applications.

The RemotingConfiguration Class

The `RemotingConfiguration` class contains static class methods for interfacing with configuration settings and register objects so that they can be remotely invoked.

The following snippet of code registers the class `TBankManager`:

```
RemotingConfiguration.RegisterWellKnownServiceType(
  typeOf(TBankManager),
  'BankManager.soap',
  WellKnownObjectMode.Singleton);
```

More about this method is explained in the section "Server Activation."

Remoting settings can be programmatically set or can be read from external configuration files.

The `RemotingConfiguration.Configure()` method allows developers to configure the Remoting infrastructure through the use of XML formatted configuration files.

This is how you would use it:

```
RemotingConfiguration.Configure('MyConfiguration.config');
```

The configuration files can contain information such as the networking protocol to use for remote communication, the TCP or HTTP port used, the message formatting type (SOAP or binary), and more.

> **NOTE**
>
> Refer to the section called "Remoting Settings Schema" in the MSDN Online Library for more information at:
>
> http://msdn.microsoft.com/library/default.asp?url=/library/en-
> us/cpgenref/html/gnconRemotingSettingsSchema.asp

The ChannelServices Class

The `ChannelServices` class provides static class methods to register remoting channels, and it's used in both clients and servers.

The following snippet of code shows how to create and register an HTTP communication channel listening on port 9088 for use on the server side:

```
var Channel : HttpChannel;
begin
  Channel := HttpChannel.Create(9088);
  ChannelServices.RegisterChannel(Channel);
```

Clients do not specify a port number when registering channels. The URI information necessary to access remote objects is specified in the call to the Activator object at a later time, and this will also include a port number.

The following snippet of code shows how to create a client channel and acquire a reference to the remote service from the client application:

```
  fChannel := HttpChannel.Create();
  ChannelServices.RegisterChannel(fChannel);

  fBankManager := Activator.GetObject(
    typeof(IBankManager),
    'http://localhost:8099/BankManager.soap');
```

Remotable Objects

Objects intended to be accessed by different domains are called remotable objects. Two types of remotable objects exist in .NET: Marshal-By-Reference, and Marshal-By-Value.

> **NOTE**
>
> A third type, Context-bound is also available, but it won't be covered in this book because of the length and complexity of the topic. You can think of a .NET context as a subdivision of an application domain in which context-bound objects live. For more information about Contexts, refer to the .NET Framework SDK Documentation at `"ms-help://MS.NETFrameworkSDKv1.1/ cpguidenf/html/cpconremotableobjects.htm"`.

Marshal-By-Reference Objects

Simply put, instances of this type can be seen as a collection of methods that can be invoked from remote clients.

Marshal-By-Reference objects are created on the server where they live for the duration of a method call (see "Single-call Instantiation" later) or are shared among different clients (see "Singleton Activation" later) for the duration of a lease (see "Leases and Sponsors" later).

In order to create a Marshal-By-Reference object, you need to make its class descend from `MarshalByRefObject`, which is defined in the System namespace.

The following is an example of a Marshal-By-Reference class:

```
type
  TCalculator = class(MarshalByRefObject, ICalculator)
  private
  protected
```

29

```
// ICalculator
function Sum(A,B : integer): integer;

public
end;
```

The methods of this type of objects can have any kind of simple data type (that is, integers, strings, and so on) or object parameters(as long as they are Marshal-By-Value objects).

Marshal-By-Value Objects

Instances of this type cross application domain boundaries after being serialized in a transportable format.

When they reach the target domain, they are deserialized and a new instance of the original class is created in the target application domain.

In order to create a serializable object, you need to mark its class with the [Serializable] attribute like this:

```
{ TAccount }
  [Serializable]
  TAccount = class
  private
    fNumber : integer;
    fBalance: double;
    fName: string;

  public
    constructor Create(const aNumber : integer;
                       const aName : string;
                       const aBalance : double);

    property Number : integer read fNumber;
    property Name : string read fName;
    property Balance : double read fBalance write fBalance;
  end;
```

The purpose of these types of objects is generally to share data between applications in a structured manner. They are usually used as input or output parameters of remote methods.

Object Activation

Before you can acquire a reference to a remote object running in a different application domain, the object needs to be created on the remote machine.

There are two ways to create an instance of a remotable object: using server activation and using client activation.

Server Activation

Server-activated objects are referred to as well-known because they are registered in the .NET remoting system and published at a specific and well-known endpoint or URI.

Well-known objects can be activated in two ways: singleton and single-call.

Singleton Activation   Singleton activated means only one instance of an object will be created and be accessible at any given time. If two clients request a reference to a singleton-mode–configured object, they will both receive the same reference and their calls will be serialized.

The following code shows how to register a singleton-mode–configured object:

```
RemotingConfiguration.RegisterWellKnownServiceType(
    typeOf(TBankManager),
    'BankManager.soap',
    WellKnownObjectMode.Singleton);
```

Single-call Activation

Single-call instantiation is the most scalable activation mode because it best fits stateless systems. When you register an object as single-call, an instance will be created upon each client's request and, once the call is completed, it will be released for garbage collection.

The following code shows how to enable single-call instantiation:

```
RemotingConfiguration.RegisterWellKnownServiceType(
    typeOf(TBankManager),
    'BankManager.soap',
    WellKnownObjectMode.SingleCall);
```

Client Activation

Client-activated objects are activated on a per-client basis. Each client will have his own unique reference that can also remain active between method calls (stateful).

Although client-activation offers some advantages and is simpler to use than server-side instantiation, it is less scalable. It uses more resources on the server, ties clients to one server, and, because of this, doesn't work in Web farms.

To enable for this kind of activation, your server will have to include a call similar to the following:

```
RemotingConfiguration.RegisterActivatedServiceType(typeof(TBankManager));
```

And corresponding code on the client would look like this:

```
RemotingConfiguration.RegisterActivatedClientType(typeof(TBankManager),
'http://someurl');
```

You will see more in detail how to create client-activated objects in the section "Client Activation" in Chapter 30.

Leases and Sponsors

A remote object's lifetime is managed by lease-based garbage collection. Each application domain contains its own lease manager and tracks access to objects. If an object is not accessed for a certain amount of time, it's then handed to the garbage collector that destroys it.

Object lifetime management in .NET is radically different from how DCOM handles object lifetimes. In DCOM, a combination of reference counting and network pinging was used to determine when objects could be destroyed. This led to network congestion and other side effects that were less-than-optimal in large installations. .NET remoting was designed to resolve those problems.

Leases are used for server-activated singleton objects and client-activated objects. After the .NET Framework creates an instance of those, it calls the virtual method `InitializeLifeTimeServices` (inherited from `MarshalByRefObject` and possibly overridden), which returns an object that implements the interface `ILease`. This object will then be queried to determine if the lease on the object has expired and it can be destroyed.

Leases can be renewed by sponsors. You can define a class that acts as a sponsor by implementing the `ISponsor` interface. You then need to associate the sponsor to a lease by calling the method `ILease.Register`.

The .NET Framework defines the `ClientSponsor` class, which provides a default implementation for a lifetime sponsor class.

Proxies

Clients communicate with remote objects by using proxies. A proxy is an object that resides in the address space of the client and acts as a surrogate for the remote object.

In .NET, we have two types of proxies: transparent and real.

The transparent proxy is the object we directly acquire when writing code such as

```
fBankManager := Activator.GetObject(
    typeof(IBankManager),
    'http://localhost:8099/BankManager.soap');
```

After a method call is issued, the transparent proxy packages the name and parameters into a message object and hands this to the real proxy.

The real proxy then dispatches the message object to the .NET Framework, which will then use a remoting channel to deliver it.

Channels

Remoting channels transport messages across application domains. The .NET SDK provides two types of channels you can use: TCP/IP and HTTP.

You would use a TCP/IP channel mostly in local area networks or where communication has to be as fast as possible.

You would instead use the HTTP channel for Internet or, in general, firewall-friendly type of communication.

Both channels can be used independently of the messaging format. This means that you can decide to use SOAP or Binary formatting over either TCP/IP or HTTP.

Your First .NET Remoting Application

Developing Delphi applications that make use of .NET remoting is a relatively easy process, and, if you used COM, you will find that it's conceptually very similar to developing OLE automation servers. Luckily, registration of remotable objects is much simpler. It can be done programmatically (RemotingConfiguration method calls) or declaratively (using an XML configuration file). You no longer have to deal with type libraries.

The following example, although simple, shows how to best structure .NET Remoting projects and contains a certain amount of real-world business logic.

The server of this example represents a bank service. It contains a list of bank accounts (two to be precise) and allows to query for the details of these (account number, name of the person associated with it, and its balance) and to do a money transfer.

Setting Up the Project

We'll start the development of our bank system by creating a project group and three empty projects (a Package, a Console Application, and a Windows Forms Application) that we will complete in the following sections.

Select File, New, Other. Click Other Files and select Project Group, as shown in Figure 29.7.

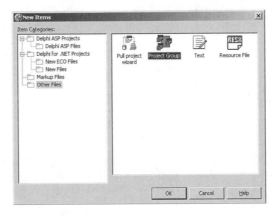

FIGURE 29.7   Setting up a project group.

Save the project group as **BankExample**.

It's very convenient to use project groups when developing distributed applications, especially at early stages. Project groups provide you with an immediate look at all the elements of your systems and allow you to switch between them more efficiently than with individual projects.

Add the Package to the group by clicking the New button inside the Project Manager panel and then selecting Package, as shown in Figure 29.8.

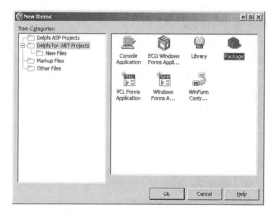

FIGURE 29.8   Selecting a Package.

Repeat the operation and add a Console Application and a Windows Forms Application to your project group.

Once done, save and name the projects as shown in Table 29.1.

TABLE 29.1   Project Names in the Project Group

Project Type	Project Name
Package	BankPackage.dll
Console Application	BankServer.exe
WinForms Client	BankClient.exe

Adding References

In order for applications to make use of Delphi packages, the package itself and the applications using it must include a reference to the Borland.Delphi assembly.

This is automatically added for you by Delphi, but in case you removed the reference, simply go inside the Project Manager, right-click on the node Requires under the project BankPackage.dll and select Add Reference.

When the Add Reference dialog box appears, select the Borland.Delphi assembly, as shown in Figure 29.9.

Click OK, compile the package, and select the Server project.

The server application will need references to the Borland.Delphi assembly, the BankPackage. dll itself, and System.Runtime.Remoting.

Reopen the Add Reference dialog box and select the assemblies shown in Figure 29.10. You will have to browse to the directory containing BankPackage.dll to select it. Once done, you will see it in the Project References page of this dialog box. The .NET Assemblies page only contains GAC'ed assemblies.

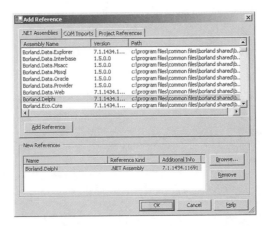

FIGURE 29.9   Adding the Borland.Delphi reference.

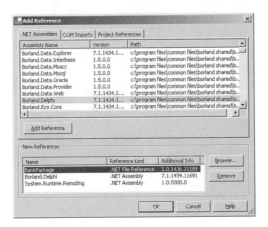

FIGURE 29.10   Adding the Assembly reference to the BankServer project.

Once you're done adding these references, your project group should look like that shown in Figure 29.11.

BankPackage.dll: Contract Between Clients and Servers

If you're familiar with COM, you'll be accustomed to creating type libraries. The type library is a standardized binary resource linked in your server's executable or DLL that Windows requires to enable for interprocess communication. The type library represents the contract between your server and clients: It tells clients what they can do and what complex data types they will be using, but it contains no implementation.

When you develop .NET Remoting servers, type libraries are not necessary anymore: .NET's metadata included inside the compiled package will serve this purpose. The BankPackage.dll we just created is a .NET assembly that will contain the shared interfaces and classes used by the server and the client application.

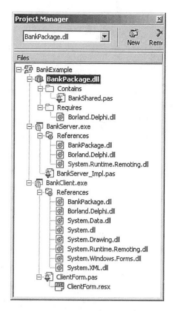

FIGURE 29.11   The BankExample project group.

We've added a new unit to BankPackage.dll and saved it as BankShared.pas. This unit is shown in Listing 29.1.

LISTING 29.1   The BankShared.pas Unit

```
1:    unit BankShared;
2:
3:    interface
4:
5:    type
6:      { TAccount }
7:      [Serializable]
8:      TAccount = class
9:      private
10:       fNumber : integer;
11:       fBalance: double;
12:       fName: string;
13:
14:     public
15:       constructor Create(const aNumber : integer;
16:                          const aName : string;
17:                          const aBalance : double);
18:
19:       property Number : integer read fNumber;
20:       property Name : string read fName;
21:       property Balance : double read fBalance write fBalance;
22:     end;
23:
24:     { IBankManager }
25:     TAccountNumberArray = array of integer;
```

LISTING 29.1   Continued

```
26:
27:    IBankManager = interface
28:      function GetAccountNumbers : TAccountNumberArray;
29:      function GetAccount(const AccountNumber : integer) : TAccount;
30:      procedure TransferMoney(const Origin, Destination : integer;
31:                              const Amount : double);
32:    end;
33:
34:  implementation
35:
36:  { TAccount }
37:
38:  constructor TAccount.Create(const aNumber : integer;
39:                              const aName : string;
40:                              const aBalance : double);
41:  begin
42:    inherited Create;
43:
44:    fNumber := aNumber;
45:    fName := aName;
46:    fBalance := aBalance;
47:  end;
48:
49:  end.
```

▶ Find the code on the CD: \Code\Chapter 29\Ex01.

In Listing 29.1, the IBankManager interface is a critical aspect of this unit (lines 24–32). As you can see, there isn't any class implementing it. This package is going to be shared between server and client, but the client doesn't need to know about (or contain) any implementation details. All it needs to know is what and how to call it.

The only class defined and implemented in this unit is TAccount (lines 6–22 and 38–47). In addition to this, the array TAccountNumberArray is also declared (line 25).

Because these two types are referenced by the methods of IBankManager, they need to be included in the shared assembly.

The interface IBankManager is implemented in the server project.

The other important thing to notice is the use of the attribute [Serializable] above the class TAccount (line 7). If TAccount was not marked as serializable, IBankManager.GetAccount would fail at runtime when called remotely.

TAccount is used as a Marshal-By-Value object. When the remote client calls GetAccount, a copy of the object is passed across application domain boundaries.

Implementing the Server

The server is composed of two parts:

- The project source file in which we will open an HTTP remoting channel and register the class that implements the IBankManager interface.

- A unit that contains the class TBankManager. This class implements the IBankManager interface.

We've added a new unit to the server project and saved it as BankServer_Impl.pas. This unit is shown in Listing 29.2.

LISTING 29.2   The BankServer_Impl.pas Unit

```
1:   unit BankServer_Impl;
2:
3:   interface
4:
5:   uses
6:     BankShared;
7:
8:   type
9:     TBankManager = class(MarshalByRefObject, IBankManager)
10:    private
11:      fAccount1,
12:      fAccount2 : TAccount;
13:    protected
14:      // IBankManager
15:      function GetAccountNumbers : TAccountNumberArray;
16:      function GetAccount(const AccountNumber : integer) : TAccount;
17:      procedure TransferMoney(const Origin, Destination : integer;
18:                             const Amount : double);
19:    public
20:      constructor Create;
21:    end;
22:
23:  implementation
24:
25:  { TBankManager }
26:
27:  constructor TBankManager.Create;
28:  begin
29:    inherited Create;
30:    fAccount1 := TAccount.Create(1, 'John Smith', 1999);
31:    fAccount2 := TAccount.Create(2, 'Jack Rockwell', 249);
32:  end;
33:
34:  function TBankManager.GetAccount(const AccountNumber: integer): TAccount;
35:  begin
36:    case AccountNumber of
37:      1 : result := fAccount1;
38:      2 : result := fAccount2;
39:      else raise Exception.Create('Invalid account number!');
40:    end;
41:
42:    Console.WriteLine('A client requested account
➥'+result.Number.ToString+
43:                    ' ('+result.Name+')');
44:  end;
45:
```

LISTING 29.2   Continued

```
46:  function TBankManager.GetAccountNumbers: TAccountNumberArray;
47:  begin
48:    SetLength(result, 2);
49:    result[0] := fAccount1.Number;
50:    result[1] := fAccount2.Number;
51:
52:    Console.WriteLine('A client requested the list of accounts');
53:  end;
54:
55:  procedure TBankManager.TransferMoney(const Origin, Destination: integer;
56:    const Amount: double);
57:  var origin_acct, destination_acct : TAccount;
58:  begin
59:    origin_acct := GetAccount(Origin);
60:    destination_acct := GetAccount(Destination);
61:
62:    if (origin_acct.Balance<Amount) or (Amount<0)
63:      then raise Exception.Create('Insufficient funds or
➥invalid amount specified');
64:
65:    destination_acct.Balance := destination_acct.Balance+Amount;
66:    origin_acct.Balance := origin_acct.Balance-Amount;
67:
68:    Console.WriteLine('Transferred ${0} from account {1} to account {2}',
69:      Amount.ToString, origin_acct.Number.ToString,
70:      destination_acct.Number.ToString);
71:  end;
72:
73:  end.
```

▶ Find the code on the CD: \Code\Chapter 29\Ex01.

Pay attention to the declaration of TBankManager at line 9. MarshalByRefObject is the base class for objects that communicate across application domain boundaries by exchanging messages using a proxy.

The proxy is created the first time the object is accessed. Subsequent calls on the proxy are marshaled back to the object residing in the server application domain.

Classes must inherit from MarshalByRefObject when their instances need to be used across application domains, and their state doesn't need to be or cannot be copied.

In the project source file (see Listing 29.3 later), we've added the namespaces System.Runtime.Remoting, System.Runtime.Remoting.Channels, and System.Runtime.Remoting.Channels.HTTP. The project source file now contains

```
uses
  BankServer_Impl in 'BankServer_Impl.pas',
  System.Runtime.Remoting,
  System.Runtime.Remoting.Channels,
  System.Runtime.Remoting.Channels.HTTP;
```

We've also defined a variable of type HTTPChannel called Channel and initialized it as follows:

```
var def_HTTPPort : integer = 8099;
    Channel : HttpChannel;
Begin
[..]
  Channel := HttpChannel.Create(def_HTTPPort);
  ChannelServices.RegisterChannel(Channel);
```

Finally, we registered the type TBankManager by using the RemotingConfiguration class:

```
RemotingConfiguration.RegisterWellKnownServiceType(
  typeOf(TBankManager),
  'BankManager.soap',
  WellKnownObjectMode.Singleton);
  // Starts accepting requests
  Writeln('Waiting for requests...');
  Readln;
```

The complete source for the BankServer.dpr file is shown in Listing 29.3.

LISTING 29.3   BankServer.dpr File

```
1:    program BankServer;
2:
3:    {$APPTYPE CONSOLE}
4:
5:    {%DelphiDotNetAssemblyCompiler 'BankPackage.dll'}
6:    {%DelphiDotNetAssemblyCompiler [..]}
7:    {%DelphiDotNetAssemblyCompiler [..]}
8:
9:  uses
10:    BankServer_Impl in 'BankServer_Impl.pas',
11:    System.Runtime.Remoting,
12:    System.Runtime.Remoting.Channels,
13:    System.Runtime.Remoting.Channels.HTTP;
14:
15: var def_HTTPPort : integer = 8099;
16:     Channel : HttpChannel;
17: begin
18:    Console.WriteLine('Initializing server...');
19:
20:    // Initializes the server to listen for HTTP requests on a specific port
21:    Channel := HttpChannel.Create(def_HTTPPort);
22:    ChannelServices.RegisterChannel(Channel);
23:    Console.WriteLine('HTTP channel created. Listening on port '+
24:            System.Convert.ToString(def_HTTPPort));
25:
26:    // Registers the TBankManager service
27:    RemotingConfiguration.RegisterWellKnownServiceType(
28:      typeOf(TBankManager),
29:      'BankManager.soap',
30:      WellKnownObjectMode.Singleton);
31:
32:    // Starts accepting requests
```

LISTING 29.3   Continued

```
33:    Console.WriteLine('Waiting for requests...');
34:    Console.ReadLine;
35: end.
```

▶ Find the code on the CD: \Code\Chapter 29\Ex01.

Lines 21–22 show how to make the server application create a remoting channel that listens for HTTP messages on port 8099. Lines 27–30 register the object TBankManager as a singleton ready to be remotely accessed.

Notice how you do not need to associate a class to a channel. If you have other remote classes, you would just need to register them as we did with TBankManager (lines 27–30). The HTTP channel that was previously created listens for any type of remoting message coming from clients and forwards it to the correct target object.

At this point, you can compile the server application and launch it outside the IDE. It will display the contents as shown in Figure 29.12.

FIGURE 29.12   Server application output.

Implementing the Client

In the client project, the main form's uses clause contains the following namespaces:

```
uses
  System.Drawing, System.Collections, System.ComponentModel,
  System.Windows.Forms, System.Data,
  // Remoting and Bank related
  BankShared,
  System.Runtime.Remoting,
  System.Runtime.Remoting.Channels,
  System.Runtime.Remoting.Channels.HTTP;
```

The form's OnLoad event handler contains the following code:

```
fChannel := HttpChannel.Create();
ChannelServices.RegisterChannel(fChannel);
```

```
fBankManager := Activator.GetObject(
  typeof(IBankManager),
  'http://localhost:8099/BankManager.soap');
```

As you probably guessed, the preceding code creates an instance of the remote object
BankManager, which we can now use from inside the client application.

It is now possible to test the remote methods. Figure 29.13 shows the form of the example
application that does this at design-time.

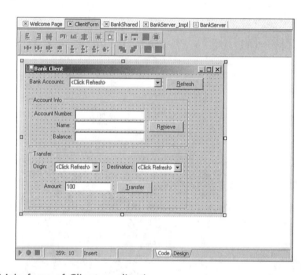

FIGURE 29.13   Main form of Client application.

The Refresh button's Click event handler contains code shown in Listing 29.4.

LISTING 29.4   Refresh Button's Click Event Handler

```
1.    procedure TWinForm2.bRefresh_Click(sender: System.Object;
2.            e: System.EventArgs);
3.    var accountarray : TAccountNumberArray;
4.        i : integer;
5.    begin
6.      accountarray := fBankManager.GetAccountNumbers;
7.      cbBankAccounts.Items.Clear;
8.      cbOrigin.Items.Clear;
9.      cbDestination.Items.Clear;
10.
11.     for i := 0 to High(accountarray) do begin
12.       cbBankAccounts.Items.Add(accountarray[i].ToString);
13.       cbOrigin.Items.Add(accountarray[i].ToString);
14.       cbDestination.Items.Add(accountarray[i].ToString);
15.     end;
```

LISTING 29.4   Continued

```
16.    cbBankAccounts.SelectedIndex := 0;
17.  end;
```

▶ Find the code on the CD: \Code\Chapter29\Ex01.

As you can see from the first line of this method, the use of the remote object pointed by fBankManager is not any different from using a local copy. We declared a variable of type TAccountNumberArray at line 3, and we use it at line 6.

Keep in mind that the similarities end at the code level, especially when it comes to performance.

When the code

```
accountarray := fBankManager.GetAccountNumbers;
```

is executed, the client application is creating a SOAP message, sending it to the server via HTTP and unpacking the response. This overhead is not obvious when making a single method call, but you will immediately see a big difference in performance as soon as you put that code inside a loop.

The Retrieve button's Click event handler contains the code shown in Listing 29.5.

LISTING 29.5   Retrieve Button's Click Event Handler

```
1.    procedure TWinForm2.bRetrieve_Click(sender: System.Object;
2.      e: System.EventArgs);
3.    var acctnumber : integer;
4.        account : TAccount;
5.    begin
6.      acctnumber := System.Convert.ToInt32(cbBankAccounts.Text);
7.      account := fBankManager.GetAccount(acctnumber);
8.      tbAcctNumber.Text := account.Number.ToString;
9.      tbAcctName.Text := account.Name;
10.      tbAcctBalance.Text := account.Balance.ToString;
11.    end;
```

▶ Find the code on the CD: \Code\Chapter29\Ex01.

At line 6, we grab the selected account number from the combo box cbBankAccounts and assign it to the integer variable acctnumber. We then pass acctnumber to the BankManager.GetAccount method (line 7), which will generate a remote call to the BankManager object running on the server. Finally (lines 8–10), we display the information contained in the account returned by the server.

Finally, the Transfer button's Click event handler contains

```
procedure TWinForm2.bTransfer_Click(sender: System.Object;
  e: System.EventArgs);
var originacct_acct, destination_acct : integer;
    amount : double;
```

```
begin
  originacct_acct := System.Convert.ToInt32(cbOrigin.Text);
  destination_acct := System.Convert.ToInt32(cbDestination.Text);
  amount := System.Convert.ToDouble(tbAmount.Text);
  fBankManager.TransferMoney(originacct_acct,
                             destination_acct,
                             amount);
  MessageBox.Show('Transfer completed');
end;
```

The client, when launched, displays the form shown in Figure 29.14.

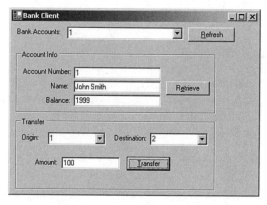

FIGURE 29.14   Client application—remoting in action.

CHAPTER 30

.NET Remoting in Action

by Alessandro Federici

IN THIS CHAPTER

- Template Project
- Tracing Messages
- Analyzing the SOAP Packets
- Client Activation
- Lifetime Management
- Failing to Renew the Lease
- Configuration Files
- Switching from HTTP to TCP Communication
- Switching from SOAP to Binary Remoting
- Differences Between SOAP and Binary Encoding.

The examples presented in this chapter illustrate various features of the .NET remoting framework. Each example will help you reach a good understanding of the concept being discussed.

Template Project

The project group contains a shared assembly, a server, and a client console application ready to be compiled and launched.

Figure 30.1 shows how the template project looks.

The service included in the template is very basic, and it implements the following interface:

```
ISimpleServer = interface
  function GetValue : integer;
  procedure SetValue(Value : integer);
  property Value : integer read GetValue write SetValue;
end;
```

▶ Find the code on the CD: \Chapter 30\Ex01.

This template will save you precious time while doing your first tests with .NET remoting.

To start a new remoting application, just copy the template folder, rename its files, and extend it with your own custom code.

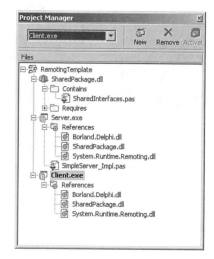

FIGURE 30.1   Template project.

Tracing Messages

When developing distributed applications, it's often useful to see what goes across the wire. By seeing the size of the data packets, their contents, and so on, you will gather a better understanding of the technology you are using and be in a better position to understand what is going wrong if problems occur.

> **TIP**
>
> There are different ways to do it, but the simplest is probably to use a packet capture tool such as `tcpTrace`.
>
> You can download this free utility from www.pocketsoap.com.
>
> `tcpTrace` captures TCP packets sent by client applications over a certain port, displays them in a window, and then forwards them to a specified destination. Once the destination receives and processes the packet, `tcpTrace` captures the response and forwards it back to the client.

The server for this example was built in Chapter 29, ".NET Remoting and Delphi." It listens for HTTP messages sent to port 8099.

This is depicted in Figure 30.2.

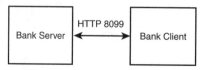

FIGURE 30.2   BankSample HTTP messaging.

In order to log the traffic using tcpTrace, we need to change from the original listening port 8099 to a different one (that is, 8231). This is illustrated in Figure 30.3.

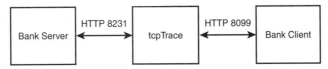

FIGURE 30.3   Rerouting for HTTP messages sent from port 8099 to port 8231.

On the project, the line

```
const def_HTTPPort : integer = 8099;
```

must be changed to

```
const def_HTTPPort : integer = 8231;
```

before recompiling and running it.

To have tcpTrace capture packets, you must launch it and enter the values, as shown in Figure 30.4, in the tcpTrace Settings dialog box.

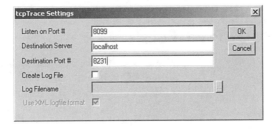

FIGURE 30.4   tcpTrace Settings dialog box.

After clicking OK, tcpTrace is ready to capture packets.

After launching BankClient.exe and clicking the Refresh button, tcpTrace will display the information shown in Figure 30.5.

The ListBox on the left shows the currently open connections. The panes on the left instead show the outgoing (top) and incoming (bottom) data for the client.

After clicking the Refresh button (or any other for that matter) in the bank client, you will not see new entries in the ListBox because the TCP connection is being kept open. tcpTrace will keep adding data to the memo boxes on the right. In order to see the new data, simply select the memo and scroll down.

30

FIGURE 30.5   tcpTrace window.

Analyzing the SOAP Packets

As you might have guessed by looking at the logged data, the client and server in the Bank project are using SOAP as messaging protocol. This is the default encoding .NET uses for remoting. You will see how to switch to binary encoding later in this chapter.

A SOAP message is an XML document formally called `Envelope` having the structure shown in Figure 30.6.

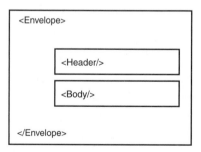

FIGURE 30.6   Envelope structure.

The SOAP Header part is optional and pretty much open for any use as of today. You can use headers to pass additional information related to the processing of the message and allow a SOAP message to be extended in an application-specific manner.

> **NOTE**
>
> Future uses of SOAP headers might include multiserver messaging (that is, server A receives the packet, does something, and then forwards the message to server B).

The SOAP Body is mandatory and basically describes the remote procedure call (the target service and method name along with its parameters).

Select the bank account 1 and click the button Retrieve. Listing 30.1 shows the SOAP envelope that will be generated and will result in a call to the method `BankManager.GetAccount()`.

LISTING 30.1   The SOAP Request

```
1:   <SOAP-ENV:Envelope xmlns:xsi="http://www.w3.org/2001/XMLSchema-instance"
➥xmlns:xsd="http://www.w3.org/2001/XMLSchema" xmlns:SOAP-
➥ENC="http://schemas.xmlsoap.org/soap/encoding/" xmlns:SOAP-
➥ENV="http://schemas.xmlsoap.org/soap/envelope/"
➥xmlns:clr="http://schemas.microsoft.com/soap/encoding/clr/1.0" SOAP-
➥ENV:encodingStyle="http://schemas.xmlsoap.org/soap/encoding/">
2:       <SOAP-ENV:Body>
3:         <i2:GetAccount id="ref-1"
➥xmlns:i2="http://schemas.microsoft.com/clr/nsassem/
➥BankShared.IBankManager/BankPackage">
4:           <AccountNumber>1</AccountNumber>
5:         </i2:GetAccount>
6:       </SOAP-ENV:Body>
7:   </SOAP-ENV:Envelope>
```

As you can see, SOAP Envelopes contain information such as the remote method name (line 3) and its parameters (line 4) along with their values. This information will be used by the server to locate the right server object and the right method to invoke.

The response message is another SOAP Envelope that contains the results. Listing 30.2 shows an example of a response message.

LISTING 30.2   The SOAP Response

```
1:   <SOAP-ENV:Envelope xmlns:xsi="http://www.w3.org/2001/XMLSchema-instance"
➥xmlns:xsd="http://www.w3.org/2001/XMLSchema" xmlns:SOAP-ENC="http://
➥schemas.xmlsoap.org/soap/encoding/" xmlns:SOAP-ENV="http://
➥schemas.xmlsoap.org/soap/envelope/" xmlns:clr="http://schemas.
➥microsoft.com/soap/encoding/clr/1.0" SOAP-ENV:encodingStyle="http://
➥schemas.xmlsoap.org/soap/encoding/">
2:     <SOAP-ENV:Body>
3:       <i2:GetAccountResponse id="ref-1" ➥xmlns:i2="http://
➥schemas.microsoft.com/clr/nsassem/
➥BankShared.IBankManager/BankPackage">
4:         <return href="#ref-4"/>
5:       </i2:GetAccountResponse>
6:     <a1:TAccount id="ref-4"
➥xmlns:a1="http://schemas.microsoft.com/clr/nsassem/BankShared/
➥BankPackage%2C%20Version%3D1.0.1436.24713%2C%20Culture%3Dneutral
➥%2C%20PublicKeyToken%3Dnull">
7:       <fNumber>1</fNumber>
```

30

LISTING 30.2   Continued

```
 8:    <fBalance>1999</fBalance>
 9:    <fName id="ref-5">John Smith</fName>
10:    </a1:TAccount>
11:    </SOAP-ENV:Body>
12:    </SOAP-ENV:Envelope>
```

If you look closely at Listing 30.2 you will see an XML representation of a TAccount instance and the value of its properties (lines 6 to 10). That instance is referenced at line 4 and associated with the return value of the call to the method GetAccount (line 5).

Finally, if an exception occurs, SOAP defines a special type of envelope that follows the structure shown in Figure 30.7.

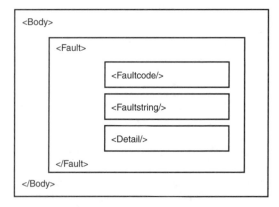

FIGURE 30.7   Envelope with exception.

To generate an error, simply type "13333" in the Bank Accounts ComboBox and click Refresh. The server will raise an exception because there isn't any account matching that code. The exception will then be wrapped in an SOAP error message and will be reraised on the client side.

Just as a reminder, the server-side method that returns account information and raised the exception was as simple as

```
function TBankManager.GetAccount(const AccountNumber: integer): TAccount;
begin
  case AccountNumber of
    1 : result := fAccount1;
    2 : result := fAccount2;
    else raise Exception.Create('Invalid account number!');
  end;

  with result do
    Writeln('A client requested account '+result.Number.ToString
➥+' ('+result.Name+')');
end;
```

As you can see, the SOAP formatting and exception propagation is done entirely outside the "business" code.

> **NOTE**
>
> If you're interested, you can read more about the SOAP specification at `http://www.w3c.org/2000/xp/Group/`.

Client Activation

The BankManager service shown in Chapter 29 is an example of a Server Activated Object (SAO).

Although SAOs are sufficient for most uses, they have a number of restrictions:

- SAOs don't enable clients to control when they are created.

- They are either just shared (singleton) or created on demand (per-call).

- SAOs don't enable per-client state to be preserved between subsequent method calls.

- You can only create SAOs using the default constructor.

There are cases in which these limitations are too restrictive.

Client activated objects (CAOs) provide you with an alternative solution. Client activation allows you to

- directly control when remote objects are created

- provide each client with a unique copy of the object and thus allow per-client state on the server

- issue subsequent method calls and be sure state is preserved between each

- create the remote objects with any constructor

The Factory Pattern

Client activated objects are best created using the factory pattern.

The factory pattern is a common approach used to help decouple object creation from a client. The basic idea is that clients invoke a method of a specialized object (the factory) whose purpose is to create and return other objects (the CAO in our case) to them. The method in the factory method can have any number of parameters, which generally match those of the constructor of the CAO class.

The example ClientActivated contained in the folder CAO contains an example of a factory object and how you can use it to create two separate instances of client activated TSimpleServer objects.

The project group for this example is shown in Figure 30.8.

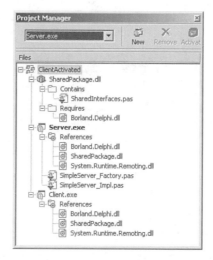

FIGURE 30.8   ClientActivated example project group.

The factory class is contained in the new unit `SimpleServer_Factory.pas` and is declared as follows:

```
TSimpleFactory = class(MarshalByRefObject, ISimpleFactory)
protected
  function NewInstance: ISimpleServer;
  function NewInstanceWithValue(Value: Integer): ISimpleServer;
end;
```

The interface `ISimpleFactory` had been previously declared and added to the `SharedPackage` as

```
ISimpleFactory = interface
  function NewInstance : ISimpleServer;
  function NewInstanceWithValue(Value : integer) : ISimpleServer;
end;
```

The client will use a remote instance of the factory object (SAO, singleton) to explicitly create instances of `SimpleServer` by using either one of the two `NewInstanceXXX` methods.

To enable the client to access the `SimpleFactory` object, we will need to register as a well-known service as we did in the BankExample with regard to `TBankManager`.

This code registers `TSimpleFactory`:

```
RemotingConfiguration.RegisterWellKnownServiceType(
  typeOf(TSimpleFactory),
  'SimpleFactory.soap',
  WellKnownObjectMode.Singleton);
```

Notice that we did not put any registration code for the class `TSimpleServer`. The remoting infrastructure doesn't need to be made aware of its existence because `SimpleFactory` will be the one that instantiates `SimpleServer(s)` objects.

This is instead the client code:

```
SimpleFactory := Activator.GetObject(
  typeof(ISimpleServer),
  'http://localhost:8099/SimpleFactory.soap');

SimpleSrv1 := SimpleFactory.NewInstanceWithValue(5);
SimpleSrv2 := SimpleFactory.NewInstance;
```

As you can see, the syntax necessary for using CAOs is identical to those for local objects.

Listings 30.3–30.7 show the full code of the most important units in the project group.

Listing 30.3 contains the definitions of the ISimpleServer and ISimpleFactory interfaces that are needed and referenced by both client and server applications.

LISTING 30.3   The Shared Interfaces

```
1:    unit SharedInterfaces;
2:
3:    interface
4:
5:    type
6:       ISimpleServer = interface
7:          function GetValue : integer;
8         procedure SetValue(Value : integer);
9:
10:        property Value : integer read GetValue write SetValue;
11:      end;
12:
13:      ISimpleFactory = interface
14:         function NewInstance : ISimpleServer;
15:         function NewInstanceWithValue(Value : integer) : ISimpleServer;
16:      end;
17:
18:   implementation
19:
20:   end.
```

▶ Find the code on the CD: \Chapter 30\Ex02.

Listing 30.4 contains the TSimpleServer implementation. The only difference from the original TSimpleServer unit contained in the RemotingTemplate is the console outputs, which will allow us to track what's happening when we create instances of the class and assign an integer value to the Value property. This output is shown later in Figure 30.9.

LISTING 30.4   TSimpleServer Implementation

```
1:    unit SimpleServer_Impl;
2:
3:    interface
4:
5:    uses
6:       SharedInterfaces;
7:
```

30

LISTING 30.4   Continued

```
 8:    type
 9:      { TSimpleServer }
10:      TSimpleServer = class(MarshalByRefObject, ISimpleServer)
11:      private
12:        fValue : integer;
13:
14:      protected
15:        function GetValue: Integer;
16:        procedure SetValue(Value: Integer);
17:
18:      public
19:        constructor Create; overload;
20:        constructor Create(Value : integer); overload;
21:      end;
22:
23:    implementation
24:
25:    { TSimpleServer }
26:
27:    constructor TSimpleServer.Create;
28:    begin
29:      inherited;
30:
31:      Console.WriteLine('Creating TSimpleServer with empty constructor');
32:    end;
33:
34:    constructor TSimpleServer.Create(Value: integer);
35:    begin
36:      inherited Create;
37:
38:      fValue := Value;
39:
40:      Console.WriteLine('Creating TSimpleServer with value '+
    ➥Int32(Value).ToString);
41:    end;
42:
43:    function TSimpleServer.GetValue: Integer;
44:    begin
45:      result := fValue;
46:
47:      Console.WriteLine('Getting value '+Int32(result).ToString);
48:    end;
49:
50:    procedure TSimpleServer.SetValue(Value: Integer);
51:    begin
52:      fValue := Value;
53:
54:      Console.WriteLine('Setting value '+Int32(Value).ToString);
55:    end;
56:
57:    end.
```

▶ Find the code on the CD: \Chapter 30\Ex02.

Listing 30.5 contains the implementation of the class TSimpleFactory that is registered as well known type.

LISTING 30.5   TSimpleFactory Implementation

```
1:   unit SimpleServer_Factory;
2:
3:   interface
4:
5:   uses
6:     SharedInterfaces;
7:
8   type
9:    TSimpleFactory = class(MarshalByRefObject, ISimpleFactory)
10:    protected
11      function NewInstance: ISimpleServer;
12:       function NewInstanceWithValue(Value: Integer): ISimpleServer;
13:
14:    end;
15:
16:
17:  implementation
18:
19:  uses SimpleServer_Impl;
20:
21:  { TSimpleFactory }
22:
23:  function TSimpleFactory.NewInstance: ISimpleServer;
24:  begin
25:    result := TSimpleServer.Create;
26:  end;
27:
28:  function TSimpleFactory.NewInstanceWithValue(
29:    Value: Integer): ISimpleServer;
30:  begin
31:    result := TSimpleServer.Create(Value);
32:  end;
33:
34:  end.
```

▶ Find the code on the CD: \Chapter 30\Ex02.

The concrete class TSimpleFactory is used only in the server application, and it is responsible for creating instances of the CAO TSimpleServer. Instances of TSimpleServer are returned as ISimpleServer by the methods NewInstance and NewInstanceWithValue.

Listing 30.6 contains the DPR file of the server project and shows how to register the TSimpleFactory object in the remoting infrastructure (see line 27).

As previously said, the class TSimpleServer is never registered.

The only things clients need in order to create CAOs using the factory pattern are: (1) their interface (included in the shared package), and (2) a class factory (registered as WellKnownServiceType as shown at line 28).

LISTING 30.6   Server DPR File

```
1:    program Server;
2:
3:    {$APPTYPE CONSOLE}
4:
5:    {...}
6:    {...}
7:    {%DelphiDotNetAssemblyCompiler 'SharedPackage.dll'}
8:
9:    uses
10:     SharedInterfaces,
11:     SimpleServer_Impl in 'SimpleServer_Impl.pas',
12:     System.Runtime.Remoting,
13:     System.Runtime.Remoting.Channels,
14:     System.Runtime.Remoting.Channels.HTTP,
15:     SimpleServer_Factory in 'SimpleServer_Factory.pas';
16:
17:    const def_HTTPPort : int32 = 8099;
18:    var Channel : HttpChannel;
19:    begin
20:      Writeln('Initializing server...');
21:
22:      // Initializes the server to listen for HTTP requests on a specific port
23:      Channel := HttpChannel.Create(def_HTTPPort);
24:      ChannelServices.RegisterChannel(Channel);
25:      Console.WriteLine('HTTP channel created. Listening on port '+
➥int32(def_HTTPPort).ToString);
26:
27:      // Registers the TSimpleFactory service
28:      RemotingConfiguration.RegisterWellKnownServiceType(
29:        typeOf(TSimpleFactory),
30:        'SimpleFactory.soap',
31:        WellKnownObjectMode.Singleton);
32:
33:      // Starts accepting requests
34:      Writeln('Waiting for requests...');
35:      Readln;
36:    end.
```

▶ Find the code on the CD: \Chapter 30\Ex02.

Listing 30.7 contains the DPR file of the client application. It shows how to register an HTTP channel to enable remote communication with the server (lines 21 and 22) and how to acquire a reference to the SimpleFactory object (lines 24–26).

LISTING 30.7   The Client DPR File

```
1:    program Client;
2:
3:    {$APPTYPE CONSOLE}
4:
5:    {..}
6:    {..}
7:    {%DelphiDotNetAssemblyCompiler 'SharedPackage.dll'}
```

LISTING 30.7   Continued

```
 8:
 9:   uses
10:     SysUtils,
11:     SharedInterfaces,
12:     System.Runtime.Remoting,
13:     System.Runtime.Remoting.Channels,
14:     System.Runtime.Remoting.Channels.HTTP;
15:
16:   var SimpleFactory : ISimpleFactory;
17:       SimpleSrv1,
18:       SimpleSrv2 : ISimpleServer;
19:       Channel : HttpChannel;
20:   begin
21:     Channel := HttpChannel.Create(0);
22:     ChannelServices.RegisterChannel(Channel);
23:
24:     SimpleFactory := Activator.GetObject(
25:       typeof(ISimpleFactory),
26:       'http://localhost:8099/SimpleFactory.soap');
27:
28:     SimpleSrv1 := SimpleFactory.NewInstanceWithValue(5);
29:     SimpleSrv2 := SimpleFactory.NewInstance;
30:
31:     Writeln('SimpleServer1''s value is '+IntToStr(SimpleSrv1.Value));
32:     Writeln('SimpleServer2''s value is '+IntToStr(SimpleSrv2.Value));
33:     Writeln('Setting simpleServer2''s value to 2');
34:     SimpleSrv2.Value := 2;
35:     Writeln('SimpleServer2''s value is '+IntToStr(SimpleSrv2.Value));
36:     Writeln('SimpleServer1''s value is '+IntToStr(SimpleSrv1.Value));
37:     Writeln('Press enter to terminate');
38:     Readln;
39:   end.
```

▶ Find the code on the CD: \Chapter 30\Ex02.

SimpleFactory will then be used to create instances of SimpleServer CAOs using the two NewInstanceXXX methods (lines 28 and 29).

Finally, the code will demonstrate how the two variables SimpleSrv1 and SimpleSrv2 are really pointing to two separate server-side instances and the assignment to the Value property results in different readings (lines 31–37).

The Example at Runtime

The following screenshots show you what happens when the server and client applications are executed.

Figure 30.9 shows the output of the server application.

Compare the screen output with the code shown in Listings 30.4 and 30.6.

30

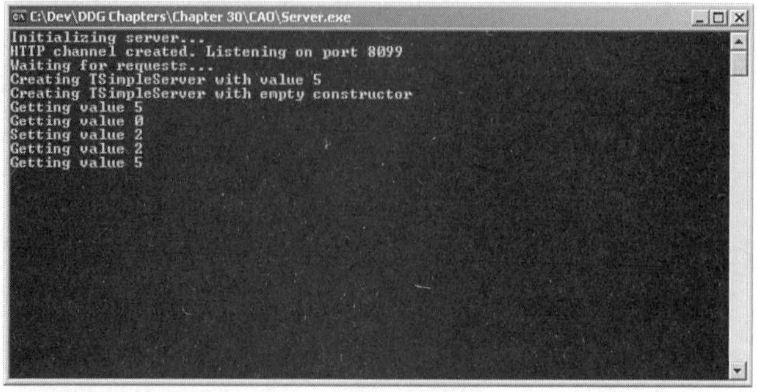

FIGURE 30.9   The server at runtime.

Figure 30.10 shows the output of the client application. Refer to the code shown in Listing 30.7 when looking at this screen.

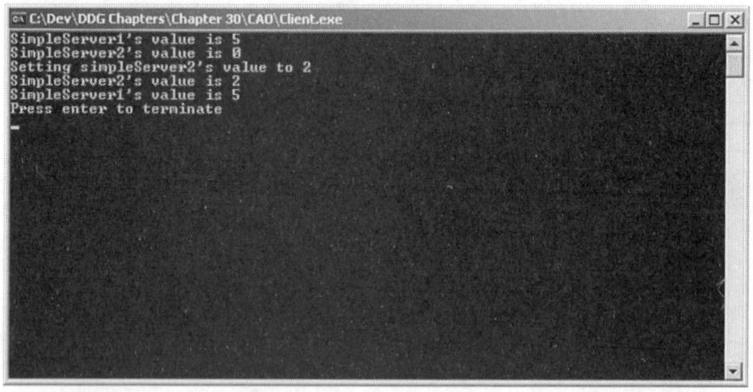

FIGURE 30.10   The client at runtime.

Notice how the values are correctly preserved by the two separate instances of SimpleServer.

Problems of CAOs

CAOs are simple to write and use, but—from a server perspective—they can be very resource intensive.

To illustrate this, imagine if you had 1,000 concurrent users each running the client application: The server would need to create 2,000 instances of TSimpleServer none of which would be destroyed until: (1) their lease is expired, and (2) the .NET garbage collector decided to kick in.

A simple example similar to that shown in this chapter would likely not have problems even with 2,000 clients. However, if you start to use database connections, allocate memory in each CAO, and so on, performance and responsiveness will be quickly affected.

Distributed systems based on CAOs (or stateful objects in general) are not scalable. Each CAO is bound to a particular server until it is destroyed, and subsequent method calls cannot be load balanced.

Be conservative when using CAOs and try to avoid using them except when strictly necessary or you have a small number of concurrent clients.

Lifetime Management

Managing the lifetime of a remote object is complex, but having control over when to release server resources is essential to the scalability and efficiency of any distributed system.

Historically, DCOM used a combination of reference counting and network pinging in order to determine when to free objects. While this technique worked decently enough in LAN's with few clients, it resulted in problems when the number of clients increased (think in thousands) and was practically unfeasible over the Internet.

.NET uses a completely different approach and gives you direct control of the lifetime of your objects.

Whenever a MarshalByRefObject object is created, the .NET Framework calls its virtual method InitializeLifetimeService(), which, in turn, returns an object implementing the interface ILease.

ILease is declared as

```
ILease = interface
  function get_CurrentLeaseTime: TimeSpan;
  function get_CurrentState: LeaseState;

  procedure set_InitialLeaseTime(value: TimeSpan);
  function get_InitialLeaseTime: TimeSpan;

  function get_RenewOnCallTime: TimeSpan;
  procedure set_RenewOnCallTime(value: TimeSpan);

  function get_SponsorshipTimeout: TimeSpan;
  procedure set_SponsorshipTimeout(value: TimeSpan);

  procedure Register(obj: ISponsor; renewalTime: TimeSpan); overload;
  procedure Register(obj: ISponsor); overload;
  function Renew(renewalTime: TimeSpan): TimeSpan;
  procedure Unregister(obj: ISponsor);

  property CurrentLeaseTime: TimeSpan read get_CurrentLeaseTime;
  property CurrentState: LeaseState read get_CurrentState;
  property InitialLeaseTime: TimeSpan read get_InitialLeaseTime
    write set_InitialLeaseTime;
  property RenewOnCallTime: TimeSpan read get_RenewOnCallTime
    write set_RenewOnCallTime;
  property SponsorshipTimeout: TimeSpan read get_SponsorshipTimeout
    write set_SponsorshipTimeout;
end;
```

The ILease interface contains all the methods necessary for the remoting infrastructure to determine when a remote object is ready to be garbage collected. Each application domain embeds a lease manager that is aware of every lease in the domain and periodically checks its expiration time. Whenever a lease is expired, the remoting infrastructure will ask a sponsor (an object implementing ISponsor such as TSimpleFactory in our example) to renew the lease by invoking the method Renewal.

ISponsor instead is declared as

```
ISponsor = interface
  function Renewal(lease: ILease): TimeSpan;
end;
```

If the call to Renewal doesn't result in a lease renewal, the ILease object is removed from the list of leases managed by the lease manager. This will ensure that the remote object is garbage collected.

Sponsors are objects that are periodically asked to renew their leases. If that doesn't happen and the lease expires, the sponsored object is disconnected from the remoting infrastructure. After that, it will be available for garbage collection.

The SponsorAndLease project shows how to add ISponsor support to MarshalByRefObjects.

The SimpleServerFactory_Impl.pas unit contains the following changes:

```
uses
  SharedInterfaces,
  SimpleServer_Impl,
  System.Runtime.Remoting.Lifetime; // Contains the definition of ISponsor

type
  TSimpleFactory = class(MarshalByRefObject, ISimpleFactory, ISponsor)
[..]
  public
    function InitializeLifetimeService: System.Object; override;
    function Renewal(lease: ILease): TimeSpan;
  end;
```

▶ Find the code on the CD: \Chapter 30\Ex03.

This is the implementation of InitializeLifetimeService() in which we get a reference to a lease and initialize it to last five minutes:

```
function TSimpleFactory.InitializeLifetimeService: System.Object;
var lease : ILease;
begin
  Writeln('Initializing lifetime service for TSimpleFactory');
  lease := inherited InitializeLifetimeService() as ILease;
  if (lease.CurrentState = LeaseState.Initial) then begin
    lease.InitialLeaseTime := TimeSpan.FromMinutes(5);
    lease.Register(Self);
  end;
  result := lease;
end;
```

▶ Find the code on the CD: \Chapter 30\Ex03.

The following code is the implementation of the method `Renewal` in which we constantly renew the lease for an extra five minutes at a time:

```
function TSimpleFactory.Renewal(lease: ILease): TimeSpan;
begin
  writeln('Request for renewal for TSimpleFactory');
  lease.Renew(TimeSpan.FromMinutes(5));
end;
```

▶ Find the code on the CD: `\Chapter 30\Ex03`.

Similar code is added to the implementation of the CAO `TSimpleServer`.

Figure 30.11 shows the output from this server.

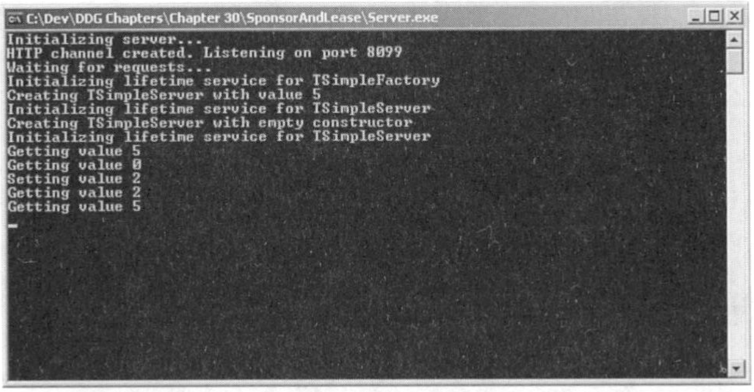

FIGURE 30.11   Server output.

Notice how the lifetime service initialization is performed immediately after the creation of the objects.

Figure 30.12 shows the client activity.

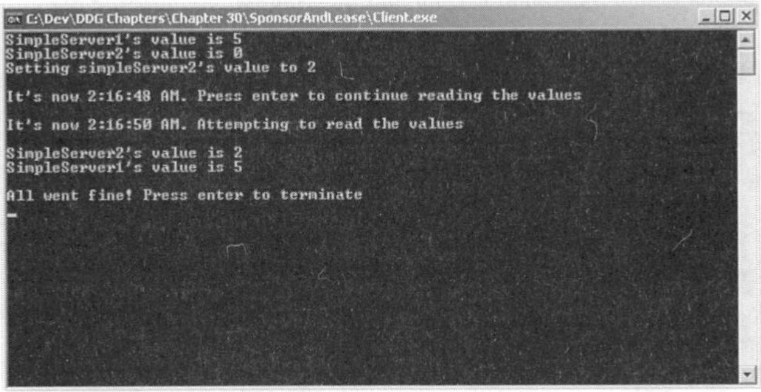

FIGURE 30.12   Client activity.

Notice how waiting for two seconds before rereading the `SimpleServer(s)` values didn't result in any destruction or re-initialization. Those two instances will remain alive and will keep renewing their leases every five minutes.

30

Failing to Renew the Lease

As previously said, if you fail to renew a lease, the remote object is removed from the remoting infrastructure and released for garbage collection.

Although this doesn't ensure that the object will be freed immediately, it guarantees that any subsequent call to it will fail.

To illustrate this, you can modify the unit SimpleServer_Impl.pas, by commenting out the line where it renews the lease. It will look as shown below:

```
function TSimpleServer.Renewal(Lease: ILease): TimeSpan;
begin
  writeln('Request for renewal for TSimpleServer');
  // Comment the following line to prevent lease renewal
  // Lease.Renew(TimeSpan.FromMinutes(LeaseDurationInMinutes));
end;
```

▶ Find the code on the CD: \Chapter 30\Ex03.

By doing this, the lease for the CAO SimpleServer now will not be renewed. If you now wait five minutes (or modify your clock time to simulate this), when the client prompts you to click Enter to read the values, it will raise an exception.

Figure 30.13 demonstrates this.

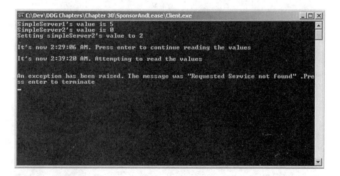

FIGURE 30.13   Client exception.

Configuration Files

Although it's simple to specify the HTTP and TCP settings you want to use with .NET remoting, production systems often need to be configurable.

.NET remoting includes support for so-called configuration files. These are XML files formatted according to the structure shown in Listing 30.8.

LISTING 30.8   The Structure of .NET Remoting Configuration XML Files

```
<configuration>
  <system.runtime.remoting>
    <application>
```

LISTING 30.8 Continued

```
                <lifetime>
                <channels> (Instance)
                    <channel> (Instance)
                        <serverProviders> (Instance)
                            <provider> (Instance)
                            <formatter> (Instance)
                        <clientProviders> (Instance)
                            <provider> (Instance)
                            <formatter> (Instance)
                <client>
                    <wellknown> (Client Instance)
                    <activated> (Client Instance)
                <service>
                    <wellknown> (Service Instance)
                    <activated> (Service Instance)
                <soapInterop>
                    <interopXmlType>
                    <interopXmlElement>
                    <preLoad>
        <channels> (Template)
            <channel> (Template)
                <serverProviders> (Instance)
                    <provider> (Instance)
                    <formatter> (Instance)
                <clientProviders> (Instance)
                    <provider> (Instance)
                    <formatter> (Instance)
        <channelSinkProviders>
                <serverProviders> (Template)
                    <provider> (Template)
                    <formatter> (Template)
                <clientProviders> (Template)
                    <provider> (Template)
                    <formatter> (Template)
        <customErrors>
        <debug>
```

> **NOTE**
>
> Refer to http://msdn.microsoft.com/library/default.asp?url=/library/en-us/cpgenref/
> html/gnconRemotingSettingsSchema.asp for a detailed description of each element.

The various nodes in these files allow you to configure all the aspects of remoting—from the channels you want to use (HTTP or TCP for instance), the services you want to expose or access, their lifetime settings, and so on.

You can apply XML configuration files by calling the `RemotingConfiguration.Configure()` method and specifying the name of a file as parameter.

The example `ConfigFiles` shows how to use remoting configuration files on both server and client ends.

The example will also illustrate how to use configuration files on the client.

Server Configuration

Listing 30.9 shows the XML document with the contents of the file `Server.Config.xml` contained in the project's folder.

LISTING 30.9   Server Configuration File

```
1:   <configuration>
2:     <system.runtime.remoting>
3:       <application>
4:         <channels>
5:           <channel ref="tcp"  port="8231" />
6:           <channel ref="http" port="8099" />
7:         </channels>
8:         <service>
9:           <wellknown type="SimpleServer_Factory.TSimpleFactory, Server"
10:                 mode="Singleton"
11:               objectUri="SimpleFactory.soap" />
12:         </service>
13:       </application>
14:     </system.runtime.remoting>
15:  </configuration>
```

▶ Find the code on the CD: \Chapter 30\Ex04.

When used, this configuration file will instruct the remoting infrastructure to create a TCP and a HTTP channel listening respectively on port 8231 and 8099.

It will also register the class TSimpleFactory as the WellKnown, singleton object that handles requests sent referencing the URI "SimpleFactory.soap".

Listing 30.10 shows how simpler the server becomes when using configuration files similar to the one shown in Listing 30.9.

LISTING 30.10   Server DPR Using Configuration Files

```
1:   uses
2:     SharedInterfaces,
3:     SimpleServer_Impl in 'SimpleServer_Impl.pas',
4:     System.Runtime.Remoting,
5:     System.Runtime.Remoting.Channels,
6:     System.Runtime.Remoting.Channels.HTTP,
7:     SimpleServer_Factory in 'SimpleServer_Factory.pas';
8:
9:   begin
10:    Writeln('Initializing server by reading the configuration file');
11:    RemotingConfiguration.Configure('Server.config.xml');
12:
13:    // Starts accepting requests
14:    Writeln('Waiting for requests...');
15:    Readln;
16:  end.
```

▶ Find the code on the CD: \Chapter 30\Ex04.

Compare this code with the one shown in Listing 30.6 to see the advantages of using configuration files.

It's worth noticing that configuration files don't necessarily have to contain both service and channel information. You could use them to configure just what you need to make dynamic.

For instance, you could omit the `"<service>"` node from the XML configuration file and still register it as we did at line 29 of Listing 30.6.

You can now start the client of the Client Activation example against this server and it will work just fine, as with the original server.

Client Configuration

Client configuration files are structurally similar to those used server side, but they contain slightly different information.

Listing 30.11 shows the XML configuration file used client side.

LISTING 30.11   Client Configuration File

```
1:  <configuration>
2:     <system.runtime.remoting>
3:        <application>
4:           <client>
5:              <wellknown type="SharedInterfaces.ISimpleFactory, SharedPackage"
6:                         url="http://localhost:8099/SimpleFactory.soap" />
7:           </client>
8:        </application>
9:     </system.runtime.remoting>
10: </configuration>
```

▶ Find the code on the CD: `\Chapter 30\Ex04`.

The first thing to notice is that the client configuration registers the interface type `ISimpleFactory` rather than the class `TSimpleFactory` like the server did.

Clients don't have any knowledge of the actual class implementing remote interfaces. To make them aware of the existence of classes such as `TSimpleServer`, we would have to deploy their assemblies on the clients.

Although doable, that would violate the most basic principle of distributed architectures, which is strongly recommended against.

Before we continue, we must take a step back and look at following code taken from the client's `.dpr` file of the Client Activation example:

```
var SimpleFactory : ISimpleFactory;
[..]
    Channel : HttpChannel;
begin
  Channel := HttpChannel.Create(0);
  ChannelServices.RegisterChannel(Channel);
```

```
SimpleFactory := Activator.GetObject(
  typeof(ISimpleFactory),
  'http://localhost:8099/SimpleFactory.soap');
```

In this code, the method `Activator.GetObject()` creates a proxy for a server-activated, well-known object implementing `ISimpleFactory`, which then gets assigned to the variable `SimpleFactory`.

Activator defines two overload versions of the method `GetObject()`.

The one we use has the following declaration:

```
function GetObject(type : System.Type; url : string) : System.Object;
```

The second instead is defined as

```
function GetObject(type : System.Type; url : string;
➥state : System.Object) : System.Object;
```

The problem with both versions is that they require the URL parameter to be specified. Setting the URL as an empty string will generate an exception, and the application will terminate.

The goal in this example is to remove the need for the URL parameter and have that read from the configuration file.

There doesn't seem to be a direct way to do this using the `Activator` class, and the solution for this problem is to create and use a helper class: `TRemotingHelper`.

How to Create Proxies without Specifying URLs Using the TRemotingHelper Class

When you call the method `RemotingConfiguration.Configure`, the remoting infrastructure is updated and is made aware of the configuration settings specified in your XML file.

By using the properties and methods of `RemotingConfiguration`, you can then access this information dynamically from your application.

`TRemotingHelper` extends the functionality of the standard `Activator` class by accessing the remoting configuration and allows us to create proxies without specifying any URL thanks to the method `GetRemoteObjectRef()`.

`GetRemoteObjectRef()` is declared as follows:

```
function GetRemoteObjectRef(aType : system.type) : TObject;
```

Client applications will invoke this method by just specifying the type of interface they need (in this case, `ISimpleFactory`) and by typecasting the resulting `TObject` to that interface. This is an example of its use:

```
SimpleFactory := RemotingHelper.GetRemoteObjectRef(
    typeof(SharedInterfaces.ISimpleFactory));
```

The `TRemotingHelper` class is very simple. To use it, simply issue a `RemotingConfiguration.Configure` call, create an instance of `TRemotingHelper`, and invoke the method `GetRemoteObjectRef()`.

The following code illustrates this:

```
RemotingConfiguration.Configure('Client.Config.xml');
RemotingHelper := TRemotingHelper.Create;
SimpleFactory := RemotingHelper.GetRemoteObjectRef(
  typeof(SharedInterfaces.ISimpleFactory));
```

The first time you call the method GetRemoteObjectRef(), TRemotingHelper will read the list of the names and URLs of all the remoting types known to the client (in this case, it would be ISimpleFactory and 'http://localhost:8099/SimpleFactory.soap') and store both entries (system.type and URL) in an IDictionary field called fWellKnownTypes.

fWellKnownTypes will then be used to locate the target URL by using the system.type parameter specified in the call to GetRemoteObjectRef.

After GetRemoteObjectRef() collects this information, TRemotingHelper has all the information required to call the original Activator.GetObject(), specifying the needed URL on our behalf.

Listing 30.12 shows the code of the server DPR file. (The file Server.config.xml was previously shown in Listing 30.9.)

LISTING 30.12   The Server DPR File

```
1:    program Server;
2:
3:    {$APPTYPE CONSOLE}
4:
5:    {...}
6:    {...}
7:    {%DelphiDotNetAssemblyCompiler 'SharedPackage.dll'}
8:
9:    uses
10:     SharedInterfaces,
11:     SimpleServer_Impl in 'SimpleServer_Impl.pas',
12:     System.Runtime.Remoting,
13:     System.Runtime.Remoting.Channels,
14:     System.Runtime.Remoting.Channels.HTTP,
15:     SimpleServer_Factory in 'SimpleServer_Factory.pas';
16:
17:   var args : System.Array;
18:       filename : string = 'Server.Config.xml';
19:   begin
20:     // Reads the command line arguments
21:     args := Environment.GetCommandLineArgs;
22:     if args.Length>1 then
23:       filename := args.GetValue(1).ToString+filename;
24:
25:     // Configures the remoting infrastructure
26:     Console.WriteLine('Initializing the server by reading the file '+filename);
27:
28:     RemotingConfiguration.Configure(filename);
29:
30:     // Starts accepting requests
31:     Console.WriteLine('Waiting for requests...');
```

30

LISTING 30.12   Continued

```
32:    Console.ReadLine;
33:  end.
```

▶ Find the code on the CD: \Chapter 30\Ex04.

As you can see, the registration of the HTTP channel and TSimpleFactory has been completely replaced by the call to RemotingConfiguration.Configure('Server.config.xml').

Listing 30.13 contains the full source code of the TRemotingHelper class.

LISTING 30.13   The RemotingHelper Class

```
1:    unit RemotingHelper;
2:
3:    interface
4:
5:    uses
6:      System.Collections,
7:      System.Runtime.Remoting;
8:
9:    type
10:     { TRemotingHelper }
11:     TRemotingHelper = class
12:     private
13:       fIsInitialized : boolean;
14:       fWellKnownTypes : IDictionary;
15:
16:       procedure InitTypeCache;
17:     public
18:       function GetRemoteObjectRef(aType : system.type) : TObject;
19:     end;
20:
21:
22:    implementation
23:
24:    { TRemotingHelper }
25:
26:    function TRemotingHelper.GetRemoteObjectRef(aType: system.type): TObject;
27:    var entry : WellKnownClientTypeEntry;
28:    begin
29:      if not fIsInitialized
30:        then InitTypeCache;
31:
32:      entry := fWellKnownTypes[aType] as WellKnownClientTypeEntry;
33:
34:      if (entry=NIL)
35:        then raise Exception.Create('Type not found!');
36:
37:      result := Activator.GetObject(entry.ObjectType,entry.ObjectUrl);
38:    end;
39:
40:    procedure TRemotingHelper.InitTypeCache;
41:    var i : integer;
```

LISTING 30.13   Continued

```
42:       arr : array of WellKnownClientTypeEntry;
43:       entry : WellKnownClientTypeEntry;
44:  begin
45:     fWellKnownTypes := Hashtable.Create;
46:
47:     arr := RemotingConfiguration.GetRegisteredWellKnownClientTypes;
48:     for i := 0 to Length(arr)-1 do begin
49:       entry := arr[i];
50:       fWellKnownTypes.Add(entry.ObjectType, entry);
51:     end;
52:
53:     fIsInitialized := TRUE;
54:  end;
55:
56:  end.s
```

▶ Find the code on the CD: \Chapter 30\Ex04.

This class makes use of a standard .NET IDictionary (private field fWellKnownTypes) to represent the collection of System.Type and url pairs associated with the remote services. The dictionary is created by using the class HashTable at line 45, which implements IDictionary.

The values stored in the dictionary are read directly from the remoting configuration through the call to RemotingConfiguration.GetRegisteredWellKnownClientTypes at line 47.

GetRegisteredWellKnownClientTypes is declared as

```
Function RemotingConfiguration.GetRegisteredWellKnownClientTypes :
array of WellKnownClientTypeEntry:
```

Keep in mind that in order to use this class, you need to first call RemotingConfigure. Configure. This is done in the client DPR file shown in line 30 of Listing 30.14.

Listing 30.14 shows the full source of the client application. Notice how we read the configuration file; we never need to create a channel and don't directly use the Activator class anymore.

This remoting parameters used by the client application are entirely contained in the XML file shown in Listing 30.11.

LISTING 30.14   The Client DPR Files

```
1:   program Client;
2:
3:   {$APPTYPE CONSOLE}
4:
5:   {..}
6:   {..}
7:   {%DelphiDotNetAssemblyCompiler 'SharedPackage.dll'}
8:
9:   uses
10:     SharedInterfaces,
11:     System.Runtime.Remoting,
```

30

LISTING 30.14   Continued

```
12:     System.Runtime.Remoting.Channels,
13:     System.Runtime.Remoting.Channels.HTTP,
14:     RemotingHelper in 'RemotingHelper.pas';
15:
16:  var SimpleFactory : ISimpleFactory;
17:      SimpleSrv1,
18:      SimpleSrv2 : ISimpleServer;
19:      RemotingHelper : TRemotingHelper;
20:  var args : System.Array;
21:      filename : string = 'Client.Config.xml';
22:  begin
23:     // Reads the command line arguments
24:     args := Environment.GetCommandLineArgs;
25:     if args.Length>1 then
26:       filename := args.GetValue(1).ToString+filename;
27:
28:     // Configures the remoting infrastructure
29:     Console.WriteLine('Initializing the client by reading the file '+
➥filename);
30:     RemotingConfiguration.Configure(filename);
31:
32:     RemotingHelper := TRemotingHelper.Create;
33:
34:     SimpleFactory := RemotingHelper.GetRemoteObjectRef(
35:       typeof(SharedInterfaces.ISimpleFactory));
36:
37:     SimpleSrv1 := SimpleFactory.NewInstanceWithValue(5);
38:     SimpleSrv2 := SimpleFactory.NewInstance;
39:
40:     Console.WriteLine('SimpleServer1''s value is '+Int32(SimpleSrv1.Value).
➥ToString);
41:     Console.WriteLine('SimpleServer2''s value is '+Int32(SimpleSrv2.Value).
➥ToString);
42:     Console.WriteLine('Setting simpleServer2''s value to 2');
43:     SimpleSrv2.Value := 2;
44:     Console.WriteLine('SimpleServer2''s value is '+Int32(SimpleSrv2.Value).
➥ToString);
45:     Console.WriteLine('SimpleServer1''s value is '+Int32(SimpleSrv1.Value).
➥ToString);
46:     Console.WriteLine('Press enter to terminate');
47:     Console.ReadLine;
48:  end.
```

▶ Find the code on the CD: \Chapter 30\Ex04.

It is important to notice that we also made a small change to the units
SimpleServer_Factory.pas and SimpleServer_Impl.pas by adding the compiler directives:

```
[assembly: RuntimeRequiredAttribute(TypeOf(TSimpleFactory))]
```

and

```
[assembly: RuntimeRequiredAttribute(TypeOf(TSimpleServer))]
```

These directives were added right below the implementation keyword in the respective units and instruct the Delphi linker not to remove the references to the classes TSimpleServer and TSimpleServerFactory even if the classes were never directly or indirectly referenced in the .dpr file.

Switching from HTTP to TCP Communication

The HTTP protocol is ideal when trying to send data through firewalls or over the Internet, but when your goal is to achieve the maximum communication speed, TCP communication will probably be a better candidate. .NET remoting allows you to switch communication channels by simply changing a few configuration parameters.

> **NOTE**
>
> The server configuration file shown in Listing 30.16 instructs the server to listen for HTTP messages on port 8099 and TCP messages on port 8231.

The client is instead configured to use HTTP messages because of the value of the url attribute in the well-known node (http://localhost:8099/SimpleFactory.soap).

To make it use a TCP channel, simply change that to "tcp://localhost:8231/SimpleFactory.soap" as in Listing 30.15.

LISTING 30.15   Client Configuration File Using a TCP Channel on Port 8231

```
1:   <configuration>
2:     <system.runtime.remoting>
3:       <application>
4:         <client>
5:           <wellknown type="SharedInterfaces.ISimpleFactory, SharedPackage"
6:                      url="tcp://localhost:8231/SimpleFactory.soap" />
7:         </client>
8:       </application>
9:     </system.runtime.remoting>
10:  </configuration>
```

▶ Find the code on the CD: \Chapter 30\Ex04.

> **TIP**
>
> If you would like to stop the server from listening on the TCP channel, simply remove the node "<channel ref="tcp"   port="8231"   />" from the *server* configuration file.

Switching from SOAP to Binary Remoting

Through the use of configuration files, we can also switch from SOAP encoding (the default one used by the .NET Framework) to the more efficient binary one.

In order to do this, we need to register the binary provider under the node "channels" in both configuration files.

30

The new server configuration file is shown in Listing 30.16.

LISTING 30.16   Server Configuration File for Binary Encoding

```
1:  <configuration>
2:    <system.runtime.remoting>
3:      <application>
4:        <channels>
5:          <channel ref="tcp"  port="8231" />
6:          <channel ref="http" port="8099">
7:            <serverProviders>
8:              <formatter ref="binary" />
9:            </serverProviders>
10:         </channel>
11:       </channels>
12:       <service>
13:         <wellknown type="SimpleServer_Factory.TSimpleFactory, Server"
14:               mode="Singleton"
15:               objectUri="SimpleFactory.soap" />
16:       </service>
17:     </application>
18:   </system.runtime.remoting>
19: </configuration>
```

▶ Find the code on the CD: \Chapter 30\Ex04.

As you can see, parameters such as port numbers (line 5 and 6), the activation mode (line 14), and more can be easily specified by just using XML configuration files.

The matching client configuration file is shown in Listing 30.17.

LISTING 30.17   Client Configuration File for Binary Encoding

```
1:  configuration>
2:    <system.runtime.remoting>
3:        <application>
4:        <channels>
5:          <channel ref="http">
6:              <clientProviders>
7:              <formatter ref="binary" />
8:            </clientProviders>
9:            </channel>
10:       </channels>
11:
12:       <client>
13:         <wellknown type="SharedInterfaces.ISimpleFactory, SharedPackage"
14:                 url="http://localhost:8099/SimpleFactory.soap" />
15:       </client>
16:       </application>
17:     </system.runtime.remoting>
18: </configuration>
```

▶ Find the code on the CD: \Chapter 30\Ex04.

Differences Between SOAP and Binary Encoding

It's worth examining the differences between SOAP and binary encoding using `tcpTrace` now.

The example folder contains two configuration file pairs (`Binary*.Config.xml` and `SOAP*.Config.xml`).

You can instruct the server and client application to load either one by specifying the command-line argument `"SOAP"` or `"Binary"`.

These files will instruct the client to send messages via HTTP using port 8001 and the server to listen on ports 8099 as usual.

Configure `tcpTrace` to use the options shown in Figure 30.14 and launch the applications to see the exchanged data.

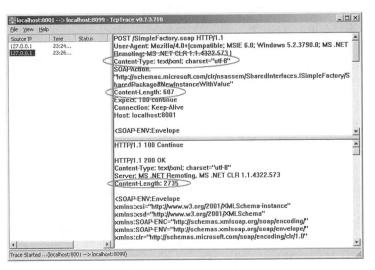

FIGURE 30.14   tcpTrace settings dialog box.

Figure 30.15 is a screenshot of a SOAP data exchange.

FIGURE 30.15   SOAP data exchange screenshot.

Compare the circled Content-Type and Content-Length values with those of Figure 30.16 to understand the overhead of SOAP messaging.

Figure 30.16 is a screenshot of a data exchange done using binary messaging.

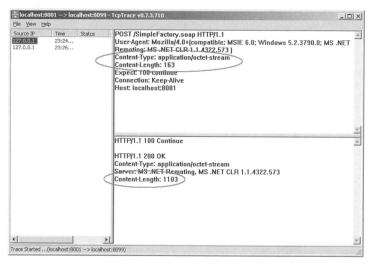

FIGURE 30.16   Binary data exchange screenshot.

Compare the circled Content-Type and Content-Length values with those of Figure 30.15 to see how binary messaging can help you save bandwidth.

The difference in size between the two data packets (see Content-Length header) is significant: 607 bytes versus 163 for the request and 2735 versus 1103 for the response.

The choice of the correct formatter is crucial in developing efficient .NET applications. Although SOAP might be fast enough in local area networks, its overhead will most likely create problems when using modem connections.

Similar considerations apply to TCP versus HTTP channels: TCP is faster than HTTP and can provide a better solution to performance critical systems. HTTP instead is better suited to systems in which firewalls are monitoring network traffic.

In general, it is good practice to make your own .NET clients use binary messaging over TCP and use SOAP over HTTP whenever your services need to be accessed from Java, Win32, or any other non .NET application.

Because the server applications can have more than one channel active at the same time, it really isn't difficult to get the best of both worlds at the same time.

TIP

Given the constraints of Chapters 29 and 30, we can't diverge in to more advanced topics. However, if you want to become more knowledgeable about the subject, you can use the following resources:

The MSDN Online at www.msdn.microsoft.com

Advanced .NET Remoting by Ingo Rammer, APress and his Web site at http://www.ingorammer.com

Microsoft .NET Distributed Applications: Integrating XML Web Services and .NET Remoting by Matthew Macdonald, Microsoft Press

---

CHAPTER 31

Securing ASP.NET Applications

IN THIS CHAPTER

- ASP.NET Security Methods
- Authentication
- Authorization
- Signing Off

Security is a major topic, particularly as it relates to Web-based applications. Web applications that aren't secure are highly vulnerable to IP theft, network attacks, data corruption, and more. These are only a few of the potential hazards that can occur when your security layers have been breached. Several layers of security should be employed, and this chapter touches on one of them—that is, securing your ASP.NET applications.

> **NOTE**
>
> For information on the various security measures that you can take beyond just writing secure applications, visit www.microsoft.com/security.

ASP.NET Security Methods

Two primary aspects of ASP.NET security exist that you should know about—authentication and authorization. Authentication is the process of discovering and verifying the identity and roles of a user. Through authentication, the user either has or does not have access to the resource. Authorization uses a user's identity and roles to determine what resources and at what level the user has access to.

> **NOTE**
>
> For the purpose of this discussion, I am referring to user access to external systems. We developers tend to write applications for ourselves, and security is an often overlooked or deferred feature. When developing applications that aren't going to run on just your box, it is paramount that security is a feature that is dealt with up front in the design and implementation and not left on the back burner until there's more time.

Authentication

Three forms of authentication exist in ASP.NET. These are Integrated Windows Authentication, Forms Authentication, and Passport Authentication. A forth, which is not really an authentication mode, is none. This chapter primarily discusses the first two methods. It will only touch on the Passport authentication model.

Configuring ASP.NET's Authentication Model

You can specify the authentication model that your ASP.NET application will use in the `web.config` file as shown here:

```
<configuration>
  <system.web>
    <authentication mode="Windows" />
  </system.web>
</configuration>
```

Windows Authentication

Before getting into how to secure your application through ASP.NET, now is a good time for a primer on the Windows role-based security model.

In Windows, you grant users access to the system via an identity. Some refer to this as a user account. You have the ability to grant an identity access to various resources within the system or to the system itself (authentication). After access is granted, you can give each identity varying capabilities (authorization). For instance, an identity may have access to a certain directory on a system, but this identity may only be able to read files from that directory. On the other hand, another identity may have read/write access to the same directory. This represents different levels of authorization.

Rather than granting users' capabilities within the system based on their identities, it is preferred to assign an identity to a role or to multiple roles. Figure 31.1 shows the User dialog box, which contains the Group in which they belong.

Three forms of Windows authentication exist—Basic, Digest, and NTLM. This section discusses each of these options.

Windows NTLM authentication is only valid for Internet Explorer. Therefore, it is only suitable when you can control the users who will hit your site. NTLM authentication is widely used with intranets because it does not work across proxy servers.

Under Windows authentication, when IIS receives a request from a client, it can handle the authentication itself or it can defer authentication to ASP.NET. The former is what this section is about. When IIS handles the authentication, it uses the Window's user accounts to determine user access.

To configure your site for Windows authentication, you must first modify the `web.config` file for your site as shown here:

```
<configuration>
  <system.web>
    <authentication mode="Windows" />
```

```
    </system.web>
</configuration>
```

▶ Find the code on the CD: \Code\Chapter 31\Ex01.

FIGURE 31.1   Users dialog box.

Additionally, you must disable anonymous access to the site through IIS by launching the properties dialog box for your site. You must select the Directory Security tab. From there, you click the Edit button in the Anonymous Access and Authentication tool section. This launches the Authentication Methods dialog box (see Figure 31.2).

FIGURE 31.2   Authentication Methods dialog box.

You must uncheck the Anonymous Access check box. You must also check the Basic Authentication and uncheck the Integrated Windows Authentication check boxes.

After performing these steps, when trying to hit the Web site, you will be presented with the dialog box shown in Figure 31.3.

After the user enters the correct credentials, he is allowed to view the Web page requested. The credentials that the user enters are compared against those that exist within the user accounts maintained on the server hosting the Web site.

FIGURE 31.3   Dialog box requesting username and password from a Web site.

What actually occurs with Basic authentication is this. When the browser requests a page from IIS on the server, IIS responds with a "401 Unauthorized" code. The browser understands this and presents the user with the login dialog box shown in Figure 31.3. If the user enters the correct credentials, he is granted access to the Web page. If the user's credentials are incorrect, the browser displays the login dialog box again.

A drawback to Basic authentication is that the information is sent from the client browser to the server in text format. This is an unacceptable level of security in many circumstances. An alternate form of authentication would be to use Digest authentication. This form of authentication is similar to Basic, but it has the advantage of the user credentials being hashed prior to being sent to the server.

Enabling Digest authentication involves checking the Digest Authentication for Windows Domain Servers check box in the Authentication Methods dialog box shown in Figure 31.2. This option will be disabled if you are not connected to a domain.

The last form of Windows authentication is NTLM authentication. This method takes the user login information that the user used when logging in to his computer. The user is not presented with a login dialog box because the credential information is already known. This method requires that both the user and the server are running Windows operating systems. Also, in Figure 31.2, the Integrated Windows authentication check box must be checked to enable NTLM.

Forms-Based Authentication

Now that I've explained Windows-based authentication, I can say that Windows-based authentication is realistically impractical for any real production-level Web application. First, it imposes requirements on the user such as having to use Internet Explorer in the case of NTLM and/or being on a computer with Windows as the operating system. The most glaring problem with IIS-based authentication is that server-side checking is based on Windows users accounts. Although it might serve well in some simple deployments, a real Web application requires more control on security and less constraints on the user's environments. ASP.NET brings Forms-based authentication to address this.

An advantage of Forms-based authentication is that it gives you, the developer, the ability to customize the form used to retrieve the user's credentials. It also gives you flexibility in how to authenticate the user in terms of where users credentials are stored and what type of security model to be utilized (user/role, for instance).

In order for Form-based authentication to be effective, you must authenticate the user by his credentials on every page of your Web applications. This does not mean that you must ask the user for his credentials on every page. It means that you use credentials that the user has already entered from a login form. Ideally, if for some reason the user hits a page and the login credentials are incorrect or not present, the user should be redirected back to the login form where he can reenter his username and password (the typical elements of a user's credentials).

When the user enters his login information, this information is not only used to validate the user against known/stored credentials, but it is also returned back to the user as a cookie. This cookie is then used to validate the user's credentials on subsequent pages of the Web application. If the user's browser had cookies disabled, ViewState is used. Let's look at a simple example of this model.

Entries in web.config

First, it is necessary to put the proper entries in the web.config file. The settings are entered in the <authentication> section of the web.config file as shown here:

```
<authentication mode="Forms">
  <forms
     name="logincookie"
     loginUrl="LoginForm.aspx"
     timeout="30">
  </forms>
</authentication>
```

Table 31.1 lists the various attributes that can appear in the <forms> section.

TABLE 31.1   <forms> Section Attributes

Attribute	Description
name	Name of the cookie to use for authentication. This defaults to .ASPXAUTH.
loginUrl	URL to which a request is redirected when no authentication cookie is found. This defaults to default.aspx.
protection	Specifies type of encryption to use for the authentication cookie. Valid values are All, None, Encryption, and Validation.
timeout	Specifies the time period in minutes after which the authentication cookie expires.
path	Specifies a path for cookies issued by the ASP.NET application.
requireSSL	Specifies whether SSL is required for the transmission of the cookie.
slidingExpiration	When true, the cookie's expiration is reset upon each request.

Authenticating Individual Pages

Once again, the idea to authenticating an application is that the user's authentication is checked upon every request on every page. If authenticated, the user is granted access to the requested page. Otherwise, the user is redirected to the login dialog box. The following is a simple example of the code that might appear in the Load event for each Web Form:

```
procedure TWebForm2.Page_Load(sender: System.Object;
  e: System.EventArgs);
begin
  if not User.Identity.IsAuthenticated then
    Response.Redirect('LoginForm.aspx');
end;
```

An authenticated user's information is represented by the IIdentity interface, implemented by the FormsIdentity class. The preceding code illustrates how to access this class through the User.Identity property. One of the properties of this class is IsAuthenticated, which returns a Boolean value representing whether a user has been authenticated. You would execute code similar to this in every page of the ASP.NET application. Listing 31.1 shows a longer example that displays information about the user from the FormsIdentity class.

LISTING 31.1   Checking for User Authentication

```
 1:    procedure TWebForm2.Page_Load(sender: System.Object;
 2:      e: System.EventArgs);
 3:    var
 4:      formsId: FormsIdentity;
 5:    begin
 6:      if not User.Identity.IsAuthenticated then
 7:        Response.Redirect('LoginForm.aspx')
 8:      else
 9:      begin
10:        Response.Write('Welcome: '+User.Identity.Name+'<br>');
11:        Response.Write('Authentication Type: '+
12:          User.Identity.AuthenticationType+'<br>');
13:        formsId := FormsIdentity(User.Identity);
14:        Response.Write('Cookie Path: '+ formsId.Ticket.CookiePath+'<br>');
15:        Response.Write('Expiration: '+
16:          Convert.ToString(formsID.Ticket.Expiration)+'<br>');
17:      end;
18:    end;
```

▶ Find the code on the CD: \Code\Chapter 31\Ex02.

Listing 32.1 shows the use of some of the properties of the FormsIdentity class. One of these properties is the Ticket property, which represents the authentication ticket. This class is the FormsAuthentication class. It basically represents the cookie that gets created when the user logs in.

Now that you understand how to check for user authentication on each page, let's see how you actually authenticate the user.

This is typically handled through a login form. The following code is a response to a Login button. The form used here has two TextBox controls into which the user enters his username and password combination.

```
procedure TLoginForm.btnLogin_Click(sender: System.Object;
  e: System.EventArgs);
begin
  if UserLoginValid(txbxUserName.Text, txbxPassword.Text) then
    FormsAuthentication.RedirectFromLoginPage(txbxUserName.Text,  False);
end;
```

▶ Find the code on the CD: \Code\Chapter 31\Ex02.

In the preceding code, the UserLoginValid() function is a method I wrote that executes the code to authenticate the user. It returns a Boolean value based on whether the user successfully authenticated. The following example is just a placeholder used to demonstrate the execution logic:

```
function TLoginForm.UserLoginValid(aUserName, aPassword: &String): Boolean;
begin
  Result := (aUserName = 'Elvis') and (aPassword = 'Presley');
end;
```

I will show realistic examples of this function. Certainly, you can just place the same code in the btnLogin_Click() event handler. However, having it in a separate method allows me to demonstrate the various possibilities of authenticating users by using this same example.

The FormsAuthentication class provides static helper methods for working with the authentication ticket. One of these methods is RedirectFormLoginPage(). This method redirects an authenticated user back to the page that he had originally requested. This method has two overloaded versions. The version shown here passes the username as the first parameter, which is stored in the authentication ticket. Listing 31.1 displays this information from the user object. The second parameter determines whether to create a cookie that persists across browser sessions. A second form of the RedirectFormLoginPage() method takes a third string parameter that specifies the cookie path.

Using the <credentials> Section

Continuing on the example provided previously, I will illustrate how you can store username and password definitions in the web.config file. I will also demonstrate a version of the UserLoginValid() function that validates a user based on the entries contained within web.config.

You can modify the web.config file to store the username and password combinations by doing so within the <credentials> section as illustrated here:

```
<authentication mode="Forms">
  <forms
     name="AuthCred" loginUrl="LoginForm.aspx" timeout="30">
     <credentials passwordFormat="Clear">
        <user name="Bobby" password="87pizza"/>
        <user name="Marsha" password=" bi45rd"/>
        <user name="Greg" password="Greg"/>
     </credentials>
  </forms>
</authentication>
```

The `<credentials>` element contains a single attribute, `passwordFormat`. This element specifies the encryption format for the stored passwords. The support formats are

- `Clear`—No encryption performed on passwords
- `MD5`—Passwords encrypted using the MD5 hashing algorithm
- `SHA1`—Passwords encrypted using the SHA1 hashing algorithm

The `<user>` subtag of the `<credentials>` section defines the usernames and passwords for users who are to be given access to the system. Had I specified an encryption scheme for the `passwordFormat` attribute of the `<credentials>` section, the passwords would have to be in their encrypted format.

TIP

The `FormsAuthentication.HashPasswordForStoringInConfigFile()` method can be used to produce hashed passwords.

NOTE

The idea of storing users in the `web.config` file is convenient and useful to demonstrate the capabilities of ASP.NET. However, it is highly impractical to store them here except with some simple deployments. You really don't want administrators to have to edit `web.config` files whenever you want to add/remove a user from the system. Better approaches exist that are illustrated in this chapter.

Once users are defined in the `web.config` file, all that is necessary is to rewrite the `UserLoginValid()` method from the last example. This is a one-liner statement:

```
function TWebForm1.UserLoginValid(aUserName, aPassword: &String): Boolean;
begin
  Result := FormsAuthentication.Authenticate(aUserName, aPassword);
end;
```

▶ Find the code on the CD: `\Code\Chapter 31\Ex03`.

The `FormsAuthentication.Authenticate()` function conveniently authenticates the username and password strings entered by the user against those maintained in the `web.config` file.

Using an XML File to Host Credentials

Another area in which you can store user information is within a separate XML file. Given the `.xml` file shown here

```
<root>
  <user>
    <username>mary</username>
    <password>marypassword</password>
  <user>
    <username>joe</username>
    <password>joepassword</password>
  </user>
</root>
```

We can change the UserLoginValid() function to that shown in Listing 31.2.

LISTING 31.2   UserLoginValid() Using an XML File

```
 1:  function TLoginForm.UserLoginValid(aUserName, aPassword: String): Boolean;
 2:  var
 3:    dsUsers: DataSet;
 4:    fsUsers: FileStream;
 5:    srUsers: StreamReader;
 6:    drArray: array of DataRow;
 7:    pwString: String;
 8:  begin
 9:    fsUsers := FileStream.Create(Server.MapPath('users.xml'),
10:      FileMode.Open, FileAccess.Read);
11:    try
12:      dsUsers := DataSet.Create;
13:      srUsers := StreamReader.Create(fsUsers);
14:      dsUsers.ReadXml(srUsers);
15:      drArray := dsusers.Tables[0].Select(
16:        System.String.Format('username=''{0}''', aUserName));
17:
18:      if (System.Array(drArray).Length > 0) then
19:      begin
20:        pwString := String(drArray[0]['password']);
21:        Result := System.String.Compare(pwString, aPassword) = 0;
22:      end
23:      else
24:        Result := False;
25:
26:      if Result = False then
27:        Label4.Text := 'Invalid username or password.';
28:
29:    finally
30:      fsUsers.Close;
31:    end;
32:  end;
```

▶ Find the code on the CD: \Code\Chapter 31\Ex04.

In this example, the method loads the .xml file into a stream and then reads it into a DataSet (line 14). The user is located by invoking the Select() method on the table within the DataSet. If a row is located, the password string is extracted and compared against that which the user entered (lines 20–21).

This technique has the same drawbacks as storing the username/password combinations in the web.config file. It requires that an administrator manages entering users and passwords into this text file. This becomes especially problematic if the passwords stored are in some sort of encrypted format such as MD5. Certainly, one could develop a tool that would make this data entry easier and generate the encrypted form of the password.

Using SQL Server to Host Credentials
A preferred approach to authenticate users is to store usernames and passwords within a database. The following UserLoginValid() function demonstrates how this can be done. It

also demonstrates using one of the classes from the `System.Security.Cryptography` namespace for encrypting the user's password using the MD5 hashing algorithm. This example assumes the existence of a database in SQL Server named `ddg_users` with a table generated from the following script:

```
CREATE TABLE ddgusers (
    user_name VARCHAR(40),
    password VARCHAR(100)
)
GO
```

You will find the `create.sql` and `populate.sql` scripts in the example on the CD. Listing 31.3 illustrates this technique.

LISTING 31.3   UserLoginValid() Using SQL Server

```
 1:   function BytesToHex(hash: array of Byte): String;
 2:   var
 3:     sb: StringBuilder;
 4:     i: integer;
 5:   begin
 6:     sb := StringBuilder.Create(Length(Hash)*2);
 7:     for i := Low(hash) to High(hash) do
 8:       sb.Append(hash[i].ToSTring('X2'));
 9:     Result := sb.ToString.ToLower;
10:   end;
11:
12:   function TLoginForm.UserLoginValid(aUserName, aPassword: String): Boolean;
13:   const
14:     cn  = 'server=XWING;database=ddg_users;Trusted_Connection=Yes';
15:     sel = 'select password from ddgusers where user_name = ''{0}''';
16:   var
17:     sqlCn: SqlConnection;
18:     sqlCmd: SqlCommand;
19:     dbPwStr: String;
20:     selStr: String;
21:
22:     encoder: UTF8Encoding;
23:     md5Hasher: MD5CryptoServiceProvider;
24:     HashedBytes: array of byte;
25:   begin
26:     sqlCn := SqlConnection.Create(cn);
27:     selStr := System.String.Format(sel, aUserName);
28:     sqlCmd := SqlCommand.Create(selStr, sqlCn);
29:
30:     sqlCn.Open;
31:     try
32:       dbPwStr := sqlCmd.ExecuteScalar as System.String;
33:     finally
34:       sqlCn.Close;
35:     end;
36:     encoder := UTF8Encoding.Create;
37:     md5Hasher := MD5CryptoServiceProvider.Create;
38:
```

LISTING 31.3   Continued

```
39:    // Hash the password passed in.
40:    HashedBytes := md5Hasher.ComputeHash(encoder.GetBytes(aPassword));
41:    aPassword := BytesToHex(HashedBytes);
42:
43:    Result := System.String.Compare(dbPWStr, aPassword) = 0;
44:  end;
```

▶ Find the code on the CD: \Code\Chapter 31\Ex05.

Lines 1–10 are a helper function that converts an array of bytes to a hexadecimal string. You'll see where this comes into play in a moment. In this version of the UserLoginValid() function, there are two primary portions. Lines 26–35 involve extracting the user's password from the database. This password is assumed to be encrypted using the MD5 algorithm.

Lines 36–41 involve using the MD5CryptoServiceProvider class to hash the password that was passed in by the users. The class returns an array of bytes representing the hashed password. The database stores the bytes as a string in hexadecimal form. In order to convert the originating array of bytes into a hex string, the method uses the BytesToHex() helper function.

Surely other ways exist that you can authenticate. Those shown here are the common ways that you will encounter.

Passport Authentication

Microsoft has its own centralized authentication mechanism named Passport. This service allows participants to subscribe to the passport initiative. When users log in to one of the participating sites, they are authenticated for other Passport participants.

In addition to authentication information, Microsoft hosts certain information about you that would be useful on other participating sites. The idea is to give you a cleaner experience as you navigate between participating sites without having to re-authenticate and enter user information.

Passport uses security technologies such as SSL and Triple DES encryption for managing user's authentication tickets.

To enable passport support for your application, the use of the Passport SDK is required. .NET fully supports passport through PassportAuthenticationModule and is enabled with the following entry in the web.config file:

```
<configuration>
  <system.web>
    <authentication mode="Passport"/>
  </system.web>
</configuration>
```

Passport operates in a fairly straightforward way. A user makes a request to a Passport-enabled site. This site determines whether the user has a valid Passport ticket. If so, the user is given access to the site. If not, a status code of 302 is returned and the user is redirected to the Passport login service. This service, through SSL, retrieves information about the user, authenticates him, and redirects him back to the originating site if authentication was successful.

> **NOTE**
>
> The latest version of the Passport SDK can be downloaded at `http://www.microsoft.com/net/services/passport/`.

You should be aware that the whole Passport initiative has been a controversial one. Many are skeptical about the reliability and what Microsoft's intensions are with your personal information. Do a simple Google search on "Microsoft+Passport+controversy". You'll find an article covering technical flaws to various types of conspiracy theories. Controversial as it might be, it is a very fascinating technology with many participants.

Authorization

Authentication identifies a user. Authorization determines the level of access a user has to a resource or set of resources. I discuss four forms of authorization in the following sections.

File Authorization

File authentication is based on the Windows accounts, NTFS and Access Control Lists (ACL). You provide access to users of a system through the Security tab of the Folder Properties dialog box. You can access this dialog box by right-clicking on any folder and selecting Properties. Figure 31.4 shows this form.

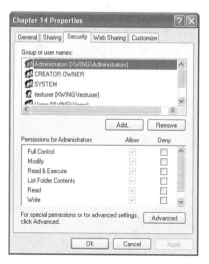

FIGURE 31.4   Security tab of the File Properties dialog box.

When the user attempts to access a resource that resides in a folder in which he has no access, he is presented with an error message: 403.2 Access Denied.

31

This technique is in contained environments in which network file security is sufficient for controlling access to resources security. You might find an intranet application in this scenario. The drawback to this technique is that managing ACLs is cumbersome and requires much administration.

URL Authorization—The <authorization> Section

URL authentication is controlled by the web.config file. Therefore, it controls access to the Web application based on how pages are defined with the directory structure. Client access at each level is controlled via the <authorization> section. The following code is an example of how this section might look:

```
<configuration>
  <system.web>
    <authorization>
      <allow users="bob, martial, gabriel, robin, amanda"/>
      <deny users="sam orie, blake, jones"/>
    </authorization>
  </system.web>
</configuration>
```

Within the <authorization> section are the subtags <allow> and <deny>. The <allow> subtag supports a comma-separated list of usernames, roles, or verbs that specifies who has access to the system governed by this web.config file. The <deny> subtag supports a similar list, but it specifies who does not have access to the resources governed by this web.config file. Therefore, in this example, the users bob, martial, and so on have access to all directories governed by this web.config file provided that no lower level web.config file overrides these settings.

Note that both subtags may contain role names as well, as shown here:

```
<authorization>
  <allow roles="manager, admins, technicians"/>
  <deny roles="executives, employees, contractors"/>
</authorization>
```

Two additional identities exist that might appear within both subtags—a question mark (?) and an asterisk (*). The question mark denotes anonymous users. The asterisk denotes all users. For example, consider the following <authorization> section:

```
<authorization>
  <allow users="?">
</authorization>
```

This setting specifies that anonymous users are allowed access to the resources governed by this web.config file. The following,

```
<authorization>
  <deny users="*">
</authorization>
```

specifies that all users are denied access to the resource.

You can also control the HTTP methods of accessing the resources through the <authorization> section. Basically, you use the verbs attribute followed by a comma-delimited list of HTTP methods. Valid verbs are shown in the following example:

```
<authorization>
  <allow verbs="GET, HEAD, POST, DEBUG">
</authorization>
```

Role Based Authorization

A role based authorization model would give users entry into the system but would limit their access so that the pages they view would differ based on their role.

How roles are stored is really a matter of the system requirements. A typical approach is to store users and roles in a database. The idea is that the ASP.NET application retrieves that information from the database and modifies the pages based on the roles that a user has.

We'll examine a simple example that performs this type of logic. We'll use the previous example's users.xml file to store users. Listing 31.2 illustrates the routine to validate users. After users are validated, the page they are requesting will be changed based on their role. The default page is a form containing four buttons, as shown in Figure 31.5.

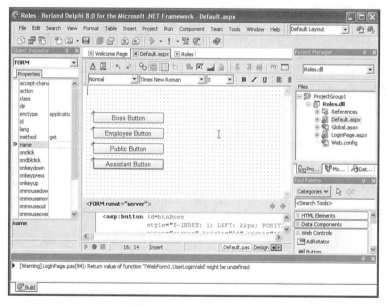

FIGURE 31.5   Default page for Role example.

Listing 31.4 shows the Page_Load() event handler for this page.

LISTING 31.4   Page_Load(), Which Checks for Role

```
1:    procedure TWebForm1.Page_Load(sender: System.Object; e: System.EventArgs);
2:    begin
3:      if not User.Identity.IsAuthenticated then
```

LISTING 31.4   Continued

```
4:        Response.Redirect('LoginPage.aspx')
5:     else begin
6:        btnBoss.Visible := User.IsInRole('Boss');
7:        btnEmp.Visible  := User.IsInRole('Employee');
8:        btnAsst.Visible := User.IsInRole('Asst');
9:        btnPub.Visible  := User.IsInRole('Public');
10:    end;
11:  end;
```

▶ Find the code on the CD: \Code\Chapter 31\Ex06.

After determining that the user is authenticated (line 3), Listing 31.4 then evaluates which roles the user belongs to by invoking the `User.IsInRole()` function (lines 6–9). The `IsInRole()` function is implemented by the `GenericPrincipal` class, `User`. The `GenericPrincipal` class represents the security context of the user for whom the ASP.NET application is running. `WindowsPrincipal` is another class that implements `IPricipal`. You would work with a `GenericPrincipal` class when you want to create authorization logic that is independent of the Windows domain security. Listing 31.3 is capable of determining to which roles the user belongs. To add the uers's roles to the `GenericPrincipal` class, you must modify the `TGlobal` class in the `Globals.pas` file. Specifically, you want to modify the `Applications.AuthenticateRequest` event handler. Listing 31.5 shows an example of what this code looks like.

LISTING 31.5   AuthenticateRequest Event

```
1:    procedure TGlobal.Application_AuthenticateRequest(sender: System.Object;
2:      e: EventArgs);
3:    var
4:      ra: TRoleArray;
5:    begin
6:      if Request.IsAuthenticated then
7:      begin
8:        ra := GetUserRoles(User.Identity.Name);
9:        if ra <> nil then
10:         Context.User := GenericPrincipal.Create(User.Identity, ra);
11:    end;
12:  end;
```

▶ Find the code on the CD: \Code\Chapter 31\Ex06.

This code simply populates a `TRoleArray` with the roles to which the user belongs. `TRoleArray` is simply an array of `String`. It is defined as

```
TRoleArray = array of String;
```

When the array is populated from the `GetUserRoles()` function (line 8), a new `GenericPrincipal` is created that contains these new roles associated with the user. `GetUserRoles()` is a function that hard-codes the array of users. It is shown in Listing 31.6.

LISTING 31.6   GetUserRoles() Function

```
 1:    function TGlobal.GetUserRoles(aUserName: &String): TRoleArray;
 2:    begin
 3:      if aUserName = 'mary' then
 4:        Result := TRoleArray.Create('Boss', 'Public')
 5:      else if aUserName = 'joe' then
 6:        Result := TRoleArray.Create('Employee', 'Public')
 7:      else if aUserName = 'mike' then
 8:        Result := TRoleArray.Create('Asst', 'Public', 'Boss')
 9:      else
10:        Result := nil;
11:    end;
```

▶ Find the code on the CD: \Code\Chapter 31\Ex06.

GetUserRoles() hard-codes the roles for specific users. Realistically, you would retrieve such roles from a database or some other external store.

When running the application, the Web Form, based on the user's roles, will contain different controls.

Impersonization

When ASP.NET executes applications, it does so using the identity "ASPNET" on Windows 2000 and Windows XP or "NETWORK SERVICE" under Windows 2003 Server. For non-ASP.NET applications (.html files or ISAPI/CGI scripts), the "IUSR_MACHINENAME" account is used. The security level for this particular account is one that has limited access to files and folders required to enable ASP.NET to run properly.

Developers of the application are expected to use some form of authentication to prohibit access to various resources.

Impersonation enables ASP.NET to execute the application under the identity of the person for whom the app is running. This enables ASP.NET to base the access level on the ACL of the user on whose behalf the application is running. This relies on NTFS-level permissions granted to the impersonated user account. Consider the following code:

```
procedure TWebForm1.Page_Load(sender: System.Object; e: System.EventArgs);
var
  fAry: array of String;
  i: integer;
begin
  Response.Write('hello');
  fAry := Directory.GetFiles(MapPath('\'), '*.*');
  for i := Low(fAry) to High(fAry) do
    Response.Write(fAry[i]+'<br>');
end;
```

▶ Find the code on the CD: \Code\Chapter 31\Ex07.

This code will work fine with impersonation disabled. That is because the default ASP.NET identity will have access to the IIS root directory (typically `c:\inetpub\wwwroot`). However, when you make the following change to the `web.config` file,

```
<configuration>
  <system.web>
    <identity impersonate="true"/>
  <\system.web>
<\configuration>
```

the file list will display only if the user has access to the IIS root directory.

Impersonation is fine if your application is working in a controlled intranet type of scenario. It is not preferred that user access is controlled through ACLs and such because this can be quite a bit of administration for a complex application.

Signing Off

Using Forms authentication, you can enable the user to sign off from the application by invoking the `FormsAuthentication.SignOut` method as shown here:

```
FormsAuthentication.SignOut;
Server.Transfer.("LoginPage.aspx");
```

IN THIS CHAPTER

- Deploying ASP.NET Applications
- Configuration Tips
- Adding/Retrieving Custom Configuration Settings

CHAPTER **32**

ASP.NET Deployment and Configuration

An ASP.NET application or Web Service has little use to anybody until you compile and deploy it. Of course, I don't mean to undermine the immediate gratification developers get from simply compiling and seeing their applications run—even in a test environment. Still, applications are written for the end user; therefore, they must be deployed when they are production ready. This chapter discusses a simple deployment approach. It also discusses configuration options that you will likely need to modify in a production environment.

Deploying ASP.NET Applications

In many situations, the deployment of an ASP.NET application is simple enough to use the XCOPY command to move from your development location to the deployment location. However, most applications are complex enough that they require an installation/setup program. Because of the varying complexities of the latter applications, I won't get into the many ways you can set them up. I will say that tools exist that you can use to simplify the process of creating robust setup applications. One of these is the Windows Installer.

Simple Deployment Considerations

When you create an ASP.NET application in Delphi for .NET, it automatically creates a virtual directory under IIS (if you opt for the IIS Server). The configuration created here is most likely in the layout that you will deploy. The directory structure is such that your application resides in an IIS virtual directory. These virtual directories refer to a physical directory somewhere on the system. To keep it simple, I'll describe the setup in my machine, a vanilla case.

Figure 32.1 shows the management console for my IIS directories.

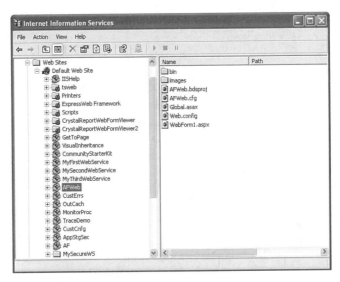

FIGURE 32.1   IIS Management Console.

You see that there are several virtual directories such as MyFirstWebService and MySecondWebService. These were created automatically in Chapter 28, "Building Web Services," when I demonstrated creating Web Services.

These virtual directories refer to a physical directory. You see this when right-clicking on a virtual directory and selecting Properties. This brings up the Properties dialog box for the virtual directory (see Figure 32.2).

FIGURE 32.2   Virtual Directory Properties dialog box.

I need to point out some items here. First, notice the radio buttons on the top of the dialog box. Through these radio buttons, you specify the physical location as being from one of three sources; it is local on your machine, it is on a network share, or it is from another URL. Changing the option changes the contents in the other portions of this dialog box (see Figure 32.3).

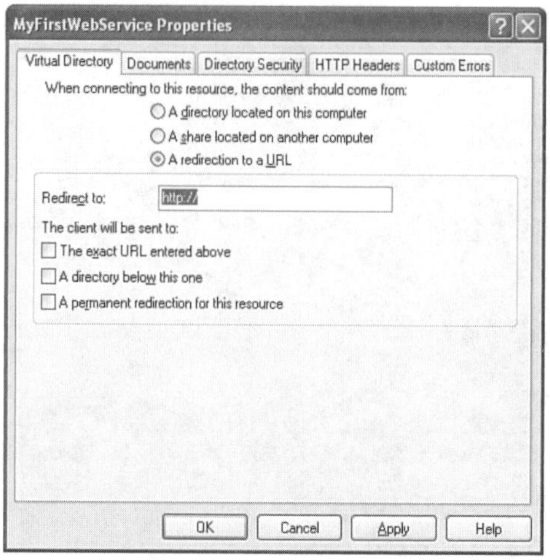

FIGURE 32.3   A virtual directory based on a redirection URL.

Back in Figure 32.2, you'll see a text box labeled as Local Path. This specifies the physical directory where your ASP.NET application resides. I will also point out a few other items in this dialog box. The various check boxes allow you to specify certain access rights on this directory from the Web. You'll want to make sure that only Read is checked. Doing otherwise dangerously exposes your directory to potential attack from the outside. Additionally, you'll want to make sure that the Execute Permissions drop-down says Scripts only. The other two options are None and Scripts and Executables. None would prevent any scripts from being run on the site. In other words, only static HTML pages could be seen. Scripts and Executables could be too open to the outside. For instance, it could be disastrous if you accidentally gave write and executable access to your directory. Not only could someone write a file to your directory, but he could also execute it.

When a user requests a page from your site with a URL such as,

```
www.xapware.com/AF/WebForm1.aspx
```

IIS resolves the alias AFWeb to the physical location on the machine.

> **NOTE**
>
> Although this chapter describes the deployment layout in the context of IIS, other Web Servers already exist that might have their own configuration specifics, such as the Cassani Web Server. You'll need to understand how those operate. For instance, Chapter 8, "Mono—A Cross Platform .NET Project," discusses the deployment of an ASP.NET application under Mono and Apache, running on a Linux box. This is obviously different from what is discussed here.

This physical location will be a directory where your ASP.NET application resides. The location to which the alias refers is considered the root of your application.

> **NOTE**
>
> In simplistic terms, the notion of an application residing in a single directory is sufficient for this discussion. In reality, an ASP.NET application can be composed of numerous subcomponents that might themselves be full-fledged applications residing in their own area. This is certainly true of applications that are composed of Web Services.

Consider, for example, the following directory structure for the AFWeb alias:

```
\AFWeb
    \bin
    \images
```

This particular structure is simple. It contains only a \bin directory and an \images directory.

The \bin directory is the location in which the compiled code-behind module resides. You can have other directories as part of your directory structure.

For example, when setting up an ASP.NET application for deployment, you might have specific directories within the root that hold various files you need in the application. The \images subdirectory here holds the images for this application. It's entirely possible that two different applications refer to the same images within their pages. In this scenario, instead of replicating the \images directory, you would place a common directory under the IIS Web Server and make those images accessible to other applications. What's key is that you refer to those images appropriately within the .aspx files as shown here:

```
<asp:image id=Image1
    style="Z-INDEX: 1; LEFT: 6px; POSITION: absolute; TOP: 6px"
    runat="server" imageurl="./images/ActiveFocusSplash.jpg">
</asp:image>
```

Note the use of the dot-slash notation so that the HTML refers to the appropriate directory, which in this case is relational. When the page is run, the image is displayed correctly as shown in Figure 32.4.

The base directory of your ASP.NET application is the starting point from which you expand to support other needs. Depending on how extensive this application is, you can deploy with a simple XCOPY deployment. Others will require an installation routine. For example, you might be deploying an application that installs a database server.

XCOPY Deployment

The whole idea of XCOPY deployment is not only for ASP.NET applications. It refers to how you should be able to install all .NET applications. Prior to .NET, anybody who has had to write an installation program knows the pain and agony involved in just getting started. For the most part, installation is a configuration nightmare. Microsoft dealt with this in how .NET applications are designed. .NET applications, being self-describing, only need to reside in an area from which they can be executed. They maintain information about themselves within their metadata or in configuration files that reside in the same directory in which they reside. It's like going back to the .ini file, but better.

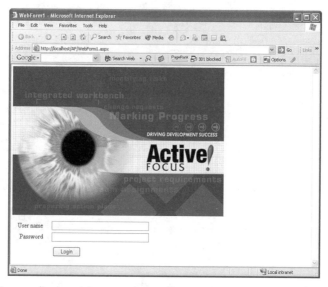

FIGURE 32.4   Image displayed from a relative directory.

To illustrate this, you would be able to deploy an ASP.NET application to a remote machine by entering the following XCOPY command within the console:

```
[c:\]XCOPY c:\Inetpub\wwwroot\AFWeb
   \\ProductionBox\c\inetpub\wwwroot\afweb /E /K /R /H /I /Y
```

The XCOPY options used are described as follows:

/E	copy all subdirectories, even empty ones
/K	copy attributes
/R	overwrite read-only files
/H	copy hidden and system files
/I	assume destination is directory
/Y	overwrite files without prompting

That's it! At this point I can type the following into my browser:

```
http://ProductionBox/AFWeb/
```

and I will see the page shown in Figure 32.4.

The remaining chapters discuss the various ways you can configure your ASP.NET application.

Configuration Settings

There are two areas that you need to be concerned with regarding configuration. First, you should understand the server-wide configurations so that you can know that the server can properly support your application. Second, you need to understand how to properly configure your own application. This is done by changing settings in two XML formatted files—`machine.config` and `web.config`.

The configuration structure in ASP.NET is hierarchical. First, all applications inherit the global configuration settings that are specified in a `machine.config` file. From there, they assume the configuration settings from the `web.config` file, which can reside in any of the directories that are part of the ASP.NET applications. For example, consider the following directory structure:

```
\AFWeb
    \bin
    \files
        \in
        \out
    \images
```

In this directory structure, all the directories inherit the settings specified in `machine.config`. If the `AFWeb` directory contains a `web.config` file, this file can override/augment some of the settings from `machine.config`. The directories below `AFWeb` will then inherit the `AFWeb.config` settings. You can place another `web.config` file in any of the sub-directories of `AFWeb` and also override/augment the settings from the parent directory. This setup gives you maximum flexibility in how you configure your ASP.NET Web applications.

ASP.NET prevents external access to these files. If someone were to try to access a `web.config` file from a browser, the server would return an error. HTTP access to `.config` files is strictly forbidden.

The machine.config File

The `machine.config` file is located in the following directory:

```
%WINDIR%\Microsoft.NET\Framework\<version>\CONFIG
```

This file is quite large. To examine it, I usually copy it to another directory and rename it so that it has an XML extension. This allows me to open it with Internet Explorer, which makes browsing XML files easier. Normally, when changing this file for ASP.NET configuration, you will be modifying the `system.web` section of the file. Of course, you cannot actually edit the file using IE. A good XML Editor, such as `notepad.exe`, is probably nice to have in this case.

It is beyond the scope of this chapter to cover the elements contained within `machine.config`. We will cover those that apply to environment configurations in the `web.config` file. What you need to know is that when a systemwide setting must be made, it should be applied within the `machine.config` file. `machine.config` is documented on the MSDN Web site or within the online SDK documentation.

The web.config File

The `web.config` file, like the `machine.config` file, holds specific settings that apply to a specific ASP.NET application. You can also add your own settings to this file that would be needed by the application, such as database connection strings. In a sense, you can think of the web.config file as you would an .ini file. The web.config file is nowhere as wieldy as the machine.config file. The schema for the web.config file is shown in Listing 32.1 with the main sections in bold font.

LISTING 32.1   web.config File Schema

```
<configuration>
    <location>
        <system.web>
            <authentication>
                <forms>
                    <credentials>
                <passport>
            <authorization>
                <allow>
                <deny>
            <browserCaps>
                <result>
                <use>
                <filter>
                    <case>
            <clientTarget>
                <add>
                <remove>
                <clear>
            <compilation>
                <compilers>
                    <compiler>
                <assemblies>
                    <add>
                    <remove>
                    <clear>
            <customErrors>
                <error>
            <globalization>
            <httpHandlers>
                <add>
                <remove>
                <clear>
            <httpModules>
                <add>
                <remove>
                <clear>
            <httpRuntime>
            <identity>
            <machineKey>
            <pages>
            <processModel>
            <securityPolicy>
                <trustLevel>
            <sessionState>
            <trace>
            <trust>
```

LISTING 32.1 Continued

```
        <webServices>
            <protocols>
                <add>
                <remove>
                <clear>
            <serviceDescriptionFormatExtensionTypes>
                <add>
                <remove>
                <clear>
            <soapExtensionTypes>
                <add>
                <clear>
            <soapExtensionReflectorTypes>
                <add>
                <clear>
            <soapExtensionImporterTypes>
                <add>
                <clear>
            <WsdlHelpGenerator>
        </webServices>
    </system.web>
  </location>
</configuration>
```

I will touch on a few these sections that are most likely to be modified. This chapter is not intended to document each section of this file. However, you should have a general under-standing of where in the `web.config` file you should modify various settings. For extended documentation, the best place to go is `www.msdn.microsoft.com`. Once there, search for the string "ASP.NET Configuration." You can also type in the following URL:

```
http://msdn.microsoft.com/library/en-us/cpguide/html/
➥cpconaspnetconfiguration.asp
```

You can also find this information in the online .NET SDK help. (Look up "ASP.NET, configuration section schema" in the index.)

The <location> Section

The `<location>` section of a configuration file allows you to specify settings for a Web Application globally or to a specific resource. It also allows you to prevent configuration setting overrides to that resource. There are two attributes to the `<location>` section. These are `path` and `allowOverride`.

- `path`—Specifies the resource to which the configuration setting(s) applies. If the path is empty, the settings apply to the current and child directories.

- `allowOverride`—Indicates whether the configuration settings can be overridden in the `web.config` files residing in child directories. This value is either `True` (the default) or `False`.

The following example establishes a maximum file size that can be uploaded to the specified page:

```
<configuration>
   <location path="GetFilePage.aspx">
      <httpRuntime maxRequestLength="128"/>
   </location>
</configuration>
```

The limit for `maxRequestLength` is 128Kb.

The following sets the same file size limit but on the entire site. It also prevents this setting from being modified by the `web.config` files in child directories.

```
<configuration>
   <location allowOverride="false" >
      <httpRuntime maxRequestLength="128"/>
   </location>
</configuration>
```

The <authentication> Section

The `<authentication>` section configures ASP.NET authentication support. This can only be done at the machine level (`machine.config`) or at the site level. Attempts to declare this at the subdirectory level result in a parser error. This section's `mode` attribute determines one of the authentication modes listed in Table 32.1.

TABLE 32.1   <authentication> Section Modes

Mode	Description
Windows	Sets `Windows` authentication as the default authentication mode.
Forms	Sets ASP.NET `Forms` as the default authentication mode.
Passport	Sets `Passport` as the default authentication mode.
None	Sets no authentication mode. Under this mode, anonymous users are accepted or the application handles its own authentication.

The `<authentication>` section uses two tags—`<forms>` and `<passport>`. When using the `<forms>` tag, optional attributes exist that you should include in the declaration. The attributes are too lengthy to show here, but they are well documented at `www.msdn.microsoft.com` and in the online SDK help. At a minimum, you should provide the `name` and `loginUrl` attributes. The `name` attribute refers to an HTTP cookie that sends the login information from the client. The `LoginUrl` attribute is the URL to which the authentication request is directed. Here is an example:

```
<configuration>
   <system.web>
      <authentication mode="Forms">
         <forms name="AppLogin" loginUrl="/login.aspx">
            <credentials passwordFormat = "SHA1">
               <user name="AppUser"
                     password="ADD A PASSWORD"/>
            </credentials>
         </forms>
```

Configuration Tips

The following sections illustrate some recommended configuration settings that you might consider in developing your ASP.NET applications.

Handling Errors Redirection

During development, it is useful that when an error occurs in a page, you are redirected to a page that includes a stack trace, which might include the offending code. Figure 32.5 shows an example of this page.

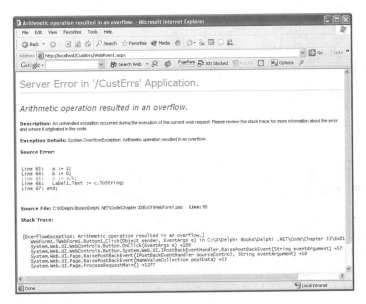

FIGURE 32.5   Error Page.

This, however, is not what you would want exposed when in a product application. This is not to say that you don't want your users to know that an error occurred—they should know this. You don't want to be exposing your code to them unnecessarily. A better option would be to redirect the users to another page. This is done by modifying the `<customErrors>` section of the web.config file. The following change in the `<customErrors>` section redirects the user to another page when an error occurs:

```
<customErrors
    mode="On"
    defaultRedirect="ErrWebForm.aspx">
</customErrors>
```

The `mode` attribute can be one of three values: `On`, `Off`, or `RemoteOnly` (the default). `On` enables custom errors and displays them to everyone. `Off` prevents customer errors from being displayed at all. `RemoteOnly` displays custom errors to users not on the server. When `mode` is `On`, you can display friendlier and less code-revealing screens to your users, such as that shown in Figure 32.6.

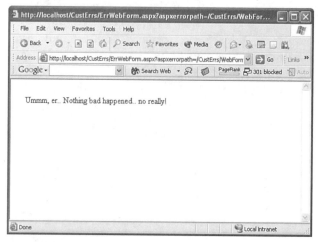

FIGURE 32.6 Redirected Error page.

▶ Find the code on the CD: \code\Chapter 32\Ex01.

Worker Process Restarting

Being what it is, software is not perfect, and occasionally a Web application will cause the ASP.NET worker process (aspnet_wp.exe) to crash or hang. To fix this, an administrator would have to shut down IIS and possibly the server. This, of course, can take an enormous amount of time. This scenario is particularly annoying for developers. During the development stages of an application, it's common that apps will hang.

The <processModel> section in the machine.config file allows you to specify some settings that will alleviate many of these problems. You can only make these changes in the machine.config file, as this is a machine setting and not a Web Application setting.

> **NOTE**
>
> In native mode, IIS 6.0 does not use this processModel section. Also, this section is read by unmanaged code in the aspnet_wp.exe; changes are not applied until IIS is restarted.

Table 32.4 lists the various properties that can be set within the <processModel> section.

TABLE 32.4 <processModel> Attributes

Attribute	Description
clientConnectedCheck	Species the time period that a request remains queued before ASP.NET does a client connection check.
comAuthenticationLevel	Specifies authentication security level for DCOM.
comImpersonationLevel	Specifies the impersonation level for COM security.
cpuMask	Specifies the CPU processors that are allowed to run ASP.NET processes in a multiprocessor machine.
enable	Specifies whether the process model is enabled.

TABLE 32.4   Continued

Attribute	Description
idleTimeout	Specifies the period of inactivity in the string format hr:min:sec after which ASP.NET ends the worker process. Infinite is the default value.
logLevel	Specifies the event types that are to be logged.
maxIoThreads	Specifies maximum number of I/O threads a process can use on a per-CPU basis.
maxWorkerThreads	Specifies maximum number of worker threads a process can use on a per-CPU basis.
memoryLimit	Specifies the maximum memory size as a percent of the total system memory that can be consumed by the worker process. The default is 60%. When exceeded, ASP.NET launches a new process and reassigns requests to that process.
password	Works in conjunction with the userName attribute.
requestLimit	Specifies a number of requests permitted prior to ASP.NET launching a new worker process.
requestQueueLimit	Specifies the number of requests allowed in the Queue. When exceeded, ASP.NET will return error 503 "Server Too Busy".
responseDeadlockInterval	Time interval after which a process will be restarted. This is conditioned upon there being requests queued and no response during the interval. The default is three minutes.
shutdownTimeout	Specifies the number of minutes within which a worker process must shut itself down. When elapsed, ASP.NET will shut the process down.
timeout	Specified number of minutes until ASP.NET starts a new worker process. Default value is infinite.
username	Specifies which user (Windows identity) runs the ASP.NET worker processes. This value is set to ASPNET by default. This is a special account created by the ASP.NET setup.
webGarden	Used in conjunction with the cpuMask attribute. When this value is True, cpuMask specifies which CPUs are eligible to run ASP.NET processes. When False, the OS makes that determination.

The attribute timeout is one you should consider changing. By default, the worker process will never restart. You can change timeout so that it will restart after the specified interval. You should do this to ensure that memory leaks do not eat up available memory.

idleTimeout specifies how long ASP.NET waits prior to restarting the worker process when requests are queued. Additionally, shutdownTimeout determines how long it allows a process to shut down before it gets killed by ASP.NET. This setting is good to change if a process is hung during its shutdown. These three settings allow you to deal with problems such as deadlocks, memory leaks, crashing (access violations), and so on.

Another type of problem you might have to deal with is excessive memory consumption by the process. Three additional settings allow you to restart the worker process and to transfer any pending requests to the new process. requestLimit, by default, is set so that it is unlimited. You can set this to a value that, upon being reached, will restart the process.

requestQueueLimit and memoryLimit are other settings that you can modify to provide a more resilient setup than going with the default settings.

Output Caching for Performance

When serving Web pages that never change, the best option is to use a standard .html file. However, some pages are still dynamically generated, but they might retain their content for a period of time. Rather than having ASP.NET regenerate .html every time the page is requested, performance would be improved if you cache the page on the server. When a new request is made, the cache is served to the requestor until a specified timeout period—at which time, a new page is generated upon the next request. You can accomplish caching by adding the @OutputCache directive to the .aspx file as shown here:

```
<%@ OutputCache Duration="20" Location="Any" VaryByParam="none" %>
```

An example provided on the CD demonstrates this. It contains a page with a Label and a Button control. When the button is pressed, the following code is executed:

```
procedure TWebForm1.Button1_Click(sender: System.Object;
  e: System.EventArgs);
begin
  Label1.Text := System.String.Format('Time on the Server is: {0}',
    [System.DateTime.Now.ToLongTimeString]);
end;
```

▶ Find the code on the CD: \code\Chapter 32\Ex02.

Basically, it just outputs the system time. When the @OutputCache directive is absent, you can continually press the button and you will see a new time being generated every second. When the @OuputCache directive is present, the time will not change until 20 seconds has elapsed. Basically, the page from the original request was cached on the first request and gets served on subsequent requests. Some of the other settings for the @OutputCache directive are shown in Table 32.5.

TABLE 32.5   @OutputCache Settings

Setting	Description
Duration	Specifies the duration in seconds that the page is cached.
Location	Specify the cacheability of the page. It can be one of the following enumerations values:
	Any—browser client, proxy server, or server where request was processed
	Client—output cache located on the browser client
	Downstream—Stored in any HTTP 1.1 cache-capable device but not the server
	None—Caching disabled
	Server—Cache located on the server
	ServerAndClient—Cache located on the server or the requesting client (but not on proxy servers)
Shared	Specifies whether the output of a user control can be shared on multiple pages.
VaryByCustom	Specifies whether to store diverse cache versions for different browsers, allowing for various output for different browsers.

TABLE 32.5   Continued

Setting	Description
VaryByHeader	Specifies whether to store different cache versions for different HTTP request headers.
VaryByParam	Specifies whether to store a different cache by parameters in a form or query string list.
VaryByControl	Caches user controls on the server so that they are not re-rendered upon page requests.

Monitoring the ASP.NET Process

The previous section discusses how you can change various settings that determine how the worker process operates. Specifically, you establish thresholds that cause the process to shut down for various reasons. It would be helpful if you could monitor this activity. Fortunately, you can by using the `ProcessInfo` class, which is from the `System.Web` namespace. The `ProcessInfo` class has members that are useful for telling you certain status information about the ASP.NET process. Table 32.6 lists these properties.

TABLE 32.6   ProcessInfo Properties

Property	Description
Age	The length of time the process has been running
PeakMemoryUsed	Maximum memory process has used
ProcessID	ID of the process
RequestCount	Number of requests executed by the process
ShutdownReason	Reason why the process has been shut down
StartTime	The time at which the process started
Status	Current status of the process

Another class, `ProcessModelInfo`, can be used to obtain information about worker process, including worker process history. To do this, you would invoke the `ProcessModelInfo.GetHistory()` method. This method takes an integer parameter specifying the number of elements the resulting array returns. `GetHistory()` returns an array of `ProcessInfo` class instances. The following code illustrates how you can call the `GetHistory()` method that will be bound to `DataGrid`:

```
DataGrid1.DataSource := ProcessModelInfo.GetHistory(20);
DataGrid1.DataBind;
```

▶ Find the code on the CD: `\code\Chapter 32\Ex03`.

Figure 32.7 shows the output of this code.

Tracing the Application

Tracing can be referred to as a poor-man's debugger. Actually, it is one of the most valuable capabilities developers have as they develop their applications. It is a way that lets you examine the execution of your code and also write out custom states about your code during the execution. There are two forms of tracing—page level and application level tracing.

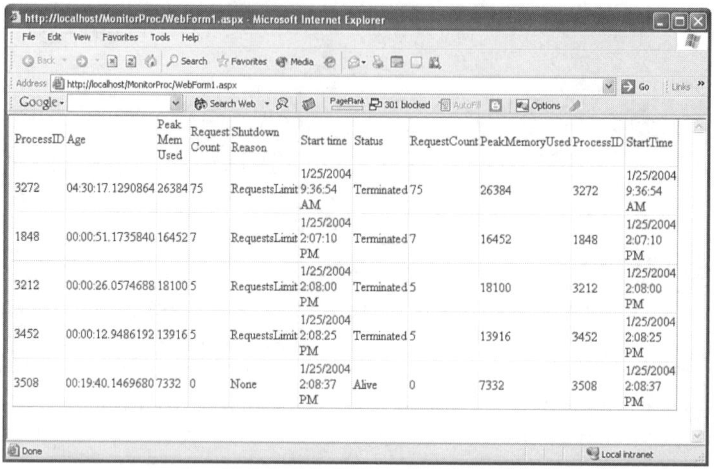

ProcessID	Age	Peak Mem Used	Request Count	Shutdown Reason	Start time	Status	RequestCount	PeakMemoryUsed	ProcessID	StartTime
3272	04:30:17.1290864	26384	75	RequestsLimit	1/25/2004 9:36:54 AM	Terminated	75	26384	3272	1/25/2004 9:36:54 AM
1848	00:00:51.1735840	16452	7	RequestsLimit	1/25/2004 2:07:10 PM	Terminated	7	16452	1848	1/25/2004 2:07:10 PM
3212	00:00:26.0574688	18100	5	RequestsLimit	1/25/2004 2:08:00 PM	Terminated	5	18100	3212	1/25/2004 2:08:00 PM
3452	00:00:12.9486192	13916	5	RequestsLimit	1/25/2004 2:08:25 PM	Terminated	5	13916	3452	1/25/2004 2:08:25 PM
3508	00:19:40.1469680	7332	0	None	1/25/2004 2:08:37 PM	Alive	0	7332	3508	1/25/2004 2:08:37 PM

FIGURE 32.7 Process Monitoring screen.

Page Level Tracing

Page level tracing lets you trace the execution of individual pages. You enable page level tracing by adding the trace attribute to the `@page` directive in the `.aspx` file as shown here:

```
<%@ Page language="c#" Codebehind="WebForm1.pas" AutoEventWireup="true"
Inherits="WebForm1.TWebForm1" Trace="true" %>
```

When you launch using a simple page, it will look as shown in Figure 32.8.

▶ Find the code on the CD: `\code\Chapter 32\Ex04`.

With tracing enabled, you will see the trace information appended to the bottom of the page. The trace information is separated into the possible sections, which are listed in Table 32.7.

TABLE 32.7 Tracing Sections

Tracing Section	Description
Request Details	Displays information about the client's request.
Trace Information	Displays execution details of the page.
Control Tree	Displays control hierarchy on the page.
Session State	Displays data stored in the `Session` state.
Application State	Displays data stored in the `Application` state.
Cookies Collection	Displays cookie name/value pair data.
Headers Collection	Displays headers from the client browser.
Form Collection	Displays the name/value pairs of form entries.
QueryString Collection	Displays the name/value pairs contained in the querystring.
Server Variables	Displays the server variables such as those in HTTP headers, environment, and so on.

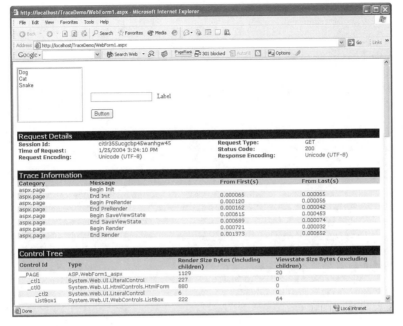

FIGURE 32.8   A page with tracing information.

In addition to this standard information, you can write your own data to the Trace Information section by executing the `Trace.Write()` method as shown here:

```
Trace.Write('Debug Session', TextBox1.Text);
```

This would result in the output shown in Figure 32.9. Notice the added entry to the Trace Information list.

The great thing about the `Trace.Write()` method is that it is ignored by your page when tracing is turned off. Therefore, when you take your application to production, you do not need to clean up all the `Trace.Write()` statements from your code.

Another thing you can do with tracing is to write out error information as a result of an exception. For example, the following code

```
try
  raise Exception.Create('An Error occurred.');
except
  on E: Exception do
  begin
    Trace.Write('My Errors', E.Message, E);
  end;
end;
```

would result in the output shown in Figure 32.10.

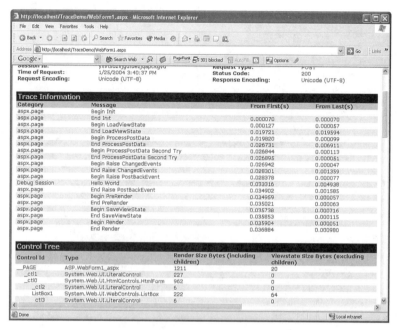

FIGURE 32.9   A Trace screen with custom information.

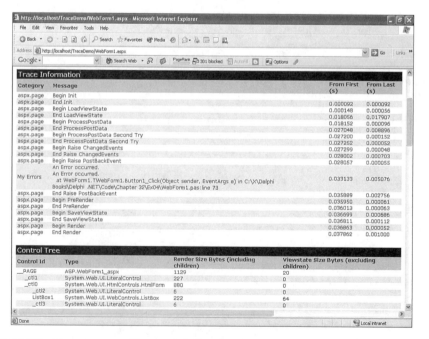

FIGURE 32.10   Trace screen with error information.

Here, notice the My Errors category.

Application Level Tracing

Page level tracing is great when you want to trace a single page. However, it would be a lot of work if you needed to trace the entire application, especially if the application consisted of hundreds of pages as many do. In this situation, you would use application level tracing. To enable application level tracing, you must add the <trace> entry to either your machine.config or web.config file. An example is provided here:

```
<trace
    enabled="true"
    requestLimit="10"
    pageOutput="false"
    traceMode="SortByTime"
    localOnly="true"
/>
```

The attributes within the <trace> directive are explained in Table 32.8.

TABLE 32.8   <trace> Attributes

Attribute	Description
enabled	Specifies whether tracing is enabled. The default value is False.
requestLimit	Specifies the number of requests to list in the trace.axd page, which is discussed later.
pageOutput	Specifies whether detailed trace information is included at the bottom of each page. This defaults to False.
traceMode	Specifies the order by which messages are displayed. This value may be SortByTime (the default) or SortByCategory.
localOnly	Specifies whether trace messages are displayed only on the local computer or also on remote computers.

With this setting, you can view a special page named trace.axd, which contains trace information for requests made to your application. Figure 32.11 shows what this page looks like.

Clicking on the View Details link shows the detailed trace information for each request.

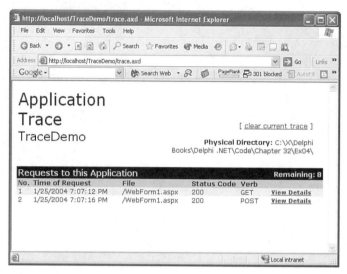

FIGURE 32.11   Application tracing.

Adding/Retrieving Custom Configuration Settings

Often, you'll need to store information into the configuration file that is not part of the standard sections. There are two places you can store information in the `web.config` file. One is in the `<appSettings>` section. The other is in your own custom section.

Adding and Reading <appSettings>

You can add custom entries to the `web.config` file. In fact, there's a section specifically for customized application settings. This section is `<appSettings>`, and it occurs outside of the `<system.web>` section. A typical entry in this section is a connection string to a database. The following shows how this might appear in the `<appSettings>` section:

```
<configuration>
  <appSettings>
    <add
        key="ConnectionString"
        value="server=XWING;database=Northwind;Trusted_Connection=Yes"  />
  </appSettings>
  <system.web>
    ...
  </system.web>
</configuration>
```

The entries in the `<appSettings>` section are based on a key/value pair. Here, you see the key as being `"ConnectionString"` and the value being the actual connection string.

To read this entry in an application, you use the `ConfigurationSettings` class, which is defined in the `System.Configuration` namespace. You can access entries in the `<appSettings>` section by referring to the `AppSettings` array property as shown here:

```
SqlConnection1.ConnectionString :=
  ConfigurationSettings.AppSettings['ConnectionString'];
```

▶ Find the code on the CD: \code\Chapter 32\Ex05.

Adding and Reading Custom Configuration Sections

When you need several items in the web.config file, you can create your own section. The following example shows what this might look like:

```
<configuration>
  <configSections>
    <section name="NewSection"
      type="System.Configuration.NameValueSectionHandler, System,
➥Version=1.0.5000.0, Culture=neutral,
➥PublicKeyToken=b77a5c561934e089"/>
  </configSections>
  <NewSection>
    <add key="ConnectionString"
     value="server=XWING;database=Northwind;Trusted_Connection=Yes"/>
  </NewSection>
…
</configuration>
```

As shown in this example, you first declare your sections in the <configSection> section of the web.config file. When declaring a section, you must specify the section name and a configuration handler. In this example, the handler used is the System.Configuration.NameValueSectionHandler. It is possible to create a custom handler. For this example, this handler is sufficient and the same used to read the <appSettings> section items. To read the value, the code would resemble that shown here:

```
var
  nvc: NameValueCollection;
begin
  if not IsPostBack then
  begin
    nvc := (ConfigurationSettings.GetConfig('NewSection') as
      NameValueCollection);
    SqlConnection1.ConnectionString := nvc['ConnectionString'];
…
end
```

▶ Find the code on the CD: \code\Chapter 32\Ex06.

IN THIS CHAPTER

- Caching ASP.NET Applications
- State Management in ASP.NET Applications

CHAPTER **33**

Caching and Managing State in ASP.NET Applications

This chapter discusses two related, but separate, topics on ASP.NET programming—caching and state management. Caching is used to improve performance by persisting commonly accessed data in the Web server. When users request the data, it is retrieved from the Web server rather than the originating data source. State management deals with the issue of Web applications being stateless—knowing nothing about previous requests. State management provides a way for the Web application to maintain information about a user's interaction with the Web application.

Caching ASP.NET Applications

This section discusses how caching works in ASP.NET applications. There are primarily three forms of caching. These are page caching, page fragment caching, and data caching.

Page Caching

Page caching is the process of persisting an entire page on the server, proxy server, or the client browser so that the next time it is retrieved, it does not have to be generated by ASP.NET.

Using the @ OutputCache Directive

Page caching is enabled by including the directive in bold (line 2) in the .aspx file shown in Listing 33.1.

LISTING 33.1   .aspx File Containing Page Caching Directive

```
 1:    <%@ Page language="c#" Debug="true" Codebehind="WebForm1.pas"
➥AutoEventWireup="false" Inherits="WebForm1.TWebForm1" %>
 2:    <%@ OutputCache Duration="20" Location="Any" VaryByParam="none" %>
 3:    <!DOCTYPE HTML PUBLIC "-//W3C//DTD HTML 4.0 Transitional//EN">
 4:
 5:    <html>
 6:      <head>
 7:        <title></title>
 8:        <meta name="GENERATOR" content="Borland Package Library 7.1">
 9:      </head>
10:
11:      <body ms_positioning="GridLayout">
12:      <form runat="server">
13:        <asp:label id=Label1
14:                  style="Z-INDEX: 1; LEFT: 62px; POSITION: absolute;
15:                  TOP: 14px" runat="server">Label</asp:label>
16:        <asp:button id=Button1
17:                   style="Z-INDEX: 2; LEFT: 70px; POSITION: absolute;
18:                   TOP: 46px" runat="server" text="Button">
19:        </asp:button>
20:      </form>
21:    </body>
22:    </html>
```

▶ Find the code on the CD: \Code\Chapter 33\Ex01.

In this example, the @ OutputCache directive includes three attributes. The first, Duration, specifies how long (in seconds) the cache will retain the page before regenerating its HTML. The second attribute, Location, determines where the cache is stored. The third allows you to create a different version of the resulting page based on values provided in the comma-separated list following the VaryByParam attribute. These and other attributes are more fully explained in Table 33.1. Some of these attributes pertain to page or control caching or both.

TABLE 33.1   @ OutputCache Attributes

Attribute	Description
Duration	Specifies the time in seconds that the page is cached. By specifying a value, an expiration policy is established for the page or control being cached. This is a required attribute.
Location	Location allows you to specify where the page is cached. It can be one of the following values. Any—The item can be cached on any of the following locations. This is the default setting. Client—The item is cached in the client's browser. Downstream—The item is cached on a downstream server. None—There is not page caching performed. Server—The item is cached on the server.

TABLE 33.1　Continued

Attribute	Description
Shared	Shares deals with user controls and determines whether the control's cache can be shared with other pages.
VaryByCustom	Semicolon separated strings that allow varying pages based on browser type or custom strings.
VaryByHeader	Semicolon separated list of headers that can be used for serving different pages based on header information.
VaryByParam	Semicolon separated list of strings representing parameters that are used in determining varying page output. These strings correspond to attributes sent with a GET method or parameters sent with the POST method. This attribute is required and might contain an empty string.
VaryByControl	Semicolon separated list of user-control property names. This is only valid for control caching (fragment caching).

The example in Listing 33.1 illustrates how page caching works. It is a page that contains a Button and a Label control. The code-behind for the Button's Click event performs the following:

```
procedure TWebForm1.Button1_Click(sender: System.Object;
  e: System.EventArgs);
begin
  Label1.Text := System.String.Format('Time on the Server is: {0}',
    [System.DateTime.Now.ToLongTimeString]);
end;
```

When running the application, clicking the button will reveal that the page is being cached. The time that is written to the page does not change until the cache has expired, as determined by the Duration attribute of the @ OutputCache directive.

Varying by Parameters

I will illustrate one of the varying attributes, specifically the VaryByParam attribute. This attribute can have one of three possible values, including none, an asterisk *, and a valid string that represents a GET method attribute or a POST parameter name. VaryByParam results in a different page being cached for each distinct request (as determined by the parameters being passed). When using the * as shown next, all parameters are taken into account.

```
<%@ OutputCache Duration="20" Location="Any" VaryByParam="*" %>
```

You can also spell out a specific parameter by name, causing only the specified parameters to be taken into account by distinguishing a separate request needing to be cached. This is illustrated here:

```
<%@ OutputCache Duration="20" Location="Any" VaryByParam="FirstName" %>
```

To illustrate this, Listing 33.2 is the .aspx file for an example similar to that shown in Listing 33.1. Notice that the VaryByParam attribute now contains an asterisk.

LISTING 33.2   Varying by Parameter Example

```
1:   <%@ Page language="c#" Debug="true" Codebehind="WebForm1.pas"
➥AutoEventWireup="false" Inherits="WebForm1.TWebForm1" %>
2:   <%@ OutputCache Duration="120" Location="Any" VaryByParam="*" %>
3:   <!DOCTYPE HTML PUBLIC "-//W3C//DTD HTML 4.0 Transitional//EN">
4:
5:   <html>
6:     <head>
7:       <title></title>
8:       <meta name="GENERATOR" content="Borland Package Library 7.1">
9:     </head>
10:
11:    <body ms_positioning="GridLayout">
12:    <form runat="server">
13:     <asp:label id=Label1
14:                style="Z-INDEX: 1; LEFT: 38px; POSITION: absolute;
15:                TOP: 14px" runat="server">Label</asp:label>
16:    </form>
17:   </body>
18:   </html>
```

▶ Find the code on the CD: \Code\Chapter 33\Ex02.

When entering a URL such as

```
http://localhost/PgCshByParam/WebForm1.aspx?FirstName=Bob
```

the output written will be

```
"Bob, the time on the Server is: 8:46:04 a.m."
```

Changing the URL to

```
http://localhost/PgCshByParam/WebForm1.aspx?FirstName=Sam
```

results in the output

```
"Sam, the time on the Server is: 8:46:17 a.m."
```

Assuming that VaryByParam="FirstName" and using Bob as the parameter, you will see that the original output is returned with the time appearing to move backward at 8:46:04 a.m. What's happening here is that there are two versions of this page being cached—one for when the FirstName parameter equals Bob, and the other for when FirstName is Sam. As another interesting point, consider the following two URLs:

```
http://localhost/PgCshByParam/WebForm1.aspx?FirstName=Bob&LastName=Jones
http://localhost/PgCshByParam/WebForm1.aspx?FirstName=Bob&LastName=Archer
```

Both would result in the same cached page being returned. However, changing the @ OutputCache directive to the following would have different results:

```
<%@ OutputCache Duration="120" Location="Any" VaryByParam="FirstName" %>
```

With this directive, only requests in which the FirstName parameter is different will result in different cached pages. The previous two URLs containing the same FirstName but different LastName parameters will be served the same cached page.

Varying by Headers

Incertain situations, you'll want your ASP.NET applications to take advantage of browser capabilities. However, you won't want to serve pages to browsers that use capabilities not supported by the target browser. Therefore, when using caching, it doesn't make any sense to be caching a page that won't be supported by the client's browser. The following @ OutputCache directive shows how you can create a different page depending on HTTP header information—specifically the User-Agent header by including the VaryByHeader attribute.

```
<%@ OutputCache Duration="120" Location="Any" VaryByParam="*"
➥VaryByHeader="User-Agent" %>
```

The client's browser can be identified by the User-Agent HTTP header. You can specify other HTTP headers in the VaryByHeader or multiple headers separated by semicolons.

Varying by Custom Strings

You can get very specific about the requirements that determine cached page variations by using the VaryByCustom attribute of the @ OutputCache directive.

There are two ways to use this attribute. The first and simplest is to specify a value of "Browser" as shown here:

```
<%@ OutputCache Duration="120" Location="Any" VaryByParam="*"
➥VaryByCustom="Browser" %>
```

This causes behavior similar to the VaryByHeader example previously explained. It differs in that VaryByCustom="Browser" only uses the browser type and major version rather than the additional information that might be included in the User-Agent header.

Another way to use the VaryByCustom attribute is to specify a user-defined string. In doing so, you must override the GetVaryByCustomString() method of the HttpApplication class in Globals.pas. This would look like the following code:

```
function TGlobal.GetVaryByCustomString(Context: HTTPContext;
  custom: &String): System.String;
begin
  if custom = 'Country' then
    Result := GetCountry(Context)
  else
    Result := GetVaryByCustomString(Context, custom);
end;
```

This illustrates a way that you might cache pages based on the country of the user originating the request. This assumes that the GetCountry() method returns a string that would be used as the string by which to vary cached pages.

Page Fragment Caching

Page fragment caching is similar to page caching but instead of caching the entire page, you are caching specific elements of the page. This can be accomplished by caching user controls, which are covered in Chapter 34, "Developing Custom ASP.NET Server Controls." User controls can be used with the @ OutputCache directive just like pages can. Some attributes aren't supported because they make no sense since user controls exist in the context of the page. These are Location and VaryByHeader. The following .ascx file defines a user control that uses such caching:

```
<%@ Control Language="c#" AutoEventWireup="false" Codebehind=
➥"WebUserControl1.pas" Inherits="WebUserControl1.TWebUserControl1"%>
<%@ OutputCache Duration="20" VaryByParam="*" %>
<asp:label id=Label1
    style="Z-INDEX: 101; LEFT: 38px; POSITION: absolute; TOP: 38px"
    runat="server">Label</asp:label>
```

▶ Find the code on the CD: \Code\Chapter 33\Ex03.

This control simply displays the system time. To illustrate the partial page caching, it is included on a page that also displays the system time but is not cached. Figure 33.1 shows the output after refreshing the browser several times. You can see that that user control retains its original time and will do so until the cache has expired.

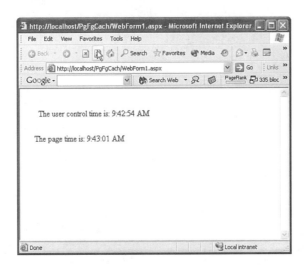

FIGURE 33.1   Caching a user control.

Data Caching

Data caching is a way to cache data of any type. This is particularly useful for obtaining a performance boost by not having to request data from a data source. Instead, this can be done once to fill a DataSet that you then cache. Subsequent requests for this DataSet will then retrieve it from the cache. To illustrate this, we'll need to examine the Cache class.

The Cache Class

The Cache class is defined in the System.Web.Caching namespace and provides the capability to store information to memory at the application level, which can be retrieved upon different requests. This works similarly to the Application class, which I discuss later in this chapter.

There are two properties and four methods of interest regarding the Cache class that are described in Table 33.2.

TABLE 33.2   Cache Class Properties and Methods

Property/Method	Description
Count	This property returns the number of items that are currently stored in the Cache.
Item	This property is an indexer array that returns the item by a specified key.
Add()	This method allows you to add an item to the Cache. You can specify as parameters dependencies, an expiration policy, a priority policy, and a remove callback method. Add() fails if an item already exists in the Cache for a given key.
Get()	This method returns an item from the Cache by the specified key.
Insert()	This method inserts an item into the Cache, replacing any item that exists with the same key. You can include the same parameters as with the Add() method.
Remove()	This method removes an item from the Cache with the specified key.

As indicated for the Cache.Add() and Cache.Insert() methods, there are several parameters that pertain to the item being placed in the Cache. These are discussed in Table 33.3 in the order that they appear as parameters.

TABLE 33.3   Cache Class Properties and Methods

Property/Method	Description
Key	The string key used to refer to the cached item.
Value	The item (a System.Object parameter) that is added to the Cache.
Dependencies	A single or multiple files, directories, or the keys to another cached item on which this new item depends. When either the file or cached item changes, this cached item is removed from the Cache.
AbsoluteExpiration	The time at which the item is removed from the Cache.
SlidingExperation	The time interval at which the item is removed from the Cache if it has not been accessed during this time. If the item is accessed, the expiration is set to be the access time plus the time specified by this value.
Priority	A CacheItemPriority enumeration value that is used by the Cache when evicting objects.
OnRemoveCallback	A delegate (event handler) that gets invoked whenever a cached item is removed.

The following code illustrates the use of the Cache class:

```
if Cache['DateToday'] <> nil then
  Response.Write('From Cache: '+
    DateTime(Cache['DateToday']).Today.ToLongDateString)
else begin
  Response.Write('From System: '+
```

```
      System.DateTime.Today.ToLongDateString);
   Cache.Add('DateToday', System.DateTime.Today, nil, GetMidnight,
      Cache.NoSlidingExpiration, CacheItemPriority.Default, nil)
end;
```

This code displays today's date retrieved from the system or the Cache if today's date exists in the Cache. The call to Cache.Add() illustrates using the AbsoluteExpiration parameter, which is set to midnight through the helper function GetMidnight(). In case you're wondering, the GetMidnight() function simply returns a DateTime value for tomorrow by adding 1 day to today's date:

```
function GetMidnight: System.DateTime;
begin
  Result := System.DateTime.Today.AddDays(1);
end;
```

Data Caching Example

Caching simple data types can be useful. The real value in performance is gained when you Cache data that would otherwise be retrieved from another resource such as a database. Listing 33.3 shows an excerpt from an example that illustrates this technique.

LISTING 33.3 Caching Data

```
1:    const
2:      c_cnstr = 'server=XWING;database=Northwind;Trusted_Connection=Yes';
3:      c_sel   = 'select * from products';
4:
5:    procedure TWebForm1.Page_Load(sender: System.Object;
6:      e: System.EventArgs);
7:    begin
8:      if not IsPostBack then
9:        GetData;
10:   end;
11:
12:   procedure TWebForm1.GetData;
13:   var
14:     sqlcn: SqlConnection;
15:     sqlDa: SqlDataAdapter;
16:     Ds: DataSet;
17:     dtView: DataView;
18:   begin
19:
20:     dtView := Cache['dvProducts'] as DataView;
21:     if dtView = nil then
22:     begin
23:       sqlcn := SqlConnection.Create(c_cnstr);
24:       sqlDA := SqlDataAdapter.Create(c_sel, sqlcn);
25:       Ds := DataSet.Create;
26:       sqlDA.Fill(Ds);
27:       try
28:         dtView := DataView.Create(Ds.Tables['Table']);
29:         Cache['dvProducts'] := dtView;
30:         Label1.Text := 'From Database';
```

LISTING 33.3   Continued

```
31:      finally
32:        sqlcn.Close;
33:      end;
34:    end
35:    else
36:      Label1.Text := 'From Cache';
37:
38:    DataGrid1.DataSource := dtView;
39:    DataBind;
40:  end;
41:
42:  procedure TWebForm1.DataGrid1_PageIndexChanged(source: System.Object;
43:    e: System.Web.UI.WebControls.DataGridPageChangedEventArgs);
44:  begin
45:    GetData;
46:    DataGrid1.CurrentPageIndex := e.NewPageIndex;
47:    DataGrid1.DataBind;
48:  end;
```

▶ Find the code on the CD: \Code\Chapter 33\Ex04.

The GetData() procedure (lines 12–40) is the one we'll want to examine closely. Line 20 attempts to retrieve a DataView from the Cache. If it does not exist, it will be nil. That being the case, the data is obtained from the Northwind database. In addition to extracting this data from the database, it gets added to the Cache (line 29). Upon subsequent requests for this page, line 20 should not return nil but instead the cached DataView.

This technique works well for data that will not change, such as lookup information. It will also work for data that does change—in which case, you will need to develop code to synchronize data stored in the Cache and the database. This could be as simple as refreshing the entire DataView when a change is made. It can also increase in complexity, such as updating both the Cache and database with only the modified data. Another useful solution is to cache the information until some specific time (for instance, midnight). This works nicely for rarely updated data. Several factors will determine approaches you should take, such as scalability and system requirements to name a few. For instance, you wouldn't want to expend system memory by caching huge DataSets, which would defeat any performance benefits you intended to gain.

Cache File Dependencies

It is possible to make a cached item dependent on single or multiple associated files, directories, or other cached items. When the associated entity is modified, the dependant item is removed from the Cache. Listing 33.4 shows how to establish such a dependency using the Cache.Insert() method.

LISTING 33.4   Establishing a Dependency on a Cached File

```
1:    procedure TWebForm1.Button1_Click(sender: System.Object;
2:      e: System.EventArgs);
3:    var
```

LISTING 33.4   Continued

```
 4:     str: String;
 5:   begin
 6:     str := Cache['MyData'] as System.String;
 7:     if str = nil then
 8:     begin
 9:       Label1.Text := 'Not in Cache';
10:       Str := 'Now in Cache';
11:       Cache.Insert('MyData', Str,
12:         CacheDependency.Create(MapPath('cache.txt')));
13:     end
14:     else
15:       Label1.Text := Str;
16:   end;
```

▶ Find the code on the CD: `\Code\Chapter 33\Ex05`.

Lines 11–12 associate the file `cache.txt` as the dependency for the cached `'MyData'` item. When `cache.txt` is modified, `'MyItem'` will be removed from the `Cache`. This allows you to establish an external mechanism by which you can invoke a refresh of the cached information. The following section illustrates a practical example of this technique.

> **TIP**
>
> Use the `MapPath()` method to translate virtual paths to physical paths as used in Listing 33.4.

In this example, when the file, `'cache.txt'` is modified or deleted, the item keyed by `'MyData'` is also removed from the `Cache`.

You can also establish a key dependency. A key dependency is one in which a cached item is dependent on another cached item. This is done by using the INSERT statement as

```
keyAry[0] := 'Item1';
keyAry[1] := 'Item2';
Cache.Insert('MyData', Str, CacheDependency.Create(nil, keyAry));
```

In this example, the item with the key `'MyData'` becomes dependant on the items keyed as `'Item1'` and `'Item2'`.

The technique of creating an array of items can also be used in establishing a dependency on multiple files or directories by creating a string array of file or directory names.

Extending File Dependencies for Use in SQL Server

This section illustrates a realistic example of using cache dependencies.

Listing 33.5 shows a `GetData()` method similar to that seen in Listing 33.3.

LISTING 33.5   GetData() with a Cached Dependency

```
1:   procedure TWebForm1.GetData;
2:   var
3:     sqlcn: SqlConnection;
```

LISTING 33.5   Continued

```
4:      sqlDa: SqlDataAdapter;
5:      Ds: DataSet;
6:      dtView: DataView;
7:    begin
8:      dtView := Cache['dvEmp'] as DataView;
9:      if dtView = nil then
10:     begin
11:       sqlcn := SqlConnection.Create(c_cnstr);
12:       sqlDA := SqlDataAdapter.Create(c_sel, sqlcn);
13:       Ds := DataSet.Create;
14:       sqlDA.Fill(Ds);
15:       try
16:         dtView := DataView.Create(Ds.Tables['Table']);
17:         Cache.Insert('dvEmp', dtView,
18:           CacheDependency.Create(MapPath('cache.txt')));
19:         Label1.Text := 'From Database';
20:       finally
21:         sqlcn.Close;
22:       end;
23:     end
24:     else
25:       Label1.Text := 'From Cache';
26:     DataGrid1.DataSource := dtView;
27:     DataBind;
28:   end;
```

▶ Find the code on the CD: \Code\Chapter 33\Ex06.

Lines 17 and 18 are where the dependency is established. When the file 'cache.txt' is modified or deleted, the DataView is removed from the Cache. You would want to do this when the data in the database is modified, making the cached information out of sync. The question this raises is how to modify cache.txt. If the underlying database is modified through an external program, this external program can modify the file. If the database is modified by this same ASP.NET application, it too can modify the file; however, one must wonder why we wouldn't just refresh the data without dealing with the file at all.

The idea here is to invoke a refresh of the cached data whenever the data stored in the table that the DataView represents gets changed. It really doesn't matter where the data was modified. The way to do this is to create a trigger on the SQL table that modified the file. An example is shown here:

```
CREATE TRIGGER EMP_UPD_CACHE
ON Employees
FOR UPDATE, DELETE, INSERT
AS
  DECLARE @ShCmd VARCHAR(100)
  SELECT @ShCmd = 'echo '+ Cast(GetDate() as VARCHAR(25))+' >
➥"C:\Data\cache.txt"'
  EXEC master..xp_cmdshell @ShCmd, no_output
```

This trigger will write information to the `cache.txt` file when a record is updated deleted or added to the Employees table, which will effectively invoke the refresh we desire.

Cache-Callback Methods

This section illustrates how you can associate a callback method with an item added to the `Cache`. This callback method gets invoked whenever the items with which it is associated gets removed from the `Cache`. The callback method takes the three parameters listed here:

- `key`—String index for the cached item.

- `value`—Value of the item removed from the `Cache`.

- `reason`—Reason item was removed from the `Cache`. This value is one of the `CacheItemRemovedReason` enumeration values.

Valid values for the `reason` parameter are

- `DependencyChanged`—A dependency on the item was modified.

- `Expired`—The item reached its expiration period.

- `Removed`—The item was removed from the `Cache` through the `Remove()` or `Insert()` method.

- `Underused`—The item was removed by the system to free up memory.

Listing 33.6 demonstrates how to use the callback method with cached items.

LISTING 33.6   Cache-callback Example

```
1:    procedure TWebForm1.Page_Load(sender: System.Object; e: System.EventArgs);
2:    var
3:      keyAry: array[0..0] of String;
4:    begin
5:      if not IsPostBack then
6:      begin
7:        Cache.Insert('Item1', 'Item 1', nil,
8:          System.DateTime.Now.AddSeconds(10), Cache.NoSlidingExpiration,
9:          CacheItemPriority.Default, CacheItemRemoved);
10:        Cache.Insert('Item2', 'Item 2', nil,
11:          System.DateTime.Now.AddSeconds(10), Cache.NoSlidingExpiration,
12:          CacheItemPriority.Default, CacheItemRemoved);
13:        keyAry[0] := 'Item2';
14:        Cache.Insert('Item3', 'Item 3', CacheDependency.Create(nil, keyAry),
15:          System.DateTime.Now.AddSeconds(10), Cache.NoSlidingExpiration,
16:          CacheItemPriority.Default, CacheItemRemoved);
```

LISTING 33.6   Continued

```
17:     end;
18:   end;
19:
20:   procedure TWebForm1.CacheItemRemoved(Key: System.String; Value: TObject;
21:     Reason: CacheItemRemovedReason);
22:   begin
23:     FItemArray := Application['Log'] as ArrayList;
24:     if FItemArray = nil then
25:     begin
26:       FItemArray := ArrayList.Create;
27:       Application['Log'] := FItemArray;
28:     end;
29:     FItemArray.Add(Key+': '+Enum(Reason).ToString());
30:   end;
31:
32:   procedure TWebForm1.btnRemove_Click(sender: System.Object;
33:     e: System.EventArgs);
34:   begin
35:     Cache.Remove('Item2');
36:     btnGetLog_Click(nil, nil);
37:   end;
38:
39:   procedure TWebForm1.btnGetLog_Click(sender: System.Object;
40:     e: System.EventArgs);
41:   begin
42:     if Application['Log'] <> nil then
43:     begin
44:       DataGrid1.DataSource := Application['Log'];
45:       DataGrid1.DataBind;
46:       DataBind;
47:     end;
48:     Label1.Text := 'Items cached: '+Cache.Count.ToString
49:   end;
```

▶ Find the code on the CD: \Code\Chapter 33\Ex07.

In this example, lines 7–16 inserts three items to the Cache. The item inserted at line 14 (Item3), is also associated with Item2 through a dependency. This means that when Item2 is changed or removed, Item3 will be removed from the Cache.

Lines 20–30 show the callback method that is used when items are removed from the Cache. This method adds the item name and reason to an ArrayList that is stored in the HttpApplicationState object. This list is used by the btnGetLog_Click() event handler, which binds the ArrayList to a DataGrid. The btnRemove_Click() event handler removes Item2 from the Cache and calls the btnGetLog_Click() method to display the results. Because Item3 is dependent on Item2, removing Item2 should also result in Item3 being removed. This is verified in Figure 33.2.

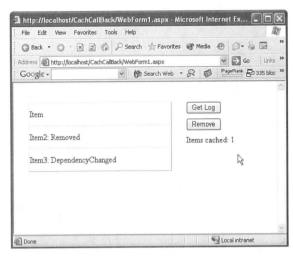

FIGURE 33.2   Results of the CacheItemRemoveCallback.

State Management in ASP.NET Applications

State management is related to caching—whereas caching keeps global state for multiple clients, session state keeps state for a single client. Web applications are stateless; therefore, they don't inherently track user information between requests. Each request is viewed as a distinct request entirely unrelated to previous requests.

ASP.NET provides several levels at which state can be managed. These are cookies, ViewState, Session, and Application.

The following sections cover each of these different state management mechanisms.

Managing State with Cookies

Cookies are basically text that the Web server can place in the client's browser. They are transferred via HTTP headers. As the user hits various pages within a Web site or application, the server can examine the content of these cookies. A cookie is associated with the domain of the server that initiated its creation. Therefore, a cookie can never be transferred to other domains. A cookie can be temporary in that it lasts for the current session only. It can also be persistent across multiple sessions. This is one mechanism that the server can use to maintain state information.

Creating a Cookie

Creating a cookie is simple. The cookie itself is encapsulated by the HTTPCookie class defined in the System.Web.HttpCookie namespace. The following code shows how to create a cookie whose value contains the text entered from a TextBox control:

```
var
  MyCookie: HttpCookie;
begin
  MyCookie := HttpCookie.Create('MyName', TextBox1.Text);
```

```
  Response.Cookies.Add(MyCookie);
  Response.Redirect('WebForm2.aspx')
end;
```

▶ Find the code on the CD: \Code\Chapter 33\Ex08.

This code creates a cookie with the name `'MyName'` and adds it to the collection of cookies in the `HttpResponse` object. This is the server's way of telling the browser to maintain the cookie specified. To illustrate how the cookie is available in a separate request, the user is redirected to another page that will retrieve the cookie.

Retrieving Cookie Values

When the browser makes a request to a Web server, it sends along its collection of cookies for that domain. They can be retrieved through the `HttpRequest.Cookies` collection as shown here:

```
procedure TWebForm2.Page_Load(sender: System.Object; e: System.EventArgs);
begin
  if Request.Cookies['MyName'] <> nil then
    Label1.Text := System.String.Format('Hello {0}, Welcome to the site',
      Request.Cookies['MyName'].Value)
  else
    Label1.Text := 'I don''t know you';
end;
```

▶ Find the code on the CD: \Code\Chapter 33\Ex08.

This code demonstrates how the cookie has been transferred by the browser as part of the request. The server can then obtain the cookie's value and, in this example, use it as part of a string displayed to the user.

Creating Persistent Cookies

A persistent cookie is one that the browser places on the user's hard drive in a directory that the browser knows about. The server can initiate this by adding an expiration date to the `HTTPCookie.Expires` property. The following code illustrates this procedure:

```
var
  MyCookie: HttpCookie;
begin
  MyCookie := HttpCookie.Create('MyName', TextBox1.Text);
  if cbxRemember.Checked then
    MyCookie.Expires := System.DateTime.Today.AddDays(30);
  Response.Cookies.Add(MyCookie);
  Response.Redirect('WebForm2.aspx')
end;
```

In this example, a `CheckBox` on the Web From determines whether the server will tell the browser to create a persistent cookie. If it does, the cookie is set to expire 30 days from today.

Now suppose that a user were to revisit a site with this code after having added a persistent cookie. The code in Listing 33.7 demonstrates how to use the cookie value to present a welcome message and to pre-populate `TextBox` so the user wouldn't have to reenter her name.

LISTING 33.7 Using a Cookie to Pre-populate Controls

```
procedure TWebForm1.Page_Load(sender: System.Object; e: System.EventArgs);
begin
  if not IsPostBack then
    if not Request.Browser.Cookies then
      lblNoCookie.Text := 'Your browser does not support cookies.'
    else begin
      if Request.Cookies['MyName'] <> nil then
      begin
        lblWelcome.Text := System.String.Format('Welcome back {0}',
          Request.Cookies['MyName'].Value);
        TextBox1.Text := Request.Cookies['MyName'].Value;
      end;
    end;
end;
```

▶ Find the code on the CD: `\Code\Chapter 33\Ex08`.

To delete a cookie from the user's machine, you can do one of two things:

- You can add another cookie of the same name that is session based; it has no assignment to the Expires property.

- You can add a cookie with System.DateTime.Now assigned to the Expires property, causing the cookie to be removed from the user's machine.

Cookie Drawbacks

Although convenient and easily implemented, cookies do have their drawbacks. They can only contain a small amount of data, 4KB specifically. Additionally, they can only store string data. Therefore, you would have to convert data such as dates, integers, floats, and so on to strings prior to storing them in cookies. Cookies are also browser dependant, and some browsers do not support them. Last, they require that the user permits your application to store files on her machine. Cookies have gotten a bad rep because they consume space on users' machines without them knowing about it. Therefore, many users opt for disabling cookie support in their browsers.

Cookies are great to use for some circumstances. However, when it comes to managing state in more complex scenarios, ASP.NET has other means for doing this, which I discuss next.

Working with ViewState

ViewState is the component of ASP.NET pages that keeps track of information such as server control properties. It is handled automatically; you typically do nothing with it other than to disable it if you don't need it. It merits discussion here because there are things you can do to improve performance of your Web applications by making adjustments to ViewState. Plus, you can use that state bag to store custom information for these round-trips.

Here's how ViewState works. When you fill out a Web form, the data entered into the form is sent to the server as part of the POST/GET commands. The server, in turn, packages this information into a hidden field, ViewState, and sends them back to the client along with the rest of the response. The client doesn't do anything with this information. ViewState is supplied to the client so that it is sent back to the server to use upon subsequent requests. This is referred to as round-tripping. The simple case is that the server uses the information to set controls properties upon a post-back of the page.

> **NOTE**
>
> The actual name of the ViewState hidden field is __ViewState. I refer to it as simply ViewState in this section.

In many examples that I have seen to demonstrate ViewState, you're asked to create an ASP.NET application with a few form fields and a Submit button. You're told to fill out the fields and click the Submit button. The page will post-back, and the fields will be populated with the information you originally entered. If you click the Back button on your browser, the fields will retain their values. This is credited to ViewState.

It is true that the properties of controls, such as the Text property of the TextBox control, are added to the ViewState. However, control properties that are sent to the server as part of the POST command are used to generate the HTML in the response instead of those values contained in the ViewState. You can see this by disabling ViewState for the entire page of an application similar to that just described. You will see that the controls retain their values. In other words, the page is still stateful, even without ViewState.

So why bother with ViewState at all? Remember that the server uses values passed as part of the POST command to initialize controls with data in generating the HTML. The only properties that get initialized as such are those that were included in the POST command. Other properties rely on ViewState. For example, consider the page shown in Figure 33.3.

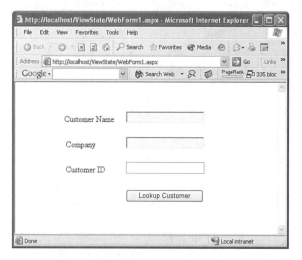

FIGURE 33.3   Example customer lookup form.

▶ Find the code on the CD: \Code\Chapter 33\Ex09.

Imagine that this is a customer lookup form. The Lookup Customer button is disabled by default. The Page_Load() event handler contains the following code:

```
if not IsPostBack then
  btnLookup.Enabled := LoggedIn;
```

LoggedIn() simply returns True. It simulates some form of test for user authentication.

With ViewState enabled for the page, the page works as you would expect. When the user first goes to the page, btnLookup.Enabled is set to True. When clicking the Lookup Customer button, it retains its enabled state. However, when disabling ViewState for the page, clicking the Lookup Customer button reveals that it will be disabled on the post-back. This is because the LoggedIn() method is not invoked since this is a post-back. The server generates the HTML for the button based on its design-time property values. The server has no information in the POST command properties, nor is there any state information in ViewState from which it can determine a different property value for the button's Enabled property.

You can see where ViewState serves a good purpose. However, more often than not, you really do not need ViewState. It is generally recommended that you disable ViewState on all pages that do not need it. This will prevent performance loss resulting in the extra bytes being tagged along in your HTML documents.

Disabling ViewState on the Page
You can disable ViewState for an entire page by adding it to the @ Page directive. This is shown here:

```
<%@ Page language="c#" EnableViewState="False" Codebehind="WebForm1.pas"
➥AutoEventWireup="True" Inherits="WebForm1.TWebForm1" %>
```

Disabling ViewState for a Control
You can disable ViewState for a specific control by simply setting its EnableViewState property to False in the Object Inspector. You can also edit the .aspx file directly as shown here:

```
<asp:button id=btnLookup
    style="Z-INDEX: 9; LEFT: 222px; POSITION: absolute;
    TOP: 206px" runat="server" enableviewstate="False"
    enabled="False" text="Lookup Customer">
</asp:button>
```

Adding Values to the State Bag
If you recall from the section on cookies, some browsers do not support cookies or the feature has been disabled by the user. You can store the same type of information in the ViewState by adding them to the state bag (or ViewState property of each control). Adding a value to the state bag is simple, as shown in the following line:

```
ViewState.Add('MyData', 'MyDataText');
```

This adds the item 'MyDataText' keyed off the string 'MyData'. To reference an item in the state bag, simply index it by its string key:

```
Response.Write(ViewState['MyData']);
```

▶ Find the code on the CD: \Code\Chapter 33\Ex10.

> **NOTE**
>
> Unlike cookies, which are restricted to storing only strings, ViewState supports storing arbitrary objects.

Session State Management

Session state management occurs during the course of a user's visit to a site. It typically begins once the user visits the site and ends when the user leaves the site.

When a user first enters a site, ASP.NET creates a unique session for that user. This session is an instance of the HttpSessionState class. The session consumes a certain amount of memory for this user. Additionally, the user is given a unique ID, which is passed to the user's browser and returned to the server on each request during the run of the session. By default, this is all done via a cookie.

The session remains in memory until the user leaves the site or until the session has timed out, which, by default, occurs after 20 minutes of inactivity.

You can store information in the HttpSessionState class instance that can be retrieved upon subsequent requests.

Session information is maintained by a session state provider. This provider is run in one of three modes: InProc, StateService, or SQLServer.

- InProc—Session data is maintained within the same domain as the ASP.NET application. It is within the context of aspnet_wp.exe. This is the default setting.

- StateServer—Session data is maintained within the context of a Windows NT Service aspnet_state.exe. This service can be run on the same or on a different machine.

- SQLServer—Session data is maintained in a predefined SQL Server database.

- Off—Session state is disabled.

Storing and Retrieving Information Using the Session Object

The following code demonstrates how to add data to the Session object:

```
Session.Add('UserName', TextBox1.Text);
```

To retrieve this same information, you would issue a statement such as

```
Response.Write('Welcome '+Session['UserName'].ToString);
```

You can add any object to the Session class. For instance, the following code adds a DataSet to the Session class:

```
Session.Add('MyData', DataSet1);
```

To remove an item from the Session object, simply call its Remove() method as

```
Session.Remove('MyData');
```

Changing the Default Session Timeout

You can change the session's default timeout by modifying the `web.config` file. The default timeout is 20 minutes. The following modification to `web.config` sets the timeout to 60 minutes:

```
<configuration>
  <system.web>
    <sessionState timeout="60"/>
  </system.web>
</configuration>
```

Making Sessions Cookieless

Earlier, I stated how the `SessionID` is passed between the server and browser via a cookie. When discussing cookies in this chapter, I pointed out some drawbacks to cookies, such as the user disabling cookie support in her browser. This would render the `Session` cookie unusable for an ASP.NET site. Therefore, you can change how ASP.NET transfers the `SessionID`. It entails modifying the `web.config` file as shown here:

```
<configuration>
  <system.web>
    <sessionState cookieless="true" />
  </system.web>
</configuration>
```

When this is done, the `SessionID` is passed as part of the URL. This is called cookie munging. A URL with the `SessionID` would look something like the one here:

```
http://www.xapware.com/SessionEx/(kxn1f555r4xgbe45j1r4wcyf)/WebForm1.aspx
```

The `SessionID` is the portion in bold.

Using this technique has a few drawbacks. First, you cannot place absolute links to pages within your site. All links must be relative to the current page. If you can live with that, this is a great way to get around cookie limitations on the client side. Second, it reduces the usefulness of client and proxy-side caching of complete HTML pages. URLs change for each session, so yesterday's cached pages will not be used today, for instance.

Storing Session Data in a Session State Server

By default, the ASP.NET applications use an in-process Session State Server. This ties session information directly to the ASP.NET application in that they are both running in the same process. If the ASP.NET application were to be shut down, all session information would be lost. This is the disadvantage of the `InProc` mode. The advantage is one of performance. With the session information existing within the same process and machine for that matter, data retrieval is faster. The following `web.config` setting shows the `Session`'s default `InProc` setting:

```
<configuration>
  <system.web>
    <sessionState  mode="InProc"/>
  </system.web>
</configuration>
```

To configure for an Out-of-Proc Session State Server, the `web.config` file would contain something similar to

```
<configuration>
  <system.web>
    <sessionState mode="StateServer"
      stateConnectionString="tcpip=192.168.0.20:42424"/>
  </system.web>
</configuration>
```

`tcpip` refers to the IP address of the machine hosting the session state server. In this example, the port used is `42424`. You can change this and be sure to make it a port unused by other processes on the machine.

To start the session state server on the machine that will be hosting it, you simply have to issue `net start aspnet_state` on the command line as shown here:

```
C:\>net start aspnet_state
The ASP.NET State Service service is starting.
The ASP.NET State Service service was started successfully.
C:\>
```

By storing session information out of process, you gain the benefit of reducing the chances of session data being lost. If the ASP.NET application or if the Web server were to be shut down, the session information would be retained by the session state server on another machine most likely. Again, the performance here is reduced and not only because of network transfer of data, but also because of the serialization/deserialization operations that must take place.

Storing Session Data in SQL Server

It is possible to store session information in SQL Server using a set of predefined tables. This approach comes with the greatest robustness, but also with the least performance. However, for applications needing robust failover, this is the best option because you can take advantage of database clustering to deal with database failures.

To get set up for storing state information in SQL Server, you must

1. Create the predefined database in SQL Server.

2. Configure the `web.config` file to point to that SQL Server.

Creating the SQL Server State Database

This first step involves running Enterprise Manager and running a ready-made script to create the database and tables needed. There are two sets of script pairs:

- `InstallSqlState.sql`—Creates the ASPState and TempDB databases. State information is maintained in the TempDB database, which only holds this information temporarily. If SQL Server is shut down, the data is lost.

- `UninstallSqlState.sql`—Uninstalls the database created with `InstallSqlState.sql`.

- `InstallPersistSqlState.sql`—Installs the ASPState database. This version of the database stores state information in the same database, and therefore state data is persistent.

- `UninstallPersistSqlState.sql`—Uninstalls the database created with `InstallPersistSqlState.sql`.

You will find these scripts located in the following directory:

```
%SystemRoot%\Microsoft.NET\Framework\[Framework Version]\
```

Depending on which install script you chose to run, you should find the ASPState and possibly the TempDB databases in SQL Server through the Enterprise Manager.

Modifying web.config for SQLServer State Management

Once your database is set up, you need to modify the `web.config` file to point the ASP.NET application to the database for state management. The `web.config` should look similar to that shown here:

```
<configuration>
  <system.web>
    <sessionState mode="SQLServer"
        sqlConnectionString="data source=localhost;user id=sa;pwd=somepwd" />
  </system.web>
</configuration>
```

Note the setting of the mode attribute to `SQLServer`. Additionally, you'll see the connection information provided so that a connection can be made to the database.

Session Events

Two events related to `Sessions` exist that you can handle. These are the `Session_Start` and `Session_End` events. The `Session_Start` event occurs when a user first visits the site. The `Session_End` event occurs when the user leaves the site or when the session times out. Both events are declared under the `TGlobal` class. This class is found in the `Global.pas` file included with your project.

One way to use these events is to maintain a running user count on your site. When a user visits, you up the count. When a user leaves, you decrement the count. Listing 33.8 shows how you might do this.

LISTING 33.8   Storing a User Count in Session_Start

```
procedure TGlobal.Session_Start(sender: System.Object; e: EventArgs);
begin
  Application.Lock;
  try
    if Application['NumUsers'] = nil then
      Application['NumUsers'] := System.Object(Integer(1))
    else
      Application['NumUsers'] :=
        System.Object(Integer(Application['NumUsers'])+1);
```

LISTING 33.8   Continued

```
  finally
    Application.UnLock;
  end;
end;
```

▶ Find the code on the CD: \Code\Chapter 33\Ex12.

Conversely, you would decrement the user count in the Session_End event as shown in Listing 33.9.

LISTING 33.9   Storing a User Count in Session_End

```
 1:    procedure TGlobal.Session_End(sender: System.Object; e: EventArgs);
 2:    begin
 3:      Application.Lock;
 4:      try
 5:        if Application['NumUsers'] <> nil then
 6:          Application['NumUsers'] :=
 7:            System.Object(Integer(Application['NumUsers'])-1)
 8:        else
 9:          Application['NumUsers'] := System.Object(Integer(0));
10:      finally
11:        Application.UnLock;
12:      end;
13:    end;
```

▶ Find the code on the CD: \Code\Chapter 33\Ex12.

You might have noticed that both these event handlers make use of the Application object, which I discuss in the next section.

Application State Management

Application state is different from session state in that data stored at the application level is available to all users of the application. In session state, session data is stored for the user of the session only. Figure 33.4 depicts this difference.

Application state is maintained by the HttpApplicationState class. This class is a dictionary, and it is created upon the first request to the application. This is unlike the HttpSessionState class, which is created upon each user's visit to the site.

The HttpApplicationState class works very much like the HttpSessionState class.

Information you would store in the HttpApplicationState class needs to be available to all users of the applications. For instance, connection strings to the database and number of users signed on are examples of application-wide information.

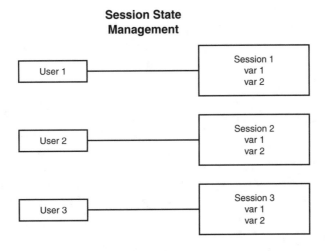

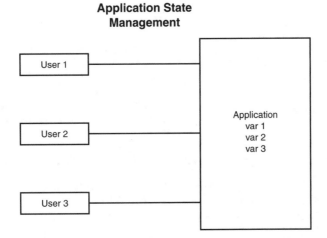

FIGURE 33.4   Difference between application and session state.

Storing Information Using the Application Object

You can add, access, and remove data similarly to how you do so with the `HttpSessionState` class.

To add an item, simply do the following:

```
Application['NumUsers'] := System.Object(Integer(1));
```

To remove an item, call the `HttpApplicationState.Remove()` function like this:

```
Application.Remove('MyItem');
```

Accessing an item is equally as simple:

```
MyItem := Application['MyItem'];
```

You can clear the contents of the Application object by calling its RemoveAll() method:

```
Application.RemoveAll;
```

Synchronizing Access to State Data in the Application Object

The operations of the HttpApplicationState class are thread-safe, but if you intend to perform a group of operations, you might want to lock writing access to the application state until you are finished with your set of operations. Listings 33.8 and 33.9 illustrate using the Application.Lock() and Application.UnLock() methods for locking and unlocking write access to the data maintained by the Application object.

Note that it is necessary to match every Lock() call with an UnLock() call that is protected by a try-finally clause.

By doing this, you can prevent concurrent access, which can cause deadlocks, race conditions, and other problems.

Using Cache Versus Application

It might appear that there are close likenesses between the Cache and HttpApplicationState classes. Both have the capability to store data in an application-wide context, and the syntax for dealing with them is basically identical. The differences, however, are great.

Both the Cache and HttpApplicationState classes provide a mechanism for storing application-wide data and can be used for managing state because of this. This is where the likenesses end.

The Cache class takes management of this data further than that of the HttpApplicationClass.

First, accessing data in the Cache class is fully thread-safe. This is unlike the HttpApplicationState class, which requires you to surround data access with synchronization methods Lock() and UnLock().

Second, the Cache class, based on a prioritization scheme, can free data from the Cache when it has not been used in order to free up memory when resources are low.

Also, you get more control over the items added to the Cache by setting absolute and sliding expiration policies.

Last, you can associate items with the Cache to other cached items or to a file, which will result in the cached items being removed from the Cache.

The HttpApplicationState class serves well as a general state store for information needing to be available application-wide and needing to exist during the life of the application.

The Cache class is better suited for complex state management in which greater control over the cached data is required.

CHAPTER 34

Developing Custom ASP.NET Server Controls

by Nick Hodges

One of ASP.NET's greatest strengths is the capability to create powerful components for use in your Web sites. Delphi developers have long known of the power and convenience of using components in their Windows applications. Now with ASP.NET, you can bring those component building skills to the world of Web application development. The Framework Class Library (FCL) provides a feature rich framework for developing custom components that will do almost anything that the limits of HTML and JavaScript will allow you to do. Web developers no longer have to envy Windows developers for having a powerful and rich set of controls to build professional looking applications.

Two main types of controls exist that you can build for your Web applications. The first type is user controls. User controls are simple to build and use in your Web pages. They function very similarly to regular pages and allow you to build up sections of a Web site using the WYSIWYG page designer. If you are familiar with frames in the VCL, you already have an understanding of what a user control is.

The other type of ASP.NET component is Web controls. Web controls are more like the traditional Delphi components. They are installed into the component palette and drag-n-dropped on to your forms like regular components.

This chapter focuses on two areas: the development and use of user and Web controls.

User Controls

This section discusses user controls and shows you how to build and add a user control to a Web page—both via the IDE and in code.

A user control is server-side control that you design in the page designer and save as a text file with the extension *.ascx. In Delphi for .NET, a user control will consist of the *.ascx file and an associated *.pas file that will be compiled into the resulting ASP.NET-based DLL. The *.ascx page is deployed and controlled along with the DLL on the server, so you as the developer can manage the control and make changes to it as needed and desired.

User controls are inserted into other pages either via the designer itself or manually by additions in code. The user control simply becomes part of the page to which it is added, like any other control. If you view user controls simply as a chunk of HTML that gets "injected" into a specific spot in a Web page, you have a good idea of how they work.

Normally, a Web page on a Web site will consist of collections of user controls that are pieced together to create a whole page. Items such as left and right panels, headers and footers, and the main body of pages can be set up as user controls, and then pieced together to create a single page. Because user controls are discreet "chunks" of HTML code, you can better manage a site as a collection of user controls rather than a set of monolithic pages. User controls divide a site into discreet sections that can be better controlled and managed.

You should also note that user controls are more powerful than simply server-side includes. User controls can have code attached that make them more robust than simply inserting HTML into a page. User controls can contain any amount of HTML, other user controls, and Web controls. All the controls can have code attached to them, increasing the functionality from simple HTML to full-fledged components. User controls represent a real instance of a class with code and data attached to it.

A Very Simple User Control

Creating a user control in Delphi for .NET couldn't be simpler. First, create a new ASP.NET application by selecting File, New, ASP.NET Web Application. Name the Application `"SimpleUserControl"`. After you have the application saved and ready to go, select File, New, Other and select the Delphi ASP Files item in the TreeView on the left. Then, in the ListView on the right, select ASP.NET User Control and click OK.

The IDE will now create a default user control. The file WebUserControl1.ascx is created for you, and it is accompanied by WebUserControl1.pas, the Pascal file that represents and defines the class for your user control. Now select File, Save As and save the user control file with the name `'ucSimpleControl'`. This will change the name of both the *.ascx and *.pas files.

What you now have should look something like that shown in Figure 34.1.

You now have an empty user control ready to be developed. From here, you can build the control using all the functionality of the designer, just as you would a full page. You can add HTML and Web controls and edit the *.ascx page directly. The IDE will manage the control for you, updating the code for both associated files.

For simplicity sake, let's just add some simple text to the control. Click on the designer and type, right on the designer, the following:

```
This is a simple user control.
```

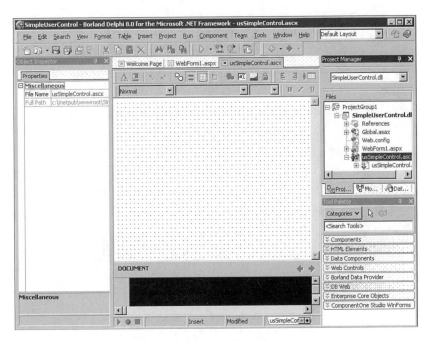

FIGURE 34.1   The IDE displaying an empty user control.

Now, go back to the WebForm1 page and add the following text:

```
This page demonstrates how to use and display a simple user control
```

Click Return after typing that, and then select Insert, Insert User Control from the menu bar. In the dialog box, click Browse, and select the ucSimpleFile.ascx control. Your dialog box should look like that shown in Figure 34.2.

FIGURE 34.2   The Insert User Control dialog box with the user control selected.

After you click OK, the IDE will insert the user control into the page, representing it with a small, gray box that has the word UserControl in it, followed by the value for the ID (or name) property. At this point, you can select the control in the designer and set some of its properties in the Object Inspector. For now, change its ID property to **SimpleUserControl**. Your form will now look like that shown in Figure 34.3.

Now run the application, and you should see the user control in the resulting page in Internet Explorer as shown in Figure 34.4.

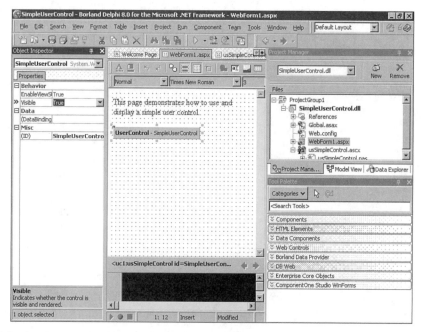

FIGURE 34.3   Setting properties in the user control.

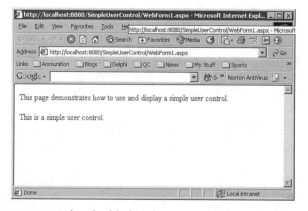

FIGURE 34.4   The user control embedded in the page and shown in Internet Explorer.

Examining the Simple Control

Now we can take a look at exactly what is going on behind-the-scenes of our user control. First, take a look at the `ucSimpleControl.pas` file. The code there declares a class for the user control as shown in Listing 34.1.

LISTING 34.1   The Simple Control Declaration

```
1:   type
2:     TWebUserControl1 = class(System.Web.UI.UserControl)
```

LISTING 34.1   Continued

```
 3:    strict private
 4:      procedure InitializeComponent;
 5:    strict private
 6:      procedure Page_Load(sender: System.Object; e: System.EventArgs);
 7:    strict protected
 8:      procedure OnInit(e: System.EventArgs); override;
 9:    private
10:      { Private Declarations }
11:    public
12:      { Public Declarations }
13:    end;
```

▶ Find the code on the CD: \Code\Chapter 34\ControlExamples.

Note that the class descends from the `System.Web.UI.UserControl` class (line 2). This class is the basis for all user controls. The class also declares a `Page_Load()` event handler (line 6), which you can implement to perform any initialization for the user control. (The next section covers doing that.) You can, of course, add methods, fields, and properties to this class as you would any other regular Delphi class.

The other half of the control is the `*.ascx` file. The file should look something like this:

```
<%@ Control Language="c#" AutoEventWireup="false"
➥Codebehind="ucSimpleControl.pas"
➥Inherits="ucSimpleControl.TWebUserControl1"%>

This is a simple user control.
```

The first line is an ASP.NET-specific tag that defines the control. The rest of the code in this unit is just normal HTML. You can edit this code as desired, and your changes will be reflected in the IDE as well as the application itself. The code can also contain normal ASP.NET control tags, as you will see when we build a slightly more complicated control in the next section.

Table 34.1 discusses the attributes of the `<@ Control %>` tag.

TABLE 34.1   `<@ Control @>` Attributes

Attribute	Description
Language	This tag defines the scripting language that the page will use. Delphi for .NET doesn't include a Delphi language scripting compiler, so the default is set to C#.
AutoEventWireup	This attribute determines whether the event handlers in your code are automatically "wired up" to the associated delegates. For applications developed in Delphi for .NET, the IDE generates code in the `*.pas` file to automatically hook up the event handling code, so this parameter should always be set to False.
CodeBehind	This attribute is used at design time to ensure that the Delphi for .NET IDE properly connects the `*.aspx` file with the code from the correct `*.pas` file.
Inherits	This attribute names the class that defines the code for the user control.

34

Note that this table only describes the existing attributes in the code. See the .NET SDK documentation for a complete description of attributes that can be used in the <@ Control @> tag.

Also important in the use of a user control is the tags and other code added to the page that uses the control. Right now, the WebForm1.aspx file should look something like that shown in Listing 34.2.

LISTING 34.2   BasicUserControlPage .aspx File

```
1:    <%@ Page language="c#" Debug="true" Codebehind="BasicUserControlPage.pas"
[ic.ccc]AutoEventWireup="false" Inherits="BasicUserControlPage.TWebForm2" %>
2:    <%@ Register TagPrefix="uc1" TagName="BasicUserControl"
[ic.ccc]Src="BasicUserControl.ascx" %>
3:    <!DOCTYPE HTML PUBLIC "-//W3C//DTD HTML 4.0 Transitional//EN">
4:
5:    <html>
6:      <head>
7:      <title></title>
8:      <meta name="GENERATOR" content="Borland Package Library 7.1">
9:      </head>
10:
11:     <body ms_positioning="GridLayout">
12:       <form runat="server">
13:         <p>
14:             This page demonstrates how to use and display a simple user control.
15:         </p>
16:          <uc1:basicusercontrol id="UserControl1" runat="server">
17:          </uc1:basicusercontrol>
18:       </form><br>
19:     </body>
20:   </html>
```

▶ Find the code on the CD: \Code\Chapter 34\ExamplePage.

The key part of this is the <% Register %> tag at the head of the file and the ASP.NET tag in the body of the HTML tag that represents the control itself. Table 34.2 discusses the meaning of the attributes for the <%@ Register %>.

TABLE 34.2   <%@ Register %> Attributes

Attribute Name	Description
TagPrefix	This parameter defines a prefix that will be used to label an ASP.NET tag in the *.aspx page.
TagName	This parameter gives the name of the control that will be referenced by the TagPrefix.
Src	This parameter names the file where the ASP.NET code for the user control resides.

The actual control is added to the *.aspx page as follows:

```
<uc1:ucsimplecontrol id=SimpleUserControl runat="server">
</uc1:ucsimplecontrol>
```

Note that the tag defining it starts with the value from the `TagPrefix` parameter in the `<%@ Register %>` tag—in this case, `uc1`. Then the control type is named—again, in this case, `ucsimplecontrol`. The rest of the tag is normal, just like any other tag representing an ASP.NET control in an `.aspx` page.

Thus, creating, adding, and using a user control is quite easy using ASP.NET and Delphi for .NET. Now let's try a slightly more complicated example

A User Login User Control

Most Web sites these days want users to identify themselves by logging in. Once logged in, users can be identified, and custom content, settings, and so on can be provided. This necessitates a system for logging in the user. Chances are you will need a small control that contains `TextBox` controls for username/password input. A user control is perfect for this.

To build a login interface control, create a new ASP Application. As shown previously, add a new Web User Control to the project. Save the project with the name **LoginControlTest**. Save the user control file with the name '**ucLogin.ascx**'.

From there, take the following steps:

1. From the Web Controls tab in the Component Palette, drop a `Panel` on the user control. Set its `ID` property to **LoginLabel**. Double-click on the panel and use the Backspace key to remove the word Panel from the control.

2. Deselect the Absolute Position speed button on the designer's toolbar. This will cause the `Panel` to be positioned relative to the upper left of whatever tag it is placed within. Note that the controls inside the `Panel` should remain absolutely positioned.

3. Drop two `Labels` and two `TextBox` controls from the Web Controls tab in the `Panel`. (Don't use the ones from the HTML tab.) Note that these controls, and any placed in the `Panel`, will be "owned" by the `Panel`—that is, they will move with the `Panel` rather than be independent of it. Set their ID property values to **UserNameTextBox** and **PasswordTextBox**, respectively.

4. Name the `Labels` **UsernameLabel** and **PasswordLabel**, respectively.

5. Set the `Labels`' `Text` properties to **Username:** and **Password:**, respectively.

6. Set the `TextMode` property of the `PasswordTextbox` control to **Password**.

7. Organize them as shown in Figure 34.5.

8. Drop a check box below the `TextBox` controls, name it **RememberMeCheckbox**, and set its `Text` property to **Remember Me On This Computer**.

9. Place a button below the check box, change its `ID` to **LoginButton**, and set its `Text` property to **Login**.

10. Arrange the items to your satisfaction inside the `LoginPanel`. `LoginPanel` should end up looking similar to Figure 34.5.

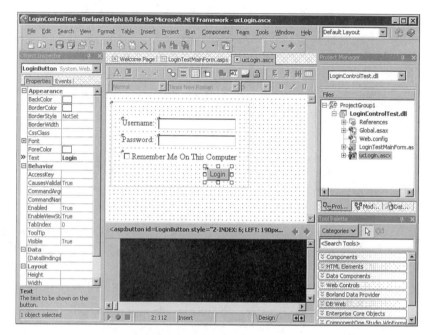

FIGURE 34.5   Login User Control in the designer.

A user control can and does have code behind it, just like a regular Web page. In this case, as seen previously, Delphi creates and manages for you a class that descends from System.Web.UI.UserControl. This class contains any code that you want to add to the control. For instance, you can add the following method to handle the user logging in:

```
procedure TWebUserControl1.DoLogin(aUsername, aPassword: &string;
  aRememberUser: Boolean);
begin
  // Do whatever login logic your application requires.
end;
```

You can then double-click on the Login button and add the following to the resulting event handler:

```
procedure TWebUserControl1.LoginButton_Click(sender: System.Object;
  e:    System.EventArgs);
begin
  DoLogin(UsernameTextBox.Text, PasswordTextBox.Text,
    RememberMeCheckbox.Checked);
end;
```

> **NOTE**
>
> One further thing to note is the actual HTML used by the control. The HTML is actually a single "chunk" of HTML code that defines an HTML form—which, of course, is exactly what the control is. This means that it should fit seamlessly within any other container tag on the Web page where it is inserted.

Now your control is ready to be used and reused in any Web page in your application. You can add it to your application wherever you like using the Insert, Insert User Control menu item. An application that shows how a simple Web page might look is included in the code for this chapter.

Web Controls

You've seen how user controls can be easily and quickly built and used to reuse HTML and Delphi code within your Web applications. However, there are times when user controls aren't sufficient. User controls are normally useful when you need a collection or composite of HTML and Web controls. Of course, sometimes you are going to want to create custom Web controls. This section covers building, installing, and using Web controls.

Just as user controls were analogous to developing custom TFrame descendents or user controls in WinForms, Web controls are analogous to developing descendents from TComponent in the VCL. Web controls can be installed into the Component Palette and dropped onto Web pages or user controls. In the following section, we'll develop a very simple Web control, discuss how it works, and then gradually adding features and functionality in order to illustrate the various capabilities of the ASP.NET component model.

Building a Very Simple Web Control

Listing 34.3 shows the code for an extremely simple Web control. It does nothing but display whatever its DisplayText property is set to. However, it does illustrate the basics of building a Web control. We'll look at this control, and then build on it, adding functionality while discussing the features of Web control development. Note that all the code for these components can be found on the accompanying CD.

LISTING 34.3   A Simple Web Control

```
1:    unit uSimpleTextControl;
2:
3:    interface
4:
5:    uses
6:      System.Web, System.Web.UI, System.ComponentModel;
7:
8:    type
9:      [DefaultProperty('DisplayText')]
10:     TSimpleTextControl = class(System.Web.UI.Control)
11:     strict private
12:       FDisplayText: string;
13:     strict protected
14:       procedure Render(Writer: HtmlTextWriter); override;
15:     public
16:       constructor Create;
17:     published
18:       function GetDisplayText: string;
19:       procedure SetDisplayText(const Value: &string);
20:     published
21:       [
```

LISTING 34.3   Continued

```
22:        DefaultValue('<Your Text Here>'),
23:        Description('The text that will be displayed in the control.'),
24:        Category('Appearance'),
25:        Bindable(True)
26:        ]
27:      property DisplayText: string read GetDisplayText write SetDisplayText;
28:    end;
29:
30:  implementation
31:
32:  constructor TSimpleTextControl.Create;
33:  begin
34:    inherited Create;
35:    // TODO: Add any constructor code here
36:  end;
37:
38:  function TSimpleTextControl.GetDisplayText: string;
39:  begin
40:    Result := FDisplayText;
41:  end;
42:
43:  procedure TSimpleTextControl.Render(Writer: HtmlTextWriter);
44:  begin
45:    Writer.Write(DisplayText);
46:  end;
47:
48:  procedure TSimpleTextControl.SetDisplayText(const Value: &string);
49:  begin
50:    if FDisplayText <> Value then
51:    begin
52:      FDisplayText := Value;
53:    end;
54:  end;
55:
56:  end.
```

▶ Find the code on the CD: \Code\Chapter 34\ControlExamples.

If you create a new package, put this control in the package, and then install the package into the IDE, you can use this control in an ASP.NET page or user control. It doesn't do much at all—it simply displays the text inline with the HTML on the page. You can't position the control, alter its format, or anything actually. However, it does illustrate the basics, so let's examine it.

First, note that the control descends from the System.Web.UI.Control class (line 10). This is the base class for all Web controls, and it would be analogous to System.ComponentModel. Component in the FCL or TComponent in the VCL. System.Web.UI.Control provides the basic functionality for putting a control on an ASP.NET surface. TSimpleTextControl adds a single published property, DisplayText, which stores a string that is then displayed (line 27).

Second, note that the component implements an "empty" constructor that does nothing but call inherited (lines 32–36). This is required by the ASP.NET framework. In the VCL, Delphi relies on virtual constructors to create and manage components at design time. In the FCL, each class must have a parameter-less constructor. That constructor cannot be inherited; it must be explicitly declared for each individual class.

The actual "work" of the control, if you can call it that, gets done in the overridden Render() method (lines 43–46). The Render() method is called when it comes time to actually render HTML for the control. The method has a single parameter of type HTMLTextWriter. HTMLTextWriter is an FCL class designed to build up HTML for rendering onto an HTML design surface. We'll cover HTMLTextWriter a bit more a little later in the chapter. Notice that the overridden Render() method simply calls HTMLTextWriter.Write(), sending along the DisplayText property as a parameter.

Thus, when this control is dropped on a page, it simply adds a line of text into the HTML wherever the control ends up in the flow of the page. Note that the control has no properties, allowing the text to be formatted or located anywhere on the page. In addition, because the control cannot be positioned, it can't even be moved around on a page's design surface in the page designer—instead, it sticks right in the flow location of the HTML.

The only property that affects the display of the control is the DisplayText property, which is declared as follows:

```
published
  [
  DefaultValue(''),
  Description('The text that will be displayed in the control.'),
  Category('Appearance'),
  Bindable(True)
  ]
  property DisplayText: string read GetDisplayText write SetDisplayText;
```

DisplayText is a simple string property, but is declared with a number of attributes. Those attributes are discussed in Table 34.3.

TABLE 34.3   Web Control Property Attributes

Attribute	Description
DefaultValue	This is the default value for the property—in this case, an empty string.
Description	This is the description for the property which will be displayed in the Object Inspector when the property is selected there.
Category	When the Object Inspector is sorted by category, the property will be placed in the 'Appearance' category.
Bindable	The Bindable attribute makes a property bindable to a dataset field.

Persistent Values

The control in the previous section did nothing other than to display unformatted text. Though you might not have noticed it, it wouldn't even maintain any values that you set for its DisplayText setting at runtime. If you set the DisplayText property and then do a post-back to the page, the original design-time value will be returned. That, of course, isn't a very valuable or even desired behavior. You almost certainly will want your controls to maintain values between post-back. A control with this capability is shown in Listing 34.4.

LISTING 34.4   A Persistent Control

```
1:   unit uPersistentTextControl;
2:
3:   interface
4:
5:   uses
6:        System.Web
7:      , System.Web.UI
8:      , System.ComponentModel
9:      ;
10:
11:  type
12:    [DefaultProperty('DisplayText')]
13:    TPersistentTextControl = class(System.Web.UI.Control)
14:    strict protected
15:      procedure Render(Writer: HtmlTextWriter); override;
16:    public
17:      constructor Create;
18:    published
19:      function GetDisplayText: string;
20:      procedure SetDisplayText(const Value: &string);
21:    published
22:      [
23:       DefaultValue(''),
24:       Description('The text that will be displayed in the control.'),
25:       Category('Appearance'),
26:       Bindable(True)
27:      ]
28:      property DisplayText: string read GetDisplayText write SetDisplayText;
29:    end;
30:
31:  implementation
32:
33:  constructor TPersistentTextControl.Create;
34:  begin
35:    inherited Create;
36:    ViewState['DisplayText'] := '';
37:  end;
38:
39:  function TPersistentTextControl.GetDisplayText: string;
40:  begin
41:    Result := String(ViewState['DisplayText']);
42:  end;
43:
44:  procedure TPersistentTextControl.Render(Writer: HtmlTextWriter);
45:  begin
46:    Writer.Write(DisplayText);
47:  end;
```

LISTING 34.4   Continued

```
48:
49:   procedure TPersistentTextControl.SetDisplayText(const Value: &string);
50:   begin
51:     ViewState['DisplayText'] := Value;
52:   end;
53:
54:   end.
```

▶ Find the code on the CD: \Code\Chapter 34\ControlExamples.

TPersistentTextControl uses the ViewState feature of ASP.NET to ensure that any changes to the DisplayText property are persistent between page requests. ViewState is a dictionary class that can store objects based on a string index. It specifically stores objects and information related to the view state for a given server control. ViewState information is streamed out with your page's HTML, so it shouldn't be used to store large amounts of information. It should be used, however, to store information about the display state of your control—in this case, the value of the DisplayText property.

Now if you place this control on a page and change its value as part of a post-back, the value that you set will be retained and displayed between page requests. This is obviously an important feature, as you will certainly want to maintain the state of your controls as a user clicks through your Web site.

Adding Some Custom Rendering

TPersistentTextControl allows you to maintain changes to the DisplayText property, but it still doesn't allow you to do any formatting of that text. The following control, TBoldTextControl, adds a UseBoldText property to allow you to display the text in bold if the property is set to True. This is done by adding code to the Render() method as shown in Listing 34.5.

LISTING 34.5   Adding a Render() Method

```
1:   procedure TBoldTextControl.Render(Writer: HtmlTextWriter);
2:   begin
3:     if UseBoldText then
4:       Writer.RenderBeginTag(HTMLTextWriterTag.B);
5:     Writer.Write(DisplayText);
6:     if FUseBoldText then
7:       Writer.RenderEndTag;
8:   end;
```

▶ Find the code on the CD: \Code\Chapter 34\ControlExamples.

As previously mentioned, the HTMLTextWriter class allows you to render HTML when the control is asked for it. In the previous case, we add a bold tag to the DisplayText property if the UseBoldText property is set to True.

But who wants to render HTML the hard way? HTML is pretty varied, and you don't want to have to write all your own code for handling the many different ways that HTML can be rendered. Luckily, you don't have to. The ASP.NET framework provides all that functionality for you via the System.Web.UI.WebControls.WebControl class. This class, unlike its ancestor Control that we've been using, includes all the functionality to apply HTML formatting and locating on the control. Thus, if we inherit from it instead, we can get a control similar to the previous TSimpleTextControl, but that can be formatted with all of HTML's capabilities. This is shown in Listing 34.6.

LISTING 34.6   Better HTML Rendering

```
 1:   unit uSimpleWebControl;
 2:
 3:   interface
 4:
 5:   uses
 6:        System.Web
 7:      , System.Web.UI
 8:      , System.Web.UI.WebControls
 9:      , System.ComponentModel
10:      ;
11:
12:   type
13:     [DefaultProperty('DisplayText')]
14:     TSimpleWebControl = class(System.Web.UI.WebControls.WebControl)
15:     strict protected
16:       procedure RenderContents(Writer: HtmlTextWriter); override;
17:     public
18:       constructor Create;
19:     published
20:       function GetDisplayText: string;
21:       procedure SetDisplayText(const Value: &string);
22:     published
23:       [
24:        DefaultValue(''),
25:        Description('The text that will be displayed in the control'),
26:        Category('Appearance'),
27:        Bindable(True)
28:       ]
29:       property DisplayText: string read GetDisplayText write SetDisplayText;
30:     end;
31:
32:   implementation
33:
34:   constructor TSimpleWebControl.Create;
35:   begin
36:     inherited Create;
37:     ViewState['DisplayText'] := '';
38:   end;
39:
40:   function TSimpleWebControl.GetDisplayText: string;
41:   begin
42:     Result := string(ViewState['DisplayText']);
43:   end;
44:
45:   procedure TSimpleWebControl.RenderContents(Writer: HtmlTextWriter);
```

LISTING 34.6   Continued

```
46:  begin
47:    Writer.Write(DisplayText);
48:  end;
49:
50:  procedure TSimpleWebControl.SetDisplayText(const Value: &string);
51:  begin
52:    ViewState['DisplayText'] := Value;
53:  end;
54:
55:  end.
```

▶ Find the code on the CD: `\Code\Chapter 34\ControlExamples`.

The code for this control is basically the same as the TPersistentTextControl except it descends from System.Web.UI.WebControls.WebControl (line 14). Instead of overriding the Render method, it overrides the RenderContents method.

The RenderContents method is called when the actual text to be displayed is needed by the control. A WebControl does all the HTML rendering for you based on your property settings, but it has to know what the specific content to be displayed is. So, in this case, we simply send along the value of the DisplayText property, just as we did for TSimpleTextControl. The difference now is that we can move the control around on the design surface and format the text with a host of HTML tags via the control's properties, as shown in Figure 34.6.

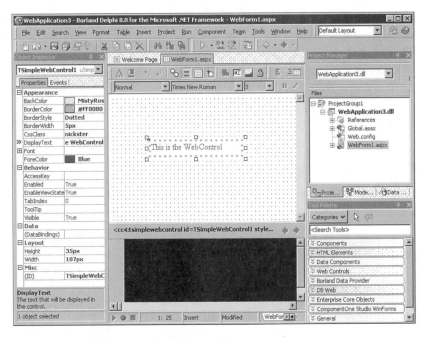

FIGURE 34.6   A basic Web control with formatting properties set.

Determining the HTML Block Type

At this point, you've developed a basic Web control that can display text and decorated it with the full spate of HTML and CSS style sheets. By default, such controls are rendered as <span> tags by ASP.NET. But you might not want a <span> tag. You might want a <div> or a <p> tag.

Web controls allow you to control what tag is placed in the HTML by your control via the TagKey property. We can augment our control at this point and call it TBlockTextWebControl. The TBlockTextWebControl allows you to put your text in either a division, span, or paragraph tag. It defines the TBlockType type as follows:

```
type
  TBlockType = (ttDivision, ttSpan, ttParagraph);
```

It then adds the following property:

```
property BlockType: TBlockType read GetBlockType write SetBlockType;
```

The value for BlockType will determine which of the three common text tags will be used for the control. The property that determines that is the TagKey property. This property needs to be overridden to return the proper value. Delphi doesn't allow you to override properties, but you can override the control's get_TagKey() method, returning the property value from the HTMLTextWriterTag enumeration. This is shown in Listing 34.7.

LISTING 34.7   Overriding the get_TegKey() Method

```
1:   strict protected
2:     function get_TagKey: HTMLTextWriterTag; override;
3:     ...
4:
5:   function TBlockTextWebControl.get_TagKey: HTMLTextWriterTag;
6:   begin
7:     case FBlockType of
8:       ttDivision: Result := HTMLTextWriterTag.Div;
9:       ttSpan    : Result := HTMLTextWriterTag.Span;
10:      ttParagraph: Result := HTMLTextWriterTag.P;
11:    else
12:      Result := HTMLTextWriterTag.Div;
13:    end;
14: end;
```

▶ Find the code on the CD: \Code\Chapter 34\ControlExamples.

Handling Post-back Data

Sometimes a control that you build might need to react to a post-back. Post-back occurs when the page is called as a result of an HTML form, such as when the user clicks a Submit button. When post-back occurs, the ViewState information is examined, and the page is redisplayed using any new information entered into the page's controls by the user. For instance, if a user enters information into an edit box and clicks the Submit button, the information in the edit box is "posted back" to the page, and your application can take action on it.

For a control to participate in the post-back process, it needs to implement the IPostBackEventHandler interface. That interface is declared as follows:

```
IPostBackEventHandler = interface
  procedure RaisePostBackEvent(eventArgument: string);
end;
```

You should implement the RaisePostBackEvent method to perform whatever code you want to be called when a post-back event occurs. You should use the IPostBackEventHandler interface if your control doesn't need to retrieve data input by the user, but still needs to participate in the post-back event. Normally, in this method, you'd call code that fires a custom event for the control. This allows you to implement and call server-side events based on client-side actions.

Oftentimes, however, your control will receive user input; thus, it will need to be capable of processing that input. In order for a Web control to handle post-back data, it must implement the IPostBackDataHandler interface, which is declared as follows:

```
IPostBackDataHandler = interface
    function LoadPostData(postDataKey: string;
      postCollection: NameValueCollection) : boolean;
    procedure RaisePostDataChangedEvent;
end;
```

IPostBackDataHandler has two methods that enable you to handle post-back data for your control. When post-back occurs, each control on the form is checked to see if it handles this interface: If so, the LoadPostData() method is called. Your implementation of LoadPostData() should process the new data as desired, returning True if the state of the control has changed and False if not. If the function returns True, the framework will in turn call the second method, RaisePostDataChangedEvent(), which works basically the same as the RaisePostBackEvent() method in the IPostBackEventHandler interface. In this method, you can fire a server-side event to allow consumers of your control to do what they need to when the data in the control has changed.

The LoadPostData() parameters contain the posted information for the control. The first parameter, postDataKey, is a string value that represents the proper string-indexed value in the collection passed in the second parameter, postCollection. Thus, in order to retrieve the posted information, you'd do something similar to

```
Var
   NewValue: string;
begin
  NewValue := postCollection[postDataKey];
  ...
end;
```

Note, too, that there might be times when you want to implement both of these interfaces in a single control.

TPostBackInputWebControl

The TPostbackInputWebControl example shown in Listing 34.8 illustrates how to create a control that handles post-back data.

LISTING 34.8   The TPostbackInputWebControl Example

```
 1:   unit uPostBackTextWebControl;
 2:
 3:   interface
 4:
 5:   uses
 6:         System.Web
 7:       , System.Web.UI
 8:       , System.Web.UI.WebControls
 9:       , System.ComponentModel
10:       , System.Collections.Specialized
11:       ;
12:
13:   type
14:     TTextChangedEvent = procedure(e: EventArgs) of object;
15:
16:   type
17:     [DefaultProperty('DisplayText')]
18:     TPostBackInputWebControl = class(WebControl, IPostBackDataHandler)
19:     private
20:       FOnTextChanged: TTextChangedEvent;
21:       function GetDisplayText: string;
22:       procedure SetDisplayText(const Value: &string);
23:     strict protected
24:       procedure AddAttributesToRender(Writer: HTMLTextWriter); override;
25:       function get_TagKey: HTMLTextWriterTag; override;
26:       procedure DoTextChanged;
27:       procedure Render(Writer: HTMLTextWriter); override;
28:
29:       // IPostBackDataHandler
30:       function LoadPostData(PostDataKey: string;
31:         PostCollection: NameValueCollection) : boolean;
32:       procedure RaisePostDataChangedEvent;
33:     public
34:       constructor Create;
35:     published
36:       [
37:        DefaultValue(''),
38:        Description('The text that will be displayed in the input control'),
39:        Category('Appearance'),
40:        Bindable(True)
41:       ]
42:       property DisplayText: string read GetDisplayText write SetDisplayText;
43:       [
44:       Category('Action'),
45:       Description('Fired whenever the user changes the text in the' +
46:           ' input control')
47:       ]
48:       property OnTextChanged: TTextChangedEvent
```

LISTING 34.8   Continued

```
49:        add FOnTextChanged remove FOnTextChanged;
50:    end;
51:
52: implementation
53:
54: constructor TPostBackInputWebControl.Create;
55: begin
56:    inherited Create;
57:    ViewState['DisplayText'] := '';
58: end;
59:
60: function TPostBackInputWebControl.GetDisplayText: string;
61: var
62:    Obj: TObject;
63: begin
64:    Obj := ViewState['DisplayText'];
65:    if Obj <> nil then
66:      Result := ViewState['DisplayText'].ToString
67:    else
68:      Result := '';
69: end;
70:
71: function TPostBackInputWebControl.LoadPostData(postDataKey: &string;
72:    PostCollection: NameValueCollection): boolean;
73: var
74:    NewValue: string;
75: begin
76:    NewValue := PostCollection[PostDataKey];
77:    Result := not DisplayText.Equals(NewValue);
78:    if Result then
79:      DisplayText := NewValue;
80: end;
81:
82: procedure TPostBackInputWebControl.RaisePostDataChangedEvent;
83: begin
84:    DoTextChanged;
85: end;
86:
87: procedure TPostBackInputWebControl.SetDisplayText(const Value: &string);
88: begin
89:    ViewState['DisplayText'] := Value;
90: end;
91:
92: function TPostBackInputWebControl.get_TagKey: HTMLTextWriterTag;
93: begin
94:    Result := HTMLTextWriterTag.Input;
95: end;
96:
97: procedure TPostBackInputWebControl.DoTextChanged;
98: begin
99:    if Assigned(FOnTextChanged) then
100:     FOnTextChanged(EventArgs.Empty);
101: end;
```

34

LISTING 34.8   Continued

```
102:
103: procedure TPostBackInputWebControl.AddAttributesToRender(Writer:
104:     HTMLTextWriter);
105: begin
106:   inherited;
107:   Writer.AddAttribute(HTMLTextWriterAttribute.Name, Self.UniqueID);
108:   Writer.AddAttribute(HTMLTextWriterAttribute.Type, 'Text');
109:   Writer.AddAttribute(HTMLTextWriterAttribute.Value, DisplayText);
110: end;
111:
112: procedure TPostBackInputWebControl.Render(Writer: HTMLTextWriter);
113: begin
114:   if Page <> nil then
115:     Page.VerifyRenderingInServerForm(Self);
116:   inherited;
117: end;
118:
119: end.
```

▶ Find the code on the CD: \Code\Chapter 34\ControlExamples.

TPostBackInputWebControl provides the basic functionality of an HTML input control, as well as providing a server-side event, OnTextChanged (lines 48–49), that is fired whenever the user changes the text in the input control and posts that change to the server. This code introduces a couple of new features of the Web control component model, so let's examine it more closely.

First, note that TPostBackInputWebControl descends from WebControl (line 18), so it provides all the style sheet properties that allow you to format the control as desired. In addition, the control declares that it will implement the IPostBackDataHandler interface (line 18), enabling it to participate in the post-back of a form and process changes made to the page by the user.

Next, the unit declares an event type, TTextChangedEvent, declared as follows:

```
type
  TTextChangedEvent = procedure(e: EventArgs) of object;
```

This event will be fired when the post-back data indicates that a change has been made to the control's DisplayText property. It is fired in the DoTextChanged() method (line 99), and that is in turn called in the RaisePostDataChangedEvent() (line 82), which is called when the LoadPostData() function returns True, indicating that the data in the control has changed.

The LoadPostData() function simply gets the old and new values of the control, compares them, and returns True if they are different. In addition, if they are different, the new version is saved in the DisplayText property.

This is also the first control that we've looked at that actually required a bit of more sophisticated rendering. The control will render a single input tag, and that is determined by overriding the get_TagKey() function:

```
function TPostBackInputWebControl.get_TagKey: HTMLTextWriterTag;
begin
  Result := HTMLTextWriterTag.Input;
end;
```

In addition, because the HTML `<input>` tag is a single tag that carries all its data in attributes, we need to override the `AddAttributesToRender()` method to add the proper attributes to the resulting HTML tag. The `AddAttributesToRender()` method, which follows, is called during the rendering process to gather up all the attributes, or `name="value"` pairs, to be included in the tag:

```
procedure TPostBackInputWebControl.AddAttributesToRender(Writer:
  HTMLTextWriter);
begin
  inherited;
  Writer.AddAttribute(HTMLTextWriterAttribute.Name, Self.UniqueID);
  Writer.AddAttribute(HTMLTextWriterAttribute.Type, 'Text');
  Writer.AddAttribute(HTMLTextWriterAttribute.Value, DisplayText);
end;
```

In this case, we add the `UniqueID` name for the control as the `'name'` attribute, the type of the input control that it will be, and the actual text to display in the control. The `UniqueID` value is needed by ASP.NET in order to uniquely identify the control during the process of calling all `postback` methods for all the controls on a page. The `AddAttributesToRender` function gathers these attributes and renders them properly into the `<input>` tag as the control is rendered to the page.

In addition, the `TPostBackInputWebControl` should never be placed on a page unless it is inside a `<form runat=server>` tag. The ASP.NET framework provides a means to ensure that. The control overrides the `Render` method as follows:

```
procedure TPostBackInputWebControl.Render(Writer: HTMLTextWriter);
begin
  if Page <> nil then
    Page.VerifyRenderingInServerForm(Self);
  inherited;

end;
```

The `Page` class includes a method called `VerifyRenderingInServerForm()` which checks to see if the control is currently being rendered inside a `<form runat=server>` tag. If not, it raises an `HttpException`. If no exception is raised, the control renders normally by calling the inherited method.

Composite Controls

Earlier in this chapter, we looked at user controls, which consist of a text-based way of putting groups of controls into a single entity. Sometimes, however, you might want to achieve the same functionality in a binary-based Web control. The ASP.NET framework allows you to build composite controls that can contain other controls in a way similar to user controls. Composite controls use the parent/child control model to manage the events, rendering, and post-back functionality of contained controls to create a single entity.

In order to create a composite control, you can descend from either `System.Web.UI.Control` or `System.Web.UI.WebControls.WebControl`, depending on the features you need for your control. Either way, your control must do two things:

First, it must override `CreateChildControls()` to create the controls that will be contained within it. The `CreateChildControls()` method is called by the framework at the point in the rendering process when these controls are needed. This helps to ensure that they properly provide post-back data. The framework, via the `EnsureChildControls()` method, keeps track of whether the child controls have been created, ensuring that they are only created once and at the proper time. If your control needs to access the child controls in any way, you should call `EnsureChildControls()` to ensure that the child controls exist.

Second, a composite control must implement the `System.Web.UI.INamingContainer` interface that will manage the naming of the subcontrols within your control. Interestingly, `INamingContainer` is an empty interface. However, when it is included as part of a composite control's class declaration, its presence will ensure that controls contained within the composite control will have unique names on the page. Think about what might happen if a user placed two instances of your composite control on a page. If the control didn't create unique names for contained controls, there would be a name clash on the page.

Implementing a Composite Control—TNewUserInfoControl

Often, a Web site will want to register users, allowing them to give an email address and a password. Such a need is common enough that it seems worth it to build a composite control that will provide the user interface for such input in a reusable form. Listing 34.9 shows the declaration and implementation of `TNewUserInfoControl`; a composite control will provide input `TextBox` controls for a user email, a password, and a verification of the password, as well as a Submit button. A partial listing of the implementation of this control is shown in Listing 34.9.

> **NOTE**
>
> Listing 34.9 only shows the key code. The entire code is available on the CD.

LISTING 34.9   Composite Control Implementation

```
1:   unit uNewUserInfoControl;
2:
3:   interface
4:
5:   uses
6:        System.Web
7:      , System.Web.UI
8:      , System.Web.UI.WebControls
9:      , System.ComponentModel
10:     ;
11:
12:  type
13:    TSubmitInfoEvent = procedure(Sender: TObject; e: EventArgs) of object;
14:
15:  type
```

LISTING 34.9   Continued

```
16:      TNewUserInfoControl = class(WebControl, INamingContainer)
17:      private
18:        FAlignLabelsToRight: Boolean;
19:        FOnSubmitInfo: TSubmitInfoEvent;
20:        SubmitButton: Button;
21:        EMailLabel: System.Web.UI.WebControls.Label;
22:        EmailTextBox: TextBox;
23:        PasswordLabel: System.Web.UI.WebControls.Label;
24:        PasswordTextBox: TextBox;
25:        VerifyLabel: System.Web.UI.WebControls.Label;
26:        VerifyTextBox: TextBox;
27:        EmailValidator: RequiredFieldValidator;
28:        PasswordValidator: RequiredFieldValidator;
29:        VerifyValidator: RequiredFieldValidator;
30:      strict protected
31:        procedure Click(Sender: TObject; E: EventArgs);
32:        procedure Render(Writer: HTMLTextWriter); override;
33:        procedure CreateChildControls; override;
34:        procedure DoSubmitInfo(Sender: TObject; e: EventArgs); virtual;
35:        procedure set_AlignLabelsToRight(const Value: Boolean);
36:        function get_AlignLabelsToRight: Boolean;
37:      public
38:        constructor Create;
39:        function get_Password: string;
40:        function get_VerifyPassword: string;
41:        function get_Controls: ControlCollection; override;
42:        [
43:        DesignerSerializationVisibility
44:          (DesignerSerializationVisibility.Hidden)
45:        ]
46:        property Password: string read get_Password;
47:        [
48:        DesignerSerializationVisibility
49:          (DesignerSerializationVisibility.Hidden)
50:        ]
51:        property VerifyPassword: string read get_VerifyPassword;
52:        function get_ButtonText: string;
53:        procedure set_ButtonText(const Value: &string);
54:        function get_UserEmail: string;
55:        procedure set_UserEmail(const Value: &string);
56:        function get_MissingEmailErrorMessage: string;
57:        procedure set_MissingEmailErrorMessage(const Value: &string);
58:        function get_EmailLabelText: string;
59:        procedure set_EmailLabelText(const Value: &string);
60:        function get_MissingPasswordErrorMessage: string;
61:        procedure set_MissingPasswordErrorMessage(const Value: &string);
62:        function get_PasswordLabelText: string;
63:        procedure set_PasswordLabelText(const Value: &string);
64:        function get_VerifyLabelText: string;
65:        procedure set_MissingVerifyErrorMessage(const Value: &string);
66:        function get_MissingVerifyErrorMessage: string;
67:        procedure set_VerifyLabelText(const Value: &string);
68:      published
```

34

LISTING 34.9   Continued

```
69:     [
70:        Bindable(True), Category('Appearance'), DefaultValue(''),
71:        Description('The text to be displayed on the Submit Button')
72:     ]
73:     property ButtonText: string read get_ButtonText write set_ButtonText;
74:     [
75:        Bindable(True), Category('Appearance'), DefaultValue(''),
76:        Description('The user's email address.')
77:     ]
78:     property UserEmail: string read get_UserEmail write set_UserEmail;
79:     [
80:        Bindable(True), Category('Appearance'), DefaultValue(''),
81:        Description('The error message for the email field validator')
82:     ]
83:     property MissingEmailErrorMessage: string read
➥get_MissingEmailErrorMessage
84:           write set_MissingEmailErrorMessage;
85:     [
86:        Bindable(True), Category('Appearance'), DefaultValue(''),
87:        Description('The text for the label that goes with the' +
88:            ' email textbox')
89:     ]
90:     property EmailLabelText: string  read get_EmailLabelText
91:          write set_EmailLabelText;
92:     [
93:        Bindable(True), Category('Appearance'), DefaultValue(''),
94:        Description('The error message for the Password validator')
95:     ]
96:     property MissingPasswordErrorMessage: string
97:          read get_MissingPasswordErrorMessage write
➥set_MissingPasswordErrorMessage;
98:     [
99:        Bindable(True), Category('Appearance'), DefaultValue(''),
100:       Description('The text for the label that goes with the' +
101:          ' password textbox')
102:    ]
103:    property PasswordLabelText: string read Get_PasswordLabelText
104:        write set_PasswordLabelText;
105:    [
106:       Bindable(True), Category('Appearance'), DefaultValue(''),
107:       Description('The text for the label that goes with the' +
108:          'verify password textbox')
109:    ]
110:    property VerifyLabelText: string read get_VerifyLabelText
111:         write set_VerifyLabelText;
112:    [
113:       Bindable(True), Category('Appearance'), DefaultValue(''),
114:       Description('The error message for the verify password validator')
115:    ]
116:    property MissingVerifyErrorMessage: string read
➥get_MissingVerifyErrorMessage
117:         write set_MissingVerifyErrorMessage;
118:    property AlignLabelsToRight: Boolean read get_AlignLabelsToRight
```

LISTING 34.9   Continued

```
119:         write set_AlignLabelsToRight;
120:      property OnSubmitInfo: TSubmitInfoEvent add FOnSubmitInfo
121:         remove FOnSubmitInfo;
122:    end;
123:
124: ...
125:
126: procedure TNewUserInfoControl.CreateChildControls;
127: begin
128:    Controls.Clear;
129:
130:    // Email controls
131:    EMailLabel := System.Web.UI.WebControls.Label.Create;
132:
133:    EmailTextBox := TextBox.Create;
134:    EmailTextBox.ID := 'EmailTextBox';
135:
136:    EmailValidator := RequiredFieldValidator.Create;
137:    EmailValidator.ID := 'EmailValidator';
138:    EmailValidator.ControlToValidate := EmailTextBox.ID;
139:    EmailValidator.Text := MissingEmailErrorMessage;
140:    EmailValidator.Display := ValidatorDisplay.Static;
141:
142:    // Password Controls
143:    PasswordLabel := System.Web.UI.WebControls.Label.Create;
144:
145:    PasswordTextBox := TextBox.Create;
146:    PasswordTextBox.TextMode := TextBoxMode.Password;
147:    PasswordTextBox.ID := 'PasswordTextBox';
148:
149:    PasswordValidator := RequiredFieldValidator.Create;
150:    PasswordValidator.ID := 'PasswordValidator';
151:    PasswordValidator.ControlToValidate := PasswordTextBox.ID;
152:    PasswordValidator.Text := MissingPasswordErrorMessage;
153:    PasswordValidator.Display := ValidatorDisplay.Static;
154:
155:    // VerifyPassword Controls
156:    VerifyLabel := System.Web.UI.WebControls.Label.Create;
157:
158:    VerifyTextBox := TextBox.Create;
159:    VerifyTextBox.TextMode := TextBoxMode.Password;
160:    VerifyTextBox.ID := 'VerifyTextBox';
161:
162:    VerifyValidator := RequiredFieldValidator.Create;
163:    VerifyValidator.ID := 'VerifyValidator';
164:    VerifyValidator.ControlToValidate := VerifyTextBox.ID;
165:    VerifyValidator.Text := MissingVerifyErrorMessage;
166:    VerifyValidator.Display := ValidatorDisplay.Static;
167:
168:    //Submit Button
169:    SubmitButton := Button.Create;
170:    SubmitButton.ID := 'SubmitButton';
171:    Include(SubmitButton.Click, Self.Click);
```

34

LISTING 34.9   Continued

```
172:
173:    Controls.Add(EmailLabel);
174:    Controls.Add(EmailTextBox);
175:    Controls.Add(EmailValidator);
176:
177:    Controls.Add(PasswordLabel);
178:    Controls.Add(PasswordTextbox);
179:    Controls.Add(PasswordValidator);
180:
181:    Controls.Add(VerifyLabel);
182:    Controls.Add(VerifyTextBox);
183:    Controls.Add(VerifyValidator);
184:
185:    Controls.Add(SubmitButton);
186: end;
187:
188: procedure TNewUserInfoControl.Render(Writer: HTMLTextWriter);
189: begin
190:    AddAttributesToRender(Writer);
191:
192:    Writer.AddAttribute(HTMLTextWriterAttribute.Cellpadding, '1', False);
193:    Writer.RenderBeginTag(HTMLTextWriterTag.Table);
194:
195:    // Email Controls
196:    Writer.RenderBeginTag(HtmlTextWriterTag.Tr);
197:    if FAlignLabelsToRight then
198:      Writer.AddAttribute(HTMLTextWriterAttribute.Align, 'right');
199:    Writer.RenderBeginTag(HtmlTextWriterTag.Td);
200:    EmailLabel.RenderControl(Writer);
201:    Writer.RenderEndTag;  // Closes the TD tag
202:    Writer.RenderBeginTag(HtmlTextWriterTag.Td);
203:    EmailTextBox.RenderControl(Writer);
204:    Writer.RenderEndTag;   // Closes the TD tag
205:    Writer.RenderBeginTag(HtmlTextWriterTag.Td);
206:    EmailValidator.RenderControl(Writer);
207:    Writer.RenderEndTag;  // Closes the TD tag
208:    Writer.RenderEndTag;  // Closes the TR tag
209:
210:    // Password Controls
211:    Writer.RenderBeginTag(HtmlTextWriterTag.Tr);
212:    if FAlignLabelsToRight then
213:      Writer.AddAttribute(HTMLTextWriterAttribute.Align, 'right');
214:    Writer.RenderBeginTag(HtmlTextWriterTag.Td);
215:    PasswordLabel.RenderControl(Writer);
216:    Writer.RenderEndTag;  // Closes the TD tag
217:    Writer.RenderBeginTag(HtmlTextWriterTag.Td);
218:    PasswordTextBox.RenderControl(Writer);
219:    Writer.RenderEndTag;  // Closes the TD tag
220:    Writer.RenderBeginTag(HtmlTextWriterTag.Td);
221:    PasswordValidator.RenderControl(Writer);
222:    Writer.RenderEndTag;  // Closes the TD tag
223:    Writer.RenderEndTag;  // Closes the TR tag
224:
```

LISTING 34.9   Continued

```
225:    //Verify Controls
226:    Writer.RenderBeginTag(HtmlTextWriterTag.Tr);
227:    if FAlignLabelsToRight then
228:      Writer.AddAttribute(HTMLTextWriterAttribute.Align, 'right');
229:    Writer.RenderBeginTag(HtmlTextWriterTag.Td);
230:    VerifyLabel.RenderControl(Writer);
231:    Writer.RenderEndTag;  // Closes the TD tag
232:    Writer.RenderBeginTag(HtmlTextWriterTag.Td);
233:    VerifyTextBox.RenderControl(Writer);
234:    Writer.RenderEndTag;  // Closes the TD tag
235:    Writer.RenderBeginTag(HtmlTextWriterTag.Td);
236:    VerifyValidator.RenderControl(Writer);
237:    Writer.RenderEndTag;  // Closes the TD tag
238:    Writer.RenderEndTag;  // Closes the TR tag
239:
240:    // Submit Button
241:    Writer.RenderBeginTag(HTMLTextWriterTag.Tr);
242:    Writer.AddAttribute(HTMLTextWriterAttribute.Colspan, '2');
243:    Writer.AddAttribute(HTMLTextWriterAttribute.Align, 'right');
244:    Writer.RenderBeginTag(HTMLTextWriterTag.Td);
245:    SubmitButton.RenderControl(Writer);
246:    Writer.RenderEndTag;  // Closes the TD tag
247:    Writer.RenderBeginTag(HTMLTextWriterTag.Td);
248:    Writer.Write(' ');
249:    Writer.RenderEndTag;  // Closes the TD tag
250:    Writer.RenderEndTag;  // Closes the TR tag
251:    Writer.RenderEndTag;  // Closes the TABLE tag
252:
253: end;
254:
255:  ...
256:
257: procedure TNewUserInfoControl.DoSubmitInfo(Sender: TObject; e: EventArgs);
258: begin
259:   if Assigned(FOnSubmitInfo) then
260:     FOnSubmitInfo(Sender, e);
261: end;
262:
263: procedure TNewUserInfoControl.Click(Sender: TObject; E: EventArgs);
264: begin
265:   DoSubmitInfo(Sender, E);
266: end;
267:
```

▶ Find the code on the CD: \Code\Chapter 34\ControlExamples.

If you refer to the full code on the CD, you will note that in each getter and setter for the properties that refer to a child control, a call is made to EnsureChildControls(), making sure that the controls are properly created before accessing any of the properties in them. These calls prevent your component from trying to access a not yet created child control, causing a NullReferenceException.

The control implements the INamingContainer interface (line 16). Again, this interface is empty, but the fact that the control supports the interface will ensure that the child controls all get unique names. You can illustrate this by dropping two of the controls on a single page and checking out the resulting HTML. The child controls are given names based on the parent control's ID along with their own ID.

The control also uses the Render() method (lines 188–253) to do all the HTML rendering. It creates a simple table to hold the controls, causing them to line up. It includes a Boolean property, AlignLabelsToRight, to allow you to align the labels to the left or the right as desired.

The individual controls are all created at runtime in the overridden CreateChildControls() method (lines 126–186). The method first clears any existing controls from the array. Each control is created, and its appropriate properties are assigned. One property to note is the ControlToValidate property on the validators, which obviously must point to a valid, existing control. After all the controls are created, they are added to the Controls array. In addition, the SubmitButton's Click event handler is assigned in this method.

> **NOTE**
>
> Note, too, that the password values are never stored on the server at all—they are merely made read-only from the controls themselves. This ensures that they are not sent back to the client control as part of a post-back response. If a user fails to meet the validation criteria, the password fields are left blank after the post-back.

The component provides an OnSubmitInfo (line 120–121) event for handling the clicking of the Submit button. Note that this event is only fired when the validators all agree that the form has been properly filled out. Until then, the validators will display the error messages assigned to them in the object inspector if the form isn't properly filled in.

> **TIP**
>
> MSDN has complete documentation on the ASP.NET framework. It also includes numerous coding examples and descriptions of component building techniques.
>
> MSDN is quite complete, but no ASP.NET component builder should be without a copy of *ASP.NET Server Controls and Components* by Nikhil Kothari and Vandana Datye. This excellent, exhaustive book thoroughly covers all aspects of ASP.NET component building. All the examples are written in C#, but a Delphi developer should have no problem following along. If you are going to be doing any type of ASP.NET control development, you really should get this book.

Index

Symbols

& (ampersand), 241

:= (assignment) operator, 53

* (asterisk), 54, 456, 711, 740

@ (at) symbol, 67, 418

{} (braces), 47, 230

, (comma), 233

// comment notation, 47

(* *) comment notation, 47

= (equal sign), 53

: format specifier, 237

<> (inequality) operator, 53

() (parenthesis), 48

% (percent sign), 233, 456

. (period), 41, 43, 233

+ (plus sign), 29, 54, 67, 456

(pound sign), 233

? (question mark), 711

; (semicolon), 233

<< (shift-left) operator, 55

>> (shift-right) operator, 55

- (minus sign), 29, 54, 67, 456

/ (slash), 54-55, 237, 243, 456

0 format specifier, 233

2-dimensional arrays, 62

2-tier architecture, 647

3-tier architecture, 648

A

AAA format specifier, 233

Aborted thread state, 317

AbortRequested thread state, 317

AboveNormal thread priority, 316

AbsoluteExpiration property (Cache class), 744

AcceptChanges() method, 443

AcceptRejectRule property (ForeignKeyConstraint), 443

access to Web Services, 5

AccessKey property (WebControl class), 566

accessor properties, 86

AcquireReaderLock() method, 325

AcquireWriterLock() method, 325

ActivateFile() method, 294

activating objects, 654-655

Active Server Pages. *See* ASP.NET

Adapter() method, 206

Add Reference dialog box, 658

Add To-Do Item dialog box, 35

Add Web Reference dialog box, 630-631

Add() method, 199, 419, 436, 440, 447, 463, 466, 634, 744

AddAttributesToRender() method, 783

Added RowState, 448

Added value (DataViewRowState), 458

AddEmployeeRow() method, 518-521

AddEmUp() method, 80

AddInts() method, 49

addition operator (+), 54, 67, 456

AddNew() method, 453, 470

AddRange() method, 206, 439-440

address of operator (@), 67

AddType directive, 185

ADO.NET, 401. *See also* databases; WinForms

  BDP (Borland Data Provider)

    architecture overview, 523-524

    BdpCommand class, 526-527

    BdpConnection class, 525-526

    BdpDataAdapter class, 528

    BdpDataReader class, 527-528

    BdpParameter class, 529-530

    BdpParameterCollection class, 529-530

    BdpTransaction class, 530

    Command Text Editor, 531

    Connections Editor, 531

    Data Adapter Configuration dialog box, 532-533

    Parameter Collection Editor, 531-532

  commands, executing against databases

    CommandBuilder class, 421-422

    DDL (Data Definition Language) commands, 416-417

    ExecuteScalar() method, 415-416

    IDbCommand interface, 412-413

    non-query commands, 413-415

    parameters, 417-422

    single values, retrieving, 415-416

    stored procedures, 419-421

  connected environments, 402

  connections (Connection class)

    closing, 408-409

    events, 409-411

    IDbConnection interface, 406-407

    OdbcConnection.ConnectionString, 408

    OleDbConnection.ConnectionString, 408

    opening, 408-409

    pooling, 411

    SqlConnection.ConnectionString, 407-408

  data binding, 463

    BindingContext class, 464

    BindingManagerBase class, 464

    complex binding, 464

    CurrencyManager class, 465

    data formatting, 472-474

    data modification, 469-472

    data parsing, 472-474

    event handling, 467-469

    IBindingList interface, 464

    IDataErrorInfo interface, 464

    IEditableObject interface, 464

IList interface, 464

lists, 465-466

master detail, 474-475

navigation, 467-469

simple binding, 464

single value binding, 466-467

data sources, updating

concurrency issues, 497-501

refreshing data after updates, 501-503

SQLCommand class, 479-486

SQLCommandBuilder, 479

SQLCommandBuilder class, 476-478

SQLDataAdapter class, 486-490

stored procedures, 491-497

DataAdapters, 403-404

BDPDataAdapter, 429

BdpDataAdapter class, 528

composition of, 429-431

creating, 431-432

IDBDataAdapter interface, 429

query results, 432-436

SQLDataAdapter, 429

SqlDataAdapter class, 486-492

transaction processing, 508

DataReaders, 404, 422

BdpDataReader class, 527-528

BLOB data, retrieving, 425-426

IDataReader interface, 423

multiple resultsets, querying, 424-425

schema information, retrieving, 426-428

single resultsets, querying, 423-424

SQLDataReader class, 423-424

DataSets, 404

adding tables, 439

cloning, 439

composition of, 437

consuming from Web services, 635-637

copying, 439

creating, 439

DataRelationCollection, 438

DataTableCollection, 438

DataTables, 438

DataViewManager, 438

defined, 436

indexing tables, 440

populating, 432-433

removing tables, 439

returning with Web services, 627

strongly typed DataSets, 437, 511-521

untyped DataSets, 437

DataTables, 405, 438-440

adding to DataSets, 439

columns, 440-441

constraints, 405, 442-444

DataColumns, 405

DataRelations, 405, 445-447

DataRows, 405, 447-450

DataTableCollection, 405

EmployeeDataTable, 515-517

indexing, 440

methods, 518

populating, 433

primary keys, 441-442

properties, 518

removing from DataSets, 439

searching, 449-450

DataViews, 405, 451-452

compared to DataSources, 452

data binding, 453-455

DataView class, 451

DataViewManager class, 453

filtering, 455-461

joins, 462-463

methods, 453

properties, 452

    searching, 461-462

    sorting, 461

design principles, 401-402

disconnected environments, 402

Mono ADO.NET applications, 181-184

    btnSubmit_Click() event handler, 182

    Page_Load() event handler, 182-183

    Web controls, 181

transaction processing

    BeginTransaction() method, 504

    Commit() method, 504-505

    DataAdapters, 508

    isolation levels, 508-510

    nested transactions, 510-511

    Rollback() method, 504-505

    savepoints, 510

    simple example, 505-508

    SqlTransaction class, 504

    transaction reads, 509

Advanced .NET Remoting, 698

Age property (ProcessInfo class), 731

aggregate functions, 460-461

AlarmClock control, 279-281

aliases, 45, 72

Align toolbar, 26

AllocateDataSlot() method, 328

AllocateNamedDataSlot() method, 328

allocating memory, 68-69

<allow> section (web.config file), 711, 725

AllowDBNull property (DataColumns), 441

AllowDefaultSort property (DataViews), 452

AllowDelete property (DataViews), 452

AllowEdit property (DataViews), 452

AllowNew property (DataViews), 452

allowOverride attribute (<location> tag), 723

AllPaintingInWmPaint ControlStyle enumeration value, 305

ALM (Application Lifecycle Development), 23

AlternatingItemStyle property

    DataGrid control, 604

    DataList control, 599

AlternatingItemTemplate template, 595

ampersand (&), 241

ancestor classes, 263-264

And operator, 53-55, 456

Animate_Click() event handler, 163

animation

    animation demo implementation, 161-165

    main form declaration, 160

    sprite declaration, 159

Ansi value (CharSet enumeration), 384

AnsiChar type, 58

Apache Mono, 184-186

ApartmentState class, 317

APIs. *See* Reflection API

AppDomains, 310-311, 651

Append file mode, 247

Append() method, 229, 248

AppendFormat() method, 229

Application Domains, 651

application-level tracing, 735

Application Lifecycle Development (ALM), 23

Application Name dialog box, 621

application root (XSP), 179

applications. *See also* databases; WebForms; WinForms controls

    Application object, 761-762

    BankExample

        BankServer.dpr file, 664-665

        BankServer_Impl.pas unit, 662-663

        BankShared.pas unit, 660-661

        client implementation, 665-668

        IBankManager interface, 661

references, 658-659

setting up, 657-658

TAccount class, 661

circular unit references, 41-42

collaborating applications, 6

console applications, 7

database-driven ASP.NET applications

binding expressions, evaluating, 597

CheckBoxList control, 586

complex data binding, 586

DataGrid control, 603-611, 613-614

DataList control, 598, 600-603

download request application, 614-619

DropDownList control, 588-590

ListBox control, 590-592

RadioButtonList control, 593-594

Repeater control, 595-598

simple data binding, 581-586

download request application

code listing, 614-618

GetData() method, 618

SaveUserInfo() method, 618-619

SendEmail() method, 618

EmitDemo, 352-355

globalization, 226

Hello.exe, 172-173

InvMemb, 348-350

InvProject, 345-346

localization, 226

main modules, 37

Mono ADO.NET applications, 181-184

Mono ASP.NET applications, 177-179

ASP.NET deployment to Mono, 179

Button1_Click event handler, 178

portability, 180-181

Web controls, 178

XSP configuration, 179

XSP runtime parameters, 179-180

MonoMenu .NET console application, 174-175

partitioning, 112

skeleton program files, 37-38

state management, 762

TransEx (transaction processing example), 505-508

units

aliases, 45

finalization section, 40

generic units, 43

headers, 39

implementation section, 40

initialization section, 40

interface section, 39

MyUnit.pas example, 38-39

uses clause syntax, 38, 40-41

ApplyStyle() method, 568

appRequestQueueLimit attribute (<httpRuntime> tag), 725

<appSettings> section (ASP.NET web.config), 736-737

architecture, 646-647

BDP (Borland Data Provider), 523-524

client/server architecture, 647

multitier architecture, 648-651

.NET Remoting, 651

peer-to-peer architecture, 647-648

Archived FileAttribute, 243

args parameter (InvokeMember() method), 347

arithmetic operators, 54-55

ArithmeticException class, 106

ArrayList collection, 206-209

arrays, 62-63

array of statements, 64

ArrayList collection, 206-209

binding CheckBoxLists to, 586-587

binding DropDownLists to, 589

binding ListBoxes to, 591

binding RadioButtonLists to, 593

declaring, 62

dynamic arrays, 63-64

iterating through, 62

multiple dimensions, 62

properties, 273-276

as operator, 73

ASP.NET, 534. *See also* **.NET Remoting;
WebForms**

.aspx file extension, 537, 540

authentication

configuring, 700

defined, 699

forms-based authentication, 702-709

Passport authentication, 709-710

Windows authentication, 700-702

authorization

defined, 699

file authorization, 710-711

role-based authorization, 712-714

URL authorization, 711-712

browser/Web server communication, 537

caching

cache file dependencies, 746-749

cache-callback methods, 749-750

data caching, 743-746

page caching, 738-742

page fragment caching, 743

CSS (Cascading Style Sheets), 567

database-driven applications

binding expressions, 597

CheckBoxList control, 586

complex data binding, 586

DataGrid control, 603-614

DataList control, 598-603

download request application, 614-619

DropDownList control, 588-590

ListBox control, 590-592

RadioButtonList control, 593-594

Repeater control, 595-598

simple data binding, 581-586

deployment

virtual directories, 716-719

XCOPY deployment, 719-720

errors redirection, 727-728

HTTPCookie class, 548-549

HTTPRequest class, 547-548

HTTPResponse class, 544-547

impersonization, 714-715

machine.config file, 720-721

monitoring, 731

Mono ASP.NET applications, 177-179

ASP.NET deployment to Mono, 179

Button1_Click event handler, 178

portability, 180-181

Web controls, 178

XSP configuration, 179

XSP runtime parameters, 179-180

output caching, 730-731

Page class, 549-550

server controls, 551-552

data-bound controls, 552

HTML controls, 552

list controls, pre-populating, 557-558

user controls, 552

validation controls, 552, 559-565

Web server controls, 552

WebControl strongly typed properties,
566

state management

application state management, 760-762

cookies, 751-753

session state management, 756-760

SQL Server, 759

ViewState, 753-755

tracing, 731
   application level tracing, 735
   page level tracing, 732-735
user controls, 763-764
   *.ascx files, 767
   <@ Control %> tag, 767-768
   creating, 764-765
   declaring, 766-767
   LoginControl, 769-771
   <@ Register %> tag, 768-769
   SimpleUserControl example, 764-769
   UserControl class, 767
validation, 558
   BaseValidator class, 559
   client-side validation, 559
   CompareValidator class, 560-561
   CustomValidator class, 564
   RangeValidator class, 563-564
   RegularExpressionValidator class, 562-563
   RequiredFieldValidator class, 559-560
   server-side validation, 559
   ValidationSummary class, 565
Web controls
   ASP.NET Server Controls and Component (italic), 790
   composite controls, 783-790
   creating, 771-773
   custom rendering, 775-777
   HTML block type, 778
   persistent values, 773-775
   post-back data, 778-783
   properties, 773
   TNewUserInfoControl, 784-790
web.config file, 721-723
   <appSettings> section, 736-737
   <authentication> section, 724-725
   <authorization> section, 725
   custom configuration sections, 737

   <customErrors> section, 727
   file schema, 722-723
   <httpRuntime> section, 725-726
   <location> section, 723-724
   <pages> section, 726
   <processModel> section, 728-730
   <sessionState> section, 726
   <trace section>, 735
worker processes, 537, 728-730
ASP.NET Server Controls and Component, 790
aspnet_wp.exe, 537
.aspx file extension, 537, 540, 767
assemblies, 14
   advantages of, 112-113
   application partitioning, 112
   Borland.Delphi.dll, 109
   building with libraries, 117-120
   building with packages
      assembly attributes, 115
      contains clause, 115
      file types, 115
      package directive, 115
      package installation, 122
      requires clause, 115
      sample package file, 113-115
      test package project, 115-117
   calling from C#, 121-122
   component containment, 112
   core assemblies, 109
   defined, 84, 109
   dependencies, 109
   deploying, 111
   distribution, 112
   GAC (Global Assembly Cache), 111-112
   Interop Assemblies, 364-365
      components of, 366-367
      Copy Local option, 365
      creating, 366

customizing, 371-372

RCWs (Runtime Callable Wrappers), 366

loading dynamically, 123-124

manifests, 110

methods, 340

mscorlib.dll, 109

PIAs (Primary Interop Assemblies), 369-372

properties, 340

referencing, 120-121

reflection, 338-341

registering, 373

running under Mono, 173

compiler errors, 176-177

MonoFuncs unit, 175

MonoMenu .NET console application, 174-175

strong naming, 122

viewing contents of, 109-111

AssemblyBuilder class, 352

AssemblyKeyFile attribute, 122

AssemblyTitle attribute, 115

AssemblyVersion attribute, 115

assignment operators, 53

asterisk (*), 54, 456, 711, 740

asynchronous stream access, 251-253

asynchronously invoking Web services, 638-639

at (@) symbol, 67, 418

Attachments property (MailMessage class), 575

Attributes property

FileSystemInfo class, 244

NotifyFilters enumeration, 255

Authenticate() method, 641-642, 706

AuthenticateRequest event, 713

authentication

configuring, 700

defined, 699

forms-based authentication, 702-703

individual pages, authenticating, 703-705

SQL Server, 707-709

web.config file, 703-706

.xml files, 706-707

Passport authentication, 709-710

Web services, 639-641

Windows authentication, 700-702

<authentication> section (web.config file), 703, 724-725

authorization

defined, 699

file authorization, 710-711

role-based authorization, 712-714

URL authorization, 711-712

<authorization> section (web.config file), 725

Auto value (CharSet enumeration), 384

AutoEventWireup attribute (<@ Control %> tag), 767

autoEventWireup attribute (<pages> tag), 541, 726

AutoIncrement property (DataColumns), 441

AutoIncrementSeed property (DataColumns), 441

AutoIncrementStep property (DataColumns), 441

automation

Automation object, 359

early bound COM, 362, 364

late bound automation, 358-360, 374-375

Microsoft Word, 359-360

registering .NET assemblies for, 373

AutoResetEvent class, 327

B

BackColor property (WebControl class), 566

Background thread state, 316

backward compatibility, 52

BankExample application

   BankServer.dpr file, 664-665

   BankServer_Impl.pas unit, 662-663

   BankShared.pas unit, 660-661

   client implementation, 665-668

   IBankManager interface, 661

   references, 658-659

   setting up, 657-658

   TAccount class, 661

BaseValidator class, 559

Basic authentication, 702

BasicUserControlPage .aspx file, 768

Bcc property (MailMessage class), 575

BDP (Borland Data Provider), 523-525

   architecture overview, 523-524

   BdpCommand class, 526-527

   BdpConnection class, 525-526

   BdpDataAdapter class, 528

   BdpDataReader class, 527-528

   BdpParameter class, 529-530

   BdpParameterCollection class, 529-530

   BdpTransaction class, 530

   Command Text Editor, 531

   Connections Editor, 531

   Data Adapter Configuration dialog box, 532-533

   Parameter Collection Editor, 531-532

bdpCn_StateChange() event handler, 526

BdpCommand class, 526-527

BdpConnection class, 525-526

BDPDataAdapter class, 429, 528

BdpDataReader class, 527-528

BdpParameter class, 418, 529-530

BdpParameterCollection class, 529-530

BdpTransaction class, 530

.bdsproj file extension, 115

Begin SeekOrigin value, 248

begin statement, 74

Begin() method, 510

BeginEdit() method, 447-448, 521

BeginGetEmployees() method, 637-638

BeginInvoke() method, 320, 331-332, 500

BeginRead() method, 253

BeginTransaction() method, 407, 504, 530

BeginWrite() method, 253

BelowNormal thread priority, 316

Bezier splines, 135-138

\bin directory, 719

binary encoding

   compared to SOAP, 697-698

   configuring, 695-696

binary file streams, 249-251

Binary Large Objects (BLOBs), 425-426

BinaryFormatter class, 257

BinaryReaders, 240, 249-251

BinarySearch() method, 206

BinaryWriters, 240, 249-251

Bindable property (Web controls), 773

binder parameter (InvokeMember() method), 347

binding. *See* data binding

BindingContext class, 464

BindingManagerBase class, 464

BitBlt() method, 159

Bitmap class, 148

bitmaps, 148

bitwise operators, 55

blittable types, 378

BLOBs (Binary Large Objects), 425-426

blocks of code, 29-31

body

   HTTP response packets, 537

   SOAP packets, 673

Body property (MailMessage class), 576

BodyEncoding property (MailMessage class), 576

BodyFormat property (MailMessage class), 576

BorderColor property (WebControl class), 566

BorderStyle property (WebControl class), 566

BorderWidth property (WebControl class), 566

Borland Data Provider. *See* BDP

Borland Web site, 23

Borland.Delphi.dll, 109

Borland.Delphi.System unit, 38

Borland.Vcl.ComObj unit, 390

Borland.Vcl.SysUtils unit, 390

Both value (UpdatedRowSource property), 501

BoundColumn column type, 604

boxing, 56-57

braces ({}), 47, 230

break statement, 77

browsers

    browser/Web server communication, 535-537

    redirecting, 547

browsing code, 32

Brush classes, 128-130

btnLogin_Click() event handler, 705

btnSubmit_Click() event handler, 182

buffer attribute (<pages> tag), 726

Buffer parameter (BeginRead() method), 253

BufferedStreams, 240

BufferResponse property ([WebMethod]), 629

Button1_Click event handler, 178, 538

ButtonColumn column type, 604

BytesToHex() method, 709

C

C format specifier, 231

C# assemblies, calling, 121-122

c_cnstr constant, 183, 433

c_sel_emp constant, 433

C#-to-Delphi type comparison, 57

Cache class, 744-745, 762

CacheDuration property ([WebMethod]), 629

CacheText ControlStyle enumeration value, 305

caching

    Cache class, 744-745, 762

    cache-callback methods, 749-750

    cache file dependencies, 746-749

    data caching, 743-746

    GAC (Global Assembly Cache), 111-112

    output caching (ASP.NET), 730-731

    page caching

        @ OutputCache directive, 738-740

        varying by custom strings, 742

        varying by headers, 742

        varying by parameters, 740-742

    page fragment caching, 743

Callback parameter (BeginRead() method), 253

calling assemblies from C#, 121-122

Cancel() method, 413

CancelCommand event, 599

CancelCurrentEdit() method, 470

CancelEdit() method, 448, 521

canceling DataRow changes, 448

CanExtend() method, 295-296

CAOs (Client Activated Objects), 675

    factory pattern

        client DPR file, 680-681

        defined, 675

        ISimpleFactory interface, 676-677

        ISimpleServer interface, 677

        server DPR file, 679-680

        TSimpleFactory class, 676, 679

        TSimpleServer class, 677-678

    problems of, 682-683

Capacity property

    ArrayList collection, 206

    StringBuilder class, 228

capitalization, 50

Caption property (DataColumns), 441

cardinal splines, 134

Cascading Style Sheets (CSS), 553, 567

case sensitivity, 50

case statement, 75

Category property (Web controls), 773

Cc property (MailMessage class), 576

CCWs (COM Callable Wrappers), 372

.cfg file extension, 115

Change() method, 319

Changed event, 255

ChangeDatabase() method, 407

channels, 656

ChannelServices class, 652-653

Chaos isolation level, 509

Char type, 58

Chars property (StringBuilder class), 228

CharSet enumeration, 384

CheckBoxList control

    binding to arrays, 586-587

    binding to database tables, 587-588

    properties, 586

CIL (Common Intermediate Language), 14-16

circular unit references, 41-42, 84

class libraries, 6

    FCL (Framework Class Library), 18

    VCL for .NET, 6-8

class statement, 86, 92

class var block, 88

classes. See also names of individual classes

    ancestor classes, 263-264

    class completion, 30

    class references, 91-92

    constructors, 192

    declaring, 71

    defined, 86

    deserialization, 256

    fields, 87-88, 95-96

    friend classes, 97

    helper classes, 97-98

    properties, 92

    proxy classes, 630-637

    serialization, 255-256

        example, 257-260

        formatters, 257

        ISerializable interface, 256-257

        object graphs, 256

        [Serializable] attribute, 256

    thread-safe classes, 328-329

Classic desktop layout, 26

ClassIDToProgID() method, 390

Clear() method, 199, 439

ClearCanvas() method, 128

Click event hander, 666-668

Client Activated Objects. See CAOs

clientConnectedCheck attribute
  (<processModel> tag), 728

ClientDataSet class, 437

clients

    BankExample application, 665-668

    client DPR files, 693-694

    client/server architecture, 647

    client-side WebForm validation, 559

    .NET Remoting configuration, 689-690

    Web Service clients, 10-11

    writing text to, 544

clipping regions, 144-146

Clone() method, 200, 439

cloning DataSets, 439

Close() method, 248, 407-408, 525

closing connections, 408-409

CLR (Common Language Runtime), 6

    assemblies, 14

    CLR-to-Delphi type comparison, 57

    headers, 13

load/compile/execute sequence, 15

managed code, 14

managed modules, 13

    circular unit references, 41-42

    main modules, 37

    skeleton program files, 37-38

    units, 38-40, 43-45

    uses clause syntax, 38-41

unmanaged code, 14

CLS (Common Language Specification), 18

CLSIDFromProgID() method, 389

clusters, 649

code-behind forms, 542-543

code blocks

    collapsing/expanding, 29

    indenting, 31

    regions, 30

code browsing, 32

Code Editor, 29-32

Code Explorer, 34-35

code folding, 29

code snippets, 28

CodeBehind attribute, 541, 767

collaborating applications, 6

collapsing code blocks, 29

Collect() method, 191

CollectionBase class, 212-215

collections, 197

    ArrayList, 206-209

    Cookies, 548

    DataColumnCollection, 440

    DataRelationCollection, 438

    DataTableCollection, 405, 438

    HashTable, 209-212

    interfaces

        ICollection, 198-199

        IComparer, 198

        IDictionary, 198-199

        IDictionaryEnumerator, 198

        IEnumerable, 198

        IEnumerator, 198-200

        IHashCodeProvider, 198

        IList, 198-199

    Queue, 203-205

    Stack, 200-203

    strongly typed collections, 212-216

    strongly typed dictionaries

        descending from DictionaryBase, 216-219

        sample application, 219-220

    TableMappings, 429-431, 436

colon (:), 237

columns. *See* **DataColumns**

COM Callable Wrappers (CCWs), 372

COM Interop, 645

    advantages of, 356-357

    COM objects in .NET code

        COM events, 367-369

        COM lifetime control, 369

        early bound COM, 362-364

        error handling, 369

        Interop Assemblies, 364-367, 371-372

        late bound automation, 358-360

        optional parameters, 360-362

        PIAs (Primary Interop Assemblies), 369-372

        RCWs (Runtime Callable Wrappers), 366

        reference parameters, 360-362

        value parameters, 360-362

    common interoperability issues, 357-358

    defined, 358

    .NET objects in COM code

        assembly registration, 373

        CCWs (COM Callable Wrappers), 372

        error handling, 381

        interface implementation, 376-377

        Interop Type Libraries, 375-376

late bound automation, 374-375

marshaling, 378-380

parameter types, 378-380

.NET routines in Win32 code, 395-396

import declarations, 400

marshaling, 397-400

parameter types, 397-400

traditional Delphi syntax, 396-397

Win32 DLL exports in .NET code, 381-382

custom attribute syntax, 383-384

error handling, 387-388

HResult error codes, 389-391

marshaling, 384-387

parameter types, 384-387

performance issues, 391-395

traditional Delphi syntax, 382-383

Win32 error codes, 388-389

comAuthenticationLevel attribute (<processModel> tag), 728

CombineMode enumeration, 145

comImpersonationLevel attribute (<processModel> tag), 728

comma (,), 233

Command class, 404

Command Text Editor, 531

CommandBuilder class, 421-422

commands

BdpCommand class, 526-527

BdpDataAdapter class, 528

BdpDataReader class, 527-528

executing against databases

CommandBuilder class, 421-422

DDL (Data Definition Language) commands, 416-417

ExecuteScalar() method, 415-416

IDbCommand interface, 412-413

non-query commands, 413-415

parameters, deriving, 421-422

parameters, specifying with IDbParameter, 417-419

single values, retrieving, 415-416

stored procedures, 419-421

File menu commands, 27

mcs, 172

rcd, 170

rpm, 170

Run menu, Run Without Debugging, 623

su, 170

XCOPY, 719-720

CommandText property (IDbCommand interface), 412

CommandTimeout property (IDbCommand interface), 413

CommandType property (IDbCommand interface), 413

comments, 47

Commit() method, 504-505, 530

common data representation, 402

Common Intermediate Language (CIL), 14-16

Common Language Runtime. See CLR

Common Language Specification (CLS), 18

Common Object Request Broker Architecture (CORBA), 644

Common Type System (CTS), 17-18

Compare() method, 224-225

CompareOrdinal() method, 224-225

CompareValidator class, 560-561

comparing strings, 224-225

comparison operators, 53, 456-457

compiler

directives

$define, 52

$IFDEF, 47

$J, 52

$UNSAFECODE ON, 67, 120

$WRITEABLECONST, 52

%DelphiDotNetAssemblyCompiler, 120

@ OutputCache, 730-731, 738-740

errors, 176-177

JIT (just-in-time) compilation, 15

complex data binding, 464, 586

Component class, 263

composite formatting, 230

composite Web controls, 783-790

Compressed FileAttribute, 243

ComVisibleAttribute parameter, 375

Concat() method, 226

concatenating strings, 226

concurrency

managing, 497-501

OnRowUpdated() event handler, 499

sample code listing, 498-499

configuration

authentication, 700

binary encoding, 695-696

errors redirection, 727-728

machine.config file, 720-721

.NET Remoting

client configuration, 689-690

proxies, creating, 690-695

server configuration, 688-689

XML file structure, 686-687

output caching, 730-731

process monitoring, 731

tracing, 731

application level tracing, 735

page level tracing, 732-735

web.config file, 721-723

<appSettings> section, 736-737

<authentication> section, 724-725

<authorization> section, 725

custom configuration sections, 737

<customErrors> section, 727

file schema, 722-723

<httpRuntime> section, 725-726

<location> section, 723-724

<pages> section, 726

<processModel> section, 728-730

<sessionState> section, 726

<trace> section, 735

Windows authentication, 700-702

worker processes, restarting, 728-730

XSP, 179

<configuration> sections (ASP.NET web.config), 737

ConfigurationSettings class, 736

Configure() method, 652

connected classes, 403-404

connected environments, 402

Connection class, 404

Connection property (IDbCommand interface), 413

connections, 406

BdpConnection class, 525-526

closing, 408-409

events, 409-411

IDbConnection interface, 406-407

OdbcConnection.ConnectionString, 408

OleDbConnection.ConnectionString, 408

opening, 408-409

pooling, 411

SqlConnection.ConnectionString, 407-408

Connections Editor, 531

ConnectionString property, 406-408

BdpConnection class, 525

IDbConnection interface, 406

console applications, 7

const statement, 51, 80, 380

constant parameters, 80

constants

backward compatibility, 52

c_cnstr, 183, 433

c_sel_emp, 433

declaring, 51-52

type safety, 51

ValParam, 361

constraints, 405, 442-444

ConstructorBuilder class, 352

constructors, 86, 192, 283-284

ArrayList collection, 206

HashTable collection, 209-210

Queue collection, 203-204

Stack collection, 201

consuming Web services, 630-637

ContainerControl ControlStyle enumeration value, 305

contains statement, 115

Contains() method, 199, 440-441

ContainsKey() method, 210

ContainsValue() method, 210

Context-bound objects, 653

continue statement, 77-78

<@ Control %> tag, 767-768

Control class, 263, 329-330

BeginInvoke() method, 331

CreateGraphics() method, 332-334

EndInvoke() method, 331-332

Invoke() method, 330

InvokeRequired property, 330-331

controls (ASP.NET), 551-552

ASP.NET Server Controls and Component, 790

CheckBoxList, 586-588

data-bound controls, 552

DropDownList, 589-590

HTML controls, 552

HtmlInputFile, 574-575

list controls, pre-populating, 557-558

ListBox, 466, 591-592

Panel, 572-573

RadioButtonList, 593-594

user controls, 552, 763-764

*.ascx files, 767

<@ Control %> tag, 767-768

creating, 764-765

declaring, 766-767

LoginControl, 769-771

<@ Register %> tag, 768-769

SimpleUserControl example, 764-769

UserControl class, 767

validation controls, 552

BaseValidator, 559

CompareValidator, 560-561

CustomValidator, 564

RangeValidator, 563-564

RegularExpressionValidator, 562-563

RequiredFieldValidator, 559-560

ValidationSummary, 565

Web controls, 552

composite controls, 783-790

creating, 771-773

custom rendering, 775-777

HTML block type, 778

persistent values, 773-775

post-back data, 778-783

properties, 566, 773

TNewUserInfoControl, 784-790

controls (WinForms), 261-262

AlarmClock, 279-281

ancestor classes, 263-264

component icons, 285

component units, 264-266

component writing steps, 263

design-time behavior, 284-285

events

creating, 279-280

defined, 277

event handlers, 277

event properties, 277-282

event-dispatching methods, 277-278

ExplorerViewer example

    ActivateFile() method, 294

    code listing, 286-293

    ExtractIcon() method, 294

    FillListView() method, 293

    FillTreeView() method, 293

    GetDirectories() method, 293

    RefreshNode() method, 293

    SHGetFileInfo() method, 294

methods, 282-284

PlayingCard example

    class declaration, 299-300

    code listing, 301-305

    ControlStyles enumeration values, 305-306

    InitComp() method, 305

    OnPaint() method, 306

    SetStyle() method, 305

properties, 266

    array properties, 273-277

    default values, 276

    enumerated properties, 268

    object properties, 269-273

    simple properties, 267

SimpleStatusBars example, 295-298

testing, 285

TypeConverter implementation, 271, 273

when to use, 262

ControlStyles enumeration values, 305-306

ControlToCompare property (CompareValidator class), 561

ControlToValidate property (BaseValidator class), 559

ConvertAssemblyToTypeLib() method, 375

ConvertFrom() method, 271

converting strings to lowercase/uppercase, 227

ConvertTo() method, 271

ConvertTypeLibToAssembly() method, 366, 370

cookieless sessions, 757

cookies (HTTPCookie class), 548-549

    creating, 751-752

    defined, 751

    deleting, 549

    drawbacks, 753

    evaluating contents of, 549

    persistent cookies, 752-753

    retrieving cookie values, 752

Cookies collection, 548

coordinate systems, 126-128, 157-158

Copy Local option (Interop Assemblies), 365

Copy() method, 64, 227, 439

CopyDirectory() method, 242

copying

    DataSets, 439

    directories, 241-243

    files, 245

    strings, 227-228

CopyTo() method, 199, 453

COR_E_FILENOTFOUND error message, 369

CORBA (Common Object Request Broker Architecture), 644

core assemblies, 109

Count property

    BeginRead() method, 253

    Cache class, 744

    DataTable class, 518

    DataView class, 452

    ICollection interface, 199

Count() method, 461

cpuMask attribute (<processModel> tag), 728

Create file mode, 247

Create() method, 86, 148, 241, 247, 314, 350, 439, 445, 467-469, 474

CreateChildControls() method, 784, 790

CreateCommand() method, 407

Created event, 255

CreateDirectory() method, 241

CreateGraphics() method, 332-334

CreateInstance() method, 350, 359

CreateInstanceFrom() method, 347

CreateOleObject() method, 358

CreateParameter() method, 413

CreateProcess() method, 384-385

CreateProcessA() method, 384

CreateProcessW() method, 384

CreateText() method, 245

CreateWLCall() method, 354

CreationTime property

    FileSystemInfo class, 244

    NotifyFilters enumeration, 255

CreationTimeUtc property (FileSystemInfo class), 244

creative round tripping, 371-372

<credentials> section (web.config file), 705-706, 725

CSS (Cascading Style Sheets), 553, 567

CssClass property (WebControl class), 566

CTS (Common Type System), 17

culture parameter (InvokeMember() method), 347

CultureInfo class, 226

CurrencyManager class, 465

CurrencyStringToDecimal() method, 474

Current DataRowVersion, 448

Current property (IEnumerator interface), 200

Current SeekOrigin value, 248

CurrentChanged event, 469

CurrentRows value (DataViewRowState), 458

curves, drawing

    Bezier splines, 135-138

    cardinal splines, 134

custom attribute syntax, 383-384

custom configuration sections (ASP.NET web.config), 737

custom date/time format specifiers, 236-237

custom numeric format specifiers, 232-233

custom rendering, 775-777

custom updating logic

    concurrency issues, 497-501

    SQLCommand class, 479-486

        DELETE statement, 484-486

        INSERT statement, 481

        sample code listing, 479-480

        SubmitAddedRow() method, 481-482

        SubmitUpdates() method, 480

        UPDATE statement, 482-484

    SQLDataAdapter class

        GetDataAdapterDeleteCommand() method, 489-490

        GetDataAdapterInsertCommand() method, 487-488

        GetDataAdapterUpdateCommand() method, 488-489

        main block example, 486-487

    stored procedures

        DeleteProduct, 497

        GetDataAdapterDeleteCommand() method, 496-497

        GetDataAdapterInsertCommand() method, 492-493

        GetDataAdapterUpdateCommand() method, 494-495

        InsertProduct, 493-494

        SelectProduct, 492

        SqlDataAdapter example, 491-492

        UpdateProduct, 495-496

custom WinForms controls. See WinForms controls

CustomAttributeBuilder class, 352

<customErrors> section (ASP.NET web.config), 727

CustomValidator class, 564

D

D format specifier, 231, 234-237

D8DG.LibU.pas, 119-120

D8DG.PkgUnit, 116-117

D8DG.TestLib.dpr, 117-119

D8DG.TestPkg, 115-116

Data Adapter Configuration dialog box, 532-533

data binding, 463, 581

    to arrays

       CheckBoxList control, 586-587

       DropDownList control, 589

       ListBox control, 591

       RadioButtonList control, 593

    binding expressions, evaluating, 597

    BindingContext class, 464

    BindingManagerBase class, 464

    CheckBoxList control, 586-588

    complex binding, 464, 586

    CurrencyManager class, 465

    data formatting, 472-474

    data modification, 469-472

    data parsing, 472-474

    to database tables

       CheckBoxList control, 587-588

       DropDownList control, 589-590

       ListBox control, 592

       RadioButtonList control, 594

    DataGrid control

       adding items to, 613

       column types, 603-604

       editing, 607-613

       paging, 604-607

       sorting, 613-614

    DataList control, 598-603

       declaration, 600

       events, 599

       example, 600-601

       image rendering, 602

       properties, 599

       templates, 598

    DataViews, 453-455

    DropDownList control, 588-590

    event handling, 467-469

    IBindingList interface, 464

    IDataErrorInfo interface, 464

    IEditableObject interface, 464

    IList interface, 464

    ListBox control, 590-592

    lists, 465-466

    master detail, 474-475

    navigation, 467-469

    RadioButtonList control, 593-594

    Repeater control, 595-598

    simple binding, 464, 581-586

    single value binding, 466-467

data caching. *See* caching

Data Definition Language (DDL) commands, 416-417

Data Explorer, 33-34

data members, 85

Data Provider. *See* BDP (Borland Data Provider)

data providers, 405

data sources, updating, 476

    concurrency issues, 497-501

    refreshing data after updates

       INSERT statement, 501-502

       RowUpdated event, 503

       UPDATE statement, 502

       UpdatedRowSource values, 501

    SQLCommand class, 479-486

       DELETE statement, 484-486

       INSERT statement, 481

       sample code listing, 479-480

SubmitAddedRow() method, 481-482

SubmitUpdates() method, 480

UPDATE statement, 482-484

SQLCommandBuilder class, 476-479

SQLDataAdapter class, 486-490

GetDataAdapterDeleteCommand()
method, 489-490

GetDataAdapterInsertCommand() method,
487-488

GetDataAdapterUpdateCommand()
method, 488-489

main block example, 486-487

stored procedures, 491-497

GetDataAdapterDeleteCommand()
method, 496-497

GetDataAdapterInsertCommand() method,
492-493

GetDataAdapterUpdateCommand()
method, 494-495

SqlDataAdapter example, 491-492

data types

aliases, 72

AnsiChar, 58

arrays, 62-64

blittable types, 378

boxing/unboxing, 56-57

Char, 58

comparison of, 57

CTS (Common Type System), 17-18

disambiguating, 40

nesting, 98

non-blittable types, 378

PAnsiChar, 70

PChar, 70

pointers, 68-70

PWideChar, 70

records, 64-65, 70-71

Reference Types, 17

reflection, 342-343

sets, 65-67

strings, 221-222

clipping, 146

comparing, 224-225

concatenating, 226

converting to lowercase/uppercase, 227

copying, 227-228

date/time format specifiers, 234-237

enumeration format specifiers, 237-238

finding length of, 227

formatting, 230-231

immutability, 222-224

inserting, 227

null-terminated strings, 70

numeric format specifiers, 231-233

padding, 228

removing characters from, 227

replacing, 227

splitting, 227

string resources, 73-74

StringBuilder class, 228-229

trimming, 228

type conversion, 72

typecasting, 72-73

unsafe code, 67-68

Value Types, 17

Variant, 58-59

expressions, 60-61

Null, 61

typecasting, 59-60

Unassigned, 61

WideChar, 58

DataAdapters, 403-404

BDPDataAdapter, 429, 528

composition of, 429-431

creating, 431-432

IDBDataAdapter interface, 429

query results

mapping, 434-436

retrieving, 432-434

SQLDataAdapter, 429, 486-490

GetDataAdapterDeleteCommand()
method, 489-490

GetDataAdapterInsertCommand() method,
487-488

GetDataAdapterUpdateCommand()
method, 488-489

main block example, 486-487

stored procedures, 491-492

transaction processing, 508

database-driven ASP.NET applications, 581

binding expressions, evaluating, 597

CheckBoxList control, 586

complex data binding, 586

DataGrid control

adding items to, 613

column types, 603-604

editing, 607-613

paging, 604-607

sorting, 613-614

DataList control, 598-603

declaration, 600

events, 599

example, 600-601

image rendering, 602

properties, 599

templates, 598

download request application

code listing, 614-618

GetData() method, 618

SaveUserInfo() method, 618-619

SendEmail() method, 618

DropDownList control, 588-590

ListBox control, 590-592

RadioButtonList control, 593-594

Repeater control, 595-598

simple data binding, 581-586

databases. *See also* **queries**

command execution

CommandBuilder class, 421-422

DDL (Data Definition Language) commands, 416-417

ExecuteScalar() method, 415-416

IDbCommand interface, 412-413

non-query commands, 413-415

parameters, deriving, 421-422

parameters, specifying with IDbParameter,
417-419

single values, retrieving, 415-416

stored procedures, 419-421

connections

BdpConnection class, 525-526

closing, 408-409

events, 409-411

IDbConnection interface, 406-407

OdbcConnection.ConnectionString, 408

OleDbConnection.ConnectionString, 408

opening, 408-409

pooling, 411

SqlConnection.ConnectionString, 407-408

data sources, updating

concurrency issues, 497-501

refreshing data after updates, 501-503

SQLCommand class, 479-486

SQLCommandBuilder, 479

SQLCommandBuilder class, 476-478

SQLDataAdapter class, 486-490

stored procedures, 491-497

DataAdapters, 403-404

BDPDataAdapter, 429, 528

composition of, 429-431

creating, 431-432

IDBDataAdapter interface, 429

query results, 432-436

SQLDataAdapter, 429, 486-492

transaction processing, 508

database-driven ASP.NET applications

binding expressions, evaluating, 597

CheckBoxList control, 586

complex data binding, 586

DataGrid control, 603-614

DataList control, 598-603

download request application, 614-619

DropDownList control, 588-590

ListBox control, 590-592

RadioButtonList control, 593-594

Repeater control, 595-598

simple data binding, 581-586

DataReaders, 404, 422

BdpDataReader class, 527-528

BLOB data, retrieving, 425-426

IDataReader interface, 423

multiple resultsets, querying, 424-425

schema information, retrieving, 426-428

single resultsets, querying, 423-424

SQLDataReader class, 423-424

DataSets, 404

adding tables, 439

cloning, 439

composition of, 437

copying, 439

creating, 439

DataRelationCollection, 438

DataTableCollection, 438

DataTables, 438

DataViewManager, 438

defined, 436

indexing tables, 440

populating, 432-433

removing tables, 439

strongly typed DataSets, 437

untyped DataSets, 437

DataTables

adding to DataSets, 439

binding CheckBoxLists to, 587-588

binding DropDownLists to, 589-590

binding ListBoxes to, 592

binding RadioButtonLists to, 594

Constraints, 405, 442-444

DataColumns, 405, 440-441

DataRelations, 405, 445-447

DataRows, 405, 447-450

DataTableCollection, 405

indexing, 440

navigating from Web pages, 583-585

populating, 433

primary keys, 441-442

removing from DataSets, 439

searching, 449-450

DataViews, 451-452

compared to DataSources, 452

data binding, 453-455

DataView class, 451

DataViewManager class, 453

filtering, 455-461

joins, 462-463

methods, 453

properties, 452

searching, 461-462

sorting, 461

monetary fields, 474

rendering images from, 602

resultsets

multiple resultsets, 424-425

single resultsets, 423-424

DataBind() method, 582

DataColumnCollection, 440

DataColumns, 405, 440-441

DataGrid control, 603-604

adding items to, 613

column types, 603-604

editing, 607-613

EditCommandColumn type, 607

GetData() method, 609-610

Page_Load() event handler, 609-610

TemplateColumn declaration, 608-609

Update command, 611-613

paging, 604-607

sorting, 613-614

DataList control, 598, 600-603

DataMember property

ListControl, 586

Repeater control, 595

DataReaders, 404, 422

BdpDataReader class, 527-528

BLOB data, retrieving, 425-426

IDataReader interface, 423

multiple resultsets, querying, 424-425

schema information, retrieving, 426-428

single resultsets, querying, 423-424

SQLDataReader class, 423-424

DataRelationCollection, 438

DataRelations, 405, 445-447

DataRows, 405

adding, 447, 520-521

canceling changes to, 448

deleting, 448, 521

editing, 521

finding, 521

modifying, 447

RowState values, 448-450

DataSet property (DataViewManager), 453

DataSets, 404

adding tables, 439

cloning, 439

composition of, 437

consuming from Web services, 635-637

copying, 439

creating, 439

DataRelationCollection, 438

DataTableCollection, 438

DataTables, 438

DataViewManager, 438

defined, 436

indexing tables, 440

populating, 432-433

removing tables, 439

returning with Web services, 627

strongly typed DataSets, 437

adding rows to, 520-521

advantages/disadvantages, 511-512

creating, 512-513

DataRow definitions, 518-520

DataTable definitions, 515-517

DataTable properties/methods, 518

deleting rows in, 521

editing rows in, 521

finding rows in, 521

hierarchical data, 521

.pas files, 513-520

sample code listing, 513-515

.xsd files, 513

untyped DataSets, 437

DataSnap, 403

DataSource property

ListControl, 586

Repeater control, 595

DataTableCollection, 405, 438

DataTables, 405, 438-440

adding to DataSets, 439

binding CheckBoxLists to, 587-588

binding DropDownLists to, 589-590

binding ListBoxes to, 592

binding RadioButtonLists to, 594

constraints, 405, 442-444

DataColumns, 405, 440-441

DataRelations, 405, 445-447

DataRows, 405, 447-450

DataTableCollection, 405

EmployeeDataTable, 515-517

indexing, 440

methods, 518

navigating from Web pages, 583-585

populating, 433

primary keys, 441-442

properties, 518

removing from DataSets, 439

searching, 449-450

DataTextField property (ListControl), 586

DataTextFormatString property (ListControl), 586

DataType property (DataColumns), 441

DataValueField property (ListControl), 586

DataView class, 405

DataViewManager class, 438, 453

DataViewManager property (DataView class), 452

DataViewRowState property (DataView class), 458-459

DataViews

compared to DataSources, 452

data binding, 453-455

DataView class, 451

DataViewManager class, 453

filtering, 455-456

aggregate functions, 460-461

by column values, 456

comparison operators, 456-457

DataViewRowState property, 458-459

functions, 458

LIKE operator, 457-458

RowFilter property, 455

RowStateFilter property, 459-460

joins, 462-463

methods, 453

properties, 452

searching, 461-462

sorting, 461

DataViewSettings property (DataViewManager), 453

date separator (/), 237

date/time format specifiers, 234-237

DateToStr() method, 180

Datye, Vandana, 790

DCOM (Distributed Component Object Model), 645

.dcpil file extension, 115

.dcuil file extension, 115

dd format specifier, 236

ddd format specifier, 236

dddd format specifier, 236

DDL (Data Definition Language) commands, 416-417

de Icaza, Miguel, 167

Debug attribute (ASP.NET pages), 541

Debug desktop layout, 26

*-debuginfo package, 172

Dec() function, 55-56

DecimalToCurrencyString() method, 474

declaration/execution blocks, 38

declaring

arrays, 62

classes, 71

constants, 51-52

dynamic arrays, 63

interfaces, 100

methods, 88-89

namespaces, 42-43

objects, 86

pointers, 68

sets, 65-66

sprites, 159

threads, 311-312

variables, 49-51

decrement procedures, 55-56

default AppDomains, 310

Default DataRowVersion, 448

Default desktop layout, 26

default directive, 276

default session timeout, 757

default.htm file, 25

DefaultValue property

DataColumns, 441

Web controls, 773

$define compiler directive, 52

DefineDynamicAssembly() method, 354

DefineDynamicModule() method, 354

DefineMethod() method, 355

delegates, 278

defined, 312, 320

executing asynchronously, 320-322

ThreadStart, 314

WaitCallback, 318

Delete queries

DeleteProduct stored procedure, 497

GetDataAdapterDeleteCommand() method, 489-490

SqlCommand class, 484-486

Delete() method, 241, 245, 448, 453

DeleteCommand object, 429, 599

Deleted event, 255

Deleted RowState, 448

Deleted value (DataViewRowState), 458

DeleteProduct stored procedure, 497

DeleteRule property (ForeignKeyConstraint), 443

deleting

cookies, 549

DataColumns, 441

DataRows, 448, 521

DataTables, 439

directories, 241

files, 245

string characters, 227

Delphi Guru Web site, 23-24

Delphi IDE. *See* IDE (Integrated Development Environment)

%DelphiDotNetAssemblyCompiler compiler directive, 120

<deny> section (web.config file), 711, 725

dependencies (cache file), 746-749

Dependencies property (Cache class), 744

deployment

advantages of .NET, 5

ASP.NET applications

virtual directories, 716-719

XCOPY deployment, 719-720

assemblies, 111

multitier architecture, 650-651

Dequeue() method, 203

dereferencing pointers, 69

DeriveParameters() method, 422

deriving parameters, 421-422

deserialization, 256-260

Deserialize() method, 259

design-time behavior (WinForms controls), 284-285

Designer, 25, 27

desktop layouts, 26

Destroy() method, 196, 284

destroying objects, 87

destructors, overriding, 284

Detached RowState, 448

development, 12

advantages of .NET, 4-5

development environments, 402

multitier architecture, 650-651

Device FileAttribute, 243

dictionaries, strongly typed

    descending from DictionaryBase, 216-219

    sample application, 219-220

DictionaryBase class, 216-219

Digest authentication (Windows), 702

directives

    $define, 52

    %DelphiDotNetAssemblyCompiler, 120

    $IFDEF, 47

    $J, 52

    @ OutputCache, 738-740

    @Page, 540

    $UNSAFECODE ON, 67, 120

    $WRITEABLECONST, 52

directories

    \bin, 719

    copying, 241-243

    creating, 241

    deleting, 241

    Directory class, 239

    directory information, viewing, 243-244

    DirectoryInfo class, 239-241

    \images, 719

    monitoring, 253-255

    moving, 241-243

    virtual directories, 716-719

Directory class, 239

Directory FileAttribute, 243

DirectoryInfo class, 239-241

DirectoryName value (NotifyFilters enumeration), 255

Dirty Reads, 509

disabling ViewState, 755

disambiguating types, 40

disconnected classes, 404-405

disconnected data architecture, 401

disconnected environments, 402

discovery process (Web services), 630

Display property (BaseValidator class), 559

DisplayMode property (ValidationSummary class), 565

dispose pattern, 193-196

Dispose() method, 194-195, 284

distributed architecture, 646-647

    client/server architecture, 647

    multitier architecture, 648-649

        deployment, 650-651

        development, 650-651

        fault tolerance, 649-650

        scalability, 649-650

        security, 651

    peer-to-peer architecture, 647-648

Distributed Component Object Model (DCOM), 645

distribution, 112

division operators, 54-55, 456

.dll file extension, 115

DllImportAttribute, 383

DLLs (dynamic link libraries). *See also* assemblies

    Borland.Delphi.dll, 109

    HResult DLL exports in .NET code

        HResult error codes, 389-391

        performance issues, 391-395

    mscoree.dll, 373

    mscorlib.dll, 109

    Win32 DLL exports in .NET code, 381-382

        custom attribute syntax, 383-384

        error handling, 387-388

        marshaling, 384-387

        parameter types, 384-387

        traditional Delphi syntax, 382-383

        Win32 error codes, 388-389

do-and-assign operators, 56

documentation

CLS (Common Language Specification), 18

.NET Framework, 6

domains, AppDomains, 651

DoSomething() method, 396

DoSomethingElse() method, 396

DoTextChanged() method, 782

DotNETClassForCOM class, 376

DoubleBuffer ControlStyle enumeration value, 305

download request form, 552

code listing, 614-618

creating, 553-554

event processing order, 557

GetData() method, 618

list controls, pre-populating, 557-558

Load events, 554-555

page layout, 553

SaveUserInfo() method, 618-619

saving information from, 555-557

SendEmail() method, 618

.dpk file extension, 115

DPR files

client DPR files, 680-681, 693-694

server DPR files, 679-680, 691-692

DrawAngle() method, 131

DrawBezier() method, 136

DrawEllipse() method, 139

DrawImage() method, 150, 164

drawing, 125

curves

Bezier splines, 135-138

cardinal splines, 134

ellipses, 139

GDI+ namespaces, 125-126

Graphics class, 126

GraphicsPath class, 142-143

images, 150-151

lines

Brush classes, 128-130

ClearCanvas() method, 128

GraphicsPath class, 132-133

joining lines, 132-133

line caps, 130-132

Pen class, 128

sample code listing, 128-130

pies, 140

polygons, 139-140

rectangles, 21, 138

regions

clipping, 144-146

sample code listing, 143-144

Windows coordinate system, 126-128

DrawLine() method, 129, 157

DrawPath() method, 143

DrawPolygon() method, 139

DrawSaucerTrans() method, 165

DropDownList control, 588-590

Duration setting (@OutputCache), 730, 739

dynamic arrays, 63-64

dynamic methods, 89

dynamically loading assemblies, 123-124

E

e format specifier, 231

/E option (XCOPY), 720

early bound COM, 362, 364

EditCommand event, 599

EditCommandColumn column type, 604

editing

DataGrid control

EditCommandColumn type, 607

GetData() method, 609-610

Page_Load() event handler, 609-610

TemplateColumn declaration, 608-609

Update command, 611-613

rows, 521

EditItemIndex property (DataList control), 599

EditItemStyle property

DataGrid control, 604

DataList control, 599

EditItemTemplate template, 598

editors

Code Editor, 29-32

Command Text Editor, 531

Connections Editor, 531

gedit, 172

Parameter Collection Editor, 531-532

ellipses, drawing, 139

email, 575-576

Emit namespace, 351-352

Emit() method, 355

EmitDemo application, 352-355

emitting MSIL through reflection, 351-355

EmitWriteLine() method, 355

EmployeeDataTable class, 515-518

EmployeeRow class, 518-520

empty variants, 61

EmptyParam variable, 362

Enable attribute

<httpRuntime> tag) 725

<processModel> tag, 728

EnableClientScript property

BaseValidator class, 559

ValidationSummary class, 565

enabled attribute (<trace> tag), 735

Enabled property (BaseValidator class), 559

EnableKernelModeCache attribute (<httpRuntime> tag), 725

EnableNotifyMessage ControlStyle enumeration value, 305

EnableSession property ([WebMethod]), 629

enableSessionState attribute (<pages> tag), 726

enableViewState attribute (<pages> tag), 726

enableViewStateMac attribute (<pages> tag), 726

encapsulation, 85

Encrypted FileAttribute, 243

encryption, 122

End SeekOrigin value, 248

end statement, 38, 74

End() method, 545

EndCurrentEdit() method, 470

EndEdit() method, 447, 521

EndGetEmployees() method, 637-639

EndInvoke() method, 331-332, 500

Enqueue() method, 203

EnsureCapacity() method, 229

EnsureChildControls() method, 784

Enter() method, 324

EnumBuilder class, 352

enumerations

CharSet, 384

CombineMode, 145

ControlStyles, 305-306

DataRowEnumeration, 448-449

enumerated properties, adding to WinForms controls, 268

FileAttributes enumeration values, 243

format specifiers, 237-238

LineCap, 130-132

NotifyFilters, 255

OleDbType, 419

RotateFlipType, 151-152

SequentialAccess, 428

SqlDbType, 419

TSpriteDirection, 160

UnmanagedType, 378

VarEnum, 379

environment variables, PATH, 366

Equals() method, 229

ErrorMessage property (BaseValidator class), 559

errors. *See also* exceptions

COM Interop, 369, 381

COR_E_FILENOTFOUND, 369

ERROR_FILE_NOT_FOUND, 369

errors redirection, 727-728

HResult error codes, 389-391

Win32 error codes, 387-389

ERROR_FILE_NOT_FOUND error message, 369

Eval() method, 597

EVariantTypeCast exception, 60

event-dispatching methods, 277-278

event-driven communication, 541-542

EventBuilder class, 352

events, 92

AuthenticateRequest, 713

CancelCommand, 599

Changed, 255

COM events, 367-369

connections, 409-411

Created, 255

creating, 279-280

CurrentChanged, 469

defined, 277

DeleteCommand, 599

Deleted, 255

EditCommand, 599

event-dispatching methods, 277-278

event-driven communication, 541-542

InfoMessage, 409, 411

ItemChanged, 469

ItemCommand, 595, 599

ItemCreated, 595, 599

ItemDataBound, 595, 599

Load, 554-555

MetaDataChanged, 469

multicast events, 94-95

multithreaded applications, 326-327

PositionChanged, 469

postback events, 549-550

ProcessExit, 40

properties, 277-282

Renamed, 255

RowUpdating, 477

Session_End, 759-760

Session_Start, 759-760

singleton events, 93-94

SortCommand, 613

StateChange, 409-411

UpdateCommand, 599

WebForm event processing order, 557

Evolution, 167

Exception class, 105-106

exceptions (Structured Exception Handling), 103. *See also* errors

ArithmeticException, 106

EVariantTypeCast, 60

Exception class, 105-106

file I/O exception handling, 103-104

FileNotFoundException, 369

flow of execution, 106-108

reraising, 108

SOAP (Simple Object Access Protocol), 674-675

SynchronizationLockException class, 337

ThreadAbortException class, 334-337

ThreadInterruptedException class, 337

ThreadStateException class, 337

try, except block, 104-105

Exclude() function, 67

ExecuteNonQuery() method, 413-415, 508

ExecuteReader() method, 413, 423-428, 526-528

ExecuteScalar() method, 413-416

ExecuteXMLReader() method, 413

executing

  commands

    CommandBuilder class, 421-422

    DDL (Data Definition Language) commands, 416-417

    ExecuteScalar() method, 415-416

    IDbCommand interface, 412-413

    non-query commands, 413-415

    parameters, 417-422

    single values, 415-416

    stored procedures, 419-421

  delegates, 320-322

ExecutionTimeout attribute (<httpRuntime> tag), 725

Exists property (FileSystemInfo class), 244

Exists() method, 241

Exit() method, 324

expanding code blocks, 29

ExplorerViewer control

  ActivateFile() method, 294

  code listing, 286-293

  ExtractIcon() method, 294

  FillListView() method, 293

  FillTreeView() method, 293

  GetDirectories() method, 293

  RefreshNode() method, 293

  SHGetFileInfo() method, 294

exports statement, 120

expressions

  binding expressions, 597

  Variant types, 60-61

Extensible Markup Language. *See* XML

Extension property (FileSystemInfo class), 244

ExtractIcon() method, 294

F

f format specifier, 231, 234, 237

f-fffff format specifier, 236

factory pattern

  client DPR file, 680-681

  defined, 675

  ISimpleFactory interface, 676-677

  ISimpleServer interface, 677

  server DPR file, 679-680

  TSimpleFactory class, 676, 679

  TSimpleServer class, 677-678

failing to renew leases, 686

fault tolerance, 649-650

FCL (Framework Class Library), 18. *See also* **namespaces**

FClearSkyImage object, 160

FieldBuilder class, 352

fields, 87-88

  defined, 85

  private, 96

  protected, 96

  public, 96

  published, 96

  strict private, 96

  strict protected, 96

  VIEWSTATE, 542

  visibility specifiers, 95-96

file authorization, 710-711

File class, 240

File menu commands, 27

FileAccess values, 248

FileAttributes enumeration values, 243

FileInfo class, 240

FileMode values, 247

FileName value (NotifyFilters enumeration), 255

FileNotFoundException, 369

files. *See also names of individual files*

    copying, 245

    creating, 245

    deleting, 245

    file access values, 248

    File class, 240

    FileAttributes enumeration values, 243

    FileInfo class, 240

    FileSystemInfo class, 240, 243-244

    modes, 247

    monitoring, 253-255

    moving, 245

    Path class, 240

    uploading from clients, 574-575

    viewing file information, 245-246

FileStreams, 240

    binary data, 249-251

    creating, 246-250

    FileAccess values, 248

    FileMode values, 247

    reading, 248-250

    SeekOrigin values, 248

    writing to, 246-249

FileSystemInfo class, 240, 243-244

FileSystemWatcher class, 253-255

Fill() method, 433, 439, 443

FillEllipse() method, 139

FillListView() method, 293

FillPath() method, 143

FillPolygon() method, 139

FillSchema() method, 443-444

FillTreeView() method, 293

filtering

    DataViews

        aggregate functions, 460-461

        by column values, 456

        comparison operators, 456-457

        DataViewRowState property, 458-459

        functions, 458

        LIKE operator, 457-458

        RowFilter property, 455

        RowStateFilter property, 459-460

    output (ASP.NET), 545-546

    RowState, 450

finalization, 40, 83, 192-193, 196

finalization statement, 83

Finalize() method, 87, 192-193, 196

Find() method, 449-450, 453, 461-462

FindByEmployeeID() method, 518

finding

    rows, 453, 461-462, 521

    string length, 227

FindRows() method, 453, 461-462

FindTableNameByID() method, 521

FirstReturnedRecord value (UpdatedRowSource property), 501

FixedHeight ControlStyle enumeration value, 305

FixedSize() method, 206

flipping images, 151-153

floating-point division operator, 54-55

flow of execution, 106-108

Flush() method, 248

Folder Properties dialog box, 710

Font property (WebControl class), 566

Foo() function, 79

FooterStyle property

    DataGrid control, 604

    DataList control, 599

FooterTemplate template, 595

for loop, 76

ForeColor property (WebControl class), 566

ForeignKeyConstraint class, 442-443

<form> tag, 536

format specifiers

    date/time format specifiers, 234-237

    defined, 231

enumeration format specifiers, 237-238

numeric format specifiers, 231-233

Format() method, 230

FormatMessage() method, 387

formatting

data binding, 472-474

format specifiers

date/time format specifiers, 234-237

defined, 231

enumeration format specifiers, 237-238

numeric format specifiers, 231-233

formatters, 257

strings, 230-231

WebForms, 566

CSS (Cascading Style Sheets), 567

Style class, 568

WebControl strongly typed properties, 566

forms. *See* **WebForms; WinForms controls**

<forms> section (web.config file), 703, 724

forms-based authentication, 702-703

individual pages, authenticating, 703-705

SQL Server, 707-709

web.config file

<authentication> section, 703

<credentials> section, 705-706

<forms> section, 703

.xml files, 706-707

FormsAuthentication class, 704

FormsIdentity class, 704

Framework Class Library. *See* **FCL**

Framework. *See* **.NET Framework**

Free() method, 192, 196

freeing resources

Finalize() method, 192-194

Free() method, 192

performance issues, 196

friend classes, 97

friend statement, 97

From property (MailMessage class), 576

FSaucer object, 160

FSection, 193

FSkyGraphics object, 160

FSkyImage object, 160

FStep object, 161

FullName property

Assembly class, 340

FileSystemInfo class, 244

FullyQualifiedName property (Module class), 342

functions. *See names of individual functions*

FxCop utility, 18, 267

G

G format specifier, 231, 234-237

GAC (Global Assembly Cache), 111-112

GC (Garbage Collector), 187-189

generational garbage collection, 189-190

invoking, 191

multithreaded applications, 337

roots, 187

System.GC class, 191

GDI+ library, 125

animation example

animation demo implementation, 161-165

main form declaration, 160

sprite declaration, 159

Brush classes, 128-130

curves

Bezier splines, 135-138

cardinal splines, 134

ellipses, 139

Graphics class, 126

GraphicsPath class, 142-143

images, 147
  bitmaps, 148
  drawing, 150-151
  flipping, 151-153
  interpolation, 151
  metafiles, 148
  mirror effect, 151-153
  resolution, 149-150
  rotating, 151-153
  thumbnails, 156-157
  transformations, 153-156
  world coordinates, 157-158
lines
  Brush class, 128
  Brush classes, 128
  GraphicsPath class, 132-133
  joining lines, 132-133
  line caps, 130-132
  Pen class, 128
  sample code listing, 128-130
namespaces, 125-126
Pen class, 128
pies, 140
polygons, 139-140
rectangles, 138
regions, 143-146
Windows coordinate system, 126-128
gedit editor, 172
GenerateThumbs() method, 578-579
generational garbage collection, 189-190
generic namespaces, 44-45
generic units, 43
Get() method, 535, 744
GetAccount() method, 674
GetBytes() method, 426
GetCallingAssembly() method, 340
GetChanges() method, 439
GetChars() method, 426

GetChildRow() method, 446
Get*ChildTableName*Rows() method, 522
GetCommandLine() method, 387
GetConstructor() method, 348
GetCountry() method, 742
GetCustomAttributes() method, 340-342
GetData() method, 606, 609-610, 618, 746-749
GetDataAdapterDeleteCommand() method, 489-490, 496-497
GetDataAdapterInsertCommand() method, 487-488, 492-493
GetDataAdapterUpdateCommand() method, 488-489, 494-495
GetDAUpdateCommand() function, 500
GetDeclareString() method, 343
GetDirectories() method, 293
GetDotNETVersion() method, 398
GetEmployees() method, 627, 637
GetEnumerator() method, 198, 206
GetEvent() method, 348
GetField() method, 348, 585
GetFields() method, 342
GetFirstName() method, 585
GetGeneration() method, 191
GetHistory() method, 731
GetInput() method, 175-176
GetInsertCompanyCmd() method, 507
GetInsertContactCmd() method, 507
GetLastError() method, 387-388, 391
GetLastName() method, 585
GetMembers() method, 343
GetMethod() method, 347-348, 355
GetMethods() method, 342
GetModules() method, 340
GetMyName() method, 582
GetObject() method, 690
GetObjectData() method, 210
Get*ParentTableName*Row() method, 522

GetPlanePosition() method, 276

GetPlanetName() method, 276

GetPrimaryInteropAssembly() method, 370

GetProperty() method, 348

GetRange() method, 206

GetReferencedAssemblies() method, 340

GetRemoteObjectRef() method, 690-691

gets operator (:), 53

GetSchemaTable() method, 426

GetStateInfo() method, 215

GetThumbNailImage() method, 577

GetTitle() method, 585

GetTotalMemory() method, 191

GetType() method, 360

GetTypeFromProgID method, 359

GetTypes() method, 340-342

GetUserName() method, 385, 388, 392

GetUserRoles() method, 714

GetVaryByCustomString() method, 742

get_DefaultSize() method, 300

get_TagKey() method, 778, 782

Global Assembly Cache (GAC), 111-112

global process data, 307

global variables, initializing, 50-51

GlobalAssemblyCache property (Assembly class), 340

Globalization namespace, 226

globally unique identifiers (GUIDs), 100

GNOME Project, 167

goals of .NET, 4-6

goals of Mono Project, 168-169

graphics. *See* GDI+ library

Graphics class, 126

GraphicsPath class, 132-133, 142-143

graphs, 256

GridLines property (DataList control), 599

GUIDs (globally unique identifiers), 100

H

h format specifier, 236

/H option (XCOPY), 720

HasDefVal() function, 48

HashPasswordForStoringInConfigFile() method, 706

HashTable collection, 209-212

HatchBrush class, 130

headers

    HTTP, 536

    program files headings, 38

    SOAP, 672-673

    unit headers, 39

Headers property (MailMessage class), 576

HeaderStyle

    DataGrid control, 604

    DataList control, 599

HeaderTemplate template, 595

HeaderText property (ValidationSummary class), 565

heavyweight processes, 308

Height property (WebControl class), 566

Hello.exe application, 172-173

HelloWorld() method, 623, 634, 641

helper classes, 97-98

hh format specifier, 236

Hidden FileAttribute, 243

hierarchical data, 521

High() function, 62

Highest thread priority, 316

history of Mono Project, 167

HTML block type, 778

HTML controls, 552

HtmlInputFile control, 574-575

HTTP (Hypertext Transfer Protocol)

    HttpApplicationState class, 760-762

    HTTPCookie class, 548-549

HTTPRequest class, 535-536, 547-548

HTTPResponse class, 536-537, 544-547

RFC 2616, 534

HttpApplicationState class, 760-762

HTTPCookie class, 548-549

HTTPRequest class, 535-536, 547-548

HTTPResponse class, 536-537, 544-547

<httpRuntime> section (ASP.NET web.config), 725-726

HttpSessionState class, 756

HyperLinkColumn column type, 604

Hypertext Transfer Protocol. *See* **HTTP**

I

/I option (XCOPY), 720

I/O (input/output)

   deserialization, 256-260

   directories, 240

      copying, 241-243

      creating, 241

      deleting, 241

      Directory class, 239

      directory information, viewing, 243-244

      DirectoryInfo class, 239-241

      monitoring, 253-255

      moving, 241-243

   files

      copying, 245

      creating, 245

      deleting, 245

      file access values, 248

      File class, 240

      file modes, 247

      FileAttributes enumeration values, 243

      FileInfo class, 240

      FileSystemInfo class, 240, 243-244

      monitoring, 253-255

      moving, 245

      Path class, 240

      viewing file information, 245-246

   serialization, 255-256

      example, 257-260

      formatters, 257

      ISerializable interface, 256-257

      object graphs, 256

      [Serializable] attribute, 256

   streams

      asynchronous stream access, 251-253

      BinaryReaders, 240, 249-251

      BinaryWriters, 240, 249-251

      BufferedStreams, 240

      FileStreams, 240, 246-251

      MemoryStreams, 240

      NetworkStreams, 240

      Stream class, 240

      StreamReaders, 240

      StreamWriters, 240

      StringReaders, 240

      StringWriters, 240

      TextReaders, 240

      TextWriters, 240

   System.IO namespace, 239-240

IAsyncResult interface, 638

IBankManager interface, 661

IBar interface, 366

IBindingList interface, 464

ICloneable interface, 200

ICollection interface, 198-199

IComparer interface, 198

icons, 285

IDataErrorInfo interface, 464

IDataReader interface, 423

IDbCommand interface, 412-416

IDbConnection interface, 406-407

IDBDataAdapter interface, 429

IDbParameter interface, 417-419

IDE (Integrated Development Environment)

    Code Editor, 29-32

    Code Explorer, 34-35

    code snippets, 28

    Data Explorer, 33-34

    Designer, 25, 27

    forms, 27-28

    keyboard shortcuts, 30

    Model View, 33

    Object Inspector, 29

    Object Repository, 34

    Project Manager, 32

    To-Do list, 35

    Tool Palette, 28

    Welcome page, 24-25

IDictionary interface, 198-199

IDictionaryEnumerator interface, 198

IDispatch interface, 358, 374

IDisposable interface, 193-196

IdleTimeOut attribute

    <httpRuntime> tag, 725

    <processModel> tag, 729

IDotNETClassForCOM interface, 376-377

IEditableObject interface, 464

IEnumerable interface, 198

IEnumerator interface, 198-200

IErrorInfo interface, 369

IExtenderProvider interface, 296

if statement, 74-75

$IFDEF compiler directive, 47

IFF() method, 458

IFoo interface, 366

IHashCodeProvider interface, 198

IIdentity interface, 704

IIS management console, 716

ILease interface, 683

ILGenerator class, 352, 355

IList interface, 198-199, 464

ImageButton1_Click() event handler, 580

images, 147. *See also* GDI+ library

    bitmaps, 148

    drawing, 150-151

    flipping, 151-153

    interpolation, 151

    metafiles, 148

    mirror effect, 151-153

    rendering from databases, 602

    resolution, 149-150

    rotating, 151-153

    thumbnails, 156-157

    transformations, 153-156

    WebForms, 577

    world coordinates, 157-158

\images directory, 719

immutability of strings, 222-224

impersonization, 714-715

implementation keyword, 39-40, 82

implicit parameters, 278

in operator, 66-67, 456

INamingContainer interface, 784

Inc() function, 55-56

Include() function, 67

IncludeTrailingPathDelimiter() method, 243

increment procedures, 55-56

indenting code blocks, 31

index components, 230

indexing DataTables, 440

IndexOf() method, 199

individual pages, authenticating, 703-705

inequality operator (<>), 53

InfoMessage event, 409, 411

inheritance, 543

inherited statement, 195

Inherits attribute (<@ Control %> tag), 767

How can we make this index more useful? Email us at indexes@samspublishing.com

Inherits attribute (ASP.NET pages), 541

Init() method, 270, 284

InitComp() method, 300, 305-306

initialization statement, 40, 83

InitializeComponent() method, 284

InitializeLifetimeService() method, 683-684

InProc mode (session state), 726

input/output. *See* I/O

Insert queries

    GetDataAdapterInsertCommand() method, 487-488

    InsertProduct stored procedure, 493-494

    SQLCommand class, 481

Insert() method, 199, 223, 227-229, 744

InsertCommand object, 429

InsertCompany() method, 508

InsertContact() method, 508

inserting strings, 227

InsertProduct stored procedure, 493-494

InsertRange() method, 206

installation. *See also* configuration

    Mono, 170

    packages, 122

InstallPersistSqlState.sql, 759

InstallSqlState.sql, 758

instance methods, 312-314

instantiating objects, 86, 654

    Automation object, 359

    client activation, 655

    single-call activation, 655

    singleton activation, 655

integer division operator, 54-55

Integrated Development Environment. *See* IDE

interdependencies, 282-283

interface statement, 39, 82

interfaces. *See also names of individual interfaces*

    declaring, 100

    defined, 99

    implementing, 100-102, 376-377

    interface variables, 102-103

    methods, 101

Interlocked class, 322, 325-326

Interop Assemblies, 364-365

    components of, 366-367

    Copy Local option, 365

    creating, 366

    customizing, 371-372

    PIAs (Primary Interop Assemblies), 369-372

    RCWs (Runtime Callable Wrappers), 366

Interop Type Libraries, 375-376

interoperability

    advantages of, 356-357

    COM objects in .NET code

        COM events, 367-369

        COM lifetime control, 369

        early bound COM, 362-364

        error handling, 369

        Interop Assemblies, 364-367, 371-372

        late bound automation, 358-360

        optional parameters, 360-362

        PIAs (Primary Interop Assemblies), 369-372

        RCWs (Runtime Callable Wrappers), 366

        reference parameters, 360-362

        value parameters, 360-362

    common interoperability issues, 357-358

    .NET objects in COM code

        assembly registration, 373

        CCWs (COM Callable Wrappers), 372

        error handling, 381

        interface implementation, 376-377

        Interop Type Libraries, 375-376

        late bound automation, 374-375

        marshaling, 378-380

        parameter types, 378-380

    .NET routines in Win32 code, 395-396

import declarations, 400

marshaling, 397-400

parameter types, 397-400

traditional Delphi syntax, 396-397

Win32 DLL exports in .NET code, 381-382

custom attribute syntax, 383-384

error handling, 387-388

HResult error codes, 389-391

marshaling, 384-387

parameter types, 384-387

performance issues, 391-395

traditional Delphi syntax, 382-383

Win32 error codes, 388-389

interpolation, 151

Interprocess Communications (IPC), 308, 328, 651

Interrupt() method, 337

intersection, 67

IntPtr variable, 387

InvMemb application, 348-350

Invoke() method, 320, 330, 360, 635

invokeAttr parameter (InvokeMember() method), 347

InvokeMember() method, 347, 350, 360

InvokeRequired property (Control class), 330-331

InvokeType() method, 346

invoking

GC (Garbage Collector), 191

members

CreateInstanceFrom() method, 347

GetConstructor() method, 348

GetEvent() method, 348

GetField() method, 348

GetMethod() method, 347-348

GetProperty() method, 348

InvMemb sample code listing, 348-350

InvokeMember() method, 347

InvokeType() method, 346

InvProject sample code listing, 345-346

WriteMessage() method, 347

Web services, 624, 638-639

InvProject application, 345-346

IPC (Interprocess Communications), 308, 328, 651

IPostBackDataHandler interface, 779

IPostBackEventHandler interface, 779

IsAuthenticated property (FormsIdentity class), 704

ISerializable interface, 256-257

IsFixedSize property (ICollection interface), 199

ISimpleFactory interface, 676-677

ISimpleServer interface, 677

isolation levels, 508-510

ISpeechVoice interface, 367

ISpeechVoiceEvents interface, 367

ISponsor interface, 656, 684

IsPositive() function, 78

IsPostBack property (Page class), 549-550

ISpVoice interface, 362, 367

IsReadyOnly property (ICollection interface), 199

IsResource() method, 342

IsSynchronized property, 199, 329

IsValid property (BaseValidator class), 559

Item property

Cache class, 744

DataTable class, 518

DataView class, 452

ICollection interface, 199

ItemChanged event, 469

ItemCommand event, 595, 599

ItemCreated event, 595, 599

ItemDataBound event, 595, 599

Items property

DataList control, 599

ListControl, 586

Repeater control, 595

ItemStyle property
>   DataGrid control, 604
>   DataList control, 599
ItemTemplate template, 595
iterative controls
>   DataGrid control
>>   adding items to, 613
>>   column types, 603-604
>>   editing, 607-613
>>   paging, 604-607
>>   sorting, 613-614
>   DataList control
>>   declaration, 600
>>   events, 599
>>   example, 600-601
>>   image rendering, 602
>>   properties, 599
>>   templates, 598
>   Repeater control
>>   declaration, 596-597
>>   events, 595
>>   example, 595-596
>>   output, 597-598
>>   properties, 595
>>   templates, 595
IUnknown interface, 358

J-K

$J compiler directive, 52
Java RMI, 644
JIT (just-in-time) compilation, 15
Join() method, 330
joins
>   DataViews, 462-463
>   lines, 132-133
JustWorthless sample control, 265-267, 280

/K option (XCOPY), 720
Key property (Cache class), 744
keyboard shortcuts, 30
keys pairs, 122
Keys property (ICollection interface), 199
keywords. *See names of individual keywords*
Kothari, Nikhil, 790

L

language attribute (ASP.NET pages), 540, 767
language neutrality, 11
LastAccess value (NotifyFilters enumeration), 255
LastAccessTime property (FileSystemInfo class), 244
LastAccessTimeUtc property (FileSystemInfo class), 244
LastIndexOf() method, 206
LastWrite value (NotifyFilters enumeration), 255
LastWriteTime property (FileSystemInfo class), 244
LastWriteTimeUtc property (FileSystemInfo class), 244
late binding, 344-345
late bound automation, 358-360, 374-375
layouts (desktop), 26
leases, 655-656, 686
LEN() method, 458
length of strings, finding, 227
Length property (StringBuilder class), 228
libraries. *See assemblies; DLLs*
library statement, 112
lifetime control (COM), 369
lifetime management, 683-685
lightweight threads, 309
LIKE operator, 456-458
LinearGradientBrush class, 130, 141

LineCap enumerations, 130-132

LineJoin property (Pen class), 133

lines, drawing

Brush classes, 128-130

ClearCanvas() method, 128

DrawLine() method, 129

GraphicsPath class, 132-133

joining lines, 132-133

line caps, 130-132

Pen class, 128

sample code listing, 128-130

ListBox control, 466, 590-592

lists

CheckBoxList control, 586-588

data binding, 465-466

DropDownList control, 588-590

list controls, pre-populating, 557-558

ListBox control, 590-592

RadioButtonList control, 593-594

Load event, 554-555

loading

assemblies, 123-124

bitmaps, 148

LoadModule directive, 185

LoadPostData() method, 779, 782

local storage, 328

LocalBuilder class, 352

localization, 226

localOnly attribute (<trace> tag), 735

Location property (Assembly class), 340

<location> section (ASP.NET web.config), 723-724

Location setting (@OutputCache), 730, 739

Lock() method, 762

Locking Control, 26

locking mechanisms, 322

Interlocked class, 325-326

Monitor class, 324-325

Mutex class, 323-324

ReaderWriterLock class, 325

WaitHandle class, 323

LoggedIn() method, 755

logical operators, 53-54, 456

logical threads, 309-310

LoginControl, 769, 771

loginUrl attribute (web.config <forms> section), 703

logLevel attribute (<processModel> tag), 729

loops, 75

break statement, 77

continue statement, 77-78

for loop, 76

repeat...until loop, 77

terminating, 77

while loop, 76-77

Low() function, 62

lowercase, converting strings to, 227

Lowest thread priority, 316

M

m format specifier, 234-236

Macdonald, Matthew, 698

machine.config file, 720-721

MailMessage class, 575-576

main modules, 37

managed modules, 13-14

circular unit references, 41-42

main modules, 37

skeleton program files, 37-38

units

aliases, 45

finalization section, 40

generic units, 43

headers, 39

implementation section, 40

initialization section, 40

interface section, 39

MyUnit.pas example, 38-39

uses clause syntax, 38-41

managed providers. *See* **data providers**

managed resources, 187

management console (IIS), 716

manifests, 110

manually created threads, 312-315

ManualResetEvent class, 326-327

.map files, 632

MapPath() method, 747

mapping

query results, 434-436

tables, 429-431, 436

MarshalAsAttribute parameter, 378

marshaling, 372, 378-380, 384-387, 397-400

Marshall-By-Reference objects, 653-654

Marshall-By-Value objects, 654

master detail, 474-475

math operators, 54-55

MaxCapacity property (StringBuilder class), 228

maxIoThreads attribute (<processModel> tag), 729

MaxLength property (DataColumns), 441

MaxRequestLength attribute (<httpRuntime> tag), 725

maxWorkerThreads attribute (<processModel> tag), 729

mcs command, 172

MD5CryptoServiceProvider class, 709

member invocation

CreateInstanceFrom() method, 347

GetConstructor() method, 348

GetEvent() method, 348

GetField() method, 348

GetMethod() method, 347-348

GetProperty() method, 348

InvMemb sample code listing, 348-350

InvokeMember() method, 347

InvokeType() method, 346

InvProject sample code listing, 345-346

WriteMessage() method, 347

memory

allocating, 68-69

caching

cache-callback methods, 749-750

Cache class, 744-745, 762

cache file dependencies, 746-749

cache-callback methods, 749-750

data caching, 743-746

GAC (Global Assembly Cache), 111-112

output caching (ASP.NET), 730-731

page caching, 738-742

page fragment caching, 743

dispose pattern, 193-196

finalization, 192-193, 196

GC (Garbage Collector), 187-189

generational garbage collection, 189-190

invoking, 191

multithreaded applications, 337

roots, 187

System.GC class, 191

memoryLimit attribute (<processModel tag), 729

MemoryStreams, 240

message statement, 90

MessageBeep method, 381

MessageName property ([WebMethod]), 629

message tracing, 670-671

metadata, 13, 340

MetaDataChanged event, 469

Metafile class, 148

MethodBuilder class, 352, 354

MethodBuilder() method, 355

methods. *See also names of individual methods*

cache-callback methods, 749-750

class methods, 89

constructors, 192, 283-284

declaring, 88-89

defined, 47, 85, 88

destructors, overriding, 284

dynamic methods, 89

event-dispatching methods, 277-278

instance methods, 312-314

interdependencies, 282-283

overloading, 90

overriding, 90

passing parameters to, 79-81

private methods, 96, 283

protected methods, 96, 283

public methods, 96, 283

published methods, 96, 283

regular methods, 89

reintroducing method names, 90-91

static methods, 89, 314-315

strict private methods, 96, 283

strict protected methods, 96, 283

thread-safe methods, 328-329

virtual methods, 89

visibility specifiers, 95-96

Microsoft Developers Network (MSDN), 6, 698

Microsoft Intermediate Language. *See* MSIL

Microsoft .NET Distributed Applications: Integrating XML Web Services and .NET Remoting, 698

Microsoft Speech API. *See* SAPI

Microsoft Word automation, 359-360

MIDAS technology, 403

minFreeLocalRequestFreeThreads attribute (<httpRuntime> tag), 725

minFreeThreads attribute (<httpRuntime> tag), 725

mirror effect, 151-153

mm format specifier, 236

MMM format specifier, 236

MMMM format specifier, 236

mobile computing, 16

mod-mono package, 172, 184

mod-mono-server package, 184

mod operator, 54

mode attribute (<sessionState> tag), 726

Model view, 33

Modified RowState, 448

ModifiedCurrent value (DataViewRowState), 458

ModifiedOriginal value (DataViewRowState), 458

modifiers parameter (InvokeMember() method), 347

Module() method, 395

ModuleBuilder class, 352, 354

modules

managed modules, 13, 37

circular unit references, 41-42

main modules, 37

skeleton program files, 37-38

units, 38-40, 43, 45

uses clause syntax, 38, 40-41

Modules class

methods, 342

properties, 342

reflection, 341-342

modulus operator (%), 54, 456

monetary fields, 474

Monitor class, 324-325

monitoring ASP.NET, 731

Mono, 28

ADO.NET applications, 181-184

advantages of, 167-168

Apache, 184-186

ASP.NET applications, 177-179

ASP.NET deployment to Mono, 179

Button1_Click event handler, 178

portability, 180-181

Web controls, 178

XSP configuration, 179

XSP runtime parameters, 179-180

assemblies, running, 173

compiler errors, 176-177

MonoFuncs unit, 175

MonoMenu .NET console application, 174-175

defined, 166

FAQ Web site, 167

features of, 166

Hello.exe sample application, 172-173

history of, 167

installing with Red Carpet, 170

Mono 1.0, 168-169

Mono 1.2, 169

Mono 1.4, 169

objectives, 167

open source community, 186

packages, 171-172

SWF (System.Window.Forms), 186

Web site, 186

mono package, 171

mono-wine package, 171

MonoADO application, 181-184

MonoASP application, 177-179

ASP.NET deployment to Mono, 179

Button1_Click event handler, 178

portability, 180-181

Web controls, 178

XSP configuration, 179

XSP runtime parameters, 179-180

monodoc package, 171

MonoFuncs unit, 175

MonoMenu .NET console application, 174-175

Move() method, 241, 245

MoveNext() method, 200

MoveSaucer() method, 163-165

moving

directories, 241-243

files, 245

mscoree.dll, 373

mscorlib.dll, 109

MSDN (Microsoft Developers Network), 6, 698

MSIL (Microsoft Intermediate Language), emitting through reflection, 14-16, 46

AssemblyBuilder class, 352

ConstructorBuilder class, 352

CustomAttributeBuilder class, 352

emitting process, 352

EnumBuilder class, 352

EventBuilder class, 352

FieldBuilder class, 352

ILGenerator class, 352

LocalBuilder class, 352

MethodBuilder class, 352

ModuleBuilder class, 352

ParameterBuilder class, 352

PropertyBuilder class, 352

sample application, 352-355

System.Reflection.Emit namespace, 351-352

TypeBuilder class, 352

msw.Free statement, 39

MTA apartment state, 317

multicast events, 94-95

multidimensional arrays, 62

multiform simulation, 572-573

multiple resultsets, querying, 424-425

multiplication operator (*), 54, 456

MultiplyTransform() method, 154-156

multithreaded applications

control methods, 329-330

BeginInvoke(), 331

CreateGraphics(), 332-334

EndInvoke(), 331-332

Invoke(), 330

InvokeRequired property, 330-331

delegates

    defined, 312, 320

    executing asynchronously, 320-322

    ThreadStart, 314

    WaitCallback, 318

events, 326-327

exceptions, 334-337

garbage collection, 337

locking mechanisms, 322

    Interlocked class, 325-326

    Monitor class, 324-325

    Mutex class, 323-324

    ReaderWriterLock class, 325

    WaitHandle class, 323

producer threads, 326

System.Threading namespace

    ApartmentState class, 317

    AutoResetEvent class, 327

    Interlocked class, 325-326

    ManualResetEvent class, 326-327

    Monitor class, 324-325

    Mutex class, 323-324

    ReaderWriterLock class, 325

    SynchronizationLockException class, 337

    Thread class, 311-316

    ThreadAbortException class, 334-337

    ThreadInterruptedException class, 337

    ThreadPool class, 317-319

    ThreadPriority class, 316

    ThreadState class, 316-317

    ThreadStateException class, 337

    Timer class, 319-320

    WaitHandle class, 323

thread-safe classes/methods, 328-329

threads

    apartment states, 317

    AppDomains, 310-311

    creating with instance methods, 312-314

    creating with static methods, 314-315

    declaring, 311-312

    defined, 309

    lightweight threads, 309

    local storage, 328

    logical threads, 309-310

    pools, 317-319

    priorities, 316

    thread states, 307, 316-317

    timers, 319-320

    Win32 interprocess communications, 328

multitier architecture, 648-649

    deployment, 650-651

    development, 650-651

    fault tolerance, 649-650

    scalability, 649-650

    security, 651

mutable strings, 228-229

Mutex class, 323-324

MyUnit.pas file, 38-39

N

N format specifier, 231

name property

    InvokeMember() method, 347

    FileSystemInfo class, 244

    web.config <forms> section, 703

named parameters, 383

namedParameters parameter (InvokeMember() method), 347

namespaces, 18, 42-44, 82-83

creating, 117

declaring, 42-43

namespaces clause, 44

project default namespaces, 42

resolving, 44-45

System, 18

System.CodeDOM, 19, 351

System.Collections, 19, 197

  ArrayList collection, 206-209

  HashTable collection, 209-212

  interfaces, 198-200

  Queue collection, 203-205

  Stack collection, 200-203

  strongly typed collections, 212-216

  strongly typed dictionaries, 216-220

System.ComponentModel, 19

System.Configuration, 19

System.Data, 19, 406

System.DirectoryServices, 19

System.Drawing, 19-21, 125

System.EnterpriseServices, 19

System.Globalization, 226

System.IO, 19, 239-240

System.Management, 19

System.Messaging, 19

System.Net, 19

System.Reflection, 19

System.Reflection.Emit, 351-352

System.Resources, 19

System.Runtime.CompilerServices, 19

System.Runtime.InteropServices, 19

System.Runtime.Remoting, 19, 651-653

System.Runtime.Serialization, 19

System.Security, 19

System.ServiceProcess, 19

System.Text, 19

System.Threading, 19

ApartmentState class, 317

AutoResetEvent class, 327

Interlocked class, 325-326

ManualResetEvent class, 326-327

Monitor class, 324-325

Mutex class, 323-324

ReaderWriterLock class, 325

SynchronizationLockException class, 337

Thread class, 311-312, 314, 316

ThreadAbortException class, 334-337

ThreadInterruptedException class, 337

ThreadPool class, 317-319

ThreadPriority class, 316

ThreadState class, 316-317

ThreadStateException class, 337

Timer class, 319-320

WaitHandle class, 323

System.Timers, 19

System.Web, 19

System.Windows.Forms, 19-21

System.XML, 19

namespaces clause, 44

NameValueSectionHandler configuration handler, 737

naming PIAs (Primary Interop Assemblies), 371

navigating between WebForms, 568

HttpResponse.Redirect() method, 569-570

POST method, 569

Server.Transfer() method, 570-571

session variables, 571-572

nesting

comments, 47

transactions, 510-511

types, 98

.NET components, 7

.NET Framework, 3-4. *See also* **ADO.NET; assemblies; managed modules; namespaces; .NET Remoting**

class libraries, 6-8

  CLR (Common Language Runtime), assemblies, 14

  load/compile/execute sequence, 15

  managed code, 14

  unmanaged code, 14

CLS (Common Language Specification), 18

CTS (Common Type System), 17

data providers, 405

documentation, 6

FCL (Framework Class Library), 18

GC (Garbage Collector), 187-191

goals

  access to services, 5

  collaborating applications, 6

  faster, easier development, 4-5

  seamless deployment of applications, 5

JIT (just-in-time) compilation, 15

locking mechanisms, 322

  Interlocked class, 325-326

  Monitor class, 324-325

  Mutex class, 323-324

  ReaderWriterLock class, 325

  WaitHandle class, 323

mobile computing, 16

MSIL (Microsoft Intermediate Language), 14, 16

P/Invoke, 381-382, 392-395

Reflection API

  assemblies, 338-341

  late binding, 344-345

  member invocation, 345-351

  metadata, 340

  modules, 341-342

  MSIL, emitting through reflection, 351-355

  Reflector utility, 340

  types, 342-343

Web Services

  consuming, 630-637

  creating, 621-626

  example, 622-623

  invoking, 624, 638-639

  returning data from, 627

  security, 639-642

  SOAP (Simple Object Access Protocol), 620

  UDDI (Universal Description, Discovery, and Integration), 621

  WSDL (Web Service Description Language), 620

  XML (Extensible Markup Language), 620

  [WebMethod] attribute, 627-629

  [WebService] attribute, 626-627

.NET Reflector, 262

.NET Remoting

  Advanced .NET Remoting, 698

  AppDomains, 651

  architectural overview, 651

  BankExample application

    BankServer.dpr file, 664-665

    BankServer_Impl.pas unit, 662-663

    BankShared.pas unit, 660-661

    client implementation, 665-668

    IBankManager interface, 661

    references, 658-659

    setting up, 657-658

    TAccount class, 661

  binary encoding

    compared to SOAP, 697-698

    configuring, 695-696

  CAOs (Client Activated Objects)

    factory pattern, 675-682

    problems of, 682-683

  channels, 656

  ChannelServices class, 652-653

  client/server architecture, 647

COM-Interop, 645

configuration

    client configuration, 689-690

    server configuration, 688-689

    XML file structure, 686-687

CORBA (Common Object Request Broker Architecture), 644

DCOM (Distributed Component Object Model), 645

defined, 643, 646

Java RMI, 644

leases, 655-656, 686

lifetime management

    ILease interface, 683

    InitializeLifetimeService() method, 683-684

    ISponsor interface, 684

    Renewal() method, 685

    SponsorAndLease project, 684-685

message tracing, 670-671

Microsoft .NET Distributed Applications: Integrating XML Web Services and .NET Remoting, 698

multitier architecture, 648-649

    deployment, 650-651

    development, 650-651

    fault tolerance, 649-650

    scalability, 649-650

    security, 651

object activation, 654-655

peer-to-peer architecture, 647-648

proxies, creating, 656, 690-695

    client DPR files, 693-694

    GetRemoteObjectRef() method, 690-691

    server DPR files, 691-692

    TRemotingHelper class, 690-693

remotable objects, 653-654

RemotingConfiguration class, 652

RPC (Remote Procedure Call), 644

SAOs (Server Activated Objects), 675

SOAP (Simple Object Access Protocol), 645-646

    compared to binary encoding, 697-698

    exceptions, 674-675

    packet structure, 672-673

    requests, 673

    responses, 673-674

    specification, 675

sockets, 643-644

sponsors, 655-656

TCP (Transmission Control Protocol), 695

template project, 669

XML-RPC, 645

NetworkStreams, 240

New Items dialog box, 264, 621

NewEmployeeRow() method, 518

NewRow() method, 447

NextResult() method, 425

nil pointers, 70

NLTM authentication (Windows), 700

nodefault directive, 276

non-blittable types, 378

non-query commands, 413-415

Non-repeatable reads, 509

None value

    AcceptRejectRule property, 443

    CharSet enumeration, 384

    DataViewRowState, 459

    DeleteRule property, 443

    UpdatedRowSource property, 501

    UpdateRule property, 443

Normal FileAttribute, 243

Normal thread priority, 316

NOT operator, 54-55, 456

not-equal operator (<>), 53

NotContentIndexed FileAttribute, 243

NotifyFilters values, 255

NTLM authentication, 702

null pointers, 70

null-terminated strings, 70

Null variant types, 61

numeric format specifiers, 231-233

O

Object class, 87

object graphs, 256

Object Inspector, 29

object-oriented programming (OOP), 84-85

object properties, 269-273

Object Repository, 34

objects, 71. *See also names of specific objects*

    COM objects in .NET code

        COM events, 367-369

        COM lifetime control, 369

        early bound COM, 362-364

        error handling, 369

        Interop Assemblies, 364-367, 371-372

        late bound automation, 358-360

        optional parameters, 360-362

        PIAs (Primary Interop Assemblies), 369-372

        RCWs (Runtime Callable Wrappers), 366

        reference parameters, 360-362

        value parameters, 360-362

    CORBA (Common Object Request Broker Architecture), 644

    DCOM (Distributed Component Object Model), 645

    declaring, 86

    defined, 86

    destroying, 87

    instantiating, 86

    lifetime management, 683-685

    .NET objects in COM code

        assembly registration, 373

        CCWs (COM Callable Wrappers), 372

        error handling, 381

        interface implementation, 376-377

        Interop Type Libraries, 375-376

        late bound automation, 374-375

        marshaling, 378-380

        parameter types, 378-380

    Object Inspector, 29

    Object Repository, 34

    remotable objects, 653-655

    roots, 187

OCI (Oracle Call Interface), 405

ODBC (Open Database Connectivity), 405, 408

OdbcConnection object, 408

Off mode (session state), 726

Offline FileAttribute, 243

Offset parameter (BeginRead() method), 253

OLE DB, 405, 408

OleCheck() method, 391

OleDbConnection object, 408

OleDBParameter class, 418

OleDbType enumeration, 419

OnDeserialization() method, 210

OnJump() method, 277-278

OnLoad event hander, 665

OnPaint() method, 300, 306

OnRemoveCallback property (Cache class), 744

OnRowUpdated() event handler, 499

OOP (object-oriented programming), 84-85

Opaque ControlStyle enumeration value, 305

OpCodes, 352

open array parameters, 80-81

Open Database Connectivity (ODBC), 405, 408

Open file mode, 247

Open Group Web site, 644

Open() method, 407-408, 525

opening

    connections, 408-409

    Object Repository, 34

OpenOrCreate file mode, 247

Operator property (CompareValidator class), 561

operators, 52

    address of, 67

    arithmetic operators, 54-55

    as, 73

    assignment operators, 53

    bitwise operators, 55

    comparison operators, 53, 456-457

    decrement, 55-56

    do-and-assign, 56

    in, 66-67

    increment, 55-56

    LIKE operator, 457-458

    logical operators, 53-54

    overloading, 98-99

OR operator, 53-55, 456

Oracle, 405, 408

Oracle Call Interface (OCI), 405

Original DataRowVersion, 448

OriginalRows value (DataViewRowState), 459

out parameters, 79-80

output caching, 730-731

@OutputCache directive, 730-731

OutputParameters value (UpdatedRowSource property), 501

overload statement, 48, 90

overloading

    functions, 48

    methods, 90

    operators, 98-99

override statement, 90

overriding

    destructors, 284

    methods, 90

P

p format specifier, 231

P/Invoke (Platform Invocation Service), 381-382, 392-395

package statement, 112, 115

packages

    assembly attributes, 115

    compared to libraries, 120

    contains clause, 115

    defined, 84

    file types, 115

    installing, 122

    Mono packages, 171-172

    package directive, 112, 115

    Red Carpet packages, 170

    requires clause, 115

    sample package file, 113-115

    test package project

        D8DG.PkgUnit, 116-117

        D8DG.TestPkg, 115-116

packets

    HTTP

        request packets, 535-536

        response packets, 536-537

    SOAP, 672-673

padding strings, 228

PadLeft() method, 228

PadRight() method, 228

page caching

    @ OutputCache directive, 738-740

    varying by custom strings, 742

    varying by headers, 742

    varying by parameters, 740-742

Page class, 549-550

@Page directive, 540

page fragment caching, 743

page level tracing, 732-733, 735

Page_Load() event handler, 712

Page property (BaseValidator class), 559

pageBaseType attribute (<pages> tag), 726

pageOutput attribute (<trace> tag), 735

PagerStyle (DataGrid control), 604

<pages> section (ASP.NET web.config), 726

paging DataGrid control, 604-607

Panel control, 572-573

PAnsiChar type, 70

Parameter class, 404

Parameter Collection Editor, 531-532

ParameterBuilder class, 352

parameterized queries, 417-419, 433-434

ParameterModifier structure, 360

parameters

    BdpParameter class, 529-530

    BdpParameterCollection class, 529-530

    COM (Component Object Model), 360-362

    deriving, 421-422

    functions, 48-49

    parameter types, 378-380

    parameterized queries, 417-419, 433-434

    passing to functions/procedures

        constant parameters, 80

        open array parameters, 80-81

        out parameters, 79-80

        reference parameters, 79

        value parameters, 79

        variable parameters, 79

    specifying with IDbParameter, 417-419

Parameters property (IDbCommand interface), 413

parentheses (), 48

parsing, 472-474

partitioning assemblies, 112

.pas files, 115, 513-520, 543, 632

    DataRow definitions, 518-520

    DataTable definitions, 515-517

    DataTable properties/methods, 518

    sample code listing, 513-515

passing parameters to functions/procedures

    constant parameters, 80

    open array parameters, 80-81

    out parameters, 79-80

    reference parameters, 79

    value parameters, 79

    variable parameters, 79

Passport authentication, 709-710

<passport> section (web.config file), 724

Passport SDK, 710

PassportAuthenticationModule, 709

password attribute (<processModel tag), 729

passwords, 639

path attribute

    <forms> tag, 703

    <location> tag, 723

Path class, 240

PATH environment variable, 366

PathGradientBrush class, 130

paths, GraphicsPath class, 142-143

PChar type, 70

PE headers, 13

PeakMemoryUsed property (ProcessInfo class), 731

Peek() method, 200, 203, 249

peer-to-peer architecture, 647-648

Pen class, 128

percent sign (%), 233

period (.), 41-43, 233

persistent cookies, 752-753

persistent Web controls, 773-775

phantom reads, 509

PIAs (Primary Interop Assemblies), 369-372

pies, drawing, 140

PInvoke (Platform Invoke), 328

Planets component, 273-276

Platform Invocation Service. *See* P/Invoke

PlayingCard control

   class declaration, 299-300

   code listing, 301-305

   ControlStyles enumeration values, 305-306

   InitComp() method, 305

   OnPaint() method, 306

   SetStyle() method, 305

plus sign (+), 29

pointers, 68-70

polygons, drawing, 139-140

pooling

   connections, 411

   threads, 317-319

Pop() method, 200

PopulateDdlFromFile() method, 557

populating DataSets/DataTables, 432-433

portability of Mono ASP.NET applications, 180-181

ports, 180

Position toolbar, 26

PositionChanged event, 469

post-back data, 549-550, 778-783

POST method, 536, 569

pound sign (#), 233

pre-populating list controls, 557-558

Pred() function, 56

Prelink() method, 392, 395

PrelinkAll() method, 392

Prepare() method, 413

preprocessors, 52

PreserveSigAttribute property, 381

Primary Interop Assemblies (PIAs), 369-372

primary keys, 441-442

PrintItems() method, 215

priority of threads, 316

Priority property

   Cache class, 744

   MailMessage class, 576

private methods, 283

private statement, 96

procedures. *See also names of specific procedures*

   default value parameters, 48-49

   defined, 47, 78

   example, 78

   parentheses, 48

   passing parameters to, 79-81

   stored procedures

      data sources, updating, 491-497

      DeleteProduct, 497

      executing, 419-421

      InsertProduct, 493-494

      SelectProduct, 492

      UpdateProduct, 495-496

<processModel> section (ASP.NET web.config), 728-730

processes

   global process data, 307

   heavyweight processes, 308

   IPC (Interprocess Communications), 308

   single-threaded processes, 309

   worker processes, restarting, 728-730

ProcessExit event, 40

ProcessID property (ProcessInfo class), 731

ProcessInfo class, 731

Processing Transaction dialog box, 172

processing transactions. *See* transaction processing

producer threads, 326

programs. *See* applications

project default namespaces, 42

project groups, 32

Project Manager, 32

properties. *See also names of individual properties*

accessor properties, 86

defined, 85

event properties, 277-282

PropertyBuilder class, 352

Proposed DataRowVersion, 448

protected methods, 283

protected statement, 96

protection attribute (web.config <forms> s ection), 703

protocols, 308

COM-Interop, 645

CORBA (Common Object Request Broker Architecture), 644

DCOM (Distributed Component Object Model), 645

HTTP (Hypertext Transfer Protocol), 534-535

HTTPCookie class, 548-549

HTTPRequest class, 535-536, 547-548

HTTPResponse class, 536-537, 544-547

RFC 2616, 534

Java RMI, 644

RPC (Remote Procedure Call), 644

SOAP (Simple Object Access Protocol), 9, 620, 645-646

compared to binary encoding, 697-698

exceptions, 674-675

packet structure, 672-673

requests, 673

responses, 673-674

specification, 675

stateless protocols, 535

TCP (Transmission Control Protocol), 695

UDDI (Universal Description, Discovery, and Integration), 9, 621

WSDL (Web Service Description Language), 620

XML-RPC, 645

ProvidePropertyAttribute class, 295

providers. *See* **data providers**

proxies, 656, 690-695

client DPR files, 693-694

GetRemoteObjectRef() method, 690-691

proxy classes

creating, 630-632

examples, 632-637

server DPR files, 691-692

TRemotingHelper class, 690-693

public methods, 283

public statement, 96

published methods, 283

published statement, 96

Pulse() method, 325

Push() method, 200

PWideChar type, 70

Q

queries

commands, executing against databases

CommandBuilder class, 421-422

DDL (Data Definition Language) commands, 416-417

ExecuteScalar() method, 415-416

IDbCommand interface, 412-413

non-query commands, 413-415

parameters, deriving, 421-422

parameters, specifying with IDbParameter, 417-419

single values, retrieving, 415-416

stored procedures, 419-421

Delete

DeleteProduct stored procedure, 497

GetDataAdapterDeleteCommand() method, 489-490

SqlCommand class, 484-486

Insert

GetDataAdapterInsertCommand() method, 487-488

InsertProduct stored procedure, 493-494

SQLCommand class, 481

multiple resultsets, querying, 424-425

parameterized queries, 417-419, 433-434

query strings, 536

results, mapping, 434-436

results, retrieving with DataAdapters, 432-434

Select, 492

single resultsets, querying, 423-424

Update

GetDataAdapterUpdateCommand() method, 488-489

SqlCommand class, 482-484

UpdateProduct stored procedure, 495-496

QueryPerformanceCounter, 381

QueryPerformanceFrequency, 381

question mark (?), 711

Queue collection, 203-205

QueueUserWorkItem() method, 318

R

R format specifier, 231, 234

/R option (XCOPY), 720

RadioButtonList control, 593-594

RaiseLastOSError() method, 388

RaiseLastWin32Error() method, 388

RaisePostBackEvent() method, 779

RaisePostDataChangedEvent() method, 782

Rammer, Ingo, 698

RangeValidator class, 563-564

rcd command, 170

rcd-{version}.{arch}.rpm package, 170

RCWs (Runtime Callable Wrappers), 366

Read file access, 248

Read() method, 249, 423-424

ReadBlock() method, 249

ReadChars() method, 251

ReadCommitted isolation level, 509

readers

BdpDataReader class, 527-528

BinaryReaders, 240, 249-251

DataReaders, 422

BLOB data, retrieving, 425-426

IDataReader interface, 423

multiple resultsets, querying, 424-425

schema information, retrieving, 426-428

single resultsets, querying, 423-424

SQLDataReader class, 423-424

StreamReaders, 240

StringReaders, 240

TextReaders, 240

ReaderWriterLock class, 325

ReadLine() method, 249, 500

ReadOnly FileAttribute, 243

ReadOnly property (DataColumns), 441

ReadOnly() method, 206

ReadToEnd() method, 249

ReadUncommitted isolation level, 509

ReadWrite file access, 248

real proxies, 656

ReBind() method, 586

records, 64-65, 70-71

Rectangle class, 138

rectangles, drawing, 21, 138

Red Carpet, 170-172

red-carpet-{version}.{arch}.rpm package, 170

Redirect() method, 569-570

RedirectFormLoginPage() method, 705

redirection

ASP.NET error redirection, 727-728

browser redirection, 547

reference parameters (COM), 360-362

reference, passing parameters by, 79

Reference Types, 17

ReferenceEquals() method, 224

referencing assemblies, 120-121

ReflectAssembly() method, 340-342

Reflection API

   assemblies, 338-341

      FullName property, 340

      GetCallingAssembly() method, 340

      GetCustomAttributes() method, 340

      GetModules() method, 340

      GetReferencedAssemblies() method, 340

      GetTypes() method, 340

      GlobalAssemblyCache property, 340

      Location property, 340

      ReflectAssembly() method, 340

      sample code listing, 338-339

   late binding, 344-345

   member invocation

      CreateInstanceFrom() method, 347

      GetConstructor() method, 348

      GetEvent() method, 348

      GetField() method, 348

      GetMethod() method, 347-348

      GetProperty() method, 348

      InvMemb sample code listing, 348-350

      InvokeMember() method, 347

      InvokeType() method, 346

      InvProject sample code listing, 345-346

      WriteMessage() method, 347

   metadata, 340

   modules, 341-342

   MSIL, emitting through reflection

      AssemblyBuilder class, 352

      ConstructorBuilder class, 352

      CustomAttributeBuilder class, 352

      emitting process, 352

      EnumBuilder class, 352

      EventBuilder class, 352

      FieldBuilder class, 352

      ILGenerator class, 352

      LocalBuilder class, 352

      MethodBuilder class, 352

      ModuleBuilder class, 352

      ParameterBuilder class, 352

      PropertyBuilder class, 352

      sample application, 352-355

      System.Reflection.Emit namespace, 351-352

      TypeBuilder class, 352

   Reflector utility, 340

   types, 342-343

Reflector utility, 340, 368

ReflectType() method, 343

RefParam variable, 361

Refresh button (BankExample application), 666-667

Refresh() method, 470

refreshing data after updates

   INSERT statement, 501-502

   RowUpdated event, 503

   UPDATE statement, 502

   UpdatedRowSource values, 501

RefreshNode() method, 293

RefreshSchema() method, 477

regasm.exe tool, 370, 373

regions, 30

   clipping, 144-146

   sample code listing, 143-144

<@ Register %> tag, 768-769

registering

   .NET assemblies, 373

   PIAs (Primary Interop Assemblies), 370

RegisterWellKnownServiceType() method, 652, 655

RegistrationServices class, 373

regular methods, 89

RegularExpressionValidator class, 562-563

reintroduce statement, 90-91

reintroducing method names, 90-91

ReleaseComObject() method, 369

ReleaseMutex() method, 323-324

remotable objects

    activation, 654-655

    Context-bound, 653

    Marshall-By-Reference objects, 653-654

    Marshall-By-Value objects, 654

    well-known objects, 654

Remote Procedure Call (RPC), 644

RemoteAt() method, 439

RemotingConfiguration class, 652

Remove() method, 199, 227-229, 439, 744, 761

RemoveAll() method, 762

RemoveAt() method, 199, 439, 470

RemoveEmployeeRow() method, 518

RemoveRange() method, 207

Remove*TableName*Row() method, 521

removing. *See* deleting

Renamed event, 255

Render() method, 775

RenderContents() method, 775-777

rendering

    images from databases, 602

    Web controls, 775-777

Renewal() method, 685

ReparsePoint FileAttribute, 243

Repeat() method, 207

repeat...until loop, 77

RepeatableRead isolation level, 509

RepeatColumns property (DataList control), 599

RepeatDirection property (DataList control), 599

Repeater control

    declaration, 596-597

    events, 595

    example, 595-596

    output, 597-598

    properties, 595

    templates, 595

RepeatLayout property (DataList control), 599

Replace() method, 223, 227-229

replacing strings, 227

RequestCount property (ProcessInfo class), 731

requestLimit attribute

    <processModel> tag, 729

    <trace> tag, 735

requestQueueLimit attribute (<processModel> tag), 729

requests

    HTTP, 535-536, 547-548

    SOAP, 673

RequiredFieldValidator class, 559-560

requires statement, 115

requireSSL attribute (web.config <forms> section), 703

reraising exceptions, 108

Reset() method, 200, 327

ResetAbort() method, 334

ResizeRedraw ControlStyle enumeration value, 305

resolution, 149-150

resolving namespaces, 44-45

Resourcer, 285

resources

    freeing

        Finalize() method, 192-194

        Free() method, 192

        performance issues, 196

    managed resources, 187

    unmanaged resources, 187

resourcestring statement, 73

responseDeadlockInterval attribute (<processModel> tag), 729

responses

    HTTP, 536-537, 544-547

    SOAP, 673-674

restarting worker processes, 728-730

Result variable, 78

results of queries

    mapping, 434-436

    multiple resultsets, querying, 424-425

    retrieving with DataAdapters, 432-434

    single resultsets, querying, 423-424

Resume() method, 312

ResumeBinding() method, 470

.resx files, 285

Retrieve button (BankExample application), 667

reusability of Web Services, 11

Reverse() method, 207

RFC 2616, 534

roadmap (Mono), 168-169

Roeder, Lutz, 262, 285, 340, 368

role-based authorization, 712-714

Rollback() method, 504-505, 510, 530

roots, 187

RotateFlip() method, 151

RotateFlipType enumeration, 151-152

RotateTransform() method, 152-155

rotating images, 151-153

round tripping, 371-372

Round() function, 73

routines. *See* functions; procedures

RowFilter property (DataView class), 452, 455

rows. *See* DataRows

RowState values, 448-450

RowStateFilter property (DataView class), 452, 459-460

RowUpdating event, 477

RPC (Remote Procedure Call), 644

rpm command, 170

RTTI (runtime type information), 338

rug-{version}.{arch}.rpm package, 170

Run menu commands, Run Without Debugging, 623

Run Without Debugging command (Run menu), 623

running assemblies under Mono, 173

    compiler errors, 176-177

    MonoFuncs unit, 175

    MonoMenu .NET console application, 174-175

Running thread state, 316

Runtime Callable Wrappers (RCWs), 366

runtime parameters (XSP), 179-180

runtime type information (RTTI), 338

S

s format specifier, 234-236

SAOs (Server Activated Objects), 655, 675

SAPI (Microsoft Speech API)

    COM events, 367-368

    downloading, 362

    Interop Assemblies, 365

    sample code listing, 363-364

Save() method, 510

savepoints, 510

SaveUserInfo() method, 555-557, 618-619

saving WebForm information, 555-557

scalability, 649-650

ScaleTransform() method, 154

schema information, retrieving, 426-428

scope, 81-82

SDKVars.bat file, 366

searching
    DataTables, 449-450
    DataViews, 461-462
security
    authentication
        configuring, 700
        defined, 699
        forms-based authentication, 702-709
        Passport authentication, 709-710
        Web services, 639-641
        Windows authentication, 700-702
    authorization
        defined, 699
        file authorization, 710-711
        role-based authorization, 712-714
        URL authorization, 711-712
    impersonization, 714-715
    multitier architecture, 651
    Web services, 639-642
Security value (NotifyFilters enumeration), 255
Seek() method, 248
SeekOrigin values, 248
SEH (Structured Exception Handling).
    See exceptions
Select queries 492
Select() method, 450, 707
Selectable ControlStyle enumeration value, 305
SelectCommand object, 429, 433
SelectCommand property (BdpDataAdapter
    class), 528
SelectedIndex property
    DataList control, 599
    ListControl, 586
SelectedItem property
    DataList control, 599
    ListControl, 586
SelectedItemStyle
    DataGrid control, 604
    DataList control, 599

SelectedItemTemplate, 598
SelectedValue property (ListControl), 586
SelectProduct stored procedure, 492
Self variable, 91
semicolon (;), 233
SendEMail() method, 576, 618
SeparatorStyle property (DataList control), 599
SeparatorTemplate template, 595
SequentialAccess enumeration, 428
[Serializable] attribute, 256
Serializable isolation level, 509
serialization, 255-256
    example, 257-260
    formatters, 257
    ISerializable interface, 256-257
    object graphs, 256
    [Serializable] attribute, 256
Serialize method, 259
Server Activated Objects (SAOs), 655, 675
server controls. See user controls; Web controls
server DPR files, 679-680, 691-692
server-side WebForm validation, 559
servers, 11
    Apache, 184-186
    clusters, 649
    .NET Remoting configuration, 688-689
    server DPR files, 691-692
    Session State Server, 757-758
    SQL Server
        forms-based authentication, 707-709
        storing session data in, 758-759
    Web Server Survey, 184
    XSP, 179-180
services. See Web Services
Session_End event, 759-760
Session object, 756
Session_Start event, 759-760

session state management
    cookieless sessions, 757
    default session timeout, 757
    session events, 759-760
    Session object, 756
    Session State Server, 757-758
    SQL Server, 758-759

Session State Server, 757-758

session variables, 571-572

<sessionState> section (ASP.NET web.config), 726

set of statement, 65-66

set properties, 268

Set() method, 327

SetClip() method, 145

SetEntryPoint() method, 354

SetLastError() method, 387

SetLength() function, 63-64

SetMode() method, 472

SetRange() method, 207

SetResolution() method, 149-150

SetRowNum() method, 585-586

sets
    addition operator, 67
    assigning values to, 66
    declaring, 65-66
    in operator, 66-67
    intersection, 67
    membership, 66
    subtraction operator, 67
    union, 67

SetSomeProp() method, 281

SetStateInfo() method, 215

SetStyle() method, 305

SetWindowText() method, 385

SetWindowTextW() method, 385

shapes, drawing
    curves
        Bezier splines, 135-138
        cardinal splines, 134
    ellipses, 139
    GraphicsPath class, 142-143
    lines
        Brush classes, 128-130
        ClearCanvas() method, 128
        DrawLine() method, 129
        GraphicsPath class, 132-133
        joining lines, 132-133
        line caps, 130-132
        Pen class, 128
        sample code listing, 128-130
    pies, 140
    polygons, 139-140
    rectangles, 138
    regions
        clipping, 144-146
        sample code listing, 143-144

Shared attribute (@ OutputCache), 740

Shared setting (@OutputCache), 730

SHGetFileInfo() method, 294

shift-left operator (<<), 55

shift-right operator (>>), 55

ShowMessageBox property (ValidationSummary class), 565

ShowSummary property (ValidationSummary class), 565

ShutdownReason property (ProcessInfo class), 731

shutdownTimeout attribute (<processModel> tag), 729

simple data binding, 464, 581-586

Simple Object Access Protocol. *See* SOAP

SimpleStatusBars control

  code listing, 296-298

  IExtenderProvider interface, 296

  ProvidePropertyAttribute class, 295

SimpleUserControl, 764-765

  .ascx file, 767

  BasicUserControlPage .aspx file, 768

  <@ Control %> tag, 767-768

  declaration, 766-767

  <@ Register %> tag, 768-769

single-call object activation, 655

single resultsets, querying, 423-424

single value data binding, 466-467

single values, retrieving from databases, 415-416

singleton events, 93-94

singleton object activation, 655

Size value (NotifyFilters enumeration), 255

SizeOf() function, 58

skeleton program files, 37-38

slash (/), 47, 237, 243

SlidingExperation property (Cache class), 744

slidingExpiration attribute (web.config <forms> section), 703

Smart Clients, 11

smartNavigation attribute (<pages> tag), 726

SmtpMail class, 576

sn.exe utility, 122

SOAP (Simple Object Access Protocol), 9, 620

SoapHttpClientProtocol class, 635

SolidBrush class, 130

Some_Func() method, 382

SomeObject class, 269

SomeProc() function, 82

sort criteria (Select() method), 450

Sort property (DataView class), 452

Sort() method, 207

SortCommand event, 613

sorting

  DataGrids, 613-614

  DataViews, 461

Spacing toolbar, 26

SparseFile FileAttribute, 243

Speech API. *See* **SAPI**

splines

  Bezier splines, 135-138

  cardinal splines, 134

Split() method, 227, 558

splitting strings, 227

SponsorAndLease project, 684-685

sponsors, 655-656

sprites, 159

SQL (Standard Query Language).
  See also **queries**

  SQLCommand class, 479-486

    DELETE statement, 484-486

    INSERT statement, 481

    sample code listing, 479-480

    SubmitAddedRow() method, 481-482

    SubmitUpdates() method, 480

    UPDATE statement, 482-484

  SQLCommandBuilder class, 476-479

    limitations, 476-477

    saving updates with, 477-478

  SQLDataAdapter class, 429

    GetDataAdapterDeleteCommand() method, 489-490

    GetDataAdapterInsertCommand() method, 487-488

    GetDataAdapterUpdateCommand() method, 488-489

    main block example, 486-487

    stored procedures, 491-492

SQL Server, 405

  connections

    connection strings, 407-408

    events, 409-411

    opening and closing, 408-409

forms-based authentication, 707-709

storing session data in, 758-759

SQLCommand class, 479-486

DELETE statement, 484-486

INSERT statement, 481

sample code listing, 479-480

SubmitAddedRow() method, 481-482

SubmitUpdates() method, 480

UPDATE statement, 482-484

SQLCommandBuilder class, 476-479

limitations, 476-477

saving updates with, 477-478

SqlConnection object, 407-408

SQLDataAdapter class, 429

GetDataAdapterDeleteCommand() method, 489-490

GetDataAdapterInsertCommand() method, 487-488

GetDataAdapterUpdateCommand() method, 488-489

main block example, 486-487

stored procedures, 491-492

SQLDataReader class, 423-424

SqlDbType enumeration, 419

SqlParameter class, 418-419

SQLServer mode, 726

SqlTransaction class, 504. *See also* **transaction processing**

Src attribute (<@ Register %> tag), 768

ss format specifier, 236

STA apartment state, 317

Stack collection, 200-203

StandardClick ControlStyle enumeration value, 306

StandardDoubleClick ControlStyle enumeration value, 306

StartFigure() method, 142

StartTime property (ProcessInfo class), 731

state management (ASP.NET)

application state management, 760-762

cookies

creating, 751-752

defined, 751

drawbacks, 753

persistent cookies, 752-753

retrieving cookie values, 752

session state management, 756

cookieless sessions, 757

default session timeout, 757

session events, 759-760

Session object, 756

Session State Server, 757-758

SQL Server, 758-759

ViewState, 753-755

State property

BeginRead() method, 253

IDbConnection interface, 406

StateChange event, 409-411

stateful, 655

stateless protocols, 535

statements. *See names of individual statements*

states

apartment states, 317

RowState values, 448-450

thread states, 307, 316-317

StateServer mode (session state), 726

static fields, 87

static methods, 89, 314-315

status line (HTTP response packets), 536

Status property (ProcessInfo class), 731

stdcall calling convention, 396

Step1_Click() event handler, 163

Step1_DrawSaucerTrans() event handler, 163

Step1_Erase() event handler, 163

Step2_Click() event handler, 163

Step2_DrawSaucerTrans() event handler, 164

Step3_DrawSaucerPos() event handler, 165

Stopped thread state, 316

StopRequested thread state, 316

stored procedures

    data sources, updating, 491-497

        GetDataAdapterDeleteCommand() method, 496-497

        GetDataAdapterInsertCommand() method, 492-493

        GetDataAdapterUpdateCommand() method, 494-495

        SqlDataAdapter example, 491-492

    DeleteProduct, 497

    executing, 419-421

    InsertProduct, 493-494

    SelectProduct, 492

    UpdateProduct, 495-496

Stream class, 240

StreamReaders, 240

streams

    asynchronous stream access, 251-253

    BinaryReaders, 240, 249-251

    BinaryWriters, 240, 249-251

    BufferedStreams, 240

    FileStreams, 240

        binary data, 249-251

        creating, 246-250

        FileAccess values, 248

        FileMode values, 247

        reading, 248-250

        SeekOrigin values, 248

        writing to, 246-249

    MemoryStreams, 240

    NetworkStreams, 240

    Stream class, 240

    StreamReaders, 240

    StreamWriters, 240

    StringReaders, 240

    StringWriters, 240

TextReaders, 240

TextWriters, 240

StreamWriters, 240

strict private methods, 283

strict private statement, 96

strict protected methods, 283

strict protected statement, 96

string resources, 73-74

String type. *See* strings

StringBuilder class, 228-229

StringReaders, 240

strings, 221-222

    clipping, 146

    comparing, 224-225

    concatenating, 226

    converting to lowercase, 227

    converting to uppercase, 227

    copying, 227-228

    date/time format specifiers, 234-237

    enumeration format specifiers, 237-238

    finding length of, 227

    formatting, 230-231

    immutability, 222-224

    inserting, 227

    null-terminated strings, 70

    numeric format specifiers, 231-233

    padding, 228

    removing characters from, 227

    replacing, 227

    splitting, 227

    string resources, 73-74

    StringBuilder class, 228-229

    trimming, 228

StringWriters, 240

strong naming assemblies, 122

strongly typed aliases, 72

strongly typed collections, 212-216

strongly typed DataSets, 437

    adding rows to, 520-521

    advantages/disadvantages, 511-512

    creating, 512-513

    DataRow definitions, 518-520

    DataTable definitions, 515-517

    DataTable properties/methods, 518

    deleting rows in, 521

    editing rows in, 521

    finding rows in, 521

    hierarchical data, 521

    .pas files, 513-520

    sample code listing, 513-515

    .xsd files, 513

strongly typed dictionaries, 216-220

Structured Exception Handling. *See* **exceptions**

Style class, 568

Style property (WebControl class), 566

su command, 170

Subject property (MailMessage class), 576

SubmitAddedRow() method, 481-482

SubmitDeletedRow() function, 485

SubmitUpdates() method, 480

SubString() method, 458

subtraction operator (-), 54, 67, 456

Succ() function, 56

SupportsTransparentBackColor ControlStyle enumeration value, 306

SuppressFinalize() method, 194-195

Suspend() method, 312

SuspendBinding() method, 470

Suspended thread state, 316

SuspendRequested thread state, 316

SWF (System.Window.Forms), 186

switch statement, 75

SynchronizationLockException class, 337

synchronized() method, 328-329

Syncronize() method, 203

Syncronized() method, 200, 207, 210

SyncRoot property, 199, 329

SysErrorMessage() method, 387-388

System FileAttribute, 243

System namespace, 18

System.CodeDOM namespace, 19, 351

System.Collections namespace, 19, 197

    ArrayList collection, 206-209

    HashTable collection, 209-212

    interfaces

        ICollection, 198-199

        IComparer, 198

        IDictionary, 198-199

        IDictionaryEnumerator, 198

        IEnumerable, 198

        IEnumerator, 198-200

        IHashCodeProvider, 198

        IList, 198-199

    Queue collection, 203-205

    Stack collection, 200-203

    strongly typed collections, 212-216

    strongly typed dictionaries, 216-220

System.ComponentModel namespace, 19

System.Configuration namespace, 19

System.Data namespace, 19, 406

System.DirectoryServices namespace, 19

System.Drawing namespace, 19-21, 125

System.EnterpriseServices namespace, 19

System.GC class, 191

System.GC.MaxGeneration, 191

System.Globalization namespace, 226

System.IO namespace, 19, 239-240

System.Management namespace, 19

System.Messaging namespace, 19

System.Net namespace, 19

System.Object class, 87

System.Reflection namespace, 19

System.Reflection.Emit namespace, 351-352

System.Resources namespace, 19

System.Runtime.CompilerServices namespace, 19

System.Runtime.InteropServices namespace, 19

System.Runtime.Remoting namespace, 19, 651-653

System.Runtime.Serialization namespace, 19

System.Security namespace, 19

System.ServiceProcess namespace, 19

System.Text namespace, 19

System.Threading namespace, 19

    ApartmentState class, 317

    AutoResetEvent class, 327

    Interlocked class, 325-326

    ManualResetEvent class, 326-327

    Monitor class, 324-325

    Mutex class, 323-324

    ReaderWriterLock class, 325

    SynchronizationLockException class, 337

    Thread class, 311-316

    ThreadAbortException class, 334-337

    ThreadInterruptedException class, 337

    ThreadPool class, 317-319

    ThreadPriority class, 316

    ThreadState class, 316-317

    ThreadStateException class, 337

    Timer class, 319-320

    WaitHandle class, 323

System.Timers namespace, 19

System.Web namespace, 19

System.Window.Forms (SWF), 186

System.Windows.Forms namespace, 19-21

System.XML namespace, 19

T

T format specifier, 234, 236

Tab Order (Designer), 26

TabIndex property (WebControl class), 566

Table Mappings dialog box, 512

Table property (DataView class), 452

TableMappings collection, 429-431, 436

tables. *See* DataTables

TAccount class, 661

TagName attribute (<@ Register %> tag), 768

TagPrefix attribute (<@ Register %> tag), 768

target parameter (InvokeMember() method), 347

TClientDataSet component, 403

TCP (Transmission Control Protocol), 695

tcpTrace utility, 670-671

TCriticalSection class, 193-195

TDataSetProvider component, 403

TemplateColumn column type, 604

templates

    AlternatingItemTemplate, 595

    EditItemTemplate, 598

    FooterTemplate, 595

    HeaderTemplate, 595

    ItemTemplate, 595

    .NET Remoting, 669

    SelectedItemTemplate, 598

    SeparatorTemplate, 595

Temporary FileAttribute, 243

terminating loops, 77

testing conditions, 74-75

testing WinForms controls, 285

text

    text file streams

        creating, 246-249

        reading, 248-250

        writing to, 246-249

    writing to clients, 544

Text property (BaseValidator class), 559

TextReaders, 240

TextureBrush class, 130

TextWriters, 240

Thread class, 311-316

thread-safe classes/methods, 328-329

thread-safe code, writing

events, 326-327

locking mechanisms, 322

Interlocked class, 325-326

Monitor class, 324-325

Mutex class, 323-324

ReaderWriterLock class, 325

WaitHandle class, 323

thread local storage, 328

thread-safe classes/methods, 328-329

Win32 interprocess communications, 328

ThreadAbortException class, 334-337

ThreadInterruptedException class, 337

ThreadMePlease() method, 314

ThreadPool class, 317-319

ThreadPriority class, 316

threads

apartment states, 317

AppDomains, 310-311

control methods, 329-330

BeginInvoke(), 331

CreateGraphics(), 332-334

EndInvoke(), 331-332

Invoke(), 330

InvokeRequired property, 330-331

creating with instance methods, 312-314

creating with static methods, 314-315

declaring, 311-312

defined, 309

delegates

defined, 312, 320

executing asynchronously, 320-322

ThreadStart, 314

WaitCallback, 318

events, 326-327

exceptions, 334-337

garbage collection, 337

lightweight threads, 309

locking mechanisms, 322

Interlocked class, 325-326

Monitor class, 324-325

Mutex class, 323-324

ReaderWriterLock class, 325

WaitHandle class, 323

logical threads, 309-310

pools, 317-319

priorities, 316

producer threads, 326

System.Threading namespace

ApartmentState class, 317

AutoResetEvent class, 327

Interlocked class, 325-326

ManualResetEvent class, 326-327

Monitor class, 324-325

Mutex class, 323-324

ReaderWriterLock class, 325

SynchronizationLockException class, 337

Thread class, 311-316

ThreadAbortException class, 334-337

ThreadInterruptedException class, 337

ThreadPool class, 317-319

ThreadPriority class, 316

ThreadState class, 316-317

ThreadStateException class, 337

Timer class, 319-320

WaitHandle class, 323

Thread class, 311-316

thread local storage, 328

thread states, 307, 316-317

thread-safe classes/methods, 328-329

timers, 319-320

Win32 interprocess communications, 328

ThreadsStart delegate, 314

ThreadState class, 316-317

ThreadStateException class, 337

threadvar keyword, 328

three-tier architecture, 648

thumbnail-based image viewer, 577-580

thumbnails, 156-157

time separator (:), 237

time/date format specifiers, 234-237

timeout attribute
   <forms> tag, 703
   <processModel> tag, 729

timeouts, 757

Timer class, 319-320

Timer1_Tick() event handler, 160

Timer1_Timer() event handler, 163

TlbImp.exe tool, 366, 370

TMyStringWriter class, 39

TMyType class, 41, 350

TNewUserInfoControl, 784-790

To property (MailMessage class), 576

To-Do list, 35

ToArray() method, 200, 203, 207

TObject class, 263

ToLower() method, 227

Tool Palette, 28

ToolTip property (WebControl class), 566

ToString() method, 229, 244

ToUpper() method, 227

TPostbackInputWebControl, 780-783

<trace> section (ASP.NET web.config), 735

traceMode attribute (<trace> tag), 735

tracing, 731
   application level tracing, 735
   messages, 670-671
   page level tracing, 732-735

Transact-SQL queries. *See* queries

Transaction class, 404

transaction processing, 476
   BdpTransaction class, 530
   BeginTransaction() method, 504
   Commit() method, 504-505
   DataAdapters, 508
   isolation levels, 508-510
   nested transactions, 510-511
   Rollback() method, 504-505
   savepoints, 510
   simple example, 505-508
   SqlTransaction class, 504
   transaction reads, 509

Transaction property (IDbCommand interface), 413

TransactionOption property ([WebMethod]), 629

TransEx application, 505-508

Transfer button (BankExample application), 667-668

Transfer() method, 570-571

transformations, 153-156

TranslateTransform() method, 154-157

Transmission Control Protocol (TCP), 695

transparent proxies, 656

TRemotingHelper class, 690-693

Trim() method, 228

TrimEnd() method, 228

trimming strings, 228

TrimStart() method, 228

TrimToSize() method, 203, 207-209

Trunc() function, 73

Truncate file mode, 247

try..finally blocks, 409

try, except block, 104-105

TryEnter() method, 324

TSimpleFactory class, 676, 679

TSimpleServer class, 677-678

TSpriteDirection enumerations, 160

TStateInfoCollection, 212-216

TStateInfoDictionary class, 216-219

tt format specifier, 236

TWebService1 class, 623

TWinForm.ReflectAssembly() method, 340

two-dimensional arrays, 62

two-tier architecture, 647

Type Library to Assembly Converter tool, 366

Type property (CompareValidator class), 561

Type statement, 62, 98

TypeBuilder class, 352

typecasting, 59-60, 72-73

TypeConverter class, 271-273

typed constants, 51

typed pointers, 68

TypeLibConverter class, 375

types. *See* data types

U

u format specifier, 234

UDDI (Universal Description, Discovery, and Integration), 9, 621

Unassigned variants, 61

unboxing, 56-57

Unchanged RowState, 448

Unchanged value (DataViewRowState), 459

Unicode value (CharSet enumeration), 384

UninstallPersistSqlState.sql, 759

UninstallSqlState.sql, 758

unions, 67

Unique property (DataColumns), 441

UniqueConstraint class, 442

unit keyword, 39

units, 82-84
    aliases, 45
    circular unit references, 41-42, 84

    finalization section, 40, 83

    generic units, 43

    headers, 39

    implementation section, 40, 82

    initialization section, 40, 83

    interface section, 39, 82

    MonoFuncs, 175

    MyUnit.pas example, 38-39

    uses clause syntax, 38-41

    uses statement, 83-84

Universal Description, Discovery, and Integration (UDDI), 9, 621

Unknown apartment state, 317

UnLock() method, 762

unmanaged code, 14

unmanaged exports, 395-396
    import declarations, 400
    marshaling, 397-400
    parameter types, 397-400
    traditional Delphi syntax, 396-397

unmanaged resources, freeing, 187
    Finalize() method, 192-194
    Free() method, 192
    performance issues, 196

UnmanagedType enumeration, 378

$UNSAFECODE ON compiler directive, 67, 120

unsafe code, 67-68

unsafe statement, 67

Unspecified isolation level, 509

Unstarted thread state, 316

untyped DataSets, 437

Update queries, 611-613
    GetDataAdapterUpdateCommand() method, 488-489
    SqlCommand class, 482-484
    UpdateProduct stored procedure, 495-496

Update() method, 477, 508

UpdateCommand object, 429, 599

UpdatedRowSource property (SqlCommand class), 501

UpdateProduct stored procedure, 495-496

UpdateRowSource property (IDbCommand interface), 413

UpdateRule property (ForeignKeyConstraint), 443

updating data sources, 476
  concurrency issues, 497-501
  refreshing data after updates, 501-503
  SQLCommand class, 479-486
  SQLCommandBuilder, 479
  SQLCommandBuilder class, 476-478
  SQLDataAdapter class, 486-490
  stored procedures, 491-497

uploading files from clients, 574-575

UpperCase() method, 38

uppercase, converting strings to, 227

URL authorization, 711-712

useFullyQualifiedRedirectUrl attribute (<httpRuntime> tag), 725

user controls, 552, 763-764
  *.ascx files, 767
  <@ Control %> tag, 767-768
  creating, 764-765
  declaring, 766-767
  LoginControl, 769-771
  <@ Register %> tag, 768-769
  SimpleUserControl example, 764-765
      .ascx file, 767
      <@ Control %> tag, 767-768
      <@ Register %> tag, 768-769
      BasicUserControlPage .aspx file, 768
      declaration, 766-767
  UserControl class, 767

user-defined types. *See also* strings
  aliases, 72
  arrays, 62-64
  pointers, 68-70

records, 64-65, 70-71

sets
  addition operator, 67
  assigning values to, 66
  declaring, 65-66
  in operator, 66-67
  intersection, 67
  membership, 66
  subtraction operator, 67
  union, 67

unsafe code, 67-68

User dialog box, 700

<user> section (web.config file), 706

UserControl class, 263, 767

userControlBaseType attribute (<pages> tag), 726

UserLoginValid() method, 705-709

UserMouse ControlStyle enumeration value, 306

username attribute (<processModel> tag), 729

UserPaint ControlStyle enumeration value, 306

uses statement, 38-41, 83-84, 174

V

Validate() method, 559

validateRequest attribute (<pages>tag), 726

validating WebForms, 558
  BaseValidator class, 559
  client-side validation, 559
  CompareValidator class, 560-561
  CustomValidator class, 564
  RangeValidator class, 563-564
  RegularExpressionValidator class, 562-563
  RequiredFieldValidator class, 559-560
  server-side validation, 559
  ValidationSummary class, 565

validation controls, 552

>BaseValidator, 559

>CompareValidator, 560-561

>CustomValidator, 564

>RangeValidator, 563-564

>RegularExpressionValidator, 562-563

>RequiredFieldValidator, 559-560

>ValidationSummary, 565

ValidationSummary class, 565

ValParam constant, 361

value parameters (COM), 360-362

value, passing parameters by, 79

Value property (Cache class), 744

Value Types, 17

Values property (ICollection interface), 199

ValueToCompare property (CompareValidator class), 561

var statement, 38, 50, 79

VarEnum enumeration, 379

variable parameters, 79

variables

>declaring, 49-51

>initializing, 50-51

>interface variables, 102-103

>session variables, 571-572

variant record, 70-71

Variant types, 58-59

>expressions, 60-61

>Null, 61

>typecasting, 59-60

>Unassigned, 61

Variant variable, 358

VaryByControl attribute (@ OutputCache), 731, 740

VaryByCustom attribute (@ OutputCache), 730, 740-742

VaryByHeader attribute (@ OutputCache), 731, 740, 742

VaryByParam attribute (@ OutputCache), 731, 740-742

varying by custom strings (page caching), 742

varying by headers (page caching), 742

varying by parameters (page caching), 740-742

VCL for .NET, 6-8, 390

VCL Forms, 28

VerifyRenderingInServerForm() method, 783

VerifyType() method, 215

versionHeader attribute (<httpRuntime> tag), 725

viewing

>assembly contents, 109-111

>assembly dependencies, 109

>directory information, viewing, 243-244

>file information, 245-246

views. See DataViews

ViewState, 753-755

VIEWSTATE field, 542

virtual address space, 307

virtual directories, 716-719

Virtual Directory Properties dialog box, 717

Virtual Method Table (VMT), 89

virtual methods, 89

visibility specifiers, 95-96

Visual Component Library, 6-8, 390

VMT (Virtual Method Table), 89

W

W3C (World Wide Consortium), 9

Wait() method, 325, 337

WaitAll() method, 323, 327

WaitAny() method, 323, 327

WaitCallback delegate, 318

WaitHandle class, 323

WaitOne() method, 323, 327, 639

How can we make this index more useful? Email us at indexes@samspublishing.com

WaitSleepJoin thread state, 316

Web browsers. *See* **browsers,**

Web controls

composite controls, 783-790

creating, 771-773

custom rendering, 775-777

HTML block type, 778

persistent values, 773-775

post-back data, 778

IPostBackDataHandler interface, 779

IPostBackEventHandler interface, 779

LoadPostData() method, 779

RaisePostBackEvent() method, 779

TPostbackInputWebControl, 780-783

properties, 773

TNewUserInfoControl, 784-790

Web pages, building with ASP.NET WebForms

creating pages, 553-554

dynamically adding controls, 577-580

email responses, sending, 575-576

event processing order, 557

files, uploading from clients, 574-575

formatting, 566-568

images, 577

list controls, pre-populating, 557-558

Load events, 554-555

multiform simulation, 572-573

navigating between WebForms, 568

HttpResponse.Redirect() method, 569-570

POST method, 569

Server.Transfer() method, 570-571

session variables, 571-572

page layout, 553

panels, 572-573

saving information from, 555-557

server controls, 551-552

data-bound controls, 552

HTML controls, 552

user controls, 552

validation controls, 552, 559-565

Web server controls, 552

WebControl strongly typed properties, 566

thumbnail-based image viewer, 577-580

validation, 558

BaseValidator class, 559

client-side validation, 559

CompareValidator class, 560-561

CustomValidator class, 564

RangeValidator class, 563-564

RegularExpressionValidator class, 562-563

RequiredFieldValidator class, 559-560

server-side validation, 559

ValidationSummary class, 565

WebForms, 552

Web root (XSP), 179

Web server controls, 552

Web Service Description Language (WSDL), 9, 620, 632

Web Services, 8, 620

access to, 5

clients, 10-11

communication benefits, 9-10

consuming

through Add Web Reference dialog, 635-637

discovery process, 630

proxy classes, 630-637

creating, 621-626

defined, 7-9

example, 622-623

invoking, 624, 638-639

language neutrality, 11

returning data from, 627

reusability, 11

security, 639-642

servers, 11

SOAP (Simple Object Access Protocol), 9, 620

UDDI (Universal Description, Discovery, and Integration), 9, 621

[WebMethod] attribute, 627-629

[WebService] attribute, 626-627

WSDL (Web Service Description Language), 9, 620

XML (Extensible Markup Language), 9, 620

web.config file, 721-723

<appSettings> section, 736-737

<authentication> section, 703, 724-725

<authorization> section, 725

<credentials> section, 705-706

custom configuration sections, 737

<customErrors> section, 727

file schema, 722-723

<forms> section, 703

<httpRuntime> section, 725-726

<location> section, 723-724

<pages> section, 726

<processModel> section, 728-730

<sessionState> section, 726

<trace> section, 735

WebControl class, 566

WebForms, 28, 552

adding controls to, 538

code-behind, 542-543

creating, 538, 553-555

defined, 7

design/programming separation, 543

dynamically adding controls, 577-580

email responses, sending, 575-576

event-driven communication, 541-542

event handlers, 538

event processing order, 557

files, uploading from clients, 574-575

formatting, 566-568

images, 577

list controls, pre-populating, 557-558

Load events, processing, 554

multiform simulation, 572-573

navigating between, 568

HttpResponse.Redirect() method, 569-570

POST method, 569

Server.Transfer() method, 570-571

session variables, 571-572

page inheritance, 543

page layout, 553

page structure, 538-541

panels, 572-573

postback events, 549-550

saving information from, 555-557

server controls, 551-552

data-bound controls, 552

HTML controls, 552

user controls, 552

validation controls, 552, 559-565

Web server controls, 552

WebControl strongly typed properties, 566

state maintenance, 542

thumbnail-based image viewer, 577-580

validation, 558

BaseValidator class, 559

client-side validation, 559

CompareValidator class, 560-561

CustomValidator class, 564

RangeValidator class, 563-564

RegularExpressionValidator class, 562-563

RequiredFieldValidator class, 559-560

server-side validation, 559

ValidationSummary class, 565

VIEWSTATE field, 542

webGarden attribute (<processModel> tag), 729

[WebMethod] attribute (Web services), 627-629

[WebService] attribute (Web services), 626-627

Welcome page, 24-25

well-known objects, 654

while loop, 76-77

WideChar type, 58

Width property (WebControl class), 566

Win32 applications

error codes, 388-389

interprocess communications, 328

.NET routines in Win32 code, 395-396

import declarations, 400

marshaling, 397-400

parameter types, 397-400

traditional Delphi syntax, 396-397

Win32 DLL exports in .NET code, 381-382

custom attribute syntax, 383-384

error handling, 387-388

HResult error codes, 389-391

marshaling, 384-387

parameter types, 384-387

performance issues, 391-395

traditional Delphi syntax, 382-383

Win32 error codes, 388-389

Win32Check() method, 388-389

Windows authentication, 700-702

Windows coordinate system, 126-128

Windows Forms. *See* WinForms controls

Windows Services, 7

WinForms controls, 261-262

AlarmClock, 279-281

ancestor classes, 263-264

component icons, 285

component units, 264-266

component writing steps, 263

design-time behavior, 284-285

events

creating, 279-280

defined, 277

event-dispatching methods, 277-278

event handlers, 277

event properties, 277-282

ExplorerViewer example

ActivateFile() method, 294

code listing, 286-293

ExtractIcon() method, 294

FillListView() method, 293

FillTreeView() method, 293

GetDirectories() method, 293

RefreshNode() method, 293

SHGetFileInfo() method, 294

methods, 282-284

PlayingCard example

class declaration, 299-300

code listing, 301-305

ControlStyles enumeration values, 305-306

InitComp() method, 305

OnPaint() method, 306

SetStyle() method, 305

properties, 266

array properties, 273-277

default values, 276

enumerated properties, 268

object properties, 269-273

simple properties, 267

SimpleStatusBars example

code listing, 296-298

IExtenderProvider interface, 296

ProvidePropertyAttribute class, 295

testing, 285

TypeConverter implementation, 271-273

when to use, 262

Word automation, 359-360

Worker Processes (ASP.NET), 537, 728-730

world coordinates, 157-158

World Wide Consortium (W3C), 9

wrappers

  CCWs (COM Callable Wrappers), 372

  RCWs (Runtime Callable Wrappers), 366

Write file access, 248

Write() method, 248-250, 316, 545, 733, 773

$WRITEABLECONST compiler directive, 52

WriteLine() method, 222, 248, 316, 355

writeln procedure, 315

WriteMessage() method, 347

writers

  BinaryWriters, 240, 249-251

  StreamWriters, 240

  StringWriters, 240

  TextWriters, 240

WriteSomething() method, 350

WSDL (Web Service Description Language), 9, 620, 632

y format specifier, 234, 236

/Y option (XCOPY), 720

yy format specifier, 236

yyyy format specifier, 236

z format specifier, 236

zz format specifier, 236

zzz format specifier, 237

X-Z

x format specifier, 231, 237

XCOPY deployment, 719-720

Ximian Red Carpet, 170-172

XML (Extensible Markup Language), 9, 620

  ADO.NET integration, 402

  authentication, 706-707

  .NET Remoting configuration files

    client configuration, 689-690

    server configuration, 688-689

    structure of, 686-687

XML-RPC, 645

Xor bitwise operator, 55

.xsd files, 513

XSP, 179-180

xsp package, 172

Other Related Titles

**Delphi 6
Developer's Guide**
*Xavier Pacheco and
Steve Teixeira*
0-672-32115-7
$58.50 USA/ $84.50 CAN

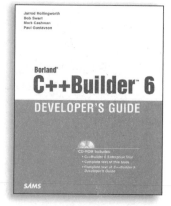

**Borland C++Builder 6
Developer's Guide**
*Jarrod Hollingworth,
Bob Swart, Mark
Cashman, and Paul
Gustavson*
0-672-32480-6
$59.99 USA/$93.99 CAN

**Microsoft Windows
Server 2003 Unleashed**
Rand Morimoto
0-672-32667-1
$59.99 /$86.99 CAN

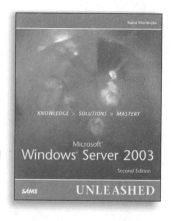

C#Builder Kick Start
Joe Mayo
0-672-32589-6
$34.99 USA/$52.99 CAN

**Microsoft .NET
Kick Start**
Hitesh Seth
0-672-32574-8
$34.99 USA/$52.99 CAN

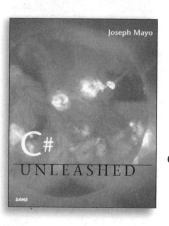

C# Unleashed
Joseph Mayo
0-672-32122-X
$49.95 USA/$74.95 CAN